DICTIONARY OF ARTIFICIAL INTELLIGENCE

DICTIONARY OF
ARTIFICIAL INTELLIGENCE

Dennis Mercadal

VNR VAN NOSTRAND REINHOLD
New York

Copyright © 1990 by Van Nostrand Reinhold

Library of Congress Catalog Number 90-38646
ISBN 0-442-00451-6

All rights reserved. No part of this work covered by the copyright hereon may be reproduced or used in any form by any means—graphic, electronic, or mechanical, including photocopying, recording, taping, or information storage and retrieval systems—without written permission of the publisher.

Printed in the United States of America

Van Nostrand Reinhold
115 Fifth Avenue
New York, New York 10003

Chapman and Hall
2-6 Boundary Row
London, SE1 8HN, England

Thomas Nelson Australia
102 Dodds Street
South Melbourne 3205 Victoria, Australia

Nelson Canada
1120 Birchmount Road
Scarborough, Ontario M1K 5G4, Canada

16 15 14 13 12 11 10 9 8 7 6 5 4 3 2 1

Library of Congress Cataloging in Publication Data

Mercadal, Dennis, 1943–
    Dictionary of artificial intelligence / Dennis Mercadal.
      p.   cm.
    Includes bibliographical references.
    ISBN 0-442-00451-6 (pbk.)
    1. Artificial intelligence—Dictionaries. I. Title.
Q334.2.M47 1990
006.3′03—dc20   90-38646
                                    CIP

Designer: M.R.P. Design.

To Pam and Helen,
without whom this book would never have been started.

Contents

Preface	ix
Dictionary of Terms and Concepts	1
Signs, Symbols, and Numbers	308
Expert System Shells/Tools	309
References	318

Preface

The main goal I had in writing this book was for you, the reader, to find the large majority of terms you are looking for in this book. I use the words "large majority" because I know this dictionary cannot include all the terms and concepts in this dynamic field. Once you find the term, my hope is that you will find the information accurate and useful.

I wrote this dictionary for the novice and for the professional in artificial intelligence. I placed emphasis not just on defining terms but in giving numerous concrete examples. For the more experienced professional, I included contrasts with other terms and spent time pointing out the implications of the concept.

The languages of artificial intelligence have received special attention. Trying to understand artificial intelligence without knowing LISP, PROLOG, or Smalltalk is like visiting a foreign country without knowing the language. You cannot obtain a true appreciation of the country without knowing the language.

Terms from related fields, such as logic, are included because concepts from other fields have much to offer to the field of AI.

Some terms not specific to artificial intelligence are included because they are frequently used in the AI literature. Examples include data types and pointers.

Many terms have multiple definitions. A given term may have definitions that are related, unrelated, or even contradictory. Rather than simply giving you the "correct" definition of a term, I have often provided a full range of definitions.

Expert systems are highlighted because most people reading this text will be looking for information on expert systems and related areas. An appendix of expert systems is provided.

Many new areas of AI are included. You will find information on genetic algorithms, neural networks, model-based reasoning, case-based reasoning, object-oriented programming, intelligent data bases, and more.

The many references included can steer you onto further information about a subject.

My final goal is to make the text interesting so that readers will use it as more than a reference book. I hope this book helps open insights into this exciting field.

Acknowledgments

All of the professionals cited in the references have contributed greatly to this work and their efforts are greatly appreciated.

Dictionary of Terms and Concepts

A* algorithm A heuristic search that is an enhanced version of branch-and-bound search. The A* algorithm is an optimal type of heuristic search, in that it finds the optimal goal and the optimal path to the goal rather than just any goal, or just any path. It does not, however, guarantee that the effort put forth in the search is minimized. It is a search algorithm in which the next node chosen is based on the cost thus far from the beginning and on heuristics that estimate the future cost to the final goal. Estimates are made of the current accumulated cost and the estimated cost to finish. These two costs are combined in a final result called A'. The different A's for each alternative are then compared and the most promising one is chosen. This approach prevents the exploration of paths that are too time consuming. The other alternatives are kept in case the most promising path does not turn out to be the best path after all. If the most promising path turns out not to be the best path, the A* algorithm searches the next most promising path. The A* method works well as long as the future cost is not overestimated. As long as the A* procedure does not overestimate the correct future cost, it is guaranteed to discover the best route in comparison with other search methods that have the same information. The A* algorithm is much more efficient than breadth-first search. When the heuristic for estimating distance to the goal is trivial, the A* algorithm reduces to branch-and-bound/uniform cost search. Like all best first-search techniques, it is memory hungry. *See also* Beam search for a type of search that cuts down on the memory required (Forsyth and Naylor 1985, 155–159; Flamig 1987, 18–26; Wolfgram 1987, 66–67; Barr and Feigenbaum 1981 vol. 1, 64–73; Chabris 1989, 159–162, 285; Luger and Stubblefield 1989, 166–167; Smith 1989, 1; Winston 1984, 113–114).

AAAI *See* American Association for Artificial Intelligence.

AAL *See* Adventure Authoring Language.

Aaron An artificial intelligence program devoted to drawing. The three concepts the program uses are the differences between inside and outside, closed and open, and figure and ground. The program consists of different experts capable of carrying out different tasks. The architecture is reminiscent of Hearsay II (Johnson 1986, 211–223).

a-list An association list (Winston and Horn 1988, 574; Townsend and Feucht 1986, 243).

A^q algorithm An algorithm used in propositional logic for selecting training instances that are considerable distances from one another in the instance space (Smith 1989, 12).

Abduction An illegal inference that generates explanations for a phenomenon. The explanations generated may not be correct. Example: If X implies Y and Y is found to be true then by deduction X is true. Deduction is a much sounder computation. Medical diagnosis is a form of abduction. Another example: For all X, X is having a heart attack if X is having chest pains. Abduction may be considered the first part of the generate-and-test process. *Compare with* Deduction. *See also* Plausible reasoning (Charniak and McDermott 1985, 21; Chabris 1989, 285; Smith 1989, 1; Olsen et al 1987, 118).

Abductive inference The generation of hypotheses to explain a phenomenon. *Contrast with* Deduction (Jackson 1986, 117).

Absolute rule A rule that evaluates a circumstance. For example, in a problem-solving process an absolute rule may detect the velocity of a particle that has been computed and the absolute rule then calculates the acceleration (Hunt 1986, 41).

Abstract class A class that holds the methods of all its subclasses. A class that spawns subclasses, not instances. A class whose members consist of other classes. Example: The animal class is an abstract class because it consists of other classes—mammals, birds, carnivores, and so on (Miller 1989, 64; Thomas 1989, 238).

Abstract data type A data type and the operations relevant to the objects in the domain of the data type. It describes the representation of objects. It hides the details of the operations of the data type. Examples of abstract data types are classes in Smalltalk. Each class in Smalltalk has operations called methods. Another example would be an abstract data type called animal. Methods for communication are associated with each animal. A dog in the animal class barks when a message requesting it to bark is passed to it. A cat meows when a message to talk is passed to it (Olan 1988, 37; Miller May 1988, 45; Pountain 1986, 227; Swaine June 1989, 114–116).

Abstraction 1. The technique of using simplified assumptions to cope better with large solution spaces (for example, instead of analyzing all the subtle details of different types of interest rates, simply looking at the general classes of interest rates). When a general class of interest rate candidates is established, then the specific interest rate computations in that class can be examined. Human experts routinely use abstraction, and it is one reason why they can quickly solve problems without having to go through extended logic computations. In expert systems involved in planning, hierarchical planning is regularly used. That is, an abstract plan is first formulated. Then more detailed implementations of the plan are generated. Such planning forms a hierarchical structure of the plan from the more abstract to the more specific. All expert system factbases employ abstractions of the real world to some degree. 2. The process of hiding implementation details. Such abstraction can take place with data and with flow of control. *See also* Data abstraction (Hayes-Roth et al 1983, 70, 85; Walters and Nielsen 1988, 281–283, 326–327; Barr and Feigenbaum 1981 vol 3, 516–518, 528–530).

Abstraction barrier   A protective layer concealing lower-level details, which can be created using either procedure or data abstraction (Winston and Horn 1988, 437).

Abstract object type   An object/class used to spawn other objects/classes that are not instances. For example, the object animal may be used to spawn mammals and birds. Neither mammals nor birds are specific concrete objects. Abstract superclass (Duntemann 1989, 132).

Abstract operator   An operator used to delineate abstract actions in planning systems. Once the abstract operations have been delineated the planning system works on filling in the details of the plan (Smith 1989, 2).

Abstract superclass   *See* Abstract object type (Duntemann 1989, 132).

ABSTRIPS   A successor program to STRIPS. It is a robot-planning program that uses hierarchical planning. In the more abstract plans only the essential conditions are considered. It then moves to more concrete plans, where the less important conditions are considered. All conditions are assigned criticality scores that are used to decide how important a given detail is. Its use of hierarchical planning results in less search and less backtracking than its predecessor, STRIPS. It carries out a length-first search which forms a complete overall plan first before carrying out actions (Hayes-Roth et al 1983, 104–106; Barr and Feigenbaum 1981 vol 3, 517–518, 523–530).

Access-oriented method   A computational method that is triggered by the reading of data or changes in data (Hunt 1986, 41; Smith 1989, 2).

Access procedure   A LISP procedure that includes constructors, readers, and writers. *See also* San Marco LISP Explorer.

Accidental property   The property of an object that may be possessed by all objects in a class, but which is not crucial to the definition of the object. *Compare with* Essential properties and Typicality (Jackson 1986, 67).

Accuracy   **1.** The measurement of expert systems achieved by comparing the actual correct predictions with the expected number of correct predictions. There are statistical techniques such as Chi Square that help in measuring accuracy. Other important measures of the value of an expert system are adequacy, validity, reliability, breadth, practicability, adaptability, credibility, and generality.   **2.** The difference between the calculated location of a robot arm and the real location of the arm in robotics (Hunt 1986, 41; Marcot 1987, 44).

ACE   An expert system that detects problems in telephone systems and makes recommendations for repairs. It is a rule-based forward-chaining system (Hunt 1986, 41–42).

ACES   A program that places labels on maps and uses information about locations on the map to label the point with the correct label size and type font. It is implemented in LOOPS (Hunt 1986, 42).

ACRONYM   A model-based vision program that uses geometric matching and algebraic consistency checking to interpret three-dimensional interpretations of images. The user tells the system what images to expect and the program attempts to find those images in the data it receives. It employs a powerful generate-and-test procedure. ACRONYM has been used in aerial photograph interpretation. It makes a clear distinction between image domain and scene domain (Mishkoff 1986, 5–13; Barr and Feigenbaum 1981 vol 3, 313–321; Townsend and Feucht 1986, 183; Waldrop 1987, 105–106; Winston 1984, 164–166).

ACT   A computer model of human cognition; a successor program to HAM. ACT includes both short-term and long-term memory. Its long-term memory is made up of nodes and arcs. The nodes represent concepts and the arcs represent relations between concepts. The short-memory also consists of nodes, but the nodes represent more active concepts. There is a separate production rule component. The production rules examine short-term memory and based on the results initiate changes in long-term memory by activating nodes in long-term memory and placing the nodes in short-term memory. The placing of nodes in short-term memory is the process that is responsible for ACT's ability to shift attention readily. ACT can be programmed to demonstrate a variety of cognitive tasks (Barr and Feigenbaum, 1981 vol 3, 50–55).

Act One of the four cycles in the recognize act cycle of OPS5 expert systems. Act is responsible for firing the commands found in the right-hand side of the production rule after conflict resolution has taken place. The four cycles in the recognize act cycle are conflict resolution, act, match, and halt.

Action An action carried out on the right-hand side of a production rule in a production system. The actions vary depending on the production system. Some actions may include making, deleting, or modifying a working memory element, building a rule, writing to the screen, opening and closing a file, and binding a value to a variable (Brownston et al 1986, 51–60).

Activation A number representing the degree of attention an entity may receive in an artificial intelligence program. A rule with a high activation number is more likely to be used than one with a low activation number (Brownston et al 1986, 284–285; Hunt 1986, 42).

Activation accommodation The use of sensory feedback and control mechanism in robotics to manage the movement of a robot in a changing environment; analogous to the human nervous system, which allows us to sense and adjust to objects in our environment (Hunt 1986, 42).

Activation cycle The time it takes for activation to be spread to adjacent objects in an activation network. More than one activation cycle may take place during a single recognize-act cycle (Hunt 1986, 42).

Activation environment The environment in force when the procedure needing the free variable values is called (Winston, and Horn 1984, 54).

Activation filtering A type of data filtering in which the datum is assigned a number that determines the relevancy of the datum for a particular part of the problem-solving process. *See also* Certainty filtering for another type of data filtering (Brownston et al 1986, 310).

Activation function A function that computes the neural net output based on the input to the system and the system's current state (Obermeier and Barron 1989, 219).

Activation network A network of nodes and arcs. The arcs represent relationships between the nodes. The nodes represent objects and each arc may have a number that represents the strength of the relationship. When an object is processed its activation level can be altered and it can, in turn, alter the activation level of adjacent objects (Brownston et al 1986, 441).

Activation time constant A constant used in the instar activation equation which determines the rate of decay of learning over time (Caudill Nov 1988, 60).

Active data structure A data structure that both represents and processes data. Active data structures are found in the connection machine. This type of data structure receives instructions from an external source. It then uses its own built-in procedures to carry out the request. This structure differs from conventional passive data structures which are manipulated by external procedures. Active data structures include objects, frames, sets, trees, butterflies, strings, arrays, and graphs (Hillis 1985, 18).

Active illumination A means of increasing the amount of information from a scene by varying the lighting (Rosenberg 1986, 3).

Active image A demon that can be used to call an image which can then be used to choose from a set of options. Example: An image with five buttons can be called. Each button represents a choice. A mouse can be used to press one of the buttons to execute a procedure (Luger and Stubblefield 1989, 549).

Active instance selection The search of the instance space in learning programs to find active instances, which can be used to produce rules (Smith 1989, 4).

Active object An object that can take action without having to be called by another object. The object may, for example, take action in response to a change in data (Wegner 1989, 246).

Active value 1. A value in an artificial intelligence program which, when added, deleted, scanned, or modified, can trigger a procedure called a demon. The demon may carry out such procedures as requiring a password to access the value, modify another value, place constraints on any modification of the value, display a graph of the variable being reasoned about, or trigger-rule sets. Active values can be used in building truth maintenance systems. They can be used to implement nonmonotonic reasoning. 2. Procedural attachment and demons. That is, active value can refer to the procedure which is activated when a value is somehow accessed (Tello 1989, 28, 190; Shepard 1987, 76; Rauch-Hindin 1988, 58; Walters and Nielsen 1988 138–139; Harmon and King 1985, 58, 126; Rosenberg 1986, 3; Waterman 1986, 388).

Actor 1. An object that carries out actions in conceptual dependency theory. 2. The fundamental entity in Carl Hewitt's actor theory. Actors differs from the standard Smalltalk approach in that actors take an intermediate value as a message and continue processing. In Smalltalk the object always returns a value in response to a message (Chabris 1989, 286; Smith 1989, 4).

ACTOR An object-oriented language developed by the Whitewater group which supports inheritance and is similar to Smalltalk. ACTOR's code is closer to C than standard implementations of Smalltalk. One feature of ACTOR is that it uses windows (Tello 1989, 115).

Actor language An object-based language that is capable of concurrency, but does not support inheritance and classes. Its promise is in open systems that use parallel processing. Actor languages should not be confused with the ACTOR language from the Whitewater Group which does support inheritance (Tello 1989, 285; Wegner 1989, 249).

Actor theory A theory developed by Carl Hewitt consisting of subprograms called actors. Each actor is able to respond to messages, change its internal state, send messages, or create a new actor. Each actor gains control of an artificial intelligence program at different times depending on the circumstances. It is somewhat reminiscent of Freud's id, ego, and superego theory in which each of these actors gains control at different times. Hewitt is currently developing APIARY, an implementation of actor theory.

Actual parameter An actual value that replaces the formal parameter, for example, Max(A, B,C). The procedure decides which of the three numbers represented by A, B, and C is the maximum number. A, B, and C are formal parameters for the procedure Max. The actual parameters are the numbers A, B, and C represent (Hunt 1986, 192).

Actuator The mechanism that powers the movement of a robot; the three common types are pneumatic, hydraulic, and electric (Mishkoff 1986, 5–17).

Acyclic data base A data base in a PROLOG program obtained from the original data base through queries and deduction (Shmueli et al 1986, 248).

Acyclic graph A graph in which a descendant may have more than one parent.

ADA A general-purpose, strongly typed computer language which, while not usually used in artificial intelligence, has certain characteristics that make it attractive for AI applications: Its memory management is the type needed in real-time expert systems. ADA uses recursion and allows for the possibility of object-oriented programs. The language permits a compile time version of polymorphism and multitasking. It has the ability to carry out parallel processing. It is portable, readable, has good error-handling capabilities, and is able to implement real-time programming. ADA is an object-based language, but it is not a class-based language. ADA should be considered especially in very complex applications (Tello 1988, 397–398; Wegner 1989, 247; Roland 1987, 55).

Adaline A single-neuron system which can learn to recognize a single letter, even if the orientation of the letter is rotated; it uses the Delta learning rule (Caudill Feb 1988, 56; Tank and Hopfield 1987, 104; Caudill June 1988, 53).

Adaptability The ability of an expert system to deal with different hardware and software, and different types of information. Other important measures of the value of an expert system are adequacy, accuracy, reliability, breadth, practicability, validity, credibility, and generality (Marcot 1987, 45).

Adaptive Having the ability of a robot to alter its control system in response to a changing environment (Hunt 1986, 43).

Adaptive control theorist A researcher interested in obtaining a synthesis of learning theory and control theory (Jorgensen and Matheus 1986, 31).

Adaptive learning Learning employed in artificial intelligence for dealing with noisy environments. The program builds a model that correctly approximates the inputs and outputs; examples include automata learning, parameter learning, statistical algorithms, and structural learning (Smith 1989, 4–5).

Adaptive linear element A single-neuron system capable of learning to discriminate patterns even if the spatial orientation or size of the pattern is changed. It could, for example, recognize an "A" even though the "A" is upside down or half the original size; developed by Widrow.

Adaptive linear network See Adaline.

Adaptive pattern-recognition processing A pattern-recognition procedure used in the SAVVY front end that makes educated guesses about the user input. See also Adaptive query recognition (Tello 1988, 27).

Adaptive production system A production system that can modify its production rules with experience (Smith 1989, 5).

Adaptive query recognition A language-recognition process that is used in the natural language front-end Savvy; a holistic approach to pattern matching. Adaptive query recognition avoids analysis of the sentence. It matches the query with the statement in its data base that most closely resembles the query. It answers the question of which statement in the data base best approximates the query. Contrast with the logic-based approach found in Clout (Rubin 1985, 46).

Adaptive resonance theory (ART) A self-organizing neural network noted for its autonomy, complexity, and power; based on outstar learning. It has the capabilities of categorizing input patterns without outside feedback, learning new patterns, recategorization, and immediate recall (Caudill May 1989, 57; Caudill Aug 1989, 61–67).

Adaptive robot A robot that can make adjustments to changes in its environment. It possesses enough artificial intelligence programming to process sensory information and use that information to give motor commands (Rosenberg 1986, 4).

Adaptive systems researcher A researcher interested in the properties of living organisms, particularly properties that contribute to adaptation such as self-modification and organization. These researchers have given impetus to the study of neural networks (Jorgensen and Matheus 1986, 31).

Adder The process that keeps track of information from filters and demons in a perceptron (Reece 1987, 52).

Address-induced representation The connecting of cells of a data structure by the addresses of the cells (Hillis 1985, 91).

ADEPT A battlefield management expert system developed by TRW using the expert system language ROSIE (Hunt 1986, 4).

Adequacy A measure of the number of different conditions in the knowledge domain with which an expert system can cope. In a medical expert system, the number of symptoms the expert system can handle is a measure of adequacy. Other important measures are breadth, accuracy, reliability, validity, practicability, adaptability, credibility, and generality (Marcot 1987, 44).

Ad-hoc polymorphism The polymorphism found in Common Lisp Object Oriented systems. It differs from standard polymorphism in that the system is more sensitive to argument types than is standard polymorphism (Gabriel Sep/Oct 1989, 41).

Admissibility theorem A means of ascertaning whether or not A*, in conjunction with a given heuristic, will always find the optimal solution to a problem. To find the optimal path it must be guaranteed that calculations of the remaining distance to the goal state be underestimates of the correct distance (Bratko 1986, 284; Chabris 1989, 286).

Admissible A property of search. When a search procedure is admissible, it means the procedure always finds the best solution path, not just any solution path (Luger and Stubblefield 1989, 165–166; Smith 1989, 1; Chabris 1989, 286; Bratko 1986, 273, 284).

Adventure Authoring Language A language designed for writing text adventure games, which is a combination of object-oriented programming, logic programming, and LISP (Amsterdam 1988, 18–39).

Advice taking The ability of some artificial intelligence programs to learn from instructions (Hayes-Roth et al 1983, 153; Barr and Feigenbaum 1981 vol 3, 345–349).

ADVISOR An advisory system for users of MACSYMA. It analyzes what the user is attempting to do, diagnoses the user's mistakes and gives the user advice on how to achieve his goal (Hunt 1986, 44).

Advisory system An expert system that emphasizes the use of advice rather than commands; used to make recommendations, not to make final decisions. Advisory systems also stress detailed explanation systems. "Advisory system" may be a more appropriate term than "expert system" for many applications (Hunt 1986, 44; Walters and Nielsen 1988, 165).

After inheritance The function in a frame-based system stored in an object's slot and applied after the inherited function is applied. In this arrangement the object function may be used to massage the data further after the more general inherited function has completed generating data. The object function may also be used simply to record the data produced by the inherited function. *Contrast with* Before inheritance (Walters and Nielsen 1988, 242–243).

After-when-modified demon A type of demon summoned after the value of a slot is altered (Matthews 1987, 80).

AGE An expert system tool developed at Stanford. AGE stands for attempt to generalize. Its development was influenced by Hearsay II. It is capable of using either a backward-chaining paradigm or a blackboard paradigm (Johnson 1986, 145; Hayes-Roth et al 1983, 196–198, 203–209; Harmon and King 1985, 140).

Agenda 1. A means of organizing goals in expert systems. A listing of prioritized activities waiting to be acted on. A means of control. A variation of a queue, with the exception that individual goals can be assigned priorities over other goals. This structure is useful in a situation in which goal priorities are subject to frequent change. The goal priorities are usually controlled by a rule set. An agenda can be reasoned about by an expert system. Other data structures used in organizing goals are tree structures, queues, and stacks. **2.** Agenda is also used to refer to conflict sets (Matthews 1987, 82; Hayes-Roth et al 1983, 16–17, 399; Brownston et al 1986, 281–282; Barr and Feigenbaum 1981 vol 1, 338–339; Tello 1988, 311; Harmon et al 1988, 173; Smith 1989, 7).

Agenda-based system A system that uses an agenda as a means of central control. The agenda can control which set of rules may be executed next. The agenda is a series of tasks that are not static, but may change throughout a program run. Tasks may be added or removed from the agenda because of the execution of other tasks, or as the result of the execution of a rule. There is an intense interaction between the agenda and the rest of the system as each influences the other. It is easier to follow the logic of an agenda-based system than a pure production system. Examples of agenda-based systems include CENTAUR, DENDRAL, and AM (Aikins 1990, 3–4).

Agenda element A decision element used to record the future sequence of knowledge-based rules which will be scrutinized in a blackboard system. One of three types of decision elements in a blackboard system; the other two are plan elements and solution elements.

Agenda manager A mechanism in an artificial intelligence application for scheduling events against a real or simulated clock.

AI/COAG A medical expert system that analyzes and interprets blood coagulation. It assists the physician in diagnosing diseases of hemostasis. AI/COAG was developed at the University of Missouri School of Medicine (Hunt 1986, 45).

AIMDS An expert system language developed at Rutgers University using LISP. A frame-based system that uses multiple inheritance, deductive and nondeductive reasoning, belief maintenance, analogical inference, and procedural attachment. AIMDS has a set of procedures to detect inconsistencies in the knowledge base and is capable of procedure oriented representation (Hunt 1986, 45).

AI/MM A medical expert system that makes interpretations of data in the area of renal physiology, which understands physiology, physics, and anatomy and uses this knowledge to interpret conditions. A rule-based system developed at Stanford University using MRS (Hunt 1986, 45).

AI representation language A language that must include the ability to deal with qualitative data, represent abstractions, and infer facts. It must be able to handle both general principles and details. Metalevel reasoning and complex meaning must be handled effectively (Luger and Stubblefield 1989, 30).

AI/RHEUM A medical expert system that does differential diagnoses of diseases of rheumatology. A rule-based system developed at the University of Missouri School of Medicine using EXPERT (Hunt 1986, 45).

AIRID An expert system used to identify aircraft. An amalgamation of a rule-based and semantic network representation. It was developed at the Los Alamos National Laboratory using KAS (Hunt 1986, 46).

AIRPLAN An expert system used to help carrier based aircraft avoid such problems as running out of fuel by warning the air operations officer of a potential problem and making recommendations for avoiding the problem. It was developed at Carnegie Mellon using OPS7 (Hunt 1986, 46).

AI system A program capable of knowledge acquisition, goal-directed behavior, and skill acquisition (Firdman 1986, 81).

AI workstation A computer designed specifically for artificial languages such as LISP, sometimes called a LISP machine (Mishkoff 1986, G-1).

AKO A Kind Of. A link used in object-oriented languages. A link between classes and superclasses. The values of slots are inherited through this link. *Contrast with* an Is-a (Amsterdam 1987, 15; Jackson 1986, 76).

AL A robotics control language developed at Stanford.

ALADIN An expert system that assists in finding currently existing alloys, or in designing alloys that will fit specific requirements (Hunt 1986, 46).

ALDOUS A human-simulation program that takes on a variety of personalities, including decisive ALDOUS, hesitant ALDOUS, radical ALDOUS, and saint ALDOUS. The program was designed by John Loehlin (Frude 1983, 170–171).

AlgebraLand A computer-aided instruction program that keeps an audit trail of the student's problem-solving process, which can be examined later (Waldrop 1987, 205–206).

Algorithm An abstract description of a procedure or a program. A step-by-step procedure that if followed will lead to a correct answer. Artificial intelligence programs rely less on algorithms than do conventional programs. Instead, they use heuristics, a procedure which does not guarantee a correct answer (Johnson 1986, 83–84; Brownston et al 1986, 441; Townsend, 1987b, 376; Winston and Horn 1984, 17; Townsend and Feucht 1986, 26).

Algorithmic solution A sequential fixed procedure for arriving at a solution, associated with procedural programming and guarantees a specified output. It is faster than a heuristic state space search and should be employed when possible. Heuristic state space search can be used for many problems that do not have algorithmic solutions.

Aliasing A distortion found in computer-produced images. It is produced by inadequate sampling of the signal (Tanimoto 1987, 392–394).

ALICE A logic-based experimental language developed at the Institut de Programmation in Paris (Hunt 1986, 47).

Allophone A unit of speech that stands for a unique sound in a word.

Alpha notation An extension of the LISP function FUNCALL, which is used in CmLISP and which allows parallel mapping (Hillis 1985, 37–41).

Alpha-beta algorithm *See* Alpha-beta pruning.

Alpha-beta pruning An algorithm used in game search, with two parameters, alpha and beta, which are used to prune a search tree. It prunes the search tree by cutting off branches that are known not to be useful. Example: In a game situation, assume an opponent has a devastating response to a move the home player is considering. Once this response is discovered, there is no need to waste time looking at other possible responses the opponent could make to that move. It is used to augment the minimaxing algorithm by eliminating those portions of the search space that cannot possibly give a good solution. Under certain conditions it has the capability of searching twice as deep as MINIMAX when both procedures are limited to the same number of static evaluations (Chabris 1989, 179–185; Forsyth and Naylor 1985, 183–188; Winston 1979, 115–122; Barr and Feigenbaum 1981 vol 1, 88–93; Townsend and Feucht 1986, 42; Winston 1984, 117–126; Knuth and Moore 1975, 293–297).

Alpha-testing Testing of an expert system after a successful prototype has been developed and before it is placed on site. In alpha-testing the adequacy, accuracy, and reliability of the system is tested. *Contrast with* Beta-testing (Marcot 1987, 44).

Alternate worlds reasoning A sophisticated what-if capability found in some expert systems.

Copies of the knowledge base are made with some changes to see how these changes would alter the solution (Schuler 1987, 101).

Alvey project   An AI project sponsored by the United Kingdom which is a response to the Japanese fifth-generation project (Hunt 1986, 47).

AL/X   A knowledge-engineering language using frames, rules, semantic nets, forward and backward chaining, truth maintenance, and certainty factors. It is built by Intelligent Terminals, Ltd., using PASCAL (Hunt 1986, 47).

AM   Automated Mathematician—developed by Doug Lenat for discovering mathematical concepts without outside help. It has the capability of learning from experience. Lenat calls the type of learning involved "discovery learning." Frames and rules are used for representing knowledge. It uses frames and slot filling to represent and modify concepts. It includes about 250 rules of thumb, which work in conjunction with the knowledge in the frames. It utilizes a survival-of-the-fittest process. Old frames are mutated and scores are assigned to the new frames. The low-scoring frames are dropped while the high-scoring frames end up with greater attention. Eventually these frames are used to develop new concepts. Example: Starting with general heuristic rules, a few primitive set concepts like equality and the empty set, it is able to derive mathematical operations like addition and subtraction. It goes even further by being able to assert, for example, that any even number can be expressed as the sum of two prime numbers. The author of AM holds that the flexibility available in LISP is one of the key reasons AM is able to show such originality. EURISKO is the successor program to AM (Johnson 1986, 191–193; Barr and Feigenbaum 1981 vol 1, 195–197; Waldrop 1987, 57–59; Forsyth and Naylor 1985, 212–214).

Ambiguity   The doublespeak found in human language, Example: "I hit the man with the ball." Did I hit the man with a ball, or did the man I hit have a ball in his hand? Dealing with ambiguity is a major challenge for language-understanding programs (Rubin 1985, 44; Barr and Feigenbaum 1981 vol 1, 208–211).

American Association for Artificial Intelligence (AAAI)   The society for artificial intelligence. The society publishes the *AI Magazine*. Its address and phone number are 445 Burgess Drive, Menlo Park, CA 94025, (415) 328-3123 (Harmon and King 1985, 250).

AML   A computer language used for programming robots. It was developed by IBM and is based on AL (Mishkoff 1986, 5–19; Rosenberg 1986, 7).

AMORD   A rule-based knowledge-engineering language using a forward-chaining paradigm. It uses truth maintenance and discrimination networks. It was developed at MIT using MACLISP (Hunt 1986, 47).

AMUID   A battlefield expert system. A realtime, rule-based system with certainty factors, it uses incoming information to identify enemy units (Hunt 1986, 48).

Analogical inference   The process of inferring similarities between two objects and using information about the known object to solve a problem concerning the unknown object. Example: Tigers have fur. Lions are like tigers. Lions probably have fur. Patrick Winston designed two programs, Macbeth and a cup-learning program, which used analogical inference. Both programs use a semantic network representation (Johnson 1986, 161; Barr and Feigenbaum 1981 vol 1, 146; Rosenberg 1986, 7).

Analogical means-end analysis   The process of using a previously solved problem to solve a new, somewhat similar problem. Operators are used to reduce differences between the two problems. *Refer to* Analogical problem-space (Rosenberg 1986, 7).

Analogical problem-space   A representation of a problem space in which each node represents a problem solution. The different problem solutions possess a degree of similarity. An operator transforms one problem solution to another similar problem solution. *Refer to* Analogical means-end analysis (Rosenberg 1986, 7).

Analogical reasoning A method of reasoning employing two separate systems that have some type of resemblance. One system is well understood. A characteristic of the well-understood system which somehow resembles the second system is applied to the second system to enhance understanding of the less understood system. Comparing love to a rose is an example of analogical reasoning. Both are beautiful, but both eventually wither away. There has been little success in employing this type of pattern matching in artificial intelligence. Frames are a prime candidate for dealing with analogical reasoning. An analogy can be made with frames by filling empty slots in a frame with corresponding attribute values from another frame. Assume a system with many different concepts that are represented as frames in a hierarchy. Assume another frame which represents a current problem to be solved. Now assume a rule base that actively compares the problem frame with the concept frames, and derives a best-fit score for each higher-level concept frame. The higher-level concept frame with the best score can be investigated further to see if a specialization of that frame produces an even better fit. The best-fit concept frame is then used to fill the slots on the problem frame. It is proposed by Doug Lenat that analogical reasoning rests not only on having a good representational technique, but more important on having access to a great deal of knowledge which can be efficiently searched for analogies. *See also* Analogical inference, a synonym (Lenat 1988, 73–74; Fischler and Firschein 1986, 44).

Analogical representation Representation found in some artificial intelligence programs that is somehow analogous to the structure it is representing in the real world. The structure of the representation gives information about the structure itself. An example of an analogical representation is a map of a city. The geometry theorem prover uses analogical representation. Diagrams of angles and figures are used to direct the reasoning process. Different types of knowledge representation differ in the degree to which they are analogical representations. A frame is closer to an analogical representation than is a propositional representational scheme. A propositional representational scheme is more of an analogical representation than is a procedural program which uses arrays of numbers and computations to represent objects. Direct representation is used interchangeably with analogical representation (Hayes-Roth et al 1983, 120; Barr and Feigenbaum 1981 vol 1, 200–206).

Analogy approach Machine learning that relies on learning through analogies. Other approaches to machine learning include empirical induction and discovery systems. CYC is an example of the analogy approach (Tello 1988, 509, 517).

Analysis by synthesis An image-comprehension procedure. *See also* Bottom-up comprehension (Forsyth and Naylor 1985, 86–87).

Analysis expert system An expert system that breaks down a problem in order to study or analyze a given situation. Example: MYCIN. *Contrast with* Synthesis expert system (Floyd 1988, 64).

ANALYST A real-time battlefield expert system that uses both frames and rules to interpret battlefield situations, which was developed by Mitre Corporation using FRANZ LISP (Hunt 1986, 48).

Anaphoria Using replacements in language. Pronouns are examples. Anaphoria is a problem with which computer language processors must cope.

Anaphoric reference A reference to an earlier word or phrase (Smith 1989, 10).

Ancestor A class from which an object inherits methods, slots or values. A parent is an immediate ancestor of an object.

Ancestor class A class that is related to and higher in the hierarchy than the class under consideration (Duntemann 1989, 132).

AND A logic operator that implies both statements it connects must be true in order for a consequent then to be true. Example: If X and Y then Z. Both X and Y must be true for Z to be true (Rosenberg 1986, 8).

AND elimination The ability to ascertain the truth of any of a set of conjuncts from the truth value of a conjunctive sentence. Example: If $A \wedge B$ is true, then both A and B are true. *See also* AND introduction (Luger and Stubblefield 1989, 61).

AND introduction The ability to ascertain the truth of a conjunction from the truth of its components. Example: If A and B are true, then $A \wedge B$ is true. *See also* AND elimination (Luger and Stubblefield 1989, 61).

AND/OR tree A graphic representation of problem reduction. A proof tree consisting of AND, OR nodes. For an AND node, each of the child nodes must be proved true for the parent node to be true. For an OR node, any one of the child nodes that is proved to be true is sufficient to prove the parent node true. This approach can be used for problems that can be decomposed into independent subproblems. *Compare with* State space, an alternative method of representing problems (Winston 1979, 102–105; Barr and Feigenbaum 1981 vol 1, 38–41; Levi and Sirovich 1976, 243–259).

AND-parallelism A parallelism employed in PROLOG-based systems in which each microprocessor is assigned a list of clauses and each microprocessor receives a subgoal from a goal list. Each subgoal must succeed for the supergoal to succeed. The different microprocessors must coordinate because all of the subgoals must be evaluated true for the supergoal to succeed. *Contrast with* OR-parallelism (Townsend and Feucht 1986, 179; Eadline 1989, 36).

Android A robot resembling a human being (Rosenberg 1986, 8).

AND-THEN A clause found in the expert system shell Goldworks which is in the consequent part of a rule and is only fired after the initial consequent has been fired. Example: Assume a set of rules consisting of both backward and bidirectional rules. During the backward-chaining process the AND-THEN components are not referenced. That is, no attempts are made to prove the AND-THEN components. After backward chaining is successful, the AND-THEN consequents are executed (Tello 1988, 309; Tello Jul/Aug 1989, 57).

ANGY A medical expert system used to diagnose coronary heart disease by the visual interpretation of angiograms (Hunt 1986, 49).

Animism The tendency to interpret animal and physical objects such as computers as having human characteristics like a soul. Joseph Weizenbaum, the developer of ELIZA, warns fiercely of this tendency. He feels it could eventually rob us of our humanism. He believes such terms as "understanding" and "love" characterizing human beings should not be attributed to computers (Frude 1983, 103–123).

ANNA A medical expert system that assists physicians in giving digitalis. Once the initial dosage has been given, ANNA monitors the patient's response to see if the predicted response is achieved. If the response is not as predicted, ANNA then makes further recommendations concerning dosage levels. It was developed at MIT using LISP (Hunt 1986, 49).

Annealing *See* Simulated annealing.

Answer extraction Producing the desired answer in a resolution-based procedure by finding the necessary substitutions for the original query so that the original query is proved true (Luger and Stubblefield 1989, 423, 431).

Antecedent A condition in a rule (Hunt 1986, 49).

Antecedent-consequent rule If-then-rule (Winston and Horn 1988, 580).

Antecedent-driven production system A forward-chaining production system (Michaelsen et al 1985, 307; Townsend and Feucht 1986, 40).

Antecedent reasoning   Forward chaining.

Anthropomorphize   The tendency to regard an inanimate object such as a computer as a human being.

APES   A PROLOG-based expert system shell that uses a number of types of inexact reasoning (Jackson 1986, 212).

APIARY   An artificial intelligence system developed by Carl Hewitt based on actor theory. Actor theory is based on independent entities that send and receive messages. It is an object-oriented system that uses an open-system architecture (Waldrop 1987, 124).

APL   A programming language best known for modeling and decision support, possessing a number of characteristics that make it suitable for artificial intelligence programming. Character strings may be treated as atoms or nested arrays. It possesses Boolean and numeric functions. It has a good interactive environment. APL is useful for building business applications that require a combination of numeric and symbolic processing. It is highly interactive. Structures may be created at run time. It uses a functional programming style (Brown et al 1987, 72–84).

APLICOT   A PROLOG-based knowledge-engineering language developed at the University of Tokyo. It has backward and forward chaining and certainty factors (Hunt 1986, 49–50).

Append   A function found in LISP that concatenates (joins) two lists.

Applicative language   A language that applies functions to objects, in which nested function calls are emphasized instead of sequences of statements, which are used in procedural languages. Side effects and assignment statements like $X = X + 1$ are avoided. Functional language. It is sometimes used loosely for the term declarative language. LISP is an applicative language (Eisenbach and Sadler 1985, 186; Brownston et al 1986, 442; Barr and Feigenbaum 1981 vol 2, 6; Hung 1986, 49; Allen 1985, 29).

Approximate pattern matching   The ability of an expert system to find a match even though the match may not be perfect with respect to certain less important attributes. This is a very important characteristic since most matches in the real world are not perfect. The Holland classifier and neural nets are examples of approximate pattern-matching expert systems. In a Holland classifier data are represented as a string of digits of 1's and 0's. Assume a pattern with a string of 12 digits. The first eight digits must be an exact match, but perhaps the last four digits of the string need only match more of the last four digits than any other competing pattern. An expert system that can fire a rule based on any four of possibly six conditions is another example of approximate pattern matching. The term partial pattern matching is roughly equivalent (Frey 1986, 163).

Approximate reasoning   1. The use of probabilities, fuzzy logic, and certainty factors in reasoning. A synonym for inexact reasoning.   2. Sophisticated inexact reasoning. Approximate reasoning can take into account the use of factors that measure the importance of a finding, the cost/risk ratio of obtaining a finding, the cost/risk ratio of carrying out a recommendation, and the frequency of association between a finding or symptom and a particular conclusion (Jackson 1986, 118; Forsyth and Naylor 1985, 5–6).

Approximate string matching   The attempt to match two strings that are similar in some way, but not exactly alike (Roach et al 1989, 24–27).

AQ   A machine language algorithm with the capacity to generalize rules instead of decision trees. AQ uses a single example and continues to generalize it until it begins to conflict with other examples. Then, the STAR procedure is used in an iterative fashion until all examples are generalized (Parsaye 1989, 29).

AQ11   An induction expert system that learns from examples. It uses the examples to build rules and classification schemes. The rules are then used to discriminate new patterns of data. In one test AQ11 was able to compete successfully with an expert system that was built by a knowledge engineer interviewing experts (Barr and Feigenbaum 1981 vol 3, 423–425).

AQUINAS An induction system that was probably the first to use hierarchical repertory grids (Parsaye 1988, 51).

Arc A directed link between nodes. Example: the link between New York and Los Angeles, which may be represented by distance or cost. An arc is a type of link that allows movement in only one direction. One may fly from New York to Los Angeles, but not from Los Angeles to New York. There is some disagreement in the literature as to whether or not an arc is required to have the quality of directedness. It is best to speak of a directed arc when speaking of an arc that can be traversed in only one direction (Chabris 1989, 286; Rettig Mar 1987, 15; Winston and Horn 1984, 169; Winston and Horn 1988, 574).

ARCHES A program written by Patrick Winston, which illustrates concept learning. *See also* Arch learning program (Hunt 1986, 50).

Arch learning program A program written by Patrick Winston which was able to learn concepts by being presented with examples. The program is given descriptions of various types of structures that are arches and other kinds of structures that are not arches. The program uses both types of examples to build the concept of an arch (Johnson 1986, 88–91, 157–158).

Architecture 1. The basic design of a computer program. 2. The fundamental underlying structure of an artificial intelligence system. Some of the more common expert system architectures include blackboard, production, backward-chaining, forward-chaining, frame-based, and hybrid systems (Hayes-Roth et al 1983, 20–23; Brownston et al 1986, 442; Chabris 1989, 286).

Argument 1. A conclusion and its premises in logic. 2. In PROLOG, terms that follow the predicate and are enclosed in parentheses. In the statement likes(john, mary), john and mary are arguments for the predicate likes. Sometimes arguments are referred to as objects. 3. The elements a procedure uses to complete its designated computation in LISP (Harrison and Tribble 1986, 66; Townsend 1987a, 32; Dos Reis 1988, 50; Winston and Horn 1984, 17).

Argument from informality of behavior An argument that holds that a program cannot be designed which will tell a human being what to do under all possible circumstances (Luger and Stubblefield 1989, 12).

ARGUS A computer program developed by Mildred Shaw that allows individuals to gain insight into their multiple selves (Frude 1983, 178–179).

Arity The number of objects or arguments in a PROLOG predicate. In the predicate likes(john, mary) the arity is two because there are two arguments—john and mary. If the predicate were, likes(john mary susan), the arity would be three because there are three arguments (Harrison and Tribble 1986, 66).

Arm That portion of a robot that connects the body and hand or effector. The portion of the robot that positions the effector. (Rosenberg 1986, 9).

Array 1. A data structure that uses coordinates to store and find data objects. 2. An active data structure used in connection machines. It is used to represent matrices and in image processing. It is much more efficiently utilized on connection machines than on conventional computers. Other active data structures include trees, butterflies, sets, strings, and graphs (Hillis 1985, 111–113; Hunt 1986, 51).

ART *See also* Adaptive resonance theory.

Articulate expert The part of an intelligent computer-aided instructional system that explains the reasoning behind the problem-solving steps taken (Smith 1989, 12).

Articulated joint A robot arm that has either a sliding or a rotary joint.

Artificial intelligence 1. An interdisciplinary approach to understanding human intelligence that has as its common thread the computer as an experimental vehicle. This definition emphasizes the fact that many disciplines contribute to the field of artificial intelligence. These professions include computer science, psychology, mathematics, physics, philosophy, engineering, and business. 2. The aspect of computer science that is concerned with building computer systems that emulate what is commonly associated with human intelligence. 3. An area of computer science that focuses on symbolic, nonalgorithmic methods of problem solving. 4. The building of programs that are characterized by symbolic representation, symbolic inference, and heuristic search. 5. Using symbolic pattern-matching methods to describe objects, events, or processes, and to make inferences. 6. The study of mental faculties through the use of computational models. This definition ensures the inclusion of vision and natural language processing. Major areas of artificial intelligence include robotics, general problem solving, machine learning, pattern matching, pattern recognition, logic programming, theorem proving, expert systems, game playing, decision making, planning, automatic programming, intelligent computer-aided instruction, natural language processing, vision, speech recognition, search, knowledge representation, knowledge acquisition, expert data base systems, neural networks, understanding systems, and uncertainty (Mishkoff 1986, 1–4 to 1–12, 1–15 to 1–18; Townsend 1987a, 243; Schildt 1987, 10–12; Charniak and McDermott 1985, 6; Townsend 1987b, 376; Parsaye and Chignell 1988, 9–10; Jackson 1986, 3; Waldrop 1987, 1).

Artificial intelligence language A computer language that excels in symbol manipulation, pattern matching, and flexibility in constructing knowledge structures. The flexibility in knowledge structures allow AI languages to handle the frequently unpredictable information packets found in artificial intelligence applications. The ideal AI language allows deferment of key decisions like amount of memory required and data typing until runtime. Artificial intelligence languages usually follow an applicative or declarative style of programming as opposed to the sequential style of programming found in conventional languages. This style of programming allows the greater flexibility needed in dealing with nonalgorithmic problems. The languages that generally fit these criteria include LISP, PROLOG, and Smalltalk. There are certain specialized expert system programs such as OPS5 which are called languages. These expert systems have enough built-in flexibility to qualify as languages. When does an expert system tool qualify as a language? There is no hard and fast rule but there are guidelines. A language should have flexible input/output capabilities, including the ability to print reports to a printer, the screen, or the disk, and access data from a file; basic knowledge structures, such as lists available which can be used to build more complex knowledge representation structures; a variety of iterative control structures and higher-level control features such as metarules. In speaking specifically of expert systems is it possible to do such things as enter your own procedure for computing confidence factors, or alter the explanation procedures to suit your needs? At the other extreme is a simple expert system shell that allows input of rules only through a menu system, and which permits little flexibility in output (Barr and Feigenbaum 1981 vol 2, 3–76).

Artificial life 1. A discipline concerned with the analysis and synthesis of artificial systems exhibiting the characteristics necessary for survival in a complicated and changing environment. 2. The study of artificial systems that have the behavior characteristics of natural systems (Goldberg 1988, 63).

Artificial neural system Neural network (Caudill Dec 1987, 46).

Artificial vision The branch of artificial intelligence devoted to the understanding of vision. Vision research is important in robotics and military applications (Rosenberg 1986, 10).

Askable flag   The predicate used in some expert systems to tell the computer that if the inference system cannot compute the value of a fact to ask the user for the value.

Assembly robot   A robot that has a relatively fixed task of putting together parts. Such robots are usually immobile (Rosenberg 1986, 11).

Assertion   A fact or belief in a data base or an expert system (Charniak and McDermott 1985, 321).

Assertion relation   A type of fact that allows a series of assertions for a given object. Example: The object "car" can have more than one assertion —car (Oldsmobile, red), car (Buick, green). *Contrast with* Functional assertion relation.

Assertion-time inference   Forward chaining (Charniak and McDermott 1985, 344).

Assimilation   The process of relating incoming data to previously known data.

Associationist theory   A theory that holds the underlying assumption that meaning is derived from an interconnection of related terms. The semantic network was originally devised to explore associationistic meaning (Luger and Stubblefield 1989, 338).

Association list   A list with a set of sublists. The first element of the sublist is a key that can be used to find and return the given sublist. It is possible to construct an association list in which one key is "grocery," and the associated sublist is made up of groceries that must be purchased. Another key may be "friends" and the associated sublist the names of the friends. It is sometimes called an a-list. *Contrast with* Property list. *See also* San Marco LISP Explorer (Winston and Horn 1984, 93–94; Townsend and Feucht 1986, 122).

Associative access   A search in object-oriented programming of a group of related objects dependent on the internal condition of the objects. Clustering, hashing, and B-tree indexing are techniques that greatly enhance associative access. Example: finding all airplanes that are scheduled to land in Chicago within the next day (Stein 1988, 33).

Associative analog inference   A set of techniques designed to find a path through an associative network (Charniak and McDermott 1985, 400).

Associative law   A law in logic that states (X AND Y) AND Z is equivalent to X AND (Y AND Z) (Schildt 1987, 225; Luger and Stubblefield 1989, 46).

Associative learning   Learning that takes place in neural nets. The system is trained on a set of patterns by fixing the visible units to represent the different patterns. Later, when only a partial pattern is presented the system is able to recall the previously learned pattern that most closely resembles the partial pattern. Two subtypes of associative learning are auto-association, and pattern-association. *Contrast with* Regularity detector (Ingraham et al 1988, 17).

Associative memory   **1.** The ability to access an object by name rather than by its address. Linked lists, arrays, balanced search trees, and hash tables are some of the means of implementing associative memory. It is employed in database searches and it uses a search that can find the necessary information by using a keyword or a pattern of keywords. Generally the memory searched is a two-dimensional array.   **2.** Memory that recalls information through the association of one stimulus with another. Human memory is associative in nature. Each memory is stored as a pattern of nodes. Related memories have patterns with nodes in common. When one memory pattern is activated the related memories become partially activated. Associative memory can perform parallel search. Example: when one remembers a name of someone a set of associations comes to mind. The associations may include the person's behavior, dress, or physical features. There is no single address in the brain that holds this information. This process is called associative memory. Currently, researchers are attempting to duplicate associative memory using neural nets. Associative memory is common to living organisms. An associative memory is reconstructive in nature. That is, one may recall an entire memory from a single association. Example: Recall an actor president. Contrast this with the type of memory found in computers. In computers information is usually recalled through the use of addresses. The term "content-addressable memory" is used interchangeably with "associative memory." There is a difference, however. Associative memory is more likely to be associated with human memory, whereas content-addressable memory is more likely to be associated with computer memory. Also, associative memory is able to find matches using more fragmented patterns than is possible with content-addressable memory (Chabris 1989, 47; Hillis 1985, 28; Tank and Hopfield 1987, 112; Josin 1987, 184; Kosko 1987, 137–144; Jorgensen and Matheus 1986, 36; Townsend and Feucht 1986, 179; Hunt 1986, 52; Lipvoski 1990, 16–18; Minker 1971, 453–504).

Associative memory model A neural network model that lends itself to such operations as visual processing (Josin 1987, 184–188).

Associative net Semantic net. The term "associative net" is less misleading than the term "semantic net" (Jackson 1986, 52; Charniak and McDermott 1985, 23, 400–405).

Associative triple The object attribute value. A type of knowledge representation that consists of an object along with its associated attributes and values. Example: The object "plane" with an attribute of type, and the value of the attribute type is "fighter" (Barr and Feigenbaum 1981 vol 2, 188).

Assume-mode choose One of two methods of choosing an alternative from a choice set in HEARSAY-III. This mode is chosen when there is a reasonable possibility that the choice could be withdrawn later. *Contrast with* Deduce-mode choose (Hayes-Roth, et al 1983, 311).

Assumption-based system A methodology used in belief-revision systems to keep track of the origin of propositions, which holds information about the nonderived propositions that generated it.

Assumption-based truth maintenance Hypothetical reasoning. This truth maintenance reasons with all the contexts in parallel. All the potential solutions are found and an evaluation function is used to find the best solution. Example: Assume a spreadsheet model. If there are 10 different versions of the spreadsheet in memory, all with different assumptions, then there are 10 different contexts. The assumption-based truth maintenance system reasons with all 10 contexts until it finds the context that is most appropriate. *Contrast with* Justification truth maintenance (Walters and Nielsen 1988, 271–272; Matthews Sep 1987, 84).

ASTA A knowledge-based consultation system that combines inferencing with distributed database management. It is able to work with external data bases (Cromarty et al 1986, 505–524).

Asynchronous computer A computer that can be used to solve a problem consisting of tasks the order of completion of which cannot necessarily be predicted. The asynchronous computer waits until specific prior tasks are completed before beginning subsequent tasks that require input from the prior tasks (Hunt 1986, 53).

Asynchronous design A design found in connection machines in which different components of the system do not have to be in synchrony. Such an architecture makes it easier to emulate asynchronous real-world phenomena. *Contrast with* Synchronous design.

Asynchrony Having the characteristic of open systems in which different parts of the system are sometimes required to run out of phase with other parts of the system and, at times, with the outside world. This is necessary in open systems because the requirement of synchronicity slows down the system greatly. Other characteristics of open systems include concurrency, decentralized control, ability to deal with inconsistent information, arms-length relationships, and continuous operations (Hewitt Premier Issue 1986, 45).

ATNS *See* Augmented transition network.

Atom **1.** Indivisible items in LISP. An atom may be numeric or symbolic. Examples: 15, food, and left-hand. In LISP an atom can have properties associated with it. **2.** A constant data symbol in PROLOG. Atoms are used to represent objects, or concepts. **3.** Atomic sentence (Luger and Stubblefield 1989, 50; Smith 1989, 14; Harrison and Tribble 1986, 66; Townsend 1987a 119–120; Charniak and McDermott 1985, 45; Winston and Horn 1984, 4, 19; Townsend and Feucht 1986, 243).

Atomic expression Atomic sentence (Luger and Stubblefield 1989, 50).

Atomic formula The sentences or propositions of logic. In PROLOG it is a predicate. Example: likes(john,mary). The objects john and mary are usually referred to as arguments, or objects (Charniak and McDermott 1985, 16, 321; Townsend and Feucht 1986, 59; Amsterdam Oct 1986, 18).

Atomic sentence A predicate along with its arguments in predicate calculus (Luger and Stubblefield 1989, 49).

Atomic symbol The predicate and its arguments in predicate calculus. Atomic formula.

Attached procedure A procedure that is attached to a slot of a frame. The procedure may be activated by a move to read the value of the slot, change the slot value, or delete the value. The procedure may do such things as ensure authorized access, ensure the new value is within a legal range, or compute the value. Attached procedures are a type of demon (Townsend 1987a, 126).

Attempt A structure found in the expert system tool Goldworks used to control backward chaining. Example: An attempt may be used to find one match or all possible matches for a goal (Tello 1989, 170).

Attenuation A term used in MYCIN that expresses the reliability of a rule. It is an expression of the confidence the expert has in the rule. Attenuation is a certainty factor for a rule. A rule with an attenuation of .90 is more reliable than a rule with an attenuation of .50 (Brownston et al 1986, 283).

Attribute A property or quality of an object that helps define the object. Color may be considered an attribute of a car. If the color of the car is red, then red is the value of the attribute color. An attribute in an expert system differs from attributes or variables in conventional programs. In artificial intelligence an attribute represents the concept with which the program reasons rather than being a memory location. An ai attribute generally has a nonnumeric value. An attribute in an ai program may have more than one value at a given time as opposed to a variable in a standard program that can have only one value at a given time. The advantage is that the inference engine in an expert system automatically reasons with all of the values to find a solution. *See also* Attribute value pairs; Multivalued attribute; Object attribute value triplets (Townsend 1987a, 119–123; Schildt 1987, 61–67; Harmon and King 1985, 54; Brownston et al 1986, 442).

Attribute-value element Working-memory element (Brownston et al 1986, 442).

Attribute-value pair A means of representing knowledge in which attributes can be assigned values. Example: The color of the car is red. The attribute is color and the value is red. This is a very simple type of knowledge representation. Expert system shells that use this type of knowledge representation are limited to only one object. In this there can only be one car represented. *Compare with* other more sophisticated types of knowledge representation, Frame; Object attribute-value; Semantic network (Townsend 1987a, 124; Townsend and Feucht 1986, 49).

Audio-response The portion of an artificial intelligence device that responds with a verbal reply to requests (Rosenberg 1986, 11).

Audit trail In an expert system the record of reasoning steps used to reach a conclusion (Wolfgram et al 1987, 299).

Augmented conceptual ranking An approximate ranking procedure used to rank facts according to certainty. It produces a uniform ranking of the facts. The procedure can be used to cut down on the time taken up by the expert having to constantly adjust and readjust the certainty ordering of objects (Parsaye and Chignell 1988, 245–249).

Augmented-term rewriting An important method found in the Bertrand language used to interpret rules that contain constraints. It is more sophisticated than most other constraint problem solvers. There are some problems that have constraint rules with so many unknown variables that most constraint problem solvers cannot handle the problem. The augmented-term rewriting method can often solve such problems (Rettig 1988, 16–17).

Augmented transition network (ATNS) A means of representing the syntactic structure of complex languages, which were invented to parse sentences efficiently. An ATN is used to decide if a sentence is grammatical. It tests to see what kind of word or phrase it encounters. An ATN asks what role a word may play in the sentence—subject, verb, object, and so on. An augmented transition network remembers what it learned about the sentence. This ability to remember allows ATNS to make fewer mistakes and to avoid the excessive inefficiency found in its predecessor, recursive transition networks (RTNS). Example: An ATN remembers the characteristics of the part of the sentence already parsed. The ATN is able to recall the number of the subject when parsing the verb phrase to ensure they match. This ability enhances the ability of the ATNS to accept or reject a sentence as grammatical quickly. An RTN does not have this ability and is less efficient. Although ATNS are primarily considered to be parsers, they also have the ability to carry out actions. Another characteristic sets ATNS apart from RTNS. ATNS were first used in Wood's LUNAR. *Compare with* its predecessors, Recursive transition networks; Template matching. ATNS, like recursive transition networks, make heavy use of recursive programming. Though ATNS are very expressive they are still inefficient. Their complexity makes it difficult to follow the program logic (Amsterdam Premier Issue 1986, 15; Johnson 1986, 105–109; Charniak and McDermott 1985, 206–209; Winston 1979, 169–173; 169–173; Barr and Feigenbaum 1981 vol 1, 263–267; Waldrop 1987, 68–71; Tello 1988, 410–411; Chabris 1989, 89–94, 286–287; Winston 1984, 303; Woods 1973; Obermeier 1987, 230).

Auto-association A learning paradigm used in neural nets. A type of associative learning in which each pattern presented associates with itself. That is, during the training phase the different patterns are presented and the net generates an internal pattern that is associated with the input pattern. This is continued until the net reliably responds to the different input stimuli. That is, it has learned all of the patterns and is able to discriminate among the different patterns. Later, the neural net is expected to identify the different patterns. For example, each input pattern during the learning phase may be a different type of plane. It is hoped that later it will be able to recognize the different planes even though the later patterns may not be exactly like the original. *Contrast with* Classification builder; Pattern-association; Regularity detector (Ingraham et al 1988, 17; Rumelhart and McClelland 1986, 161; Bayle 1988, 44).

Auto-associative (memory system) Having the ability to recall a previously stored memory based on data input that is somehow associated with the stored memory. The data input may be only a fragment of the stored memory (Obermeier and Barron 1989, 219).

Automata A machine-learning system. Automata systems are more expressive when compared to parameter learning systems. They also do not necessitate a unique least criterion. Automata are slower than parameter-based systems (Smith 1989, 16).

Automated knowledge acquisition The use of computers to acquire knowledge. Machine learning. *See also* Concept learning; Discovery learning; Knowledge elicitation; Neural network (Parsaye and Chignell 1988, 346–363).

Automated Mathematician *See* AM.

Automated Reasoning A program that uses clear notations, precise inference rules, and strategies to control those rules. It uses weak problem-solving methods. Some characteristics of automated reasoning include sound inference rules, general search strategies, and a uniform representation. It is also referred to as theorem proving (Luger and Stubblefield 1989, 409–410; Wos and Veroff 1990, 894).

Automated Reasoning Assistant An automated reasoning program that is used to explore problems in formal logic, mathematics, circuit design, and puzzles (Tello 1988, 420).

Automated testing A facility available in some expert systems that will automatically call into play all test cases that could possibly be affected by a revision in the rule base. EXPERT and EMYCIN are two expert system tools with this facility (Hayes-Roth et al 1983, 152–153).

Automate network One of a large number of interconnected components, which are used to build neural networks (Soulie and Mejia Dec 1988, 58).

Automatic classification The procedure of classifying knowledge and checking for possible errors in a kbms when a knowledge base is being modified (Brodie and Matthias 1986, 21).

Automatic deduction 1. The field of logic programming that is concerned with how to get computers to draw deductions automatically. Reasoning with incomplete information. The use of formal logic as a representational scheme and deductive logic as a means of inference. Logic Theorist, Advice Taker, the Boyer-Moore Theorem Prover, resolution-based systems, non-resolution-based theorem provers, logic programming, higher-order logic, and nonmonotonic logic fit under the rubric of automatic deduction. Almost any artificial intelligence system that deals with incomplete information owes some debt to automatic deduction. 2. The process of drawing conclusions using an inferencing method and a means of knowledge representation (Barr and Feigenbaum 1981 vol 3, 76–123; Smith 1989, 16).

Automatic discovery The use of AI procedures known as discovery programs to discover relation ships in data in a data base (Parsaye et al 1990, 40–42).

Automatic error detection A characteristic of an intelligent data base in which constraints are enforced by expressing the constraints in terms of pattern-matching rules. Such constraints are more comprehensive and easier to modify than constraints in ordinary data bases (Parsaye et al 1990, 42–43).

Automatic generalization The ability of organisms to extend a property of an object to other similar objects. Example: after noting that a number of species of birds fly assuming that all birds fly. A neurological explanation is the following: It is thought that each species of bird has a number of memory locations in common—wings, feathers, and so on. Since most of the species have these nodes in common, when a new species is introduced with these nodes it will also generalize to the node for flying. Automatic generalization is an emergent property of the thought processes of living organisms and of neural nets. In neural nets each connection strength is involved in storing many related patterns. The generalized associations are produced by the firing of these units which are responsible for multiple related memories (Rumelhart and McClelland 1986, 82; Zeidenberg 1987, 242).

Automatic goal generation The ability of an expert system to generate alternative goals automatically when attempting to solve a problem. Example: In medicine a physician may want to inquire about the possibility of a particular disease. The bare-bone response of an expert system is to give a yes or no answer to the user concerning the presence of the disease. The preferred alternative is for the expert system to be able to generate alternative possible diseases.

Automatic inspection An application of image-understanding programs in which objects are scrutinized for defects and the defective parts are discarded (Lawrence 1985, 47).

Automatic object An object found in C++ that is local to a given block of code and abandoned when the program exits from the block of code. When automatic objects are in use C++ is acting more like a functional language. *Contrast with* Static objects, where C++ treats objects more as they are treated in Smalltalk (Stroustrup 1987, 250).

Automatic programmer A programmer dedicated to developing computerized machine-learning systems, but not necessarily interested in emulating human learning. *Compare with* Cognitive model of learning (Jackson 1986, 205).

Automatic programming The area of artificial intelligence involved in constructing software that can produce programs from a user's specifications. Computer programs that can derive programs from being told what is wanted rather than how to accomplish the task. PSI, CHI, SAFE, DEDALUS, The Programmer's Apprentice, NLPQ, LIBRA, and PECOS are examples of automatic programs. The four general approaches to automatic programming are the deductive approach, the transformational approach, the high-level language approach, and the knowledge-based approach. Though PROLOG does not actually derive programs from user specifications, PROLOG is declarative in nature and does automate some of the procedural aspects of programming. *Contrast with* Induction expert systems, which build programs from examples and not from the user's specifications. *Contrast with* High-level language approach, which does give high-level specifications, and compiles these high-level specifications into lower-level programs, but which generally still follow the "how to" procedure of programming (Johnson 1986, 15–16, 94–95; Hayes-Roth et al 1983, 321; Mishkoff 1986, 1–18; Harmon and King 1985, 219; Barr and Feigenbaum 1981 vol 1, 9; Barr and Feigenbaum 1981 vol 2, 297–379; Tello 1988, 420–421).

Automatic storage management Procedures that allow the programmer to avoid having to deal with managing memory. Example: garbage collection. Automatic storage management is found in object-oriented systems and LISP (Pascoe 1986, 144).

Automatic theory formation The derivation of rules from examples (Smith 1989, 17).

Automatic writing The use of computers to write coherent stories. Unlike a word processor, the user of the program gives minimal input. The program is responsible for producing the output (Forsyth and Naylor 1985, 219–220).

Automaton A processing system that accepts signals and alters the internal state of the system as a result of a transfer function (Soulie and Mejia 1988, 58).

Autonomous learning Learning that is hinted at in some advanced neural networks like adaptive resonance networks. Its characteristics include the ability to categorize without outside help, associative parallel recall, the ability to learn and remember complex patterns, the ability to discriminate between significant and insignificant information, the avoidance of newly learned material interfering with previously learned material, the capability of reorganizing categories, generalization, and a large storage capability (Caudill Aug 1989, 62).

Autonomous robot A robot designed to operate in more uncontrolled environments than do most industrial robots. Autonomous robots must be more intelligent, more flexible, and more complex than industrial robots. Sensors, natural language capability, and problem-solving capability are characteristics of autonomous robots (Schildt 1987, 175–176).

Auxiliary function A function used as an argument to another function, a common practice in LISP (Hasemer 1984, 39).

Auxiliary objects Special knowledgeable objects found in some expert systems to handle special situations which may arise. This is in contrast to most objects which stand for a real-world object or concept (Jackson 1986, 194).

Availability heuristic A cognitive bias in which an individual is likely to assign a higher confidence level to an event which can more easily be recalled (Parsaye and Chignell 1988, 241).

Average of minimums A method for calculating confidence factors. Assume a set of rules with the same conclusion. Each rule has confidence factors for each premise and a confidence factor for its conclusion. Find the minimum confidence factor for each rule. Take all the minimums and find their average. The result is the average of minimums. Other methods of calculating confidence factors include confirmative of minimums, confirmative of products, maximum of minimums, maximum of products, average of products, and weighted average. The problem at hand dictates the most appropriate method for computing confidence factors (Shafer May/Jun 1989, 71).

Average of products A method of calculating confidence factors. Assume a set of rules with the same conclusion. Each rule has confidence factors for each premise and a confidence factor for its conclusion. Multiply all the confidence factors in rule one and save the result. Repeat this procedure for each subsequent rule. Compute the average of these products to find the average of products. Other methods of calculating confidence factors include confirmative of minimums, confirmative of products, maximum of minimums, maximum of products, average of minimums, and weighted average. The problem at hand dictates the most appropriate method of computing confidence factors (Shafer May/Jun 1989, 71).

Avl-tree A balanced binary tree in which the left and right subtrees can have a height difference of at most one. Each subtree must also be an avl-tree (Bratko 1986, 241).

Axiom The initial facts in a predicate calculus system. *Contrast with* Theorem (Charniak and McDermott 1985, 20).

Axiomization The use of sentences of first-order logic to represent a problem (Smith 1989, 17).

Axon The output portion of a neuron or neural net processing unit. The part of a nerve cell that carries the nerve impulse away from the cell body (Obermeier and Barron 1989, 219; Stevens 1985, 288–289).

B

Backed-up value The value assigned to a node in a game tree, which is derived from the values below it (Forsyth and Naylor 1985, 188).

Back propagation A learning algorithm that changes the weights in the system by means of an error signal that travels backward from the outputs to the inputs. *See also* Back propagation rule (Obermeier and Barron 1989, 219).

Back-propagation network A neural network that is based on the back propagation rule (Caudill Jun 1988, 54–59).

Back-propagation rule A learning algorithm found in neural networks that uses a generalized version of the gradient descent procedure. A more powerful version of the delta rule. Back-propagation networks consist of three or more layers of processing units. In contrast with the Delta rule, it is capable of computing deltas for hidden units. The back-propagation rule can be divided into two phases: The first phase is called the forward phase and consists of the stimulus being presented and propagated through the network to compute the output value y for each unit. This output is then compared to the target value and the difference is computed. In the second phase, the backward phase, the differences (errors) are computed for all output units and these differences (errors) are propagated back through the neural network until all differences (errors) are computed. Then, the differences are used to compute the weights at the synapses. The importance of the third, hidden layer of the neural network is that it allows the system to develop internal representations of the input stimuli. Such systems are then capable of doing such things ashandling the exclusive-OR. The draw backs of the back propagation rule are that it requires a large number of training trials, it is slow, it is unstable over time, and it is susceptible to finding false minima. A momentum term is added to the equation to reduce the problem of false minima. The back propagation rule is used in supervised networks. *Contrast with* the Kohonen self-organizing network, which is used in unsupervised learning. *Contrast with* Hebb's rule. The back-propagation rule is being used in both speech and vision systems. It is also referred to as the "generalized delta learning rule." *See also* Generalized delta rule for more information (Rumelhart and McClelland 1986, 328–330; Jones and Hoskins 1987, 155–162; Caudill Feb 1988, 61; Bayle 1988, 43; Caudill Jun 1988, 54, 58)

Backtracking A part of the search procedure of a number of artificial intelligence languages. It is a means by which an algorithm can recover from blind alleys. PROLOG is the best known example of languages that use backtracking. When a portion of a multiple goal fails, the search mechanism of PROLOG backs up in the data base it is searching and finds alternative values for the variables in the goal. Backtracking is one of the primary features of PROLOG that distinguishes it from conventional procedural computer languages. Backtracking is often very useful when the knowledge is not well understood. As the user gains greater understanding of the knowledge base, he or she can begin to eliminate some of the backtracking, so as to make the program more efficient. Backtracking can be very time consuming. It is frequently desirable to employ complex pattern matching to cut down on excessive backtracking. Backtracking may be considered a type of nonmonotonic reasoning. Backtracking is employed in some sophisticated expert system tools. *Contrast with* Chronological backtracking, which is backtracking to the most recent state, not simply an earlier state. *See also* Deep backtracking; Dependency-directed backtracking, Intelligent backtracking; selective backtracking; Shallow backtracking. *Contrast with* Constraint logic programming (Bharath and Sklar 1985, 51; Thompson and Thompson 1986, 25; Townsend 1987a, 50–53, 99–100; Hayes-Roth et al 1983, 399; Brownston et al 1986, 442; Sterling and Shapiro 1986, 97, 99; Townsend and Feucht 1986, 146; Jay and Knaus Mar 1989, 19–24; Luger and Stubblefield 1989, 119; Charniak and McDermott 1985, 266; Knaus 1988, 18).

Backus-Naur form (BNF) A version of context-free grammar used to delineate programming languages (Luger and Stubblefield 1989, 318).

Backward chaining A computer-implemented control strategy and problem-solving method that uses a chain of inference steps. In backward chaining one begins with an hypothesis and attempts to prove the hypothesis by proving the assumptions true that support the hypothesis. Example: To prove a person has a cold one must find the presence of the necessary symptoms—sneezing, fever, and so on. This type of inference process is frequently used in expert systems. Another way to describe backward chaining is working from a goal state to an initial state. It is most effective when there are a small number of goal states and a large number of initial states. Medical diagnosis, where there may be a large number of symptoms (initial states) and a relatively small number of diseases (goal states), is an appropriate application of backward chaining. Backward chaining is appropriate when an hypothesis or a set of hypotheses can be formulated. It is preferred over forward chaining, when a large number of rules can match the facts, thus producing combinatorial explosion. In such a situation a backward-chaining approach can greatly prune the search space. Finally, it may be preferred to forward chaining when all of the data cannot be given at the outset, but instead must be given as the problem solution progresses. Backward-chaining systems typically do not allow the complex type of pattern matching found in forward-chaining systems. Backward chaining appears to the user as more purposeful than forward chaining. Backward chaining is also known as top-down processing, consequent reasoning, and backward reasoning. Chaining refers to the chain of rules used to prove the hypothesis. The process of backward chaining can become complex. It may be worthwhile to describe a typical backward-chaining algorithm for an expert system in a bit of detail. Given a particular hypothesis, the inferencing system first checks to see if the hypothesis is a built-in clause. Then, it checks to see if the hypothesis matches a fact in the fact base. If it does the goal is proved. If not, it may find an askable fact in the fact base. If an askable fact is found, then the user is asked if the fact is true. If no askable fact can be found, then rules are checked to see if the hypothesis matches the conclusion of a rule. If the hypothesis matches the conclusion of a rule, then the inference engine attempts to prove the premises of the rule. Once the premises are proved, then the hypothesis is proved. To prove each premise it is necessary to repeat the above process of checking to see if the premise is a built-in clause, if it can be matched to a fact in the fact base, or if it can be matched to the conclusion of another rule. The depth of this process is a function of the complexity of the knowledge. Backtracking can be employed, making the process even more complex: Assume a rule with two premises and common variables in the two premises. Assume the first premise is proved but the second premise fails. With the failure of the second premise backtracking is brought into play. The backtracking mechanism will go to the first clause in the rule, attempt to find new values for the variables in that clause, and then return to the second clause with new variable bindings. If even this fails, the rule may eventually fail and another rule with the same premise may be tried. If this rule fails, and no rules with the same premise can be found then the failure could cause the initial hypothesis to fail. *Compare with* Forward chaining; Rule-value method. MYCIN and PROSPECTOR are two expert systems that employ backward chaining (Townsend 1987a, 139–142, 153–154; Schildt 1987, 64–67; Hayes-Roth et al 1983, 399; Winston 1979, 135–136; Walters and Nielsen 1988, 196–197; Parsaye and Chignell 1988, 256–257; Harmon and King 1985, 54–57; Brownston et al 1986, 15–17; Luger and Stubblefield 1989, 89; Chabris 1989, 116; Hunt 1986, 58–59; Gifoney 1986, 58).

Backward-propagation error correction A procedure used in teaching neural networks. An input produces an output. The output is compared with the desired output. Adjustments are made in the weights in the neural net so that the true output more closely resembles the desired output. The backward-propagation error correction procedure can be used to teach a neural network to discriminate different objects on an assembly line (Chabris 1989, 287).

Backward reasoning Reasoning from an initial hypothesis—proving the initial hypothesis by ascertaining the truth value of the assumptions of the initial hypothesis. *See also* Backward chaining, for a computer implementation of backward reasoning (Kowalski 1985, 161).

Backward rule A rule used exclusively for backward chaining. With a backward rule pattern matching starts with the head (conclusion) of the rule. *Constrast with* Forward rule.

BACON A series of data-driven, concept-learning programs that are used to rediscover scientific laws. These programs have been used to derive Ohm's law, Kepler's laws, and Newton's law of universal gravitation. The Bacon programs have production rules that search the data looking for patterns that will trigger the production rule. The triggering of a production rule creates a term. The term organizes and explains the relationships in the data. The quotient creation term is one example. If the quotient production rule detects a pattern in which two variables are varying monotonically and the slope is variable, the production creates a term that is the quotient of the two variables (Barr and Feigenbaum 1981 vol 3, 401–406).

Bag A class of objects in object-oriented programming in which objects of different types may be stored. The order of storage is not important and duplicate objects are allowed. Compare with sets that do not allow duplicates (Minsky 1985, 136; Barr and Feigenbaum 1981 vol 2, 39–41; Smalltalk/V 1986, 81).

B* algorithm A search procedure used in artificial intelligence applications in chess. It attempts to find the best available move and also shows that none of the other available moves can match the best available move. Two different algorithms are used to evaluate each node. One algorithm is an optimistic algorithm and the other is a pessimistic algorithm. When the optimistic value of the most promising move becomes greater than the pessimistic value of the next most promising move the most promising move is then made (Smith 1989, 17; Forsyth and Naylor 1985, 189–194).

Bandwidth search A search procedure used in an ordered state-space search. Each nongoal node n must satisfy the following two requirements: 1. $h^*(n) <= h(n) + e$. 2. $h(n) - d <= h^*(n)$ (Smith 1989, 19).

Banyan-type network A network topology used in connection machines which is a type of logarithmic network that has only one path between any input output pair. Other topologies include Clos networks, rings, trees, grids, delta networks, hashnets, shuffle-type topologies, and cross-bars (Hillis 1985, 59).

Base class A parent class (Stroustrup 1987, 9).

Base fact A fact found in the data base of a PROLOG program prior to a program run. *Contrast with* Derived fact (Shmueli et al 1986, 248).

Base relation A set of facts in PROLOG, all of which have the same head predicate (Shmueli et al 1986, 250).

Basic probability assignment The certainty value assigned a hypothesis in the Shafer-Dempster theory of evidence (Townsend and Feucht 1986, 174).

Basic resolution unit (BRU) The smallest amount of change in position that a robot can detect.

Bayesian inferencing Probabilistic inference. *See also* Bayes' theorem (Forsyth and Naylor 1985, 18–24).

Bayes' theorem A statistical method of dealing with uncertainty employed in some expert systems. Bayes' theorem states that if the user has an estimate of the probability of a hypothesis and an understanding of how some prior event can affect the probability of the conclusion, then information about the prior event can be used to modify the value of the probability of the hypothesis. Bayes' theorem is expressed in the following equation: $P(H|E) = [P(E|H)P(H)] / [P(E|H)P(H) + P(E|\text{not } H)P(\text{not } H)]$. This equation may be interpreted as the probability of the hypothesis H, given that event E has occurred. $P(E|H)$ is the probability of the event assuming the hypothesis is true. $P(H)$ is the probability of the hypothesis. Take the example of a business wanting to know the value of giving a screening test to job applicants. Of the current workers who are considered quality workers, about 80 percent passed the screening test previously. Only 40 percent of those who are considered poor quality workers could pass the screening test. About 60 percent of all workers are defined as quality workers. If only workers who pass the screening test are to be hired, what is the probability of these workers being quality workers? The following equation applies: $p(H|E) = [(.80)(.60)]/[(.80)(.60) + (.40)(.40)] = (.75)$. Notice the user has been able to go to the company computer to obtain the frequencies for workers who are considered quality or poor quality and whether or not they passed the screening test. If such frequencies are available, then using Bayes' equation may be justified. The extent to which these frequencies must be guessed is the extent to which error is introduced into the calculation. Example: In medicine the user may not know the frequencies with which people who have a particular symptom will have a given disease and how many people with the symptom will not have the disease. These frequencies will then have to be estimated. Also, in many real-world situations there may be more than one prior event. In medicine the prior events may be four or five symptoms. Bayes' equation can be applied in such cases, but the assumption is that the events of symptoms which contribute to the probability estimate are independent. What this means is that the occurrence of one symptom has nothing to do with the occurrence of another symptom. This is a tenuous assumption in the disease example. As this assumption is violated the probability estimate becomes to some extent inaccurate. In other situations the independence assumption may be less tenuous. Assume a burglary system which has three types of alarms. One is sensitive to motion, another to heat, and the third to sound. Each alarm is based on a different underlying factor and each is reasonably independent of the others. In this case Bayes' theorem is more applicable. Another necessary assumption is that if a given event is assigned a probability p, then its negation must be assigned $1-p$ as a probability. Example: The possible outcomes for predicting rain are either it is raining or it is not raining. If the probability of rain is .6, then the probability of it not raining must be .4, since the two probabilities must sum to one. There are no other unknown categories and only one category can be true at a given time. If there is a situation in which the outcome could be two categories being true at a given time or there is an unknown category, then other means of analysis may be more appropriate. (*See* Shafer-Dempster theory of evidence as an alternative.) Bayesian probability is used in the Prospector expert system with enough success to give empirical support to the use of Bayes' equation in some settings. MYCIN uses ad-hoc certainty factors because it was believed the necessary assumptions of Bayes' theorem could not be met. There is disagreement concerning when the foregoing assumptions are violated if the Bayes equation may still be better than ad-hoc approaches such as certainty factors. Certainty factors may simply be a special case of the application of the Bayesian equation. Recent empirical research indicates Bayesian inference may be superior to confidence factors even when the assumptions are being violated (Borden 1987, 50; Shepard 1988, 11; Lecot and Parker 1986, 37; Hayes-Roth et al 1983, 94; Charniak and McDermott 1985, 460–465; Townsend and Feucht 1986, 173; Parsaye and Chignell 1988, 217–223; Tello 1988, 107–110; Morawski 1989, 44–48; Duda et al 1976, 1075–1082).

Beam search An extension of breadth-first search and the A* algorithm. It is like breadth-first search in that it explores the search tree level by level. It differs from breadth-first search in that at the next level it only chooses a selected number of the most promising nodes. It differs from the A* algorithm in that it is adjusted to abandon unpromising paths. It is called the beam search because it moves through the search space by only illuminating a small area at any one time. This small area consists of a designated set of the most promising paths. An elaboration may help: A set of X training instances are randomly chosen. This set of X training instances is called the beam width. Each concept in the set is generalized by eliminating a single condition for each concept. Eliminate hypotheses that are highly unlikely. Examine each concept left to see if it handles all of the training instances. The concepts that are capable of handling all of the training instances are placed in a set of output concepts. Repeat the above steps until a specified set of concepts in the set X are left. HARPY is a natural language processing program that uses beam search. The comparison techniques HARPY uses eliminate sentences that begin correctly, but which contain a word that does not seem to fit. Using beam search, the program may not necessarily find the best interpretation of the sentence, but beam search is quick at arriving at an answer. It is most applicable in situations in which there is a good measure of distance to the goal, and in which it is probable that a good path can be found among the most likely paths at each level (Winston 1984, 96, 100; Hayes-Roth et al 1983, 122; Barr and Feigenbaum 1981 vol 1, 350–351; Winston and Horn 1984, 178; Barr and Feigenbaum

1981 vol 3, 411–415; Smith 1989, 20–21; Winston and Horn 1988, 574; Lowerre and Reddy 1980, 340–360).

Before demon A demon that is invoked when access to the value of a slot is being attempted. A before demon is frequently used to guard against unauthorized access to the value of a slot (Matthews 1987, 80).

Before inheritance The function stored in a frame-based system in a child's slot is applied before the inherited function is applied. The function in the child's slot may be used to analyze the data to determine if the inherited function may be applied. It could also be used as a preprocessor, modifying data so that the data can be used by the more general inherited function. *Contrast with* After inheritance (Walters and Nielsen 1988, 241–242).

Behavioral hierarchy Causal hierarchy. The objects in a system are represented according to their behavior. *Compare with* Structural hierarchy, which represents more shallow knowledge, and Functional hierarchy, which represents deeper knowledge (Townsend and Feucht 1986, 72–73).

Behaviorally object-oriented data base management system An object-oriented data base system that supports complex objects and procedures that are encapsulated in the objects such that data within the objects can only be accessed by sending the appropriate message which will activate one of the procedures within the object. *Contrast with* Operationally object-oriented data base management system (Manola 1990, 32).

Behavior inheritance The inheritance in object-oriented programming of the methods of a parent object. The methods of an object determine the object's behavior. Method inheritance (Gabriel Mar 1989, 55–56).

Belief A statement the validity of which is uncertain, but which is assumed to have some truth value. Certainty factors are frequently used as a measure of belief. *Contrast with* Fact which is generally considered to have more truth value than belief. Both beliefs and facts may be found to be false (Brownston et al 1986, 442).

Belief revision The ability of an expert system to be able to withdraw facts when they are found to be in error and to withdraw any conclusions that have been derived based on those facts. Dependency records are necessary to keep a record of the different inferential steps that have taken place. The information in the dependency records can then be used to withdraw the necessary fact and conclusions when it is found a given fact is invalid. The two ways a belief-revision system keeps a record of where a proposition in the knowledge base came from are through justification-based and assumption-based approaches. The term "nonmonotonic logic" is associated more with logic-based systems. Truth maintenance is a type of belief-revision system (Hayes-Roth et al 1983, 75–82; Barr and Feigenbaum 1981 vol 2, 72–76; Martins 1990, 58–62).

Belief sets The potential set of outcomes for a proposition that are available in an expert system. Some systems allow propositions to be evaluated as only true or false. This type of system is referred to as a two-element belief set. A three-element belief set includes the possibility of unknown. A four-element belief set includes uncertainty of a possible outcome (Tello 1988, 478–480).

Belief system An artificial intelligence program that serves as a model of cognition in the study of human beliefs. PARRY is an example of such a program. It consists of a group of beliefs along with procedures for deriving new beliefs. PARRY is a belief system that models paranoid thought processes (Barr and Feigenbaum 1981 vol 3, 65–74).

Bernstein, Alex The man who is noted for his development of computer programs that play chess. The heuristics he developed were a significant contribution to artificial intelligence (Mishkoff 1986, 2–14).

Bertrand A general-purpose constraint programming language. It is rule based, permits definitions of new constraints, has conditional clauses, uses recursion and Booleans, allows constraints on other constraints, and has abstract data types (Rettig Feb 1988, 15–17).

Best-first search A heuristic search that is a generalization of breadth-first search. A satisfice type of search and not necessarily an optimal type of search. The node that has the closest estimated distance to the goal is the most promising node. Best-first search maintains an open list that holds potential solution path states. Best-first search sorts these states according to their level of promise. The most promising state is chosen first. If best-first search takes a path that proves to be a dead end, it can backtrack by recalling the next best path on the open list. It is a more global type of search as compared with hill climbing. That is, in best-first search everything in the open list is sorted, not simply the children of the most recently considered node. Best-first search's ability to backtrack from blind alleys is another advantage it has over hill climbing. Best-first search is most applicable when there is a good measure of distance to the goal and when there is a high probability of blind alleys. The difference between best-first search and branch-and-bound search is that best-first search uses expected remaining cost as an estimate, not costs that have thus far been accumulated. Best-first search's path through the search tree is likely to jump around more than other types of searches. It is also reasonably likely to find shorter paths than other types of searches since it is always looking for the shortest path to the goal. The search mechanism in AM is inspired by best-first search (Haley 1987, 173–175; Wolfgram 1987, 66; Winston 1979, 99; Barr and Feigenbaum 1981 vol 1 59–60; Sterling and Shapiro 1986, 292–294; Barr and Feigenbaum 1981 vol 3, 441; Chabris 1989, 287; Luger and Stubblefield 1989, 102, 153–156; Winston and Horn 1988, 574; Winston 1984, 96–102).

Beta reduction A process found in CmLISP that changes a two-argument function into a function that reduces the elements of a Xector to one value (Hillis 1985, 41).

Beta-testing On-site testing of an expert system. *Contrast with* Alpha-testing (Marcot Aug 1987, 44).

Beta token A token used in the OPS5 language. It is made up of a number of pointers to working memory elements and a flag that tells if the list of tokens is to be added to or deleted from the system's saved state. The list of tokens represents a match for the patterns or a partial set of the patterns in a rule (Forgy and Shepard 1987, 39).

Bidirectional associative memory system A two-layer neural network characterized by stability, unsupervised encoding, and recalling binary vector pairs. Bidirectional associative memory systems can be used in real-time pattern matching and in parallel systems (Simpson 1988, 50–57).

Bidirectional chaining Switching from reasoning from facts (forward chaining) to goals (backward chaining).

Bidirectional inheritance The use of downward and upward inheritance (Epp et al, 1988, 830).

Bidirectional reasoning A control strategy that switches between forward and backward chaining as the situation warrants one or the other control strategies. A bidirectional strategy is useful in a diagnostic situation in which there are many potential problem states. The forward chaining is employed to determine which problem states are relevant for the given symptoms. Then, backward chaining is employed to test the rules that are relevant to the selected problem states. A synonym is "mixed-mode reasoning" (Wolfgram 1987, 68).

Bidirectional rule A rule that can be used in either forward- or backward-chaining mode (Hu 1989, 254).

Bidirectional search A search that starts from both ends of a search space and meets in the middle (Hayes-Roth et al 1983, 68; Barr and Feigenbaum 1981 vol 1, 51–53).

Binary dictionary A dictionary based on a binary tree, in which all left branch nodes are less than the mother branch and all right branch nodes are greater than the mother branch. Both branches order their subbranches. A binary dictionary increases search efficiency (Bratko 1986, 214).

Binary image A black and white image represented in the computer's memory as an array of 0's and 1's. Since there are no gray areas it is easier for the computer program to recognize shapes. Binary picture (Schildt 1987, 126–131; Winston and Horn 1984, 151, 153).

Binary message A message in object-oriented programs that has one argument, a receiver, and a message selector. Example: 'hello', 'there'. The object that receives the message is 'hello'. The argument is 'there'. The message selector is the comma (Rubin Aug 1985, 28; *Smalltalk/V 1986, 32).*

Binary picture *See* Binary image.

Binary resolution An inference rule that derives a new clause from two clauses through unification of the predicates that are equivalent but of the opposite sign (Tello 1988, 418).

Binary tree A tree in which each node has only two children. In LISP, a binary tree can be represented by nested lists. Each list consists of atoms or lists that represent the names of the nodes and the children of the node. The first item of the list is always an atom and represents the node, and the second and third items represent the children of the node. The children of the node may be either atoms or a list. If the child is a terminal node, the child is called a leaf and is represented by an atom. If the child is a nonterminal node, then the child is represented by a list. Binary trees are used in data bases and in mathematical optimization programs (Minasi Jun 1988, 25; Winston and Horn 1984, 74–75).

Binding 1. the process whereby a calling routine obtains the address of the called routine. 2. The process of establishing room in memory for the value of parameters. The amount of room in memory set aside is a function of the type of value. The value could be a string, an integer, real, and so on. Each of these types requires a different amount of memory. Languages vary as to the type of binding used. Two types of binding are early binding and late binding (dynamic binding). These two types of binding have important implications for the speed and flexibility of the language. 3. The process of assigning a value to a variable. This definition of binding should be avoided. The assignment of a value to a variable should be referred to as assignment (Valdex-Perez 1986, 35; Baker 1987, 41; Thompson and Thompson 1986, 26; Townsend 1987a, 39–42; Winston and Horn 1984, 42; Townsend and Feucht 1986, 59; Hunt 1986, 60; Duntemann 1989, 132).

Binding pair A variable along with a value that is assigned to that variable (Valdex-Perez 1986, 34).

Binding time The time when a variable is assigned to a type. In conventional languages variables are assigned types at compile time (early binding). In artificial intelligence languages variables are more frequently assigned to a type at run time, when the variable is assigned a value. Late binding lends flexibility to programs at the cost of speed (Bernat 1987, 42).

Binocular stereo problem The problem of how to estimate the distance from the perceiver to the scene being analyzed by employing two separate perspectives (Winston 1984, 335).

Binocular vision Stereo vision (Barr and Feigenbaum 1981 vol 3, 249).

Biological assumption The assumption that the neurons of the human brain fire in an all-or-none fashion and that information processing is digital rather than analog. Although it appears that neurons do fire in an all-or-none manner, it still does not prove that the brain processes information digitally as the modern digital computer does. There is, for example, some evidence indicating analog processing in the brain (Lawrence 1985, 161).

Bioprogram hypothesis The contention that the structure of the human brain has evolved so that it is innately receptive to the learning of language. Evidence for this comes from the fact that certain parts of the brain must be intact for language to develop, and there are critical periods of brain development during which humans are most receptive to learning. The almost effortless way children learn seems to indicate that learning human language is more than simply copying what others say (Waldrop 1987, 72).

Bitmap A two-dimensional image of a scene (Chabris 1989, 198).

Bit representation A single bit is used to mark a data structure as a member of a set. Other types of representation are tag and pointer (Hillis 1985, 92–93).

blackboard A common memory location for AI systems that use a blackboard architecture. It is used to hold intermediate results. There are independent modules that will post data to the blackboard and use data from the blackboard in new computations. These modules are sometimes referred to as a group of collaborating experts. The blackboard may consist of two parts: the domain blackboard (reasoning about the domain) and the scheduling blackboard (reasoning about scheduling). Hearsay-II, Hearsay-III, and AGE are the best known expert system tools which use a blackboard architecture. *See also* Blackboard architecture for more information (Minsky 1985, 138; Johnson 1986, 132–133, 143–146; Hayes-Roth et al 1983, 11, 16, 399; Barr and Feigenbaum 1981 vol 1, 343–346).

Blackboard architecture This type of architecture was first developed for speech-understanding systems. Hearsay I was the first speech-understanding system to use a blackboard architecture. Later, the blackboard architecture was adapted for use with expert systems. The three essential elements of a blackboard system include the blackboard, a scheduler, and knowledge sources. The knowledge sources are best thought of as a group of cooperating experts. The knowledge sources add facts to, or use facts from a common memory—the blackboard. The blackboard is partitioned so that it can be used at different levels of abstraction. The blackboard may be thought of as the mechanism for communicating intermediate results between the knowledge sources. The scheduler is responsible for scheduling which knowledge source is currently active. The flow of control, though controlled by the scheduler, is to a great extent really controlled by the data being supplied to the blackboard. The flow of control is data driven. That is, the scheduler can opportunistically cause attention to be turned to another aspect of the problem because new information has been made available. The following is an example of a three-dimensional blackboard: The horizontal axis is arranged according to the time the data are received. For example, a sentence is entered from left to right on the horizontal axis. The vertical axis represents levels of abstraction. A lower level of abstraction in analyzing sentences is the incoming sound waves. Higher levels of abstractions are words, phrases, and entire sentences. The third axis attaches certainty to each hypothesis on the blackboard. A particular knowledge source is triggered when information is posted to the part of the blackboard that the knowledge source is assigned to monitor. Problems which are suited to a blackboard architecture include: those problems that are decomposable into a hierarchical structure, those problems that require some flexibility in the calling of different sources of expertise, problems that have errorful data, problems with a large search space, interacting subproblems, and problems with incomplete information. Problems that fit this description are planning, scheduling, and speech processing. Some common related terms include opportunistic problem solving, plan elements, agenda elements, solution elements, consistency enforcer, interpreter, and justifier. *Contrast with* the other two expert system architectures, reasoning Frame-based and Production systems (Townsend 1987a, 136; Hayes-Roth et al 1983, 16–18, 21, 119; Walters and Nielsen 1988, 302–318; Harmon and King 1985, 137–139; Brownston et al 1986, 443; Barr and Feigenbaum 1981 vol 2, 31, 126–127; Townsend and Feucht 1986, 62; Lenat 1988, 71, 74–75; Parsaye and Chignell 1988, 143–147; Hayes-Roth 1990, 73–80).

Blackboard model   An expert system that uses a blackboard architecture and is useful in situations that have noisy data. Blackboard models can take advantage of islands of opportunity.

Blackboard units   The primary elements of knowledge representation found in HEARSAY—III, which are used to represent domain and scheduling knowledge (Hayes-Roth et al 1983, 310).

Black-box model of learning   An approach to learning in which the emphasis is on input and output. The programmer cares little about the mechanism of learning as long as the device learns. An example is the use of Markov chains as a mechanism of learning. Most black-box models rely on mathematical formulations. The black-box model of learning is unable to explain its reasoning. *Compare with* the Cognitive model of learning (Forsyth and Naylor 1985, 102–108).

Blind alley   A path in state-space search that does not lead to a suitable goal (Chabris 1989, 151).

Blind search   A systematic search that does not involve intelligent decision making. Breadth-first, depth-first, and bidirectional search are examples of blind search. Random search could be considered a type of blind search but the literature generally refers to blind search as a systematic type of search. *Contrast with* Heuristic state space search (Wolfgram 1987, 64–65; Schildt 1987, 40; Hayes-Roth et al 1983, 68).

Block   1. A compound statement. A set of statements surrounded by braces. Most modern languages like C, Pascal, and Smalltalk use blocks. In C and Pascal, a block may be a consequent of an if/then statement. In Smalltalk a block of code may be passed as an argument for a message.   2. A piece of modular code in which the scope of the variables in the block is limited to the block. An example of such a block is a function in C (Stroustrup 1987, 18; Rubin Aug 1985, 30, 32; *Smalltalk/V* 1986, 83; Hunt 1986, 62).

Block-structured language   A computer language in which programs are broken up into blocks of code. The scope of variables in each block is limited to the block. That is, given a block of code, outside of the block of code the program is completely unaware of the existence of the variable which is local to the block of code. This approach to programming greatly helps in reducing errors. The concept is frequently applied in large programs, including AI programs. C and PASCAL are block-structured languages (Thompson and Thompson 1986, 27).

Blocks world   Winograd's SHRDLU program. *See also* SHRDLU (Winston 1979, 158–167, 173–177; Sterling and Shapiro 1986, 221–224).

Blooming   A problem in robot vision concerning a phenomenon in which streaks fan out in the image around an area of intense illumination. It takes place when the high electrical charge in the sensor cell spills over into adjacent CCD registers. Overflow drains next to the photosensitive area can prevent this problem.

BNF production   Backus-Naur Form production, a variation of Backus-Naur Form. A formalized representation of a production rule for expert system shells. A representation describes how a rule is defined for the expert system shell. Example: <rule> ::= (DEFRULE <rule-number> If [(<conditions>)] THEN [(<actions>)]). The keywords in this rule are DEFRULE, IF, and THEN. The number of BNF keywords can vary from 5 to over 200 in expert system shells, and it is a measure of the complexity and perhaps the sophistication of an expert system (Brownston et al 1986, 442; Freedman 1987, 70).

Bobrow, Daniel The man who developed STUDENT, which reads algebraic story problems, converts them to equations, and solves the problem.

Body 1. The right-hand side of a PROLOG clause which consists of zero or more literals. 2. The set of conditions in a PROLOG clause (Shmueli et al 1986, 249; Townsend 1987b, 376).

Body literal The goals or procedure calls found in the body of a PROLOG clause (Shmueli et al 1986, 249).

Body of a procedure The forms that are to be evaluated when a procedure is entered. *See also* San Marco LISP Explorer.

Boltzmann machine A probabilistic neural network. A type of Hopfield neural network. Also a version of Markov Random Fields. It requires the use of stochastic units and symmetrical networks. The amount of thermal noise in the system is gradually reduced through the use of simulated annealing, which is a type of random search for the weights that will minimize the error in the system. The goal of a Boltzmann machine is to develop a learning procedure that can construct an internal representation which can then carry out the task to be solved. Its learning paradigm consists of two parts: In the first, a set of patterns is presented and the system responds to each in turn. In the second part the system runs without any input. The performance during the second part is subtracted out as internal noise and the remainder accounts more accurately for the input patterns. A Boltzmann machine has the capability of recognizing patterns of incomplete data. Error propagation is another method of achieving this end (Rumelhart and McClelland 1986, 43, 148–149; Zeidenberg 1987, 240–242; Jorgensen and Matheus 1986, 37; Waldrop 1987, 118–120; Hinton 1985, 269–270; Ingraham 1988, 19–26; Duntemann 1989, 113; Hinton 1990, 80–81; Ackley et al 1985, 827–832).

Boolean logic A means of deductive reasoning. Boolean logic uses the terms ONES, ZEROS, AND, OR, NOT to represent binary states. A one represents an on state while a zero represents an off state. AND, OR, and NOT are connectors (Schildt 1987, 223; Brownston et al 1986, 187–194; Hunt 1986, 62).

Boolean operators The connectives AND, OR, NOT, which are used in propositional logic (Townsend and Feucht 1986, 59–60).

Boole, George Author of the text *The Laws of Thought*. He first mechanized symbolic logic. *See also* Boolean logic (Schildt 1987, 223; Waldrop 1987, 15).

BOOPS Basic Object-Oriented Programming System adds object-oriented features to a relational data base. The advantage to this lies in adding sophisticated planning and simulation potential to the system (Gomsi and Desanti 1987, 60–66).

BORIS A story-understanding program, successor to Shank's SAM and PAM programs. Like its predecessors BORIS is based on conceptual dependency. BORIS can make inferences about five-page paragraphs and answer questions about the story based on the inferences. BORIS uses MOPS (memory organization packets) and TAUS (thematic affect units) as programming structures (Johnson 1986, 175–176; Tello 1988, 499–507).

Bottom-up comprehension An image-comprehension technique in which the computer is given substantial detailed information about what it is likely to see. It works from lower-level detail until it finds a comprehensive whole. Its advantage over controlled hallucination is that it can comprehend images it has never seen before. Analysis by synthesis (Forsyth and Naylor 1985, 86).

Bottom-up editing The ability to define and edit individual objects and then their classes in object-oriented systems. *Compare with* Top-down editing.

Bottom-up-inference Forward chaining.

Bottom-up-parsing Analyzing a sentence by evaluating the words from left to right, determining all possible sentence structures. *Compare with* Semantic-grammar parsing; Top-down parsing (Mishkoff 1986, 4–11).

Bottom-up processing An attempt to make higher-level interpretations from lower-level data. It sometimes is used as a synonym for forward chaining (Brownston et al 1986, 13, 15; Barr and Feigenbaum 1981 vol 1, 23–24).

Boundary detection A procedure in visual processing for discriminating a body's outline. It follows edge detection (Smith 1989, 23).

Boundary sets representation The information found in version spaces that determines the boundaries of the concept being learned (Jackson 1986, 200).

Bound variable 1. A variable in LISP that appears in the parameter list of a procedure. *Contrast with* Free variable 2. A variable that has been assigned a value (Winston 1979, 276; Brownston et al 1986, 443; Winston and Horn 1984, 54).

Box and arrow A diagrammatic method of illustrating how lists in LISP and PROLOG are linked. The representation consists of boxes and arrows. The boxes represent elements of the list. The elements may be atoms or lists. If the box represents an atom, an arrow points from the box to the name of the atom. If the box represents a list (a sublist), the arrow points to a box that represents the sublist. The box that represents the sublist points to a set of boxes that will represent the elements of the sublist (Charniak and McDermott 1985, 62; Winston and Horn 1984, 132).

Boyer-Moore theorem prover A theorem prover that obtains mathematical proofs through induction by means of heuristics and recursion. The theorem prover uses LISP functions rather than predicate calculus (Barr and Feigenbaum 1981 vol 3, 102–103; Smith 1989, 23).

BPA *See* Basic probability assignment (Townsend and Feucht 1986, 174).

Brainstorms: Philosophical Essays on Mind and Psychology A text by Daniel Dennett, which contends the principal contribution of artificial intelligence is that it shows a way out of the homunculus dilemma. That is, intelligent behavior can be reduced to a set of functions which can in turn be reduced to more basic processes until the individual neuron is finally reached (Johnson 1986, 60).

Branch The connection between nodes of a tree (Winston and Horn 1984 and 1988, 575).

Branch-and-bound algorithm An algorithm similar to the A* algorithm. It does not search a subtree if it estimates none of the nodes can contain an optimal solution (Smith 1989, 23).

Branch-and-bound search A type of heuristic search in which at each step the shortest path of all incomplete paths is chosen. The shortest or least expensive path is used as a bound on future candidate paths. The shortest path is expanded to the next level where more paths are generated. The search is not done until it is known that all incomplete paths are longer than the completed path. Underestimating the distance to the goal usually improves the performance of branch-and-bound search. It is an optimal type of search which requires less effort than other types of optimal search. Branch-and-bound search is only a very modest improvement over blind search. Branch-and-bound search becomes A* search when dynamic programming and calculations of remaining distance to the goal are used. Compare to best-first search, which moves forward from an estimate of the shortest path to the goal rather than the least expensive path thus far. Branch-and-bound search is also known as uniform cost search (Chabris 1989, 153–154; Wolfgram 1987, 66; Winston 1979, 99–102; Barr and Feigenbaum 1981 vol 1, 64; Luger and Stubblefield 1989, 87; Winston 1984, 102–113; Parsaye and Chignell 1988, 385).

Branching The transfer of control to a statement other than the next sequential statement in the program. Conditional branching is carried out using if/then control structures. Branching is used extensively in robot-control programs in order to enhance flexibility (Hunt 1986, 64).

Branching factor The mean number of moves available to the player at a given time in a game situation. In a single level of a game tree, it is the average number of moves available. *See also* Penetrance (Chabris 1989, 162; Winston 1979, 112; Barr and Feigenbaum 1981 vol 1, 328–329; Forsyth and Naylor 1985, 188).

Breadth The number of conditions and parameters in an expert system compared to the number of rules and facts. Other important measures of the value of expert systems are adequacy, accuracy, reliability, validity, practicability, adaptability, credibility, and generality (Marcot 1987, 45).

Breadth-first search A blind systematic search that traverses a search tree horizontally rather than in a depth-first manner. Another way of stating this is that all rules or objects at a particular level are tried first before dropping to the next lower level. It is least efficient when all the goal nodes are at the same depth. That is, a depth-first search would probably find one of the goal nodes more quickly if all of the goal nodes were at the same depth. An expert system using a breadth-first search asks questions of a user that seem disjointed, because it is checking out a number of different hypotheses at one time. Breadth-first search is favored over depth-first search when the user is concerned about committing too early to a possible solution. It is preferred over depth-first search when there is a low branching factor for the search tree. Breadth-first search is preferred over depth-first search when blind alleys present a significant problem. Breadth-first search encourages the finding of one of the best solutions, rather than any solution. In contrast to the British Museum algorithm, breadth-first search stops when it finds a solution. Breadth-first search cuts down on the possibility of infinite search paths. It requires more memory than depth-first search because it must keep track of more paths. *Contrast with* Heuristic state space search (Wolfgram 1987, 64–65; Schildt 1987, 29–32; Hayes-Roth et al 1983, 68; Winston 1979, 91–92; Harmon and King 1985, 57–58; Brownston et al 1986, 66; Chabris 1989, 151; Winston 1984, 95–96, 100).

Break package A means of halting a program so that the values of variables can be examined (Hunt 1986, 64).

Bridges of Königsberg problem The city of Königsberg consists of two islands in a river and the banks of a river. The islands are connected to each other and to both river banks with bridges. One island has two bridges to both banks. The problem is to find a path over which each bridge is crossed only once in a tour of the city. Using graph theory Euler showed that there is no solution to the problem (Luger and Stubblefield 1989, 78).

Brilliant pebbles Small rockets approximately 3 feet long and weighing about 300 pounds which are being proposed as part of the "Star Wars" antiballistic program. Each rocket is to be controlled by the equivalent of a supercomputer.

British Museum algorithm The procedure of searching the entire search space in an attempt to find the best path. Unlike depth-first and breadth-first search, this algorithm continues to search, even after a solution has been found. It is an optimal but inefficient form of search. It is a type of blind search. *See also* Brute force method (Barr and Feigenbaum 1981 vol 2, 35; Smith 1989, 24; Winston 1984, 101–102).

Broad-based partitioning In vision, the procedure of dividing an object into two or more parts for further processing (Lawrence 1985, 53–54).

Browser A sophisticated editor used in object-oriented languages like Smalltalk. The browser can call various panes. One pane may contain the methods of an object. Another pane may contain the variables and values of the variables of an object. Another pane may show where the object is located in the object hierarchy (Duntemann 1989, 132; *Smalltalk/V* 1986, 214).

BRU See Basic resolution unit.

Brute force method A means of problem solving that consists of simply trying all possible solutions without regard to using heuristics to eliminate blind paths. It is sometimes called the British Museum algorithm. It is a type of blind search (Waldrop 1987, 24).

B+ tree A data structure and a powerful indexing system for searching data bases. It is somewhat similar to a B tree, but there is more than one key string at each node. In a B+ tree all the keys will be duplicated in the leaves of the tree. All of the leaves are doubly linked. Since the keys are in the leaves as well as the node pages there's no need to have the record node pointers in the node pages as is necessary in a B− tree. A B+ tree is balanced. That is, all search paths are the same length giving rapid retrieval of data from large data bases (Shammas 1985, 11–12; Lane Sep/Oct 1988, 62; Morak 1988, 78).

B− tree A recursive data structure that is very efficient for indexing items that can be classified in a similar way. It is useful in dealing with large amounts of data. They are used in some expert systems to store data permanently in frame-like objects which can use inheritance and attached predicates (Rettig Jun 1987, 18; Sterling and Shapiro 1986, 57–61; Tello 1988, 275–276).

B*-tree search A variant of best-first search. It works as follows: It first finds evidence that a path from the root of the search tree is superior to the other paths. This information is used to fix the order of node expansions. Upper and lower bounds are furnished for these expanded nodes. The search is successfully completed where the bounds come together (Tello 1988, 404).

Bug An approach to intelligent computer-aided instruction that searches for defects or bugs in the student's reasoning. *Contrast with* the overlay approach, which makes the assumption the student does not have defects in reasoning but simply does not have the knowledge (Smith 1989, 25).

BUGGY An AI program used to diagnose mistakes students are making in solving arithmetic problems. It not only identifies mistakes but finds the faulty procedure responsible for the mistake. BUGGY actually forms a model of the student's problem-solving behavior. Three hundred and thirty possible faulty procedures in arithmetic problem solving are explored by BUGGY in an attempt to account for the student's mistakes. BUGGY is an initial version of the more advanced DEBUGGY (Mishkoff 1986, 6-4; Barr and Feigenbaum 1981 vol 2, 279–282).

Build A command in OPS5 systems used to construct rules at run time. Commands like build allow the construction of expert systems that learn (Brownston et al 1986, 218–221).

BUILD An expert system that uses some elements of common sense (Hunt 1986, 65).

Built-in predicate A predicate in PROLOG that is a part of the language. Standard predicate is used interchangeably with the term "built-in predicate" (Schildt 1987, 140).

Business systems approach An approach to expert system design in which a series of small applications rather than a large potentially overwhelming application is found. *Contrast with* Technology approach (*Knowledge-Based Systems* 1986, 2–46).

Butterfly An active data structure used in connection machines, which is made up of multiple trees that share the same leaves. This regular data structure is especially efficient in sorting operations. Other types of active data structures are trees, sets, arrays, strings, and graphs (Hillis 1985, 106).

C

C A procedural, typed language which has recently been used in the development of expert systems, originally designed as a system-programming language. The advantages of C are that it is fast, concise, flexible, and portable, and a language with which many programmers are familiar. There are a number of expert system tools being converted from LISP to C for many of these reasons. C is being used extensively in neural networks, for one reason because of its ability to interact effectively with the hardware. Some of C's disadvantages are that it does not possess dynamic binding, lists must be implemented with pointers, it has limited symbol-processing capacity, and its memory-management facility is not as well adapted for artificial intelligence as LISP. It is not capable of achieving parallel processing or coroutines (Hunt 1986, 66; Barber 1987, 30; Roland 1987, 47; Tello 1988, 399–401; Reymann 1988, 89; Dlugosz 1989, 103).

C++ An object-oriented extension of the C language, which supports multiple inheritance, encapsulation, operator overloading, function overloading, message passing, constant types, free store management operators, function argument checking, references, and inline functions. C++ uses both early and late binding. Objects can be dynamically created. Automatic memory management and symbol data types are not available. Whereas C is meant to be close to the machine, C++ is meant to be close to the problem to be solved. Of course C++ inherits many of the assets of C including portability and speed. The primary difference between C and C++ is that C++ has classes. C++ gives the user enhanced capability in defining new data types. C++ is compatible with C. It is not a pure object-oriented language like Smalltalk in which everything is an object—data types exist in C++ which are not necessarily true objects. For example, some objects do not possess inheritance capabilities. Functions can exist in C++ which are independent of objects. Objects can be accessed by other means than message passing, while in Smalltalk access to objects may only take place by messages. C++ supports multiple inheritance while Smalltalk does not. C++ is strongly typed while Smalltalk is weakly typed. Smalltalk has a more mature environment than C++; it has a large collection of built-in classes, a garbage collector, run-time debugging facilities, and a built-in user interface. The more mature environment plus the fact that Smalltalk is interpreted while C++ is compiled makes Smalltalk a better prototyping language. Since C++ is compiled it is considered faster. One authority holds that C++'s run-time binding is relatively limited and therefore that it is not an optimal language to use for learning programs, and programs that may need to deal with unanticipated circumstances. What can be passed as a parameter is more limited in C++ than in other object-oriented languages. *Compare with* Objective-C (Tello 1989, 88; Flamig 1987, 18–26; Stroustrup 1987, 245; Pohl Sep 1989, 67–77; Williams Aug 1989, 36–45).

C with classes   The original version of C++. C with classes did not include a number of facilities that were eventually included in C++.

Caching   1. The saving of intermediate results in a table so that the results do not need to be recomputed if they are needed again.   2. The saving of an answer to a question that has a high probability of being asked again. In that way the AI program can answer its own question without having to bother the user (Rosenberg 1986, 25; Sciore and Warren 1986, 298–300; Tello 1988 156–157).

CADUCEUS   An expert system used in diagnosis in internal medicine; a forward- and backward-chaining system. The basic information is input into the program and forward chaining is used to generate diagnostic hypotheses. The backward-chaining system is then used to verify a diagnosis. CADUCEUS deals with the problem of multiple diseases in a patient by using Bayesian statistics. CADUCEUS stops when all symptoms have been accounted for by a single diagnosis or by multiple diagnoses. It improves on its predecessor, INTERNIST, in that it employs causal relationships to arrive at a diagnosis (Hayes-Roth et al 1983, 40–41; Tello 1988, 109–110).

CAI   *See* Computer-assisted instruction.

Calculus   The means of calculating the truth of propositions in the predicate calculus (Schildt 1987, 228–230).

Call   The summoning of a program or subroutine. Once the program or subroutine has completed execution the system is returned to continue executing the original program (Hunt 1986, 67; Brownston et al 1986, 51–52).

Call by reference   A process whereby the value of a previously defined variable used on a function's parameter list may be altered by the function. Call by reference is more prone to programmer error than call by value (Winston and Horn 1984, 55–56).

Call by value   A method of handling procedure arguments whereby the value of a previously defined variable used on a procedure's parameter list may not be altered by the procedure. The value of the variable can be copied but the value of the variable cannot be changed. Call by value is less prone to programmer errors than is call by reference. LISP is a call by value language (Winston and Horn 1984, 55–56).

Calling in   The ability of a program to call functions in the expert system. Calling in can be used to review and modify the working memory or the objects in an expert system. Calling in can also be used to modify the inferencing process and load new knowledge bases.

Calling out   The ability of an expert system to execute external programs.

Cancellation The event that takes place in frame-based systems when a slot already contains a value and the class the frame belongs to contains a default value for the slot. The presence of the value in the slot of the frame cancels the inheritance process (Chabris 1989, 288).

Candidate elimination algorithm A version-space learning procedure for single-concept descriptions, developed by Mitchell. An algorithm that is applied to version spaces by manipulating boundary sets representations. It is an algorithm responsible for concept learning which adds and eliminates characteristics of a concept as a function of the examples presented. Example: Assume the concept being distilled is that of a bird. Objects that are birds and objects that are not birds are presented. The algorithm constricts or generalizes the concept of bird according to the characteristics of the positive or negative examples. The candidate elimination algorithm employs the least-commitment principle. That is, a characteristic of a concept is eliminated only when the presented examples force the characteristic to be eliminated. Noisy data is one problem with which the candidate elimination algorithm must cope. One means of dealing with noisy data is to use multiple concepts. Each concept is generally consistent with all of the examples, but may be inconsistent with a small subset of examples. The candidate elimination algorithm has difficulties with disjunctive concepts such as parent which is defined as a father or a mother (Barr and Feigenbaum 1981 vol 3, 386–391, 396–399; Jackson 1986, 200; Chabris 1989, 288).

Candidate generation The generation of hypotheses, diagnoses, or faults in a diagnostic expert system. In model-based diagnostic systems this procedure compares the predicted responses and the actual responses of the system, and this procedure uses the comparison to identify candidate faulty components (Chabris 1989, 288).

Candidate generation by constraint suspension An algorithm that searches for faulty components in a system by first viewing the system as a set of constraints and then selectively relaxing constraints in the system. When certain constraints are relaxed and the system begins to function as the underlying model predicts it should, then the component that has been taken out of the system because of the relaxed constraints may be considered to be the faulty component. Example: Assume an electronics system. An input voltage is entered and the subsequent output voltages are measured. The discrepancies between expected and actual voltages are measured. Records of the components that could contribute to the discrepancies are consulted. The suspect components are selectively taken out of the system one at a time until the expected and actual voltages are the same. When this occurs the component that is out of the system is identified as the faulty component. This type of system relies on a knowledge of the underlying behavior of the system being tested and is a deep-knowledge system. *See also* Constraint network; Davis' Diagnostic Reasoning System; Dependency record; Simulation rule (Chabris 1989, 125, 290).

Candidate-solution graph A solution graph in a backward-reasoning system that has been tested for consistency (Smith 1989, 25).

Canned explanation An explanation in an expert system, as to why a question is being asked or how a conclusion was reached that the developer must write. The advantage is that the developer may elaborate on the reason for the question being asked. The disadvantage is the time involved in writing the explanations. *Contrast with* Dynamic explanation (Brownston et al 1986, 323, 332).

Canned text An explanation in an expert system as to why a rule is being asked or how a conclusion was reached (Brownston et al 1986, 323, 332).

Capsule The building of a template of a complex SQL query which can then be called by a PROLOG predicate to query the data base (Rettig 1987, 24).

Car 1. A built-in LISP function that takes a list as an argument and returns only the first member on the list. 2. The first item in a list in LISP. The head of the list (Sterling and Shapiro 1986, 43).

Cardinality A facet found in frame-based systems that restricts the number of values a slot can hold (Fox et al 1986, 162–163).

Carnegie Representation Language A frame-based language that is used in the Knowledge Craft expert system tool. It has the capability of forward-chaining, backward-chaining, object-oriented programming, and event-driven programming (Schuler 1987, 99–103).

Cartesian coordinate robot A robot that uses the cartesian coordinate system to guide movement (Rosenberg 1986, 26).

Cascaded augmented transition network A series of augmented transition networks. The first ATN processes the data and passes on the modified data to the next ATN (Smith 1989, 26).

Case The part of a concept that delineates the role of the concept, a term used extensively in natural language processing. Examples: agent and object (Smith 1989, 26).

CASE Computer-Assisted Software Engineering. The goal of CASE is to automate the software development process by modeling the system to be developed and providing the necessary tools to reach the goal of a completed product, with sufficient accompanying documentation. One CASE tool that can be used with expert systems is the Information Engineering Workbench, produced by KnowledgeWare (Blackman 1990, 27–31; Morrill 1989, 206; Gibson 1989, 209–218; McClure 1989, 235–244).

Case analysis A case-study approach to the development of an expert system. Examples of the process being captured in the expert system are scrutinized to aid in development of the expert system.

Case-based reasoning Reasoning that uses learning from analogy. A problem is compared to a set of case examples and the case most similar to the problem is used as a basis for solving the problem. Case-based reasoning is the solving of problems by recognizing how the current problem is similar to a previously solved problem and adapting the solution of the previously solved problem to the current problem. Important components of case-based reasoning are retrieve, compare, adapt, repair, and generalize. Case-based reasoning is implemented with similarity networks. The analogical inference engine uses the similarity network to find cases that are somehow similar to the current case in an attempt to solve the problem at hand. Case-based reasoning is applicable to problem solving in the legal arena (Bailey et al Jul/Aug 1988, 31; Luger and Stubblefield 1989, 569).

Case-based system An artificial intelligence system used to process a number of similar cases through the use of a generic database. Case-based systems emphasize the distinction between subkind and instance links, and they make use of cross-indexing. Case-based systems are applied to large real-world problems. Frames, semantic networks, and similarity networks are used to construct case-based systems (Salzberg 1987, 32).

Case grammar A grammar in which the deep case of the word or phrase is the primary focus of attention. The term case is best thought of as a role and not as a case in the sense of nominative and objective cases. The cases are kept to a small number. Examples: agent, counteragent, object, result, instrument, source, goal, and experiencer. Many nouns and verbs can be subsumed under this small number of terms. *Compare with* Context-free grammar; Systemic grammar; Transformational grammar. Case-grammer theory is able to use a few basic cases to represent a large amount of language (Charniak and McDermott 1985, 230– 238; Winston 1979, 73–84; Barr and Feigenbaum 1981 vol 1, 252–255).

Case-management facility A facility used in some expert systems that stores and retrieves specific cases. The case may be the diagnostic data on a patient. A case-management facility gives an expert system a what-if capability, for use in a training situation, in which the symptoms may be changed and the case given to the expert system to see what effect the changes have on the diagnosis (Salzberg 1987, 35).

Case-method tutor   An intelligent computer-aided instruction program that emulates the Socratic approach to teaching (Smith 1989, 27).

CASE tool   Computer-Assisted Software Engineering tool, automatic programming (Tello 1989, 16).

CASNET   An expert medical system that uses a causal associative network to diagnose and make treatment recommendations for glaucoma. This causal associative network is a semantic network in which the link between nodes is CAUSES. Each CAUSES link is given a confidence value that represents the strength of the association between a cause and a disease. An example of such a link is increased interocular pressure causing cupping of the optic disk. CASNET begins with asking questions about the presenting symptoms and forward chains its way to final diagnoses. The questions asked are a function of the importance of the question in answering a differential diagnosis and the cost of obtaining that answer. To reach the level of a confirmed diagnosis a given diagnosis has to surpass a preset threshold level. It also makes treatment recommendations. CASNET's explanation system is a printout of the literature justifying the diagnoses. The expert system tool EXPERT evolved from CASNET. *Contrast with* MYCIN, a backward-chaining medical expert system (Brownston et al 1986, 356; Barr and Feigenbaum 1981 vol 1, 180–183, 193–196).

Categorical knowledge   Knowledge that is absolutely true or false. *Compare with* Probabilistic knowledge (Bratko 1986, 317).

Category-editor   A module found in the NEXPERT expert system tool, which is used to prioritize rules. The higher priority rules are examined first in a program run (Harmon et al 1988, 112).

Category node   A node in a neural network that fires in response to a particular pattern of feature node activity (Levine 1989, 30).

Category variable   A variable found in some expert system shells that can take on any number of string values. For example, given a variable Weather, the variable may have the values of hot, cold, cloudy, windy, and muggy. The program can then build a menu of these items for the user to choose from. Category variables are found in the ES/P ADVISOR (Tello 1988, 148).

Causal hierarchy   A hierarchy that represents a system in terms of cause-effect relations. Example: the presence of a bacteria indicating a particular disease. *Compare with* a Functional hierarchy which represents deeper knowledge. *Compare with* Structural hierarchy, which represents more shallow knowledge. A causal hierarchy is also called a "behavioral hierarchy" (Townsend and Feucht 1986, 72–73).

Causal model   **1.** A knowledge base that possesses causal relationships.   **2.** An expert system that relies on an underlying cause-effect relationship as opposed to most expert system models, which rely on shallow rule-of-thumb knowledge. One important advantage of such a knowledge base is that it can more effectively answer why and how questions concerning the conclusion. *See also* CASNET (Barr and Feigenbaum 1981 vol 1, 193–195).

Causal reasoning   Making inferences so as to explain past behavior and predict future behavior (Kuipers 1990, 827–832).

CCD camera   A camera that changes a light image into a digital image. The type of scan pattern it uses is line by line (Rosenberg 1986, 27).

cdr   **1.** A built-in LISP function that takes as an assignment a list and returns all but the first member on the list.   **2.** The remainder of the items in a list in LISP after the car has been removed. Example: The cdr of the list (John Mary Susie) is (Mary Susie). It is sometimes called the tail of the list (Barr and Feigenbaum 1981, vol 2, 16; Sterling and Shapiro 1986, 43).

Cell   **1.** The underlying structure of a list. Each cell has two parts. One part has a pointer which points to a piece of data and the other part contains a pointer which points to other cells. Cell is frequently referred to as a cons cell. 2. A manufacturing section which is made up of a series of workstations, which are coordinated in carrying out a manufacturing process (Barr and Feigenbaum 1981 vol 2, 16–17; Rosenberg 1986, 27).

Censor A rule that stops another rule or rules from being executed (Winston 1984, 430).

CENTAUR An expert system tool that uses both frames and rules, which was used to build the expert system PUFF (Jackson 1986, 142).

Center A series of cells that are coordinated in carrying out a manufacturing process (Rosenberg 1986, 27).

Centralized architecture A parallel architecture in which the microprocessors are in a hierarchy and one processor is the executive, controlling the overall process. This type of architecture is used in the Connection Machine. *Contrast with* Decentralized architecture.

Centralized control scheme A control scheme for parallel processing systems in which the processors are in a hierarchy. One processor controls the entire system. *Compare with* Decentralized control scheme (Waldrop 1987, 116).

Certainty factor An ad-hoc approach to inexact reasoning. It is used in expert systems to express the confidence in a conclusion, a fact, or rule. The assignment of a numerical value to a fact, conclusion, or rule indicating the level of confidence of that conclusion, fact, or rule. The numerical value may range from 0 to 100, -1 to $+1$, -100 to $+100$, 0 to 10, or 0 to 1, depending on the system being used. The upper endpoint of the interval stands for full confidence, while the lower endpoint of the scale means the entity is false, or that there is complete ignorance concerning the validity of the entity. While the use of certainty factors is debated, certainty factors appear to contribute to the effectiveness of expert systems such as MYCIN. Certainty factors may be simply a special case of the Bayesian equation. There are a number of ways to combine certainty factors to achieve an overall certainty factor rating. One common way is as follows: Assume the certainty factor of one piece of evidence is .3. The certainty factor of the second piece of evidence is .5. In order to arrive at the overall certainty factor the equation used is $CF = .3 + (1 - .3) * .5$. The final confidence factor of .65 is cumulative in nature. With this equation the final confidence factor can never exceed one. The use of negative certainty factors allows for decrements in the final certainty factor. The ability to make decrements in certainty factors may be critical in some applications. Some certainty factor systems allow the certainty factor to be locked in, if an extreme certainty factor is chosen. That is, assume that a certainty range of 0 to 10 is being used. If 0 or 10 is chosen, then that minimum or maximum certainty value is locked in regardless of what is found in subsequent rules. Certainty factors can be used to resolve the problem of multiple answers. That is, certainty factors can be used to order multiple answers from the best to the poorest answer. Some systems use thresholds. That is, any conclusion below a certainty factor threshold is ignored. Certainty factors are not probabilities. A confidence factor of .80 does not mean a statement has an 80 percent probability of being true. There are about 30 different methods of computing certainty factors. Methods of calculating certainty factors include confirmative of minimums, confirmative of products, maximum of minimums, maximum of products, average of minimums, and average of products. The problem at hand dictates the most appropriate method for computing certainty factors. A synonym for certainty is confidence factor. Certainty should not be confused with probability (Townsend 1987a, 168–172; Hayes-Roth et al 1983, 399; Winston 1979, 243–244; Harmon and King 1985, 50–52; Brownston et al 1986, 443; Barr and Feigenbaum 1981 vol 2, 188–191; Tello 1988 257–259; Chabris 1989, 113; Shafer May/Jun 1989, 71).

Certainty filtering Data filtering based on the assignment of a reliability value to the data. If a datum falls below a given reliability it is filtered out of the examination process. *See also* Activation filtering (Brownston et al 1986, 309–310).

Certainty theory   A theory, like fuzzy logic, that focuses on degree of belief that a fact or rule is true rather than the relatively greater emphasis on probability found in the Bayesian approach (Parsaye and Chignell 1988 228–233).

Chaining   A control strategy used in expert systems, which refers to the chain of inferences from one rule to the next. *See also* Backward chaining; Forward chaining (Walters and Nielsen 1988, 196–197).

Chain rule   An extension of modus ponens (Smith 1989, 29).

Change-driven inference   Any change in the data base that causes a designed rule to fire. This type of inference is found in ROSIE, an expert system tool. *Constrast with* Goal-driven expert system; State-driven inference (Hayes-Roth et al 1983, 187).

Chaos   The investigation of nonlinear dynamics (Obermeier and Barron 1989, 219).

Chart   The data structure used to portray the grammar and the input sentence in the General Syntactic Processor (Smith 1989, 29).

Checker player   An artificial intelligence program developed by Arthur Samuels that plays checkers and is capable of learning by remembering board positions. Checker player makes efficient use of minimax look-ahead search in conjunction with remembered board positions. When the program encounters a board position that fits a previously seen board position, it recalls the evaluation score for the board position rather than having to recompute the score (Barr and Feigenbaum 1981 vol 3, 332–333, 339–344, 457–464).

Child   The object that inherits characteristics from a parent object in object-oriented programming. Example: the parent object cat passing characteristics like four legs and mammal to the lion and tiger objects.

Child class   A class that inherits characteristics from another class (Duntemann 1989, 132).

Chinese room   A hypothetical situation which is used as a vehicle in the debate over whether or not computers can think. It goes as follows: Assume a man is locked in a room and given Chinese writings. He knows no Chinese. He is, however, given rules (a program) to manipulate the symbols so as to translate from Chinese to English. He learns to translate faithfully from Chinese to English, but understands nothing of what he is translating, and never learns a single word of Chinese. It is argued the computer is in a similar position in that it can manipulate symbols, but understands nothing about what it is doing (Waldrop 1987, 136–137).

Choice sets   A unit which stands for an unresolved decision in HEARSAY-III (Hayes-Roth et al 1983, 310).

Chomsky hierarchy   The hierarchy of the different classes of formal languages. The hierarchy, from most restrictive to least restrictive, consists of regular languages, context-free languages, context-sensitive languages, and recursively enumerable languages (Luger and Stubblefield 1989, 389).

Chomsky, Noam   The man responsible for developing the theory of formal grammar. The theory of formal grammar states that at the heart of a sentence lies a deep structure. Certain transformations or rules are applied to the deep structure to produce what Chomsky called a surface structure.

Chronological backtracking   That form of backtracking that retreats to the last decision made or most recent state. Contrast with the definition of backtracking that is a retreat to an earlier state, not necessarily to the most recent state. A commonly used but inefficient form of backtracking. It is inefficient because data are automatically abandoned when failure is met.

Some of the abandoned information could be of value in eventually reaching the solution. In this type of blind backtracking it is possible for the program to repeat the same mistakes again. An example is a robot that touches a hot object that damages its arm. The chronological backtracking mechanism would then cause the robot to back up and touch the hot object again with its other arm. *Contrast with* Dependency-directed backtracking (Hayes-Roth et al 1983, 75; Barr and Feigenbaum 1981 vol 2, 9, 72; Chabris 1989, 287; Smith 1989, 31; Charniak and McDermott 1985, 266).

Chunk Information stored and retrieved as a single entity. The information is somehow related, although the different pieces of information in the chunk may be of different data types. Miller found people learn most effectively by dealing with chunks of meaningful information. The chunks may be fairly large pieces of organized information. They are a collection of facts stored and retrieved as a single unit. In chess a chunk may be the placement pattern of the entire chessboard. Research has indicated that one important difference between an advanced chess player and a beginner is the experience which allows the advanced player to have more chunks. This insight points out the importance of attempting to organize information in chunks. When we do this we are employing more of a holistic approach rather than a strictly logical approach. Sometimes rules are referred to as chunks. Frames are used to organize chunks of information (Johnson 1986, 199–200; Townsend 1987a 120; Harmon and King 1985, 24–25; Townsend 1987b, 377; Barr and Feigenbaum 1981 vol 3, 5; Townsend and Feucht 1986, 243).

Chunking The storing of information about a topic or object so that information is easily accessed. A process that takes place in learning in which information is abstracted in chunks. These chunks of information are stored, recalled, compared, and matched with patterns found in subsequent situations. *See also* Chunk (Chabris 1989, 288; Jackson 1986, 172).

Church-Rosser theorem One of a group of theorems that show why the rule order is a trivial factor in commutative and decomposable production systems (Smith 1989, 31).

Church-Turing thesis The proposition that computers have the ability of carrying out any clearly described symbolic process. This thesis contends that if a function is computable then it can be determined with a standard computer (Luger and Stubblefield 1989, 28; Zeidenberg, 1987, 237).

Circumscription A type of nonmonotonic reasoning that assumes all objects, qualifications, and assumptions concerning the problem have been specified. It is really a procedure for augmenting predicate calculus with nonmonotonic reasoning. The primary advantage circumscription has over other types of nonmonotonic reasoning is that the reasoning capacity of predicate calculus is available to the system. The following is an example of nonmonotonic reasoning to which circumscription may be applied: Imagine a program in which the assumption is made that all objects, qualifications, and assumptions concerning the problem have been specified. Assume in solving a problem with this program that we have an unknown substance which resembles the compound magnesium oxide. Since magnesium oxide is the compound the program knows most resembles the unknown substance, the unknown compound is identified as magnesium oxide. It could, however, be a different compound which is not known by the program. If new facts are introduced, the circumscription mechanism can be applied to withdraw the faulty facts and conclusions from the data base. Circumscription has kept track of the reasoning process so that the faulty data can be withdrawn. Predicate calculus usually does not keep track of the reasoning process. *Compare with* Default reasoning (Barr and Feigenbaum 1981 vol 3, 115–119; Smith 1989, 30; Nutter 1990, 843; McCarthy 1980, 27–40).

Class 1. A definition for a set of objects. In an object-oriented language a class is a template for a group of objects with common characteristics. The objects in a class have common variables and common methods for responding to messages. A class is an abstract object that defines the character and behavior of other objects. It may be thought of as an object characterized by encapsulation and inheritance. The class can be used to spawn other objects. Depending on the class in question, the other objects may be instances or other classes. Types are to records as classes are to objects. Example: sports cars, which have certain characteristics which are unique. These unique characteristics are represented by methods and variables. Specialized versions of sports cars such as Jaguar and Spitfire may be created.   2. A user-defined type in C++ and other object-oriented languages. A class specifies how objects of a class can be created, destroyed, manipulated, accessed, how they behave, and how they are represented. A class contains the different types of data needed to represent an object, and procedures that are used to handle the object. A class in C++ is like an ordinary C structure in that both structures can contain heterogeneous information. A class in C++ differs from the kinds of data items found in ordinary C structures because unlike an ordinary C structure a class can include functions that can only be accessed through the use of messages. This is known as data hiding. In C++ a class provides data hiding, operator overloading, data typing, implicit type conversions, guaranteed initialization of data, user-controlled memory management, reference types, and dynamic typing.   3. An object and its attributes in OPS5. In OPS5 the types of values for attributes are not specified ahead of time, thus allowing an attribute to take on the value of a variety of different data structures and values at runtime. In OPS5 there is no hierarchy of classes as there is in object oriented languages. The term "object type" is used in place of class in Turbo Pascal (Duntemann 1989, 132–133; Stein 1988, 20, 30; Meyer 1988, 82; Skelly 1987, 82; Walters and Nielsen 1988, 210; Brownston et al 1986, 39–40; *Smalltalk/V* 1986, 51; McGregor 1987, 50; Stroustrup 1987, 23–24, 136; Flamig 1987, 21; Hu 1989, 187; Lane 1989, 11; Pohl 1989, 68).

Class-based language   An object-based language with classes. Examples: Smalltalk and Flavors. ADA is an object-based language but it is not a class-based language because it does not support classes (Wegner 1989, 247–248).

Class hierarchy   The organization of related classes in a hierarchy in which the more abstract classes are at the top of the hierarchy and the less abstract classes are at the bottom, and in which the less abstract classes inherit characteristics from the more abstract classes (Duntemann 1989, 134).

Class hierarchy browser   A system browser found in Smalltalk V, in which the screen can be divided into the windows that show the classes and subclasses, methods, and the source code (Tello 1988, 387).

Classification   1. Categorizing objects according to their characteristics.   2. The process of assigning an image to a predefined category in vision.   3. Attributing behavior or characteristics to a class of objects rather than to individual objects (Gabriel Sep/Oct 1989, 40; Gabriel Mar 1989, 55).

Classification builder   A type of learning paradigm used in neural nets in which there is a clearly delineated set of classes in which the input pattern can be classified. *Contrast with* Auto association; pattern associator; Regularity detector (Bayle 1988, 44).

Classification table   A procedure used in the expert system CASNET to classify a disease as present or absent for a given patient (Smith 1989, 31).

Classification tree   Decision tree (Thompson and Thompson Nov 1986, 149).

Classifier   A bit-string pattern used to classify patterns in a bitmapped classifier. Each bit in the string represents attributes of the object to be classified. If the bit is a 1, then the attribute is present. If the bit is a 0, then the attribute is not present. If the object to be classified has a pattern close enough to the Classifier, then the match is successful. *See also* Holland classifier (Frey 1986, 162).

Classless language   An object-based language that does not use classes. Two types of classless languages are proptypical languages and actor languages (Wegner 1989, 249).

Class scope   The limiting of the scope of a name to a class of objects (Tello 1989, 85).

Class tree   Class hierarchy (Duntemann 1989, 137).

Class variables   Variables in an object-oriented program that are shared by all objects in the class (Rubin Aug 1985, 30).

Clausal form   A syntactic scheme employed in logic programming; a conjunction of clauses. It is like a conjunctive normal form except that the positive and negative literals in each conjunction are placed together on the opposite sides of an arrow and the negation symbols are eliminated. It is easier to read than the conjunctive normal form. It differs from the horn clause subset in that more than one atom is allowed on the left-hand side. It is produced by applying prenex normal form, skolemization, and conjunctive normal form. Some authorities use clausal form and conjunctive normal form interchangeably (Bratko 1986, 397; Jackson 1986, 77–79; Smith 1989, 31).

Clause   1. In logic a syntactic construction consisting of a predicate and a subject. A well-formed clause that may be a single literal, a disjunction of literals, or empty. Some examples are [], x, not$x$, x or not$y$, not$x$ or y or z. In order to use resolution, clausal forms must be used.   2. A fact, query, or rule in the PROLOG language. A PROLOG program consists of a set of clauses. In a clause the existential and universal quantifiers are not explicitly stated.   3. A condition element in production systems in the left-hand side of a rule.   4. A test-result element in LISP in the conditional procedure COND (Amsterdam Oct 1986, 18; Townsend 1987a, 36; Dos Reis 1988, 50; Brownston et al 1986, 13–15; Townsend 1987b, 377; Sterling and Shapiro 1986, 9, 17; Winston and Horn 1984, 51; Barr and Feigenbaum 1981 vol 3, 87–94; Townsend and Feucht 1986, 142; Hunt 1986, 70; Bratko 1986, 61).

Clause schema   The name of a predicate and a number that stands for the number of arguments of the predicate (Parsaye and Chignell 1988, 204).

Cleanup   The process of deleting objects that are no longer needed. Destructor is the cleanup function in C++ (Stroustrup 1987, 140–141).

Client relationship   How a class inherits characteristics from a superclass. Example: The superclass animals pass certain characteristics to the class cats. An alternative way of looking at inheritance is to see the superclass as a client of the class. That is the superclass animal serves the classes like cats, dogs, and so on (Swaine Jun 1989, 116).

Closed-world assumption   A concept adopted in many expert systems in which it is assumed all relevant knowledge is present. This closed-world assumption allows for the implementation of negation as failure which holds: All relationships that are not explicitly stated to be true are considered false. While George Bush may be president, if that fact is not in the data base, then the assertion is thought to be false. Negation as failure is a strong version of the closed-world assumption, and negation as failure is used in the PROLOG language. That is, negation as failure is a basic assumption of the PROLOG language (Walters and Nielsen 1988, 202; Barr and Feigenbaum 1981 vol 3, 115; Townsend and Feucht 1986, 168; Hewitt Apr 1985, 235–236).

Clos network   A type of crossbar network topology found in connection machines that requires fewer switches than are found in a full implementation of a crossbar topology. Other topologies include rings, trees, banyan-type networks, grids, delta networks, hashnets, shuffle-type topologies, and crossbars (Hillis 1985, 57).

Closure A function and its set of bindings in LISP (Graham Apr 1989, 28).

Clout A natural-language front end for the popular data base RBase. A logic-based system that consists of a set of rules which process the query. It handles grammatically incorrect queries. It will give a list of choices if it is not sure of the query. *Contrast with* Savvy (Rubin Jul 1985, 47).

CLS A predecessor of the ID3 algorithm (Barr and Feigenbaum 1981 vol 3, 406–408).

CLUSTER A machine-learning algorithm that assembles data in groups and finds structure (Parsaye 1989, 29).

Cluster analysis A type of analysis that applies a distance function to different objects so as to group the objects in clusters (Bailey et al Jul/Aug 1988, 29).

Clustered information Related information placed together. Much information we know comes in clusters. Example: the mention of a dog automatically connotes four legs, barking, meat eater, and so on. Because information comes in such clusters it may be most efficient to assume the characteristics of the objects unless specifically told otherwise. This is default reasoning. Frame-based expert systems are equipped to handle such clustered information (*Knowledge-based systems* 1986, 1–26).

Clustering 1. The use of a table of conditions and conclusions. The conditions are the rows and the conclusions are arranged in columns. Clustering can be an effective aid in obtaining an overall view of a body of knowledge. Clustering can be used to help decide which rules are most capable of pruning the largest amount from the search tree. 2. A process in object-oriented programming of placing objects that are likely to be called together near each other on the disk. This increases efficiency. 3. Organizing data so that related information is together. Frames naturally cluster related data (Stein 1988, 33; Walters and Nielsen 1988, 217–218, 282; Townsend 1987b, 245–249).

Clustering techniques Algorithms used in neural nets that classify incoming patterns of information. The clustering algorithm may be supervised or unsupervised (Townsend and Feucht 1986, 196).

Clyde the Claw A robot that resides in Chicago. Its most famous claim to fame is that its fellow workers sent it get well cards when it broke down (Frude 1983, 82–83).

CmLISP *See* ConnectionMachine LISP (Hillis 1985, 31).

Coaching A teaching strategy found in a number of intelligent computer-aided instruction programs. This strategy involves the student in some type of game situation in which the student learns the desired skill as a by-product of playing the game (Smith 1989, 32).

Coalesce A heuristic that, when it has an equation with two variables, will set both variables equal to the same value. Using this heuristic EURISKO discovered the concepts of doubling, squaring, and recursion (Lenat 1988, 72).

Coarse grain Analyzing a problem in such a way that fine details are ignored.

Coarse-grained parallelism A parallel processing in which there are only a few, relatively large microprocessors, and there exists a degree of centralized control. *Contrast with* Massive parallelism (Waldrop 1987, 113–114; Hillis 1985, 23–24).

COCOMO1 An expert system program built with Insight 2+ which is used for planning development project costs (Williamson 1986, 52–57).

Cognition The use of perception and ideas to acquire knowledge (Hunt 1986, 71).

Cognitive compatibility A principle of knowledge engineering that holds that the way the problem is presented to the user on the screen should conform to the user's conceptualization of the problem (Parsaye and Chignell 1988, 33).

Cognitive economy 1. The representation of concepts and their associated properties in the most economical way possible. 2. A principle that holds to avoiding the storage of redundant information. Nevertheless, the information can be accessed from different parts of the program when necessary. Inheritance is a method of achieving cognitive economy (Hayes-Roth et al 1983, 122–123; Jackson 1986, 55; Parsaye and Chignell 1988, 143; Chabris 1989, 52).

Cognitive learning The application of reasoning to evaluate, organize, correlate, and classify information (Schildt 1987, 202).

Cognitive model of learning Learning that makes explicit the procedure used in learning. Example: the derivation of rules in a rule-based expert system. *Compare with* the Black-box model of learning (Forsyth and Naylor 1985, 102–118).

Cognitive modeling 1. The development of theories of how the human mind works. 2. The approach to artificial intelligence that emphasizes copying how the brain functions. 3. The modeling of human cognition. Cognitive modeling can include thinking, memory, and perception (Chabris 1989, 15–16; Hunt 1986, 71; Townsend and Feucht 1986, 243).

Cognitive-modeling school A school of thought that holds that artificial intelligence research should attempt to model itself after human cognitive functioning. Production systems have been used regularly by cognitive scientists to study human mental faculties. GRAPES and PRISM are two languages that have been developed by this approach. This approach is fruitful, but not the only approach. *Contrast with* the Intelligent artifacts school (Johnson 1986, 55; Brownston et al 1986, 364–368).

Cognitive psychology The branch of psychology that emphasizes the study of human memory and views information processing as a metaphor for thought. Cognitive psychologists make heavy use of computer programs to gain insight into human thought process rather than rely on true theories of psychological cognition. In contrast, information-processing psychology sees computer programs as theories of human thinking. Allen Newell and Herbert Simon are identified with information-processing psychology and they implemented their theory of cognition with the artificial intelligence program, General Problem Solver (Barr and Feigenbaum 1981 vol 3, 4–7).

Cognitive science The study of human information processing. The area of science dedicated to the understanding of the process of human thought. In cognitive science both humans and computer programs are used as objects of study to better understand human thought processes (Mishkoff 1986, 1–6; Barr and Feigenbaum 1981, vol 3, 4; Jackson 1986, 3).

Cognitivists Researchers who are interested in emulating psychological phenomena such as learning by using computer programs. *Contrast with* Automatic programmer (Jackson 1986, 205).

Cold War Idealogue A natural language understanding program that modeled a conservative philosophy. It was guided by a master script that assumed all good events were attributed to the West and all bad events were the fault of the Communists. The Idealogue interpreted new events according to its conservative philosophy (Waldrop 1987, 79–85).

Collections A collection is a group of related objects in object-oriented languages. Three major types of collections are dictionaries, sets, and bags (*Smalltalk/V* 1986, 80–82, 174).

Collective computation Computation which is parallel rather than sequential. This type of computation process is the basis of neural networks. An analogy is a group of people attempting to reach a decision by interchanging ideas and then gradually coming to a consensus. Contrast with the group of people solving the problem in such a manner that each person makes a contribution in a sequence, and each person only knows the contributions of those who preceded him or her (Tank and Hopfield 1987, 106).

Collective decision circuits Decision circuits that employ the collective computation principle (Tank and Hopfield 1987, 105).

Coloration The specific details of a scene in a MOP (Schank and Hunter 1985, 150).

Combinatorial explosion The exponential increase in the number of ways the objects in a set can combine as the number of objects increases. A major problem in artificial intelligence because the rapid increase in different combinations causes such a large increase in the search space that it is not practical to be able to search the search space within a reasonable period of time (Schildt 1987, 16–18; Barr and Feigenbaum 1981 vol 1, 27; Barr and Feigenbaum 1981 vol 3, 519; Hunt 1986, 72).

Combinatorics Probability (Parsaye and Chignell 1988, 213).

Combining certainties The process of deriving a certainty factor from two or more confidence factors. Example: If two inexact rules with the same premise of "Diagnosis is epilepsy" and with certainties of A and B were fired, the combined certainty could be achieved with the formula: Combined certainty = $(A + B) - (A * B) / 100$ (Glasgow and Graham 1988, 31).

Combining confidence Blending different confidences from different rules to produce an overall confidence level for a conclusion. It is equivalent to combining certainties.

Commit operator The operator used for the guarded clause. It is represented as a colon (Luger and Stubblefield 1989, 483).

Common LISP The commonly accepted standard of LISP. It is lexically scoped, contains 700 built-in functions, and has automatic memory management (Allen 1987, 54).

CommonLoops A version of LISP that has object-oriented capabilities. It is capable of multiple inheritance, a characteristic not found in Smalltalk (McGregor 1987, 56).

Common sense The ability to cope with situations based more on experience than reasoning ability (Hunt 1986, 73).

Common-sense reasoning **1.** Reaching practical conclusions concerning common events using everyday knowledge. **2.** The ability to reach conclusions from incomplete and contradictory information, and to revise conclusions in the light of new information. Common-sense reasoning uses default reasoning and must have the ability to represent and manipulate both intensional and extensional concepts. It is difficult to come by in expert systems. Some experts believe common-sense reasoning is a combination of inductive and analogical reasoning (Fischler and Firschein 1986, 44; Hayes-Roth et al 1983, 73–74; Barr and Feigenbaum 1981 vol 3, 84; Chabris 1989, 65; Davis 1990, 131–151).

Commutative production system A production system in which the order in which rules are executed is trivial (Smith 1989, 33).

Commutativity law A law of propositional logic that states A AND B is equivalent to B AND A (Schildt 1987, 222; Luger and Stubblefield 1989, 46).

Competence A desirable characteristic of expert systems which means the expert system avoids asking irrelevant questions (Rovira 1988, 68).

Competence model The modeling of the underlying principles of a knowledge domain. *Contrast with* Performance model (Luger and Stubblefield 1989, 598).

Competence reasoning In the HEARSAY III expert system tool one of two types of reasoning carried out on the blackboard. It is reasoning about the knowledge in the domain. *Contrast with* Performance reasoning (Hayes-Roth et al 1983, 310).

Competition An important principle in neural networks. Certain nodes, if activated, can inhibit other nodes which are in competition with the activated nodes. This inhibition principle helps to ensure the input data are quickly identified. The human brain uses this principle as well as the associative learning principle (Levine 1989, 29).

Competitive bidding A procedure in some expert systems which assures that rules that frequently succeed will be paid greater attention in the future. This procedure is characteristic of self-organizing systems.

Competitive learning A nonassociative, statistical learning scheme used in neural nets. It consists of feature detectors in which each one can respond uniquely to different stimulus patterns. These feature detectors then compete with one another to respond to different patterns. Eventually a particular feature detector will be the one that responds most intensely to a given pattern. Competitive learning is used in multilayer neural nets. A given feature detector (processor unit) in a layer can receive input from all units in a lower level layer. The same unit can send output to all units in the next higher level. Each layer consists of clusters of units. They are connected in such a way that they can inhibit one another. In that way a given unit in a cluster competes with other units in the cluster and then becomes dominant for a particular pattern of input. A type of unsupervised learning, used to discriminate different letters of the alphabet through the process of successive presentations of the letters (Rumelhart and McClelland 1986, 147, 151–153, 162–163; Zeidenberg 1987, 240).

Compilation The changing of one type of knowledge representation into another. This is important since the transformation increases the speed of the program. Most expert systems must execute quickly, since they are frequently dealing with very large knowledge bases. The availability of a compiler can be an important factor in choosing a language or an expert system tool, and it allows for the production of runtime copies of an expert system. That is, the user of a runtime version does not need to have the complete expert system development tool available in order to run the expert system (Hayes-Roth et al 1983, 121; Harmon and King 1985, 108–109).

Compiled knowledge 1. Knowledge that is transformed in some way so that the system runs more efficiently. Some expert system tools allow the expert system to run in either a compiled or a noncompiled form. The noncompiled form is helpful during program development because the program can be edited and rerun quickly. The compiled form is best for production versions of the expert system since a compiled version usually runs faster and the compiled version can function without the full expert system environment. 2. Knowledge that has been extracted from a domain expert, organized, and entered into an expert system. 3. The mental model of the domain expert. Such compiled knowledge can be very abstract and it can be difficult to translate this knowledge to an expert system. Some compiled knowledge may be more in the form of heuristics and is more readily translated into an expert system (Harmon and King 1985, 30–31; Brownston et al 1986, 17–18, 443; Townsend and Feucht 1986, 244; Hunt 1986, 73).

Compiled language A language that must compile or transform a program into a more efficient representation before it can be run. The final product is faster than a comparable interpreted language product, but development time is longer. C is a compiled language. BASIC is generally considered an interpreted language.

Complementary pair A variable and its negation in logic. Example: p and not$p$ (Dos Reis 1988, 50).

Complete Being able to derive all possible inferences from the set of propositions. When a strategy can guarantee a refutation when used with a set of clauses which is unsatisfiable. Breadth-first search is complete since it will eventually find a refutation if one exists. Depth-first search is not complete (Luger and Stubblefield 1989, 59, 426).

Completeness A property of a logic system that states the system is able to reach the necessary conclusion if all required information is present (Smith 1989, 35).

Completeness property 1. A property of propositional calculus that states that if X is a theorem of propositional calculus then it can be deduced by using the rules of inference. 2. The ability of the theorem prover to find a proof if there is one. Assume a set of axioms known to be true and a theorem which is to be tested for its truth value. The negation of the theorem is taken and inferences are made by combining the negation with the axioms. Completeness is the property that if the theorem is true a contradiction will be found using resolution based inference. Other properties of propositional calculus are soundness and decidability. Completeness in an AI system may sometimes need to be partially sacrificed for the sake of speed (Jackson 1986, 74; Lenat 1988, 68–69; Parsaye and Chignell 1988, 408).

Completeness theorem The theorem proved by Godell: First-order logic will, from an initial set of axioms, correctly produce all statements that are valid instances of the initial set of axioms. *See also* Soundness (Ladkin 1987, 59; Barr and Feigenbaum 1981 vol 3, 91).

Component-structured approach An approach to designing an expert system that emphasizes breaking up the program in terms of the structure under scrutiny. The components are described in terms of their connections with one another. Example: Breaking up an airplane diagnostic system into the elements of the electrical system, the fuel system, and so on. This is more of a deep-knowledge approach when compared with the device-specific symptom/cause rule set method (Merritt 1987, 54).

Composite object An object composed of other objects. The ability to handle composite objects exists in some expert system tools like Goldworks. Goldworks is able to handle composite objects because a slot of one object may hold the value of another object (Tello 1988, 307).

Compositional semantics The meaning of an expression as it hinges on the meaning of its parts and nothing else. Predicate calculus has compositional semantics (Charniak and McDermott 1985, 322).

Composition rule The use of fuzzy connectives and fuzzy predicates to build rules. Example: "The stock is quality IF the Price Earnings Ratio is low AND the Cash Flow is very good" (Suits 1988, 41).

Compound clause A clause consisting of a series of simple clauses connected by the logical connectives AND, OR, NOT (Parsaye and Chignell 1988, 77).

Compound data structure type Data structure that consists of simpler data structures, possibly of different types. Example (in OPS5): (Person !name Joe Smith !birthday June 18, 1943, !weight 175). A compound data structure is similar to a record in conventional languages (Winston and Horn 1984, 99).

Compound goal A goal with two or more subgoals (Townsend 1987a, 39–40).

Compound object Compound structure (Townsend 1987a, 377; *Turbo PROLOG* 1986, 38).

Compound structure An object in PROLOG that is contained in another object in a hierarchical relationship. It consists of a functor and arguments surrounded by parentheses and separated by commas. A compound structure is not a PROLOG statement, fact, or rule. Consider the statement owns(John, book("Expert Systems," Harmon)). The part of this fact which is a compound structure is, book("Expert Systems," Harmon). Such compound structures permit hierarchical definitions. They can be used as a means of reducing the number of rules in an expert system. Such structures are very helpful when there are many complex objects. A synonym is compound object. A compound structure is also referred to simply as a structure (Townsend 1987a 83–87, 244; Townsend 1987b, 377; Young 1987, 370).

Compound term One of the three terms of a logic program. A compound term consists of a functor and one or more arguments which are terms. An example of a compound term is author (smith, mike). Author is the functor and smith and mike are the terms. Constants and variables are the other two types of terms in a logic program (Sterling and Shapiro 1986, 4, 16).

Computation A deduction in PROLOG made from the program statements. The calculation of an instance from a query and a logic program. PROLOG computations may be either deterministic or nondeterministic (Sterling and Shapiro 1986, 17, 76, 88).

Computational energy The energy found in a collective decision circuit. Example: Assume a surface with hills and valleys. The energy eventually settles from the hills to the more stable state in the valleys. An incomplete memory may be thought of as energy on a hill. The energy settling into the nearest surrounding valley corresponds to the process of completing the memory with the best possible associations (Tank and Hopfield 1987, 105, 107).

Computationalism A philosophy that holds thinking is information processing, and information processing is the computational processing of symbols, and symbols describe the external world. *Contrast with* Holistic (Waldrop 1987, 135–140).

Computational linguistics The use of computers to investigate language (Barr and Feigenbaum 1981 vol 1, 226, 229; Ballard and Jones 1990, 133–151).

Computational logic Applying logic in a computer program. The use of the language PROLOG is an example of the use of computational logic (Hunt 1986, 10).

Computational paradox The insight that the more scientists attempt to model the brain and mind with linear computers the more they realize how nonlinear and complex the brain and mind are.

Computational theory of vision A theory of vision pioneered by David Marr, which focuses on the importance of finding and concentrating on the critical aspects of the scene (Waldrop 1987, 91–104).

Computer-aided manufacturing A manufacturing process controlled by a computer (Rosenberg 1986, 35).

Computer-assisted instruction A programmed learning procedure based on Skinnerian principles of reinforcement and implemented on computers. Programs employing this approach present information to the user and then ask specified questions. If the user answers correctly, the user is informed the answer is correct, and the program moves on to the next set of information. If the user responds incorrectly, the program repeats the information, or gives remedial instruction and then repeats the questions. It is also called "frame-base-cai." *Contrast with* Intelligent computer-aided instruction, which is more sophisticated (Barr and Feigenbaum 1981 vol 2, 225–294; Mishkoff 1986, 6-1 to 6-2).

Computer control Controlling robots through the use of a programming language. Computer languages used to control robots include WAVE, AL, AML, and AL. *Contrast with* Playback control (Mishkoff 1986, 5-18).

Computerized Pastoral Counseling System A counseling program that gives advice based on Christ's teachings. It was developed by Russell Cassell (Frude 1983, 86–87).

Computer vision The area of artificial intelligence dedicated to endowing computers with the ability to see.

Concatenate To join.

Concept An abstraction. A description that states properties that delineate the instances of the concept. A concept is used to describe a class of objects and the attributes of the objects. Concepts are frequently represented by frames or sets of rules (Hayes-Roth et al 1983, 399; Townsend 1987b, 288; Jackson 1986, 197).

Concept acquisition   1. The building of a concept by the process of positive and negative examples.   2. A type of concept learning, sometimes referred to as learning from examples (Rosenberg 1986, 104).

Concept attainment   *See* Concept acquisition.

Concept learning   The procedure of acquiring abstractions in artificial intelligence by processing information. Very frequently this process is implemented by using examples of a domain of information to build a rule set. The ID3 algorithm is frequently used to process examples and build a rule set. Patrick Winston uses the principle of hit and near miss to build a concept. The concept can then be used to classify objects. Repertory grids are another means of concept learning. Concept learning may be viewed as a search problem. The search space consists of possible solutions to the problems. The search is guided by the constraints of the examples. *See also* Automated knowledge acquisition; Induction learning (Jackson 1986, 197; Kolokouris 1986, 226; Townsend and Feucht 1986, 182).

Conceptual bug   A defect in reasoning that leads to an incorrect answer (Smith 1989, 35).

Conceptual clustering   Arranging objects in sets according to concepts the objects have in common (Rosenberg 1986, 36).

Conceptual dependency   A theory of natural language processing developed by R. Schank and C. R. Riesback, which focuses on semantic analysis. It states that a very small set of primitive actions called semantic primitives can account for most of what must be represented in the world. Example: Schank used only 11 verbs to replace the hundreds of verbs in the English language. "Ptrans" is one such verb; it means moving an object from one place to another. "Ptrans" took the place of "fly," "move," "transfer," "transport," and so on. Conceptual dependency is used in the computer programs MARGIE, SAM, PAM, and BORIS, and it reduces the necessity of syntactic considerations (Fischler and Firschein 1986, 46; Johnson 1986, 172–173; Mishkoff 1986, 4–11; Winston 1979, 192–199; Barr and Feigenbaum 1987 vol 1, 211–215; Schank 1972, 185–192).

Conceptual graph   A knowledge-representation formalism. A finite connected, bipartite graph. Each conceptual graph stands for a single proposition. A conceptual graph consists of nodes connected by arcs. The arcs of a conceptual graph are not labeled. The two kinds of nodes in a conceptual graph are concept nodes and relation nodes. Two concept nodes and two relation nodes cannot be directly connected. A conceptual graph can be used to determine if an instance belongs to a type or to find its properties through inheritance. It has a high degree of expressive power and is readily translated into the predicate calculus. It is capable of dealing with fuzzy logic and multimodal logics. It has been proposed as a means of connecting expert systems with neural networks (Lendaris 1988, 7–13; Luger and Stubblefield 1989, 349–359).

Conceptualization   One of five phases in developing an expert system. In this phase the key concepts, relations, strategies, tasks, and constraints are identified. The five phases, in order, are identification, conceptualization, formalization, implementation, and testing (Hayes-Roth et al 1983, 24, 143–144).

Conceptual object   An object that is the general equivalent of a frame in the KRL language (Jackson 1986, 60).

Conclusion   The expression in logic that logically follows from the set of expressions referred to as the premises (Dos Reis 1988, 50).

Concurrency   The processing of information in parallel—at the same time. An object-oriented approach naturally complements concurrency (Swaine Jun 1989, 116; Hewitt 1986, 44; Eisenbach and Sadler 1985, 184).

Concurrency control   Methods of simultaneously executing a set of subqueries. Concurrency control is an important means of increasing the efficiency of queries. Currently researchers are attempting to enhance PROLOG so that the subcomponents of a given query are executed simultaneously, or so that queries from different users can be executed simultaneously. Enhancing PROLOG in this way is important if PROLOG is to be used with large data bases (Carey et al 1986, 271–291).

Concurrent PROLOG A version of PROLOG that uses an independent procedure to deal with each part of the OR graph. It opens the door to parallel programming. Constructs that characterize concurrent PROLOG are read-only variables, the guarded clause, and the otherwise command (Luger and Stubblefield 1989, 482–485).

Concurrent protocols The recording of information as the task is being performed (Wolfgram et al 1987, 300).

Condition The portion of a rule that must be satisfied before the action portion of the rule can be executed (Rosenberg 1986, 36).

Condition-action rule Production rule (Jackson 1986, 31).

Conditional A statement whose truth is based only on the truth value of another statement. If/then statements, case statements, loop/exit statements are conditional statements (McMillan 1987, 50; Schildt 1987, 231; Barr and Feigenbaum 1981 vol 2, 31).

Conditional plan A plan whose execution is contingent on the existence of certain conditions (Smith 1989, 36).

Conditional probability The probability of an event given a prior event. Example: the probability of rain given a cloudy day. Conditional probabilities are used in Bayes' theorem. They are also called posterior probabilities. *Contrast with* Unconditional probability (Charniak and McDermott 1985, 457).

Conditional rule application A control strategy that restricts the application of a rule unless certain conditions are met (Smith 1989, 36–37).

Conditional substitution A substitution that holds a conditional expression; it is used in resolution (Smith 1989, 37).

Condition element A condition element in an OPS5 production system that appears in the left-hand side of the rule and is a pattern that is satisfied when it is correctly matched with an element in working memory. A production rule may consist of a number of condition elements which may need to be satisfied in order for the actions of the right-hand side to be executed (Neiman and Martin 1986, 56; Brownston et al 1986, 45–51).

Confidence factor Certainty factor.

Confirmative of products A method of calculating confidence factors. Assume a set of rules with the same conclusion. Each rule has confidence factors for each premise and a confidence factor for its conclusion. Multiply the confidence factors in the first rule, and do the same for all of the other rules. Take the result for the first rule (CF1-PROD) and second rule (CF2-PROD) and combine them using the following formula: (CF1-PROD + CF2-PROD) − (CF1-PROD * CF2-PROD/100). The result from this computation and the product computation for rule three are then used with the above equation to obtain a new result. This is continued until all rules in the set have been included and a final confidence factor is computed. Other methods of calculating confidence factors include confirmative of minimums, maximum of minimums, maximum of products, average of minimums, average of products, and weighted average. The problem at hand dictates the most appropriate method for computing confidence factors (Shafer 1989, 71).

Confirmative of minimums A method of calculating confidence factors. Assume a set of rules with the same conclusion. Each rule has a confidence factor for each premise and a confidence factor for its conclusion. The minimum confidence factor in the first rule (MIN-CF1) is combined with the minimum confidence factor in the second rule (MIN-CF2) using the following equation: (MIN-CF1 + MIN-CF2) − (MIN-CF1 * MIN-CF2/100). The result is then combined with the minimum confidence factor of the next rule using the same formula. This continues until all relevant rules are used and a final confidence factor is computed. Other methods of calculating confidence factors include confirmative of products, maximum of minimums, maximum of products, average of minimums, average of products, and weighted average. The problem at hand dictates the most appropriate method of computing confidence factors (Shafer 1989, 71).

Conflict resolution   1. A means of deciding which of a set of rules to utilize when all the rules in a set can satisfy a given pattern. Example: in an expert system it is possible for a set of rules to match the data in working memory. Conflict resolution is the strategy which decides which of the matched rules to execute. The choice is made in OPS5 systems on the basis of recency, specificity, complexity, or it is made arbitrarily. Conflict resolution is one of the four cycles found in the recognize-act cycle in OPS expert systems. The four cycles in the recognize-act cycle are conflict resolution, act, match, and halt. The input the conflict resolution cycle receives is the conflict set which is the output of the Rete algorithm. The conflict resolution strategy in OPS5 can be used to implement backward chaining. PECOS has 12 different conflict resolution strategies it can employ. If none of the 12 strategies is able to narrow the choice to one rule, PECOS can work with each of the rules in parallel and give a separate implementation for each rule.
2. The strategy that will decide on the next rule to be examined. Under this definition, some types of conflict resolution that may be included are DoOne, Do in Sequence, and DoAll (Parsaye and Chignell 1988, 273–275; Moskowitz Nov 1986, 221; Forgy and Shepard 1987, 36–37; Neiman and Martin 1986, 57; Brownston et al 1986, 60–71, 444; Barr and Feigenbaum 1981 vol 2, 350–351).

Conflict set   Rules in OPS expert systems that have been chosen to be further examined for possible firing. All these rules have been matched to working memory elements and the variables in the rules have been instantiated. The rule that will be chosen to be executed will be a function of the conflict strategy being used (Matthews Sep 1987, 82; Brownston et al 1986, 7, 9–11, 444; Townsend and Feucht 1986, 172).

Confusion matrix   A method of examining the performance of expert systems by scrutinizing the incorrect answers. It typically consists of a table in which the cells record the percentage of incorrect answers. One column may represent a diagnosis of neuroses which was made by the expert system. A given row may represent the actual diagnosis for psychosis. The cell that intersects this row and column contains the percentage of neurotic diagnoses made which really should have been psychotic diagnoses. A total confusion score is obtained by summing the rows and columns of the matrix and dividing by the total number of filled cells. The confusion matrix measures the degree to which different conditions are confused and how important it is to avoid confusing conditions. Confusion matrices can be used in expert systems to avoid excessive costs in making errors. The cost of a misdiagnosis in medicine could be, in one case, only mild continued pain, but in another case it may be the patient's life (Parsaye 1988, 61–62; Parsaye and Chignell 1988, 370–372).

CONGEN   CONstrained GENerator. A successor to DENDRAL in which, in contrast to DENDRAL, constraints can be specified by the user (Barr and Feigenbaum 1981 vol 2, 111–115).

Conjecture of inconsistency   The position that any body of knowledge contains inconsistencies. (Hewitt 1985, 230).

Conjunction   1. The logical AND.   2. The requirement in PROLOG that a given goal can be satisfied only if all subgoals are satisfied. The subgoals are connected with the AND connector as opposed to the use of the OR connector. The AND conjunction is a necessity in expert systems (Harrison and Tribble 1986, 66; Winston 1979, 148; Brownston et al 1986, 48–50).

Conjunctive normal form A syntactic scheme employed in logic programming in which conditionals and biconditionals are deleted in favor of disjunction and negation. A conjunction of disjunction of literals. It takes the form of ($X1$ OR $X2$ OR ....) AND ($Y1$ OR $Y2$ OR $Y3$ OR ....) AND .... Conjunctive normal form is used in the resolution process. Conjunctive normal form is sometimes simply referred to as clause form, but for others clause form has a related but unique meaning. Horn clause subset is a related syntactic scheme (Jackson 1986, 77; Smith 1989, 37; Bratko 1986, 397).

Conjunctive query A goal that is a set of goals separated by the conjunction AND. Example (in PROLOG): likes(john, mary) AND likes(bill, sue). Both goals must be computed from the logical database for the program to return true for the query (Sterling and Shapiro 1986, 7–8).

Conjunctive subgoal A subgoal connected to other subgoals with the AND connective. As a result, each conjunctive subgoal must be satisfied for the overall goal to be satisfied (Smith 1989, 37).

Connected graph A graph in which every node has a path to every other node (Bratko 1986, 228).

Connected-word recognition A strategy of speech recognition that recognizes spoken words in a context in which there are not significant pauses between words. This is in contrast to the much simpler goal of recognizing words in isolation. In the latter the problem of telling where one word ends and the next word begins is avoided. *Compare with* the more sophisticated Continuous-speech recognition (Mishkoff 1986, G-1, 5-5).

Connection The point of attachment between processing elements in a neural net, more commonly called the "synapse" (Obermeier and Barron 1989, 219).

Connection graph A control structure used in backward-chaining systems. The connection graph finds the connections between all of the rules' antecedents and consequents. This enhances performance (Smith 1989, 38).

Connectionism An approach to artificial intelligence that holds that one must go deeper than simply working on the symbolic level. Instead, one must attempt to duplicate intelligent behavior by designing systems that emulate the neural processes of the brain. This computational paradigm consists of simple computing elements that communicate with each other and pass their information along in a parallel processing structure. Connectionism is also referred to as parallel distributed processing and the neural network approach (Feldman 1985, 277).

Connectionist A person in the artificial intelligence community who opposes the symbolists and suggests that one must move to a more neural level, and who uses the central nervous system as a model and focuses on parallel processing. A connectionist bases his or her models on nodes, the strength of connections between nodes, and algorithms that change the weights of the connection strengths as a function of the input data. One of the best known connectionists is Geoffrey Hinton (Waldrop 1987, 177–120; Levine 1989, 29).

Connectionist learning Learning that appears to take place through a change in the connection strengths of the connected units in the brain and in neural nets (Salzberg 1988, 50).

Connectionist system Neural networks (Caudill 1987, 46).

Connection machine A parallel processing computer that permits the connections between microprocessors to be programmable, allowing for construction of a variety of different networks. The Connection Machine consists of 64,000 microprocessors. The microprocessors are capable of interacting with one another. LISP is the language used to program the Connection Machine (Zeidenberg 1987, 238; Waldrop 1987, 114; LaGrow 1986, 81–86; Johnson 1986, 297–298).

ConnectionMachine LISP A version of common LISP that can be used on parallel computers. The program control procedures are like common LISP. It differs from common LISP in that operations can be carried out simultaneously at each element of a large data structure (Hillis 1985, 31).

Connection modulation schemes Schemes that adjust the strengths of connections between units on the basis of information that is locally available to the units. Examples: delta rule, competitive learning rule, stochastic parallel models. These models learn by training themselves —adjusting the right interconnections in the course of processing information.

Connective 1. The boolean operator AND, OR or NOT, which is used to describe how information in the conditional if/then statement should be used. 2. Truth functional predicate (Hayes-Roth et al 1983, 62; Charniak and McDermott 1985, 16).

Connectivity The ability of an expert system to communicate with other programs (Ketonen 1989, 44).

Conniver An artificial intelligence language that pioneered the development of higher-level control constructs and data types. It had the capability of putting on hold work on one part of a solution and starting work on a more promising part of the solution. This procedure is called coroutining. It was capable of different kinds of search through coroutining. Conniver employed procedural knowledge. It was the first program to use tree of contexts (choice points) in the data base and it had a powerful pattern matcher to access the data base. It used recursion instead of the backtracking found in its predecessor Planner. It was hoped that it would become a successor language to LISP. It is no longer used because it is too inefficient. In some ways PROLOG may be considered a successor language to Planner and Conniver (Winston 1979, 393; Barr and Feigenbaum 1981 vol 2, 8–10).

Cons-cell A LISP structure used to represent lists. It consist of two parts, a head and a tail. The head has a pointer that points to an atom of the list. The tail of the cons-cell also points to another cons-cell, which has pointers that point to the rest of the list (Charniak and McDermott 1985, 64; Barr and Feigenbaum 1981 vol 2, 16–17).

Consequent The conclusion of a rule. In an OPS5 expert system the consequents make up the right-hand side of the rule. In PROLOG the consequent is the left-hand side of the rule. Sometimes the consequent is an inference. At other times it may be an action such as writing data to a file (Brownston et al 1986, 444).

Consequent-driven production system A backward-chaining production system (*Byte* Apr 1985, 307; Townsend and Feucht 1986, 40).

Consequent reasoning Backward chaining.

Consequent rule Backward-chaining rule (Tello Oct 1987, 242).

CONSIGHT An object-recognition system in industry that uses lighting to produce silhouette images to discriminate images. It was developed by General Motors Research Laboratories (Barr and Feigenbaum 1981 vol 3, 303–305).

Consistency The property of a logic system that all deductions are correct and therefore all consequents logically follow from their premises (Smith 1989, 39).

Consistency-checking function A function in object-oriented programs found in some object structures whose purpose is to check to see that other necessary objects are available in the environment and that the existing environment is one that is compatible with the object (Walters and Nielsen 1988, 134–135).

Consistency enforcer The procedure in blackboard expert systems responsible for keeping the system on the track of a plausible solution. It may also do truth maintenance (Hayes-Roth et al 1983, 18).

Consistency-management system Truth-maintenance system (Walters and Nielsen 1988, 265).

Consistent bindings 1. The acquisition of a set of values that satisfy all variables in all parts of a rule. The bindings that satisfy the conditions between and within each pattern. 2. The property whereby the value for a variable is the same in all appearances in a rule (Brownston et al 1986, 48, 444; Hunt 1986, 77).

Consistent match Consistent binding (Brownston et al 1986, 48).

Constant 1. An entity that does not change in a program run, as contrasted to a variable that can change in a program run. 2. One of the three terms of a logic program. It may be a number or a symbol for an object in the real world (Brownston et al 1986, 13–14).

Constraint 1. A fact that places restrictions on the solutions to a problem. 2. A characteristic used to screen possible solution candidates. 3. A relation among objects that sets a limit on the values the objects can achieve. A constraint defines objects by inclusion or exclusion or by delineating relationships among objects. Example: X > 5 AND X < 10 (constraint by inclusion). Example: "use high detergent oil only for high performance engines" (constraint among objects). Constraints are used in vision programs. They can be used to preserve the integrity of a knowledge base. In a frame-based system a constraint limits the values allowed in a slot. Constraints are used in the least-commitment approach to problem solving. *See also* Forbidden constraints; Required constraint (Jackson 1986, 21; Lassez 1987, 171; Rettig Dec 1987, 17; Voda May/Jun 1988 26; Rettig 1988, 15; Hayes-Roth et al 1983, 77–80; Barr and Feigenbaum 1981 vol 3, 292–300; Parsaye and Chignell 1988, 136; Tello 1988, 308; Shepherd and Kerschberg 1986, 309).

Constraint language A language that expresses a program as a set of constraints (Rettig 1988, 15–17).

Constraint logic programming The use of constraints in logic programming to solve a set of complex problems that are not solvable using ordinary PROLOG. Constraint logic programming requires a special version of PROLOG. Queries can be made using constraints. The variables in the equations being utilized to solve a problem do not have to be instantiated as they do in ordinary PROLOG. The answers may also be in the form of constraints. Constraint logic programming can help to avoid blind bactracking thus greatly enhancing efficiency. Examples: PROLOG II, PROLOG III, and TRILOGY (Lassez 1987, 171–178).

Constraint management The specification, distribution, update, mapping, and reasoning on constraints, which ensure that each object in the knowledge base satisfies certain restrictions. Constraint management helps to ensure the stability of a body of knowledge (Shepherd and Kerschberg 1986, 309–331).

Constraint network A description of the system that is being analyzed in Davis's Diagnostic Reasoning System. It describes the system as a combination of restrictions on the inputs and outputs of each device in the circuit (Chabris 1989, 124).

Constraint propagation 1. The continuing accumulation of a set of constraints on values until the remaining values are reduced to the point where a reasonable solution is reached. For example, in vision the different parts of an image are described in greater detail until the different potential values of the different parts of the image are reduced. Then the image can be identified. 2. Defining a structure so that it is dependent on the value of another structure. Example: The length of time of a project is a function of the number of goals to be achieved. A rule is devised so that as the number of goals is increased the length of time estimated for the project is increased proportionally. The time necessary to complete a project is constrained by the number of goals to be achieved. 3. The use of constraints in developing high-level data bases and expert systems. It is used in semantic network data bases to improve retrieval. It consists of constraints that are represented by labels on the nodes of the semantic network. The labels are spread to other nodes through the use of the laws of logic. It is an alternative to rule-based expert systems. 4. The use of constraints to ensure that subproblems are solved in an order that will yield a reasonable solution to the total problem. The range of values for the various parameters are made available so that the subproblems will be solved within this set of constraints. The problem-solving problem is therefore able to pursue a least-commitment style of programming. This procedure is used in configuration and design of expert systems. The output data are a function of specified constraints. That is, an expert system configuring a computer system may have constraints that include cost, floor space, memory size, speed, and so on. For example, the limited amount of money may prevent the use of a mainframe computer. 5. The use of constraints to limit a search space. Constraints that are connected to each node along with a subset of arcs linked to the node are used to compute the values for other linked arcs. Constraint propagation is considered to be one approach to constraint satisfaction. Constraint satisfaction is often used interchangeably with constraint propagation (Winston and Horn 1988, 576; Hunt 1986, 77; Harmon et al 1988, 148; *Knowledge-Based Systems* 1986, 2-16 to 2-18; Barr and Feigenbaum 1981 vol 2, 146; Townsend and Feucht 1986, 173; Arcidiacono 1988, 114; Hunt 1986, 34–35).

Constraint resolution A procedure used in PROLOG III based on the use of constraints, which is used in place of the standard pattern-matching unification procedure found in PROLOG (Rettig 1988, 17).

Constraint rule 1. A rule that may limit the range of application. 2. A rule that uses constraints to prune the search space. Example: one that allows the use of only those metals with melting points within a certain range (Hunt 1986, 77).

Constraint satisfaction A problem-solving method that uses constraints as a means of quickly finding a solution. In constraint satisfaction only a certain range of values can be assigned to variables because of constraints placed on the variables. That is, the variable X may only be allowed the range of all positive integers up to and including 100. In neural networks lateral inhibition is a means of implementing local constraints. Other methods of implementing constraint satisfaction include backtracking, constraint propagation, and cooperative algorithms (Chabris 1989, 290; Nachsheim 1989, 31).

Constraint structured planning A problem-solving procedure that uses depth-first search and backtracking when it encounters a constraint to which it cannot conform (Smith 1989, 40).

Constraint suspension *See* Candidate generation by constraint suspension.

Constrictor A finding that narrows the search for a solution to hypotheses in broad categories (Jackson 1986, 121).

Constructive bug A defect in problem-solving behavior in intelligent computer-aided instruction that can be identified with the help of the program (Smith 1989, 40).

Constructive dilemma A rule of inference that is a special case of resolution (Dos Reis 1988, 51).

Constructive search Search that avoids backtracking. Constructive search can greatly enhance the execution speed of a program.

Constructor 1. The means of initializing objects in C++. 2. A procedure that creates an object. *See also* San Marco LISP Explorer (Reymann 1988, 89; Flamig 1987, 23–24).

Consultation mode Interaction between a user and an expert system by answering or asking questions (Townsend and Feucht 1986, 18).

Consultation paradigm 1. The part of an expert system that interacts with the user by asking the user questions, giving conclusions, and explaining conclusions. Some consultation paradigms accept unknown as an answer. Others allow multiple choice or free-form input. 2. A conceptualization of a particular type of problem-solving process. Examples: diagnosis/treatment, planning, monitoring, and configuration (Townsend 1987a, 9–11, 157–158; Harmon and King 1985, 92–99; Hunt 1986, 77).

Consultation system An expert system and a knowledge system.

Contact sensor The sensor in a robot that detects when a robot hand has contacted an object. Contact sensors vary from very simple to sophisticated (Mishkoff 1986, 5–19).

Content addressability 1. The ability to retrieve a memory based on a description of the memory or its meaning rather than using the memory location or its name. Example: retrieving the name of a person based on the information that she is a female politician who is known as the "iron lady." Content addressability is a natural by-product of parallel-distributed processing, in which each memory is represented by a unit with mutually excitatory interactions with units standing for each of its properties. Then, whenever any property of the memory is stimulated, the entire memory and all its contents tend to be activated. This type of structure produces content addressability. Associative memory is similar, though associative memory is associated more with human memory than computer memory. 2. Pattern matching. Example: loves(john,X). The data base is searched for data which will match the variable X, and mary is found. The result returned is X = mary. 3. A type of memory in which memory items are accessed by name rather than by address. Linked lists, arrays, balanced search trees, and hash tables are some of the means of implementing content addressable memory (Chabris 1989, 47, 190; Barr and Feigenbaum 1981 vol 2, 58; Rumelhart and McClelland 1986 25–29, 79–80;

Hunt 1986, 78; Jorgensen and Matheus 1986, 36).

Context 1. The state of the solution at a given point in time in a problem-solving process. The state of the solution in a production system is really working memory, because that is where the assumptions and inferred facts are located. 2. The different components into which the domain of an expert system is divided. Example: A set of rules used to solve a particular subproblem is a context. 3. Alternative means of solving a problem. A planning expert system may generate different contexts to find the best way of solving the problem. 4. A conceptual entity or an object in the MYCIN expert system. Examples: a patient or a microorganism. 5. A frame in a frame-based system. 6. A set of bindings of variables and functions in the Scheme programming language which are essentially considered to be a functional whole. 7. A set of facts or conditions that delineate a circumstance in which a particular set of knowledge is applicable. Example: A rocket launch may be carried out in the context of rainy weather, or in the context of an emergency situation. Such contexts can greatly affect the decision to launch, even though the state of the rocket prior to launch is the same for each context. 8. The text surrounding the text which is currently being analyzed in natural language processing. *See also* Multiple contexts (Jackson 1986, 143; Hayes-Roth et al 1983, 288; Mishkoff 1986, 4-5 to 4-6; Winston 1979, 386–390; Walters and Nielsen 1988, 254; Brownston et al 1986, 87–90, 444; Barr and Feigenbaum 1981 vol 1, 190–192; Barr and Feigenbaum 1981 vol 2, 35–36; Rosenberg 1986, 37; Parsaye and Chignell 1988, 14; Tello 1988, 358; Wolfgram et al 1987, 300; Hunt 1986, 78).

Context-based system Structured rule tool (approximate synonym) (Harmon et al 1988, 55–58, 119).

Context element A special type of working memory element in production systems that signals when a particular subproblem is complete and work on the next subproblem may begin. Its function is to control when to move from one context rule set to another. A type of control element (Rosenberg 1986, 37).

Context free   A term used in natural language processing meaning that the analysis of the sentence takes place independently of the context. Example: The phrase, "man writes hurriedly" is analyzed independently of words surrounding it.

Context-free grammar   A grammar in which all production rules consist of terminal and nonterminal symbols. The production rules must have only one nonterminal symbol on their left-hand side. The right-hand side of the rule can can have terminal and nonterminal symbols. The production rules are referred to as rewrite rules. The grammar is context free because the rules only tell how to replace a nonterminal without any reference to the surrounding context. Example: Assume a grammar consisting of two nouns and a verb—boy, writes, book. This context-free grammar has only one primary rule. A sentence is made up of a subject, a verb, and an object. The rule is represented as: Sentence —> <subject> <verb> <object>. The other rules are <subject> —> boy. <object> —> book. <verb> —> writes. Sentence, subject, object, and verb are nonterminal symbols. Boy, book, and write are terminal symbols. The grammar can consist of only one meaningful sentence: "boy writes book." This is a context-free grammar. A context-free grammar cannot take into account the surrounding context. Frequently, the context is critical in understanding what a sentence means. Example: "I hit the man with the bat." Did I hit the man who was holding a bat, or did I hit the poor fellow with a bat I was holding? A more sophisticated grammar such as transformational grammar is context sensitive and has rules that take into account the context. Context-free grammars have been used in limited environments but they cannot deal with the complexities and ambiguities of languages used in everyday life. *Compare with* Case grammar; Systemic grammar; Transformational grammar. Context-free grammar is the simplest of the four and is also the easiest of the four to implement. *See also* Context free (Barr and Feigenbaum 1981 vol 1, 242–243; Thompson and Thompson Dec 1986, 24; Brittain 1987, 37; Charniak and McDermott 1985, 179–188; Clinger 1988, 80–81; Brownston et al 1986, 444; Chabris 1989, 89, 290; Obermeier 1987, 226).

Context-free language   A formal language in which each sentence is produced by a grammar in which the left-hand side of each rewrite rule is made up of one nonterminal symbol. *See also* Context-free grammar (Brownston et al 1986, 444).

Context-free parser   1. A form of a definite-clause grammar parser. The parsing is independent of the surrounding context.   2. A language parser that analyzes sentences in terms of phrases and then breaks down the phrases into its components. Since the parser analyzes sentences in terms of phrases rather than words, as does the state-machine parser, the context-free parser is more apt to attain a degree of comprehension. The rules of the language are represented in the computer program as if/then rules. The draw-back of the context-free parser is that the rules of English grammar are so complex it is extremely difficult to build a system to handle all the variants of the language. Context-free parsers that make heavy use of recursion are called context-free, recursive descent parsers (Schildt 1987, 105–116).

Context mechanism   1. A module found in some expert systems that allows for the use of multiple hypothetical situations.   2. The breaking up of a knowledge base into components to solve the subproblems of the problem (Smith 1989, 41; Harmon et al 1988, 153).

Context-parameter triplets   An object, its parameters, or its values in the expert system MYCIN (Hunt 1986, 78).

Context-restricted rule filtering   The organization of rules into contexts so as to restrict the number of rules that need to be examined at a given time in the problem-solving process. OPS production systems use contexts by making each rule have as a condition element the name of the goal it is designed to help solve. In this way only those rules that have the condition element corresponding to the current active goal are examined. Other expert systems physically separate rules into contexts by placing the different rule contexts into separate files. *See also* Controlled-rule filtering; Goal-restricted rule filtering.

Context-sensitive grammar A grammar that is similar to a context-free language except that the left-hand side of the rewrite rules contain both terminal and nonterminal symbols. The symbols on the right hand side must outnumber the symbols on the left side. Therefore, the context in which the rule is permitted to be used can be delineated. *Compare with* the less complex Context-free grammar (Chabris 1989, 290; Luger and Stubblefield 1989, 389; Obermeier 1987, 226).

Context tree 1. An arrangement of objects in a structured manner. Context trees are used in the expert system EMYCIN. 2. The facts and the values of variables in the expert system MYCIN, which apply to a given program run. This information may be supplied by the user or deduced from previously known facts. The context tree is found in working memory (Chabris 1989, 112; Walters and Nielsen 1988, 260–261; Barr and Feigenbaum 1981 vol 1, 197).

Contextual link A link that connects sets of rules among which shifts can be made to solve the problem at hand.

Contextual rule sets A subset of rules so divided that at a given time the expert system need only search through a small rule set in order to reach a given subgoal or goal. The ability to avoid searching an entire rule base can greatly increase the efficiency of an expert system. The term is interchangeable with context-restricted rule filtering. Contextual rule sets are frequently referred to simply as rule sets (Tello 1988, 207; Tello, Jun 1987, 266).

Context-value-parameter triplets Object-attribute-value.

Continuation A control procedure found in the Scheme programming language. A continuation waits for the results being computed by another part of the program before continuing with a computation. It puts on temporary hold the execution of the rest of the program along with the environment. Continuation functions can be used in building backtracking mechanisms (Maxwell and Riggle 1989, 30–34; Tello 1988, 359).

Continuous boolean function A method for combining closeness values. It has boolean properties and at the same time it takes as input and produces as output, values between 0 and 1. Continuous boolean functions are used to implement fuzzy data base queries. For example, assume you have a data base with information about important events in computer science. One text field includes a description of the event, another text field comments on the importance of the event, and another comments on the time the event took place. A continuous boolean function can take approximate information about each field and combine the approximate information to build a fuzzy query which will return appropriate information. The user must derive distance measures for each field in his data base (Kimbrell 1988, 56–61).

Continuous-path control A type of playback control in which the robot is moved in a continuous motion through the different positions required to carry out the task. It remembers these positions and is later able to duplicate them. Continuous-path control is used for robots which must carry out tasks that require smooth, continuous motion. *Contrast with* Point-to-point control (Mishkoff 1986, 5-18).

Continuous-speech recognition The study of speech that emphasizes the understanding of speech under normal conditions. *Contrast with* Connected-word recognition, which cannot cope with the velocity of normal speech (Mishkoff 1986, 5-5).

Contradiction The condition in which the antecedents of two rules are the same, but the consequents produce different results (Thompson and Thompson Jan 1987, 25).

Contrapositive The process of interchanging the antecedent with the consequent (Smith 1989, 42).

Contrapositive law $(P \Longrightarrow Q) = (\text{NOT } Q \Longrightarrow \text{NOT } P)$ (Luger and Stubblefield 1989, 46).

Control 1. The way an artificial intelligence program chooses between its internal means of solving a problem. The boundary between control and search is fuzzy. Search emphasizes how an AI program explores the problem space. 2. A procedure that governs that order of problem-solving activities. 3. One of the two basic aspects of an inference engine, the other of which is inference. Control determines where to start, the order in which rules and sets of rules are examined, the type of conflict resolution to be employed, and when to stop. Example: In the OPS5 production system which set of rules will next be considered is controlled by choosing either the LEX or MEA conflict resolution strategy. In production systems in general the primary source of control is that exerted by the state of working memory. Some expert systems have a top file which directs which goal will next be sought, or which rule set to use next. Other expert systems use metarules as a means of control. Rule ordering can be critical with respect to control concerning some expert systems, and less important for others like OPS5. With respect to when to stop, some expert systems allow the option of stopping after finding one answer, or after finding all possible answers. The type of inferencing strategy (forward or backward chaining) has a great deal to do with control since the next rule chosen is, in part, a function of the inferencing strategy being used. Active values, activation, procedural attachment, backtracking, coroutining, island driving, and certainty factors are important control factors for different expert systems. For some, search is considered under the rubric of control (Hayes-Roth et al 1983, 306–307, 400; Winston 1979, 87; Harmon and King 1985, 53–58; Hunt 1986, 78; Brownston et al 1986, 12, 15–21).

Control component The part of the expert system that decides the sequence in which rules are to be examined. The term control component is frequently used interchangeably with inference engine and rule interpreter.

Control element A working memory element in an OPS production system whose function it is to control the direction the system takes in problem solving. It is able to pass information from one rule to another. One type of control element is a context element: It is used to enable or disable all rules in a given context. In a production system the right-hand side of a rule makes a working memory element (a control element) which can then be matched to the left-hand side of another rule. In this way, the control element encourages or discourages the firing of a rule or a set of rules (Brownston et al 1986, 152; Rosenberg 1986, 39).

Control expert system A type of expert system that manages the behavior of a complex situation. Such a system must be capable of interpreting, diagnosing, predicting, planning, and monitoring the actions taken. Air traffic control is an example of a situation in which a control expert system can be applied.

Control hierarchy A hierarchy of control elements in which the higher-level elements control the lower-level elements.

Control knowledge Knowledge used to direct the sequence of problem-solving steps to solve a problem (Rosenberg 1986, 39).

Controlled hallucination A method of dealing with the problem of overlapping objects in vision. An image-comprehension technique in which the incoming information is being continually compared with internal models of images. The assumption about what the object could be is made much more quickly than in bottom-up comprehension. Its advantage over bottom-up comprehension is that it can discover what the image is before all information is processed. Top-down comprehension (Forsyth and Naylor 1985, 87–88).

Controlled laziness A technique in vision research in which the image is scanned for key features which the computer program can use to interpret the image quickly. It is similar to the keyword technique used in the Eliza program. While it may quickly identify images, it can easily be fooled (Forsyth and Naylor 1985, 91, 97, 138).

Controlled production system The use of a finite-state machine to control the problem-solving process rather than the normal control mechanisms available in the production system (Hunt 1986, 79).

Controlled-rule filtering A procedural program written to specify which rule set is to be used at a particular time in the problem-solving process. *See also* Context-restricted rule filtering; Goal-restricted rule filtering.

Controlled search A type of heuristic search used with multiple contexts. A combination of depth-first and breadth-first search. The search process starts out in a depth-first mode but, depending on conditions, can switch to a breadth-first search. This type of search keeps a history of the paths it traverses. As a result, it can abandon its current path if the outlook for that path becomes bleak. It can then pursue an earlier path. A variety of evaluation functions such as branch-and-bound search can be used to control the paths chosen (Walters and Nielsen 1988, 277–278).

control pattern A pattern that can initiate or disable an entire set of rules (Tello 1989, 176).

Control rule A rule that controls other rules, also called a metarule (Firdman, Oct 1986, 76).

Control schema The control strategy found in production expert systems. The control schema matches rules and data elements, schedules the rules for some form of conflict resolution by placing them in a conflict set, selects the appropriate rule from the conflict set by means of a conflict resolution strategy, and then executes the rule (Michaelsen et al 1985, 307).

Control strategy A reasoning strategy used in artificial intelligence programs. The best-known control strategies are forward chaining, backward chaining, bidirectional, and means-end. Choosing the best control strategy for the problem at hand greatly enhances the efficiency of the program. *See also* Control schema for a type of control strategy. Of course, control strategies are used in conventional programs. Some experts suggest adding the type of procedural control found in conventional programs can enhance artificial intelligence programs (Firdman 1986, 76; Thompson and Thompson Nov 1986, 25–29; Wolfgram 1987, 67–68).

Control structure The structure a computer language uses to control where it will go next. 1. The control structures in conventional languages are loops, case statements, and if/then statements. Conventional computer languages are relatively sequential in nature. The next program statement is probably the next statement to be executed. 2. The functions that make up the program and the data in a language like LISP, rather than conventional control structures. A LISP program is much less sequential in nature than a conventional program. That is, it is much more difficult to predict which statement will next be executed in LISP. This type of flexibility is helpful when dealing with artificial intelligence applications. Coroutines are important control structures in LISP. 3. The definition for control structure in ai is generally the same as in conventional programming. The types of control structures are different: backward-chaining, forward-chaining, metarules, superlogical quantifiers, productions, attached procedures, agendas, recursion, backtracking, means-end analysis, and pattern-directed invocation. 4. Inference engine (Mishkoff 1986, 3–5; Winston and Horn 1984, 63, 90–91).

Cooperating knowledge source A component of a blackboard expert system, which takes data from the blackboard, analyzes the data and then deposits the results to the blackboard so that the data are available for other cooperating knowledge sources to use. It is also referred to as a cooperating specialist and an independent knowledge source (Rosenberg 1986, 40).

Cooperating specialist A module in the HEARSAY II program that has specialized knowledge about the domain, and uses this knowledge to draw conclusions which are then posted to the blackboard. It is also referred to as an independent knowledge source and a cooperative knowledge source (Hayes-Roth et al 1983, 11).

Cooperative response A type of response to a data base query which in failing to find an answer that strictly fits the query will look for the best fit response to the query (Smith 1989, 43).

Coordination problem The problem in parallel processing of assigning work to a set of microprocessors over a period of time so as to maximize performance (Gasser 1989, 29).

Copycat project A project that works with analogies. Example: *abc* is to *abd* as *cde* is to *X*. It uses subcognitive processes called enzymelike codelets to direct random shuffling, which will find the appropriate answer. The author of Copycat is Douglas Hofstadter (Johnson 1986, 291–292).

Coroutine A program unit that solves problems by working with other program units of equal stature by passing control back and forth between coroutines until the designated problem is solved. The use of coroutines encourages program abstraction (Brownston et al 1986, 197–198).

Coroutining The use of a set of routines that can pass control to any routine, wait until the other routine has finished, and then continue its operation. In LISP the difference between ordinary LISP procedures and coroutining is that the coroutine can pass control to another routine, suspend itself, and preserve its environment. It is somewhat like nested subroutines except that the coroutines are of equal stature and the overall structure is more flexible. That is, coroutining can respond to new information by calling up a set of functions that would not have been called if the information had been different. Subroutines in procedural programs are more likely to be called in fixed sequence regardless of the incoming information (Smith 1989, 43; Barr and Feigenbaum 1981 vol 1, 271; Barr and Feigenbaum 1981 vol 2, 45).

Correctness The measure of a program that determines whether or not a program does what it is supposed to do (Bratko 1986, 179).

Correlation matrix A set of correlations of events. The correlations can give a measure of the expectation of event *A* following event *B*. A correlation matrix can be used to generate constraints that can impose order on a set of events (Johnson 1986, 224).

Cost function A procedure used in state-space search that calculates the cost of achieving a state that has already been reached (Chabris 1989, 291).

Coupling Interfacing a data base with a computer language like PROLOG. *See also* Loose Coupling; Tight coupling.

Coverage The degree to which the expert system is able to handle all the different possible problems in the domain (Parsaye and Chignell 1988, 302).

Creativity The process of synthesizing information so that new and useful insights can be achieved. Learning can be distinguished from creativity in that creativity has discovered something nobody else has yet realized. Artificial intelligence programs that show creativity are rare. Perhaps EURISKO is one program that qualifies. Emulating creativity with computers is one of the greatest challenges facing artificial intelligence researchers (Lawrence 1985, 155; Forsyth and Naylor 1985, 210–211).

Credibility The degree to which the expert system appears to be measuring what it purports to measure. This characteristic is critical since an expert system with credibility is much more likely to encourage a user to utilize it. Credibility is also known as face validity. Other important measures of the value of an expert system are adequacy, accuracy, reliability, practicability, breadth, adaptability, and generality (Marchot 1987, 44).

Credit-assignment problem 1. The problem of ascertaining what aspect of a problem-solving procedure is responsible for solving the problem. The successful resolution of this problem allows a machine-learning algorithm to learn. **2.** A problem that arises in using neural nets. When a neural net makes a mistake, credit assignment is the difficulty of figuring out which connections are at fault. The problem of determining which procedures most contributed to solving the problem (Chabris 1989, 208, 291; Jorgensen and Matheus 1986, 32).

Critic A procedure used in some planning systems with the capability of spotting actions that might prevent the plan from succeeding. A procedure in the NOAH program that monitors potential actions and takes steps to prevent actions which could cause the plan to fail (Smith 1989, 44; Tello 1988, 481).

Criticizer The component in a learning program that scores rules or concepts (Savory 1988, 233).

CRL *See* Carnegie Representation Language.

Crossbars A type of network topology found in Connection machines which connects every microprocessor to every other microprocessor. *See also* Clos networks for a subtype of crossbars. Other topologies include rings, trees, banyan-type networks, grids, delta networks, shuffle-type topologies, and hashnets (Hillis 1985, 57).

Cross-correlation A method used in vision in which a template is compared to a scene in an effort to find key matching positions (Smith 1989, 45).

Cross-indexing The use of different attributes to retrieve a set of objects in knowledge-representation languages. Example: the retrieval of all airplanes that are older than five years and have jet engines (Salzberg 1987, 36).

Crossover A genetic operator that copies portions of two structures to build a new structure. Usually a heuristic is used to ensure the two parent structures have been successful. *See also* Genetic algorithm (Austin 1990, 49–53).

Cross-product The set of all possible matches for a sequence of working memory elements in a production system. The combination of all working memory matches to all condition elements in an expert production system. Large cross-products of working memory elements and condition elements impair the efficiency of an expert system and should be avoided (Brownston et al 1986, 251–263; Hunt 1986, 81).

Cross-reference table A debugging facility used in some expert systems, which references which rules hold which data elements (Brownston et al, 1986, 320).

Cross-validation Evaluating an expert system in a second test site to see if it maintains its ability to solve problems, after it has been evaluated in one test site.

Cryptarithmetic A problem used to test the GPS system. Each letter of an alphabet is assigned a number. The letters are put together in words and two words are added to produce a third word. That is, the sum of the letters in the first two words equals the third word. The goal for the artificial intelligence program is to find out the numerical values of the letters (Barr and Feigenbaum 1981 vol 3, 13; Forsyth and Naylor 1985, 4).

CRYSALIS An expert system used in the area of protein crystallography, which generates structural hypotheses and tests them. CRYSALIS uses a blackboard architecture. Knowledge is stored in facts, algorithms, and rules (Barr and Feigenbaum 1981 vol 2, 124–133).

Cunningham diagram A diagramming technique used in object-oriented programming, which diagrams the objects in an object-oriented system taking into account message passing, methods, and inheritance (Cunningham and Beck 1987, 53–54).

Cut An operator used in PROLOG to prune a search space so that a conclusion can more quickly be reached. The cut prevents backtracking. The cut is usually represented by the exclamation sign. In a PROLOG clause the cut freezes all choices made to the left of the cut. The cut does not stop backtracking for any potential choices to its right. The cut also prevents any subsequent clauses with the same head as the one with the cut in it from being used. Cut is frequently used in conjunction with fail to stop the search for a solution. Cuts can be used to produce if/then/else statements in PROLOG. Two classifications of cuts are red cuts and green cuts (Kenig Nov 1986, 61–62; Townsend 1987a, 75–78, 80–81; Sterling and Shapiro 1986, 157–174).

Cybernetics   A movement that began in the 1940s and was the forerunner of artificial intelligence. Its two key themes are communication and control. The three main elements are feedback, information processing, and the computer. The theory holds the transfer of information is the important factor in explaining many scientific phenomena. Cybernetics was developed by Norbert Wiener (Mishkoff 1986, 2-9; Waldrop 1987, 17; Forsyth and Naylor 1985, 2).

CYC   A recent project embarked on by Doug Lenat, creator of AM and EURISKO. His goal in this project is to design a computer program that will have common sense. He believes that the only way to do this is through the utilization of vast bodies of knowledge. CYC holds 500,000 pieces of information. CYC applies analogical reasoning to its extremely large data base to draw conclusions. CYC stands for the CYC in enCYClopedia (Luger and Stubblefield 1989, 599; Lenat Jul/Aug 1988, 35; Waldrop 1987, 60; Tello 1988, 517).

Cycle   A path that repeats itself in a graph (Luger and Stubblefield 1989, 82).

Cyclic structure   A data structure that is recursively defined. Cyclic data structures are found in PROLOG systems that permit second-order calculus. PROLOG II has cyclic data structures.

Cyclists   People who give information to artificial intelligence programs.

Cylindrical coordinate robot   A stationary robot with a vertical base component and a horizontal arm. The vertical base is capable of elevating, lowering, and rotating. The arm is capable of extension and retraction (Rosenberg 1986, 42).

D

Daemon *See* Demon.

DARPA *See* Defense Advanced Research Project Agency.

DART A diagnostic expert system, developed at IBM, which is used to diagnose equipment failure problems. It is unique in that it does not hold information about why a piece of equipment fails. Instead, it contrasts the expected behavior with the actual behavior of the equipment in order to diagnose the problem (Lawrence 1985, 43–44).

Dartmouth conference The conference at Dartmouth College in 1956 in which artificial intelligence first achieved its impetus. It was at this conference that John McCarthy popularized the term artificial intelligence.

Data abstraction 1. The structuring of data into natural units which make the understanding of the data clearer, and allows easier access. The organization of data into a meaningful format. 2. The process of constructing data types which can be used to represent higher-level concepts. These data types are sometimes referred to as generic objects because they represent the general outline of the concept. Specific instances of the generic object can then be spawned and the instances will represent detailed implementations of the generic objects. Data abstraction allows for the separation of physical details of data from their logical properties. The advantage of this is it allows the user to concentrate on the logic rather than the details of the data. Data abstraction encourages the isolation of the programmer and the user from such details as how to save, retrieve, and communicate with the data objects. Programs and languages using data abstraction are more modular and easier to understand. Less programming is required for modification. It permits the user to write generalized routines for a large class of objects without having to be concerned about the object's internal structure. Smalltalk is a language that excels in the use of data abstraction. In Smalltalk the details of how data are retrieved, saved, and modified is well concealed in objects. *See also* Message passing and Object-oriented programming for more information. In LISP defstruct is a procedure frequently used to build abstract data types. Example: (defstruct (automobile)(color nil)(has-a 'engine')(is-a 'vehicle')). The abstract data type automobile has a number of fields and values attached. In PROLOG data abstraction is produced by nested statements. Example: book (Author-last-name, Author-first-name, Publisher-name, Publisher-city, Publisher-state). Contrast with book(author(Last, First), publisher(Name, address(City, State))). This type of nesting produces a more abstract representation. The use of data abstraction can greatly reduce costly backtracking when doing pattern matching.   3. Organizing data in objects which include the procedures that access the data. The data can be accessed only by sending the object that holds the data a message. The partitioning of the representation of a data object from the instructions that control its use. This type of modular programming is supported by Smalltalk. Languages like C which can avoid messages and access objects using pointers do not fully support this type of data abstraction.   4. The process of employing user-defined data types to represent objects in the application under development. This is a definition of data abstraction which is used in C++ (Swaine 1988, 115; Hu 1989, 67; Waite et al 1987, Preface; Thomas 1989, 232; Wegner 1989, 248; Bratko 1986, 97; Sterling and Shapiro 1985, 25–28; Winston 1984, 97–100; Pugh 1986, 26; Pascoe 1986, 140; Harmon et al 1988, 144; Bratko 1986, 97; Touretszky and Pomerleau 1989, 232).

Data base   1. The facts and rules in a PROLOG program.   2. Working memory in a production system.   3. The data structures that are used to build a fact base (Charniak and McDermott 1985, 320; Brownston et al 1986, 36–37; Townsend and Feucht 1986, 244; Harrison and Tribble 1986, 66).

Data base interface   A procedure in a knowledge-based system used to extract data from a data base. An interface may consist of a program which when executed will use the data from the data base to compute a value that will be returned to the knowledge base. A number of knowledge-based systems have the ability to pass parameters to the interface program. This ability greatly enhances the communication between the knowledge base and the data base (Tello Jul 1985, 72; Hayes-Roth et al 1983, 95–96).

Data base management system   A computer system that provides a means of storage and retrieval for a domain of data. Data base management systems are being enhanced by artificial intelligence technology through the use of natural language inferfaces, improving search procedures, and by adding the ability for the program to reason about its data, thus improving on reporting capabilities and data integrity. *See also* Expert data base systems (Barr and Feigenbaum 1981 vol 2, 163–173).

Data base mining   Using a program like a neural network to find trends in a data base.

Data base rule   A rule with variables, which is derived from data base records. VP Expert uses data base rules (Harmon et al 1988, 84).

Data-centered program   Another term for object-oriented programming. In contrast to function-centered programming, each object possesses its own internal methods which work only with that object. When a new data structure is included the preexisting functions need not be altered. Instead, new functions are tailored specifically for the new data structure. *Contrast with* Function-centered programming (Fernhout 1989, 38).

Data-correction rule   A rule that corrects for errors in data. Example: think of a process in which it is common for a particular type of data to be missed by detection equipment, but it is known that the data must be present if other data are present. A data-correction rule ensures that frequently missed data are tested for in some way and then included in the analysis if the test is positive (Hayes-Roth et al 1983, 95–96).

Data-dependency A record of how assertions were placed in a data base. If the premise (*p*) of an inference that produced the assertion (*q*) were later proved to be false, the assertion (*q*) could then be found and withdrawn. Such records form the basis of truth maintenance (Charniak and McDermott 1985, 411–415).

Data-directed search control The use of heuristic rules and data to prune unproductive avenues of search (Brownston et al 1986, 445).

Data-directed inference An expert system that finds a solution by being directed by the data rather than goals. A synonym for forward chaining. *Contrast with* Goal directed (Hayes-Roth et al 1983, 38, 400).

Data driven 1. Describing programs and functions whose execution pattern is controlled by the data. The control in data-driven programs resides more in the data than in the program commands. LISP and PROLOG are two languages that are data driven. That is, where the program next goes is more a function of the data than is true in a conventional program. In data-driven programs the distinction between programs and data is small. Example (C++): Given a function for multiplication, the procedure that will be used to carry out the multiplication is a function of the type of data supplied as arguments—(times 3, 2), and (times 3.10, 2.20) will call different procedures because in the first example the numbers are integers and an integer multiplication procedure will be used. In the second example the numbers are real and a slower multiplication procedure will be called. 2. Describing a forward-chaining expert system in which the rules are fired as a function of the data in data memory. The data are in control of what will be executed next. Contrast this with conventional programs which will more likely follow a fixed sequence of program statements regardless of the data they are given (Neiman and Martin 1986, 55; Winston 1979, 304–308; Brownston et al 1986, 445; Barr and Feigenbaum 1981, vol 2, 129, 257).

Data-driven expert system Forward-chaining expert system (Brownston et al 1986, 26–27).

Data-driven language A language that does not distinguish between data and programs, and one that can carry out symbolic processing. The data are what determine how the program will be solved (Townsend 1987a, 16).

Data-driven learner A type of induction system that learns only based on the data. *Contrast with* Model-driven learner (Moskowitz 1986, 225).

Data-driven method In example-learning programs, a program that is exclusively driven by the data and not guided by an a priori model. *See also* Version-space method for an example of a data-driven method. One advantage of data-driven methods is their ability to employ incremental learning. One problem is they have difficulties in dealing with contradictory data. *Contrast with* Model-driven method (Barr and Feigenbaum 1981 vol 3, 369).

Data encapsulation The process of hiding data inside an object. The data in an object can be accessed only by using an appropriate message which will activate a function inside of the object. Only procedures inside the object can manipulate the data in the object. An important characteristic of object-oriented programming. Data encapsulation prevents accidental changes in values. *See also* Encapsulation (Skelly 1987, 82; McGregor 1987, 49; Harmon et al 1988, 37).

Data filtering Screening out data so that only a limited subset of data will be used in the problem-solving process. Limiting of the number of working memory elements in a production system that will be involved in the matching process. Data filtering avoids excessive search and improves the speed with which the expert system finds a solution. The two variants of data filtering are activation filtering and certainty filtering. *Contrast with* Rule filtering (Brownston et al 1986, 308–310, 445; Rosenberg 1986, 44).

Data-flow analysis The analysis of data in a computer program to determine which statements are dependent on other statements. That is, which statements must be executed before other statements are executed. In parallel processing data-flow analysis can determine which sets of statements are independent of one another and these independent statements can then be executed in parallel (Eisenbach and Sadler 1985, 186).

Data hiding A characteristic of object-oriented programs in which it is ensured that the only way to access a given piece of data is through the appropriate function. Any language that uses modules can implement data hiding. More conventional languages like C are less strict in allowing access to data in modules than are object-oriented programs like Smalltalk. That is, C allows access to data within a function by the use of pointers. Data hiding is used interchangeably with the term information hiding. *See also* Data encapsulation (Swaine 1988, 115).

Data memory The facts or data base of a production system. Working memory is a synonym (Hunt 1986, 84).

Data modeling The process of identifying the physical entities which need to be represented in the program. This is an important process in information engineering (Blackman 1990, 29).

Data ordering A means of control in some expert systems and PROLOG. The most critical data may be ordered in some way so that the program will pay the most attention to them. This may be done by ordering the data, or by using a tag which labels certain data as more important.

Data-procedure paradigm The process of data being acted on by procedures. The process that takes place in most conventional programs. Compare this approach with an object-oriented approach in which the objects are the focus of attention and procedures are deemphasized (Pascoe 1986, 139).

Data structure The receptacles for storing information in computer programs. A means of representing information. The term is often reserved for relatively complex structures which can represent different data types. Examples: records, semantic nets, contexts, and frames. *Contrast with* Data types (Barr and Feigenbaum 1981 vol 2, 30–31, 34–44; Townsend and Feucht 1986, 244).

Data types A kind of basic data that are recognized by a computer language. The data type delineates the size and arrangement of memory storage for an object of that type. Data types found in conventional computer languages are integers, reals, characters, arrays, strings, booleans, and records. Data types in artificial intelligence languages may also include sets, bags, tuples, vectors, classes, and lists. *Contrast with* Data structure, the receptacles of different data types. In LISP data types are expressions, atoms, numbers, symbols, lists, characters, arrays, strings, and structures. A data type also includes a set of procedures which are associated with it. The list data type, for example, has a set of procedures for manipulating lists (Winston and Horn 1988, 577). *See also* San Marco LISP Explorer (Barr and Feigenbaum 1981 vol 2, 34–35; Hansen 1988, 49).

Davis' Diagnostic Reasoning System An expert system which uses constraint satisfaction and relies on deep knowledge. Its inference engine is known as the candidate generation algorithm, and its working memory is made up of the constraint network of the system being diagnosed. The knowledge base is made up of simulation rules. It has a user interface that allows various inputs, which can then be used to calculate the outputs and compare the calculated outputs with the observed outputs (Chabris 1989, 123–126).

Dead-duck challenge A query that illustrates the shortcomings of logic programs. Example: If Charlie is a duck then Charlie can fly. But Charlie is dead. Can Charlie fly? Once a standard logic program has concluded that Charlie is a duck and can fly then there is no way to retract that conclusion even if later on the program finds out Charlie is dead. The use of truth maintenance is an attempt to remedy this kind of problem.

Debugging aid A tool used to find errors in an expert system, Examples: cross-reference tables, master-scope facilities, syntax checkers, modifying productions and data memory during execution, halting execution after a given rule has fired, the ability to print the contents of working memory, printing the conflict set, printing all matches for a given rule, and tracing (Brownston et al 1986, 18).

DEBUGGY An intelligent computer-aided instruction system that identifies and analyzes the mistakes made by mathematics students. The program can distinguish among 100 million hypotheses. DEBUGGY presents problems to the student to narrow down the possible errors the student is making. It attempts to explain why a student made a mistake, and confirms this by predicting future mistakes. Studies confirmed DEBUGGY was able to predict mistakes the students would make (Johnson 1986, 272–273; Waldrop 1987, 208–212).

Decentralized AI *See* Distributed AI.

Decentralized architecture A parallel architecture in which each microprocessor must have its own program and its own memory and in which there is no executive processor controlling all of the microprocessors. Such an approach needs relatively powerful microprocessors. This type of architecture may be preferred for complex, relatively unpredictable problems with many contradictions, or for using inference with very large data bases. The Japanese have adopted this type of architecture. *Contrast with* Centralized architecture.

Decentralized control scheme A control scheme used in parallel processing in which each microprocessor is relatively independent. There is no centralized control. Such a scheme may be best for large unpredictable problems. *Contrast with* Centralized control scheme (Waldrop 1987, 116).

Decidability A property of propositional calculus that states, for any X there is a procedure that proves whether or not X is a theorem. Other properties of propositional calculus are completeness and soundness (Jackson 1986, 74).

Decision list A tool sometimes used in building an expert system, which lists the different decisions that the expert system can make.

Decision-modeling system An artificial intelligence program involved in selecting the best solution from a number of known alternatives. These programs generally use decision trees. A decision modeling system differs from expert systems in that with decision modeling software it is a matter of choosing between one of a small number of known alternatives, as in choosing one of five different stock portfolios. Examples: Expert Choice, Lightyear, and REVEAL (Tello 1988, 65; Tello Jul 1985, 72–76).

Decision procedure An algorithm used to decide if a string of symbols belongs to a language (Chabris 1989, 291).

Decision support Specialized planning programs that assist managers in making business decisions. Examples: Expert Ease™, Expert Choice, and Arborist.

Decision table A method of holding information about the conditions in a set of rules, which is used to identify the rules with common conditions. This information is then used so that a given condition need only be evaluated once rather than every time the condition shows up in a rule (Smith 1989, 47).

Decision theory A theory to calculate the probabilities, gains, and losses that are attached to each potential decision in a set of potential decisions (Smith 1989, 47).

Decision tree   1. A knowledge structure used to make decisions and solve classification problems.   2. A map of the decision-making process of an expert system.   3. A representation in which diagnostic knowledge about faults is encoded without regard for their underlying causal relationships. The diagnostic process consists of asking and answering questions and as a result moving through the different possible decisions in the decision tree until a correct decision or classification is reached. Decision trees are implemented in decision-modeling software and example-based rule-induction programs. Decision trees are frequently implemented as one large rule. They are not used in large expert systems because of the excessive duplication of branches. The term classification tree is a synonym. In contrast to expert systems decision trees are harder to construct and modify. They do not provide explanations, and they cannot handle unknown information (Barr 1988, 47; Thompson and Thompson Nov 1986, 149; Tello Jul 1985, 72; Fischler and Firschein 1986, 44; Brynjolfsson and Loofbourrow 1988, 32; Townsend 1987, 231, 378; Tello 1988, 65–66; Chabris 1989, 291).

Declaration   The act of associating an identifier with an entity, as in declaring the variable income to be a real variable (Hunt 1986, 85).

Declaration section   The part of an OPS5 program that specifies working memory elements, indexes of attributes, vector attributes, and external functions (Hunt 1986, 85).

Declarative knowledge   1. Knowledge that emphasizes concepts and their relations with other concepts, rather than procedures that manipulate the concepts.   2. Knowledge that is a specification of a problem rather than a procedure for solving the problem. The knowledge is explicitly specified, rather than being intertwined in a procedure. Declarative knowledge must be interpreted and executed by a separate component of the program. The language best known for its use of declarative knowledge is PROLOG. *Compare with* Procedural knowledge (Townsend 1987, 378; Chabris 1989, 291; Hunt 1986, 85).

Declarative language   Languages that focus on what the problem is rather than how to solve the problem, and in which the problem is defined in such a manner that the solution can be deduced from the explicitly stated knowledge. Heuristics, as opposed to algorithms as in procedural programs, are used to solve problems in declarative programs. The flow of control in declarative languages is not specified by the programmer nor is it as rigidly controlled as it is in procedural programs. The flow of control is implicit in the declarative language and is more in the hands of the data than a specified procedure. In contrast, a procedural language's flow of control is explicit and the knowledge is generally more implicit. Declarative languages possess the property of referential transparency. That is, the computational history of the program run is not as critical as it is for a procedural program. Advantages of declarative languages are that the programs are easy to read, compact, and are relatively free of side effects. This latter characteristic makes them suitable for parallel processing. At least one authority includes functional languages like LISP as a declarative language. Others hold that LISP is a highly procedural language. Certainly, LISP can be used to build a declarative language. PROLOG is considered the prime example of a declarative language. *Compare with* Imperative language (Eisenbach 1985, 149; Eisenbach and Sadler 1985, 186; Lane 1987, 94; Voda, 1988, 25; Townsend 1987a, 17; Townsend 1987b, 378).

Declarative meaning   The relationships defined in the program. The procedure as to how the problem is solved is deemphasized. PROLOG is known for its use of declarative meaning. A PROLOG program simply defines relationships. In pure PROLOG, the order of clauses does not change the meaning of the program. Contrast the declarative approach with the procedural approach in which the order of the programming statements is more crucial. The resolution procedure is the underlying procedural part of PROLOG which goes about using the relationships to solve problems (Bratko 1986, 24, 62).

Declarative query language A query language that produces a query by placing constraints on the fields. *Compare with* Procedural query language (Graham 1989, 21–26).

Declarative representation The representation of knowledge by focusing on the description of knowledge rather than on step-by-step procedures for achieving knowledge. Examples: logic and semantic nets. *Compare with* Procedural representation (Harmon and King 1985, 43–46; Barr and Feigenbaum 1981 vol 1, 230).

Decomposition An important strategy used by knowledge engineers in which the knowledge engineer breaks up a problem into parts as an aid in designing an expert system (Walters and Nielsen 1988, 83, 281–283).

DEDALUS An automatic programming system that takes as its input a logical specification of the program and outputs a LISP-like program (Barr and Feigenbaum 1981 vol 2, 355–363).

Deduce-mode choose One of two methods of choosing an alternative from a choice set in HEARSAY-III. This mode is chosen when the evidence for the alternative is reasonably conclusive and it is doubtful there will be a reason to make a change. *Contrast with* Assume-mode choose (Hayes-Roth et al 1983, 311).

Deduction 1. A type of inference. 2. The process of using rules to find the solution to a problem. In deduction a conclusion must be true because it is a specific instance of a general case known to be true. Example: "All humans are mortal" is known to be true. The fact "John is human" can be used to deduce the specific instance "John is mortal." Deduction proceeds from the more abstract to the more specific. Deduction may be considered a type of shorthand for knowledge. Rather than place all known facts in a knowledge base, deductive rules can be used to infer a set of facts. A deduction from a true premise must give a correct conclusion. Formal reasoning is a synonym for deduction. *Contrast with* Abduction; induction (Townsend 1987a, 46; Charniak and McDermott 1985, 14; Olsen et al 1987, 118).

Deduction tree An AND/OR tree (Townsend and Feucht 1986, 155).

Deductive approach Automatic programming that uses deduction to derive the principal control structures of a program. Other approaches to automatic programming include the transformational approach, high-level language approach, and knowledge-based approach (Tello 1988, 420).

Deductive data base Knowledge-based management system (Parker Jr. et al 1986, 36).

Deductive production system A production system in which the consequents of the rules are limited strictly to inferences that can be made from the knowledge in the system. Situation-action rules—that is, rules that trigger input and output—are not permitted (Winston 1979, 144).

Deductive retrieval Pure logic programming. That is, the answering of a query by finding a match in the facts and rules of a data base. PROLOG is the language best known for its deductive retrieval capacity. In PROLOG deductive retrieval is programming without such extras as input/output commands and the cut predicate (Amsterdam 1988, 18, 22; Charniak and McDermott 1985, 369).

Deductive retriever Theorem prover (Charniak and McDermott 1985, 353).

Deep backtracking Backtracking that takes place when a program is unable to unify the goal with the last clause of a procedure, and the program attempts another goal in the computation tree. Backtracking is employed in the PROLOG language. *Contrast with* Shallow backtracking (Sterling and Shapiro 1985, 97, 193).

Deep knowledge Knowledge based on underlying principles, processes, theories, or cause-effect relations rather than simple empirical associations. Example: a medical diagnostic system based on principles of physiology. Knowledge based on cause-effect relationships is a form of deep knowledge as opposed to correlational relationships. Deep knowledge is much more reliable. Most expert systems rely on shallow knowledge. *See also* Deep representation (Townsend 1987a, 151–152; Harmon and King 1985, 33; Townsend 1987b, 378; Townsend and Feucht 1986, 74; Parsaye and Chignell 1988, 122, 127–128).

Deep meaning   Deep knowledge.

Deep representation   The use of knowledge-representation structures capable of representing underlying principles. Semantic nets and frames are two knowledge-representation structures that are capable of representing deep knowledge. Such representations are capable of relatively high levels of abstraction and analogical reasoning. Rules are more likely to represent shallow knowledge. *See also* Deep knowledge (Michaelsen et al Apr 1985, 304–309).

Deep structure   A basic underlying structure in transformational grammar that retains the essential meaning of a sentence (Smith 1989, 47).

Default reasoning   1. Making assumptions based on experience rather than empirical proof. Example: assuming a given dog has four legs even though you have never seen that dog. Such reasoning is not as sound as deductive reasoning, but default reasoning is critical in making decisions in everyday life, and it is important in many expert system applications. In a rule-based system default reasoning can be instituted by rules that draw a conclusion unless a contradiction is found in the data base.   2. A means of dealing with incomplete information (Charniak and McDermott 1985, 370; Barr and Feigenbaum 1981 vol 1, 176–177; Barr and Feigenbaum 1981 vol 2, 239; Barr and Feigenbaum 1981 vol 3, 115–116; Townsend and Feucht 1986, 168).

Default rule   1. The last clause in a set of clauses with the same head in PROLOG; this last clause is a default fact that is true if the other clauses (rules) fail. Red cuts are used to implement default rules. It is PROLOG's version of an IF/THEN/ELSE rule with the last clause being the ELSE part of the rule.   2. The rule used in the expert system shell Personal Consultant whereby, if a value is not supplied for a variable, the rule automatically supplies a default value (Sterling and Shapiro 1985, 171–173).

Default value   A value of a property that is assumed for the property unless another value is specified. Default values are used frequently in frame-based artificial intelligence systems. Demons are frequently used in frames to retrieve default values. *See also* Default reasoning, for an illustration of how default values are used; Default rule (Floyd 1988, 84; Winston 1979, 180; Harmon and King 1985, 44; Barr and Feigenbaum 1981 vol 1, 183; Winston 1984, 317).

Defense Advanced Research Project Agency (DARPA)   The government agency responsible for financially backing a number of artificial intelligence projects.

Definite-clause grammar   1. A grammar that is represented as logic statements, which is used in logic languages like PROLOG. A unique notation for PROLOG clauses which can be used to more efficiently parse sentences.   2. A generalization of a context-free grammar, which employs nondeterministic programming and difference lists. *See also* Definite-clause grammar parser; Difference lists (Clinger 1988, 80–84; Sterling and Shapiro 1985, 256–265; Knaus Jun 1989, 50).

Definite-clause grammar parser   A context-free, top-down type of parser based on the use of definite-clause grammar. A parser breaks up the input of a sentence into smaller, more digestible chunks and then tests these chunks to see if they conform to the rules of grammar. Most definite-clause grammar parsers make use of difference lists. The use of difference lists allows sentences to be divided into chunks such as noun and verb phrases. Pattern matching a sentence by phrases is much faster than pattern matching a sentence word by word. The more complex pattern matching of phrases rather than words ensures early failure of dead-end paths. A definite-clause grammar is the most common type of parser used in the PROLOG language. The context-free recursive descent parser is a limited version of a definite clause grammar—it does not allow contextual analysis (Boisen 1987, 47–55; Clinger 1988, 81–82; Townsend 1987b 318–332; Sterling and Shapiro 1985, 256–265).

Definition A set of facts or rules in a PROLOG program that have the same predicate and the same number of arguments (Young 1987, 42–44).

Definitional concept A frame that has a parent. *Contrast with* Primitive concept.

Definitional relationship A relationship that defines a value of an attribute. Example: The value of the attribute color of the car is red (Townsend 1987a, 122).

Definition environment The environment in force when the procedure needing the free variable value was defined (Winston 1984, 54).

Defun A built-in function in LISP that defines new functions.

Degree of freedom A measure of the flexibility of a robot arm. A robot arm with two degrees of freedom has two joints. One with three degrees of freedom has three joints (Mishkoff 1986, 5-14).

Delayed binding Dynamic binding (Swaine Jun 1989, 116).

Delegation A procedure followed in prototype object-based systems in which all messages sent to instance objects are delegated to a parent object. The instance objects do not have the methods to respond to the message. All methods are kept in the parent objects. *See also* Prototype systems (Thomas 1989, 238).

Deliberation A type of reasoning that does not rely on stored knowledge, and which is necessary when an unforeseen situation arises and the necessary knowledge has not been programmed into the system. In such cases the system must rely on weaker methods such as search (Chabris 1989, 28).

Delivery system The final expert system product, which has been debugged, optimized for speed, and customized for the end user.

DELTA/CATS-1 An expert system used to maintain General Electric's diesel-electric locomotives. It is a forward- and backward-chaining system which was originally designed in LISP and then converted to FORTH for reasons of portability. Its interface uses both menus and queries. It does much more than diagnosis. It emphasizes facilities for giving details concerning the engines, and help in repairs. A number of video tapes that can aid in the actual repair process can be triggered by the system (Harmon and King 1985, 160–163).

Delta-D recognizer A visual pattern recognizer that focuses on changes in direction to discriminate patterns. That is, you will change direction three times in following the path of a triangle but four times in following the path of a square. *See also* Recognition by key points, for another pattern recognition approach (Schildt 1987, 155–165).

Delta network A subtype of a banyan-type network, which is noted for its uncomplicated routing. Other topologies include clos networks, rings, trees, banyan-type networks, grids, hashnets, shuffle-type topologies, and crossbars (Hillis 1985, 59).

Delta rule A learning rule used in parallel-distributed processing systems. It has the capability of associating arbitrary input/output pairs, and it can then learn to compute artibrary input/output functions. It does this by changing the strengths of the weights at processor connection points depending on whether or not a given classification is correct. The equation is $W_{new} = W_{old} + B*Error*X/abs(X*X)$. W_{new} is the new weight.

W_{old} is the old weight. *B* is a learning constant. Error is the difference between the actual output and the desired output. *X* is the input stimulus. Its goal is to reduce the difference between the output target pattern and the actual output pattern. The delta rule minimizes the least-mean-square error in the system. It essentially maps similar-looking input patterns into similar-looking output patterns. It is used in supervised learning. That is, in addition to the input signal from the stimulus, the delta rule also uses an input signal from an outside agent which tells whether or not the stimulus is correctly classified by the network. The delta rule cannot be used in neural nets with hidden units, and it cannot compute the exclusive-OR. It has been succeeded by the more general and more powerful back propagation rule (the generalized delta rule), which can accommodate hidden units. The delta rule is sometimes called the Widrow/Hoff rule or the least-mean-square law (Jones and Hoskins Oct 1987, 156–158; Rumelhart and McClelland 1986 vol 1, 53, 417–418; Caudill Feb 1988, 57–59; Caudill Jun 1988, 53–54; Bayle Nov/Dec 1988, 42–43).

Demodulation   An inference rule that takes as input an equality expression with variables and a ground clause. Its output is a ground clause that is a combination of the two input clauses (Tello 1988, 419; Luger and Stubblefield 1989, 439).

Demodulator   A clause that carries out demodulation (Luger and Stubblefield 1989, 439).

Demon (also known as daemon)   **1.** A cell in a perceptron that monitors a set of cells and fires when a certain pattern of activity is observed. The firing of the demon signals a decision maker cell.   **2.** Procedures that lie dormant in a knowledge system, until a value is needed, being added, or modified, or until a specific pattern of data appears, a rule fires, or some other event takes place. Demons take care of procedural details and allow the overall program to be more clearly visualized; they are used to respond to emergencies, to guard data, and to compute values. Procedural attachment is a name for demons in a frame-based system. There are many types of demons. Generally demons are thought of as procedures that reside on a slot in a frame-based system. A demon can also be a rule in a rule-based system. *See also* WHENEVER as an example of such a demon. Demons can be implemented in OPS5 expert systems by using the MEA conflict resolution strategy. *See also* if-added demon; If-needed demon; If-removed demon (Amsterdam Feb 1987, 15; Minsky 1985, 138; Reece 1987, 52–53; Matthews Sept 1987, 80; Winston 1979, 379–386; Shafer Sep/Oct 1988, 54; Brownston et al 1986, 206–207; Barr and Feigenbaum 1981 vol 2, 45; Winston 1984, 317–320; Forsyth and Naylor 1985, 3; Walters and Nielsen 1988, 138–139).

DeMorgan's theorem   A theorem in propositional logic that states NOT(*A* OR *B*) is equivalent to NOT *A* AND NOT *B* (Schildt 1987, 225–227; Hayes-Roth et al 1983, 63; Luger and Stubblefield 1989, 45).

Dempster-Shafer theory of evidence   *See* Shafer-Dempster theory of evidence (Townsend and Feucht 1986, 174).

DENDRAL   An expert system developed by Feigenbaum which finds the correct structures for chemicals. It uses production rules to prune the search space. The program begins by taking the chemical in question and analyzing it by a spectrogram, which produces lists of possible structures of the compound and a list of structures that cannot possibly fit the compound. (The chemical formula for the chemical has in the meantime been derived by some other independent means which is irrelevant here.) This chemical formula is then given to DENDRAL so that it can generate all the structures which can fit the formula. DENDRAL's output of structures is limited by the structure lists produced by the spectrogram. The mass spectrogram is generated for each candidate left. The generated mass spectrograms are then compared with the actual spectrogram of the chemical and the best fit is chosen as the appropriate structure. This approach is referred to as the generate-and-test approach. It generates all the different types of molecular structures that satisfy the constraints and then tests the candidates. In contrast to most other expert systems, its explanation facilities are limited. It is also more difficult to modify than most other expert systems since it is not a pure production system. DENDRAL is considered to be a product of the intelligent artifacts school. Unlike the cognitive-modeling school, the intelligent artifacts school believes that artificial intelligence need not operate like the human mind (Hayes-Roth et al 1983, 7–9, 51; Winston 1979, 237–241; Harmon and King 1985, 134–135; Barr and Feigenbaum 1981 vol 2, 106–123; Tello 1988, 96–97).

Dendrite The part of the nerve cell that brings impulses to the nerve body (Stevens 1985, 288; Obermeier and Barron 1989, 219).

Dennett, Daniel Author of *Brainstorms: Philosophical Essays on Mind and Psychology*. His contention is that the most important contribution of artificial intelligence has been to show a way out of the homunculus dilemma by breaking up a task into smaller and smaller functions.

Dependency A chronicle of the inference process taking place while an expert system is attempting to solve a problem (Hunt 1986, 87).

Dependency-directed backtracking 1. Backtracking that returns to the point where failure occurred. The backtracking involved when one is dealing with incorrect reasoning rather than errorful information. 2. Backtracking guided by dependency records. Such backtracking is more efficient than chronological backtracking because, rather than blindly retracting the last item inferred, dependency records can be used to find and retract the item that is the cause of the failure. In some instances dependency-directed backtracking can cause infinite loops. A synonym is intelligent backtracking. *Contrast with* Truth-maintenance system (Chabris 1989, 287; Walters and Nielsen 1988, 270; Townsend and Feucht 1986, 173; Hunt 1986, 34; Winston 1984, 79–82; Hayes-Roth et al 1983, 74–77, 82).

Dependency-directed search A search that uses dependency records to decide what conclusions to withdraw.

Dependency record 1. A recording of the inferential steps taken by an expert system. Records that link conclusions and the reasons for the conclusions. Dependency records are useful in being able to implement nonmonotonic reasoning and dependency directed backtracking. 2. The record in a candidate generation by constraint suspension system that keeps track of which components contribute to which output values. The dependency record is then used to zero in quickly on the potential set of faulty components (Hayes-Roth et al 1983, 75; Brownston et al 1986, 445; Townsend and Feucht 1986, 168; Chabris 1989, 124).

Depth bound The restriction on the depth to which a search is allowed to reach (Smith 1989, 49).

Depth-first iterative deepening A combination of depth-first and breadth-first search. In the first pass a depth-first search for each path is carried out only for one level. In the second pass depth-first search is carried out for two levels for each path. On the third pass the depth level searched is three. This continues until a solution is found (Luger and Stubblefield 1989, 101).

Depth-first search A blind search in which the search tree is traversed from the left side of the search tree as deeply as possible until the goal is achieved or a terminal node is reached. If the goal is not achieved and a terminal node is reached it then starts at the next top leftmost node and goes as deeply as possible again. If the search tree has infinite depth and there is no solution in the leftmost branch, this type of search will never return a solution. Depth-first search is employed in PROLOG, though other types of search can be implemented in PROLOG. Questions posed to the user when depth-first search is employed are more focused on a particular topic and easier to follow than they are in breadth-first search. It is preferred over breadth-first search when there are a minimal number of subtrees which have only one connecting point to other nodes. Breadth-first search is preferred over depth-first search when blind alleys present a significant problem. *Contrast with* Breadth-first search (Chabris 1989, 151; Wolfgram 1987, 65; Mishkoff 1986, G-1; Harmon and King 1985 57; Sterling and Shapiro 1985, 104–105; Winston 1984, 171–175).

Derivation tree   A structure that describes how the different words in a sentence are related (Smith 1989, 50).

Derived class   A descendant of a more abstract class. A specialized version of the base class. A useful method of adding facilities of an already existing class to the new class without the problem of complete reprogramming (Waite et al 1987, 2, 30–32, 191).

Derived fact   A fact in a PROLOG program produced by queries. *Contrast with* Base fact (Shmueli et al 1986, 248).

Descriptive knowledge   Knowledge that describes a situation. A set of facts. *Contrast with* Prescriptive knowledge.

Descriptive language   A computer language that relies on the programmer to provide an explicit description of the problem. The built-in mechanisms like unification and backtracking then compute the solution. PROLOG is a descriptive language. Descriptive languages are also called declarative languages. *Contrast with* Prescriptive language (Townsend and Feucht 1986, 27).

Design expert system   An expert system that develops a plan for building an object. Design expert systems are usually constraint based and frequently must be able to reason with spatial relations. Example: a system that designs an electronic circuit (Hayes-Roth et al 1983, 84–85).

Destructive dilemma   A rule of inference that is a special case of resolution (Dos Reis 1988, 51).

Destructor   A function in C++ that is called to destroy a member of a class (Miller May 1988, 45; Flamig 1987, 23–24).

Determinate   A problem that can be broken up into subtasks at different levels, if the subtasks at each level are in a fixed order. *Compare with* Indeterminate (Jackson 1986, 133).

Deterministic   Describing a rule whose premises and conclusions are known with certainty (Keller 1987, 234).

Deterministic computation   A type of computation in PROLOG in which only one clause is capable of achieving a particular goal (Sterling and Shapiro 1985, 76).

Deterministic expert system   The category of expert systems that deals primarily with definite true-false responses. A deterministic expert system does not use fuzzy logic, certainty factors, or Bayes' theorem (Schildt 1987, 62).

Deterministic inference   An inference in which the answer is either right or wrong. *Contrast with* Probabilistic inference (Forsyth and Naylor 1985, 18).

Developer interface   The tools available to aid in developing an expert system, including an editor and a tracing system (Harmon et al 1988, 61).

Developmental efficiency   A measure of how quickly an expert system shell/tool can construct an expert system. *Contrast with* Runtime efficiency (Freedman 1987, 73).

Device-specific symptom/cause rule set method   An approach to designing an expert system that emphasizes symptoms and probable causes rather than focusing on the underlying structure of the system. This is a shallow-knowledge approach. *Contrast with* Component structured approach (Merritt 1987, 54).

DEVISER A planning system which can produce parallel plans when given time constraints. It is a temporal planning system. *See also* FORBIN, for an example of a planning program which can deal with deadline time constraints (Tello 1988, 484).

Diagnostic expert system An expert system that uses symptoms or faults to diagnose a disease or to find the fault. Examples: medical diagnosis and auto repair expert systems (Hayes-Roth et al 1983, 83).

DIAL *See* Draper Industrial Assembly Language.

Dialogue task A type of task given expert systems in which the user is involved in an ongoing dialogue with the system. Each portion of the dialogue provides the expert system with information to make a choice. In this type of task a backward-chaining approach is usually more appropriate. *Contrast with* Signal-processing task (Harmon et al 1988, 187).

Dictionary A class in object-oriented programming that stores and retrieves objects using a key. Example: using the name of a person as a key to retrieve the person's address (Rettig Jan 1987, 16; *Smalltalk/V Tutorial and Programming Handbook* 1986, 80–81).

Difference An operator in relational algebra to select records that are in one relation but not another. Each relation must have the same schema (Parsaye and Chignell 1988, 414–415).

Difference lists A difference structure in PROLOG that uses uninstantiated variables to prune search. An incomplete data structure. Example. [a, b, c, d, e] − [d, e]. The difference list is [a, b, c]. Difference lists can be used to more efficiently process data. They are used in definite-clause grammars. When difference lists are used in definite-clause grammars, sentences can be examined a phrase at a time rather than a word at a time. This greatly reduces the amount of processing. Difference lists can also be used to efficiently concatenate lists. *See also* Definite-clause grammars (Boisen 1987, 49; Clinger 1988, 82–83; Sterling and Shapiro 1985, 239–245; Bratko 1986, 192–193; Luger and Stubblefield 1989, 456).

Difference measures Calculations that estimate the difference between input and output pairs. Difference measures are used in automatic programming (Smith 1989, 51).

Difference reduction Means-end analysis (Hunt 1986, 89).

Difference table One of the two components of the General Problem Solver. The difference table holds the knowledge of the problem domain the General Problem Solver is currently exploring. The difference table is somewhat analogous to the knowledge base of an expert system (Luger and Stubblefield 1989, 410–415).

Differential modeling A principle used in some computer-aided instruction systems. The computer has a model of how the student should solve a problem. When the student's response differs from the model, the computer attempts to ascertain what the difference is between the ideal model and the student's actual response. It then uses this difference as a means of correcting the problem the student is having (Waldrop 1987, 211; Smith 1989, 51).

DIGITALIS Therapy Advisor An expert system that advises physicians on the administration of the drug digitalis and emphasizes ongoing patient management. It pays attention to both quantitative and qualitative aspects of the situation.

Digitalization The process of converting a visual image to binary data by using an analog-to-digital convertor (Mishkoff 1986, 5-9).

Digraph Directed graph (Jackson 1986, 52; Emerson 1987, 58).

Dimensionality A combinatorial explosion problem associated with expert systems that use multiple contexts. An expert system that generates a large number of contexts will be very difficult to search for a solution unless an efficient method of pruning the contexts is available (Walters and Nielsen 1988, 280).

Dimensioned variable A variable that can have multiple values at a given point in time and the values are indexed. They are very much like a one-dimensional array. Such variables are useful in dealing with spreadsheet data (Tello 1988, 128).

DIPMETER ADVISOR An expert system used to interpret geological data for oil exploration.

Directed acyclic graph A graph in which moves cannot be undone (Luger and Stubblefield 1989, 84).

Directed arc An arc in a network in which movement can take place in only one direction. Example: an arc that represents the distance that must be traveled between two cities. If this arc is directed, then movement can only take place from city A to city B, but not in the opposite direction (Forsyth and Naylor 1985, 132).

Directed graph 1. A graph of nodes with arrows connecting the nodes indicating the direction of the search. The search may take place in only one direction. That is, you may proceed from node b to c, but may not go from c to b. 2. A graph that depicts the direction of flow from processing elements in a neural network (Obermeier and Barron 1989, 219; Schildt 1987, 20-21; Sterling and Shapiro 1985, 29–30).

Directed network A network in which the arcs work in one direction only.

Direct representation Analogical representation (Smith 1989, 52).

Disabling The process whereby one rule prevents another rule from being executed. In production systems this can be accomplished by adding or removing working memory elements from working memory.

Discourse analysis Language analysis that comprehends the meaning of a sentence by taking into account the information provided by the surrounding sentences (Chabris 1989, 291).

Discovery A type of learning that was pioneered by Lenat with his programs AM and EURISKO. The process whereby a computer program derives new rules about a knowledge domain. *See also* Learning by discovery (Barr and Feigenbaum 1981 vol 1, 196).

Discovery program A program that discovers relationships among data in a data base. It characteristically relies on statistical techniques, but its output is expressed in rule form (Parsaye et al 1990, 40–42).

Discovery systems Machine learning in which the system finds or deduces new information from previously learned information. The program is able to use the newly discovered information to enhance performance. DENDRAL and PROSPECTOR are two of the best-known discovery learning systems. EURISKO may be considered a very sophisticated type of discovery system. In contrast to expert systems, discovery systems may be applied in situations in which there may not be any human experts available. Other approaches to machine learning include empirical induction and analogy (Tello 1988, 509–510; Tello 1989, 38).

Discrete type A type with a finite set of ordered values (Hunt 1986, 91).

Discrimination 1. The process of distinguishing between members and nonmembers of a concept being learned. Discrimination acts in conjunction with the process of generalization— preventing generalization from including nonmembers. 2. Recognizing differences. The procedure of specialization allows for successively finer degrees of discrimination of a concept. 3. The procedure in model-based diagnostic systems that decides on steps to take that will help to tell which of a set of candidate faulty components is responsible for a failure (Hunt 1986, 91).

Discrimination net 1. A type binary decision tree that is an efficient means of classifying objects. It continually performs tests on a search tree and each test eliminates one half of the search tree. A discrimination net can be implemented by using nested rules. 2. A procedure that categorizes objects by testing their characteristics, until a category is found that satisfies all the tests. Discrimination nets are used by natural language generation programs to decide on the best output word and to optimize retrieval from the data base (Smith 1989, 54; Chabris 1989, 292; Tello Aug 1985, 102; Barr and Feigenbaum 1981 vol 1, 278; Tanimoto 1987, 57–59).

Disjoint Describing a set that has no common elements (Savory 1988, 233).

Disjunction A series of subgoals, one of which must be true in order for the overall goal to be true. The subgoals are connected with the connector OR. Example: A IF B OR C. If either B or C is true then A is true. The OR connective is not always included in expert systems. Its absence can mean that the user may have to generate many somewhat redundant rules. With the above rule one would need two rules to achieve the same goal: A if B. A if C. In PROLOG a disjunction is represented by a set of rules with the same head—a procedure. The goal succeeds if any one of the rules in the procedure succeeds. The OR connective is implied. *Contrast with* Conjunction. *See also* Exclusive-OR; Inclusive-OR element (Harrison and Tribble 1986, 66; Townsend 1987a 173–174; Winston 1979, 148; Brownston et al 1986, 191–193; Sterling and Shapiro 1985, 11).

Disjunctive syllogism A rule of inference which is a special case of resolution (Dos Reis 1988, 51).

DISPLAY A command used in INSIGHT 2 that presents textual information to help the user understand the general workings of the expert system. In an expert system that identifies automotive engine problems, the DISPLAY command may be used to define terms in a question such as carburetion and combustion. *Contrast with* the EXPLAIN command, which is used to give an explanation as to why the expert system is asking a given question (Harmon et al 1988, 78).

Disproving Attempting to prove a given course of action cannot reach a goal to avoid a waste of time in following that course of action. The information obtained can often be used to suggest an alternative course of action (Hunt 1986, 13).

Distributed artificial intelligence The application of artificial intelligence to monitor and coordinate a set of multiple processes. Such applications use a parallel-processing architecture which consists of a relatively small number of powerful microprocessors. Each microprocessor along with its memory has unique capabilities. The data each microprocessor possesses may be unique and may contradict data possessed by other microprocessors. The goals for each microprocessor may be inconsistent with the goals of other microprocessors. Each microprocessor may interpret a given set of data differently from its brother microprocessors. Each of the microprocessors contributes its unique skills to solving the problem the system is given. It is also referred to as decentralized AI. Examples: the use of an artificial intelligence system to coordinate a large number of robots on an assembly line, or the use of an artificial intelligence system in traffic control. *See also* Parallel processing (Lawrence 1985, 79-83).

Distributed problem solving 1. The type of problem solving associated with a network of loosely connected distributed networks, which are relatively autonomous and interact with each other to solve complex problems. 2. A type of problem solving in which the problem is broken into components and a microprocessor is assigned to each component. The results for each component are posted on a blackboard so that the final solution can be achieved (Parsaye and Chignell 1988, 145).

Distributed processing Parallel processing.

Distributed representation The concept that the memory engram is not found in a single place in the brain but is distributed among many neurons. The pattern as a whole is the meaningful level of analysis. A given concept is represented by a pattern of connection strengths rather than a single location in memory. Each processing element may be involved in characterizing many different objects. That is, each processing unit in the system bears the responsibility for participating in recognizing more than one pattern. Distributed representations can retrieve an entity by using as a cue a single property of the entity. The emergent properties that flow from distributed representations include content addressability, automatic generalizations, and the choosing of the rule which best fits the current situation, but which may not be a perfect fit. In neural networks knowledge is represented by a pattern of nodes. A given node may be used to represent many patterns. Example: The activation of nodes 1, 3, 5 may represent an automobile. The activation of nodes 1, 2, 4, may represent a plane. Notice that one node may be used to represent more than one object. The ability of a given node to participate in the representation of multiple objects greatly increases the knowledge representation ability of neural networks. Because of the redundancy, distributed representations are relatively insensitive to damage (Zeidenberg 1987, 242; Rumelhart and McClelland 1986, vol 1, 79–87, 104–108).

Distributive law   p AND (q OR r) = (p AND q) OR (p AND r) (Luger and Stubblefield 1989, 45).

Divide and conquer   The strategy of breaking up a large problem into smaller problems. This strategy is frequently used in building expert systems. *See also* Problem reduction representation (Lenat 1988, 72).

DMDM   An object-oriented data base language being developed at the Oregon Graduate Center. A query in DMDM is similar to a PROLOG clause (Zaniolo et al 1986, 58–59).

DoAll   Conflict resolution that executes all matching rules with the original facts in the fact base (facts asserted in the current cycle are ignored). It then cycles through the rules a second time looking for rules that have not yet fired which can now match the original facts and the newly asserted facts in the fact base. *Contrast with* Do the Most Recent, Do the Most Specific, DoOne; Do in Sequence (Parsaye and Chignell 1988, 273).

dobefore   A command used in some expert systems which specifies that other rules be executed before the current rule (Tello Oct 1987, 243).

DOCTOR   A version of ELIZA used to demonstrate a mock conversation between a psychotherapist and his or her client, which was developed by Weinstein (Frude 1983, 83–85; Winston 1979, 333–335).

Document-understanding system   A program that takes as input text which is then analyzed and the result of the analysis is used to answer questions, or paraphrase, or draw inference about the text (Hunt 1986, 92).

DOF   *See* Degree of freedom.

Domain   A body of knowledge used by an expert system to solve problems. Example: information about pulmonary diseases (Mishkoff 1986, G-1; Harmon and King 1985, 79–81; Townsend and Feucht 1986, 244).

Domain blackboard   A component of the blackboard in HEARSAY III. The domain blackboard is where competence reasoning takes place. *See also* Scheduling blackboard.

Domain expert   An expert in a particular field of knowledge who contributes his or her knowledge to an expert system. An electronics engineer can be a domain expert in electronics (Citrenbaum et al 1987, 33).

Domain-free metarule   A metarule that holds information which is not domain specific. An example is the advice to search smaller search spaces before searching large search spaces. *Contrast with* Domain-specific metarule (Jackson 1986, 37).

Domain independence In expert systems the separation of the knowledge domain from the inference engine (Smith 1989, 55).

Domain-independent expert system A synonym for an expert system shell. An expert system without a knowledge base (Michaelsen et al 1985, 306).

Domain-independent systems An expert system shell (Michaelsen et al 1985, 306).

Domain model Mental model (Harmon et al 1988, 267).

Domain-specific knowledge representation Knowledge representation whose strategy is to encode the knowledge so that the domain expert is able to readily understand the code of the expert system because the code uses the vocabulary of the domain expert. This strategy encourages the domain expert to accept the expert system (Menzies 1989, 36).

Domain-specific metarule A metarule that holds strategic knowledge about the domain. Example: a metarule that would know individuals with a certain trait are more likely to have a certain set of diseases and the rule would tell the expert system to try the set of rules that are specific to that set of diseases. *Contrast with* Domain-free metarule (Jackson 1986, 37).

Do the Most Recent Conflict resolution that executes the rule in the conflict set that matches the most recent working memory element. The most recent working memory element refers to the working memory element that has most recently been inferred by the expert system. This type of conflict resolution is an option in OPS5 expert system languages. *Compare with* DoAll; Do the Most Specific; DoOne; Do in Sequence (Parsaye and Chignell 1988, 274).

Do the Most Specific Conflict resolution that executes the rule in the conflict set that matches the most specific working memory element. The most specific working memory element may be defined as simply the working memory element with the most facts. This type of conflict resolution is an option in OPS5 expert system languages. *Compare with* DoAll; Do the Most Recent; DoOne; Do in Sequence (Parsaye and Chignell 1988, 274).

DoOne Conflict resolution that executes the first rule to match the necessary facts in the fact base. It then goes back to the top of the rule set and starts a second cycle. *Contrast with* DoAll; Do the Most Recent; Do the Most Specific; Do in Sequence (Parsaye and Chignell 1988, 273).

Do in Sequence Conflict resolution that executes each matching rule in sequence employing both original facts and facts that have been asserted by a previous rule in the cycle. *Contrast with* DoAll; Do the Most Recent; Do the Most Specific; DoOne (Parsaye and Chignell 1988, 273–275).

Do-until A superlogical quantifier used in logic-based systems, which executes instances of a clause until a specified second clause becomes true. It can be used to simulate a for-next loop (Parsaye and Chignell 1988, 268–269).

Do Whenever Refers to the control procedures used in forward-chaining expert system languages like OPS5. The flow of control is a function of the patterns of data rather than a specific programming construct like a do-while or for-next loop (Parsaye and Chignell 1988, 25).

Draper Industrial Assembly Language A computer language developed specifically to program assembly robots (Rosenberg 1986, 49).

Drawing closed curves A technique used in eliciting data from an expert. The expert is asked to draw closed curves around objects that go together (Olson and Rueter, 1988, 25–26).

Dreyfus, Hubert A philosopher best known for his opposition to the belief computers can think. A well-known critic of artificial intelligence. His criticisms have been important in defining the current limits of artificial intelligence (Lawrence 1985, 160–167; Johnson 1986, 254–256).

DRILLING ADVISOR A backward-chaining expert system used on oil rigs to deal with the problem of "down hole sticking" (Harmon and King 1985, 163–167).

Drive-reinforcement theory A neural net learning paradigm used to model classical conditioning. It more accurately models classical conditioning than does outstar learning (Caudill 1980, 51–58).

Drunkards walk A type of dumb search. A direction is chosen at random and one step is taken in that direction. This process is repeated until the solution is reached. *Contrast with* Blind search; Heuristic search (Forsyth and Naylor 1985, 143–147).

Dual semantics **1.** The examination of a computer program from both a procedural and declarative perspective. PROLOG code can be interpreted in either a procedural or declarative manner. Example: $X :- A, B, C$ may be interpreted declaratively as X is true if A, B, and C are true. It could be interpreted procedurally as, to satisfy goal X first do A, then B, and finally C. **2.** The use of both declarative and procedural representations to represent a situation. Frames can combine both declarative and procedural representations (Harmon and King 1985, 44–46; Smith 1989, 56; Luger and Stubblefield 1989, 307; Lazarev 1988, 76).

DUCK A production expert system based on predicate calculus. DUCK stands for deDUCtive retrieval. As is true in PROLOG there is no separate data memory. Control is based on resolution and unification. DUCK is written in LISP and it is possible to mix LISP programming with relational programming. Both forward-chaining and backward-chaining rules are allowed. It uses nonmonotonic reasoning (Hunt 1986, 96; Brownston et al 1986, 368–370).

Dueling rules Rules that are in the same knowledge base and interfere with the firing of one another. Examples: duplicate rules and irregular rules (contradictory rules) (Lane Jun 1989, 303).

Due-process reasoning A property of an expert system in which the expert system can collect and debate alternatives to a given hypothesis (Hewitt 1985, 234).

Dumb search A random search. An example is the drunkard's walk. *Compare with* the more systematic Blind search and Heuristic search (Forsyth and Naylor 1985, 139).

DWIM Do What I Mean, a utility program that works with INTERLISP. Its function is to interpret and execute misspelled commands (Tello 1988, 20; Smith 1989, 56).

Dynamic allocation **1.** The allocation of memory that takes place at runtime. Reserving memory space for variables and data structures which are created during the program run. Languages like LISP use dynamic memory management in which all variables and structures are created during the program run. Other languages declare variables and data structures when the program is compiled. Both approaches have their virtues. The dynamic memory-management approach of LISP allows for greater flexibility. The declaration of variables and data structures at compile time gives programs greater speed. Modern languages like C and Pascal declare variables and data structures at compile time. However, both languages possess the property of dynamic allocation—they can create variables and data structures while the program is running. **2.** A characteristic of some data objects in which the object can expand or contract during the program run. Lists in LISP possess this characteristic (Smith 1989, 56).

Dynamical systems theory The analysis of sets of numerical variables that change as a function of time in parallel and interact through differential equations (Rumelhart and McClelland 1986 vol 1, 397–398).

Dynamic binding **1.** The ability of certain computer languages to allow an object to decide at runtime the procedure it will use in reaction to the execution of a member function. Binding which takes place after compile time. It is sometimes referred to as delayed or late binding. 2. A message in Smalltalk specifying the name of the operation rather than the address. 3. The extent to which a variable holds its binding under the condition of dynamic scoping (Rubin Aug 1985, 29; Swaine Jun 1989, 116; Hu 1989, 68).

Dynamic data Data which change over time. Time-dependent data. *Contrast with* Static data.

Dynamic data base A data base that can have rules or facts added or deleted during runtime (Townsend 1987a, 67–73; Townsend 1987b, 379).

Dynamic data management Data management in which required values are computed as needed rather than storing the values. In frame-based systems attached predicates are frequently used to calculate values or a range of legal values. Sometimes attached predicates use a set of rules to derive a set of possible values (Parsaye and Chignell 1988, 184–187).

Dynamic data structure 1. A data structure in which memory is put aside for it when the data structure is created, not at compile time. 2. A type of data structure found in expert systems whose values are subject to change in a program run. Example: the data gathered on a particular patient during a program run of a medical expert system. *Contrast with* Static data structures (Jackson 1986, 98–99; Eisenbach and Sadler 1985, 190).

Dynamic evaluation Evaluating an expert system by using test cases and examining its reasoning processes. *Contrast with* Static evaluation.

Dynamic explanation Answering a user's why or how questions in an expert system by displaying the rule the expert system is attempting to prove or displaying the rules used to reach a conclusion. The advantage of dynamic explanations is that the developer does not have to write explanations for each rule being attempted and each conclusion that could be reached. The disadvantage is the builder cannot put in the detail he may sometimes want to include in an explanation. *Contrast with* Canned explanation.

Dynamic extent The property of a variable that is bound only as long as the function that calls it continues to be executed (Steele, 37–38).

Dynamic frame A frame that can be created or changed during the course of a consultation. *Contrast with* Static frame.

Dynamic inheritance 1. The ability inherent in some object-oriented systems that allows inheritance patterns to be altered. Assume an artificial intelligence system that consists of ships. One ship which belongs to a class with diesel powered engines is outfitted with a new nuclear powered engine. Having a system that can make this exception is an example of dynamic inheritance. 2. Inheritance in which the child objects inherit slots, but not the methods. The parent objects react to the messages sent to the child objects. The advantage is the child objects can change classes during a program run. The child objects can receive the same messages as before and the messages will be sent to the new parent objects which will react differently to the messages because they hold different methods. *Contrast with* Static inheritance (Harmon et al 1988, 145; Amir 1989, 30).

Dynamic knowledge base The portion of the knowledge base in an expert system that can expand or contract during a consultation. Working memory in a production system is a dynamic knowledge base (Smith 1989, 56; Hunt 1986, 96).

Dynamic list 1. A list to which objects can be added or deleted during a program run. 2. A list that produces elements only when they are requested. Hence, infinite lists such as all whole numbers can be represented.

Dynamic memory The portion of memory that changes during the program run. Working memory is a type of dynamic memory.

Dynamic menu A menu constructed during a program run. The contents of the menu are a function of facts accumulated in the program run (Parsaye and Chignell 1988, 187).

Dynamic object 1. Object allocated on the heap as opposed to static objects, which are allocated in a program's data declaration section. Dynamic objects are objects that can be created during a program run. 2. An object whose values may be altered during a program run. An object that is allocated on the heap. *Contrast with* Static object (Duntemann 1989, 137; Harmon and King 1985, 39).

Dynamic ordering A procedure incorporated in some search programs in which the ordering of future moves is reassessed and possibly changed when a test indicates that one of the moves may be a poor one. When carried to extremes dynamic ordering becomes best-first search. Dynamic ordering can be a very time-consuming technique (Barr and Feigenbaum 1981 vol 1, 102; Smith 1989, 57).

Dynamic procedure A language in which control is a function of the data rather than such control procedures as do loops. The procedure for solving the problem is embedded in the language itself. Example: PROLOG.

Dynamic programming 1. The ability of certain computer languages like LISP and PROLOG to construct and execute program statements during runtime. These languages have this ability because they do not distinguish between programs and data. This ability allows programs to write other programs, to construct interpreters, and to modify data bases dynamically. 2. A procedure in matching that matches the input data with a flexible template so that close matches can be made. 3. The principle that holds that in attempting to move from A to the intermediate node B, all paths from A to B may be ignored, except for the minimum path (Assume a search tree with a node A, an intermediate node B, and a goal node G.) (Winston 1984, 112; Smith 1989, 57).

Dynamic representation Model-based representation in which the inputs change frequently over time. Such models are useful for simulating the effect on the internal process and the output when the inputs are altered. Dynamic-representation models are frequently employed in situations in which the real system cannot be tested. Applications would be the modeling of a complex electrical circuit with different inputs, or the modeling of a nuclear power plant under conditions of overload. A what-if type system. *Contrast with* Static representation (Walters and Nielsen 1988, 294–297).

Dynamic rule A rule that can be created, deleted, or modified during runtime. *Contrast with* Static rule (Townsend 1987a, 124).

Dynamic scoping 1. Determination of the values of free variables by their activation environment. 2. Scoping in which the free variables continue to be bound as long as the function that defined the free variables continues to be active. In dynamic scoping, a free variable which is defined inside a function maintains its value in any function the initial function calls, and any subsequent function that is called. Once the function that defined the free variable is terminated the value of the free variable is forever lost. That is, if the defining function is later called, the original value of the free variable is no longer available. Common LISP and most current versions of LISP default to lexical scoping rather than dynamic scoping. Dynamic scoping is faster than lexical scoping but it is also more prone to producing errors. A combination of indefinite scoping and dynamic extent. *Contrast with* Lexical scoping (Charniak and McDermott 1985, 74; Barr and Feigenbaum 1981 vol 2, 18, 33; Winston 1984, 54; Tello 1988, 351; Steele 1984, 38; Graham Apr 1989, 28).

Dynamic variable 1. A variable that can be declared at runtime. 2. A variable that is allocated on the heap. 3. A variable in LISP that holds its value until the construct that bound the variable terminates. When the construct terminates, the value of the dynamic variable is forever lost. *Contrast with* Lexical variable (Udell

1989, 105; Steele 1984, 55–56; Duntemann 1989, 137).

Dynamic view The ability of some natural language interfaces to do more than simply answer Englishlike questions, but also to offer to monitor a situation. Example: The user may ask, "Is phase three of the XYZ project completed?" The response can be "No, shall I inform you when it is done?" (Mays 1986, 559).

E

Eager evaluation The evaluation of an expression as soon as possible, without regard to whether or not it is needed by another expression.

Early binding 1. The calling routine obtaining the address of the called routine at compile time, not at runtime. *Compare with* Late binding. 2. The assignment of a variable to a type at compile time. Early binding has the advantage of increasing efficiency but reducing flexibility. Early binding is found in procedural languages such as C. *Contrast with* Late binding (Duff 1986, 214–216; Bernat 1987, 42; Duntemann, 1989, 137).

Early failure A strategy used in expert system programming in which the conditions of a rule most likely to fail are placed first. In that way the rule will fail early and less processing time will be spent on evaluating the rule. The principle is also used in PROLOG programs where complex pattern matching is used at the beginning of a rule to precipitate early failure, and avoid useless backtracking. Such early failure can increase the execution speed by a factor of seven (Brownston et al 1986, 264–265).

Early processing Low-level vision.

Economy principle The storing of characteristics of objects as high up in the hierarchy as possible in a hierarchical system. Example: In a hierarchy of automobiles, the characteristics of number of wheels should be stored at the level of automobile and not at the level of subclasses of automobiles such as sedans, sports cars, and so on (Barr and Feigenbaum 1981 vol 3, 39–41).

Edge Arc (Jackson 1986, 52).

Edge detection The process of finding important edges in a scene so as to discriminate objects. A segmentation process in which contrasting intensities of a scene are differentiated. An important process in helping a computer to discriminate objects and understand an image. *Compare with* Region detection (Mishkoff 1986, 5–12; Barr and Feigenbaum 1981 vol 3, 130–131, 216–224; Forsyth and Naylor 1985, 18–92; Chabris 1989, 201; Davis 1975, 248–270).

Edinburgh PROLOG A style of PROLOG that uses ":-" for "if" and ";" for "or." Facts and rules end with a period. The + and - operators are available. Variables must be capitalized. Members of lists are separated by commas. *Contrast with* Marseille PROLOG (Colmerauer 1987, 181).

Effective branching factor A measure of a search algorithm's efficiency. It describes the bushiness of the search tree. The average number of children of a node searched. An effective branching factor of 1 means the search met with no blind alleys. *See also* Branching factor; Penetrance (Chabris 1989, 162).

Efficiency The speed with which a program accomplishes its mission (Bratko 1986, 179).

EL A forward-chaining expert system used to solve complex electronic circuit problems, which employs the propagation method and can recover from mistaken assumptions (Hayes-Roth et al 1983, 111–115).

Electron A clause whose truth value is false (Dos Reis 1988, 55).

Element 1. An item in the data memory or on the left-hand side of a rule in a production system. Elements can be very complex data structures. They can be a list, a set of tuples, a set of named property lists, or a set of recursively defined records. Example: (Person^name John^occupation knowledge engineer). Person is the name of the working memory element. It holds the name of the person and his occupation. The two types of elements in an OPS5 production system are working memory elements and condition elements. 2. A single entity of a list in LISP. A list element may be a number, a symbol, or a list (Brownston et al 1986, 446; Hunt 1986, 98).

Elementary Perceiver and Memorizer An information processing model of rote learning of nonsense syllables, which is used to model paired-associate learning. It was used to emulate such learning concepts as retroactive inhibition and stimulus and response generalization. It employs a discrimination net. EPAM is given an example and it traverses the discrimination net. If the information for the example is sufficient to traverse the discrimination net to find a successful match, then no learning takes place. If traversal runs into a dead end, then EPAM uses information about the example to create a new node thus modifying the discrimination net. EPAM learns by failure. Using EPAM, it is difficult to ascertain what EPAM has learned by simply inspecting the program. Also, what is learned is too dependent on the order of training instances. *Compare with* the more sophisticated Version-space model (Chabris 1989, 209–212).

Element class A compound data structure type found in OPS expert systems (Brownston et al 1986, 39–40).

Element variable A variable which is bound to a working memory element in OPS5 (Hunt 1986, 98).

Elimination rule A rule that eliminates the implication connective (—>). Modus ponens is an elimination rule since it replaces A, and $A \rightarrow B$ with B (Barr and Feigenbaum 1981 vol 1, 163–164, 169).

Eliza A famous artificial intelligence program that mimics the advice given by a Rogerian psychotherapist. Eliza looks for certain keywords from the input and processes the input, based on the keywords, in such a way as to make what looks like a somewhat intelligent response. The response is usually a question about the user's input. The keyword approach to pattern matching used in Eliza is a very simple type of pattern matching. The keyword approach pays no attention to the ordering of the words and the surrounding context of sentences. With some unsuspecting individuals Eliza has been able to pass the Turing test. Eliza was developed by Joseph Weizenbaum (Johnson 1986, 51–55; Schildt 1987, 262; Mishkoff 1986, 2–6; Barr and Feigenbaum 1981 vol 1, 285–287; Tello 1988, 407–409).

Ellipsis 1. The exclusion of words from a sentence. The use of such shortcuts plays havoc with the syntax of a sentence even though the meaning may not be altered. Example: "Come here" rather than "You come here." A problem computer language processors must find ways with which to cope. 2. The deletion of deep structure elements in the external manifestation of a sentence (Brittain 1987, 35; Bates et al 1987, 65; Barr and Feigenbaum 1981 vol 1, 358–359; Smith 1989, 60).

Embed To write a higher-level language on top of another language (Hunt 1986, 99).

Embedded expert system An expert system that is made a part of another program so that the other program can call on the expert system when it is needed. This is a very important ability since there are many already existing programs which could benefit from the addition of reasoning. CXpert is an expert system written in the C language which can produce an expert system that can become a part of an already existing program written in C.

Embedded intelligence Integrating artificial intelligence programs into standard computer program applications (Stapleton 1988, 97).

Embedded language A higher-level language written on top of another language such as LISP, or PROLOG. This embedded language has added features that allow it to attack a particular set of problems. Some common extensions found in embedded languages include pattern matchers, access functions, and production system controllers (Luger and Stubblefield 1989, 279).

Embedding 1. The nesting of lists within lists. 2. The production of clauses as parts of a sentence. The clauses are produced from nonterminal symbols (Smith 1989, 60).

Emergent property A property of an object that appears to spontaneously emerge from the interaction of the components of the object. Automatic generalization and associative memory are emergent properties of living organisms and neural nets (Rumelhart and McClelland 1986 vol 1, 128).

Empirical induction A learning system that includes both learning by being told and learning from examples. Other approaches to machine learning include discovery systems and analogy (Tello 1988, 509).

Empty clause The clashing of two contradictory statements in resolution. The production of the empty clause proves that the original proposition is true (Luger and Stubblefield 1989, 417).

EMYCIN An expert system shell developed from the expert system MYCIN, which uses production rules as a means of knowledge representation. Certainty factors and explanation facilities are present. Its editor checks for syntax errors, contradictory rules, and rules subsumed by other rules. The shell can be used to develop expert systems that fit the backward-chaining paradigm (Hayes-Roth et al 1983, 287–291; Harmon and King 1985, 89–90; Barr and Feigenbaum 1981 vol 2, 84; Tello 1988, 104–105).

Enabling The process whereby one rule makes another rule eligible to be executed. In production systems this can be accomplished by adding or removing working-memory elements from working memory.

Encapsulation The process of hiding data and procedures that manipulate the code together inside an object. This prevents the improper examination and access of data in a module or an object. The data in an object can be accessed only by using an appropriate message which will activate a function inside of the object. An important characteristic of object-oriented programming. Encapsulation prevents unintentional value changes and makes programs easier to understand and modify. *See also* Information hiding (Udell 1989, 104; Swaine Jun 1989, 116; Skelly 1987, 82; Bharath and Sklar 1985, 49; Harmon et al 1988, 37; Thomas 1989, 232–234; Duntemann 1989, 137).

End effector The extremities of the robot that carries out an action. Examples: grippers, welding torches, and multifingered hands.

Ensemble averaging 1. The use of multiple copies of a scene to filter random noise. 2. A procedure that uses multiple copies of an image to decrease noise without losing detail (Smith 1989, 60; Barr and Feigenbaum 1981 vol 3, 214).

Entity Framelike structures. It is sometimes used to refer to a collection of objects, or a single object. Entity is frequently used as a synonym for unit, when unit is used to refer to a specific object (Hu 1989, 189; Michaelsen et al 1985, 309; Zaniolo 1986, 53).

Entropy 1. The tendency of a system to move to disorder. As new rules are added to a production system some degree of entropy is introduced. The new rules may, for instance, produce contradictions with existing rules. 2. A procedure from communications theory which is a measure of the uncertainty of the classification of objects. A process that aids in dividing data most efficiently. It helps in the process of deciding what data to look at first by choosing the data which have the least uncertainty. In this way the data which have the least uncertainty in reaching a solution are evaluated first. Entropy is used in organizing data in induction expert systems (Thompson and Thompson 1986, 152).

Entry conditions A component of a script that must be correct so that the script may be executed (Luger and Stubblefield 1989, 364).

Environment 1. Libraries of code associated with a particular computer language that can be used to develop a program. They are different from expert system tools in that tools are used specifically to build expert systems and provide a variety of knowledge-representations and inferencing strategies rather than libraries of code. An environment is more general than a tool and more flexible. A tool will likely get the job done more quickly than an environment if it happens to fit the problem nicely. INTERLISP is considered an environment because it is a language that comes with a set of procedures. 2. The set of all the current variables and their bindings in PROLOG. 3. A set of bindings in LISP. 4. A set of variables, their values, and a set of functions in SCHEME. SCHEME has the capability of placing one environment on hold and switching to another environment. *Compare with* Programming environment (Tello 1988, 358; Thompson and Thompson 1986, 26; Harmon and King 1985, 79–80, 83; Winston 1984, 54; Townsend and Feucht 1986, 157; Harmon et al 1988, 269; Maxwell and Riggle Mar 1989, 31).

Environmental approach A computer program designed as a free-style type of learning instrument. The LOGO language is the best-known example of this approach. *Contrast with* Intelligent computer-aided instruction which is more structured (Barr and Feigenbaum 1981 vol 1, 225).

Environment variable A variable whose value is set from the operating system. In some expert systems like GURU environment variables are special global variables used to control the inference engine in a variety of ways. The control may include the type of certainty factor used, the inclusion of how and why capabilities, setting the strategy for deciding on the order in which rules are to be examined, setting the threshold for certainty factors, toggling a trace facility, and controlling the rigor employed in determining the values of variables (Tello 1988, 259–261).

Envisage A computer language derived from PROLOG, with which it is possible to put on hold one line of questioning to pursue another line of questioning so that the results of the two can be compared (Rosenberg 1986, 60).

Envisioning   1. The type of human knowledge which is a mental image of a situation. The process of picturing in the mind's eye a situation. Much of what humans know may be stored in images.   2. A type of qualitative reasoning that employs causal reasoning to predict the behavior of objects (Smith 1989, 61; Waldrop 1987, 61).

Envisionment   The primary procedure in the physics expert system NEWTON. Example: a series of descriptions of an object moving through space. Each description corresponds to a given point in time. Envisionment is the set of descriptions, and how they can be used to solve a number of physics problems (Jackson 1986, 159).

EPAM   *See* Elementary Perceiver And Memorizer.

Ephemeral garbage collection   Generation scavenging in which the scavenging takes place incrementally, with two generations. *See also* Generation scavenging (Gabriel 1987, 38).

Episodic memory   Memory for a sequence of events (Chabris 1989, 57–58).

Epistemological adequacy   The ability of a knowledge structure to represent the information it is supposed to represent sufficiently (Smith 1989, 61).

Epistemological assumption   The assumption that representations and procedures can be formulated that will allow computers to emulate human thought, although these procedures may not be the same as the procedures of human thinking. Computers use rules to solve problems. It is debatable as to the true role of rules in human problem solving. Pattern matching may, for instance, be the more crucial factor (Lawrence 1985, 164–165).

Epistemological problems   The problems arising from the lack of clarity about exactly what the objects should be representing in an object-oriented program. While at times objects may stand for objects in the world, it is often necessary to have objects stand for goals, sets of rules, or hypotheses. This causes problems as to exactly what a message should say or mean. Another example of epistemological problem is the lack of a clear differentiation between essential and accidental properties of objects (Jackson 1986, 193–195, 157).

Epistemology   The study of the nature of knowledge (Barr and Feigenbaum 1981 vol 1, 151).

Equipotentiality   A concept developed by Karl Lashley which holds that the memory engram is stored in more than one place in the brain. The forerunner of the concept of distributed representation.

Equivalence operation   If-and-only-if (Rosenberg 1986, 60).

Equivalence relation   Relations that are reflexive, symmetric, and transitive (Savory 1988, 234).

Equivalent   Expressions in logic with the same truth table values (Dos Reis 1988, 50).

ESPIRIT   A joint European project that has the general goal of encouraging advanced information and technology. One of its specific goals is to facilitate the development of intelligent knowledge bases (Harmon and King 1985, 223–224).

Essential properties   The properties of an object that all objects in that class must possess. *Contrast with* Accidental property; Typicality (Jackson 1986, 67).

EURISKO   The successor program to Doug Lenat's AM. The primary difference between EURISKO and its predecessor AM is that with EURISKO the mutation and natural selection processes can act on the heuristics as well as the concepts. The language used is RLL, which uses frames for knowledge representation. Its representation system is called units—a framelike structure with slots. Everything in EURISKO is represented by units, including the heuristics. Having a uniform representation scheme is one important source of EURISKO's strength. Because of this uniform representation scheme, it can build new heuristics. EURISKO has been used in mathematics, to design computer chips. It is best known for its exceptional accomplishments in a space war game competition called Traveler. It beat all of its competitors for two straight years. In the Traveler competition, frames held information about basic concepts—gun parameters, ship speed, and so on. Other frames held heuristics. An example of one heuristic is, if a concept proves occasionally useful but usually worthless then try creating a new, more specialized version of it. EURISKO used such heuristics in refining its war machines in simulated battles. As a result, it came up with cheap, numerous, defensive, heavily armored ships which would outlast fleets of fast expensive ships. An evolution program using EURISKO came up with a smaller, whiter, light-boned creature with sharp teeth, large jaw muscles, large leg muscles, and increased brain size. It had thick stiff fur, small ears, an added layer of fat, and sought safe burrows (Johnson 1986, 242–244, 194–195, 185–189; Hayes-Roth et al 1983, 320–321; Barr and Feigenbaum 1981, vol 3, 449; Forsyth and Naylor 1985, 212–216; Tello 1988, 511–517; Waldrop 1987, 59–61).

Eval The primitive in LISP that evaluates all forms. It decides if the form is an atom, a number, a quote, or a function. It then evaluates the form according to what it is and returns the value. A universal function in LISP that can interpret any other function (Winston 1979, 271; Hasemer 1984, 10).

Evaluation 1. The computation of the value of an expression. It is the executing of a piece of computer code. The evaluation of a function or the finding of the value of a symbol, variable, or list. 2. The measuring of the value of a node in search programs. *See also* San Marco LISP Explorer (Barr and Feigenbaum 1981 vol 1, 60–73; Winston 1984, 20; Smith 1989, 62; Luger and Stubblefield 1989, 48).

Evaluation function 1. A function that evaluates the desirability of different possible moves by assigning numerical values to the different possible actions. The action with the highest value is then chosen. 2. A procedure that assesses the attractiveness of a particular goal state by calculating the state's distance to the goal state, or the cost of solving the problem from the beginning position (Chabris 1989, 292; Minasi Dec 1988, 21; Hayes-Roth et al 1983, 69–70).

Event-driven processing The idea that expert systems are driven not simply by the rules in the system but by the events which it is currently processing. A system that can temporarily halt ongoing processing because of new important information, and begin an alternative line of processing in response to the new data. The new information may be from a process, another computer, or another inference engine. It can be a value or a new goal to investigate. Event-driven expert systems are necessary in real-time monitoring expert systems. Example: an expert system that monitors conditions in a nuclear power plant. Forward-chaining paradigms are most frequently used in event-driven applications. It is similar to data-driven processing except that event-driven processing emphasizes the importance of responding to new information (Schur 1988, 32–34; Walters and Nielson 1988, 308; Barr and Feigenbaum 1981 vol 1, 198, 220; Tello 1988, 466).

Event knowledge One of three types of knowledge found in diagnostic expert systems. The behavior expected under known accident conditions. *See also* Functional knowledge; Structure knowledge (Merritt 1987, 53).

Event space A term used in probability. The set of all possible events that are related to a specific situation.

Evolutionary capacity The ability of a computer language to allow additions to a computer program with relatively little effort. Some experts argue one of the primary advantages of object-oriented programming is its evolutionary capacity. Enhancement, rather than replacement, is the keyword in object-oriented programming (Hayes-Roth et al 1983, 400; Shafer Winter 1987, 39).

Evolutionary development The process of incrementally building and refining a computer program. Expert systems and programs built with AI languages differ from standard program design in that these programs can be changed without having to modify the entire program extensively. Rule-based expert system languages also have an evolutionary capacity (Hunt 1986, 101).

Exact reasoning Standard inferential reasoning. *Contrast with* Inexact reasoning.

Example and near miss *See* Hit and near miss.

Example-driven system Induction expert system shell. It takes examples, builds a decision tree, and then constructs rules from the decision tree. An example-driven expert system is one type of machine learning (Tello Jul 1985, 72; Walters and Nielsen 1988, 308; Rosenberg 1986, 62).

Exception The assignment of a value to a slot in a frame such that the exception value overrides any inherited value.

EXCHECK An intelligent computer-aided instructional system which has as its subject material a university-level course in logic. Its reasoning emulates the reasoning of a mathematician. It can make hypotheses about the student's reasoning.

Exclusive-OR A version of OR which allows only one value of a set of values to satisfy the condition. If more than one value is present to satisfy the condition, the rule will not be executed. If the variable is Weather is cloudy OR cold the rule will fire. If Weather is both cloudy and cold the rule will not fire. *Contrast with* Inclusive-OR element (Brownston et al 1986, 191–193).

Executable data The production rules in a production system that are both data and procedures (Knaus Jan 1989, 13).

Exhaustive search A type of search in which all paths in a search tree are searched to find the best possible solution to a problem. Such a search can be very time consuming and impractical when a large search space is involved. Exhaustive search is sometimes referred to as brute force search. *Compare with* Heuristic state space search (Schildt 1987, 18; Harmon and King 1985, 58–59; Barr and Feigenbaum 1981 vol 3, 14).

Existential quantification The statement "there exists an entity with a given property" in logic. Example: "There exists a computer which has an 80386 microprocessor and a hard disk." Existential quantifiers are employed in predicate calculus. *Contrast with* Universal quantification (Sterling and Shapiro 1985, 9; Barr and Feigenbaum 1981, vol 3 88–89, 91; Charniak and McDermott 1985, 18).

Existential quantifier 1. A variable found in a PROLOG query. It means, for some variable X there exists some object which could instantiate the variable. 2. The quantifier that states a sentence is true for one value in a domain. Example: for some X has(X, wings). *Compare with* Universal quantifier (Charniak and McDermott 1985, 18; Luger and Stubblefield 1989, 51).

Exodus A program that extends a relational data base model to support complex objects. The University of Wisconsin is involved in this project (Peterson 1987, 30).

Expansion of a node The determination of all possible nodes which can be successor nodes for a given node (Smith 1989, 63–64).

Expectation-driven processing *See* Expectation-driven reasoning.

Expectation-driven reasoning 1. A type of processing that has some type of guide to direct processing. The guide is based on the nature of the structure being processed. 2. A type of reasoning used in AI programs which has a model of how to solve the problem at hand and uses this model to test hypotheses to reach a solution. 3. This control strategy uses as its basis a model of the problem area. The model guides the control strategy in choosing the knowledge source that will most likely to able to help at a particular point in the problem-solving process. 4. Reasoning that uses current data to predict, disprove, or confirm. A control procedure that builds hypotheses about unknown events or future events based on present data. The procedure then attempts to confirm whether or not the predicted events take place. It is a type of default reasoning. Expectation-driven reasoning is found in blackboard and frame-based expert systems (Barr and Feigenbaum 1981 vol 1, 216–218; Barr and Feigenbaum 1981 vol 2, 91–92, 97–101; Smith 1989, 64; Hayes-Roth et al 1983, 400; Rosenberg 1986, 63; Hunt 1986, 103).

Expected-case complexity Looking at a problem solution from the point of view of the most complex case likely to arise. *Contrast with* Worst-case complexity (Charniak and McDermott 1985, 256).

Experiential knowledge Knowledge gained from practical experience. Surface knowledge. *Contrast with* Deep knowledge (Rosenberg 1986, 63).

Expert An individual who is acknowledged to be able to solve problems efficiently in a particular field (domain). One who is able to avoid getting bogged down in irrelevant material (Michaelsen, et al 1985, 303–304; Harmon and King 1985, 31–33).

EXPERT A diagnosis/prescription expert system shell written in FORTRAN, which employs a relatively simple language. EXPERT compiles rules for the sake of efficiency. It uses categorical reasoning, and the decision procedures are such as to produce predictable results. This latter property allows the easy tracing of the behavior of the program when rules are modified. It is capable of accepting volunteered information from the user. Its data memory consists of facts which are either findings or hypotheses. Findings are observations or measurements. Hypotheses are the inferences made by the execution of the system. There are three types of rules: rules which deduce findings from findings, rules which deduce hypotheses from findings, and rules which deduce hypotheses from hypotheses. Rules can be grouped in contexts. The control strategy is a data-driven one. The rules are executed in the order of finding-finding, finding-hypotheses, and hypotheses-hypotheses. It employs certainty factors. Statistical analysis is available to assess the improvement in performance as rules are added. It can be purchased through Rutgers University (Hayes-Roth et al 1983, 180–183, 297–301; Harmon and King 1985, 110–112; Barr and Feigenbaum 1981 vol 2, 217–222).

Expert confidence One of two types of confidences found in an expert system. It is the confidence the expert has in a given rule. *See also* User confidence (Harmon et al 1988, 74).

Expert data base system A combination of a data base system and an expert system, which is most applicable when used with complex and ill-structured data. They have a flexible knowledge representation scheme. *See also* Knowledge-base management systems (Barr and Feigenbaum 1981 vol 2, 163–173).

Expert helper A software tool with inferential capability that is used to assist in the specification, usage, and maintenance of a data base system (Furtado and Moura 1986, 581–589).

Expertise module The part of an intelligent computer-aided intelligence system that propagates problems and checks that the student makes a correct answer (Smith 1989, 65).

Expert system A computer program that uses symbolic knowledge and inference to reach conclusions. It derives most of its power from its knowledge. The key components of an expert system are an inference engine and a knowledge base. The separation of control (the inference engine) from knowledge (knowledge base) is a hallmark of an expert system. Other components of an expert system include a user interface, a knowledge-acquisition module, and an explanatory inferface. An expert system derives most of its power from its knowledge rather than its inferencing ability. Expert systems are applied to the class of problems in which no simple algorithmic solution is known. To qualify as an expert system it must attain levels of performance roughly equivalent to a human expert. Most expert systems are able to explain their reasoning. Expert systems are generally able to reason about their own inference processes. Other advantages of expert systems are that they do not forget, they consider all details, they don't overlook remote possibilities, and they do not jump to conclusions. Disadvantages are that they do not have common sense, they can be slow as compared to humans, they are not good at approximate pattern matching, and they do not possess the quality of graceful degradation. At this time most expert systems use surface knowledge rather than deep knowledge. In contrast with ordinary computer programs, expert systems can be incrementally modified with little difficulty—at least as compared to conventional programs. The knowledge in an expert system is more available to scrutiny than it is in a conventional program where knowledge may be intertwined with procedure. It is better able to handle ill-defined problems. Expert systems are more robust than conventional programs —they are more likely to be able to handle unexpected situations. One day expert systems may be able to recognize an exceptional situation and synthesize rules to produce a creative response to deal with the new situation. A statistically based program is not generally considered an expert system since it does not employ symbol manipulation. A statistically based system cannot give an explanation as to how it arrived at a conclusion. There are a number of criteria for the use of expert systems: One is the existence of expertise in the area. The task should be a complex problem with multiple interacting subtasks where there appears to be no fixed order of problem solution. It is useful when the solution needs to be explained, when what-if analysis is desirable, or when it is known that the system will be frequently revised.

Expert systems are needed when it is necessary for the system to shift attention quickly, or to be able to handle unique or unexpected patterns of data. The term expert system is sometimes used to refer to an expert system tool or shell. It is best to avoid this practice, and use the term expert system only for a finished system that has a knowledge base. Three common architectures for expert systems are rule-based, frame-based, and blackboard systems. Some of the better known expert systems are MYCIN, DENDRAL, XCON, and PROSPECTOR. Some experts reserve expert system to refer to systems which can compete with experts. The term knowledge system is reserved for less competent systems. A more appropriate term for most expert systems is intelligent assistant (Townsend 1987a, 111–115; Schildt 1987, 58–67, 82–85; Hayes-Roth et al 1983, 50, 400; Mishkoff 1986, G-1; Harmon and King 1985, 4–5; Barr and Feigenbaum 1981 vol 2, 78–86; Townsend and Feucht 1986, 30; Parsaye and Chignell 1988, 1; Smith 1989, 64).

Expert system development Seven different phases: (1) front end analysis. (2) task analysis. (3) prototype development. (4) system development. (5) field testing. (6) implementation. (7) maintenance (Harmon et al 1988, 159–171).

Expert System Environment An expert system tool developed by IBM (Rosenberg 1986, 64).

Expert system kernel Knowledge-based management system (Parker Jr. et al 1986, 36).

EXPLAIN A command used in INSIGHT 2 used to display text in response to a request by the user for more information, concerning why a given question is being asked. It is a static explanation facility. *Contrast with* DISPLAY; Dynamic explanation (Harmon et al 1988, 78).

Explanation-based learning Learning that makes generalizations from a single training example. It takes the knowledge it already has and builds a reason as to why the example belongs to the target concept. This reasoning is then saved as part of the concept (Luger and Stubblefield 1989, 573).

Explanation facility The portion of an expert system that can explain the system's reasoning and justify its conclusions. It can usually answer why a question is being asked of the user and how a particular conclusion was reached. A critical facility for expert systems. It is sometimes referred to as an explanatory interface module. *See also* Canned explanations; Dynamic explanations (Hayes-Roth et al 1983, 42–43, 48–49, 400; Mishkoff 1986, 3-20; Harmon and King 1985, 62–63; Parsaye and Chignell 1988, 33).

Explanation processor The portion of an expert system that is responsible for explaining how a conclusion was reached (Hu 1989, 162).

Explicit knowledge Knowledge that is readily open to inspection. Explicit knowledge is more easily modifiable. It is easier to use explicit knowledge in multiple ways. Example: in production systems rules can be used to reason and to explain the reasoning. Explicit knowledge is used by declarative systems. *Contrast with* Implicit knowledge (Barr and Feigenbaum 1981 vol 1, 150–151, 172).

Exploratory programming The use of prototypes to investigate the best way of solving a problem. A trial-and-error process which is used when it is not possible to decide ahead of time what is the best way of designing the system. This approach is frequently necessary in expert system development (Hunt 1986, 106).

Expr A LISP function whose arguments are evaluated prior to execution of the function. This is how functions are normally evaluated in LISP. *Compare with* Fexpr.

EXPRESS A financial-modeling expert system produced by Management Decision System (Hunt 1986, 106).

Expression 1. Either an atom or a list in LISP. 2. The basic data structure in PROLOG. The arguments of a predicate. They may be constants, variables, strings, lists, structures, arithmetic expressions, and operator expressions. 3. A premise or a conclusion in a rule. *See also* San Marco LISP Explorer (Harmon and King 1985, 42–43; Winston 1984, 4, 20).

EXPRS A PROLOG-based knowledge engineering language that uses backward and forward chaining. Its rules are easily understandable since they are Englishlike. Lockheed Palo Alto Research Laboratory developed EXPRS (Hunt 1986, 106–107).

Extendability The elaboration of an object through the modification of the object's inherited methods. Override is the procedure used to carry out extendability (Duntemann 1989, 137).

Extended inference Inference outside of the boundaries of standard logic. Example: intuitionistic logic (Smith 1989, 66).

Extended-prediction problem A manifestation of the frame problem. Attempting to predict how long a valid fact remains valid (Eckert 1989, 52–54).

Extended response The attempt to focus on the intent of a user of a natural language system. Example: the query, "Give me the gross national products of all Western European nations" would be valueless if the system did not grasp that the intent of the user is also to obtain the names of all Western European nations that correspond to the gross national products (Mays 1986, 559–561).

Extensibility *See* Extensible.

Extensible Having the ability to add new features using previously defined features. This characteristic greatly increases the flexibility of a language. LISP is an extensible language because existing facilities lend themselves to adding new facilities. FORTRAN is not an extensible language (Rosenberg 1986, 64; Smith 1989, 66).

Extensional Only objects that exist can be referenced (Charniak and McDermott 1985, 373).

Extensional definition A definition of class by a listing of its members. Data bases are extensional and knowledge bases are intensional. (Chapnick Nov 1987, 7).

Extensional knowledge The set of all objects denoted by a given object (Luger and Stubblefield 1989, 335).

Extensional meaning Meaning denoted by the external referents of an object. Example: Defining chairs by referring to the set of all chairs. *Contrast with* Intensional meaning (Chabris 1989, 64–65).

Extent The length of time in which a variable or object can be referenced. For some variables the extent to which they exist is from the time the function they are in is activated to the time the function is exited. Other variables or objects maintain their identity throughout the entire program run (Tello 1987, 241).

Extra-logical feature A nonlogic feature. In LISP this refers to such features as dynamic binding, association lists, setq, and replaca (Voda 1988, 28).

Extra-logical predicate A predicate in PROLOG that produces side effects while attempting to satisfy a goal. While side effects are usually best avoided some are needed. Predicates which read input from the keyboard, communicate with the operating system, and assert and retract facts and rules all fit under this classification (Sterling and Shapiro 1985, 175–190).

Face validity The appearance that the expert system does the job it is designed to do. While this may be considered a superficial characteristic, it is important in the sense that it gives the user enough confidence in the system to continue to use it. *Contrast with* Validation (Marcot 1987, 45).

Facet A property of a slot that can elaborate or place restraints on the meaning of the slot. A facet may be a demon or values which reside in the slot of a frame and somehow controls what takes place when the slot is accessed. A facet may control the type of information allowed in a slot. That is, only text may be allowed. It may control the number of pieces of information allowed in the slot. Very often facets are constraint values that give minimum and maximum allowable values. A facet may specify default values. It may display information or a graph when the slot is accessed. It may request a password when a slot is accessed. It may be an explanation of the slot. A slot can have multiple facets (Matthews Sep 1987, 78; Walters and Nielsen 1988, 215–217; Townsend 1987a, 125–126; Hayes-Roth et al 1983, 400; Winston 1984, 312–313; Townsend and Feucht 1986, 55; Tello 1988, 308; Luger and Stubblefield 1989, 547).

Facilitator principle The tenet that artificial intelligence programs should not be used simply to give an answer to a problem, but should be used to encourage alternative solutions which may not have been ordinarily thought of in the problem-solving situation. The problem with this concept is that in some situations too many answers can prevent any action at all.

Fact 1. An assertion that a statement is true. A fact is generally accepted as being true until it is proven otherwise. 2. One of the three basic statements in logic programming. (Queries and rules are the other two kinds of statements.) It is a means of stating that a relationship holds between objects. An example of a fact in logic programming is the predicate likes(john, mary), which states the fact john likes mary. In a fact all of the arguments are usually constants. The fact is also a nonconditional clause. That is, it has an empty body. A logic statement with a body is a rule. A synonym for fact in logic programming is unit clause. 3. A knowledge structure. 4. A record in a relational data base, or an instance of a frame. Assume a predicate, book(author, title, copyright). A fact in this logic program could be book(winston, lisp, 1985). In a data base, book is the title of a table. Author, title, and copyright are field names. The values winston, lisp, 1985 are the data which make up a particular record in the data base. In a frame called book, the slots author, title, and copyright hold the values winston, lisp, 1985 (Parsaye and Chignell 1988, 41, 204–209; Bharath and Sklar 1985, 49; Townsend 1987a, 31–32; Hayes-Roth et al 1983, 400; Townsend 1987b, 379; Sterling and Shapiro 1986, 2–3; Shmueli et al 1986, 249).

Fact base The accumulated facts and/or beliefs in an expert system (Parsaye and Chignell 1988, 42; Charniak and McDermott 1985, 320).

Factorable 1. Describing the ability to reduce the size of a search space by means of a heuristic. 2. Describing the division of a speech space into separate components, which can then be processed separately (Hayes-Roth et al 1983, 101).

Factoring A variant of resolution in which two components of a clause with a common predicate are selected to produce a new clause by combining them with appropriate values (Tello 1988, 419).

Fact parameter A parameter found in some expert system shells which allows only yes or no answers (Tello 1988, 147).

Factual knowledge Knowledge pertaining to facts and the relation between facts.

Fail A predicate in PROLOG that, when used in a clause, always guarantees failure. Fail can be used to produce multiple solutions or ensure incorrect answers are pruned (Clocksin and Mellish 1984, 85–87).

Failure-driven loop An iteration in PROLOG produced by using the fail predicate, which can be used to produce multiple solutions (Sterling and Shapiro 1986, 188–189; Clocksin and Mellish 1984, 85–87).

FAITH A diagnostic expert system that troubleshoots problems in spacecraft. It includes forward and backward chaining, frames, and predicate logic. It was developed at the Jet Propulsion Laboratory (Hunt 1986, 108).

FALCON A monitoring expert system that uses input information in a chemical plant to warn of problems and interpret the cause. The knowledge is represented in forward chaining rules and a network system. FALCON was designed at the University of Delaware using the language LISP (Hunt 1986, 108).

Falk, G A computer scientist who is known for his development of the vision program.

Fan out The number of nodes attached to a given node (Barr and Feigenbaum 1981 vol 3, 50).

Fast Reading and Understanding Memory Program A research program which reads, and to a limited extent understands news stories and summarizes them (Johnson 1986, 171–172; Rosenberg 1986, 73).

Fault tolerance 1. The ability of living organisms and some computer programs to function despite defects in the system. 2. The ability of a neural network to continue to carry out previously learned tasks even though a portion of it has been destroyed. 3. The ability of a computer system to continue to function despite software failures and hardware defects. Connection machines and neural networks are noted for their fault tolerance because of the built-in redundancy. Expert systems can be designed in a redundant manner so that they can achieve a degree of fault tolerance (Josin 1987, 188; Tello 1989, 21).

Fault tree A diagrammatic, ordered representation of faults that may be found in a system. Example: a fault tree that represents the different problems that might arise in an automobile.

Feasibility analysis An evaluation of the practicality of building an expert system for a particular application. Feasibility analysis focuses on such questions as: Are there true experts in the area? Is there a reasonably stable set of knowledge? Are case histories available? Is there a domain expert available? Is the problem area too large? Is the problem area too small? Will the expert system actually be used? Will it save time and money?

Feature A characteristic of an object or a concept, equivalent to attribute (Chabris 1989, 293).

Feature detector A processing unit in a neural net that becomes specialized in detecting a particular pattern or set of patterns (Jorgensen and Matheus 1986, 34; Forsyth and Naylor 1985, 79, 94).

Feature extraction The first stage of pattern recognition, during which patterns are extracted from incoming numerical data. The second stage of pattern recognition is pattern classification (Townsend and Feucht 1986, 184).

Feature matching A procedure used in visual processing in which an image is reduced to a skeleton and examined for matches. The matched features are then stored together as a depiction of the object (Jorgensen and Matheus 1986, 34; Barr and Feigenbaum 1981 vol 3, 250–253).

Feature node A node in a neural network that fires in response to a given pattern of input node activity (Levine 1989, 30).

Feature space A graph of the different features an image analysis system has extracted from a scene (Fischler and Firschein 1986, 44; Winston 1979, 206).

Feature vector 1. The features of an object that distinguish it from other objects. 2. A representation of a concept in a machine-learning system. A feature vector consists only of intensional features, not extensional features. A frame-like object that represents a concept. The slots of the feature vector represent the attributes of the concept (Chabris 1989, 209, 293; Hunt 1986, 109).

Feedback The information in machine learning that the program receives about the correctness of the choices it makes.

Feedback loop A loop in which information is constantly injected into the network concerning the performance of the loop so that the necessary adjustments can be made and the desired output can be produced (Obermeier and Barron 1989, 219).

Feedforward perceptron A perceptron in which the information flows in only one direction —from input to output. A relatively simple version of a perceptron that is employed in pattern-recognition problems (Tank and Hopfield 1987, 114).

Feigenbaum, Ed One of the authors of the text *The Fifth Generation,* and coauthor of the *Handbook of Artificial Intelligence*. He developed Elementary Perceiver and Memorizer (EPAM) and DENDRAL.

Fexpr A LISP function whose argument is not evaluated prior to execution of the function. A fexpr takes only one argument. The argument can be a complex structure which is then passed to the function which analyzes the structure so as to carry out the task of the function. Example: the fexpr may be defined in such a way as to analyze an if/then/else structure argument. In this way users can design their own if/then/else structures if such a structure does not exist in their version of LISP. Such a task cannot be carried out by the more common exprs functions, because exprs evaluate their arguments. The more common functions in LISP are called exprs. Much of what was accomplished with fexprs is now done by macros (Winston 1979, 355; Hasemer 1984, 18–20).

Field testing   The fifth of seven stages in expert system development. In this stage the system is turned over to selected end users for on-the-job testing and revisions are made. *See also* Expert system development (Harmon et al 1988, 197–198).

Fifth generation   The Japanese government sponsored project for developing artificial intelligence technology. The chosen language for the project is PROLOG (Harmon and King 1985, 87–89).

Fifth-generation computer   A computer that uses multiple processors to process information in parallel. *Contrast with* Von Neumann machine (Townsend 1987a, 21, 234; Harmon and King 1985, 59).

Fifth-generation language   A language that has flexibility in design alternatives, the ability to emulate human problem-solving processes more easily and to model complex and not completely understood processes. Fifth-generation languages are characterized by dynamic binding of variables and types, polymorphic variables, a declarative style, an integrated programming environment, good abstraction capabilities, forward and backward chaining, resolution theorem proving, spreading activation, support for the symbol as a data type, automatic memory management, operator overloading, message passing, and backtracking. A language does not have to have all of these characteristics to qualify as a fifth-generation language. The tradeoff for the above features is speed. PROLOG, OPS5, C++, and Common LISP are considered fifth-generation languages (Matthews Jul 1987, 35; Matthews Sep 1987, 43).

File scope   The limiting of the scope of a name to a file (Tello 1989, 85).

Filler   A value found in a slot on a frame (Jackson 1986, 58).

Fillmore, Charles   The thinker who emphasized that what is invariant in a sentence is the set of roles or cases being used.

Filter   A function in LISP that tests the elements of a list. Those elements which do not pass the test are deleted (Luger and Stubblefield 1989, 267).

Filtering   A control strategy used in expert systems. The process decides which rules or data will be used to reach a goal. In production systems filtering is limiting either data or rules from the matching process to achieve solutions more quickly. *See also* Data filtering; Rule filtering (Rosenberg 1986, 69).

Filtering of images   The deletion of portions of the image in vision to enhance black and white contrasts. A method of removing noise and enhancing important features. Mathematical functions are employed in filtering. An important procedure in vision (Chabris 1989, 293; Schildt 1987, 126–127).

Fine grain   The extreme detail of a problem.

Fine-grained parallelism   A type of parallel processing in which a large number of small microprocessors are used. *Contrast with* Coarse-grained parallelism (Hillis 1985, 23–24).

Finite-state machine   A device which begins in one state and when conditions warrant it, changes to another state. The next state it moves to is a function of the current state and the conditions that can produce a change in state (Emerson 1987, 58).

Finite-state transition diagram   A diagram consisting of a set of nodes and arcs used to decide if a sentence input is accepted as correct. The nodes represent different states. The arcs represent the words which must be matched by the input to allow a transition from one state to the next. When the final state is reached the input sentence is accepted as correct input. Augmented Transition Networks were derived from finite-state transition diagrams (Barr and Feigenbaum 1981 vol 1, 263).

Fire The carrying out of actions on the right side of an if/then rule once the conditions on the left side of the rule have been satisfied (Brownston et al 1986, 7, 12–13).

First-class functions Functions treated as first-class objects. That is, they can be passed as arguments and returned by a function. *See also* First-class object (Allen 1985, 29–32).

First-class object An object with the following characteristics: It may be passed as a parameter to a function. It may be returned as a value from a function. It may be tested for equality. It may be incorporated in composite data structures. It may be stored indefinitely while still retaining its environment of definition. A first-class object is an object that can be assigned to a variable. Assume a language that allows procedures to be first-class objects. The procedures can then be assigned to a variable. The procedure can be executed by passing the necessary parameters to the variable name. A series of procedures represented as variables can be placed in a list and executed in sequence, hence producing a sophisticated control strategy. There are fewer restrictions on first-class objects than on other objects. In the language Scheme all objects are first-class objects (Tello 1988, 358; Allen 1985, 28; Maxwell and Riggle 1989, 30).

First-in-last-out A conflict resolution strategy that decides to execute the rule that has been under consideration for the shortest period of time (Hu 1989, 273).

First-level induction A classification of examples without using inexact values, ranges, or generalization. Example: in an expert system using barometric pressure, if examples used the values of 25 and 32 the induction system would not attempt to generalize beyond these values to any other values. *See also* Fourth-level induction; Second-level induction; Third-level induction.

First Operational Operationalizer (FOO) An advice-taking program that can translate advice into a series of actions. FOO uses general advice about the game of hearts and translates the advice into specific actions.

First-order language Languages that do not allow functions as arguments. *Contrast with* Higher-order language (Allen 1987, 54).

First-order logic An extension of propositional logic. The primary extensions are the use of predicates and quantified variables. A predicate states a relationship between objects. The use of quantified variables and predicates opens the door to the implementation of functions that can return values as well as true and false. A predicate in first-order logic is really a function in the sense that predicates in first-order logic can return values. In first-order logic the existential quantifiers "for all" and "there exists" are used. This quantification over symbols is the hallmark of first-order logic. First-order logic also implements the negation symbol NOT, and the equals predicate. Unification is the pattern-matching and value-substitution procedure used in first-order logic. First-order logic possesses the property of completeness. First-order logic is distinguished from second-order logic in that quantification over predicates and functions is not allowed in first-order logic. For example, such statements as, "all predicates may have a maximum of two arguments" is not allowed. PROLOG is an implementation of first-order logic. First-order logic is also referred to as first-order predicate calculus or predicate logic. *Contrast with* Propositional calculus; Second-order logic (Ladkin 1987, 58; Barr and Feigenbaum 1981 vol 1, 165–171; Sterling and Shapiro 1986, 280; Townsend and Feucht 1986, 57–62; Smith 1989, 68).

First-order predicate calculus Logic. *See also* First-order logic.

First principles Relying on the basic theory of the field rather than rules of thumb in attempting to build an expert system in a particular field. Deep knowledge. *Contrast with* Heuristic knowledge.

Fission An incremental growth by refinement used in rule-based systems. A rule is replaced by a set of rules which more accurately capture the patterns the original rule was designed to capture. *See also* Spinning off for another version of incremental growth by refinement (Brownston et al 1986, 168, 170–171).

Fixed partitioning Partitioning used in expert systems, in which the subtasks are carried out in a fixed sequential fashion (Hayes-Roth et al 1983, 102).

Flat data base A data base that has no hierarchical organization.

Flat image processing In vision the processing of an image with only two dimensions represented. Such flat image processing is used in assembly lines. Flat image processing can be used with three dimensional objects as long as the key features of the objects are not lost (Schildt 1987, 127–128).

Flat net A neural net with no hidden layers (Pao 1989, 64).

Flavor A method-bearing entity in a taxonomy of method properties. *See also* Flavor mixing (Winston 1984, 248).

Flavor mixing A term used in the frame-based program which refers to multiple inheritance and the mixing of methods. This is, the ability of some frame-based systems to allow an object to inherit a combination of methods from two objects (Jackson 1986, 64).

Flavors An object-oriented extension of ZETA-LISP. It is known for its flexible method of inheritance ability. It does not employ data abstraction and is a weakly typed language (Walters and Nielsen 1988, 91; Winston 1984, 311; Wegner 1989, 248; Smith 1989, 69).

Flexible query processing A characteristic of an intelligent data base in which partial matches of data can be used to obtain a query response. The query response can be accompanied by a confidence level (Parsaye et al 1990, 43–44).

Flexibility The measure of a robot's ability to adapt to different manufacturing duties (Rosenberg 1986, 70).

Flexigrid A program based on the repertory grid technique (Thompson and Thompson Jan 1987, 26).

Flow of control How control is exerted over the execution of artificial intelligence systems. Example: In production systems control is a function of patterns in working memory rather than such control structures as do loops. *See also* Control (Brownston et al 1986, 8, 12, 15–21).

FOLIO A rule-based forward-chaining expert system that assists in choosing stock portfolios. Forward chaining is used to ascertain the client goals and linear programming is then used to find a best fit between the goals and an actual portfolio (Hunt 1986, 111).

For-all A superlogical quantifier used in logic-based expert systems which continues to execute instances of a clause until a specified second clause becomes false. Example: "for-all 'X' is-a plane; is-true 'X' does fly." If a single instance of the clause 'X' is-a plane is found which does not fly then the clause fails (Parsaye and Chignell 1988, 270).

For-all quantifier Universal quantifier (Schildt 1987, 229).

Forbidden constraint A constraint that screens out solution candidates because it possesses certain characteristics that would not make them suitable. *Compare with* Required constraint (Jackson 1986, 21).

FORBIN A robot-planning program developed at Yale University, which is capable of planning in situations in which deadline time constraints are important. It represents a significant advance over the planning program DEVISER (Tello 1988, 493–494).

Force fitting 1. Attempts to force an expert tool to work with a problem that the tool was not designed to handle. 2. Using an expert system shell that is not truly appropriate for a particular knowledge domain. It may not be appropriate because it does not have the most appropriate knowledge representation scheme or the most appropriate inferencing technique. Such force fitting can make it difficult to complete the expert system (Walters and Nielsen 1988, 182–183).

FOREST A rule-based expert system that diagnoses problems in electronic instruments, which was designed at the University of Pennsylvania using PROLOG (Hunt 1986, 111–112).

For-every A superlogical quantifier used in logic-based expert systems which for each instance of a given clause, all instances of a second clause are executed. Example: "for-every 'Plane' in_inventory; do-write 'Plane', "is in inventory" (Parsaye and Chignell 1988, 267–268).

Forgiving environment A computer environment that compensates for the user's mistakes by guessing what the user really meant (Tello 1988, 19).

Form 1. A data object in LISP that can be evaluated. Some examples of forms are numbers, symbols that represent values, and lists. 2. A screen of fill in the blank statements used to gain information from the user. The form is in contrast to the usual type of question and answer dialogue found in expert systems. The advantage of a form is the user can see at a glance if he or she has all the necessary information at hand. *See also* San Marco LISP Explorer (Shafer Sep/Oct 1988, 58; Steele 1984, 54–55; Tello Jun 1987, 272).

Formal grammar theory The theory of formal grammar is a method of defining legal sentences in a language by using a finite vocabulary and by adhering to specified concepts. The concepts include syntactic categories (noun, adjective and so on), terminal symbols (the individual words in the grammar), rewrite rules (Sentence —> noun phrase and verb phrase), and a start symbol (Sentence). It was developed by Noam Chomsky (Brownston et al 1986, 12; Barr and Feigenbaum 1981 vol 1, 239–244).

Formalism A means of representing knowledge in expert systems. Three types of formalism used in expert systems are production rules, structured objects, and clauses (Jackson 1986, 30).

Formalist An artificial intelligence researcher who uses a theoretical approach, and who holds that one must build an underlying system which can represent such concepts as time, causality, and space before building a general knowledge base with common sense. A contrasting approach is used by the builders of CYC. They are attempting to build an artificial intelligence system which has common sense without waiting for the underlying theoretical apparatus to be developed.

Formalization One of five phases in developing an expert system. In this phase the language and type of knowledge representation are chosen. The five phases, in order, are identification, conceptualization, formalization, implementation, and testing.

Formal parameter A placeholder for the actual parameter of a procedure. Example: Max(*A*, *B, C*). The procedure decides which of the three numbers represented by *A, B,* and *C* is the maximum number. *A, B,* and *C* are formal parameters for the procedure Max. The actual parameters are the numbers *A, B,* and *C* actually represent (Hunt 1986, 192).

Formal reasoning A reasoning process that uses specified rules of inference to make inferences. The process of deriving new facts from previously known facts. This process is carried out using rules. Inference is a synonym. Deduction and induction are two types of formal reasoning (Townsend 1987a, 12–13, 115–116; Barr and Feigenbaum 1981 vol 1, 146; Smith 1989, 70).

Formal specification A type of automatic programming that relies on formal logic. Theorem-proving techniques are at the heart of this method. *Contrast with* Natural-language specification; Specification by example (Mishkoff 1986, 6-7).

Formant representation A means of encoding human speech. Particular attention is paid to the three major frequency bands of human speech when using this method. Two other methods of encoding human speech are vocorder representation and linear predictive coding (Forsyth and Naylor 1985, 43, 44, 45).

Formation problems The putting together of a complex whole using a set of constraints. The expert system R1 is used to solve formation problems. R1 is used to configure computer systems from a set of specifications. Synthesis problems (Jackson 1986, 222).

Forms feature A characteristic of some expert systems that allows the entry of data into a form rather than answering a series of questions. This feature can enhance data entry for some applications. The screen will have a large number of data entry blanks and the user can see at a glance if he or she has all the necessary data. Contrast the forms feature with the usual interview procedure in which questions are asked one at a time. In the interview method the user may have to leave the program many times to go find an answer. If the form feature is used, the user may only need to leave the computer once to find the necessary information (Shafer Sep/Oct 1988, 55–58; Tello 1988, 207).

Formula A proposition or state of affairs in logic. Example: (loves mike sue). This formula states mike loves sue (Charniak and McDermott 1985, 322).

FORTH A fourth-generation computer language, which has a number of features that make it attractive for artificial intelligence programming. It is a very fast and compact language, it is easy to extend, it has lists as a data structure, and it encourages functional programming and is modular. FORTH has excellent facilities for interacting with the hardware. It has an interactive environment. The expert system DELTA/CATS-1 was converted to FORTH (Trelease Oct 1987, 58–66; Shaw 1988, 67–75; Tello 1988, 392–393).

FORTRAN A high-level computer language best known for its use in scientific numeric programming. The expert system shell EXPERT was implemented with FORTRAN (Harmon and King 1985, 79–80, 83–85).

Fortuitous accident A heuristic that works as follows: While working on a subproblem, if a deduction is made; using that deduction to see if it will solve any higher level goals. The definition is repetitious since fortuitous means accidental (Lenat 1988, 75).

FORUM A set of modules that can be used to enhance the expert system tool Knowledge Craft. The enhancements include dependency networks, quantitative calculations, and the inclusion of knowledge which can be executed in either a backward- or forward-chaining mode (Hunt 1986, 112).

Forward-action effect A type of inference found in the expert system NEXPERT OBJECT. In this type of inference the inference mechanism propagates any new declarations that have been made in rule actions through the system. If this produces new hypotheses, they are placed on the agenda. The other types of inference found in NEXPERT OBJECT are forward-confirmed hypotheses, forward-rejected hypotheses, unconditionally forward hypotheses, and exhaustive evaluation (Tello 1988, 303).

Forward chaining A control strategy used in artificial intelligence. It is a chain of inferences that start from an initial state and moves to a goal state. The initial set of facts are compared to the condition elements of the rules in the rule base and when matches are found the eligible rules are fired, adding new facts. The new facts can in turn fire more rules. This process is continued until no more rules can be executed. Forward chaining is sometimes described as starting from an initial state and moving to a goal state. It is synonymous with forward reasoning, data-driven search, bottom-up processing, and antecedent reasoning. It is preferred over backward chaining when most of the data have been collected and the user wants to find all possible conclusions, or the user has not formulated specific hypotheses, or when there are a large number of goal states. It is most effective when the amount of initial information is small and the number of outcomes is large. Configuring a mainframe computer in which there may be an extremely large number of goal configurations is an appropriate application of forward chaining. It may also be the method of choice when a monitoring expert system is required, or in a planning situation in which no goals exist when reasoning begins. Forward chaining is the method of choice when every possible conclusion is wanted from the knowledge at hand. A drawback of forward-chaining systems is that they can have great difficulty in quickly narrowing down the search space. It is also difficult to follow the forward-chaining reasoning process. Chaining refers to the chain of rules used in the reasoning process. Forward-chaining procedures can be complex. The following is a forward-chaining algorithm in some detail: Assume a forward-chaining rule with two premises, with variables that are common to both premises, and the first premise has already been proved. In order to prove the second premise true, the algorithm first checks to see if the premise is a built-in clause. Then it checks to see if the premise is a fact in the fact base. It also checks to see if the fact is an askable fact in the fact base. If it is an askable fact, then the user is asked whether or not the fact is true. If there is no fact in the fact base that will match the premise, the algorithm then searches for a backward-chaining rule that can prove the premise. If the backward-chaining rule can be found and proved then the second premise of the forward-chaining rule can be proved and the rule can be executed. If no backward-chaining rule can be found, then backtracking may take place to the first premise in the forward-chaining rule. New values for the variables in the first and second premise may be found and the second premise may be again tried, and will meet with success. Goal-directed forward chaining is a variant of forward chaining. *Contrast with* Backward chaining; Rule-value method (Darlington 1985, 216; Reedy and Kaplan 1986, 66; Merritt 1986, 30–42; Townsend 1987a 139–142; Schildt 1987, 63–66; Charniak and McDermott 1985, 345–349; Winston 1979, 135–136; Walters and Nielsen 1988, 197–198; Parsaye and Chignell 1988, 277–278; Harmon and King 1985, 54–57; Brownston et al 1986, 13, 15–17, 24, 26); Townsend 1987b, 380; Winston 1984, 276; Luger and Stubblefield 1989, 89–90; Chabris 1989, 116; Smith 1989, 70).

Forward-confirmed hypothesis An inference found in the expert system NEXPERT OBJECT in which the inference mechanism will only go to the next knowledge island if the current hypothesis is true. The other types of inference found in NEXPORT OBJECT are forward-rejected hypotheses, unconditionally forward hypotheses, forward-actions effects, and exhaustive evaluation (Tello 1988, 302).

Forward pruning Plausible-move generation (Barr and Feigenbaum 1981 vol 1, 104).

Forward reasoning 1. Reasoning from a given set of facts to a conclusion or a series of conclusions. 2. Reasoning from an initial state to a goal state. *See also* Forward chaining for a computer implementation of forward reasoning (Kowalski 1985, 164; Smith 1989, 70).

Forward-rejected hypothesis An inference found in the expert system NEXPERT OBJECT. In this type of inference the inference mechanism will only go to the next knowledge island if the current hypothesis is false. The other types of inference found in NEXPERT OBJECT are forward-confirmed hypotheses, unconditionally forward hypotheses, forward-actions effects, and exhaustive evaluation (Tello 1988, 303).

Forward rule A rule used exclusively for forward chaining. With a forward rule, pattern matching starts with the premise of the rule.

Fourth-level induction A type of induction that produces very general rules which use inexact reasoning. *See also* First-level induction; Second-level induction; Third-level induction.

Four-value logic A type of logic that can have the values, true, false, not known, and unknown. Not known means the system has attempted to ascertain the value of an object and has failed. Unknown means the system has not yet attempted to ascertain the value of the object (Oman 1988, 100).

FP The language Functional Programming, which was developed at IBM. It is a functional/declarative language. Its emphasis is on the manipulation of functions rather than objects. The language deemphasizes the use of variables. FP programs are hierarchically structured. Rather than recursion, while loops are used. FP is an attempt at producing a fast functional language (Eisenbach and Sadler 1985, 194–195; Harrison and Khoshnevisan 1985, 219–232).

Frame A knowledge representation that can organize large and complex chunks of stereotypical information that are related. A data structure for representing stereotyped situations, objects, or concepts in which there are certain expectancies. A frame has slots which hold values of properties of an object. The slots of a frame can hold default values, pointers to rule sets, attached procedures, how to use the frame, expectations about what may happen next, what to do then, or what to do if expectancies are not met. Other frames and scripts can also be represented on the slots of a frame. A frame was originally meant to function in conjunction with many other frames in a sequential manner. The analogy of a series of frames in a motion picture is a good one. In this way frames can be used to represent a sequence of events. Example: A computer could be represented as a frame. There may be slots for certain properties of the frame. One slot may be called CPU. In this slot the type of central processing unit is kept. That value could be 8088, 80286, 68000, and so on. Other slots may stand for other properties of the computer. Frames combine declarative and procedural representations. An example of a declarative representation is a fact like the CPU for a particular computer is an 8088. The attached procedure which can compute values for a slot are examples of procedural representations. The fact that procedures can be placed on slots allows frames to become active rather than passive objects. An important property of a frame is that it can inherit properties and values from other frames. As a result, frames are most appropriate when used with hierarchically arranged information, as in an animal phylum. Frames are used to represent knowledge in natural language processing and in expert systems. Frames are also a prime candidate for dealing with analogical reasoning. In large expert systems it is easier to conceptualize the overall structure of the system when frames are used than it would be if production rules were used. Frames are somewhat like a PASCAL record in that they both hold diverse data types. They are different in many ways: (1) The slots in a frame are capable of holding procedures, constraints, and references to other frames. (2) Frames are capable of inheritance. (3) Frames can be arranged in a hierarchical structure. (4) In many frame-based systems slots can be dynamically added to frames, while fields cannot be dynamically added to records. (5) In many frame-based systems a slot is not restricted to a single data type as is a field in a record. On a more molecular level a frame, in LISP, is a generalized property list. In PROLOG, a frame can be constructed using a predicate and a single argument which is a list. The list contains the slot names and slot values. Words which refer to framelike structures include units, objects, concepts, schema, property lists and entities. Other types of knowledge representation with which frames may be contrasted are production rules, logic clauses, scripts, and semantic nets. Frames differ from scripts in that frames are used to represent a point in time. Scripts represent a sequence of events that take place in a time sequence. A frame can be viewed as a subclass of a semantic net. They improve on semantic networks by adding slots, fillers, procedural attachment, defaults, and cancellation. They are more amenable to representing complex objects than are semantic networks, and logic schemes. A frame resembles a logic clause in that the relation of the clause can be compared with the frame name, and the arguments of the clause can be compared with the slots of the frame. Marvin Minsky is credited with proposing frames as knowledge structures. Excellent examples of the applications of frames are in the programs AM and EURISKO. To use frames effectively the frame-based system should have one or both of the following capabilities—a rule syntax that is capable of referencing values in the slots of a frame, or the ability to use methods which can turn the frame hierarchy into a search space for matching generic knowledge with a dynamic real-world model (Tello 1989, 26; Tello 1988, 414–416, 319; Waldrop 1987, 49–57; Forsyth and Naylor 1985, 134–136; Walters and Nielsen 1988, 210; AI *Expert* MM 1985, 59; Floyd Mar/Apr 1988, 80, 82; Miller Jul/Aug 1988, 28; Schuler 1987, 99; Amsterdam Nov 1986, 19; Fischler and Firschein 1986, 44; Townsend 1987a, 124–127, 135–136; Hayes-Roth et al 1983, 400; Mishkoff 1986, 4-7 to 4-8; Charniak and McDermott 1985, 28; Winston 1979, 179–186; Harmon and King 1985, 44–47; Brownston et al 1986, 374–375; Barr and Feigenbaum 1981 vol 1, 216–222; Winston 1984, 311–320; Rosenberg 1986, 72; Lenat 1988, 73; Jay and Knaus 1989, 19–24; Luger and Stubblefield 1989, Chabris 1989, 68; Smith 1989, 70–71).

Frame-based CAI A computer-aided instruction based on programmed instruction. The student is given a set of material and asked questions. The next set of questions asked is based on the student's previous responses. Frame-based CAI has been referred to as a sophisticated page turner. *Contrast with* Intelligent computer-aided instruction (ICAI) (Mishkoff 1986, 6-1).

Frame-based expert system An expert system in which the primary knowledge representation is the frame. Frame-based systems are characterized by hierarchical inheritance. Frame-based systems are most useful when there are numerous complex objects arranged in a hierarchy. Any situation that consists of sets of clustered data should be considered as a possibility for frame-based representation. It is helpful if there are few exceptions in the hierarchy. An example of an exception is an animal that is a mammal which does not give milk to its young. Frame-based systems are useful in situations that require the adding of new instances on a frequent basis. In such situations the new instance automatically inherits the properties of the parent instance. A frame-based system is also useful when relationships are frequently modified, or when new relationships are added. For example, when a new characteristic is added to an object all objects which are below the object automatically inherit the new relationship. In a rule-based system extensive modification of many rules would have to be made in order to accommodate the new characteristic. It is less likely to suffer from contradictions and duplications as compared to a rule-based system. When rules are used in conjunction with frames, the rules can be more generic, hence there is less need for specialized rules. This leads to smaller rule sets. Frame-based systems provide more structure and are easier to understand and maintain than rule-based systems. In complex domains it is less likely one would lose sight of hierarchical relationships in a frame-based system as compared to a rule-based system. A frame-based expert system is similar to an object-oriented expert system. One difference is frame-based systems generally have a more flexible inheritance architecture (Townsend 1987b, 234–236).

Frame-based reasoning The different types of reasoning that are unique to frame-based systems. This can include (1) The use of facets to restrict or guard values; (2) the placement of sets of rules on a slot. The rule set is triggered when the value of the slot is requested. The purpose of the rule set is to compute the requested value. (3) Hierarchical reasoning. In a frame-based system the use of rules to eliminate entire classes of objects from the solution search process. This is one of the strengths of a frame-based system. A rule-based system would have to check out each individual object in search of a solution—a time-consuming process. (4) Inheritance hierarchies can be used in conjunction with generic rules to find values and to reason about the frames. The use of frames allows rules to be generic, greatly cutting down on the number of rules required. As a result, a system that uses frame-based reasoning is easier to understand and maintain (Walters and Nielsen 1988, 210–251).

Frame instantiation   The creation of a frame in a frame-based expert system (Harmon et al 1988, 109).

Frame language   A language in which the primary means of knowledge representation is the frame. The expert system tools KEE and Knowledge Craft both possess frame-based languages. Programming with frames is generally considered a type of object-oriented programming (Finin 1986, 44–50).

Frame problem   1. The problem of not knowing which facts must be withdrawn and which facts remain valid in a data base. This is a particularly vexing problem when AI systems must deal with time as a dimension.   2. The difficulty that representational formalisms have in modeling changes in the real world by making appropriate modifications to its data base. When new information makes invalid already existing information it is difficult for many programs to be able to alter their fact base to accommodate this change. Example: Assume a city-planning expert system that recommends the building of a particular manufacturing plant, but incorrectly estimates the water supply needs. All aspects of the plan that were based on the incorrect estimation of the water supply must now be modified (Jackson 1986, 227; Barr and Feigenbaum 1981, vol 1, 177; Barr and Feigenbaum 1981 vol 3, 337; Chabris 1989, 65–66; Luger and Stubblefield 1989, 372; Eckert 1989, 52–54; Hayes 1973, 45–59).

FRANZLISP   A version of LISP used at the University of California at Berkeley (Hunt 1986, 114).

Free variable   1. In a LISP function, a free variable is not on the parameter list of a function and may be bound within the function through the use of setq or let. Free variables should be used cautiously since it is possible they may retain their value after the function has completed execution. Whether or not the free variable retains its value after the function has completed execution is a function of the particular implementation of LISP used.   2. A variable that does not have a value. *Contrast with* Bound variable (Townsend 1987a, 40–42; Charniak and McDermott 1985, 74; Winston 1979, 276–277; Townsend 1987b, 12; Winston 1984, 54).

Friend   A nonmember function of a class in C++ that is allowed access to the data of that class. This type of function can have access to objects in more than one class (Stroustrup 1987, 149).

FRL   A frame-based knowledge engineering language. Its features include procedural attachment, defaults, constraints, indirection, preferences, abstraction, and multiple inheritance. It was developed at MIT (Hunt 1986, 114).

Front-end analysis   The first of seven stages in expert system development, in which basic questions are answered concerning the project. In this stage the problem area is delineated, cost effectiveness is determined, and management support is sought. *See also* Expert System (Harmon et al 1988, 168–169; Rosenberg 1986, 73).

FRUMP   *See* Fast Reading and Understanding Memory Program.

Fudge factor   A factor sometimes used in artificial intelligence game programs to delete borderline moves (Forsyth and Naylor 1985, 194).

Full-width searching   In a game-search situation, ensuring that all authorized moves are inspected before being eliminated (Smith 1989, 72).

FUNARG   The calling of a LISP function along with its environment. FUNARG is often used to produce generators (Smith 1989, 71).

Function 1. A rule in mathematics that characterizes the correspondence between members of two classes of objects. The two classes of objects are generally referred to as the domain and the range. Each element of the domain is paired with a unique element of the range. A mathematical entity that returns a value based on the value of one or more independent variables. 2. A function in LISP analogous to a mathematical function. A LISP program primarily consists of functions that work cooperatively. A LISP function is a set of program statements with a set of arguments and a unique name. The function uses the program statements and arguments to compute and return a single value. The value returned is a function of the set of arguments. A function in LISP does not permanently alter memory. That is, it is free of side effects. One way to think of a function is thinking pure thoughts and remembering nothing. There are three types of functions in LISP: fexpr, expr, and macros. Functions in LISP have a number of problems that prevent them from being considered pure functions. LISP functions have problems passing functions as parameters. Also, many procedures in LISP are not completely side-effect-free. That is, LISP is not a pure function language. In LISP a function may be considered a data type, because LISP functions may be created at runtime, passed as arguments to a function, stored as variables, and stored in structures. One authority defines a LISP function as any entity which will serve as the first argument to funcall and apply. 3. A set of clauses in PROLOG with the same name and the same number of parameters in the head. This set of clauses can return true, false, or a value. 4. For completeness sake the definition of function in C is included. In C, the term function is defined as a set of program statements which carries out a computation and has a name. It is a block of code that is named and can be called from different parts of the program in which it is contained. In this way it is like a subroutine. Functions provide modularization, memory conservation, and data hiding. Functions are the essential building blocks of the C language. The use of arguments and the returning of a value are optional in C. Functions in C can produce side-effects. In summary, the advantages of functions are modularity, memory conservation, and information hiding. *See also* Functional language for more information (Allen 1987, 50–51; Thompson and Thompson 1987, 22; Charniak and McDermott 1985, 37; Brownston et al 1986, 197, 201–204, 290–291; Townsend 1987b, 9–10; Winston 1984, 29; Graham Apr 1989, 23; Stroustrup 1987, 21; Savory 1988, 235; Steele 1984, 32; Morein 1986, 155).

Functional assertion relation Assertion in which only one assertion is allowed in a data base for a given object. Example: you would only want one of the following assertions in a data base at a given time: (tomorrow's-stockmarket-prediction, market goes up), (tomorrow's-stockmarket-prediction, market goes down). *Contrast with* Assertion relation (Flamig Spring 1988, 52).

Functional dependency A data dependency that can be used as an alternative to the PROLOG cut in some circumstances. It occurs over a relation in which certain arguments determine the value of the remaining argument. Assume the predicate member(lastname, firstname, rank). If lastname and firstname uniquely determine rank then lastname, firstname = = > rank is a functional dependency (Denney 1988, 44).

Functional hierarchy The type of hierarchy in which the function of each component is represented in terms of how each component is related to other components. This type of hierarchy represents deep knowledge. *Compare with* Causal hierarchy; Structural hierarchy (Townsend and Feucht 1986, 73–74).

Functional knowledge One of three types of knowledge found in diagnostic expert systems. The way the components of a system work together to carry out a task. *See also* Event knowledge; Structural knowledge (Merritt 1987, 53).

Functional language A computer language consisting of functions that are somewhat analogous to functions in mathematics. Each function takes a series of arguments, processes the arguments, and returns a single value. The values of all variables are lost once evaluation is completed. The value returned is not stored in a permanent place in memory. A function does not modify values that are already present; rather it adds new information. While this may initially appear to be a disadvantage it is actually an advantage since it prevents the possibility of a mysterious change in the values of variables in a program run. Because of the relative absence of side effects functional languages are candidates for parallel processing. A functional language is to some extent the opposite of an object-oriented language. In an object-oriented language the variables maintain their values throughout a program run. Functional languages are noted for their use of complex data structures and frequently result in shorter programs. Example: LISP (although LISP is not a pure functional language), FP, and HOPE. Functional languages are sometimes called applicative languages; that is, they apply functions to arguments. *See also* Function for more information (Allen 1985, 28–29; Steele 1987, 6, 50–61; Thompson and Thompson Apr 1987, 21, Thompson and Thompson Sep 1987, 15; Eisenbach and Sadler 1985, 186; Townsend and Feucht 1986, 82).

Functional links A type of neural net that changes the input through a nonlinear metamorphosis. This takes place before the incoming data reach the input layer. It is a method of solving supervised learning problems using neural nets without hidden layers (Pao 1989, 60–68).

Function call A program executing a function so the function can carry out a task or return a value that the program can then use (Rosenberg 1986, 74).

Function-centered program A program made up of functions that operate on data types. If a new data type is added to the program, all the functions must be altered to accommodate the new data type. *Contrast with* Data-centered program (Fernhout 1989, 38).

Function overloading The procedure in C++ of allowing a user to define two functions with the same name. They are distinguished by their argument list. Example: Given a function call of POWER(3,2) the first function that works only with integers would be called which would produce the square of 3 which is 9. If the call is POWER(3.5, 2.0), then the second, slower function is called to process the real numbers. Overloaded functions are called generic functions. Function overloading takes place at compile time. Contrast with an analogous process polymorphism that takes place at runtime. *Contrast with* Operator overloading (Waite et al 1987, 496–497; Thomas 1989, 234).

Functor 1. The portion of a predicate which expresses a relationship. 2. The parent object of a compound structure along with its arity. In the structure auto(Engine, Body-type), auto is the functor and its arity is 2 because it has two arguments—Engine and Body-type. The arity is important because auto with an arity of 2 is a completely different functor from auto with an arity of 3 (Harrison and Tribble 1986, 66; Townsend 1987a, 84; Townsend 1987b, 380; Sterling and Shapiro 1986, 4; Bratko 1986, 31; Lazarav 1988, 76).

Fundamental training theorem Perceptron convergence procedure (Brown Apr 1987, 24).

Fusing The second part of the process used in OPS5 production systems to achieve a backward-chaining system. After rules have been used to split a goal into subgoals, and the subgoals have been achieved, rules are then used to bring together the information obtained from each subgoal so as to solve a higher goal. Splitting is the first part of this process (Brownston et al 1986, 163).

Fuzzy-AND A portion of fuzzy logic that attempts to arrive at a confidence level for a given conclusion from a series of events, choosing the minimum confidence level of the events. fuzzy-AND = minimum(event-one confidence-one, event two confidence-two). If confidence-one and confidence-two are .9 and .2, respectively the overall confidence is the minimum of the two confidences - (.2). An appropriate application of the fuzzy-AND is a sickness in which you know two symptoms are always present. The consequences of deciding the disease is present is a drastic operation. The consequences of deciding the disease is not present is some continued discomfort for the patient. If the confidence in one symptom being present is .8 and the other is .1 then it would be appropriate to choose the minimum confidence of .1 as the overall confidence since you know the disease cannot possibly be present without the latter symptom and the consequences of not operating are not that severe (Olsen et al 1987, 126).

Fuzzy complement An element's membership in the complement of a fuzzy set. Example: A cat's membership in the Siamese category is (.7). The fuzz complement of not being Siamese is (.3). This operation is used to define the fuzzy-NOT (Richards 1988, 285).

Fuzzy connectives The use of the connectives OR, AND, and IF/THEN in fuzzy logic. *See also* Fuzzy-AND; Fuzzy-OR (Suits 1988, 42).

Fuzzy intersection The weakest-link approach. This operation is used to define the fuzzy-AND (Richards 1988, 285).

Fuzzy logic A type of logic that attempts to deal with imprecise information. An extension of boolean logic. In boolean logic an entity is considered to be a member of a set or it is not. In fuzzy logic membership in a set is a matter of degree. A given object may belong to different classifications with varying degrees of certainty. Consider the concept of age. It is possible to define old age arbitrarily as greater than 70. Those with an age less than 70 are excluded from this set. However, in reality, there is no general agreement on what constitutes old age. The better approximation of reality is to use fuzzy logic and assign a number between 0 and 1 to represent the degree to which an entity belongs in a class. Age 0 to 40 is assigned the number 0. Age 41 to 50 is assigned the number .7. Age 51 to 60 is assigned the number .8. This process can be continued until all ages are assigned a number between 0 and 1. The total certainty for all the classes the object belongs to does not have to sum to 1 as it does in classical probability. In fuzzy logic the probability of joint events is the minimum of the probabilities associated with each event. Contrast this with classical logic where the probability of joint events is the product of the joint events. Which approach should be used is a function of the types of data involved. Lofti Zadeh is responsible for developing fuzzy logic. *Contrast with* Certainty factor; Bayes' theorem. *See also:* Composition rules; Fuzzy-AND; Fuzzy complement; Fuzzy connectives; Fuzzy intersection; Fuzzy modifiers; Fuzzy-NOT; Fuzzy-OR; Fuzzy predicates; Fuzzy quantifiers; Fuzzy relations; Fuzzy union; Strongest-link method; Weakest-link method (Townsend 1987a 167–168; Suits 1988, 39–43; Schildt 1987, 12, 239; Hayes-Roth et al 1983, 94–95; Townsend and Feucht 1986, 175; Parsaye and Chignell 1988, 223–228; Tello 1988, 82–84; Waldrop 1987, 48; Olsen et al 1987, 126).

Fuzzy modifier Words that modify fuzzy predicates. Examples: NOT happy, VERY happy, MORE OR LESS happy, happy(confidence level squared), happy(square root of confidence level) (Suits 1988, 41):

Fuzzy-NOT The equivalent of 1 - confidence of event. Assume you are attempting to determine the desirability of living in different cities. The estimation of crime in a given city is (.8). A desirability rating is obtained by using fuzzy-NOT = 1 - .8 = (.2) (Olsen et al 1987, 126).

Fuzzy operators The use of adjectives in fuzzy logic like good, poor, reasonable, and cheap. Fuzzy operators are defined mathematically (Tello 1988, 92–94).

Fuzzy-OR A part of fuzzy logic that attempts to arrive at a confidence level for a given conclusion from a series of events. Each event has an attached confidence level. The maximum confidence level of the different events is chosen to represent the overall confidence factor. fuzzy-OR

= maximum(event-one confidence, event-two confidence). An appropriate application of the fuzzy-OR is deciding on alerting defense forces because of two pieces of evidence - radar blips (.8 confidence) and intelligence reports (.1 confidence). The consequences are so severe if the defense alert is not called that it is best to choose the maximum of the two confidences. *Compare with* Certainty factors (which use a cumulative approach); Fuzzy-AND.

Fuzzy predicate A fuzzy predicate refers to the attributes of an object in fuzzy logic. Example: Assume an accountant who has developed a method of estimating the validity of accounts receivable. The fuzzy predicate that will measure the quality of the accounts receivable is "acceptability." The accountant's method returns a value ranging from 0 to 150. She or he decides that a score ranging from 0 to 50 receives an acceptability score of 0. A score of 51 to 90 receives an acceptability score of .5. A score of 91 to 110 is .6 etc. These numbers that represent acceptability could be used in rules to combine with other estimates of the overall accounting system to arrive at an overall quality rating (Suits 1988, 41).

Fuzzy qualifiers Words used in fuzzy logic that stand for portions of a continuous mathematical function. Examples: high, low, strong, and weak. *See also* Hedge words (Tello 1988, 83).

Fuzzy quantifiers The approximate equivalent in fuzzy logic of the universal (all) and existential (at least one) quantifiers found in first-order logic. Examples: ALL, AT LEAST, and NONE (Suits 1988, 42).

Fuzzy relations Terms in fuzzy logic that express some form of approximate equality between two fuzzy predicates. Examples: ABOUT THE SAME and NEARLY THE SAME (Suits 1988, 42).

Fuzzy set A set of variables with multiple values. Each value may have its own certainty value. Day may be a variable which has the values of Sunday, Monday, Saturday (Tello 1988, 258–259).

Fuzzy-set theory A type of set theory in which an element may belong only partially to a set. There are three set operations: fuzzy intersection, fuzzy union, and fuzzy complement. These operations can be used to derive the fuzzy-AND, fuzzy-OR, and fuzzy-NOT operations. Also, *refer to* Probability-AND, and Probability-OR (Suits 1988, 40).

Fuzzy union The strongest-link approach. This operation is used to define the fuzzy-OR (Richards 1988, 285).

G

Game playing A field of artificial intelligence that specializes in using games to implement and test artificial intelligence principles (Parsaye and Chignell 1988, 10).

Game tree A type of tree structure formed by considering the moves and countermoves available in a player-opponent game situation. A tree representation of all possible moves available in a game. It is different from a state-space tree in that there are two players involved rather than a single agent. A game tree is drawn from the point of view of one of the two players. The game tree is frequently represented as an AND/OR tree (Johnson 1986, 48–49; Barr and Feigenbaum 1981 vol 1, 43–45; Forsyth and Naylor 1985, 179–200).

GAMMA An expert system used to interpret gamma-ray activation spectra so as to identify unknown substances. It uses a generate-and-test paradigm and was built by Schlumberger-Doll Research (Hunt 1986, 115).

Garbage collection 1. A means of reclaiming no-longer-needed memory cells so that these memory cells can be used for further programming efforts. This is a very important process in artificial intelligence programming because most artificial intelligence programs can use a large amount of memory and the amount of memory needed can be hard to predict. During the garbage-collection process the program is temporarily suspended so that memory elements that are still needed can be marked and all unmarked elements can be reused. This temporary suspension can cause great difficulties in real-time applications. Many artificial intelligence programs employ an automatic garbage collection procedure. *See also* Incremental garbage collection as an alternative. 2. The designing of the expert system in production systems so that obsolete information is deleted. Using garbage-collection techniques can facilitate the execution speed of some expert systems, but can actually slow down others like OPS5 (Gabriel Feb 1987, 35; Charniak and McDermott 1985, 65; Brownston et al 1986, 262–263; Barr and Feigenbaum 1981 vol 2, 18; Winston 1984, 145–148).

Garden-path sentence A type of sentence with localized ambiguity. That is, the reader follows the sentence down the garden path of one meaning until he or she reaches the end of the sentence and the true meaning of the sentence becomes clear. Garden-path sentences pose problems for language parsers. Example: "The artist painted on the wall was black" (Brittain 1987, 35).

Gatekeeper A synonym for inference engine (Charniak and McDermott 1985, 319).

Gaussian convolution Sombrero filtering (Chabris 1989, 201).

GCA A planning system that helps computer science students set up their curriculum. It was written in PROLOG at Duke University (Hunt 1986, 116).

Gemstone A program that extends the concepts of object-oriented programming to data bases (Peterson 1987, 30).

Generalist school A school of thought in artificial intelligence that focuses on machine learning, neural networks, emulating human cognitive processes, and is generally more theoretical and research oriented (Chabris 1989, 16).

Generality 1. A measure of the number of different problem areas to which an expert system can be applied. In a medical expert system, could it handle pulmonary diseases as well as cardiovascular diseases? Other important measures of the value of an expert system are adequacy, accuracy, reliability, validity, practicability, adaptability, breadth, and credibility. 2. The ability of neural nets to make a discrimination despite noise (Marcot, 1987, 44–45; Reece 1987, 53).

Generality principle If the basic structure of a problem can be constructed on a computer, then the solution can be derived by the computer. This principle is the basis of early attempts at problem solving using computers. General Problem Solver is the best-known example. The generality principle worked well with small problems, but with large problems succumbed to combinatorial explosion (Parsaye and Chignell 1988, 387).

Generalization 1. The process of discovering an abstract principle from data. 2. The process of transforming a specific concept into a more general concept. Generalization is used in learning from examples. A learning process in which a set of specific instances are used as the basis of making a general hypothesis about the set to which all of the instances belong. 3. A set of methods for revising a knowledge representation so that it may apply to a larger number of situations. 4. The propagation or inheritance of properties from an object to a class. *Contrast with* Specialization. 5. The process in rule-based programming of substituting a general rule for a set of more specific rules. The more general rule may replace constants with variables. Generalization in rules can also be achieved by dropping conditions, or by adding disjunctions. 6. Generalization is used in Winston's hit-and-near-miss procedure. In the hit-and-near-miss procedure, generalization is the expansion of the definition of a concept to include characteristics found in new examples that fit under that concept. 7. A relaxation of the constraints on a concept so that the concept can become more inclusive. *See also* Is-a; Universalization; Variabilization, for examples of methods of generalization (Schildt 1987, 202, 206; Brownston et al 1986, 172–174; Barr and Feigenbaum 1981 vol 2, 365–368; Epp et al 1988, 825; Chabris 1989, 294; Hunt 1986, 116; Smith 1989, 75).

Generalization method A method that can be used to make a rule apply to a more general set of circumstances. Example: dropping a condition from a rule (Smith 1989, 75).

Generalization rule A rule that summarizes one or more premises (Brownston et al 1986, 172–174).

Generalized AND/OR graph A type of AND/OR graph in which reduction operators can take an extra two nodes as input (Smith 1989, 76).

Generalized beta The reduction in CmLISP of portions of a Xector and the association of these reductions with indices (Hillis 1985, 46–47).

Generalized bug A demon found in the AI program HACKER, which is used to scrutinize plans for mistakes (Smith 1989, 76).

Generalized cone An approach to vision in which the object is viewed as a set of cones and cylinders. The cones and cylinders can then be used to approximate three-dimensional objects. This approach has been surprisingly useful in a variety of different situations (Waldrop 1987, 102; Chabris 1989, 294).

Generalized delta rule A learning rule that can be used to train multiple layer neural networks, associate arbitrary input/output pairs, and compute arbitrary input/output functions. The generalized delta rule changes the weights in a neural network as a function of local information so that the error in the output is minimized. It uses the gradient descent process to do this and as a result is susceptible to finding false bottoms. The units employed are deterministic rather than the stochastic units found in the Boltzmann machine and in harmony theory. The generalized delta rule is used in supervised learning situations. It is also called the back-propagation rule. *See also* Back propagation rule; Delta rule (Rumelhart and McClelland 1986, 149, 327–328, 352–362; Caudill Jun 1988, 58–59).

Generalized facility A facility found in the TIMM expert system shell that allows the shell to generate new rules based on data in the knowledge base (Tello 1988, 167).

General Problem Solver An early artificial intelligence program that used symbol manipulation and modeled itself after human thought processes. It is considered to be the original computer-based production system. General Problem Solver separated knowledge from control. The knowledge component was the difference table. The control component was the forerunner of the inference engine found in current expert systems. General Problem Solver used operators to move from one stage of the problem-solving state to another in a depth-first manner. GPS employed means-end analysis which used computed differences. That is, it would search for differences between start and goal states. The largest difference found was then reduced by the application of one of the set of operators available for solving the problem at hand. The program succeeded when it attained the goal state. GPS also used backtracking when it found itself in a blind alley. It was applied to cryptarithmetic, missionaries and cannibals, chess etc. Unlike current expert systems which use a body of domain specific knowledge to solve a problem, General Problem Solver relied more on general problem-solving techniques. As a consequence, it was inefficient. General Problem Solver can work forward from the initial state or backward from the goal state, though it is primarily forward chaining in nature. One problem with it is that it requires detailed and complete information concerning the different states and the operators that make the transition from one state to the next. Current expert systems use pattern matching rather than computed differences. More recently, General Problem Solver has been used to demonstrate planning. Newell and Simon were the developers. They proposed GPS as a theory of human problem solving. *See also* Means-end (Rettig Apr 1987, 15–19; Rettig May 1987, 17; Johnson 1986, 47–48; Winston 1979, 130–143; Barr and Feigenbaum 1981 vol 1, 113–118; Barr and Feigenbaum 1981 vol 3, 11–21; Lenat 1988, 68; Parsaye and

Chignell 1988, 13–14, 387–393; Waldrop 1987, 27–42; Luger and Stubblefield 1989, 410–415; Newell and Simon 1972).

General problem solving The field of artificial intelligence devoted to building programs which will solve a large class of problems. The programs in this category emphasized reasoning as opposed to knowledge. General Problem Solver is the best known example of this type of program. Such programs are in disfavor at this time because although they can solve a range of problems they are very inefficient. They have been supplanted by expert system programs. *See also* General Problem Solver (Parsaye and Chignell 1988, 10; Rettig 1987, 15–19).

General-purpose knowledge-engineering language A computer programming language used for building expert systems with a wide range of applications (Rosenberg 1986, 76; Hunt 1986, 117).

General rule A rule that uses variables, which can be used for a large number of facts. Synonyms are generic rule and variable rule. *Compare with* Specific rule (Parsaye and Chignell 1988, 46).

General-weighted network A method used in eliciting data from an expert. The domain expert is asked to estimate distances between the objects in the domain. The general weighted networks allow secondary paths between objects. Research has shown significant differences between the general-weighted networks of experts and less qualified personnel (Olson and Rueter 1988, 29–30).

Generate-and-test 1. The generation of a state and the testing of the state to see if it is a solution to the problem. If the state is a solution, then the program stops. Otherwise, the program generates a new state to be tested. Generate-and-test produces solutions to a problem and then tests the different possible solutions. Under this definition depth-blind search and heuristic search may be considered as subtypes of generate-and-test. Generate-and-test is sometimes called reasoning by elimination. 2. A program that DENDRAL uses in situations which require the finding of all possible solutions. This version of generate-and-test uses heuristic information and it generates only a set of solutions which fit the given constraints. It is a restrained type of generate-and-test and is efficient only in situations where pruning rules can be applied at an early stage of the search process. The term sometimes used is hierarchical generate-and-test. Generate-and-test is sometimes referred to as hypothesize and test (Wolfgram 1987, 66; Hayes-Roth et al 1983, 71–72; Barr and Feigenbaum 1981 vol 1, 30; Sterling and Shapiro 1986, 206–217; Jackson 1986, 4; Hunt 1986, 34).

Generation 1 robot A programmable-memory robot with more than one degree of freedom. Usually such robots are equipped with grippers so that it can use a variety of tools (Rosenberg 1986, 76).

Generation 1.5 robot A sensory-controlled robot that carries out tasks in a predetermined way, but which has some capability of altering the way the task is carried out based on sensory input (Rosenberg 1986, 76).

Generation 2 robot A futuristic robot that has visual perceptual abilities and can coordinate these abilities with movement to carry out tasks (Rosenberg 1986, 76).

Generation 3 robot A futuristic factory robot endowed with artificial intelligence that can problem solve a variety of tasks in an intelligent manner (Rosenberg 1986, 76).

Generation scavenging A garbage-collection strategy in which objects are assigned to groups of objects called generations. Each generation is distinguished by the length of time in memory. Objects that have been in memory the longest are the ones which will continue to be needed while newer objects are more likely to be temporary. Garbage collection therefore starts with the younger generations (Gabriel Feb 1987, 37–38).

Generative grammar A formal grammar declared as a collection of rules that can propagate all legal sentences without generating illegal sentences (Rosenberg 1986, 76).

Generator 1. A procedure that furnishes a value each time it is called and then waits in a suspended state until it is called again to produce a new value. A generator is a type of coroutine. 2. A function in LISP that manufactures a set of data objects (Luger and Stubblefield 1989, 491; Smith 1989, 76–77).

Generic concept A concept that uses a generic marker to indicate the concept node referring to an unspecified individual with reference to conceptual graphs. *Contrast with* Individual concept (Luger and Stubblefield 1989, 353).

Generic function 1. A type of function found in the C++ language that holds multiple definitions. The definition which is activated is a function of the contents of the function call. *See also* Function overloading for more information on generic functions. 2. A set of methods with the same name. They are used in Flavors and CLOS. They permit multiple inheritance and the distributed definition of functions. Generic functions allow the implementation of a form of message passing. *See also* San Marco LISP Explorer (Tello 1989, 145–146, 150–155; Thomas 1989, 234).

Generic operations An operation in an object-oriented program whose procedural details may differ depending on what object is receiving the message. A term that refers to the use of generic operations is polymorphism (Jackson 1986, 60).

Generic rule 1. A rule in expert systems that contains variables. The variables give the rule a level of abstraction, allowing the generic rule to take the place of many specific rules. The variables in the rule can be supplied with values by look-up tables or fact bases. This approach allows smaller rule sets and is essential for all but the smallest applications. Synonyms are general rule and variable rule. 2. A general rule that can apply to a variety of objects. The generic rule may be considered a jumping-off point to another more specific rule which is tailored to a specific object. Example: IF computer does not run THEN check power supply. The check power supply is not really a final recommendation. It is really a type of go-to statement in which check power supply is the conditional part of a set of rules. Each nongeneric rule represents a particular type of computer and each nongeneric rule may have a particular diagnostic procedure depending on the type of computer. Generic rules are frequently used in conjunction with frames. The generic rules are responsible for control and have no domain knowledge. The frames are where the domain knowledge is kept (Tello 1989, 31–32; Tello Aug 1985, 100; Shafer and Golden 1990, 56).

GENESIS A design expert system that devises molecular genetics experiments and procedures. It uses frames and backward and forward chaining. GENESIS actually consists of seven distinct expert systems. GENESIS is used by over 500 scientists and is licensed through IntelliCorp (Peterson 1987, 30; Harmon and King 1985, 159–160; Hunt 1986, 117).

Genetic algorithm 1. A search technique that is derived from natural population genetics and used in different problems in science. An algorithm used in learning that holds more than one competing hypothesis. As new examples are introduced the different competing hypotheses are tested. Hypotheses that are compatible with the new examples are allowed to combine and reproduce more new hypotheses. 2. An algorithm that is iterative in nature, and which maintains a set of structures that are potential solutions to a given problem. The algorithm evaluates the value of the different structures, and then takes actions eliminating poor structures and increasing the probability of use of more promising structures (Austin 1990, 49–53; Luger and Stubblefield 1989, 575; Chabris 1989, 294).

Genetic operator An operator used by genetic algorithms to encourage the survival of structures which are more likely to produce solutions to the problem at hand. Examples: reproduction, crossover, and mutation (Austin 1990, 49–53).

GEN-X A hybrid expert system that uses both rules and frames, which was written in C at the General Electric's Research and Development Center. It runs on the IBM-PC (Hunt 1986, 116).

Geometric reasoning A type of reasoning employed by robots. Example: a robot retrieving an object and moving it to another position while avoiding objects in the way.

Geometry Theorem Prover An automated theorem prover that uses diagrams to control the proof of the geometry theorem. The diagrams are a form of analogical representation. The first program to use conjunctive subgoals to utilize a problem-reduction approach (Barr and Feigenbaum 1981 vol 1, 119–122, 201–202).

GLIB A rule-based knowledge engineering language which was developed using SMALLTALK-80, which is used primarily to develop expert systems for troubleshooting electronic devices (Hunt 1986, 117).

Global free variable In LISP a symbol that does not appear in the procedure's parameter list and its definition or activation environment (depending on the use of lexical scoping or dynamic scoping). *Compare with* Global variable (Winston 1984, 55).

Global variable 1. A type of variable whose value is always in force no matter what part of the program is currently being executed. 2. A variable defined outside of a function which can be accessed at any place in the program. In LISP a global variable is defined at the top level. *Contrast with* Local variable (Charniak and McDermott 1985, 74).

Gnat robot A miniature robot that can be used for such tasks as sentinel duty. The primary advantage is that such robots would be very inexpensive (Flynn 1987, 34).

Goal The node that is the subject of a search. The end state for which an artificial intelligence program is striving. In predicate calculus, a clause whose truth value needs to be determined. In PROLOG the query is the goal. Typically, in backward-chaining expert systems the expert system starts with a goal and attempts to prove the goal by breaking by the goal into subgoals which are then proved. Once the subgoals are proved the goal is then proved. In forward-chaining expert systems like OPS5 the left-hand side of the rule may be thought of as a conjunction or disjunction of subgoals, and the right-hand side of the rule may be viewed as unattained goals. A forward-chaining expert system proves the goals in the left-hand side of the rule and then generates new goals found in the right-hand side of the rule. This process is continued until no further goals can be achieved (Harrison and Tribble 1986, 66; Schildt 1987, 15; Brownston et al 1986, 15–17; Sterling and Shapiro 1986, 3; Parsaye and Chignell 1988, 60).

Goal-directed behavior Planning to reach a goal and planning execution in artificial intelligence. The plan is constructed by means of search (Firdman 1986, 85).

Goal-directed forward chaining A type of forward chaining system that stops when a specified goal is achieved. This is in contrast to how forward-chaining systems will usually continue to cycle through the rule set until no further rules can be fired.

Goal-directed inference An expert system that finds a solution by trying one possible goal through checking to see if the necessary facts exist to support that goal. If not, it then tries another goal. Backward reasoning. *Contrast with* Data directed search control.

Goal-directed system A system that starts with an hypothesis and attempts to prove the hypothesis by verifying facts that must be true for the hypothesis to be true. Example: starting with the hypothesis of measles and checking for the symptoms that must accompany this disease. Backward chaining. *Contrast with* Forward chaining (Townsend 1987a, 139; Hayes-Roth et al 1983, 401).

Goal-driven expert system A backward chaining expert system which is most appropriate when there are a small number of goal states and a large number of initial states (Townsend 1987a, 139).

Goal outline A menu provided by some expert system shells which presents the different goals and subgoals in an expert system. The user can then choose a goal, a subgoal, or an unknown and start from the beginning. It is a time-saving method (Harmon et al 1988, 78).

Goal reduction The process in PROLOG of seeking a solution to a problem by reducing a goal to a set of subgoals.

Goal regression A procedure used in planning systems to avoid subgoal interactions. The procedure of solving one subgoal at a time and checking that each newly solved subgoal does not interfere with a previously solved subgoal. When subgoal interaction is encountered goal regression reorders the subgoals to eliminate the interaction. This approach can avoid some of the inefficiency found in some planning programs which rely on backtracking, but it must spend time evaluating subgoal interactions (Barr and Feigenbaum 1981 vol 2, 537–540); Hunt 1986, 13, 118; Smith 1989, 79).

Goal-restricted rule filtering A process by which only rules relevant to the current goal are employed in production expert systems that have an architecture organized as a hierarchy of goals. *See also* Context-restricted rule filtering; Controlled-rule filtering (Brownston et al 1986, 308–309).

Goal tree 1. A true structure in which the root node is the final goal and each node is a subgoal. The structure can be arranged in a manner similar to the AND/OR tree. 2. Another name for an AND/OR tree (Hunt 1986, 118; Winston 1984, 43).

Gödel, Kurt The thinker who proved that any formal system must always be either incomplete or inconsistent. If it is incomplete, there will be statements that can't be proved true or false. If you make it complete, you must have inconsistencies. Gödel's proofs used the ability of a system to reflect on itself—reason about itself (Johnson 1986, 281–284).

Gold's theorems Theorems that prove it is not possible to learn a context-free grammar from the use of only positive instances (Smith 1989, 79).

Goldwater machine An artificial intelligence program which was given a set of conservative beliefs. The user could interact with the program by asking it questions about how to deal with Communist aggression in a variety of situations. It is a forerunner of the artificial intelligence program Politics (Johnson 1986, 259).

Graceful degradation A gradual rather than abrupt decline in performance. The characteristic of an expert such that when he or she reaches the edge of his or her knowledge there is a gradual rather than precipitous drop in performance. Expert systems do not possess this characteristic. Proponents of neural networks claim neural networks possess the capability of graceful degradation (Shepard Feb 1988, 12; *Knowledge-Based Systems* 1986, 1–30; Barr and Feigenbaum 1981 vol 1, 336).

Graceful failure The ability to recover from failure in such a way as to continue the search for a solution to the problem. Most conventional languages do not have this property. PROLOG with its backtracking capabilities does possess graceful failure. Neural networks are also capable of graceful failure. Building redundancy into a system is a means of implementing graceful failure (Rosenberg 1986, 77).

Gradient descent A method used in neural networks to give the optimal solution within the limitations of the constraint equations. Gradient descent uses least squares to minimize errors over a set of examples. An analogy of how the gradient descent method is used, is trying to find the deepest part of a valley by beginning to walk downhill. When one finally finds the place in which all directions are uphill then the deepest valley is found. A type of hill-climbing search method. The values are changed in that direction which most reduces the cost function. It has difficulty with local minima. It is a generalized version of the delta rule. *Contrast with* Simulated annealing, which is less likely to be trapped by local minima (Rumelhart and McClelland 1986, 322–324; Bayle 1988, 43; Thompson and Thompson Jan 1988, 18; Barr and Feigenbaum 1981 vol 2, 375–380).

Gradient space A tool for reasoning about surface orientation.

Gradual refinement The process of moving from an abstract specification to a detailed, working program (Smith 1989, 80).

Grain size The degree of detail in which an object is represented in a knowledge representation scheme (Minsky 1985, 138; Barr and Feigenbaum 1981 vol 1, 147).

Grammar A means of describing legal sentences in a language. A set of rules used to specify the syntax of a language. These rules are frequently referred to as rewrite rules or productions. Parsers are used in natural language processing to decide if a sentence is grammatical *See also* Transformational grammar Context-free grammar; Definite-clause grammar; (Thompson and Thompson Dec 1986, 23; Clinger 1988, 80; Winston 1979, 168–169; Barr and Feigenbaum 1981 vol 1, 229; Chabris 1989, 294; Obermeier 1987, 225).

Grammatical inference Making inferences about the grammar of a language by using correct and incorrect examples of the language (Barr and Feigenbaum 1981 vol 2, 494–510; Rosenberg 1986, 77).

Grammatical marker A representative of such features as number and tense in transformational languages (Luger and Stubblefield 1989, 405).

Grandmother cell A processing unit in a neural network that fires only when a single specified input pattern is present. A neural network needs to be fine tuned so that grandmother cells are avoided, because the system cannot recognize inexact or incomplete stimulus patterns (Caudill Dec 1987, 52; Caudill Jun 1988, 53).

Grand tour The traveling-salesman problem.

Grand unification The unification of object-oriented programming, logic programming, and data base systems (Zaniolo et al 1986, 56).

Granularity The degree of detail in a knowledge representation. *See also* Coarse grain; Fine grain (Rosenberg 1986, 77).

Grapes A backward-chaining expert system tool. The goals are kept in a separate memory called goal memory. It has a working memory and a long-term memory. The rules are organized in groups according to goals they have in common. Its conflict resolution strategy uses refraction, recency, working-memory specificity, goal-test specificity, and arbitrary choice (Brownston et al 1986, 364–366).

Graphs 1. A network of nodes connected by arcs in artificial intelligence. A tree is a special type of graph in which there is a unique path between each pair of nodes. The arcs can be labeled and are bidirectional. Example: a graph in which each node represents a word and the arcs can be labeled as parts of speech to indicate which words can be connected. In artificial intelligence graphs are sometimes used as a synonym for networks. A graph can be used to model a state space, or forward and backward chaining. **2.** A type of active data structure used in Connection machines. A very general type of data structure that can be used to represent other active data structures such as strings, arrays, and butterflies (Hillis 1985, 116–117; Forsyth and Naylor 1985, 131–133; Chabris 1989, 294; Luger and Stubblefield 1989, 81–82).

Gray scale The brightness level of the pixels of an image (Forsyth and Naylor 1985, 76–77).

Gray-scale manipulation A technique used in image processing which alters the gray scales (brightness levels) to bring out the detail of the most interesting aspects of an image (Forsyth and Naylor 1985, 78).

Green cut A cut in PROLOG that prunes the portions of the search tree which are known not to have a solution, thus saving time. Green cuts do not change the declarative meaning of the program. *Contrast with* Red cut (Sterling and Shapiro 1986, 157–162).

Grid A network topology found in Connection machines which is most useful in simulations of electrodynamics, aerodynamics, image processing, and hydrodynamics. Other topologies include Clos networks, rings, trees, banyan-type networks, delta networks, hashnets, shuffle-type topologies, and crossbars (Hillis 1985, 58).

Gripper The hand of a robot, which is also called an end effector (Schildt 1987, 169).

Grossberg in-star A processing element in neural networks which relays information to the next processing element without altering the information (Klimasauskas Nov/Dec 1988, 28).

Ground term A term in PROLOG that does not have variables. The terms likes(john, mary) is a ground term (Sterling and Shapiro 1986, 4).

G set The most general set of hypotheses represented, given a set of hypotheses (Smith 1989, 73).

Guarded clause A clause in concurrent PROLOG used to coordinate parallel processing (Luger and Stubblefield 1989, 483).

Guessing Plausible reasoning (Hayes-Roth et al 1983, 110–115).

GUIDON An intelligent computer-aided instruction system used to instruct medical students in the diagnosis and treatment of bacteriological infections. It works in conjunction with MYCIN and other rule-based expert systems to instruct medical students. If the student asks irrelevant questions, GUIDON will gently ask why the student is asking that question or bluntly tell the student the question is irrelevant. If the student gives a diagnosis without a relevant piece of information, GUIDON will point this out to the student. GUIDON consists of 200 tutorial rules. The rules possess the means of running the mixed-initiative dialogue, building a model of the student's ability, and displaying diagnostic rules (Mishkoff 1986, 6-4; Harmon and King 1985, 242–244; Barr and Feigenbaum 1981 vol 2, 267–278).

Guzman, A. The man known for his development of SEE, an important vision program which uses heuristics rather than mathematical processing.

H

HACKER HACKER is a learning program used to build a plan for a robot which manipulates toy blocks. It repeatedly goes through the cycle of constructing a plan, testing a plan, and then making corrections to the plan. It learns two kinds of knowledge: generalized subroutines and generalized bugs. The generalized subroutine is a macro that is a sequence of actions used to reach a particular goal. The generalized bug is a demon used to find a program error and fix it. HACKER is a nonhierarchical planner. It develops a plan which consists of a series of steps. When it finds that the sequence of steps will not work it reorders the steps in an effort to find a sequence of steps that will work. After carrying out a particular task HACKER is able to examine its actions and make improvements. Much of the power of HACKER derives from its ability to reason about the task (Barr and Feigenbaum 1981 vol 3, 475–483, 531–535; Luger and Stubblefield 1989, 22).

HAL 9000 The name of the computer endowed with artificial intelligence in the science fiction books *2001* and *2010* (Tello 1988, 7).

Halt The last of four phases in the recognize act cycle found in OPS5 production systems. It returns control to the user or returns to the first cycle. The four phases are match, conflict resolution, act, and halt (Brownston et al 1986, 75–76).

HAM *See* Human Associative Memory.

Hamiltonian path An acyclic path made up of all of the nodes in the graph (Bratko 1986, 227).

Handler A function in the expert system Goldworks, which is invoked by sending a message to a frame. The rough equivalent of a method in Smalltalk (Matthews Sep 1987, 78).

Harmony theory   A mathematical theory for examining a set of dynamical systems that emulate cognitive tasks by following the subsymbolic paradigm. In harmony theory knowledge is in a set of numerical constraints. The constraints develop as a function of experience. Like the Boltzmann machine harmony theory uses binary units that are determined probabilistically through the use of the Boltzmann equation. Like the Boltzmann machine it employs simulated annealing. Although harmony theory is similar to the Boltzmann machine, their origins are different. Harmony theory grew from attempts to understand schema and the concepts of schema theory. It can be employed in intuitive problem solving and in perception (Rumelhart and McClelland 1986, 195–196, 213–220, 261–262).

HARPY   A speech-understanding system. Despite its relatively simple methodology it was able to outperform other more sophisticated speech understanding systems. Its primary contribution is that it integrates phonemic, acoustic, lexical, semantic, and syntactic knowledge into a single precompiled network. It utilizes beam search, the processing of segmented speech, and heuristics. In tests it achieved a recognition accuracy greater than 95 percent (Johnson 1986, 137–139; Mishkoff 1986, 5–9; Barr and Feigenbaum 1981 vol 1, 349–352).

Has-a   A link in a semantic net which indicates an object has a property of the node that is connected to the object by the has-a link. Example: An airplane has-a fuselage (Townsend and Feucht 1986, 56).

Hashing   1. The procedure in LISP by which LISP checks to see if there already exists a copy of the atom the user enters into the computer. If there is already a copy of the atom, LISP uses that copy. Otherwise, an error message may be received.   2. A method used in search in which the search can quickly be restricted to that part of a data base that holds the objects of interest.

The address of an object is computed to access the object. *See also* Hash table (Williams 1989, 36; Deering and Faletti 1986, 530–531; Coffee and Strauss 1988, 40; Charniak and McDermott 1985, 74).

Hashnets   A type of network topology suggested for Connection machines. This type of network is composed of random connections which can be analyzed statistically. Other topologies include Clos networks, rings, trees, banyan-type networks, grids, delta networks, shuffle-type topologies, and crossbars (Hillis 1985, 59).

Hash table   A type of data structure that can be used to access information rapidly. An object that is able to map one object to another object quickly. The entries in a hash table are accessed by using keys. Example: Assume a set of objects in which the ASCII values of the object names are computed. The ASCII values are then used as an index to store and later efficiently retrieve a given object. Each time the object is needed the ASCII value is computed and the search begins at that number. In this way the entire data base of objects does not need to be searched (Chabris 1989, 189; Steele 1984, 282).

Head   1. The conclusion portion of a rule in PROLOG.   2. The first data item in a list (Townsend 1987a, 47, 87; Townsend 1987b, 380).

HEARSAY architecture   The blackboard-type architecture first developed in the speech-understanding program HEARSAY. *See also* Blackboard architecture for more information. Hearsay architecture uses both top-down and bottom-up processing. *Contrast with* Frame-based expert system; Multiple contexts; Rule-based expert system.

HEARSAY I   A very influential speech-understanding system that gave birth to its successor, Hearsay II. Hearsay I introduced the concept of independent knowledge sources. There were three independent knowledge sources which posted information to a blackboard and used information from the blackboard to derive more information which was then posted to the blackboard.

See also Blackboard architecture (Barr and Feigenbaum 1981 vol 1, 343–348).

HEARSAY II A successor program to the speech-understanding program Hearsay I. Hearsay II uses twelve independent knowledge sources which enter their results on a common blackboard. The blackboard is partitioned. Different partitions handle words, phrases, syllables, phonemes, and so on. Word sequence expert is the most important expert function. It uses fragments and makes hunches from the fragments about what the sentence conveyed. It only passes a selected number of possibilities to the parser. As a result, the parser is not overwhelmed. Its vocabulary is over 1,000 words. *See also* Blackboard architecture for more information (Johnson 1986, 132–135; Hayes-Roth et al 1983, 20–21, 116–119, 401; Winston 1979, 152; Barr and Feigenbaum 1981 vol 1, 345–348; Waldrop 1987, 122–123; Erman et al 1980, 213–253).

HEARSAY III A knowledge-engineering tool based on HEARSAY I architecture, which can asynchronously process data and handle multiple goals. It makes a clear differentiation between domain and control blackboards. Hearsay III allows knowledge sources to write information to the blackboard to influence the scheduler (Smith 1989, 84; Hayes-Roth et al 1983, 308–314).

Hear What I Mean (HWIM) A speech-understanding system, which is more centralized than the speech-understanding program HEARSAY. There is a central processing control component through which all incoming data must pass. Control strategies are more easily manipulated with HWIM than with HEARSAY (Johnson 1986, 135–139; Mishkoff 1986, 5–9; Barr and Feigenbaum 1981 vol 1, 353–357).

Hebb, D.O. A psychologist who is known for Hebb's rule, the concept of cell assemblies, and reverberation of activation.

Hebb's rule A rule formulated by D.O. Hebb, which is used to explain learning in biological organisms. When two units are simultaneously activated the connection strengths between the two units are strengthened. This simple rule is thought to be the basis of learning in the brain. A more detailed explanation may help explain how Hebb's rule is applied in neural nets: Assume two processing units. As the activity between the two processing units continues, the weighting factor between the two processing units is strengthened. That is, as neuron A continues to fire neuron B, then neuron B becomes more sensitized and is more likely to fire by a minimal stimulation from neuron A. Most learning rules in neural networks are indebted to the Hebb's rule. Newer rules include the delta rule, the back-propagation procedure, and the Kohonen learning procedure. One problem with Hebb's rule is that it has no way of preventing the weighting factor of a neuron from becoming so strong that it completely dominates the system. Hebb did not represent his rule mathematically, but others have. Hebb's rule says nothing about the inhibitory connections found in biological systems (Bayle 1988, 42; Caudill Nov 1988, 58).

Hedge words Descriptor words used in fuzzy logic to modify fuzzy qualifiers. Examples: around, very, about, quite. The hedge word "very" can be used in conjunction with the fuzzy qualifier low in the phrase "very low" (Tello 1988, 82).

HELP A robot-control language developed by General Electric, which is characterized by the ability to manage multiple cartesian arms in manufacturing tasks (Mishkoff 1986, 5–19).

HEME A medical expert system that diagnoses hematologic diseases and uses Bayes' theorem to calculate probabilities. HEME was built at Cornell University (Hunt 1986, 124–125).

HEPAR A medical diagnostic expert system written in PROLOG. It diagnoses liver and biliary disease. It is a backward-chaining system that uses certainty factors (Van Der Gaag and Lucas 1988, 34–43).

Herbrand universe The collection in a logic program of all ground terms that can be derived from the constants and function symbols in the program (Lassez 1987, 171; Sterling and Shapiro 1986, 80–81).

Hetarchical constraint propagation The process whereby relatively equal analysis procedures pass information back and forth to each other. The passed information aids each procedure in its analysis and in limiting the set of possible answers to the problem. Hetarchical constraint propagation is used in image analysis (Winston 1984, 341).

Hetarchy A style of programming analogous to a community of cooperating experts. Each expert contributes what it can to solving the problem and then passes control to another expert. Control is distributed among the experts. This style of programming is emphasized in languages like LISP. *Contrast with* Hierarchical problem solving, which is more efficient but less flexible (Winston 1979, 298–299).

Heterogeneous abstraction space An abstraction space in expert systems that uses different vocabularies because the knowledge in it is so diverse. A blackboard-type expert system uses heterogeneous abstraction spaces. *Compare with* Uniform abstraction space (Hayes-Roth et al 1983, 117).

Heterogeneous data base A system whose purpose is to integrate separate data bases, each of which holds a wide variety of heterogeneous information, to use the information successfully from these different data bases to respond to user requests (Manola 1990, 33–34).

Heterogeneous list A list that can have objects of different data types. C++ uses pointers to implement heterogeneous lists, and PROLOG, C++, and LISP all support heterogeneous lists (Stroustrup 1987, 213).

Heuristic Having capacity to discover or invent. A shortcut or rule of thumb in artificial intelligence used to increase the efficiency with which a solution is found. At a given choice point, using a method which helps to pick one choice over another because one choice is somehow better than the other. Heuristic approaches filter out unprofitable search paths. Unlike an algorithmic approach a heuristic approach does not guarantee a solution. Heuristics can include the use of such properties as recency, certainty, least cost, maximum movement to a goal, and activation to achieve a solution. A heuristic is very frequently an educated guess. Heuristics represented a major conceptual shift in artificial intelligence research. The realization was made that an artificial intelligence program could not rely on reason alone to solve problems, but must rely heavily on knowledge that includes heuristics. For some examples of higher-level heuristics, *see also* Look at extremes; Coalesce; Fortuitous accident (Minsky 1985, 138; Schildt 1987, 15; Hayes-Roth et al 1983, 4; Winston 1979, 122–126; Harmon and King 1985, 5; Townsend and Feucht 1986, 26–27; Forsyth and Naylor 1985, 212; Waldrop 1987, 24–28; Luger and Stubblefield 1989, 38).

Heuristic continuation A heuristic function that extends a search path rather than prune search paths, which is used in games situations. Example: The choice may be made to extend search in a chess game to find out if it is fruitless to sacrifice other pieces in an effort to save the queen (Winston 1984, 129–131).

Heuristic function A function used in heuristic search to compute a value for each state. The value represents the level of difficulty for achieving the state, and also the difficulty involved in reaching the goal state from this state (Rettig Mar 1987, 17).

Heuristic knowledge Knowledge based on rules of thumb which will allow more efficient problem solving. Heuristic knowledge is not based on the underlying theory of the particular area to which the expert system is being applied. *Contrast with* Deep knowledge.

Heuristic power One of three criteria used to assess a representation language. It is the inferencing capabilities of the chosen representation. Other criteria for assessing a representation language are logical adequacy and notational convenience (Jackson 1986, 29–30).

Heuristic problem solving The planning of problem-solving activities that employ knowledge-laden shortcuts to achieve a solution (Hunt 1986, 125).

Heuristic programming Programming that uses heuristics because of incomplete knowledge, and lack of applicable algorithms. Artificial intelligence is noted for its use in heuristic programming. Heuristic programming is characterized by rapid prototyping and incremental development (Jackson 1986, 196).

Heuristic pruning The use of heuristics to avoid search of paths that are unlikely to hold a good solution (Bratko 1986, 369).

Heuristic rule A rule that prunes unproductive avenues of search. Rules that order possible solutions according to merit (Forsyth and Naylor 1985, 139, 177).

Heuristic state-space search A process that uses heuristics or shortcuts to move through the search space to quickly find the solution state. Certain kinds of problems can be perceived as a series of states in which the final state is the solution state. Examples: best-first, hill climbing, A*, B*, branch-and-bound, and beam search. It differs from generate-and-test in that the latter simply computes an element of the search space and tests it. There is no heuristic ordering of the elements computed. *Contrast with* Algorithmic solution. (Smith 1989, 85–86; Rettig Mar 1987, 15; Wolfgram 1987, 65–68; Hayes-Roth et al 1983, 68–70; Townsend 1987b, 231; Forsyth and Naylor 1985, 213–215).

Hewitt, Carl A scientist known for his development of the concept of actors, and as a proponent of open architecture. In a program which uses actors, different agents gain control of the program at different times. It is somewhat reminiscent of Freud's id, ego, superego.

Hidden unit A processing element in neural nets that is not directly connected to the environment. The hidden units in a neural network are used to represent the important features of the input data (Obermeier and Barron 1989, 219; Ingraham et al 1988, 17).

Hierarchical abstraction The ability of the mind to form hierarchical concepts (Luger and Stubblefield 1989, 188).

Hierarchical clustering *See* Johnson hierarchical clustering (Olson 1988, 28–29).

Hierarchical generate-and-test A version of generate-and-test that is able to use constraints early in the search process to prune effectively the number of solutions generated. In this type of generate-and-test entire classes of possible solutions are eliminated at one time (Hunt 1986, 34; Hayes-Roth et al 1983, 71).

Hierarchical ordering Arranging related concepts into a treelike hierarchy. The parent object is at the top of the hierarchy and the more specialized versions are at the base (Stroustrup 1987, 8).

Hierarchical planner A type of planning system that develops a plan at multiple levels of abstraction. In this approach to planning an overall abstract plan is first developed and then details are filled in. The most important features of the problem are included at the most abstract level. In this way the planner does not get mired in details at the beginning stages of development. A hierarchical planner uses various procedures, such as the least-commitment principle, to avoid the difficulty of interacting subproblems. It is sometimes referred to as top-down planning. ABSTRIPS is a hierarchical planner. *Contrast with* Opportunistic planning (Barr and Feigenbaum 1981 vol 1, 135).

Hierarchical planning and repair Devising a general plan to achieve a goal, and then continuing to refine the plan into a hierarchy of subproblems (Hunt 1986, 12).

Hierarchical problem decomposition The approach to problem solving that emphasizes breaking the problem into subproblems on an abstract hierarchical level and then breaking up each subcomponent into more detailed components (Luger and Stubblefield 1989, 20).

Hierarchical problem solving An approach to problem solving in which attempts are made to solve the problem at a more abstract hierarchical level. Then, attempts are made at progressively less abstract levels. This approach has important advantages. It allows a quick overview of the problem so that the quickest and one of the best solutions can be pursued first. This approach prevents the program from becoming bogged down in the hopeless detail of a dead end. This type of problem solving is frequently how human experts operate. Humans abstract problem spaces, quickly grasp the overall picture, and employ an optimal means of efficiently solving the problem (Hayes-Roth et al 1983, 70, 76; Walters and Nielsen 1988, 314–318).

Hierarchical reasoning The use of rules in a frame-based system to eliminate entire classes of objects from the solution search process. This is one of the strengths of a frame-based system. A rule-based system has to check out each individual object in search of a solution—a time-consuming process (Walters and Nielsen 1988, 226–228).

Hierarchical rule-based organization Top-down design in procedural programming.

Hierarchical rule building A procedure used in rule building that defines lower-level rules in such a manner that they can be used by higher-level rules to reach conclusions. Example: an expert system used to purchase an airplane. A purchase rule would use information from other rules which have been used to compute ease of maintenance, fuel economy, and safety for this particular application (Glasgow and Graham 1988, 31).

Hierarchy A network in which objects are classified as subclassifications of other objects. Example: the class of airplanes. At the top of the hierarchy is the generic concept plane. Subclasses of the concept are military plane, passenger plane, cargo plane. Subclasses of the subclasses are F16, F14, and C 47. The advantage of a hierarchy is that knowledge can be stored in a very efficient manner. Trees are a type of knowledge representation that are hierarchical in nature. Hierarchies usually include inheritance. *See also* Causal hierarchy; Functional hierarchy; Structural hierarchy; Tangled hierarchy (Townsend 1987a, 124; Schildt 1987, 210; Harmon and King 1985, 40–41; Parsaye and Chignell 1988, 38; Hunt 1986, 126).

High-church computationalism A pejorative reference to the extreme view of computationalism. The extreme view is that the computer does more than manipulate symbols. It actually thinks, is aware, and has understanding. Some critics hold that human thinking is holistic and cannot be broken down into computational entities (Waldrop 1987, 135–136).

High connectivity The presence of a high ratio of the number of operators available per state to the number of states (Chabris 1989, 152).

High-contrast imaging The technique in vision of increasing the contrast between different objects in the image so that the overall image may be better comprehended in subsequent stages of analysis (Schildt 1987, 127).

High-emphasis frequency filtering Sharpening an image by using filtering that will emphasize high-frequency components of the image (Barr and Feigenbaum 1981 vol 3, 212–213).

Higher-order function A function that accepts and returns functions as arguments. Such functions are found in declarative languages. Higher-order functions in LISP include apply, funcall, and mapcar. A synonym is first-class function (Schrodt 1986, 190; Luger and Stubblefield 1989, 267).

Higher-order language A language that uses functions as arguments. *Contrast with* First-order language (Allen Feb 1987, 54).

High-level goal The final goal in a problem-solving process (Townsend 1987b, 381).

High-level language approach Automatic programming that uses a high-level language which can then write a program in a lower-level language. This is essentially what a compiler does. Other approaches to automatic programming include the deductive approach, transformational approach, and knowledge-based approach (Tello 1988, 420).

High-level vision Processing that deals with objects and relies on domain-specific information to comprehend the scene.

Hill climbing A heuristic search that is a combination of depth-first search and a localized evaluation function. The choice of the next problem state to explore is a function of finding the problem state which has the best available score rather than the leftmost state as in depth-first search. In hill climbing the initial node is expanded and all the derivative nodes are evaluated. The best child node is kept and the others are discarded. The search procedure stops when a state is achieved that is better than any of its children. Its focus is to minimize the distance to the goal state. The accumulated cost is not taken into account. A weakness of hill climbing is that it may find local minimums or local maximums. Take the analogy of a hill. The search mechanism is looking for a maximum value as it finds its way to the top of a hill. Everywhere the search mechanism looks the surrounding ground is lower. It incorrectly concludes this is the maximum height even though there is a much higher adjacent hill. Although it is like best-first search, hill climbing retains only one node in its queue. This is why it can find false maxima. Hill climbing is a more local type of search than best-first search. Unlike best-first search, hill climbing keeps no records, and as a result it cannot backtrack from blind alleys. *Contrast with* A* algorithm; Beam search; Least-cost search (Wolfgram 1987, 65; Schildt 1987, 33–38; Winston 1979, 93–98; Sterling and Shapiro 1986, 290–292; Parsaye and Chignell 1988, 385; Chabris 1989, 294; Luger and Stubblefield 1989, 153; Winston 1984, 93–95, 100; Winston and Horn 1988, 584).

Histogram flattening A process that sharpens an image. The portion of an image that has intensities which occur relatively infrequently are emphasized by increasing frequency. Those intensities that occur more frequently are deemphasized by decreasing frequency (Barr and Feigenbaum 1981 vol 3, 209).

Hit and near miss A procedure developed by Patrick Winston. A method used to teach a computer concepts. A given concept is chosen to teach the computer. Different examples are presented, some of which fit the concept. These examples are "hits" and the computer is told they are correct examples of the concept. The computer uses information about these examples to generalize the concept. Other examples are presented that do not fit the concept and the computer is told this example does not fit. This type of "miss" information is used to limit the concept (Schildt 1987, 210–218).

HODGKINS A medical expert system used in the diagnosis of Hodgkins disease (Hunt 1986, 126).

Hofstadter, Douglas The author of *Godel, Escher, Bach: An Eternal Golden Braid*. His book focuses on logic and its relationship to artificial intelligence. He holds there are no laws of thought and we are not symbol manipulators. Instead he believes there is much randomness in human thinking. His position is a middle ground between the symbolists and the connectionists. One of his major themes in this middle ground is subcognition. In subcognition there is no formal reasoning. He uses the example of an anagram in which there is a juxtaposing of letters, experimentation, and recursion. He wrote "Waking up from the Boolean Dream, or Subcognition as Computation" which elaborates on his concept of subcognition. Hofstadter spends much time focusing on loops, paradoxes, and recursion. He describes Bach's music as recursive and believes circular recursive definitions are our reality. He is currently working on the COPYCAT PROJECT. The COPYCAT PROJECT works with letters such as abc is to abd as cde is to X. It uses subcognitive processes to call into play what he calls enzymelike codelets to guide complex shuffling (Entsminger 1988, 96; Johnson 1986, 279–294).

Holist A member of the school of thought in which it is thought that attempts to analyze the mind by breaking it down into separate parts will always leave out some important factor and fail. *Compare with* Reductionist (Entsminger 1988, 96).

Holistic Describing a philosophy that holds to the notion that thinking is indivisible, emergent, mysterious, and not computational. *Contrast with* Computationalism (Waldrop 1987, 135–140).

Holland classifier A machine language algorithm that classifies patterns based on features. It uses rules with weights to classify input. During the learning procedure the premises may be altered if there are defects in learning. It is a bitmapped classifier. Knowledge is represented as a 0 or 1. If an attribute is present a 1 is present, if absent a 0 is present. A particular situation and its attributes may, for example, be represented as 00001110010. The pattern of bits is a message. In a Holland classifier pattern recognition is the focus rather than reasoning. One of its strongest assets is that it can do partial or approximate pattern matching. That is, certain bits can be classified as not critical for a match thus allowing for a match even if these less critical bits are not in compliance, and assuming another match is not in better compliance. Competitive bidding ensures that rules that frequently succeed are more likely to be paid attention to in the future. Thus, it is a self-organizing system. It is a robust system in that the failure of a given rule does not necessarily mean a good solution will not be found. Drawbacks of a Holland classifier are that it cannot explain how it arrived at a conclusion, and it requires a large number of trial runs to attain efficient performance (Schrodt 1986, 177–192; Parsaye 1989, 30; Rozier and Shafer 1989, 40–47).

Homomorphic Describing the quality of an internal representation of an object having a one-to-one correspondence with its external referent (Luger and Stubblefield 1989, 372).

Homomorphism Structural similarity (Barr and Feigenbaum 1981 vol 1, 200).

Homunculus Dwarf. Some people have unfortunately used the idea of a little man at the controls of the brain. Authorities have argued the goal of AI is to eliminate the homunculus and to replace it with computation (Frude 1983, 171–172; Johnson 1986, 134).

HOMUNCULUS A social interaction program developed by Robert Abelson. It has a belief system and different personalities.

HOPE A functional language in which functions are declared as sets of equations. It uses polymorphic data types (Eisenbach and Sadler 1985, 195; Bailey 1985, 235–258).

Hopfield, John The scientist who demonstrated neural networks can be used to solve significant problems and is responsible for the development of Hopfield networks. He suggested that neural networks could be viewed as seeking minima in energy landscapes (Ingraham et al 1988, 17; Jorgensen and Matheus 1986, 33).

Hopfield network A neural net characterized by analog computational networks that can be used to solve difficult computational problems. The output of each amplifier or neuron can vary over a specified range, say 0 to 1. This is in contrast to other neural nets that have a digital output. Each amplifier is made up of two components. One component activates other connected amplifiers as input increases. The other component inhibits as input is increased. An external force controls the general activation level of each amplifier. Each amplifier can have multiple inputs. The connections for each neuron or amplifier are symmetric. In such a system optimal solutions can be found to a number of problems by providing the appropriate synaptic weights and input data. It reaches global optimizations by the use of a number of asynchronous, local calculations. It is able to do both global and local optimizations. It can be used for associative memory-type problems. That is, given a property of an entity as input it can find the entity and its related properties. It is frequently utilized in pattern recognition by applying local constraints. It can be used to solve such optimization problems as the traveling-salesman problem—a problem mathematicians consider to be difficult. A Boltzmann machine may be considered a sophisticated version of a Hopfield network which employs simulated annealing. One authority holds that the difference between the Hopfield network and the Boltzmann machine is that the latter learns while the former is not capable of learning (Swaine Oct 1989, 112; Ingraham et al 1988, 17; Hinton 1985, 268; Jorgensen and Matheus 1986, 36–37; Thompson and Thompson Jul 1987, 28–30; Rumelhart and McClelland 1986 vol 1, 288–289).

Hopkins beast   A robot built in the early 1960s at Johns Hopkins University. It had the capability of navigating the hallways by using sonar reflection and was capable of locating wall sockets and recharging itself (Frude 1983, 57–58).

Horizon effect   The shortsightedness that exists in a game-search program. The program cannot see far enough over the horizon to know that taking a loss is in vain, or a positive gain is not really achievable with the strategy adopted. An example is sacrificing a knight to save the queen temporarily even though the loss of the queen is inevitable (Winston 1979, 126; Barr and Feigenbaum 1981 vol 1, 99).

Horn clause   A type of predicate-logic clause that has multiple conditions and a single conclusion. A type of clause that has at most one positive literal and takes the following form: a or not b or not c ... or not y. Horn clauses are a syntactic scheme employed in logic programming. They are rules, facts, and queries in a logic program. They are sometimes simply referred to as clauses or statements. They are similar to a full clausal form with the exception that only a single atom is allowed on the left-hand side of the clause. Horn clauses are used in PROLOG. Logic programs frequently restrict clauses to horn clauses for the sake of efficiency. They have greater expressiveness than the rules used in expert system shells like EMYCIN. Other syntactic schemes used in logic are conjunctive normal form and clausal form (Jackson 1986, 77–80; Jackson 1986, 176; Sterling and Shapiro 1986, 9; Barr and Feigenbaum 1981 vol 3, 121; Bratko 1986, 61; Smith 1989, 87; Luger and Stubblefield 1989, 476; Hunt 1986, 127; Savory 1988, 235).

Hot graphics   A type of graphics that can be used as a user interface. That is, the user may click onto the screen a diagram of a motor and point to the trouble spot. The expert system then takes appropriate action (Shafer 1988, 11).

Hotline   An expert system built with Personal Consultant to diagnose printer problems with Texas Instruments printers. It is a frame-based system that generates a set of hypotheses and systematically evaluates the hypotheses. This system is based on the function of the underlying components of the printers, and not on a symptom-cause model. The approach used is called the component-structured approach (Merritt 1987, 52).

Hough transform   A representation technique and procedure for visual recognition of objects. The procedure looks for instances of a particular object. It uses a model of the object in its search for instances of the object. The Hough transform finds the desired object by checking the data against the model in an iterative fashion until a best fit for the parameters of the model is found (Fischler and Firschein 1986, 49).

House-of-cards syndrome   The brittleness of most expert systems. That is, if the input information diverges slightly from the knowledge domain of the expert system the consultation may fall apart like a house of cards (Tello 1988, 415–416).

Housekeeping   A special knowledge source in a blackboard system which deletes or archives data that are no longer needed to solve the problem at hand.

How processor A component of the explanatory part of an expert system that answers the question of how a particular conclusion was reached (Floyd 1988, 66; Sterling and Shapiro 1986, 316–317).

Human Associative Memory (HAM) An associative, strategy-free computer model of long-term memory, which parses sentences and accumulates them in memory. It is used by psychologists to investigate the laws of long-term memory (Barr and Feigenbaum 1981 vol 3, 42–49, 509–510).

Human information processing *See* Information processing (Hunt 1986, 128).

Humiliation theory The theory of paranoia applied to the artificial intelligence system PARRY. Colby, the creator of PARRY, posits the thesis that paranoid behavior comes from humiliation and oversensitivity (Smith 1989, 89).

HWIM *See* Hear What I Mean.

Hybrid expert system tool An expert system tool with multiple forms of representation of knowledge and a variety of inference and control strategies. Such a system may use a combination of applicative, rule-based, object-oriented, procedural, and logic programming. The pattern matching that takes place in hybrid systems is generally not as rich as that found in production systems (Harmon and King 1985, 9–12, 83; Brownston et al 1986, 374–381; Swaine Jun 1989, 116).

Hydraulic robot A robot that uses hydraulics to achieve movement (Rosenberg 1986, 82).

Hypergraph A graph in which the nodes are connected by more than one arc. An AND/OR graph is a variation of a hypergraph (Luger and Stubblefield 1989, 104–105).

Hyperplane A theoretical line represented by mathematical formulas that exist in models with more than two dimensions. It is used to separate an object into regions.

Hyperresolution A resolution that produces a clash between a clause with negative literals (nucleus) and a set of clauses that are made up of positive literals (satellites). The satellites must have at least one positive literal that will match with a negative literal of the nucleus. At least one satellite must be found for each negative literal of the nucleus. The net result is a clause that is made up of positive literals. Hyperresolution keeps the clause space small because the production of intermediate results is limited (Luger and Stubblefield 1989, 438; Tello 1988, 418; Wos and Veroff 1990, 897).

Hypertext A means of organizing a large text base in which links between information are automatically made. The links may be used to call definitions to explain concepts in more detail, display graphs, or find related concepts. KnowledgePro and VP EXPERT 2.0 are two expert systems that use hypertext (Shafer Jul/Aug 1988, 38; Thompson and Thompson Aug 1987, 25).

Hypothesis-driven expert system Goal-driven expert system (Hayes-Roth et al 1983, 37).

Hypothesize and test The formation of a hypothesis and the subsequent testing of the hypothesis. *See also* Backward chaining; Goal-directed inference (Hunt 1986, 118; Tello 1988, 182–183).

Hypothetical reasoning 1. A characteristic of some expert systems that keeps a number of perhaps contradictory solutions active at one time. The different possible solutions can be compared and eventually the best solution can be selected. 2. A what-if capability similar to the type of what-if process found in spreadsheets. Both pattern matching and conflict resolution are used in hypothetical reasoning. Hypothetical reasoning is also sometimes called assumption-based truth maintenance (Matthews Sep 1987, 84; *Knowledge-Based Systems* 1986, 2–63; Harris 1989, 56).

Hypothetical syllogism A rule of inference that is a special case of resolution (Dos Reis 1988, 51).

Hypothetical world Viewpoint and multiple world (Rosenberg 1986, 83).

I

I&W An expert system that attempts to predict world trouble spots. It uses a blackboard architecture with both frames and rules. The underlying language is INTERLISP-D and it was created at Stanford University (Hunt 1986, 129).

ICAI *See* Intelligent computer-aided instruction.

Iconic representation The depiction of scenes as images. *See also* Isomorphic/iconic/analogical representation analogical (Smith 1989, 91).

Identification One of five phases in developing an expert system. In this phase the problem area is delineated, resources needed are identified, and initial cost estimates are made. The five phases, in order, are identification, conceptualization, formalization, implementation, and testing (Hayes-Roth et al 1983, 23).

Identity Two logic propositions that have the same truth value. Both propositions are true, or both propositions are false (Hunt 1986, 129).

IDT A rule-based forward-chaining expert system that troubleshoots computers. The expert system language used is OPS5. IDT was developed by DEC (Hunt 1986, 129).

ID3 A machine-learning algorithm used in induction expert systems which builds a decision tree from a set of examples. This decision tree can be considered one very large rule. Products based on such decision trees are called decision tree generators. 1st-Class is one example of a decision tree generator. The decision tree can be translated into a rule set. This can be a very efficient means of building a rule set. One advantage of the ID3 algorithm being used to build a rule set is that it keeps to a minimum redundant rules. Another advantage is that it orders the rule set in such a way that the rules that can produce the most pruning of the search space are scrutinized first. Because the ID3 algorithm uses decision trees it is a very efficient form of learning. The use of decision trees also limits what can be learned. ID stands for iterative dichotomizer (Thompson and Thompson Nov 1986, 149–158; Brynjolfsson and Loofbourrow 1988, 32; Barr and Feigenbaum 1981 vol 3, 407–410; Luger and Stubblefield 1989, 569–570; Parsaye Jul/Aug 1989, 29).

If-added demon A demon that is activated if a value in a slot is added or changed (Amsterdam 1986, 21; Winston 1979, 379; Winston 1984, 317, 319).

If and only if *See* Iff.

Iff A derived connective which means if and only if. The two terms connected by iff have the same truth table. That is, if one term is true the other term is true. If one term is false, the other term is false. Given the formula (iff $p\ q$), if p is true then q is true. If q is true then p is true. If p is false then q is false. If q is false then p is false. This formula can be used to state that p and q stand for the same entity, or that one entity has been defined in terms of another entity. *Contrast with* Implication (Parsaye and Chignell 1988, 318; Charniak and McDermott 1985, 323).

If-needed demon A demon that is activated if a value in a slot is accessed (Floyd 1988, 84; Amsterdam 1986, 21; Winston 1979, 384–386; Winston 1984, 317, 318).

If-removed demon A demon that is activated if a value in a slot is removed (Amsterdam 1986, 21; Winston 1979, 379; Winston 1984, 317, 319–320).

If/then rule 1. A control structure found in most conventional computer languages, which controls program flow. The conditions in the If part of the rule trigger what statements are next executed. 2. A repository of a piece of modular knowledge in an expert system. In contrast to a rule in conventional programs, an if/then rule is not a control structure. If certain conditions are true in the If part of the rule, then certain inferences are made or certain actions are taken. An important feature in such rules is the ability to handle multiple statements in both the IF and the THEN portions of the rule. The ability to use the AND and OR operators allows the use of multiple statements. The inclusion of the AND and OR operators in the antecedents and consequents of rules decreases the number of rules needed to handle the information in the domain. The use of multiple consequents in a rule reduces program clarity and should not be used excessively. The ability to use variables in rules is another important factor in increasing the power of rules. 3. Production rule. 4. Antecedent-consequent rule. *See also* If/then/else statement; Production (Winston and Horn 1988, 580; Tello 1988, 257; Walters and Nielsen 1988, 196–200).

If/then/else statement An extension of an if/then statement. In an if/then/else statement, if the conditions are not true and the conclusion cannot therefore be inferred, then an alternative default conclusion following else is inferred. Example: IF patient is ill THEN administer treatment ELSE do nothing. If/then/else statements can be implemented in PROLOG by using multiple rules and the cut predicate. The use of else in expert system programs can greatly reduce program clarity and its use should be minimized (Sterling and Shapiro 1986, 170–171).

IJCAI International Joint Conference on Artificial Intelligence. The AAAI sponsors it (Hunt 1986, 129).

Illegal node A type of node that is off limits to a search process. In the cannibals and missionaries problem an example of an illegal node is allowing a state in which the cannibals outnumber the missionaries (Jackson 1986, 15).

Image A projection of a three-dimensional scene on a two-dimensional surface. The image is usually represented as an array of brightness values (Hunt 1986, 130).

Image analysis A more active process than image processing. In image analysis the computer program controls the process. The computer program decides how much image stretching or gray-scale manipulation is to take place. *Contrast with* Image comprehension; Image processing (Forsyth and Naylor 1985, 78–79; Chabris 1989, 295).

Image comprehension A matching of self-knowledge with the image under scrutiny. *Compare with* Image analysis; Image processing (Forsyth and Naylor 1985, 85–88).

Image domain The projection of scene domain properties on a two-dimensional surface. *Contrast with* Scene domain ((Barr and Feigenbaum 1981 vol 3, 131–135).

Image processing 1. The recognition and enhancement of a visual image. A massaging of an image. A more passive process than image analysis. Image stretching and gray-scale manipulation are two procedures generally associated with image processing.   2. Signal processing. *Compare with* Image analysis; Image comprehension (Forsyth and Naylor 1985, 74–78; Schildt 1987, 126).

Image redundancy A method of reducing the processing of real-time images by exploiting the similarities in each image. Once the program has made a decision about what the object is it can then focus its energies on how incoming images are changing (Forsyth and Naylor 1985, 90).

Image stretching A technique used in image processing in which the image is stretched to compensate for distortions introduced because of how the image was taken. A satellite photograph may correctly capture the area directly below it but it may distort the peripheral portions of the image. Image stretching may be used to correct these distortions (Forsyth and Naylor 1985, 77).

Image understanding Using a computer to analyze, classify, and attempt to understand visual images (Barr and Feigenbaum 1981 vol 3, 127–138; Rosenberg 1986, 86).

Image-understanding program A vision program that attempts the synthesis of a number of different sciences, including physics, neurophysiology, artificial intelligence, computer science, pattern recognition, and image processing, to deduce information from images (Barr and Feigenbaum 1981 vol 3, 135).

Impedance mismatch The prevention of interaction between two languages because of the differences between them. A data base and a computer language may not be able to share data because of their differences (Zaniolo et al 53–54).

Imperative language A computer language that specifies the flow of control. *Contrast with* Declarative language, in which the flow of control is implicit (Eisenbach 1985, 149).

Implementation 1. One of five phases in developing an expert system. In this phase a prototype program is built and tested. The five phases, in order, are identification, conceptualization, formalization, implementation, and testing.   2. The sixth of seven stages in expert system development. The system is ported to hardware which will be used by the end user. The end user is trained to use the system. *See also* Expert system development, for information concerning the other six stages (Harmon et al 1988, 199–200).

Implication A logical expression that connects the conditions and conclusions of a rule. Given the formula (if *p q*) it implies *p* is not true, or *q* is true. *Contrast with* If and only if (Charniak and McDermott 1985, 323; Savory 1988, 236).

Implicit grouping of rules The grouping of rules in an expert system by using a method that is in some way hidden. The rules may be grouped by an indexing system in the rule interpreter, or by the use of metarules to control which set of rules to try next. Metarules are used to implement backward chaining in OPS5 expert systems—the rules are implicitly grouped through the use of metarules. MYCIN uses indexing. *Compare with* Partitioning (of rule bases), an explicit method of dividing rules (Jackson 1986, 143–144).

Implicit knowledge Knowledge that is intertwined with the procedural aspects of a program and not easily subject to inspection (Barr and Feigenbaum 1981 vol 2, 277).

Implicit representation A representation that cannot rely on listing all objects included in it. Example: All real numbers between 0 and 1 cannot possibly be represented explicitly in a knowledge structure. The inequalities > and < are used to represent such infinite sets of objects implicitly. PROLOG II and PROLOG III were developed so as to define implicit objects through the use of constraints (Lassez 1987, 171–172).

Implies The connector in logic that associates the antecedents of a rule with the consequents (Hunt 1986, 131).

Imply A non-resolution-theorem prover, which uses inference rules similar to those used by human theorem provers. Imply searches for objects which will prove the hypothesis to be true. In contrast to a resolution-theorem prover, it does not attempt to find a proof by using a negation and then looking for a contradiction (Barr and Feigenbaum 1981 vol 3, 95–99).

Improper symbol A symbol in predicate calculus used to build expressions, which do not symbolize objects and their relationship to other objects. Examples: parentheses, commas, and periods (Luger and Stubblefield 1989, 47).

In-betweening A technique used in computer animation to generate scenes between two related images (Forsyth and Naylor 1985, 225).

Inclination shell An expert system shell that uses specialized knowledge representation and specialized inferencing techniques to build an expert system. Such shells are optimized for a particular group of applications (Chapnick Nov 1988, 7).

Inclusive-OR element The disjunctive process. Example: A is true if X OR Y is true. It is a version of "OR" that fires a rule even if more than one value of a set of values can satisfy the condition. If the variable Weather is cloudy OR cold the rule will fire. If the variable Weather is both cloudy and cold, the rule will also fire. *Contrast with* Exclusive-OR (Brownston et al 1986, 191–193; Rosenberg 1986, 87).

Incomplete data structure A data structure in PROLOG that can be used in place of such standard structures as lists. It is used to represent the partial results of a computation. Incomplete data structures can be more efficiently processed than a standard list. These structures are used extensively in constructing definite clause grammars. *See also* Difference lists (Sterling and Shapiro 1986, 239–255).

Incomplete information A problem faced by expert systems in which the information needed to solve a problem is not known. This can be handled in some expert system tools by using a default value. Other tools use approximate pattern matching (Baskin 1986, 147; Freedman 1987, 73).

Incompleteness theorem A theorem developed by Kurt Gödel, which proved that as a formal system becomes powerful enough to build its own rules it will also inevitably produce contradictions.

Incremental compilation A process that allows the compilation of a portion of an expert system or a file. A very valuable tool when building expert systems. Instead of having to compile the entire expert system when a change has been made only a portion of the system need be compiled (Michaelsen et al 1985, 311).

Incremental development A characteristic of many expert systems in which new knowledge may be easily added to the system without the need for extensive reprogramming. Example: adding a new rule to a rule-based system. If the rules in the system are not sequentially dependent, the addition of the new rule will not interfere with earlier demonstrated performance of the system.

Incremental garbage collection The elimination of no-longer-needed data structures in such a way that it is done at periodic intervals and is therefore less noticeable and less annoying. Incremental garbage collection is a necessity in expert systems which must respond immediately to changes in incoming data. Think of the problems caused when an expert system in an F-111 aircraft must pause for a significant period of time for garbage collection (Bernat Mar 1987, 43).

Incremental growth by elaboration Extending a production system by adding a new rule with conditions that will pick up patterns which have not previously been discovered. *Compare with* Incremental growth by refinement (Brownston et al 1986, 166–168).

Incremental growth by refinement The process of extending a production system by starting with an already-existing rule and elaborating on the condition part of the rule to create a new rule which is a variant of the original rule. Spinning off and fission are two variants of incremental growth by refinement. *Contrast with* Incremental growth by elaboration (Brownston et al 1986, 168–170).

Incremental learning A type of learning found in induction expert systems in which a program is able to revise its hypotheses as new training instances are introduced (Barr and Feigenbaum 1981 vol 3, 363).

Incremental rule compilation A process whereby new rules can be inserted in the expert system without having to recompile the entire system, an important time-saving feature. This characteristic is found in the expert system tools ART and INTELLIGENCE COMPILER (Newquist Apr 1987, 64).

Indefinite extent The continued existence of an entity throughout the entire program run. A variable continues to exist as long as the possibility exists that it can be referenced (Tello 1988, 351).

Indefinite scoping A process that allows a variable to be accessed anywhere in a program. *Contrast with* Lexical scoping (Tello 1987, 241).

Independent reasoning The reasoning that takes place in multiple contexts. Each context proceeds independently with its own reasoning using its basic assumptions and reaches conclusions based on the assumptions made for the context (Walters and Nielsen 1988, 255).

Independent subproblem A problem consisting of subproblems and the order of solution of the different subproblems does not affect the outcome of the solution. *See also* Interdependent subproblems.

Indeterminacy The use of more than one representational technique to represent an object (Smith 1989, 94).

Indeterminate Describing a task in a problem which can be broken up into subtasks at different levels, which are not in a fixed order. *Compare with* Determinate (Jackson 1986, 133).

Index A number used to locate information in an array or a program (Hunt 1986, 132).

Indexed instance variable An instance variable with a number rather than a name in object-oriented programming. Such variables are used in ordered collections like arrays. Example: "position" at : 5. The indexed instance variable is accessed by number rather than by name (*Smalltalk/ Tutorial and Programming Handbook* 1986, 55; Stein 1988, 20).

Indexing The use of a lookup table to locate an object in a set of objects. A procedure usually associated with data bases which greatly speeds the ability to find data. In arrays each array variable location is indexed by a subscript number, or in two-dimensional arrays by two subscript numbers. $A(3)$, $B(2,4)$ are examples of array variables. A noncomputer example is using the alphabetical index of a book to find a subject. Indexing is used in associative networks, and languages like PROLOG are beginning to increase their indexing abilities (Schildt 1987, 212; Sciore and Warren 1988, 40–41; Rosenberg 1986, 87; Charniak and McDermott 1985, 24–25).

Indirect recursion A type of recursion in which two functions continue to call each other.

Individual concept A concept that uses an individual marker to indicate that the concept node refers to an individual, in a conceptual graph. *Contrast with* Generic concept (Luger and Stubblefield 1989, 353).

Induce A model-driven concept-learning program that uses model-driven generate-and-test. It is used to learn a concept from positive examples. Induce employs beam search to refine rules. *Contrast with* Model-driven schema instantiation (Barr and Feigenbaum 1981 vol 3, 411–415).

Induction 1. An inference that proceeds from specific facts and examples to deriving abstract principles and rules. 2. Distilling of a general principle from a set of examples. 3. The process whereby hypotheses are formed from observation of specific events. The next step in the induction process is the evaluation of hypotheses. Induction can also include argument by analogy. Induction is an imperfect type of reasoning. Example: Growing up in the Far East, observing that each human has dark hair, and then making the generalization that all humans have dark hair. Induction is seen by some as equivalent to learning. There are numerous induction expert systems which to some extent automate the process of induction. Induction, as used in AI, is a type of automatic programming. Other types of learning are learning by being told and learning by analogy. *See also* Induction expert system. *Contrast with* Deduction (Salzberg Feb 1988, 45; Charniak and McDermott 1985, 22; Barr and Feigenbaum 1981 vol 1, 318–325; Barr and Feigenbaum 1981 vol 3, 333–334; Ligomenides 1988, 2; Savory 1988, 236).

Induction expert system The type of expert system that takes as input a series of examples of conditions and solutions in a problem area. The induction expert system turns these examples into a matrix with a single example or a set of rules which can solve problems related to the examples. The creation of a set of rules, rather than a matrix, is preferred, because modification of the rule base is easier. A good induction system eliminates redundant rules and creates an optimal search path by organizing the data so that the questions that will do the greatest pruning of the search space will be asked first. The rule base is usually flat. A synonym is example-expert system. It is a type of automated knowledge acquisition. Machine learning is sometimes used interchangeably with the term induction expert system, but machine learning has a more general meaning. *Contrast with* Knowledge elicitation (Parsaye and Chignell 1988, 336; Rosenberg 1986, 88).

Induction table Examples of conditions and conclusions arranged in a table format. Each row consists of the conditions and the conclusion that follows from the conditions. Induction tools frequently build such tables (Tello 1988, 127).

Inductive bias Elements that affect the choice of hypotheses in a machine-learning program. The type of representation used may place limitations on what is learned (Eliot Mar 1987, 62; Luger and Stubblefield 1989, 569).

Inductive generalization The process of building general rules from specific examples (Kolokouris 1986, 225).

Inductive inference A type of inference that proceeds from the specific to the general. Example: forming rules from examples (Johnson 1986, 90; Rosenberg 1986, 88; Dietterich and Michalski 1981, 257–294).

Inductive learning Inductive inference.

Industrial robot A robot designed to perform a small number of fixed repetitive tasks. It is currently taught how to carry out its assigned tasks either through a teach pendant or through a robotic control language (Schildt 1987, 171–175; Rosenberg 1986, 88–89).

Inertia problem   Ramification problem. (Eckert 1989, 53).

Inexact fact   A fact with a certainty factor attached.

Inexact logic   *See* Inexact reasoning.

Inexact reasoning   **1.** A version of logic that uses multivalued statements. Statements in logic generally are either true or false. An inexact reasoning system may use the values of true, false, and unknown. Inexact reasoning may be thought of as a set of techniques for dealing with uncertainty in facts and rules in expert systems. Bayesian statistics, fuzzy logic, and certainty factors are means of applying inexact reasoning. In using certainty factors the truth of a statement may vary on some numerical range from say 0 to 100. One of the primary functions in inexact reasoning is to produce a rank ordering of conclusions. Inexact logic is a synonym.   **2.** The use of heuristics may also be considered as a type of inexact reasoning (Lecot and Parker 1986, 32–43; Barr and Feigenbaum 1981 vol 1, 81; Jackson 1986, 103).

Inexact rule   A rule with a certainty factor attached. The certainty factor may vary on a numerical scale from 0 to 100, where 0 means false and 100 means that the rule is true.

Inference   The process of deriving new facts from previously known facts. Rules are a means of applying inference. An example is, IF *A* is true THEN *B* is true. *B* is inferred from *A*. Modus ponens and universal instantiation are two well-known rules of inference used in expert systems. Deduction, induction, and abduction are three broad types of inference. Inference is sometimes referred to as formal reasoning. *Contrast with* Inexact reasoning (Townsend 1987a, 46; Harmon and King 1985, 49–53; Brownston et al 1986, 448; Townsend, 381).

Inference chain   The series of inferential steps a rule-based system goes through to reach a conclusion. The inferential steps take the form of satisfying a series of rules to reach a conclusion (Rosenberg 1986, 89).

Inference engine   The part of an expert system that is responsible for inference and control. (1) It makes inferences by deriving new facts from old facts using rules in the knowledge base. The types of inference can include modus ponens, universal instantiation, uncertainty reasoning, and resolution. (2) It controls the order in which rules are examined. It selects the rule to start with, the next rule to check, and decides when a conclusion has been found, when to ask the user, and when to give up. Different aspects of control can include the choice of backward and forward chaining, the type of search, and monotonic versus nonmonotonic reasoning. The inference engine is sometimes referred to as the control structure, the rule interpreter, or the interpreter. One difference between an inference engine and a computer language interpreter is an inference engine provides for a high degree of modularity. Therefore, less debugging is necessary. A general rule of thumb concerning inference engines is that the more an inference engine is designed for a specific body of knowledge, the more efficiently it will run with that body of knowledge. The converse of this is that it will probably be unable to work well with other bodies of knowledge. Some authorities include that part of an expert system that interacts with the user as part of the inference engine (Forsyth and Naylor 1985, 14; Tello Jul 1985, 72; Townsend 1987a, 132–134; Mishkoff 1986, 3–5; Harmon and King 1985, 49–60; Brownston et al 1986, 488; Townsend 381; Barr and Feigenbaum 1981 vol 1, 189–191; Townsend and Feucht 1986, 34–36; Parsaye and Chignell 1988, 32; Thompson and Thompson Apr 1985, 317; Tello, 1989, 18).

Inference net   The set of all possible inferences that can be made from a rule-based system (Hunt 1986, 135; Rosenberg 1986, 89).

Inference tracing   A detailed listing of the inferences made by an expert system during a consultation. Inference tracing can be very useful in debugging and in understanding why a particular conclusion has been reached (Harmon et al 1988, 62).

Inference tree An AND/OR tree.

Inferential data base Knowledge-based management system (Parker, Jr. et al 1986, 36).

Inferential flow analysis A procedure used to elicit information from a domain expert. In inferential flow analysis the expert is repeatedly questioned so as to ascertain the cause-effect relationships in the domain (Olson 1988, 26–27).

Inferential search A search in expert data base systems which involves inference. It is more flexible than a query search in a standard data base system. Query searches in a standard data base are, however, more efficient.

Infinite tree A tree structure that does not terminate.

Infix notation A type of notation in which the operator is between its arguments. The expression 3 + 2 is infix notation. *Contrast with* Prefix notation (Townsend 1987a, 247).

Information hiding 1. The protection of variables and values of variables within a function or an object, by only allowing access through properly defined procedures. When the function or object is not being accessed the program is ignorant of these variables and their values. That is, the same variable name can be used in a different part of the program with no danger of conflict with the other encapsulated variable of the same name. Information hiding is an important characteristic of modern programs and object-oriented programs in particular. It decreases the probability of errors in a program. 2. The packaging of information and procedures within an object so that the information can only be accessed by a message being sent to the object which will activate the procedures in the object or procedures in the superclass of the object. Information hiding is also called data hiding, and data encapsulation (Pascoe 1986, 140; Thomas 1989, 232; Hansen 1988, 134; Swaine Jun 1989, 116).

Information processing A field of psychology that focuses on how humans think, using a computer. The thought processes hypothesized by the researcher are emulated on the computer to see if the proposed thought processes are feasible. The branch of psychology that holds that computer programs may be considered psychological theories. This latter contention is where information processing psychology and cognitive psychology part company. Cognitive psychology views computer programs as metaphors of human thinking rather than true psychological theories of cognition. Important areas of study in information processing include sensory inputs, attention, short-term memory, long-term memory, motor outputs, and problem solving (Harmon and King 1985, 22–24; Barr and Feigenbaum 1981 vol 3, 3–74; Chabris 1989, 295; Luger and Stubblefield 1989, 412).

Information processing language (IPL) A precursor of the LISP programming language. It was guided by the concept of association. Its primary data element was symbols. It handled the problem of unpredictable shapes by using lists (Mishkoff 1986, 7–6).

Information theory A precise mathematical definition of information devised by Claude Shannon. It is unable, however, to handle the concept of meaning (Waldrop 1987, 17–18; Bharath May/Jun 1988, 42–46; Johnson 1986, 36–41).

Informedness A state in which a heuristic needs to explore minimal search space to find the optimal path (Luger and Stubblefield 1989, 168–170).

Informed search A type of search that starts with information about the starting state or with information about certain constraints (Nachsheim 1989, 34).

Inheritance A characteristic of object-oriented and frame-based languages that allows objects to acquire characteristics of an object class. The ability to spawn a new object that has many of the characteristics of a previously defined object. It allows properties, values, and procedures to be shared between a class and its subclasses. Example: Once a sports car class is defined, any object which is created in that class, say, a Corvette, will automatically inherit the characteristics of the class sports car. Inheritance allows the creation of specialized objects of a class. Inheritance works through what is known as an a-kind-of slot. The advantages of inheritance are reduced programming time, reduced memory consumption, and a more easily comprehended program. It is argued that human beings store information about objects at the most abstract level possible, and this is the reason that humans can respond so quickly to questions about classes of objects and individual objects. Inheritance hierarchies have deductive reasoning capabilities. Using this automobile hierarchy, if a car in the hierarchy is named a Ferrari, one can ask if a Ferrari is a sports car. Since it is in the sports hierarchy the answer will be affirmative. If a characteristic of all sports cars is that they have four wheels, then one may ask if a Ferrari has four wheels. The system will not find the answer on the frame representing Ferrari, so it will work its way up the hierarchy until it finds the sports car frame which has a wheels slot which tells the user a sports car has four wheels. One can say it deduced the value of wheels from the hierarchy. The implicit rule is, "If a Ferrari is a sports car, then it has four wheels." The most common type of inheritance is property or slot inheritance. That is, all sports cars inherit the property of wheels. There are a number of other possible variants of inheritance. They include value, restriction, null, before method, after method, multiple, union, and intersection. *See also* Inheritance of methods; Tangled trees (Floyd 1988, 82; Brachman 1987, 7; Pascoe 1986, 142; (McGregor 1987, 52–54; Walters and Nielsen 1988, 228–233; Harmon and King 1985, 37; Barr and Feigenbaum 1981 vol 1, 181–182; Winston 1984, 318–319; *Smalltalk/ Tutorial and Programming Handbook* 1986, 63–75; Harmon et al 1988, 61; Gabriel Mar 1989, 55; Thomas 1989, 232; Duntemann 1989, 137–138).

Inheritance of methods An inheritance in Smalltalk in which an instance inherits the methods of its class. Assume a class of geometric shapes. The class of geometric shapes has a method that computes perimeters of this class of shapes. When a new shape that belongs to this class is created the new shape or instance inherits the method for computing perimeters.

Inheritance semantics The ability of a user to specify which slot values of an object can be inherited and which cannot.

Inheritance up A type of inheritance that takes place when an instance of a class is created and a unique property is assigned the instance and this property is inherited up to the parent objects. This type of inheritance is in the opposite direction from that we usually consider inheritance to be taking—from the parent object to the child object. NEXPERT is one expert system tool that employs inheritance up (Tello 1988, 301).

Initial design template A knowledge-engineering design tool. Templates include such information as recommendation categories, specific recommendations, rules, parameter tables (including parameter name, type, and possible values), and initial data (Phillips and Sanders 1988, 65–66).

Initial pruning Pruning that occurs early in the search for a solution. Example: When a domain expert first looks at a problem he or she will immediately rule out a number of possibilities which a novice would not rule out because of the novice's inexperience. This type of pruning can make the difference between the expert system's success and failure (Harmon et al 1988, 63).

Inline function A function in C++ in which the compiler produces the proper program code for the function where the function is called.

This reduces function call overhead (Stroustrup 1987, 29–30).

In principle   The generality principle.

Input connection   A connection (synapse) in which a unit in a neural net receives input from other units (Stevens 1985, 289; Jones and Hoskins 1987, 155).

Inspection   One of the four parts of a simulation. Unlike ordinary programs that focus on input and output, a simulation requires the ability to trace or inspect what is taking place during the program run. Being able to follow how different aspects of the model interact is usually more important than outcome in a simulation (Eliot and Holliday 1988, 55).

Inspector   Objects which are employed as debugging tools in Smalltalk V (Tello 1988, 387–388).

Inspector facility   A feature found in some high end expert systems that allow graphic inspections of networks of objects and rules. NEXPERT is one expert system tool with such a facility (Tello 1988, 297).

Instance   1. An object that is a product of a class.   2. An object that has a concrete counterpart in the real world. The Oldsmobile parked in front of your house is an instance. *Contrast with* Kind, which refers to an entire subclass of a class.   3. A less abstract object, such as mammals, birds, and so on (Kaehler and Patterson 1986, 155; Jackson 1986, 59; Walters and Nielsen 1988, 210; Harmon and King 1985, 39–40; Sterling and Shapiro 1986, 5; Duntemann 1989, 138).

Instance link   A link in a semantic network that connects a schema with an individual object. Example: The schema dog connected to the specific instance—Lassie. *Compare with* Subkind link (Salzberg 1987, 34).

Instance object   An object in a frame-based system which is an instance of a more general class. Example: cat, which is derived from the prototype class of mammals. *Contrast with* Prototype object; Referential object (Reimer 1986, 178).

Instance space   The set of all potential training instances in example-driven learning. *See also* Rule space; Two-space view of learning (Barr and Feigenbaum 1981 vol 3, 360–364).

Instance variable   A variable in object-oriented programs which is inside of an object and it holds its value even after the procedure which sent a message to the object has been terminated (Stein 1988, 20; Pascoe 1986, 140; Rubin 1985, 27).

Instantiate   To assign a value to a variable (Harrison and Tribble 1986, 66).

Instantiation   1. Assigning a value or values to a variable, a rule, or a frame.   2. An object that is an instance of a given class.   3. The creation of new objects in an object-oriented program.   4. The rule and the values that satisfy the variables in the left-hand side of the rule.   5. A production name along with the working memory elements that satisfy the production in an OPS5 system (Harmon et al 1988, 37–38; Hayes-Roth et al 1983, 401; Walters and Nielsen 1988, 202–203; Brownston et al 1986, 14–15, 61–72, 79–80; Townsend 1987b; 381; Forgy and Shepard 1987, 36; Keys 1989, 63).

Instar   The part of the processing unit in a neural network that receives input signals from other processing units or from the environment. *See also* Outstar; Outstar learning (Caudill Nov 1988, 58–65).

Instar activity equation   An equation that represents the level of activity of a neurode in an instar learning network. Activity increases when a stimulus is applied and decreases when a stimulus is removed (Caudill Nov 1988, 59–61).

Instructional expert system   An expert system that assesses a student's behavior, builds a model of the student's knowledge, diagnoses weaknesses, and constructs a tutorial that will help remedy the weaknesses. See ICAI, and Computer aided instruction (Hayes-Roth et al 1983, 15).

Integrated programming environment   The consolidation of a programming language with support utilities. The support utilities can include state-of-the-art debugging facilities, intelligent editors, incremental compilation, multitasking, and windowing. Smalltalk has an integrated programming environment.

Integration   The ability of an expert system to use information from other programs such as a spreadsheet, a computer language, or a data base (Pedersen May 1988, 27–34).

Integration problem   The problem in learning systems of blending new rules with existing rules. Adding new rules can have the impact of causing already existing rules to be misapplied or not to be applied at all (Barr and Feigenbaum 1981 vol 3, 331).

Integration technique   A technique used in expert systems to permit access of external resources as data files, worksheets, and programs. Integration techniques can call information from a data base rather than require the user to enter it. They can be used to update spreadsheets and data bases. A conventional language may be called to perform a procedure that is more efficiently carried out using the conventional language such as building graphs, menus, or performing complex mathematical calculations (Pedersen, May 1988, 27).

Integrity constraint   Restrictions on the knowledge structure in frame-based systems. Example: "All planes have wings." *See also* Model-dependent integrity constraints; World-dependent integrity constraint (Kowalski 1985 175; Reimer, 1986, 175).

Integrity maintenance   The procedure of ensuring data is protected from being mistakenly destroyed, incorrectly changed, or illegally retrieved. Attached procedures in frame-based systems are frequently used to carry out these objectives (Parsaye and Chignell 1988, 182–184).

INTELLECT   A natural language interface to data bases. It can be used to query data bases with Englishlike phrases. The language is based on augmented transition networks. It is an offshoot of HEARSAY II. INTELLECT was formerly known as ROBOT (Rosenberg 1986, 93).

Intelligence   **1.** The ability to bring to bear knowledge to solve problems.   **2.** A set of characteristics that contribute to the ability to adapt to new situations. One important characteristic of intelligence is to grasp quickly the point of an analogical statement. This type of pattern matching is marvelous and no computer program has yet been able to come close to duplicating it. Goal directedness, the ability to learn, and the flexibility in being able to perceive exceptions to rules are other important characteristics (Waldrop 1987, 47–48; Chabris 1989, 22).

Intelligent artifacts school   The school that believes that AI need not operate like the human mind. DENDRAL which was developed by Feigenbaum is an example of this type of expert system. *Contrast with* Cognitive-modeling school (Johnson, 1986, 230, 241).

Intelligent assistant   **1.** Expert system. In some ways the term is a better description of expert systems since it does not imply the infallibility of the term expert system. It relegates an expert system to "assistant" rather than "expert." Advisory system has roughly the same meaning.   **2.** The ability of expert systems to call to the attention of the user a problem or an alternative way of handling a problem (Brodie et al 1986, 22; Rosenberg 1986, 93).

Intelligent backtracking   Dependency-directed backtracking. *Contrast with* Chronological backtracking.

Intelligent computer-aided instruction (ICAI)   A program that attempts to teach a body of knowledge using a computer program. It has the following characteristics: It actually analyzes a student's performance and tailors an instruction program for the student based on the analysis. It takes active control of the learning process. It generally consists of three components: a problem-solving module, a student module, and a tutoring module. The problem-solving module contains the information that the student is to learn. The student module is a model of the program's perception of what the student knows. The tutoring module is responsible for choosing the teaching strategies to be followed. An ICAI uses mixed initiative dialogue and natural language processing. It is generally based on semantic networks. *See also* BUGGY; EXCHECK; GUIDON; SCHOLAR; SOPHIE; WEST; WHY; WUMPUS for examples of ICAI. *Contrast with* Environmental approach; Frame-based CAI (Barr and Feigenbaum 1981 vol 1, 225–294; Mishkoff 1986, 1–18, 6–2 to 6–4; Sleeman and Brown 1982).

Intelligent data base A data base that deals with knowledge as well as data. An artificial intelligence programming language with a data base. A combination of a data base which has a link with an expert system which can perform reasoning on the data in the data base. Such data bases, in addition, include such features as automatic discovery, automatic error detection, intelligent user interfaces, flexible query processing, hypermedia, and object orientation. *See also* Knowledge-based management system (Rettig Jun 1987, 15; Jenkins 1987, 34; Schur 1988, 26–34; Parsaye et al Mar 1990, 38).

Intelligent data base engine An inference engine with the following characteristics: the competence to handle objects, the ability to integrate data retrieval and inference, expertise in building optimized queries, the ability to explain how data were found or why the query failed, concurrency control, and proficiency in handling multimedia (Parsaye et al Mar 1990, 46–47).

Intelligent decision-support system A data base system that includes a reasoning component (Jenkins 1987, 32).

Intelligent form An alternative to the usual type of question-answer dialogue which takes place with the user of an expert system. Instead, the user is presented with an electronic form in which he or she fills in the blanks. The advantage is that most of the input the user needs to enter is on the screen, and he or she can decide if all the information is gatherable, and what needs to be done to gain the information all at one time (Shafer Sept/Oct 1989, 55).

Intelligent help A knowledge base used in some expert system shells to help the user with problems in developing an expert system (Harmon et al 1988, 84).

Intelligent interoperability The exchange of information among diverse information sources, some of which are intelligent (Manola 1990, 26).

Intelligent manual Using expert system technology as a basis for developing a manual that can employ a reasoning capability to efficiently answer the user's needs. Such manuals can use hypertext to allow the user to explore the manual in a nonlinear fashion (Burg 1988, 12).

Intelligent robot A robot with sufficient AI technology to allow it to make adaptations to its environment. It is also known as a sensor-controlled-robot. *See also* Servo robot.

Intelligent software development tool Software automation sometimes included under the rubric of artificial intelligence. It includes editors, debuggers, assemblers, compilers, interpreters, and programs such as The Programmer's Apprentice.

Intelligent system A knowledge-based system capable of making inferences (Hunt 1986, 137).

Intelligent text retrieval The process by which a computer program scrutinizes written text and creates rules from it. Example: KAM (Newquist Feb 1988, 69).

Intelligent tutoring Tutoring based on the information processing model rather than the behaviorist model on which programmed learning is based. Intelligent tutoring keeps track of the student's responses and develops a model of the student's grasp of the subject. The model is used as a guide in deciding which problem to bring up next or what information or questions should come next (Waldrop 1987, 207–208; Sleeman and Brown 1982).

Intelligent user interface A characteristic of an intelligent data base. Intelligent interfaces employ hypertext to link data in a variety of ways. Links for greater topic depth, links for related topics, links for a view of the overall hierarchy, and links for parents of the topic are but a few of the links that can be used (Parsaye et al Mar 1990, 44–46).

Intensional definition Defining a class by the use of rules. Knowledge bases are intensional, whereas data bases are extensional (Chapnick Nov 1987, 7).

Intensional knowledge What a concept means in the abstract. Intensional knowledge focuses on the characteristics of an object such as texture, shape, size, and so on (Luger and Stubblefield 1989, 335).

Intensional meaning Meaning that is denoted by the characteristics of an object. *Contrast with* Extensional meaning (Chabris 1989, 64–65).

Intensional operator An operator that uses the meanings of its arguments to produce sentences rather than simply the truth value of its arguments. Two intensional operators are believe and know (Barr and Feigenbaum 1981 vol 3, 83–84; Smith 1989, 97).

Intentionality 1. The representation of objects by a mental state. 2. A property of intelligence that allows concepts to be directed at objects in the environment. It is argued intentionality cannot be duplicated by computers (Chabris 1989, 295).

Interacting subproblem A problem that arises in AI planning systems. The requirement that a given subproblem be solved before another subproblem is started. An example is the requirement that a ladder be brought in before a ceiling of a room is painted. In some cases it is possible to break up a problem into subproblems and solve each subproblem independently. With many problems, however, subproblems are dependent on the solutions to other subproblems. The problem of interacting subproblems can be coped with by the use of constraints and the pursuit of least-commitment problem solving. Interactive subgoal is a term which is analogous to interacting subproblems (Barr and Feigenbaum 1981 vol 3, 531–540).

Interaction-activation model A perceptual type of parallel-distributed processing network which is designed to discriminate among different letters and words. A multilayered type of processing system in which each unit can take on a variety of values depending on the input. Each unit possesses a weight which is a function of the connection strengths. The weight processes the input to arrive at the value of the unit. Once the value surpasses the threshold the output value changes from 0 to the difference between the activation value and the threshold. The units are connected in excitatory and inhibitory patterns.

Interactive classifier A classifier that utilizes the data of a knowledge base and knowledge about its representation to aid the maintainer in describing new knowledge base objects and adding them to the knowledge base. It helps the user avoid adding new knowledge which would produce inconsistencies or errors. A dialogue between the user and the classifier determines where in the existing system the new object needs to be placed (Finin and Silverman 1986, 79).

Interactive environment An environment employing a language that is able to respond instantly, without the need of compilation. A rich supply of programming aids can be called on by the programmer at any time. An interactive environment is an important asset in developing AI programs (Tello 1988, 392).

Interactive graphics Hot graphics (Shafer Sep/Oct 1988, 11).

Interactive language An interpreted language. A language that does not have to be compiled before being run. An interactive language allows for faster development time because the programmer can immediately check out changes made by running the program without compiling it. LISP is an interactive language (Reedy and Kaplan 1986, 68).

Interconnection   One of the two primary elements of a neural network. Processing elements are the other (Caudill Dec 1987, 47).

Interconnections per second   A measure of the efficiency of neural nets (Obermeier and Barron 1989, 218).

Interdependent subproblem   A problem that can be broken up into subproblems whose solutions are dependent on which subproblems have already been solved. *See also* Independent subproblem (Barr and Feigenbaum 1981 vol 1, 81–83).

Interestingness   Rank ordering sets of rules so that certain sets are specified as needing to be used first in solving a given problem. The most needed rules are the most interesting rules (Smith 1989, 98).

INTERLISP   A dialect of LISP known for its excellent development and maintenance environment (Harmon and King 1985, 83–85; Rosenberg 1986, 94).

Intermediate processing   The processing of lines, regions, and shape information in vision.

Internal representation   All which takes place in a system after incoming data have been received and up to the time output is given. Internal representation includes deduction, search, planning, and learning. Most important, internal representation is a language used to describe and abstract events and objects. It is a basic concept used by Charniak in his book *Introduction to Artificial Intelligence* (Charniak and McDermott 1985, 7, 9, 12).

Internal sensor   A sensor used in robots to give readings on the movements or internal forces in the robot (Rosenberg 1986, 94).

INTERNIST   An expert system in the domain of internal medicine which later became known as CADUCEUS. It is written in INTERLISP. It is capable of diagnosing over 500 diseases. It accounts for the symptoms by producing a combination of diseases. Having more than one disease at a time is a distinct possibility in internal medicine. INTERNIST uses both forward and backward chaining. It uses forward chaining to generate possible diagnoses and then uses backward chaining to confirm the presence of the necessary symptoms for the diagnosis to apply. It has difficulties in developing a good overview of diseases that have a complex interaction of symptoms. It also spends too much time querying physicians about irrelevant diseases. Its successor CADUCEUS was developed to overcome these problems. *Contrast with* MYCIN, a backward-chaining system (Newquist May 1987, 69–71; Johnson 1986, 182; Harmon and King, 1985, 140–145; Barr and Feigenbaum 1981 vol 1, 197–201).

Interoperability   The connecting of diverse information systems. A second more advanced level of interoperability is the cooperative interaction of different information systems to achieve a given goal. A third form of interoperability is the exchange of information among diverse information sources, some of which are intelligent. This latter form of interoperability is sometimes called intelligent interoperability (Manola 1990, 26).

INTERPLAN   A type of nonhierarchical planner. As with most nonhierarchical planners, it has difficulties with interacting subproblems. It deals with interacting subproblems by reordering the sequence in which subproblems are attacked. Its ability to reorder goals is greater than HACKER, another well-known nonhierarchical planner (Barr and Feigenbaum 1981 vol 3, 535–540).

INTERPRET   A vision program that uses models as an aid in interpreting a scene. INTERPRET uses an hypothesize-and-test strategy. In contrast to earlier vision programs, INTERPRET uses a top-down approach. It emphasizes the difference between scene domain and image domain (Barr and Feigenbaum 1981 vol 3, 147–155).

Interpretation The assignment of a truth value to a proposition in logic. *See also* Semantic resolution (Dos Reis 1988, 50; Luger and Stubblefield 1989, 43, 53).

Interpreted language A language that requires an interpreter to execute programs. An interactive language. A language that does not have to be compiled before being run. An interpreted language allows for faster development time because the programmer can immediately check out changes made by running the program without compiling it. LISP and BASIC are interpreted languages (Rosenberg 1986, 95).

Interpreter 1. The part of a blackboard expert system that follows the general plan laid out by the scheduler by deciding which rule will next be scrutinized and executed. 2. The inference engine of a production expert system. The interpreter decides how to apply domain knowledge. 3. The part of a production system that executes the rules. It is sometimes referred to as the rule interpreter. 4. A program in interpreted languages that can immediately process and execute a procedure description. An interpreter allows interactive programming. *See also* Interpreted language (Neiman and Martin 1986, 62; Johnson 1986, 83; Winston 1979, 361; Brownston et al 1986, 7, 448; Townsend 1987b, 381; Winston 1984, 34, 287; Waterman 1986, 392).

Interpretive expert system An expert system that is designed to analyze and explain raw data. Example: the analysis and interpretation of data from a radio telescope. It differs from diagnostic expert systems in that it is not looking for a diagnosis or fault (Hayes-Roth et al 1983, 13).

Interrupt facility The ability of an expert system to stop its ongoing process to take in new data, or to deal with more than one goal at the same time (Hayes-Roth et al 1983, 176).

Interruption analysis A method used in eliciting data from an expert. When an expert is talking about a process, interrupting him or her and asking in detail the rationale for his or her actions (Olson and Rueter 1988, 25).

Intersecting hierarchies Two hierarchies that have objects which inherit characteristics from both hierarchies. Example: the classes of boats and cars, and the instance of an amphibious vehicle that inherits characteristics from both hierarchies (Walters and Nielsen 1988, 221–225).

Intersection multiple inheritance Inheritance from two different parent slots of those values the two different parent slots have in common (Walters and Nielsen 1988, 232–233).

Intersection node A node in semantic networks that represents a common concept for two other nodes (Luger and Stubblefield 1989, 342).

Intersection paths Two paths in a semantic network that converge on a relationship between two concepts (Luger and Stubblefield 1989, 342).

Intersection search A search which was proposed by Quillian and used in associative networks, which decides if one object or concept is related to another and finds the concept common to the two concepts. Assume a system with the two concepts cat and bird. Both terms are activated and the activation spreads until there is an intersection. The two terms may then be considered to be related. The common concept found will be that both cat and bird are animals (Jackson 1986, 56; Chabris 1989, 49, 68).

Intersect rule A rule used to find the elements that two lists have in common. This can be used in approximate pattern-matching procedures. Assume a set of lists in a data base. Each list represents a chemical compound. Each list consists of the name of the compound and a set of numbers, with each number corresponding to a physical characteristic of the compound. Introduce an unknown compound and match each list in the data base by counting the number of matching numbers and assigning a numerical score which is a function of the match. Collect all of the scores over a given threshold value in a list and sort the list. The highest score in the list is the best match. The intersect rule is a variation of Bratko's difference rule (Castle 1988, 71).

Interviewing   A type of manual knowledge acquisition in which the knowledge engineer questions a domain expert so as to obtain information to build an expert system. Guidelines for such interviews include being as specific as possible, preparing ahead of time, using the expert's language as much as possible, avoiding interrupting the expert, and recording his responses (Parsaye and Chignell 1988, 343–344).

Intrinsic characteristic   Any of the following characteristics of a scene: tilt, reflectivity, smoothness, and texture.

Intrinsic image   Orientation, reflectance, distance from the camera, and incident illumination (Barr and Feigenbaum 1981 vol 3, 238–242).

Introspection   The capacity of artificial intelligence programs to reflect on their own reasoning. Examples: being able to respond to the questions why and how (Winston 1979, 301–304; Winston 1984, 227–233).

Introspective modeling   A psychological technique of eliciting information from a domain expert, which is based on the work of the psychologist E. B. Titchener. The technique consists of the domain expert talking about the sensations, memories, feeling, and images one experiences in solving a problem. It is similar to free association. Contrast this approach with a standard question-answer interview (Evanson 1988, 36–38).

Intuition   Immediate comprehension or insight. It is argued that true experts have this ability and can immediately go to the heart of the problem, without complex reasoning. One possible way this can be approximated with an AI system is to have a system that carries out extremely powerful pruning of a search space at the beginning of the search (Johnson 1986, 255–256).

Inverse dynamics   A set of equations that delineate the necessary forces and torques for producing motion in a robot (Wang and Butner 1987, 28).

Inverse kinematics   The transformation between the cartesian coordinate system and the coordinate system peculiar to a robot (Wang and Butner 1987, 27).

Invertibility   The ability to use a query to ascertain the truthfulness of a fact (Kowalski Aug 1985, 193).

IPL   *See* Information Processing Language.

IQS   The language INTELLECT.

IRIS   A medical expert system for diagnosing diseases, which is used to experiment with different means of representing medical knowledge, different clinical strategies, and different approaches to consultation. It employs both semantic nets and production rules. The semantic net holds information about the different diseases' symptoms and treatments. IRIS was developed at Rutgers University (Hunt 1986, 140).

Irregular rules   Rules that contain contradictory information. Other types of error rules include identical rules, orphan rules, and unfireable rules (Lane Jun 1989, 305).

IRUS   A natural language data base interface that attempts to understand the user's query before answering it (Bates et al 1986, 617–630).

Is-a   A link used in object-oriented languages and semantic nets. It is a link between a class and more specific objects. Example: John is-a male. *Compare with* AKO; Has-a link (Jackson 1986, 76; Charniak and McDermott 1985, 25; Brachman 1983, 30–36).

ISA   A business-scheduling program, a forward-chaining system, developed by DEC using OPS5 (Hunt 1986, 140–141).

ISIS   A factory-planning system which is designed to produce optimal job-work schedules (Hunt 1986, 141–142).

Island driving 1. A technique used in some expert systems in which new information is found and as a result a part of a solution is pursued and extended as far as possible to another island of information. It is considered a part of what is known as opportunistic problem solving. 2. The process in speech recognition of choosing the words in a sentence that are most likely to be interpreted accurately. The program then attempts to link these words by choosing the interpretation of the remaining words which most likely will work with the previously selected words (Mishkoff 1986, 5–8; Barr and Feigenbaum 1981 vol 1, 339–340; Barr and Feigenbaum 1981 vol 3, 23, 519).

Isolated-word recognition A method of speech recognition that uses pattern-matching techniques as a means of identifying individual words. (Mishkoff 1986, 6–2).

Isolated-word system A type of speech-understanding system in which each word presented must be clearly isolated in time from its neighbors (Hunt 1986, 142).

Isomorphic/iconic/analogical representation A structure with direct structural and metric relations to some of the properties of the objects being represented. There is a direct correspondence between the scene and its representation. That is, the different aspects of the representation are not scattered throughout the computer program, but are together and organized in such a way as to resemble the real-world object. Example: a map of a city. Isomorphic representations are also referred to as iconic and analogical representations (Fischler and Firschein Dec 1986, 44; Hunt 1986, 142).

Item A linked list of records. An example of the use of linked lists is to create rule items. A rule item holds the attribute value, the rule number, and if the item is a consequent or a condition. Each clause in a rule is made up of a rule item. Rule items are linked to one another by pointers (Thompson and Thompson Apr 1985, 326–327).

Iteration To repeat. A type of control structure that allows the repeating of a process. Example: Do loop. Recursion is a repeating procedure commonly used in artificial intelligence programming, but it is usually classified separately (Winston 1984, 63).

Iterative approach A procedure of developing an expert system. At each state of development the output is compared to the desired output and the necessary adjustments are made.

Iterative deepening A method of limiting a search procedure so that the search procedure does not take up an inordinate amount of time. It is frequently used in conjunction with the ALPHA-BETA pruning algorithm which is a depth-first algorithm. Iterative deepening does a breadth-first search of the state space and checks the amount of time left to see if it has enough time to allow the ALPHA-BETA pruning algorithm to burrow deeper into the search space (Chabris 1989, 187–188).

Iterative enhancement A means of constructing expert systems. The designer starts with what is known as a set of problem scenarios. A problem scenario consists of a problem and a proposed solution. The knowledge engineer then constructs an expert system to solve the problem scenarios. After the system has been tested, more problems are added and the expert system is iteratively enhanced with problem scenarios to solve the new problems. *See also* Rapid prototyping (Brownston et al 1986, 356).

Iterative loop A characteristic of some expert systems which allows the user to enter a set of data of indeterminant size. The user has control over when all the data are entered.

JARS A robotics control language developed by the Jet Propulsion Laboratory (Mishkoff 1986, 5–19).

JIRA The Japanese Industrial Robot Association, which was the first robotics association (Rosenberg 1986, 97).

Job aids Small knowledge systems used to take the place of checklists and procedure manuals (Harmon et al 1988, 266).

Johnson hierarchical clustering A technique used in eliciting data from experts, based on the judgment of similarities among objects. The only assumption made is that an object either belongs to a class of objects or it does not belong. *Contrast with* Multidimensional scaling (Olson and Rueter 1988, 28–29).

Joining The building of a new table of data from more than one table. The records common to both tables are brought into the new table. Fields from each table may be brought into the new table or view. Such commands can be implemented in building intelligent data bases in languages like PROLOG (*IXL The Machine Learning System Users Manual* 1987, 30).

Joint The joints in a robot. The portion of the robot that allows movement of the robot's arms and legs (Rosenberg 1986, 97).

Jointed-arm robot A robot that has joints that allow the robot freedom of motion (Rosenberg 1986, 97).

Judgmental knowledge Knowledge found in production rules. That is, knowledge based on if/then decisions (Barr and Feigenbaum 1981 vol 1, 277).

Jumbo An artificial intelligence program written by Douglas Hofstadter. The program is made up of active data structures called codelets. The codelets combine syllables into words and then sentences in what at first is a random process; but gradually the randomness begins to drop out and meaningful outputs become more common (Johnson 1986, 289–292).

Justification A tracing facility in an expert system which can be used to follow the chain of inferences that led to a conclusion (Hu 1989, 300).

Justification truth maintenance A type of truth maintenance in which each fact has only one supporting statement. It uses dependency-directed backtracking to retract the supporting statement that produced the inconsistency. This type of truth maintenance system is susceptible to looping. For some, justification truth maintenance includes any system in which facts can be accumulated but not withdrawn. *Contrast with* Assumption-based truth maintenance (Walters and Nielsen 1988, 269–270).

Justifier The explanation procedure in a blackboard expert system (Hayes-Roth et al 1983, 18–19).

KAM *See* Knowledge Acquisition Module.

KANDOR A frame-based knowledge-engineering language, written in LISP and built at the Fairchild Laboratory for Artificial Intelligence Research (Hunt 1986, 144).

Karnaugh map A diagrammatic representation of a logic function, which is used to understand better the relationship among the logic variables (Rosenberg 1986, 99).

KAS An expert system tool used in the development of PROSPECTOR. Its knowledge representation consists of partitioned semantic networks. During execution it can be stopped by the user and given new information. It uses Bayesian reasoning to estimate probability values. The control mechanism is a variant of best-first search. The use of multiple instantiations in KAS is limited (Hayes-Roth et al 1983, 177–180, 291–297; Brownston et al 1986, 358–359).

KB editor A knowledge-base editor whose function is to aid in preventing inconsistencies and errors when addition or modification of a knowledge base is needed (Finin and Silverman 1986, 79).

KBMS *See* Knowledge-based management system (Brodie et al 1986, 19–27).

K-connector A hyperarc (Luger and Stubblefield 1989, 105).

Kestrel Institute A nonprofit organization that encourages research in artificial intelligence (Hunt 1986, 145).

Key One or more attributes that can be used to uniquely identify a record or relation. Keys can be used to improve the search process in PROLOG programs (Denney 1988, 46).

Keyword 1. Reserved terms in an expert system that refer to words which are used to create, access, and modify syntactic representations. The terms if, then, and else are examples of keywords. The greater the number of keywords in an expert system shell, the greater is the complexity and possibly the sophistication. The number of keywords can vary from 5 to 200 plus in expert system shells. *See also* BNF production. 2. The words paid attention to by a noise-disposal processor (Schildt 1987, 262, 265, 272).

Keyword analysis A simple language analysis used in programs like ELIZA. The program inspects input for certain keywords. When it finds the keywords it responds in some prearranged manner. Keyword analysis completely ignores context and sentence structure. As a result, it can easily misunderstand a sentence. *Compare with* Semantic analysis; Syntactic analysis (Mishkoff 1986, 4–9).

Keyword message A message in Smalltalk which has one or more arguments and multipart selectors. An example of a keyword message is "specialArray at: 5 put: IBM-PC." What this means is "put IBM-PC in position 5 of specialArray." "at:" and "put:" are the message selectors (Stein 1988, 20; Rubin Aug 1985, 28).

Killer heuristic A heuristic that stops a particular move or strategy because that move or strategy has proved unprofitable in similar previous situations (Barr and Feigenbaum 1981 vol 1, 102).

Killer-move heuristic A heuristic used in chess programs in conjunction with the ALPHA-BETA algorithm. It is employed when the program notes the opponent has a very strong move available to it. The program therefore puts the opponent's strong move at the head of the list of moves to examine. In this way search time is reduced because little time is spent on the alternative, weaker moves (Chabris 1989, 189–190).

Kind An entire subclass of a class. An example of a kind would be Oldsmobiles when Oldsmobiles are considered as a subclass of automobiles. *Compare with* Instance, which refers to a single object (Jackson 1986, 59).

KIPS *See* Knowledge Information Processing Systems.

K-line theory The theory according to Minsky, whereby a person in having an idea or solving a problem creates a K-line. A K-line is a network that is connected to all currently active agents. Each agent now has access to that information and can use it for problem-solving purposes. K-line theory is the memory portion of Minsky's theory of "agents" which he presents in his book *Society of the Mind* (Waldrop 1987, 127).

KL-One A frame-based knowledge-engineering language, written in INTERLISP-D and built at Bolt, Beranek, and Newman (Hunt 1986, 145).

KMS A knowledge-engineering language which employs both frames and rules. Some of its features include linear discriminant, the use of Bayes' theorem, and frame-based inferencing. It was written in LISP at the University of Maryland (Hunt 1986, 145).

Knights' tour A version of the traveling-salesman problem. It uses a knight on a chessboard. The goal is to have the knight visit every square on the chessboard only once and return to its starting point using the shortest possible route (Vita, 1987, 30–36).

KNOBS An expert system used by the tactical air command for mission planning. It represents knowledge in rules and frames. It is written in FRL and ZETALISP and was developed by the MITRE Corporation (Hunt 1986, 146).

KNOESPHERE A predecessor to Doug Lenat's CYC (Tello 1988, 14, 16).

Knowledge In artificial intelligence, symbolic information used by a domain expert to solve problems. Facts and relationships used to solve problems. In expert systems knowledge is stored in such structures as working memory elements, frames, clauses, and rules. Knowledge may be classified as either declarative or procedural. Most knowledge in expert systems is declarative in nature. *See also* Compiled knowledge; Deep knowledge; Dynamic knowledge base; Knowledge representation; Metaknowledge; Shallow knowledge (Hayes-Roth et al 1983, 401; Harmon and King 1985, 30–33, 39, 262; Brownston et al 1986, 448; Barr and Feigenbaum 1981 vol 1, 144; Parsaye and Chignell 1988, 35).

Knowledge acquisition The procedure in artificial intelligence of interacting with an external source, usually a domain expert, to find and organize knowledge for the purpose of transferring the knowledge to an expert system to solve problems. There are two types of knowledge acquisition—manual knowledge acquisition and automated knowledge acquisition. Manual knowledge acquisition refers to such procedures as a knowledge engineer interviewing a domain expert, and verbal protocol analysis. Manual knowledge acquisition can also be formally broken down into the stages of identification, conceptualization, formalization, implementation, and testing. Automated knowledge acquisition refers to the process of getting computers to learn from external sources, especially from experts. Two computer-automated techniques used to achieve this goal are computer interviewing of experts and entering examples into the computer. Rules can then be constructed from the knowledge gained. Other types of automated knowledge acquisition may include learning in neural nets, and learning by discovery. Machine learning is often used interchangeably with the term automated knowledge acquisition, although machine learning is a somewhat broader term. *See also* Learning (Hayes-Roth et al 1983, 24–25, 129, 401; Walters and Nielsen 1988, 34–45; Parsaye May 1988, 51; Thompson and Thompson Nov 87, 25; Harmon and King 1985, 80, 82; Brownston et al 1986, 18–19, 448; Barr and Feigenbaum 1981 vol 1, 80–83, 91–92, 145; Parsaye and Chignell 1988, 341–363; Jackson 1986, 10).

Knowledge-acquisition bottleneck The large amount of time required to develop the rules necessary for an expert system. The problems include poorly delineated knowledge, large bodies of knowledge, and the lack of availability of experts. The knowledge-acquisition bottleneck is in part being solved by the use of induction expert systems. (Thompson and Thompson Nov 1986, 150; Johnson 1986, 162, 238).

Knowledge-acquisition interface The part of an expert system used to enter data into the expert system. It includes the rule editor of an expert system. In more sophisticated systems it may include a syntax checker and methods for checking for rule conflicts.

Knowledge Acquisition Module (KAM) It is used for intelligent text retrieval. The program retrieves text based on constraints given to it by the user. It was developed by Phase Linear Inc. (Newquist Feb 1988, 69).

Knowledge-acquisition module The portion of an expert system responsible for acquiring and asserting new facts and rules into the knowledge base. In some systems the knowledge-acquisition module has the ability to scrutinize new rules to check for syntax errors and to see if they are in conflict with already existing rules (Townsend 1987a, 134).

Knowledge atoms The elements of schemata (Rumelhart and McClelland 1986, 203).

Knowledge base One of the two critical parts of an expert system. The other part is the inference engine. The portion of an expert system that consists of the rules (rule base) and the facts (fact base) of a particular domain of knowledge. A knowledge base is not considered to be a table of numerical information, nor is it an algorithmic solution to a problem. Some authorities prefer the term knowledge-based expert system to expert system (Townsend 1987a, 129; Schildt 1987, 61–62; Brownston et al 1986, 22–23; Forsyth and Naylor 1985, 11–30).

Knowledge-based approach 1. An AI program that derives its power from vast stores of knowledge as opposed to a powerful search mechanism. 2. A type of automatic programming that uses an expert system endowed with the ability of the expert programmers to produce program code. The PSI-PECOS system uses a knowledge-based approach. Other approaches to automatic programming include the deductive approach, transformational approach, and high-level language approach (Tello 1988, 420; Chabris 1989, 296).

Knowledge-based integrated information system A type of data base management system that can draw on data from multiple heterogeneous data bases, furnish relational capabilities, define object methods, combine data in novel and productive ways, provide flexible levels of integration, and provide intelligent interoperability (Manola 1990, 28–36).

Knowledge-based management system (KBMS) 1. A combination of a data base system and an expert system. That is, it has both stored knowledge and inferred knowledge. A system providing highly efficient management of large, shared knowledge bases for knowledge-directed systems. The data base portion of the KBMS provides efficient querying of large amounts of data. From expert systems it inherits deductive reasoning, backtracking, control knowledge, automatic classification, knowledge explanation, recursive queries, dynamic human intervention, and rich knowledge representation. A KBMS may have multiple types of representation available such as logic rules, frames, and production rules. The information found in a KBMS is more likely to be that expected of an expert, rather than the simple data found in most data bases. The use of such representation schemes as structured rules is what really sets a KBMS apart from a data base. A KBMS is more likely to operate on a class of objects rather than a single object as does a data base. For example, "all four-engine passenger planes" is a statement about a class of objects. "The airplane with the serial # a27" is more characteristic of a statement associated with a data base query. Heuristic search can be employed to reduce the search path. This type of heuristic search is often referred to as query optimization. Recursive queries are available. Rules can be used to provide integrity constraints on data base data. The use of a knowledge-based management system opens up the possibility of temporal reasoning. The possibility of interpretations of null answers is available. A KBMS provides intelligent assistance to the user. An example is finding alternative budgets for a manager. It should be able to apply knowledge to the data to produce reports, when the data indicate a report is necessary, as opposed to the current function in most data base systems which is to produce a standard end-of-the-month report. Object-oriented data bases are a type of KBMS. The construction of an object-oriented data base can be facilitated through an inheritance mechanism. Synonyms for KBMS include inferential data base, deductive data base, expert system kernels, intelligent data base, and expert data base. *Compare with* Expert system (shell), which does not have the data base characteristics of a KBMS. *See also* Object-oriented data bases for information on the unique advantages of such artificial intelligence data bases. 2. One of three subsystems of an expert system. Under this definition the KBMS automatically stores and organizes knowledge, and it begins the search process for information necessary for the solution of the problem. The other two parts of the KBMS are the inference engine and the human interface (Hunt 1986, 146; Firdman 1986, 82; Barr and Feigenbaum 1981 vol 2, 163–173; Brodie et al 1986, 19–27, 69).

Knowledge-based partitioning The breaking up of a set of rules into subsets. Then, when a particular state in the problem-solving process is reached, the expert system goes to the subset of rules which is relevant to solving this portion of the problem. The advantage for this kind of partitioning is efficiency in that the expert system does not have to search the entire rule set.

Knowledge-based programming Refers to the important factor of separation of program and control. This is frequently the key distinction made between conventional computer programs and artificial intelligence programs like expert systems.

Knowledge-based system Knowledge system (Tello, Jul 1985, 71).

Knowledge chunking *See* Chunking (Ricketts 1988, 51).

Knowledge crafting The process of building expert systems (Walters and Nielsen 1988, iv).

Knowledge diagramming The process of diagramming a knowledge base so as to gain a better understanding of the knowledge base. Knowledge diagramming includes top-down descriptions, objects and their attributes, links between objects, event knowledge, performance knowledge, and metaknowledge (Hillman 1988, 38).

Knowledge elicitation A type of automated knowledge acquisition which is used to elicit knowledge about the basic description of objects. These descriptions can then be used as a means of constructing rules for an expert system. Repertory grids are an example of knowledge elicitation (Parsaye and Chignell 1988, 347).

Knowledge encoding The process of entering facts, rules, objects, and other knowledge into an expert system (Harmon et al 1988, 164–165).

Knowledge engineer A professional who interacts with a domain expert in order to obtain the necessary facts and relationships among the facts from the domain expert to build an expert system. He or she should know which tools to use and how to use them; have interpersonal skills; and be able to test expert systems, design interesting interfaces, construct well-organized knowledge bases, verify knowledge bases, and avoid combinatorial explosion (Citrenbaum et al 1987, 33; Johnson 1986, 18; Schildt 1987, 86–89; Hayes-Roth et al 1983, 129; Harmon and King 1985, 5; Brownston et al 1986, 449; Waldrop 1987, 38).

Knowledge-engineering bottleneck *See* Knowledge-acquisition bottleneck.

Knowledge explanation The ability of an expert system to answer how and why questions during an expert system consultation (*Intelligence Compiler Users Manual* 1986, 56).

Knowledge frame A sophisticated form of knowledge representation that can include object frames, tables, and b-trees (*Intelligence Compiler Users Manual* 1986, 56).

Knowledge-fusion problem The problem of integrating a number of diverse sources of knowledge into a single expert system (*Knowledge-Based Systems* 1986, 1–27).

Knowledge information processing systems The computer systems being built by the Japanese in their Fifth Generation AI project, which will be able to efficiently process information in large knowledge bases. They have symbolic processing abilities and excellent human interfaces (Hunt 1986, 149; Rosenberg 1986, 100).

Knowledge island A related set of rules. The grouping of hypotheses into sets of hypotheses connected by links. The links established may be weak or strong. The links are used to guide the decision as to which knowledge island to try next. Knowledge islands are found in the expert systems Goldworks and NEXPERT. Dividing rules into knowledge islands allows for shorter search times (Arcidiacono Nov 1988, 114; Oman, Sep 1988, 100; Tello 1988, 302).

Knowledge-line theory *See* K-line theory.

Knowledge media The representation, storage, and dissemination of knowledge in society. Artificial intelligence is being touted as a new knowledge medium which will take its place alongside books and films (Tello 1989, 19–20; Luger and Stubblefield 1989, 598–600).

Knowledge modeling The procedure by which knowledge engineers organize the data they gain from domain experts (Harmon et al 1988, 163–164).

Knowledge-programming environment Tool kit (Citrenbaum et al 1987, 31).

Knowledge relevance problem The problem of an expert system asking irrelevant questions. An example is asking questions pertaining to diagnosing carburetion problems when the automobile uses fuel injection. This problem can be handled by carefully designing the rules, using a partitioned rule base, or using a frame-based system (*Knowledge-Based Systems* 1986, 1–26).

Knowledge representation A systematic means of organizing, portraying, and storing knowledge in a computer program which leads to knowledgeable behavior. The most common structures used to represent knowledge in artificial intelligence programs are attribute values, object-attribute values, frames, semantic nets, rules, analogical representations, bit patterns, conceptual dependencies, clauses, and, to a lesser extent, procedural representations. Trees and lists are also classified as methods of knowledge representation. Trees are really graphs that must be translated to a form of knowledge representation like lists before the computer can use the data in the tree. Lists are a form of knowledge representation usually found only in full-fledged languages like LISP and PROLOG. Some of the more sophisticated expert system tools do include lists as a form of knowledge representation. Knowledge-representation schemes can be judged by their ability to absorb knowledge, retrieve knowledge, and the degree to which they lend themselves to reason about knowledge. Important characteristics of knowledge representation include: logical adequacy, heuristic power, notational convenience, scope, grain size, modularity, understandability, explicitness, conciseness, the ability to hide less important details and make prominent the more important details; the ability to uncover natural constraints; the degree to which it lends itself to storage, retrieval, and computation. Another important dimension is the degree to which a knowledge-representation scheme is declarative or procedural. Though confidence factors are not used as a means of organizing knowledge as, say, a frame does, they do represent important knowledge. Most medical systems, for example, use a version of confidence factors to represent knowledge about the reliability of a symptom in indicating a particular disease process. Knowledge representation is an important subject in both artificial intelligence and cognitive science (Jackson 1986, 29; Salzberg Aug 1987, 32; Johnson 1986, 179–182; Schildt 1987, 209–212; Walters and Nielsen 1988, 320–332; Harmon and King 1985, 34–38; Barr and Feigenbaum, 1981 vol 1, 143–222, 229–232; Jackson 1986, 29; Chabris 1989, 39; Fischler and Firschein Dec 1986, 43–49; Brachman and Smith 1980, McCalla and Cercone 1983).

Knowledge-representation hypothesis An hypothesis coined by Brian Smith that states: "Any mechanically embodied intelligent process will be comprised of structural ingredients that (a) we as external observers naturally take to represent a propositional account of the knowledge that the overall process exhibits, and (b) independent of such external semantical attribution, play a formal but causal and essential role in engendering the behavior that manifests that knowledge." He is talking about the use of such structures as abstract rules to represent knowledge and manage the processing of the information in the system. Example: show-plane(Y) IF engine-size(X, Y) AND write("The plane is a") AND write(Y) AND write("The engine size is") AND write(X). This rule can be used to retrieve all planes in the data base and print their engine sizes. The rule is an explicit representation of knowledge and it can be readily understood by relatively naive observers. Notice, this rule does not have concrete knowledge in it; it instead uses the variables X and Y. The concrete knowledge is found elsewhere in the data base. The rule is an abstract representation of knowledge satisfying the first requirement. At the same time, the rule controls the processing, of the knowledge, thus satisfying the second requirement that the propositions directly cause the behavior of the system. The knowledge-representation hypothesis essentially states intelligent processes are composed of a dynamic, process-oriented component and a static component which is the repository of data. The knowledge-representation hypothesis is embodied in systems whose knowledge is represented declaratively, and which possesses the property of being able capitalize on the use of the knowledge to the extent that it is able to simulate intelligent behavior. *See also* Reflection hypothesis (Brachman and Levesque 1986, 71; Brachman 1987, 7; Luger and Stubblefield 1989, 288–289).

Knowledge-representation language (KRL)
1. A frame-based language whose primary function is to model a body of human knowledge. A type of computer language which provides data structures and control structures more flexible than those found in conventional programming languages. The provided flexibility makes them useful in approximating human intelligence. 2. A set of languages which usually employ semantic networks or frames as a means of knowledge representation. A KRL emphasizes the encoding of knowledge rather than the development of procedures to process knowledge. A pure KRL is

not meant to be used in procedural processes like iteration and recursion. KRL languages, in contrast to LISP or PROLOG, come with built-in complex data structures like frames. Examples: OPS5, frame-based languages, and semantic network-based systems. Some of the best-known knowledge-representation languages are KRL, CRL, SRL, and UNITS (Salzberg Aug 1987, 32; Brodie et al 1986, 21, 23; Luger and Stubblefield 1989, 334; Hu 1989, 179; Jackson 1986, 68; Barr and Feignbaum 1981 vol 1, 221; Tello 1988, 415–416).

Knowledge source 1. A body of knowledge relevant to solving a particular problem. The body of knowledge may be encoded in rules, frames, or other types of representation. An expert system may have multiple knowledge sources. 2. A specialized source of expertise in a blackboard system that can be called on to solve a particular part of a problem. It is used to place information on the blackboard and use information from the blackboard to compute new information and post the new information to the blackboard. There are multiple knowledge sources in a blackboard system and they are modular. The knowledge sources are relatively independent of one another. They only influence each other by what they write on the blackboard. Knowledge sources may be made up of facts, heuristics, and algorithms (Walters and Nielsen 1988, 303–317; Barr and Feigenbaum 1981 vol 1, 125–128, 336, 343–348; Barr and Feigenbaum 1981 vol 3, 25–27; Parsaye and Chignell 1988, 145; Hunt 1986, 151).

Knowledge structure Structures used to store knowledge and reason about the knowledge. Facts, frames, and rules are knowledge structures (Parsaye and Chignell 1988, 35).

Knowledge system 1. An alternative name for expert system. 2. For some the term knowledge system emphasizes a large body of knowledge in the form of rules and facts along with an inference mechanism that can be used to solve problems. The notion that the system is an expert which can take the place of a human expert is deemphasized. It is the equivalent of a large expert system. 3. Small expert systems; this meaning is not favored. 4. Induction programs, decision-modeling languages, and rule-oriented mathematical modeling systems. Another term which is a synonym for knowledge system is intelligent assistant. *Contrast with* Knowledge-based management system (Tello Jul 1985, 71; Townsend 1987a, 112; Mishkoff 1986, G-2; Harmon and King 1985, 5; Smith 1989, 107; Tello 1988, 96; Giboney 1986, 55).

Knowledge table A knowledge-engineering design tool. It includes such information as parameters, the values of the parameters, and in what rules the parameters are located. This table enables the user to locate rules that have parameters in common (Phillips and Sanders 1988, 66–67).

Knowledge transformation The transformation of knowledge that must take place when knowledge in one expert system shell must be transferred to another expert system shell, or when knowledge in two different expert systems shells must be combined, or when two expert systems must be made to communicate with each other (Rothman 1988, 28).

Knowledge utility General knowledge modules that can be used to develop customized applications. A knowledge utility consists of the following: a set of knowledge bases that concentrates on a particular area of study; a means of querying and maintaining the knowledge base; a means of modifying the knowledge base for customized applications. CYC is an example of a system that can be used to build knowledge utilities (Tello 1989).

Kohonen learning rule The learning rule for a Kohonen network, which is written as $W\_new = W\_old + a(X - W\_old)$. X is the input pattern, a is the size of the training step, and W is the weight (Caudill Aug 1988, 63–64).

Kohonen self-organizing network A neural network that is capable of unsupervised learning. That is, it is capable of learning without having a tutor telling it if its answer is right or wrong during the training period. It consists of only one layer of processing units which are connected with one another and the outside world in a very complex fashion. A given unit can excite and inhibit surrounding units by means of these rich interconnections. Only one processing unit and its neighbors become dominant. These units are the ones whose weights can be adjusted. This neural network is able to model the distribution of the incoming data. A Kohonen network can also produce topology-preserving maps. The Kohonen network requires a large training set. It also performs best with big networks. The advantages of the Kohonen network include its speed, continuous learning, and self-organization abilities. *See also* Kohonen learning rule. *Contrast with* the Back-propagation rule (Caudill Aug 1988, 61–67; Bayle 1988, 43).

Kolmogorov's theorem The theorem that states: Given a real vector of dimension X, this vector may be mapped to any other real vector of dimension Y using a hierarchical neural network. The input vector must have a range from 0 to 1. The theorem shows that a hierarchical neural network can solve linearly separable problems (Caudill Jun 1988, 57).

KRL *See* Knowledge Representation Language.

L

Labeled arc A name of an arc in a network. Examples: "a kind of" and "is found in" (Forsyth and Naylor 1985, 132).

Labeled graph A graph with descriptions attached to its nodes (Luger and Stubblefield 1989, 80).

Labeled network A type of network in which the arcs have names.

Lady Lovelace's objection The argument named after Lady Ada Lovelace that states that computers can do only what they are told to do. This argument is in dispute with the more and more frequent finding by artificial intelligence programmers, who note their programs show unexpected behavior (Luger and Stubblefield 1989, 12).

Lambda binding The process of relating arguments to parameters when a procedure is first called in LISP. Assume the function (cube (A)). When this function is called by (cube (3)) the binding of A to 3 is lambda binding (Winston 1979, 276).

Lambda calculus A mathematical formalism for studying functions. This formalism was used as a basis for LISP and also for Scheme. Given a function F an argument N may be substituted for the parameter and the value of F can then be computed. The lambda calculus allows the argument N to be a function, and it allows functions to be returned by a function. Lambda calculus follows lexical scoping. Another characteristic of lambda calculus is that it provides for a distinction between a name and the entity for which the name stands (Luger and Stubblefield 1989, 269; Thompson and Thompson May 1987, 23).

Lambda conversion The process of associating the formal parameters of a function with an actual set of arguments. *See also* San Marco LISP Explorer.

Lambda expression A special type of list in the LISP language. A procedure in LISP that does not have a name. A means of defining locally the equivalent of a function in LISP. It does this by specifying the argument names and the rule for determining the function. Lambda is used if the function is expected to be used in only one place in the program. Its use avoids the unnecessary proliferation of function names in a program. In some LISP implementations lambda executes more quickly because LISP does not have to go searching for the function (Thompson and Thompson May 1987, 23).

Lambertian surface A surface that appears of identical luminescence from different points of view (Winston 1984, 356).

Language processing The use of computer programs to analyze and understand language. There are a number of methods under this rubric. Template matching in Weizenbaum's Eliza is the simplest type of language processing. Another is the augmented transition network. ATN was invented and used to parse sentences. It decides if a sentence is grammatical. It tests to see what kind of word or phrase it encounters. It asks what role a word may play in the sentence as a whole—subject, verb, object, and so on. The A in ATN stands for augmented and means it takes notes of what it finds. ATNs were first used in Wood's LUNAR. ATNs are more powerful than templates.

Laplacian operator An operator that is used to differentiate edges in images. It does this by calculating points where the laplacian is zero (Hunt 1986, 155).

Large expert system An expert system that is the equivalent of an excess of 1,500 rules (Harmon et al 1988, 20).

Large expert system tool An expert system tool capable of building large expert systems. The systems built with such tools usually require a team of professionals to construct and maintain the system. The two types of large expert system tools are hybrid tools and large narrow tools (Harmon and King 1985, 9–12, 83, 92).

Large-grain processing Performing computations through the use of large microprocessors in a parallel computer system (Hunt 1986, 155).

Large narrow tools A type of large expert system tool that is good at building large expert systems rapidly by using a single paradigm. S-1 is such a tool and it specializes in the diagnostic/ prescription paradigm (Harmon and King 1985, 9–12, 83; Rosenberg 1986, 103).

Lashley, Karl He proposed the concept of equipotentiality, which is the forerunner of distributed representation.

Late binding 1. The calling routine obtaining the address of a called routine at the time the routine is called, not at compile time. *Compare with* Early binding. 2. The detecting of data types at runtime, rather than at compile time. Late binding can give a language the extra flexibility required in artificial intelligence applications. Late binding lets more than one class use the same message. LISP is a late-binding language. Its drawback is a loss of speed. C is an example of a language that uses early binding. Late binding is used interchangeably with the term dynamic binding (Swaine, Jun 1989, 116; Pascoe 1986, 139; Duff 1986, 214; McGregor 1987, 50; Duntemann 1989, 138).

Lateral inhibition A property found in living nervous systems and in connectionist systems, which consists of two structures that represent mutually incompatible responses; the two structures are capable of inhibiting each other (Chabris 1989, 220–222, 296).

Later processing High-level vision.

Late-variable binding The ability to sustain a variable as unbound during a program run and at the same time to manipulate the unbound variable. LISP and PROLOG are two AI language with this ability (Luger and Stubblefield 1989, 197).

Lattice A hierarchy of frames which supports inheritance (Falmig, 1988, 51).

Lazy evaluation The evaluation of an expression only when another expression needs it. *Contrast with* Eager evaluation (Eisenbach and Sadler 1985, 186).

Lazy list Dynamic list.

LEACHIM A teaching program used in New York City which has won awards from students as the most popular teacher. It regularly uses poems and jokes while teaching academic subjects to 9- and 10-year olds (Frude 1983, 91–92).

Lead through A technique of teaching a robot a task by physically moving the robot through the task. It is similar to the term teach pendant (Rosenberg 1986, 103).

Leaf A terminal node in a tree structure (Forsyth and Naylor, 1985, 129; Minasi Jun 1988, 25).

LEAP An associative retrieval formalism that is the basis of the multiple indexing that enables the quick lookup capabilities of the artificial intelligence program SAIL. Items are an important data category in LEAP. Items are object-attribute value triples. Retrieval of knowledge is based on associations rather than specifying a memory location (Kenig Aug 1986, 30–32; Barr and Feigenbaum 1981 vol 1, 11, 41, 317).

Learned features Hidden units (Touretzky, and Pomerleau 1989, 227).

Learning A procedure in artificial intelligence by which an artificial intelligence program improves its performance by gaining knowledge. Many of the terms used in artificial intelligence to describe learning are borrowed from psychology. There are two basic types of learning—rote learning and cognitive learning. Many of the different types of learning such as learning by discovery, learning by example, learning by analogy, and others can be classed under cognitive learning. In a production system, learning can take place through the automatic acquisition, modification, or deletion of rules. The acquisition of new knowledge in induction-based systems is a form of learning. There are a number of other examples of programs that learn. One is neural nets. In neural nets learning is the adjustment of weights in a neural network in response to input data. The type of learning that takes place in some neural nets is spontaneous in nature. That is, it does not require an active outside agent to tell the program when it is correct or incorrect. Patrick Winston's hit-and-near-miss procedure illustrates a type of learning —concept formation. SHRDLU is an expert system that can ask for help when it does not know the answer: "Sorry I don't know steeple please explain." Another type of learning is learning from abstractions. One example is to use an abstraction of the human body which could then develop rules based on that abstraction. Finally, Lenat's EURISKO is able to learn from experience. Dependency records are an important means of aiding learning by failure, and they allow the retraction of facts which are later shown to be false. The terms automated knowledge acquisition and machine learning are frequently used in place of the term learning in artificial intelligence and they are more appropriate terms (Schildt 1987, 10–12; Hayes-Roth et al 1983, 401; Winston 1979, 29–43; Harmon and King 1985, 59–60; Brownston et al 1986, 449; Barr and Feigenbaum 1981 vol 1, 72; Obermeier and Barron 1989, 219).

Learning by analogy The ability to recognize the similarity between two problem areas and use rules developed in one problem area to solve a problem in the second problem area (Schildt 1987, 200; Barr and Feigenbaum 1981 vol 3, 443–445).

Learning by being told A computer program that can learn from instructions. One type is the kind of program which can accept abstract instructions and turn the instructions into rules. The other is using sophisticated tools which help the expert convert what he knows into rules. These tools may be debuggers and sophisticated editors. *Compare with* Unsupervised learning (Barr and Feigenbaum 1981 vol 3, 345–359; Rosenberg 1986, 104).

Learning by discovery   A type of unsupervised learning in which incoming data are used to form rules so that the system is able to understand the phenomenon under study. It is the investigation of a body of knowledge without a systematic plan. It is a trial-and-error type of learning. In this type of learning raw data are manipulated by the program to find relationships. No outside source is present to guide the program. Learning by discovery differs from learning by experience and learning by example in that there is much less focus on exactly what is to be learned. Learning by discovery is sometimes used interchangeably with learning from observation (Salzberg Feb 1988, 50; Schildt 1987, 200; Forsyth and Naylor 1985, 214–216; Luger and Stubblefield 1989, 569).

Learning by example   An induction approach to knowledge acquisition. Examples of a problem and the solution are given to the expert system and the expert system derives rules from the examples (Schildt 1987, 200; Barr and Feigenbaum 1981 vol 3, 360–511).

Learning by experience   A type of learning that involves trial-and-error learning. *Contrast with* Learning by example, which is learning from specific examples. *Contrast with* Learning by discovery, which is a type of learning that takes place with little focus on specifically what is to be learned (Salzberg Feb 1988, 49).

Learning by induction   A type of computer learning that involves using data and examples to construct rules. *Contrast with* Learning by interaction (Parsaye May 1988, 50).

Learning by interaction   A type of learning that involves being interviewed by a computer. *Contrast with* Learning by induction (Parsaye May 1988, 50).

Learning class   Hit and near miss.

Learning element   The part of a machine learning system responsible for altering the performance component of the system (Chabris 1989, 296–297).

Learning from instruction   A type of knowledge acquisition in which the program is told the information and the system must translate what it is told into an internal representation of what it was told.

Learning from observation   Learning by discovery, learning without a teacher, and unsupervised learning (Rosenberg 1986, 104).

Learning, incremental   *See* Incremental learning.

Learning, multiple concepts   *See* Multiple-concept learning.

Learning paradigm   Models of learning. Four well-known learning paradigms used in neural networks are pattern associators, auto associators, classification builders, and regularity detectors (Bayle 1988, 44).

Learning rule   A rule used in neural networks to modify the coefficients of transfer functions. The learning rule uses incoming data to decide how the coefficients are to be modified (Ingraham et al 1988, 17; Caudill Feb 1988, 57).

Learning, unsupervised   *See* Unsupervised learning.

Learning, verbal   *See* Verbal learning.

Learning without a teacher   Unsupervised learning.

Least commitment   An approach to problem solving and planning that holds no decision should be made until there is sufficient information. The employment of least commitment necessitates the capability of knowing when there is sufficient information to make a decision, when to hold off making a decision, and when to combine information to make a decision. In least-commitment planning, steps are cultivated only if there is good evidence to indicate this path will not have to be given up later. At the same time the weakest constraints possible are employed so that there is sufficient freedom to develop an optimal solution. The principle of least commitment has been criticized because it is frequently found to be unrealistic for many real-world problems (Tello 1988, 483; Wolfgram 1987, 68; Hayes-Roth et al 1983, 79, 106, 124; Barr and Feigenbaum 1981 vol 3, 24–25, 387, 552–556; Townsend and Feucht 1986, 173).

Least-cost search A heuristic search that chooses as its next node the node which will take the path of minimal cost (Schildt 1987, 38–41).

Least-cost strategy A property of some expert systems in which the rules involving the least cost are pursued first.

Least-mean-square algorithm A learning rule used in parallel-distributed processing systems, which has the capability of associating arbitrary input/output pairs which can then be used to compute arbitrary input/output functions. It is also called the delta rule and the Widrow/Hoff rule. *See also* Delta rule (Caudill Dec 1987, 52).

Least-mean-squared training law Delta rule. (Caudill Feb 1988, 56).

Least-mean-square law Delta rule.

Left-hand side 1. The condition portion of a rule in a forward-chaining production system that must be matched to working-memory elements before the right-hand side of the rule can be executed. 2. The subgoals that must be satisfied before the goal on the right-hand side can be satisfied, when an OPS5 production system is being used in a backward-chaining mode. 3. A set of symbols in grammar rules that can be replaced by another set of symbols (Brownston et al 1986, 12–17, 449).

Left memory A data structure in the Rete match algorithm, which holds the different combinations of working-memory elements and variable bindings that make up a consistent match for the condition element currently being scrutinized and for all prior condition elements for a given node (Brownston et al 1986, 237–239, 449; Rosenberg 1986, 104–105).

Legal-analysis system An expert system used to assist lawyers in assault and battery cases. Its method of knowledge representation is a semantic net. The user presents the system with a set of facts pertaining to the case and the system makes recommendations, referencing relevant judicial decisions for justification. It was developed at MIT using PSL (Hunt 1986, 157).

Lenat, Douglas The thinker known for the development of programs that learn, including AM and EURISKO. These programs learn from experience. He is currently working on a project to give a computer common sense.

Length-first search A type of search used in ABSTRIPS that puts together a plan at a more abstract level before proceeding to a less abstract level. In this way dead ends are frequently avoided. Backtracking is employed when dead ends are discovered. No actions are carried out until the plan is complete (Smith 1989, 110; Winston 1979, 143; Barr and Feigenbaum 1981 vol 1, 138).

LEX 1. An artificial intelligence program that is a symbolic integration problem solver that learns from experience. LEX learns when to apply certain operators to a particular problem. It does not have the capability of deriving new operators. 2. One of the two conflict-resolution strategies in OPS5. The steps it uses in conflict resolution are refraction, recency, specificity, and arbitrary choice, in that order. Refraction prevents any rule that has already fired from being fired again. The recency principle chooses the rules with the working-memory elements which have most recently been added to working memory. Specificity chooses the set of rules associated with the working-memory elements that are most specific. If there is more than one rule left, then one rule is arbitrarily chosen. The other conflict resolution strategy in OPS5 is MEA (Moskowitz Nov 1986, 221; Brownston et al 1986, 62–63).

Lexical ambiguity The vagueness of meaning in language. Example: "Visiting relatives can be annoying." In this sentence are relatives visiting the speaker or is the speaker visiting relatives? Such ambiguity makes computer processing of language difficult (Brittain 1987, 33; Bates et al 1987, 65).

Lexical analysis The part of natural language processing that divides a string into words and then looks the words up in a dictionary. *Compare with* Keyword; Semantic analysis; Syntactic analysis (Rubin Jul 1985, 44; Mishkoff 1986, 4–9).

Lexical binding The extent to which a variable holds its binding under the condition of lexical scoping.

Lexical scoping In this type of scoping an entity can be referenced only by parts of the program that are textually contained in the body of the establishing construct. Lexical scoping is slower than dynamic scoping, but it is less prone to producing programmer errors. In PROLOG a lexically scoped variable's meaning is limited to a single clause. *Contrast with* Dynamic scoping (Bratko 1986, 30; Winston 1984, 54; Steele 1984, 37; Winston and Horn 1988, 581).

Lexical variable A bound variable in LISP which is restricted to the program construct that bound it. The lexical variable can only be accessed by forms which are physically within the program construct that bound the variable. There is no temporal limitation on a lexical variable in LISP. That is, the value of the variable is maintained even after the program construct is exited. If the program construct is reentered the value of the variable is still present. *See also* Lexical scoping. *Contrast with* Dynamic variable (Steele 1984, 55–56).

Lexicon The set of words used in a natural language processing system (Smith 1989, 111).

LEX2 An artificial intelligence program that solves problems in integral calculus and then uses this information to build heuristics that can be applied to general classes of integrals. It was developed at Rutgers by Thomaas Mitchell and Paul Utgoff (Lenat 1988, 73).

LHS Left-Hand Side of a production rule (Neiman and Martin 1986, 56).

LIFER A natural language processing system which is a tool used to develop natural language front ends.

Limit switch A switch whose function is to constrain the motion of a robot (Rosenberg 1986, 105).

Linear input form strategy A strategy that takes the negation of the goal and uses it to perform repeated resolution with the available axioms until the empty clause is produced (Luger and Stubblefield 1989, 429–430).

Linearly separable Being able to separate sets of training instances from one another by calculating a weight vector in learning problems (Smith 1989, 113).

Linear predictive coding A method of encoding human speech using a model of the human vocal chords. Parameters of the model are specified to produce different sounds. Two other methods of encoding human speech are vocorder representation and formant representation (Forsyth and Naylor 1985, 44–47).

Linear test and merge An algorithm used in OPS production systems that takes advantage of earlier computations in synthesizing matches.

Linear threshold unit A binary unit used in perceptrons whose activation value may only be 0 or 1. To achieve the status of 1 the weighted sum of its inputs must exceed the threshold value. A perceptron consists of linear threshold units with no feedback mechanisms (Rumelhart and McClelland 1986, 63–66).

Line detection The procedure of finding all relevant lines, surfaces, and borders in an image for a computer to analyze it (Forsyth and Naylor 1985, 79).

Link 1. The connecting element of a robot manipulator. 2. A synonym for arc. 3. The place in vision where two lines meet (Townsend 1987a, 121–122; Harmon and King 1985, 35–40; Rosenberg 1986, 106–107; Stevens 1985, 53).

Linked-data representations A data structure which consists of a set of data structures linked by pointers. Such data structures can be used in production systems like OPS5 to create very complex data structures.

Linked list A data structure that consists of a data part and a link part. A linked list is a list connected by pointers. It is used to build frames, but it produces a good bit of programming overhead, and the programming is hard to follow (Jay and Knaus Mar 1989, 19; Charniak and McDermott 1985, 64).

LIPS Logical Inferences Per Second. A measure of the speed of expert systems and the PROLOG language. A LIP is a reduction in a computation. It is difficult to compare expert systems using LIPS because styles of expert systems vary so much it is difficult to design an expert system that could be considered equivalent and could run on the different expert system shells (Johnson 1986, 232; Mishkoff 1986, G-2; Sterling and Shapiro 1986, 193).

LISP LISt Processing language. The major language of artificial intelligence in the United States. LISP was developed by John McCarthy. It is an easily extended functional, procedural language. LISP is based on recursive function theory. It is characterized by symbol manipulation as opposed to numerical manipulation. LISP is an interpreted, type-free, flexible language. In contrast to other languages, one can change the syntax of the language, add new data structures, or define new functions with little difficulty. It is able to spawn a rich variety of abstractions. Memory management is automatic. The control structure of LISP is applicative in nature. That is, control is centered in the functions that make up LISP. The more basic functions with their arguments are used in writing more complex functions. Once the program is written, which function is called is greatly dependent on the values supplied for the arguments of the functions. Contrast this type of flow of control with the more rigid type of flow of control found in conventional languages which use iterative loops, if/then statements, and case statements. LISP is able to create symbols allowing runtime modification of programs. Programs and data are both lists. Because programs and data use the same data structure, LISP can produce programs that are self-modifying. Thus, programs that learn can be constructed. It is a recursive language. The combination of lists and recursion allows greater flexibility in handling data than is permitted by arrays. Data structures using pointers are utilized implicitly, as compared with conventional languages which must manage pointers explicitly. All these characteristics are helpful in producing artificial intelligence programs. LISP is especially useful in prototyping. Its environment is characterized by excellent editing and debugging tools. It is criticized because it takes up much memory, is not as portable, and is slow as compared with a language like C. LISP has difficulty interacting with other computer languages. LISP is also not as good as UNIX systems when it comes to multitasking and multiusing applications. LISP has been criticized as not being a true functional language. This is a valid criticism, but LISP is more a functional language than are the standard programming languages. Recently, most versions of LISP have included an object oriented component. *See also* Function; Lists (Allen Jul 1985, 27–33; Barber Feb 1987, 28–31; Allen Feb 1987, 48–61; Roland 1987, 47–55; Eisenbach and Sadler Aug 1985, 190; Winston Apr 1985, 209–218; Johnson 1986, 86–95; Hayes-Roth et al 1983, 401; Amsterdam Apr 1988, 24; Charniak and McDermott 1985, 33–86; Harmon and King 1985, 85–87; Barr and Feigenbaum 1981 vol 2, 15–29; Winston 1984, 7; Hunt 1986, 158–159; Luger and Stubblefield 1989, 197–200. Newquist Jul 1987, 59).

LISP machine A computer designed specifically to run the programming language LISP.

List A type of knowledge representation. An object that consists of a sequence of elements. In LISP, a list is an open parentheses and a closing parentheses surrounding zero or more items. The underlying structure of a list is represented as an ordered set of LISP CONS-cells. A simple CONS-cell consists of two fields. The first field holds a symbol in the list, and the second field holds a pointer to the next symbol in the list. With this type of underlying structure lists can easily be spliced together with other lists simply by altering the pointer. Lists are the primary data structure in LISP. Lists are also used in PROLOG. Lists have a number of advantages and uses: A list can be treated as a single object. The user does not have to know ahead of time the size of the list. That is, the size of the list does not have to be declared prior to running the program. Lists have no fixed limit and can be dynamically expanded or decreased by adding or deleting elements. A list is unlike an array in that it is capable of holding different kinds of objects. Objects in a list can even be other lists and as a result a list can be used to represent hierarchical structures. Frames, associative networks, arrays, and tree structures may be represented as lists. The wide variety of structures that can be represented by lists is one of its primary advantages. Lists can be used to hold a set of constraints. An example of this latter use is checking a list of colors to see if a given color is a valid color. It can be used to order objects. Example: a list of the heads of rules could be kept in a list. The rules could then be called in order from the list. In this way the user can change the order of the rules called without having to rearrange the rules physically. Programs can be built so that the objects on a list can be sorted, minimum and maximum values can be found, and so on. A limitation of lists is they must be searched in a sequential manner. Arrays have an advantage over lists in that it is easier to find a value in an array or replace data in an array (Eisenbach and Sadler Aug 1985, 190; Townsend 1987a, 87–89, 97–98; Schildt 1987, 211–214; Mishkoff 1986, 7-7–7-8; Young 1987, 289–290; Sterling and Shapiro 1986, 43–51; Winston 1984, 4; Forsyth and Naylor 1985, 133–134; Steele 1984, 262; (Luger and Stubblefield 1989, 192).

List processing The procedure of going through a list and examining the objects in the list for a purpose. Example: the purpose may be to find or delete a given element, or reorder the elements. (Clocksin 1987, 154; Hayes-Roth et al 1983, 61).

Literal 1. A variable or the negation of a variable in logic. 2. A fundamental unit of a PROLOG program. An atomic formula or the negation of an atomic formula. Examples: likes(mary, john), $b(x, y)$, $X > Y$ (Shmueli et al 1986, 249; Amsterdam Oct 1986, 18; Dos Reis 1988, 50; Luger and Stubblefield 1989, 416).

Literalization A command in OPS5 which declares a class of working-memory elements (Moskowitz Nov 1986, 218).

Literalize The declaration of an element class in OPS5 systems. Example: One may literalize a plane class with the attributes of size, range, passenger capacity, and so on. Each element of that class has its unique name and characteristics (Brownston et al 1986, 39–42).

Local averaging A means of removing noise from an image. The intensity of each point in an image is replaced by a weighted-average intensity of the surrounding points. The process tends to blur the image (Barr and Feigenbaum 1981 vol 3, 214).

Locally admissible A property of a heuristic. When a heuristic is locally admissible it always locates the minimal path to each state in a search (Luger and Stubblefield 1989, 167).

Local scope The limiting of the scope of a name to a block of code (Tello 1989, 85).

Local variable 1. A variable whose binding is restricted to one routine or one routine and its subroutines. **2.** A variable defined inside of a function or procedure, which can only be accessed within that procedure and its subprocedures. The use of local variables helps to reduce errors. *Contrast with* Global variable (Charniak and McDermott 1985, 74; Rosenberg 1986, 108).

Locked tool   An expert system tool that does not allow access to the source code of the expert system (Harmon et al 1988, 65).

Logic   The science of thought and argument. A system of rules for manipulating symbols. A system whose goal is to ascertain the truth of statements. It has a clearly defined syntax for its statements. Rules of inference are used in logic to derive facts from previously known facts and rules. Common rules of inference are modus ponens and resolution. The most common operators found in logic are AND, OR, NOT, IMPLIES, and EQUIVALENT. Aristotle, Leibnitz, and Boole are three of the primary contributors to logic. Examples of logic systems include propositional logic, first order logic, and second order logic. PROLOG is a computer language which is based on logic. One advantage of logic-based systems is that the rules of inference are well understood. Both frames and semantic networks may be considered to be derived from logic. *Contrast with* Fuzzy logic; Inexact reasoning; Statistical logic (Chabris 1989, 65; Fischler and Firschein 1986, 44; Johnson, 1986, 38–39, 61–62; Schildt 1987, 222–239; Harmon and King 1985, 46–48, 52–53; Barr and Feigenbaum 1981 vol 1, 154–155; Barr and Feigenbaum 1981 vol 3, 77–122; Smith 1989, 114; Lane 1988, 92).

Logical adequacy   The ability of a formalism to depict the knowledge that is to be represented. One of three criteria used to assess a representation language. Other criteria for assessing a representation language are heuristic power and notational convenience (Jackson 1986, 29).

Logical clarity   A characteristic of a computer program that allows the viewer to understand more easily the logic of the program. Emphasis is on what rather than how. The computational history of the program is not important in understanding the program. Procedural programs lack logical clarity because they can only be understood in their historical context. That is, variables can change values at different times in a program run so it is difficult to understand the meaning of the program at any given point in time. Declarative languages are considered to possess lexical clarity (Lazarev Jul 1987, 60).

Logical expression   Any expression that includes operands and logical operators and can be evaluated to true or false. (Rosenberg 1986, 108–109).

Logical formalism   Knowledge representation based on logic. Two criticisms of logical formalism are its relatively limited expressiveness and its limited computational efficiency (Fischler and Firschein Dec 1986, 48; Sterling and Shapiro 1986, 4).

Logical inference per second   See LIPS.

Logically follows   A phrase meaning that an expression A is true for every interpretation that satisfies a set B of predicate calculus expressions (Luger and Stubblefield 1989, 58).

Logical operations   Such operations as comparing, matching, selecting, and sorting; not arithmetic operations (Rosenberg 1986, 109).

Logical programming   See Logic programming.

Logical representation schemes   The representation of a knowledge base using logic (Luger and Stubblefield 1989, 334).

Logical term   The data structure of a logic program. The three terms in a logic program are constant, variable, and compound term.

Logic-based expert system   An expert system based on such logic-based languages as PROLOG. Such systems are generally characterized by the use of clauses, backward chaining, and backtracking.

Logic grammar   Definite-clause grammar. (Szpakowicz 1987, 185–195).

Logic Machine Architecture An automated reasoning program (Tello 1988, 420).

Logic problem A class of problems in which the solution is obtained through a procedure of elimination and deduction. The classic example is the mystery story. All suspects who have an alibi are eliminated and logical deduction is then used to find the culprit.

Logic program Facts and rules. It consists of horn clauses and a nondeterministic goal-reduction procedure. Queries are used to begin the deduction process which produces the conclusions. In a logic program there is little difference between data and the program. Resolution is the control and inference mechanism. PROLOG and DUCK are used to develop logic programs. They are not pure logic languages since they incorporate many extralogical features. PROLOG, for example, uses the cut facility and I/O predicates. The use of negation as failure in PROLOG is also a departure from logic programming (Kowalski Aug 1985, 174; Brownston et al 1986, 368–374; Sterling and Shapiro 1986, 10; Barr and Feigenbaum 1981 vol 3, 120–121; Luger and Stubblefield 1989, 477, 481).

Logic programming A type of programming based on logic that is relatively independent of the underlying structure of the machine on which it is operating. The heart of logic programming is making deductions from a set of facts. Logic programming consists of objects, how the objects are related, and operators. One advantage of logic programming is that once the system is specified the user immediately has available a working program which is able to simulate the process. Logic programming is weak in organizing and connecting knowledge. This weakness can lead to programs that take an excessive amount of time to prove a goal. Logic programming is most applicable in situations in which the information base is relatively stable and noncontradictory. Logic programming works well in analyzing electronic circuits and in theorem proving. Compare logic programming to frame-based programming in which knowledge is structured in chunks of related information. PROLOG is an implementation of logic programming. *Compare with* Production system (Parsaye and Chignell 1988, 97–99; Tello 1988, 417; Smith 1989, 114).

Logic Theorist One of the first artificial intelligence programs, it was capable of proving theorems in propositional calculus and proving mathematical theorems. It used backward reasoning and heuristics. The inventors went on to develop general problem solver because they wanted a machine which could emulate human thought (Johnson 1986, 37; Barr and Feigenbaum 1981 vol 1, 109–112).

LOGLISP A computer language that possesses the properties of PROLOG, and at the same time uses the functions available in LISP.

LOGO A computer language devised by Seymour Papert which is derived from LISP. Designed to encourage children in constructive play, it is used to help them learn concepts and to encourage creativity. LOGO's emphasis is on discovery learning rather than injection learning. The child learns concepts by exploring on his own without the type of tutor found in most ICAI systems. The child is the active agent in the learning process. His or her self-exploration, rather than a tutor, is the source of learning. LOGO excels in turtle graphics (Johnson 1986, 85; Barr and Feigenbaum 1981 vol 2, 291–294; Rosenberg 1986, 109; Frude 1983, 91–92; Forsyth and Naylor 1985, 230; Stevens 1985, 76–78).

Look ahead A principle used in artificial intelligence to construct game trees. In chess the computer is programmed to look ahead to all the possible countermoves an opponent could make to a given move made by the computer. In order to use look ahead it is necessary to implement static evaluation and minimaxing (Winston 1979, 112–115; Barr and Feigenbaum 1981 vol 3, 340; Forsyth and Naylor 1985, 179, 181, 188).

Look at extremes A type of heuristic which states, pay attention to extreme examples. This heuristic is used in discovery artificial intelligence systems. Example: In the EURISKO program this heuristic was applied, and as a consequence the program paid attention to those extreme cases of numbers which had only a few divisors. As a result EURISKO discovered prime numbers (Lenat 1988, 72).

Loop A path that repeats itself in a graph (Luger and Stubblefield 1989, 82).

Loop node A type of node that can cause a return to an earlier node in the search space (Jackson 1986, 15).

Loops LISP Object-Oriented Programming System. A LISP-based multiparadigm language developed by Xerox Corporation. It is more of a programming environment than an expert system tool (Walters and Nielsen 1988, 91; Harmon and King 1985, 126–128; Brownston et al 1986, 376–377).

Loose coupling A type of coupling used to add query results from a data base to a PROLOG workspace. In loose coupling both programs hold their identity. It is more modular than tight coupling, therefore allowing easier updating. It is generally slower, requires more memory, and is harder to program than tight coupling (Missikoff and Wiederhold 1986, 388; Tzvieli 1989, 33).

Low-emphasis filtering The use of bandpass filtering in vision to remove noise that is concentrated at a particular frequency range. This type of filtering tends to blur the image.

Low-level goal An intermediate goal in a problem-solving process (Townsend 1987b, 382).

Low-level vision The processing of primitive aspects of a scene. The processing of changing intensity and edge orientation. *Contrast with* High-level vision.

Lucid A data-flow programming language. A Lucid program consists of streams of data flowing between functions (Lane Sep/Oct 1989, 28–33).

Lunar An expert system that identifies moon rocks. It was the first expert system to use augmented transition networks. LUNAR was developed by William Woods (Johnson 1986, 113–115).

Lvalue An expression in C++ that refers to an object. The name of an object is an lvalue (Stroustrup 1987, 251).

M

Macbeth A program written by Patrick Winston that uses analogical reasoning. Its goal is to take lessons learned in the play Macbeth and apply these lessons to understanding and predicting what may happen in similar situations (Johnson 1986, 158–161).

Machina speculatrix A small robot device built by the British physiologist William Walter in the 1950s. It was a very simple creature but it appeared to be very lifelike. It was attracted by lights but it would avoid excessively strong lights. It could push aside small objects in its way and find its way around large objects. It was capable of finding wall sockets so it could recharge itself. Its downfall was it could not recognize stairs (Frude 1983, 57).

Machine learning 1. Induction learning, a type of automated knowledge acquisition that makes the assumption that object descriptions are available and a computer program then uses examples concerning the objects to construct a decision tree which can then be used to produce rules. The process is based on statistical techniques and numerical algorithms. The term learning by induction should really be used instead of machine learning system when this restricted definition is used. Contrast this type of induction learning with knowledge acquisition, which includes but is not limited to induction learning. Knowledge acquisition includes the manual acquisition of knowledge through interviewing. Contrast induction learning with another type of automated knowledge acquisition, knowledge elicitation. 2. A field of artificial intelligence that attempts to build programs which learn from experience. This includes learning by induction, concept learning, learning in neural nets, discovery learning, learning by interaction, learning from instruction, learning by analogy, model-driven learning, skill refinement, and data-driven learning. In any type of machine learning the program makes improvement in its choices. All machine learning programs depend on feedback. In both vision and speech recognition, machine-learning procedures have been developed for recognizing objects and speech sounds (Thompson and Thompson Nov 1986, 149; Thompson and Thompson Nov 1987, 25; Brownston et al 1986, 25, 333–351; Forsyth and Naylor 1985, 97–118; Parsaye and Chignell 1988, 347; Carbonell et al 1983).

Machine translation The translation of text from one human language to another human language by computer. Results have been disappointing in this area (Mishkoff 1986, G–2; Barr and Feigenbaum 1981 vol. 1, 233–237; Waldrop 1987, 63–64).

Machine vision *See* Vision.

MACLISP A version of LISP known for its efficiency, which is considered to be less user friendly than INTERLISP (Hayes-Roth et al 1983, 402; Harmon and King 1985, 85–86; Barr and Feigenbaum 1981 vol 2, 8; Rosenberg 1986, 111).

Macro An entity that when executed translates into a different form, which is then executed. A macro is an abbreviation of a piece of computer code. Macro arguments are not evaluated at expansion time. This can be a valuable characteristic in some situations. For instance, macros are used in place of a function when the body of the function requires an if then statement and the then portion of the statement must be passed as a parameter. If a macro is not used in such a case, the "then" part of the statement will be evaluated regardless of the conditions in the "if" part of the "if then" statement. Macros can be used to build backtracking modules. The code for a backtracking module will consist of continuation functions, catch-throw pairs, and lambda expressions. Such combinations can make for hard-to-understand code. Enclosing such code in a macro can hide the complex details from the user and greatly improve the readability of the program. Macros allow for the creation of functions that can take a variable number of arguments. *See also* San Marco LISP Explorer (Charniak and McDermott 1985, 78–80; Winston 1984, 121, 124–126; Maxwell and Riggle Mar 1989, 28–34; Graham Mar 1988, 42–53).

Macro-operator A procedure used in STRIPS. A macro-operator is a series of primitive operators that have been successfully used to solve a problem. STRIPS remembers the macro-operator so as to be able to use it when it should again be appropriate (Barr and Feigenbaum 1981 vol. 1, 28).

MACSYMA A computer program that aids scientists, mathematicians, and engineers in performing symbolic differential and integral calculus, solving polynomial equations, and matrices. It has no explanation system and cannot do inexact reasoning. The program recognizes the type of problem and associates it with the proper solution method. It is written in the LISP language and is a rule-based system (Hayes-Roth et al 1983, 38–39, 52–53; Harmon and King 1985, 135–137; Barr and Feigenbaum 1981 vol 2, 143–149).

Magic number seven The fact that human beings can deal effectively with up to seven chunks of information at one time. Human thinking works by using semantic chunks of meaningful information (Waldrop 1987, 12).

Magnitude class A standard class found in Smalltalk which consists of objects that can be compared, measured, ordered, and counted. This includes such classes as number, date, time, and characters (Lazarav Nov 1988, 69).

Maintenance The last of seven stages in expert system development. Methods for ensuring the system will be adequately updated are put in place in this stage. *See also* Expert system development (Harmon et al 1988, 201; Rosenberg 1986, 114).

Majority A logic operator that states: Given a set of statements in which more than half the statements are true, then the majority of statements are true (Rosenberg 1986, 114).

Make 1. A command used in OPS5 systems to create working-memory elements. 2. A command usually associated with the C language which allows the programmer to recompile and link only those parts of the program that have been changed. This is an important advantage for the C language which other languages such as LISP do not ordinarily possess (Brownston et al 1986, 51–56).

MANDALA A logic-based knowledge-engineering language that emphasizes the use of objects. An object in MANDALA consists of a set of axioms which are local procedures (methods). The axioms act on messages which are received via what is known as an input stream. MANDALA possesses the properties of soundness and completeness. It promises to be more efficient than object-oriented languages, which use embedded lists and nested terms to implement objects (Jackson 1986, 187).

Manipulator The arm of a robot (Mishkoff 1986, 5-14).

Manipulator-oriented language A type of robot-control language which specifies exactly what the movements of the robot are to be. Compare with task-oriented languages, which focus on the effect of the action of the robot (Hunt 1986, 147).

Manual knowledge acquisition Gathering knowledge for use in expert systems in ways other than using a computer. Examples: interviewing and verbal protocol analysis (Parsaye and Chignell 1988, 342–346).

Manual programming Programming a robot by moving switches, by setting the cams on a rotating stepping drum, or by using some other similar physical method of controlling the robot's behavior (Rosenberg 1986, 114).

Many-valued logic Inexact logic.

Map A feature in LISP that applies a function to a sequence of data elements. It returns a list of the results (Luger and Stubblefield 1989, 267, 491).

Mapping functions Functions in the expert system tool PERSONAL CONSULTANT PLUS that are used to access and evaluate rules, frames, and parameters and to save those components which meet specified criteria on a list. The list is then used to do such things as build metarules (Tello 1988, 289).

Mapping problem A problem that can be solved through the conversion of one list to another by applying a function to the first list. Examples: routing problems, road mapping, electronic circuit diagramming, and computer networking. Recursion is usually used to aid in this conversion process. PROLOG and LISP are well suited to solving mapping problems since they both support lists and recursion (Townsend 1987b, 201–211).

MARGIE A language-understanding program developed by Roger Schank. It is claimed to have limited understanding and the ability to make inferences. It is an implementation of conceptual dependency. Conceptual dependency reduces sentences to a basic set of primitives. It uses 11 primitives. One primitive is PTRANS, which means to move an object from one place to another. This primitive can cover a large number of situations. MARGIE is a move toward giving a computer the ability to understand. SAM and PAM are successor programs to MARGIE (Johnson 1986, 173–174; Barr and Feigenbaum 1981 vol. 1, 300–305; Waldrop 1987, 76–78).

Mark and sweep A LISP memory-management procedure that marks all active cells. All unmarked cells then can be eliminated through garbage collection. *Compare with* Reference counting (Charniak and McDermott 1985, 65; Gabriel Feb 1987, 35).

Markov chain A statistical model of happenings in which the probability of an occurrence is a function only of the previously occurring event (Rosenberg 1986, 115; Forsyth and Naylor 1985, 103–107).

Markov random fields A probabilistic network that has been adapted to construct Boltzmann machines (Hinton Apr 1985, 270).

Marr, David A man who made important contributions in the field of vision and stressed the importance of viewing vision at different levels of understanding. He also pointed out the importance of understanding the hierarchy of processes that are involved in vision. He is author of the text *Vision* (Waldrop 1987, 91–104).

Marr's theory of vision The theory that places emphasis on the importance of choosing the best possible representation for different levels of vision processing. The three levels of representation used are the primal sketch, 2.5-D Sketch, and 3-D Sketch. It is a bottom-up approach which emphasizes the use of constraints (Johnson 1986, 149–150; Barr and Feigenbaum 1981 vol 3, 134–135).

MARS A rule-based knowledge-engineering language. Features include hierarchical structuring, forward and backward chaining, and symbolic simulation. It was built at Stanford University using MRS (Hunt 1986, 167).

Marseille PROLOG A version of PROLOG that differs from Edinburgh PROLOG in the following ways: The :- symbol is replaced with the -> symbol. Variables do not need to be capitalized. Comments are in quotes. List members are separated by periods. Facts end with a semicolon rather than a period. Punctuation is not used to separate terms on the right side of a clause. The ';' '+' and '-' symbols are not available, and other symbols are used in their place (Colmerauer Aug 1987, 181).

Martin's law The law that states that learning takes place in small increments (Winston 1984, 396, 407).

Massive parallelism Parallel processing in which large numbers of elementary microprocessors are used. Each microprocessor is small and has its own memory and is relatively independent of other microprocessors. The microprocessors are dependent on one another in the sense that they share information. There is an absence of hierarchical, centralized control. An analogy is a community of cooperating experts. The best-known computer of this type is the Connection machine, which employs 64,000 microprocessors. The company that built the Connection Machine hopes eventually to build a version with 1,000,000 microprocessors. *Contrast with* Coarse-grained parallelism (Waldrop 1987, 114).

Masterscope A component of some expert systems that is able to produce a dynamic self-description of some part of the program. Example: to query which predicates are capable of calling a particular predicate (Tello Feb 1988, 77; Hayes-Roth et al 1983, 238; Barr and Feigenbaum 1981 vol 2, 8).

Match 1. The comparison of expressions to see if they are equivalent. Much of the energy expended by expert systems and artificial intelligence programs is involved in the matching process. Therefore, much study has been made of match. 2. The procedure of comparing patterns with data objects or other patterns for the purpose of finding a match. 3. The procedure by which data structures are compared. If a system is capable of matching complex objects, this can reduce search considerably and avoid time consuming backtracking. 4a. The finding of an equivalence to a query in a PROLOG database. 4b. The initial stage of unification in PROLOG. (For some authorities match is used interchangeably with unification.) The use of variables in data structures during the matching process greatly enhances flexibility. That is, variables in a query may be considered wild cards which can become matched and instantiated to a variety of objects in the data base. In unification some of the objects in the data base may also include variables. *See also* Unification. In PROLOG, when match fails backtracking is used to search for other matches. 5. The type of Match found in

OPS5 production systems. It is more than simple matching. It is a search technique which compares the left-hand side of rules with data in working-memory elements, in an attempt to find the different combinations in which the rules may be satisfied by a consistent set of bindings. *See also* Pattern matching for more detail, and San Marco LISP Explorer (Brownston et al 1986, 9–15, 450; Harrison and Tribble 1986, 66; Forgy and Shepard 1987, 36; Townsend 1987a, 39–40; Hayes-Roth et al Towsend 1987a, 39–40; Hayes and Roth. 1983, 103–104; Charniak and McDermott 1985, 438; Townsend 1987b, 382; Barr and Feigenbaum 1981 vol 2, 202; Winston 1984, 253–267; Jackson 1986, 136; Bratko 1986, 36, 61);

Match cycle The part of the Rete match algorithm that is responsible for revising the Rete network and the conflict set when working memory is altered (Rosenberg 1986, 115).

Material-handling robot A robot that specializes in moving and arranging materials (Rosenberg 1986, 115).

Material-processing robot A robot that specializes in cutting, molding, welding, or in some other way altering the product in the manufacturing process (Rosenberg 1986, 115).

Mathematical representation Knowledge representation based on the constraints placed on a set of variables (Fischler and Firschein Dec 1986, 44).

MATHLAB 68 A forerunner of the mathematics expert system MACSYMA, developed at MIT using LISP (Hunt 1986, 167).

Maximum cardinality A facet that specifies the maximum number of values that can be assigned to a slot (Luger and Stubblefield 1989, 547).

Maximum of minimums A method for calculating confidence factors. Assume a set of rules with the same conclusion. Each rule has confidence factors for each premise and a confidence factor for its conclusion. Find the minimum confidence factor for each rule. The final confidence factor is the maximum of these minimum confidence factors. Other methods of calculating confidence factors include confirmative of minimums, confirmative of products, maximum of products, average of minimums, average of products, and weighted average. The problem at hand dictates the most appropriate method for computing confidence factors (Shafer May/Jun 1989, 71).

Maximum of products A method for calculating confidence factors. Assume a set of rules with the same conclusion. Each rule has confidence factors for each premise and a confidence factor for its conclusion. Multiply the confidence factors in the first rule, divide by 100 and save the result. Follow the same procedure for all of the other rules in the set. From these computations choose the maximum resulting confidence as the maximum of products confidence. Other methods of calculating confidence factors include confirmative of minimums, confirmative of products, maximum of minimums, average of minimums, average of products, and weighted average. The problem at hand dictates the most appropriate method for computing confidence factors (Shafer May/Jun 1989, 71).

MCC A corporation funded by other corporations to further artificial intelligence research, the closest equivalent in the United States to the Japanese-government-sponsored Fifth Generation Project. It is located in Austin, Texas (Hunt 1986, 168).

McCarthy, John The man who is credited with coining the term artificial intelligence; he developed the LISP language (Johnson 1986, 11–24).

McCulloch, Warren, and Walter Pitts Partners who demonstrated how a theoretical set of nerve cells can perform all the operations of logic. In an article written in 1943 they proposed that the network of neurons in the brain could be considered as analogous to a computer. They attempted to explain the brain mathematically (Johnson 1986, 42–44; Mishkoff 1986, 2-7; Waldrop 1987, 16).

MCL A robotics-control language developed by McDonnell-Douglas (Mishkoff 1986, 5–19).

MEA A conflict resolution strategy in OPS5. It is similar to the LEX strategy but it inserts an initial step which focuses on the recency of the working-memory element that matches the first condition element of the rule. The application of MEA can be used to build backward-chaining expert systems using OPS5 (Moskowitz Nov 1986, 221; Brownston et al 1986, 64, 132).

Meaning The deductions that can be made in a logic program. The instances that can be deduced from a PROLOG program (Sterling and Shapiro 1986, 15–16).

Means-end A type of control strategy that emphasizes differences and operator selection. It calculates an estimate of the difference between the current state of the problem and the goal state. The difference is then used to index an operator, which is then applied to make the greatest possible reduction between the current state and the goal state. If the operator cannot be applied, subgoals are generated. If the subgoals cannot be solved, they generate subgoals until subgoals are finally reached which can be solved. Then, the process works its way back to the original operator which can then be solved allowing movement to the goal state. The inference process is iterative in nature and proceeds from both ends of the search tree and simultaneously performs backward and forward chaining until the two paths meet, forming a single continuous path from the goal state to the initial state. It is a means of continually subdividing the difference between the goal state and the initial state until the difference is eliminated. Means-end analysis is used in General Problem Solver. Currently, expert systems do not use this approach. Most current expert systems employ a production system architecture that relies on productions being triggered by patterns of facts rather than computed differences. Current expert systems rely more on domain knowledge as compared to means-end analysis in General Problem Solver, which relies primarily on reasoning (Winston 1979 130–133, 155; Brownston et al 1986, 450; Barr and Feigenbaum 1981 vol 1, 24; Barr and Feigenbaum 1981 vol 2, 139, 317; Barr and Feigenbaum 1981 vol 3, 14–15; Parsaye, and Chignell 1988, 387; Newell et al 1960, 256–264).

Mechanical theorem prover A program that takes a set of logical statements and a goal statement and attempts to prove the goal statement from the initial statements. The order of the statements should have no effect. If there is a proof available, the program should find it. PROLOG does not satisfy the latter two statements and is not considered a good theorem prover. Mechanical theorem proving is based on resolution. It is also referred to as automated theorem proving and automated reasoning (Amsterdam Oct 86, 17; Wos and Veroff 1990, 894).

MECHO An expert system used to solve problems in Newtonian Physics, written in PROLOG (Jackson 1986, 158).

Medical expert system An expert system used to diagnose disease and advise physicians (Jackson 1986, 93).

Megassembly The advanced use of robots in which 10 or more robots are used in progressive stages of assembly of a product.

Member function A function in C++ that belongs to a class; that is, the function has access to the objects of the class (Stroustrup 1987, 134–136).

Member slot A type of slot in which the value will be inherited by children of the class. *Contrast with* Own slot (Hu 1989, 186).

MEMOD A computer program designed to be a general-knowledge representation system, although it is generally considered to be a model of long-term memory. A computer program which is able to represent and process the syntax and semantics of memory, perceive, reason, question answer, and acquire knowledge. It consists of a parser, a node space, and an interpreter. The node space holds information about the world, and procedural information for carrying out commands given by the interpreter. MEMOD uses semantic decomposition which means concepts which have comparable meanings have similar structures (Barr and Feigenbaum 1981 vol 1, 215; Barr and Feigenbaum 1981 vol 3, 56-65).

Memory bandwidth A measure of the number of bits that can be moved into and out of memory per second.

Memory engram A term used to refer to the storage of a memory in the brain.

Memory model A human cognition program that emulates human memory. Examples: Quillian's Semantic Memory System, EPAM, MEMOD, HAM, ACT, and PARRY. GPS is a cognition program, but it emphasizes human problem solving rather than memory (Barr and Feigenbaum 1981 vol 3, 8-9, 28-56).

Memory-organization packets (MOPS) Nested memory structures that learn from experience and modify themselves accordingly; MOPS was conceived by Roger Schank. A group of scenes with a common goal. There is one primary scene that holds the gist of the other scenes. MOPS can be linked to one another and can be activated by words or phrases. MOPS also contain details of scenes which are called colorations (Schank and Hunter 1985, 150; Tello 1988, 502-503; Johnson 1986, 176).

Mental models The mental constructs (symbolic networks and patterns of relationships) that experts use in problem solving. The knowledge engineer must translate the domain expert's mental model to the expert system being developed. The mental models that experts use in solving problems is still not well understood. This makes it difficult to translate these mental models to expert system representations. Cognitive psychologists are actively exploring mental models (Hunt 1986, 169; Harmon et al 1988, 267).

MES An expert system that assists in troubleshooting aircraft. A forward-chaining, rule-based system, which was built using LISP at the Air Force Institute of Technology. It runs on personal computers (Hunt 1986, 169).

Message A request made of an object that a particular action be carried out in an object-oriented language. The object then responds to the message by executing what is known as a method, which is the rough equivalent of a subroutine, or a function. The rough equivalent of a function call or a subroutine call in a procedural language. It differs from a subroutine call in that the name of the object in the message causes a method (procedure) unique to that object to be activated. That is, the same message evokes different responses depending on the nature of the object being sent the message. The messages "human talk" and "dog talk" will produce quite different responses because the methods (procedures) contained in the objects human and dog are unique to the object. A message also differs from a function call in that when a message is sent, if the object cannot carry out the task, the message is relayed to the parent object so that the parent object can carry out the request (Stein 1988, 20; Walters and Nielsen 1988, 243-244; *Smalltalk/V Tutorial and Programming Handbook* 1986, 30-39; Fernhout 1989, 39; Duntemann 1989, 132).

Message handler A method in the expert system Goldworks that is roughly equivalent to a method in object-oriented languages. A piece of program code that is attached to a frame and designed to carry out some task. A message handler can be inherited in a hierarchical system (Tello 1988, 309).

Message passing A term used in object-oriented programming which refers to sending a message to an object. The message sends information to a method inside of an object and activates the method so as to carry out an action. In object-oriented programming, message passing is the only means of accessing data and methods within an object. This procedure greatly reduces the problem of mysteriously changing values of variables. The use of encapsulation and message passing obviates the use of type-specific case statements that must be modified every time a new data type is defined since the procedures for the data type are encapsulated in the new data type. *See also* Message (Matthews Sep 1987, 78; Winston 1984, 245–246; Thomas 1989, 234).

Message selector In object-oriented programming the general equivalent of a procedure name. A message selector has arguments. A method selector is a component of a keyword message (Rubin Aug 1985, 28).

Message sending A term used in object-oriented programming which refers to one object sending another object a message on which the receiver object can then act. It is also called message passing and is analogous to parameter passing.

Metaclass A class of a class. A class whose instances are themselves classes. Animal may be a metaclass because instances of animal are the classes mammals and birds (Gabriel, Mar 1989, 63; (Thomas 1989, 238).

Metaclass definition A definition that gives the user control over the primary operations of an object-oriented system. These operations can include the inheritance mechanism, shadowing, and defaults (Amir 1989, 30).

Metacognition The ability to reflect on one's own thinking (Hayes-Roth et al 1983, 402; Hunt 1986, 170; Smith 1989, 121).

META-DENDRAL A program that derives rules concerning mass spectrometry based on data received about how compounds are broken up by a spectrometer. A learning program that formulates Mass-spectral rules from examples which can then be used by DENDRAL. It is capable of testing rules against training instances, refining rules, removing redundant rules, and detecting contradictory rules (Hayes-Roth et al 1983, 155–156; Barr and Feigenbaum 1981 vol 2, 116–123; Barr and Feigenbaum 1981 vol 3, 428–437; Lenat 1988, 72–73).

Metafact A type of fact found in the expert system shell M1 that controls the inference engine (Tello 1988, 157; Tello Aug 1985, 100).

Metainterpreter An interpreter created by employing the language in which the interpreter is to be used. It permits the construction of an integrated programming environment. It also allows access to the basic computational features of the language. A metainterpreter can be used to build a higher-level language which can more effectively solve a problem. The use of metainterpreters allows for the construction of expert systems (Sterling and Shapiro 1986, 303–330; Luger and Stubblefield 1989, 458–468).

Metaknowledge Knowledge about knowledge; a useful concept in artificial intelligence. It translates to building knowledge representations that are capable of inspecting and controlling the state of the system. Example: using metarules to inspect knowledge derived from one set of rules so as to then make the decision that sufficient information has been derived and it is now time to move to a new set of rules. Such rules reason about the reasoning process and control the system. Metaknowledge can be employed in knowing how and when to add new terms and knowledge structures. Other applications are reasoning about the limits of the expert system's knowledge, the ability to keep records of knowledge base development, and maintenance of dependency records (Schuler 1987, 100; Hayes-Roth et al 1983, 220, 402; Barr and Feigenbaum 1981 vol 1, 144–145, 147; Barr and Feigenbaum 1981 vol 2, 240–241; Sterling and Shapiro 1986, 317; Barr and Feigenbaum 1981 vol 3, 330).

Metalevel reasoning Reasoning about knowledge. The ability to imagine an alternative set of beliefs and to derive consequences from these alternative beliefs. The use of metarules is one type of metalevel reasoning (Matthews Sep 1987, 82; Kowalski Aug 1985, 172; Townsend and Feucht 1986, 171–173).

Metalinguistic abstraction Building a higher-level problem-solving language that employs unique characteristics for solving the problems with which it is to grapple (Luger and Stubblefield 1989, 458, 487).

Metalogical predicate One of a set of predicates in PROLOG that are not a part of first-order logic. They are capable of such activities as scrutinizing the state of the proof being attempted without producing an error or accidentally instantiating variables. That is, they can treat variables as objects. One metalogical predicate, Call, can change data structures to goals. var(X) is a metalogical predicate. It tests to see if X is a variable. Findall is another frequently used metalogical predicate (Hashim Mar/Apr 1988, 89–97; Sterling and Shapiro 1986, 146–150).

Metalogical programming A type of programming that permits a program to examine itself thus allowing programs to construct interpreters, build object-oriented programs, and learn. In PROLOG, metalogical programming depends on predicates being passed as arguments of other predicates and variables which can be used to represent predicates. That is, metalogical programming uses predicates as first-class objects. *See also* Metalogical predicate, for examples of predicates which are used in metalogical programming in PROLOG (Sterling and Shapiro 1986, 155; Hashim and Seyer 1988, 49–50; Hashim 1988, 89–97).

Metamethod Class methods. Class methods are brought to bear when a message is sent to a class rather than to an object (Rettig Nov 1987, 18).

Metaplanning The capacity of a planning system to make plans about its own planning (Hayes-Roth et al 1983, 81; Barr and Feigenbaum 1981 vol 3, 551).

Metapredicate 1. A type of predicate that manipulates other predicates. Examples: Predicates that determine the type of an expression, place type restrictions on logic programming, constructing and "taking apart" structures, comparing values of expressions, and changing predicates which are data to programming code which can be executed. 2. A type of predicate capable of treating equations as objects (Jackson 1986, 170; Luger and Stubblefield 1989, 450).

Metaproblem The problem of deciding the next rule that should be executed in an expert system (Lenat 1988, 72).

Metarule A rule that controls other rules. It gives an added means of controlling the search process in an expert system. A metarule usually specifies the conditions necessary for a given set of rules to be used rather than another set of rules. A metarule may decide such things as ruling out problem solutions which probably will not work, or remembering and reusing successful strategies. A metarule may be used to resolve conflicts. Example: If two rules are applicable to a solution, a metarule may choose one over the other because one rule may be simpler than the other. Metarules may also be used to choose which inferencing procedure to use depending on the circumstances present in the program. Examples (EURISKO): If a heuristic has fired less than once, generalize its IF condition. If a heuristic takes up a lot of room then a new slot should be created to shorten it. *See also* Domain-free metarule; Domain-specific metarule (Jackson 1986, 37; Tello 1988, 289; Forsyth and Naylor 1985, 215; Firdman Oct 1986, 76; Townsend 1987a, 124; Hayes-Roth et al 1983, 223–225, 402; Walters and Nielsen 1988, 201; Barr and Feigenbaum 1981 vol 2, 88, 92; Townsend and Feucht 1986, 172; Chabris 1989, 297; Hu 1989, 254).

Metaslot A slot that contains information about the slot, which can be used for the purpose of control. Some expert system tools allow a variety of possible metaslots: Meta-slots can be used to control which parent of an object has priority in inheritance. An if-change metaslot can take action if a change is made to a value in the slot. A metaslot may be a prompt string which prompts the user to enter a new value in the slot. An inference category metaslot forces the inference engine to examine rules containing the property value in order of entry. The order-of-sources metaslot gives information as to what to do next in the event that the property is in a rule the system currently is testing but the value of the property has not yet been computed. Other possibilities for metaslots may include ask the user, call an external procedure, search a database, use a default value, or use inheritance (Arcidiacono Nov 1988, 115–116).

Metavariable facility A synonym for the PROLOG predicate call(X). This predicate allows a data structure to be changed to a goal. This facility is important in building metainterpreters and expert systems (Sterling and Shapiro 1986, 155–156).

Method 1. Computer code in an-object oriented language which is inside an object and which determines the object's behavior. A method is activated by a message sent to the object. While other languages use functions and subroutines to get work done, object-oriented languages use methods. 2. The means by which a goal may be achieved, or has been achieved, in a production system (Pascoe 1986, 140; Stein 1988, 22–24; Winston 1984, 246–256; *Smalltalk/V tutorial and programming handbook* 1986, 51–56; Duntemann 1989, 132; Rubin Aug 1985, 31; Peterson 1987, 33).

Method combination A flexible means of inheritance of methods from multiple sources. The combining of methods inherited from different classes to implement a single generic function. Which of the inherited methods which will be used at a given time varies according to the circumstances. It is found in Symbolic's Flavors system (Gabriel Mar 1989, 62–63; Tello Mar 1987, 128; Tello Apr 1987, 148; Tello 1989, 123).

Method inheritance The inheritance of methods by objects which are children of a parent object in a frame-based system. *Compare with* Property inheritance *See also* After inheritance; Before inheritance (Walters and Nielsen 1988, 241–243).

Method property A type of procedure found in frame-based systems used to determine the value of a property. Example: A frame may represent a circle, and one slot on the frame may be for the area of the circle. When the area slot is accessed a method property is activated which computes the area of the circle (Shepard Mar 1987, 76).

Method selector The words in a message in object-oriented programming which tell the system which method to use (Shaw May 1988, 70).

Metonymy A problem that causes difficulty in natural language processing. It is the substitution of a part for a whole. An example is have a meeting of all of the captains in the regiment. It is not a meeting of captains. It is a meeting of people who are captains in the regiment (Bates et al May 1987, 65).

Metropolis algorithm An algorithm used in the Boltzmann machine which ensures that the possibility of changing of states is low when the Boltzmann machine is near a solution, but high when the Boltzmann machine is not near a solution (Jorgensen and Matheus 1986, 37).

MICKIE A computerized medical interview program developed by Christopher Evans of the National Physical Laboratory of Teddington near London. It is noted for its avoidance of medical jargon and its amicable nature (Frude 1983, 87–90).

Micro-Planner A higher-level language that was to become a substitute for LISP, which failed because it was too inefficient (Barr and Feigenbaum 1981 vol 1, 295–297).

Microprocessor The central processing chip of the computer. All processing that a computer does takes place in the microprocessor. This type of computer architecture is referred to as Von Neumann architecture. This sequential type of processing is rapidly becoming a bottleneck. Newer computer architectures have more than one microprocessor, which allows parallel processing.

Mid-run explanation A facility available with most expert systems which allows the temporary cessation of the program so that the user may inquire into the reasoning process. This ability is not usually available with conventional computer programs (Hunt 1986, 171).

Mid-sized expert system An expert system that is the equivalent of between 500 and 1,500 rules (Harmon et al 1988, 20).

Mid-sized expert system shell An expert system that has certain advanced characteristics including a partitioned rule base, inexact reasoning, multiple instantiation, simple inheritance, graphic displays, and a flexible user interface (Harmon et al, 105–106).

MIMD A type of parallel processing. *See also* Multiple-instruction multiple data.

Mind-body problem Explaining how the mind and body interact, a problem that has held the attention of philosophers and psychologists for centuries. One of the reasons artificial intelligence is so threatening to some is that AI can be viewed as experimental evidence that there is no need for the mind as an explanatory concept.

Minimax A means of searching and pruning a two-player game tree. Each node is evaluated according to what is of greatest value to one player and of least value to his or her opponent (Charniak and McDermott 1985, 286–290; Winston 1979, 114–115; Barr and Feigenbaum 1981 vol 1, 84–87; Forsyth and Naylor 1985, 179–188).

Minimization algorithm A class of algorithms employed in neural nets that learn. These algorithms have in common a means of adjusting a set of weights until the errors in the system are minimized and hence the performance of the task at hand is maximized. Examples: simulated annealing, back propagation, and Newton's method (Swaine Oct 1989, 112–113).

Minimum cardinality A facet specifying the minimum number of values required to be assigned to a slot (Luger and Stubblefield 1989, 547).

Minsky, Marvin The man who is best known for his development of frames (Johnson 1986, 23–24; Mishkoff 1986, 2-11).

Mirror effect The mirroring of processes between procedural languages and the basic processing of microprocessors. Procedural languages consist of a set of sequential statements which are processed one at a time. A microprocessor operates in the same sequential manner. Declarative languages are a move away from this mirror effect. The mirror effect produces a lack of logical clarity, limitations on mathematical properties like substitution, and illogical statements such as $X = X + 1$. Such problems pose particular difficulty for large, complex programs and for parallel processing (Lazarev Jul 1987, 60).

MISD See Multiple-instruction single data (Swaine May 1988, 100).

Missionaries and cannibals problem A game problem which is frequently used in artificial intelligence search. It involves transporting three missionaries and three cannibals across a river. The first constraint is that the boat can hold only two people. The second constraint is that the cannibals can never outnumber the missionaries on either bank or in the boat. If at any time the missionaries on either bank are outnumbered, the missionaries will be eaten. The problem is to get everyone across the river safely without anyone being eaten (Charniak and McDermott 1985, 257).

MITI The Japanese organization responsible for the Fifth Generation Project (Hunt 1986, 171).

Mixed formalism An expert system that uses more than one formalism. The three common formalisms in expert systems are production rules, structured objects, and clauses. Expert systems which use mixed formalisms are called hybrid systems (Jackson 1986, 31).

Mixed-initiative natural language interface A type of interface found in certain intelligent computer-aided instruction systems. A mixed-initiative interface can answer student questions or initiate questions on its own (Barr and Feigenbaum 1981 vol 2, 236–238).

Mixed initiative system 1. A type of program that shares the responsibility for solving the problem. Expert systems are generally mixed-initiative programs. At times the program computes part of the solution on its own. At times the program asks the user for help. 2. An expert system that allows the user to volunteer information at the start of a program run, or in the middle of a program run. PROSPECTOR is one well-known expert system which uses a mixed initiative approach. 3. An expert system that allows the user to have extended control over the entire environment. Example: stopping a consultation process, altering the knowledge base and then continuing the consultation procedure from the point at which the user had suspended it. 4. The combined use of forward and backward chaining (Harmon and King 1985, 145–146; Brownston et al 1986, 16; Tello 1988 17–18; Tello 1988, 304).

Mixed-mode chaining Using a combination of backward and forward chaining to solve a problem. A drawback of mixed-mode chaining is that it is possible for the two modes of reasoning to miss meeting each other (Parsaye and Chignell 1988, 65).

Mixed-mode reasoning The use of a combination of forward and backward reasoning to solve a problem.

Mixed quantification The use of both existential and universal quantifiers (Epp et al 1988, 825).

MIXER An expert system that assists in writing microprograms for VLSI chips, which was developed at Tokyo University and is used at Texas Instruments. The system was written in PROLOG and is rule based (Hunt 1986, 171–172).

Mixin A very flexible inheritance feature found in FLAVORS and SCHEME. Using a mixin does not limit inheritance of methods and variables to a single-parent class. The user may specify inheritance from other classes (Tello 1988, 360–361; Tello Mar 1987, 128; McGregor Jul 1987, 55).

Mobile robot A type of robot with the ability of self-locomotion. Such robots are being used in hazardous environments (Mishkoff 1986 5–20).

Modal logic A type of logic that uses such connectives as "entails" and "possibly." An attempt to deal with a world in which possibilities exist. Example: It is "possible" the Wall Street stock market crash could have been avoided if we had reduced the trade deficit (Charniak and McDermott 1985, 375; Fischler and Firschein 1987, 96; Luger and Stubblefield 1989, 373).

Modal temporal logic A type of logic that considers the different types of worlds that may exist as a function of time. A program based on modal temporal logic could take into account the changing inflation rate to build a model of an economy (Mays 1986, 562–563).

Modal truth criterion An algorithm the planning program TWEAK uses. It is stated as follows: "A proposition p is necessarily true in a situation s if and only if two conditions hold: there is a situation t equal or necessarily previous to s in which p is necessarily asserted; and for every step C possibly before s and every proposition q possibly codesignating with p which C denies, there is a step W necessarily between C and s which asserts r, a proposition such that r and p codesignate whenever p and q codesignate." David Chapman is the inventor of the modal truth criterion algorithm (Amsterdam Jan 1987, 31).

Model A synonym for simulation (Eliot and Holliday 1988, 55).

Model-based diagnosis Knowledge about the correct functioning of a given system is used to predict the behavior of the system. Any real-world deviations from these predictions are used to collect suspected faulty components. The suspected faulty components are successively failed by the model; and if the failed model then generates the correct fault pattern, then it is picked as the faulty component. Important subtasks in model-based reasoning are modeling, prediction, candidate generation, discrimination, and elaboration. Model-based diagnosis is also known as diagnosing from first principles. Model-based diagnostic systems are unlike rule-based systems in that they can diagnose even unanticipated failures. In order to apply model-based diagnosis there must be a good understanding of the functioning of the components of the system and how they interact. A sufficient number of sensors to monitor the system is also necessary (Fulton and Pepe Jan 1990, 48–55).

Model-based expert system A system that uses a model-based representation of the underlying structure or behavior of the entity involved. A model-based system is based on deep knowledge rather than surface knowledge. Model-based expert systems are robust. That is, they are more capable of handling unexpected situations than a heuristic-based system, which is based more on surface knowledge. A model-based expert system built to diagnose problems with one type of computer is much more likely to be able to be used with another type of computer than is a rule-based expert system. The two basic types of model-based expert systems are those based on static representations and dynamic representations. *See also* Model-based diagnosis; Model-based representation (Mishkoff 1986, 3–22).

Model-based representation The type of representation used in model-based expert systems, which mimics the underlying structure and behavior of the area to which the expert system is being applied. In a model-based representation the objects need to be described and how the objects interact with one another must be specified. Example: In an electrical circuit the function of a resistor needs to be described and how it behaves when voltage is applied to it must be specified. Contrast a model-based representation with a heuristic system. The two basic types of model-based representations are static representations and dynamic representations. *See also* Model-based diagnosis; Model-based expert system (Walters and Nielsen 1988, 286–301).

Model-based vision The use of templates that describe selected objects in terms of their digitized image patterns. These templates are used to recognize objects. This technique is most effective when there are only a limited number of objects the program must discriminate. Two examples of model-based vision are ACRONYM and VISIONS (Mishkoff 1986, 5–13).

Model building The matching of data with models to find a model that best fits the data. In the expert system PROSPECTOR the data only approximately fit the various models available. Estimates of the closest fits are made. Details from the model with the closest fit are used for asking further questions to confirm or disconfirm the initial model choice (Smith 1989, 123).

Model-dependent integrity constraint A restriction of the knowledge structure in frame-based systems which is a part of the data model and is static. *Contrast with* World-dependent integrity constraint (Reimer 1986, 175).

Model directed A synonym for backward chaining (Hunt 1986, 172).

Model-driven generate-and-test A type of model-based example-learning program that generates hypotheses from the rule space and then tests the hypotheses against the examples in the instance space. The hypotheses are further constrained by the a priori model. *Contrast with* Model-driven schema instantiation (Barr and Feigenbaum 1981 vol 3, 369).

Model-driven learner A type of induction-based system which learns by generating hypotheses and testing the hypotheses against the data. *Contrast with* Data-driven learner (Kolokouris 1986, 225).

Model-driven method A program in an example-learning program that is driven not only by the examples presented, but by an a priori model. One strength of the model-driven method is such programs are better able to live with contradictory data. One disadvantage is they have difficulty with incremental learning. *See also* Model-driven generate-and-test; Model-driven schema instantiation. *Contrast with* Data-driven method (Barr and Feigenbaum 1981 vol 3, 369).

Model-driven schema instantiation A type of model-based example-learning program that uses a set of rules to constrain the construction and refinement of rules. *Contrast with* Model-driven generate-and-test (Barr and Feigenbaum 1981 vol 3, 369, 416–419).

Model theory A theory in which queries consist of the computation of a truth value for the query over the data base. Updates to the data base do not change the underlying structure of the data base. This is the standard approach in data base programming. *Contrast with* Proof theory (Brodie and Jarke 1986, 191).

Modifiability The measure of a program that determines the ease with which a program can be changed (Bratko 1986, 179).

Modify A command in OPS production systems which can add attributes and values to the working-memory elements in working memory (Brownston et al 1986, 56–57).

Modularist A person in the school of thought that holds the mind is a collection of specialists, each of which can carry out a specific task (Eliot May 1988, 74).

Modularity The ability to break up large programs into units which are relatively independent of each other. Rules in expert systems are considered as modular chunks of knowledge. The advantage is that the user can add, delete, or modify rules without having to carry out extensive rewrites of the expert system. In production expert systems the rules are also modularized by breaking them up into contexts. Each context consists of a set of rules and is responsible for taking care of a particular subtask of the overall problem. Object-oriented programs are highly modular. Each object in an object-oriented program is an independent entity. Important characteristics of modularity include decomposability, composability, understandability, continuity, and protection (Swaine Jun 1989, 116; Brownston et al 1986, 20, 28; Barr and Feigenbaum 1981 vol 1, 149; Matthews Sep 1987, 44–45).

Modular rule A rule whose meaning is independent of its context. A rule with a single entry point and a single exit. Modular rules increase clarity and decrease debugging problems (Pedersen Apr 1989, 44).

Module 1. A subdivision in modern computer languages programs, which is relatively independent of the other modules and which is responsible for carrying out a particular task. Modules in C are functions. 2. A subdivision in the visual apparatus that carries out certain visual subtasks. There may be texture, shading, color, motion modules, and others. *See also* Modularity (Waldrop 1987, 98–99).

Modus ponens A rule of logic. It states that if X implies Y and X is true then Y is true. Most expert systems employ modus ponens. Modus ponens is not complete by itself. It needs other rules of inference to perform proofs. It cannot for instance show that not$p$ logically follows from p -> q and not$q$. The problem with modus ponens is that it can be difficult to select the correct rule of inference during each state of the proof. *Contrast with* Resolution, which is a complete rule of inference. Modus ponens is called an elimination rule because it replaces two facts, X and X implies Y, with one fact Y. *Contrast with* Abduction; Modus tollens; Universal specialization (Townsend 1987a, 132; Hayes-Roth et al 1983, 64–65; Dos Reis, 1988, 50–51; Charniak and McDermott 1985, 20; Harmon and King 1985, 49–50, 75; Barr and Feigenbaum 1981 vol 1, 162–163).

Modus tollens A rule of inference that is a special case of resolution. Assume, IF X THEN Y. If Y is false then it is correct to infer X is false. Many expert systems cannot make this inference. *Contrast with* Modus ponens (Dos Reis 1988, 51; Harmon and King 1985, 50).

MOLGEN A planning expert system that plans experiments in genetics. A hierarchical planner. Interactions among subproblems are represented by structures called constraints. MOLGEN is able to reason about the constraints and uses this to steer its planning. Planning takes place on three different levels: strategy decisions, design decisions, and decisions concerning how to instantiate the design. At the most abstract planning level MOLGEN ignores constraints. At the less abstract levels MOLGEN pays more attention to the constraints and takes steps to resolve the interaction problems which arise. MOLGEN pursues a least commitment policy. That is, it defers making decisions until sufficient constraints are present. In this way MOLGEN is able to avoid having to undo decisions because another subproblem was not solved first, and the answer from the newly solved subproblem invalidates the previously made decision. Contrast with the problem-reduction approach to planning used by HACKER and INTERPLAN. *Contrast with* NOAH, the hierarchical planner (Johnson 1986, 55; Barr and Feigenbaum 1981 vol 3, 551–562).

Momentum term A term used in back-propagation networks to avoid false minima. Example: Assume you are attempting to find the deepest valley in a stretch of land. Your algorithm goes into a relatively shallow valley which is not the deepest valley. The momentum term is a term in the algorithm which ensures the algorithm will maintain enough momentum so that it will move out of the false minima and then find the deepest valley (Caudill Jun 1988, 58–59).

Monitoring expert system Expert systems that pay attention to incoming information so as to alert the user when a situation worsens. Examples: programs that watch over patients and power plants (Townsend 1987a, 6–7, Hayes-Roth et al 1983, 15, 83; Brownston et al 1986, 23).

Monkeys-and-bananas problem A problem frequently used by artificial intelligence programmers to study and teach artificial intelligence programs. A monkey in a room faces the problem of reaching a bunch of bananas hanging from the ceiling. The monkey is provided with different objects that can help him reach his goal (Tello 1988, 230–233).

Monotonicity A property of search in which the search process is consistently finding the minimal path without taking mistaken paths. It is sometimes called locally admissible (Luger and Stubblefield 1989, 167–168).

Monotonic reasoning A type of expert system in which once a fact or conclusion is added to the fact base it cannot be withdrawn for that particular program run. Most current expert systems employ monotonic reasoning. *Contrast with* Nonmonotonic reasoning (Chapnick Mar 1988, 5; Townsend 1987a, 132; Charniak and McDermott 1985, 370–376; Harmon and King 1985, 58; Brownston et al 1986, 450).

Monte Carlo method A method that relies on random decisions. In problem solving such a method is used only in the case when there is no algorithmic approach or heuristic approach available. Examples: the random walk and the computation of integrals (Hunt 1986, 174; Forsyth and Naylor 1985, 147).

MOPS *See* Memory Organization Package.

MORE A computer program which can intelligently analyze the data in a data base. Persoft, located in Woburn, Massachusetts is the originating company (Newquist Jan 1988, 22).

More informed heuristic The more effective heuristic given two heuristics in pruning the search space (Luger and Stubblefield 1989, 168).

Morpheme A combination of phonemes that produces a valid word (Chabris 1989, 197).

Morphological analysis The part of natural language processing that finds the underlying equivalency of words which are somehow similar to each other. Example; eat, ate, eaten, and digest (Emerson 1987, 55).

Morphology The analysis of the meaning of morphemes (Luger and Stubblefield 1989, 379).

Mostlikely A function found in the M1 expert system shell, used to find the value of a particular expression that is believed with the highest certainty. Example: "mostlikely(wine) = X" will bind X to "claret" if claret has the highest confidence factor value for all of the different wines under consideration.

Motion The study of multiple images over time in vision.

MRS A PROLOG-based expert system shell (Jackson 1986, 213; Hunt 1986, 175).

MUD An expert system that assists in oil-drilling operations by maintaining the correct drilling fluids. It was developed at Carnegie Mellon University using OPS5 (Hunt 1986, 175).

Multidimensional scaling A method of eliciting information from a domain expert. In multidimensional scaling the domain expert makes judgments concerning the similarity between objects—working with two objects at a time. The similarities are on a continuum, the objects must be from a physical n-dimensional space, and the similarities are symmetrical. *Contrast with* Johnson hierarchical clustering (Olson and Rueter 1988, 27–28).

Multilevel expert system An expert system that organizes knowledge in more than one form. *See also* Hybrid expert system tool (Michaelsen et al 1985, 310).

Multilevel system An expert system that uses more than one type of knowledge representation (Michaelsen et al 1985, 310).

Multimethod A function used in CommonLoops that can be considered as a message to any number of types of objects. The objects may have been from different classes. The object to which the message is being sent is considered one of the arguments. The combination of methods necessary to carry out the message is determined by the arguments (Tello Apr 1987, 150; Tello Mar 1987, 129; Tello 1989, 124, 148–149).

Multiple-choice questions Two or more options given to the user by an expert system. An important trait that can greatly reduce the number of questions a user is required to answer.

Multiple-concept learning Describing programs that are capable of learning more than one concept. An example is presenting training instances of medical patients who suffer from more than one disease. Some programs in this class are AQ11, MetaDENDRAL, and AM (Barr and Feigenbaum 1981 vol 3, 420–451).

Multiple contexts Many different possible solutions to a problem found in sophisticated expert systems. Each context differs in that the assumptions are different. In an economic forecast problem one context may make the assumption that inflation may be minimal. Another context may make the assumption that unemployment will be high. Another application of multiple contexts is when the environment of a problem situation may change over time. The different contexts can represent different points in time. Multiple contexts generally allow for sophisticated what-if capabilities and reasoning over time. Synonyms are multiple worlds and viewpoints (Winston 1979, 386–390; Walters and Nielsen 1988, 253–284).

Multiple-experts problem Attempting to account for the knowledge of more than one expert, with perhaps conflicting advice, when more than one expert is available to construct an expert system. The use of a blackboard architecture is one means of dealing with this problem (*Knowledge-Based Systems* 1986, 1–27).

Multiple inheritance The ability of an object in object-oriented languages to inherit qualities, characteristics, methods, and instance variables from more than one class. *See also* Intersection multiple inheritance; Union (Pascoe 1986, 144; Hunt 1986, 175; Duntemann 1989, 139).

Multiple instance Presence of more than one version of an object. (*Knowledge-Based Systems* 1986, 1–27).

Multiple-instances problem The challenge to develop an expert system that can economically account for a knowledge domain that has many instances of the same object. Example: a particular type of robot found in a manufacturing plant. There may be one hundred such robots in the plant. They are very similar, but each robot has its own idiosyncracies. A language which uses inheritance is the language of choice (*Knowledge-Based Systems* 1986, 1–27).

Multiple instantiation   The use of variables to create more than one version of an object in an expert system. Some expert systems like EMYCIN allow multiple instantiations, but others do not. The ability of some expert systems to use a rule more than once in a program run. That is, each time the rule is used the variables in the rule can be instantiated to different values. PROLOG is a language that uses multiple instantiation as a basic part of its computational scheme (Hayes-Roth et al 1983, 291; Harmon et al 1988, 56; Walters and Nielsen 1988, 226).

Multiple-instruction multiple data   A parallel processing paradigm. Compared to other types of parallel processing there are relatively few processors, but they are powerful. Each microprocessor is able to run its own program. The control is decentralized and there is relatively little coordination between processing tasks. The level at which parallel processing takes place is relatively high. It is best suited for problems in which the data processing taking place at each processor is complex and data dependent. *Contrast with* Single-instruction multiple data (Swaine May 1988, 100; Hillis 1985, 24–25).

Multiple-instruction single data   A parallel processing paradigm. Multiple instructions applied to single data items (Swaine May 1988, 100).

Multiple lines of reasoning   The pursuit of more than one solution to a problem at the same time by an expert system. Hearsay II is an example of an expert system with this capability (Hunt 1986, 175).

Multiple paradigm   The use of more than one paradigm in an expert system. Example: the use of rules and frames in combination (Rauch-Hindin 1988, 55; Matthews Sep 1987, 47).

Multiple reasoning   The ability of certain expert systems to pursue one or more solutions to a problem in the same time period.

Multiple representations   The use of more than one type of knowledge representation in an expert system. Example: using both production rules and frames (Walters and Nielsen 1988, 322).

Multiple single inheritance   An instance being created from more than one class (Gabriel Mar 1989, 60).

Multiple view   *See* Slice.

Multiple worlds   A property available on advanced expert systems which allows the simultaneous consideration of two or more alternative solutions to a problem. A synonym is viewpoints (Harmon et al 1988 58–59).

Multiprocessing   Another name for parallel processing (Barr and Feigenbaum 1981 vol 2, 46).

Multivalued attribute   *See* Multivalued parameter.

Multivalued logics   Logics which can represent intermediate values between true and false (Fischler and Firschein 1987, 96; Luger and Stubblefield 1989, 373).

Multivalued parameter   An attribute with several values at the same time, each of which has different degrees of certainty. Example: Given an attribute named weather, the attribute may have the values of both hot and cloudy. The values hot and cloudy have different degrees of certainty (Hunt 1986, 176; Jackson 1986, 97).

Mutation   A genetic operator that in some way changes a copy of a structure in an effort to produce a more successful structure (Austin 1990, 51).

MYCIN   An early expert system which demonstrated that expert system technology could be used in practical situations. MYCIN was developed at Stanford and used in medical diagnosis of infectious diseases. It has a body of knowledge which is encoded in production rules. MYCIN has a backward-chaining, depth-first inferencing system, a working memory, and an explanation system. It also uses certainty factors. The development of the first expert system tool, EMYCIN, followed from MYCIN (Johnson 1986, 18–19; Townsend 1987a, 20–21; Hayes-Roth et al 1983, 9–10, 39–40; Winston 1979, 241–246; Harmon and King 1985, 15–21, 61–75; Brownston et al 1986, 283–284; Barr and Feigenbaum 1981 vol 2, 184–192; Forsyth and Naylor 1985, 5–6).

N

Named association It retains the locations of an element in a list (Hunt 1986, 178).

Named variables Variables identified by names, which can be bound to ground terms or complex structures. Examples: X, Person, or Human. *Contrast with* Wildcard variable, which can be matched with, but cannot be bound to, the ground term or complex structure (Luger and Stubblefield 1989, 273).

Narrow system building tools An expert system tool that will work with only a very narrow range of problems. The advantage of such a tool is that it is optimized for this narrow range of problems. S-1 is an example of a narrow tool. It is designed for diagnostic/prescription paradigms. *Contrast with* Hybrid expert system tool (Harmon and King 1985, 83, 92, 96).

Natural deduction A nonresolution approach to theorem proving, which uses inference rules that imitate the inferencing process used by humans in proving theorems. It must use a number of inference rules including such rules as modus ponens and universal specialization. In this type of logic two rules of inference are used for each connective. One rule introduces the connective into an expression. The second rule eliminates the connective from that expression. Example: the two expressions A and A—> B are eliminated and replaced by B. The connective —> is replaced by the elimination rule modus ponens. Natural deduction maintains a distinction between goals and antecedents. In natural deduction the goals are not lost sight of. This is helpful in situations in which a person must intervene when the program cannot reach the goal. IMPLY is a program which uses natural deduction.

Natural deduction is sometimes referred to as informal reasoning. *Contrast with* Resolution theorem provers, which use only one inference rule—resolution (Barr and Feigenbaum 1981 vol 1, 163–164; Barr and Feigenbaum 1981 vol 3, 94–95; Hunt 1986, 178; Smith 1989, 126).

Natural intelligence   Intelligence derived from neural networks. The term was coined to emphasize the difference between artificial intelligence and the intelligence derived from neural networks (Caudill Dec 1987, 46).

Natural-language front end   A natural-language system that allows the user to communicate with a data base, expert system, or other computer programs.

Natural-language generation   The subfield of natural-language processing which has the goal of having computers generate English language that is understandable to humans (Mishkoff 1986, 1–16).

Natural-language interface   A program that allows the user to interact with the computer using Englishlike phrases. A synonym is natural-language front end (Townsend 1987a, 134–135; Mishkoff 1986, 4–13).

Natural-language processing   A branch of artificial intelligence programming whose goal is to facilitate communications between humans and computers using written human language. It consists of two areas: natural language understanding and natural language generation. Three important areas of study in natural language processing are lexical analysis, syntactic analysis, and semantic analysis. Parsers are an important area of study in language understanding. Three common parsers are state-machine parsers, context-free parsers, and noise-disposal parsers. Speech synthesis and speech recognition are not considered a part of natural-language processing (Schildt 1987, 92–94; Mishkoff 1986, 1–16; Townsend 1987b, 304–306; Tennant 1981).

Natural-language specification   A type of automatic programming that allows interaction with the computer in English in order to construct the program. *Contrast with* Formal specification; Specification by example (Mishkoff 1986, 6-7).

Natural-language understanding   The subfield of natural-language processing with the goal of having computers understand instructions given in ordinary English. The other subfield is natural-language generation. *See also* LIFER; Lunar; MARGIE; PAM; Script-Applier Mechanism; and SHRDLU (Mishkoff 1986, 1–16; Harmon and King 1985, 137–139; Barr and Feigenbaum 1981 vol 1, 225–321).

Naturalness   The degree to which the user of an expert system believes he or she is interacting with an expert rather than a computer program (Parsaye and Chignell 1988, 302).

Navigation   The ordering of subgoals in PROLOG so that the subgoals which will do the most pruning will appear first. This increases search efficiency (Zaniolo 1986, 221).

NCUBE10   A parallel-processing computer that consists of 1,024 microprocessors. The microprocessors are connected to one another as though they are at the corners of a 10-dimensional cube. Each processor can communicate with 20 other microprocessors.

Nearest neighbor   A type of search strategy that follows the principle of proceeding to the closest neighboring node. This type of search is efficient but subject to mistakes (Luger and Stubblefield 1989, 87).

Near miss   *See* Hit and near miss.

Neats   A synonym for formalist (Luger and Stubblefield 1989, vii).

Negate   To change the truth value of a proposition to its converse (Hunt 1986, 180).

Negation   The predicate not in logic-based programming. When not is used the expression which follows it takes on a truth value the opposite of what the expression is. Example: not(likes(john, mary)). This statement can only be true if likes (john,mary) is false (Brownston et al 1986, 193–194; Rosenberg 1986, 124).

Negation-as-failure The assumption that if a relationship cannot be found in a data base, then the relationship is false. An inference rule that states that if a fact X cannot be inferred in a closed system then not-X can be inferred. The type of negation most frequently used in logic-based systems. Negation-as-failure can lead to incorrect answers if sufficient knowledge is not in the data base. For example, if the data base does not have the fact that a human is an animal, a query which asks this question would obtain a false response. Cut and fail are used to implement negation as failure in PROLOG. Negation-as-failure, as used in PROLOG, is based on the closed world assumption. Negation-as-failure can be inconsistent with classical logical negation. It is accepted as equivalent to classic negation as long as sufficient information is available in the system to draw the necessary conclusions (Kowalski Aug 1985, 172; Sterling and Shapiro 1986, 88–90, 165–167; Roach et al Mar/Apr 1989, 47; Hewitt Apr 1985, 237).

Negative evidence Evidence used to predict that an event will not take place (Smith 1989, 127; Henschen 1990, 823).

Negative example An example that does not fit the category and thus produces a restraint on the concept. *See also* Positive example (Rosenberg 1986, 124).

Negative feedback A primary principle in cybernetics that states that opposing mechanisms can be used to reach equilibrium. The common house thermostat works on the principle of negative feedback. If the thermostat receives feedback that the house is too cold, it turns on the heater to warm the house. If the thermostat receives information that the house is warm enough, it turns off the heater. It was proposed that intelligent behavior could be conceptualized using the principle of negative feedback but nobody has been able to implement this in a practical way (Parsaye and Chignell 1988, 7).

Negative logic A type of logic in which a positive value is represented by 0 and a negative value is represented by a 1 (Hunt 1986, 180).

Nested class A class in C++ that is declared and enclosed within another class. This is different from a derived class. A class nested within another class cannot hide data from the class that encloses it (Stroustrup 1987, 152, 284–285).

Nested-if problem The problem arising when programmers assume the nested-if in AI programming has the same meaning as the nested-if in conventional programming. In standard programming nested-if rules are used to control the flow of execution. In AI programming, rules are used to declare knowledge and controlling the flow of execution is to be avoided since that is the responsibility of the inference engine (Pedersen Jul 1989, 46).

Nested Interactive Array Language *See* NIAL.

Nested pattern A pattern of data which is contained in another pattern of data. Example: the names of different computer manufacturers, nested within which are the names of the different types of computers they manufacture (Brownston et al 1986, 298–299).

Nested rule A type of rule that calls another rule. This is common practice in PROLOG.

Net A set of arcs and nodes.

NETL A frame-based knowledge-engineering language, one feature of which is its ability to copy large portions of its knowledge base. It was built using MACLISP at MIT (Hunt 1986, 180).

Netware A software-based neural net. *See also* Neurocomputer (Obermeier and Barron Aug 1989, 218).

Network A means of organizing data in artificial intelligence systems. A type of knowledge representation in artificial intelligence. A directed graph that consists of nodes that represent objects and labeled arcs that represent relationships or attributes of an object. It is capable of handling both hierarchical and nonhierarchical knowledge. The term is used interchangeably with semantic network (Schildt 1987, 212; Brownston et al 1986, 279–280; Forsyth and Naylor 1985, 131–141; Jackson 1986).

Network architecture Architecture that includes the pattern of connections, the presence or absence of feedback, how data circulate through the network, and how the neurons compete with one another (Klimasauskas 1988, 29).

Network data base management system A hierarchical data base. A given record which may be referred to as a child can have more than one parent record in this type of system.

Network paradigm The combination of neurodynamics and network architecture in neural networks (Klimasauskas 1988, 29).

Network representational schemes Schemes in which the nodes represent objects and the arcs connecting them represent relations among the objects. Examples: semantic networks, conceptual dependencies, and conceptual graphs (Luger and Stubblefield 1989, 334).

Neural network 1. A web of nerve cells in a living organism. 2. A computer simulation of the brain, which consists of at least one neuron and synapses. The neuron has an activation level and a transfer function. The synapses are the connection points for the neurons and are made up of an input, a weight, and an output. The neurons may be connected to one another in a complex net and they work in parallel with each other. 3. Self-organizing systems of simple interconnected processing units which possess a learning rule and are capable of learning. (It should be noted that not all neural networks are self-organizing or capable of learning.) The processing units are analogous to the neuron in the human central nervous system. It is a computing system that processes information by its dynamic state response to external inputs. Learning is based on the changes in connection strength between processing elements. Most neural networks have at least two layers of processing units—an input and an output layer. Some networks have more than two layers. The processing units in the other layers are called hidden units. The processing units have an activation level. The input components for processing units have weights. Learning algorithms are employed that alter the activations and weights as a function of the input and output. The weights, activation levels, and input from the environment are used to compute the output through the use of transfer functions. The builder specifies the interconnections between processing units, the transfer function, and the learning rule. The neural network is then given input so that it may spontaneously learn. A neural net attempts to emulate the structure and function of the brain. In addition to spontaneous learning, neural networks have the properties of automatic generalization, associative memory, fault tolerance, forgetting, and graceful degradation. Most of these properties are not available in ordinary computing programs. One other advantage of neural networks over conventional expert systems is their capability of handling inexact patterns. Since a neural network can recognize patterns that approximate, but are not identical to, the patterns it was trained on, this opens the door to handling the type of inexact input found in language and vision. Neural nets are different from conventional computer programs in that they are not given a sequential set of instructions. Instead, neural networks are given a rule by which they must abide. Within the confine of the rule they have a greater degree of freedom than do conventional programs. They are also different from conventional expert systems in that the knowledge is in the strength of the connections between processing units, and not in rules. Neural networks can be based in either a supervised or unsupervised learning mode. In the supervised mode the system receives external input concerning the correctness or incorrectness of the net's response. In the unsupervised mode the neural net receives no external feedback concerning the correctness of its response. Some proposed applications include: credit approval, decision-support systems, expert systems, robotics, emulating cognitive processes like associative memory, information processing, speech processing, space exploration, battlefield management, vision, recognition, and complex simulators. Neural networks are also referred to as parallel-distributed processing systems, connectionist systems, and neurocomputers. People who employ neural networks are sometimes referred to as connectionists (Ingraham et al 1988, 16–20; Jones and Hoskins 1987, 155; Caudill Jun 1988, 53–59; Jorgensen and Matheus 1986, 32; Tank and Hopfield 1987, 104–114; Johnson 1986, 46; Josin 1987, 188–192; Zeidenberg, 1987, 238–239; Caudill Dec 87, 46–52; Caudill Feb 88, 55–57; Bailey et al Nov/Dec 1988, 33; Bayle 1988, 40–42; Forsyth and Naylor 1985, 93; Chabris 1989, 298; Colvin Apr 1989, 59–60; Obermeier and Barron Aug 1989, 217).

NEUREX A medical expert system that diagnoses neurological diseases. A rule-based forward- and backward-chaining system which uses certainty factors. The rules are organized into hierarchies. The hierarchies reflect successively greater levels of abstraction. It was built at the University of Maryland and written in LISP (Hunt 1986, 180–181).

Neurocomputer 1. Neural network. 2. A neural net in hardware. *See also* Netware (Obermeier and Barron 89, 218; Caudill Dec 1987, 46).

Neurode A processing element in an outstar neural network. It is meant to be used as the analogical counterpart of the term neuron which is the primary processing element in the brain. Each neurode consists of an instar and an outstar (Caudill Nov 1988, 58).

Neurodynamics The properties in a neural net of how the inputs are combined, the activation level equation, and the method of altering weights (Klimasauskas 1988, 28).

Neuron A nerve cell in the central nervous system (Stevens Apr 1985, 287; Obermeier and Barron Aug 1989, 219).

Newell, Alan, and Simon, Herbert The two men who demonstrated that the computer could be used to study the mind. These pioneers in artificial intelligence developed Logic Theorist, General Problem Solver, and wrote the book *Human Problem Solving*. They emphasized symbol manipulation and heuristic search (Harmon and King 1985, 4, 22, 24; Waldrop 1987, 20–28).

Newton's method A powerful minimization algorithm used in neural networks. An extension of back propagation. Mathematically it uses the second derivative of the performance measure while back propagation uses the first derivative. The price paid for the added power is increased computational overhead (Swaine Oct 1989, 115–116).

NIAL (Nested Interactive Array Language) This language has as its primary data structure nested interactive arrays, and it is a functional language. It is considered a good prototyping language (Roland Apr, 1987, 52–55; Jenkins 1987, 32).

Nilsson, Nils Author of the textbook *Principles of Artificial Intelligence*.

N-inheritance A type of search in frame-based systems. This type of search starts from the bottom of the hierarchy and moves to the top in search of a value. It then goes back down to the bottom of the hierarchy and back up to the top in search of a demon to compute the value. This N shape is the source of the name N-inheritance (Amsterdam Dec 1986, 21).

NOAH (Nets Of Action Hierarchies) It is a planning system for robots which uses as its basic data structure the procedural net. The procedural net includes both procedural and declarative knowledge. There are a number of criticisms of NOAH. Its exclusive use of the least-commitment principle prevents it from being used in many real-world situations. NOAH is capable of controlling its plans in conjunction with a deadline, or other events. It suffers from the closed world limitation (Tello 1988, 480).

No-altering principle A principle used in AI learning that holds that when one finds an exception, avoid altering the general theory, and instead build a "special-case exception model" (Winston 1984, 395).

Node 1. An object in a semantic network. 2. A processing element in a neural network which is also a record structure. Each node can receive inputs from more than one source (Thompson and Thompson May 1987, 26; Ingraham et al 1988, 17; Ai Expert 1987, 15).

No-guessing principle A principle used in AI learning that holds that if there is some doubt about what to learn then choose not to learn. This is a very conservative approach to learning, but it can be the best course of action in situations in which the learning algorithm cannot recover from mistakes (Winston 1984, 395).

Noise-disposal parser A type of language parser that focuses only on keywords and the information they convey. The structure of the sentence is not important. The sentence "give me all the stocks with a price greater than $10" would be equivalent to "give me greater than $10 price a with stocks the all" (Schildt 1987, 117–124; Townsend 1987b, 306–312).

Noisy data Data that include irrelevant or misleading information. Real-world expert systems must frequently find ways to cope with noisy data (Jackson 1986, 229).

Nonalgorithmic An approach to problem solving that does not follow a fixed sequential problem-solving procedure. Heuristic search is an example of a nonalgorithmic approach to problem solving (Mishkoff 1986, G-3).

Nonchronological backtracking Another name for dependency-directed backtracking (Winston 1984, 82–84).

Noncontact sensing A robot sensor that is able to notice objects with which it is not in physical contact. Example: use of a television camera to sense objects (Mishkoff 1986, 5–19).

Nondeterminism This term is used with slightly different but related meanings in the literature. 1. A property in a program in which there is more than one possible path it can take. 2. A property of a program that can make the correct choice at a given choice point. The choice is really made as a function of the data present. 3. A property of a program in which there are so many choice points it may be very difficult to follow how the data drive the program to make the choices it does. 4. The property enabling a program to produce multiple solutions. Artificial intelligence programs are distinguished by their nondeterministic nature. Deterministic programs, in contrast, are relatively fixed in the sequence of program statements they follow (Barr and Feigenbaum 1981 vol 1, 265; Sterling and Shapiro 1986, 75–76, 206–236; Bratko 1986, 126).

Nondeterministic finite automaton A computer program that scans as input a string of symbols and makes the determination to admit or to decline the input string (Bratko 1986, 99).

Nondeterministic operator An operator that allows more than one result (Savory 1988, 237).

Nonground term A term in PROLOG that has variables (Sterling and Shapiro 1986, 151).

Nonhierarchical planner A type of planning system that develops a plan at only one level of abstraction. This type of planning system has difficulty with interacting subproblems. That is, it would have difficulty with a project that required a given subproblem to be completed before another subproblem could be started. A problem with a large number of such constraints is difficult for a nonhierarchical planner to handle. Example: STRIPS. *Contrast with* Hierarchical planner (Mishkoff 1986, G-3).

Nonlinear text A type of artificial intelligence

approach to processing text. Rather than simply reading text in a sequential fashion, the user is able to pursue easily a concept in the text with which he or she may not be familiar. Example: A user reading about velocity comes on the related concept of acceleration and wants to know more about that concept. The user can take the option of pursuing acceleration which is located elsewhere in the text. *See also* Hypertext.

Nonlinked data representations Data representations that do not use pointers to link simpler data structures. Examples: sparse arrays, stacks, and priority queues, all of which can be implemented in some production systems.

Nonmonotonic reasoning A type of reasoning used in some expert systems in which facts and conclusions can be withdrawn from the fact base in the light of new evidence. While some expert systems have some ability to change or delete conclusions at runtime, this ability is primitive. A sophisticated system maintains dependency records to be able to withdraw a chain of facts that have been concluded, based on a fact that must now be withdrawn. Most expert system shells are not capable of this type of sophisticated nonmonotonic reasoning. Planning problems are one type of problem that require knowledge systems which are capable of nonmonotonic reasoning. Active values are used to build nonmonotonic reasoning systems. Different versions of nonmonotonic reasoning include justification-based belief revision, logic-based TMS, assumption-based belief revision, reasoning by default, and reasoning by circumscription. Nonmonotonic reasoning is also called parsimonious reasoning, dependency-network maintenance, truth maintenance, consistency maintenance, and belief revision. The backtracking ability of PROLOG may be considered a type of nonmonotonic reasoning. The use of negative certainty factors in inexact reasoning may also be considered a form of nonmonotonic reasoning (Chapnick Mar 1988, 5; Townsend 1987a, 132; Hayes-Roth et al 1983, 74, 76; Walters and Nielsen 1988, 264–270; Harmon and King 1985, 58–60; Brownston et al 1986, 450; Barr and Feigenbaum 1981 vol 3, 114–119; Barr and Feigenbaum 1981 vol 2, 74–75; Perlis 1990, 823).

Nonobligatory slot entry A type of slot entry found in a frame-based system which does not have to be filled. Example: a modem slot in a computer frame. A modem is not a necessary part of a computer. *Contrast with* Obligatory slot entry (Reimer 1986, 176).

Nonresolution theorem proving A synonym for natural-deduction theorem proving.

Nonservo robot A type of robot in which movement is controlled in a rigid fashion by mechanical methods. Used in moving objects between fixed locations (Mishkoff 1986, 5-18).

Nontail recursion A type of recursion in which the last line of the clause does not contain the recursive call. Nontail recursion takes up more memory space than tail recursion and should be avoided when possible (Townsend 1987b, 15).

Nonterminal node A node in a search tree that appears in the interior of the search tree and not at an end node. Example: "The pretty girl flirted with the young sailors." When a parser analyzes this sentence it breaks the sentence up into phrases. That is, "The pretty girl" is a nonterminal node in the search tree. Eventually the parser will break up the sentence into individual words. When the parser reaches individual words those words are designated as terminal nodes (Charniak and McDermott 1985, 180; Barr and Feigenbaum 1981 vol 3, 495).

Nonterminal symbol The symbolic classifications of a formal grammar. Examples: <SENTENCE>, <NOUN>, <VERB>. They are variables. *Contrast with* Terminal symbol (Barr and Feigenbaum 1981 vol 1, 239).

NOR A logic operator. Given a set of statements the NOR of the statements is true if all of the statements are false. The NOR of the set of statements is false if at least one of the statements is true (Rosenberg 1986, 126).

Normal forms The syntactic schemes available in logic programming. Three different types of normal forms are conjunctive normal form, clausal form, and the horn clause subset (Jackson 1986, 77).

Normalized data base A data base that can be broken down into a set of logically organized tables in such a way as to reduce updating problems. A data base is normalized by setting it up so that each field depends on the key field or fields of its table. The breaking up of a data base into separate tables eliminates redundant information. Normalized data bases can be set up in languages like PROLOG (Knaus 1988, 13).

NOT A logic operator used to represent the logical operation of negation. Given a statement X, the NOT of X is true if X is false. The NOT of X is false if X is true See also Negation (Brownston, et al 1986, 193–194; Rosenberg 1986, 127).

Notational convenience One of three criteria used to assess a representation language. The characteristic of having a streamlined representation so that the information may easily be entered and understood. Other criteria for assessing a representation language are logical adequacy and heuristic power (Jackson 1986, 30).

NOTKNOWN A value for variable that is allowed in the NEXPERT expert system. A variable that has been assigned the NOTKNOWN value is a variable the system attempted to find a value for and could not. This differs from an UNKNOWN value in that with the variable with the UNKNOWN value there has been no attempt to ascertain the value of the variable. Having the information that a value is NOTKNOWN rather than UNKNOWN can be useful. The information can be used in the decision to assign a default value to the variable (Tello 1988, 303).

Not-node A type of node used by the Rete algorithm. It is used in the processing of negated patterns (Forgy and Shepard 1987, 39).

Nucleus 1. A clause whose truth value is true. 2. A set of regions in an image that belong to the same object (Dos Reis 1988, 55).

Null inheritance A function that prevents a particular slot from being inherited. In some cases it is undesirable for a particular characteristic to be inherited (Walters and Nielsen 1988, 230–231).

Number parameter A type of variable found in some expert system shells which allows only numerical values (Tello 1988, 148).

Nyquist limit The upper limit of spatial resolution based on the spatial frequency of the placement of sensor elements.

O

OAV *See* Object-attribute-value.

Object **1.** Either a physical or conceptual entity which has attributes. Examples: John, human, animal. All of the subsequent definitions fit under this general definition of object. **2.** An instance of a data type in LISP. **3.** An argument of a predicate in PROLOG. An object can be an atom, number, variable, or a structured object. In the predicate likes(john, mary), john and mary are objects. **4.** In object-oriented languages objects are represented by pieces of computer code that are capable of receiving messages, exhibiting behavior in response to the message, and returning a message. A collection of data and procedures which are grouped together. Objects are active, independent, and have the characteristics of persistence, encapsulation, and information hiding. One author describes an object as a lexically scoped subroutine with multiple entry points and persistent state. **5.** A frame in a frame-based system. **6.** Records in standard programming. **7.** An object in C++ differs from a C structure in that functions are included in the definition of the object. In a structure, functions are not allowed. **8.** Working-memory elements in production systems. In the expert system MYCIN an object is called a context. *See also* Object-oriented; Object-oriented programming (Stein 1988, 20; Lane Nov/ Dec 1987, 95; McGregor 1987, 49; Eliot and Holliday 1988, 55; Townsend 1987a, 119–123; Harmon and King 1985, 35–41; Brownston et al 1986, 6; Townsend 1987b, 229; *Smalltalk/V Tutorial and Programming Handbook*, 1986, 29–39; Bratko 1986, 27; Smith 1989, 130; Flamig Winter 1987, 20; Kaehler and Patterson 1986, 148; Rapaport 1988, 92; Winston and Horn 1988, 582; Manola

1990, 29; Guthery 1989, 80; Newton and Watkins 1988, 7).

Object-attribute-value (OAV) A type of knowledge representation. An object that has one or more attributes with values. Many expert systems may have a large number of OAVs that they may use for reasoning. In an OAV system the links between objects and attributes are has-a links. The links between the attribute value relationships are definitional links. Example: An Olds 88 has-a color. The color is an attribute of an Olds 88. The color is red. The link "is" is a definitional link. It defines the color of the Olds 88. The OPS5 production system languages use OAV triplets. Simpler expert systems may consist of attribute value pairs. These simpler systems assume the existence of only one object in the domain. Other types of knowledge representations are frames, semantic nets, and logic rules. An OAV is also referred to as context-parameter-value triplets (Townsend 1987a, 122–123; Harmon and King 1985, 38–39; Rosenberg, 1986, 129).

Object based Describing a language that possesses objects which have internal operations and a persistent internal state. Under this definition classless languages such as Actor and ADA are included. Also included are the class languages Smalltalk, Flavors, and Simula67. *See also* Object oriented (Wegner 1989, 245).

Object frame A synonym for object or frame. It allows for inheritance and attached predicates.

Objective-C An object-oriented language that is a preprocessor for C. It is derived from the C language. In many ways it is closer to Smalltalk than it is to C++. For example, Objective-C includes collections, sets, bags, and containers just as Smalltalk does. It has the ability to model complex real-world situations (Gomsi and Desanti 1987, 60; Skelly 1987, 81–86).

Object oriented 1. Referring to a language in which programs are constructed by describing objects and the relations between objects. In this sense PROLOG may considered an object-oriented language. An object in PROLOG may be described as john(intelligent, motivated). The relationship between this object and other objects can be expressed in PROLOG rules. This is perhaps the loosest definition of object oriented. It should also be noted PROLOG can be used to build object-oriented programs as delineated in subsequent definitions. 2. Having the presence of inheritance. 3. Showing inheritance and classes. Data abstraction and concurrency are optional features. Under this definition weak or strong typing is allowed. Object-oriented languages allowed under this definition include Smalltalk, Simula67, ZetaLISP, LUCID, KRL, FLAVORS, and C++. C++ is an object-oriented language that employs classes, inheritance, operator overloading, and function overloading. Object-oriented languages under this definition are subsumed under the broader category of object based, which includes classless languages like Actors and Self. 4. Requiring data encapsulation, abstraction, and polymorphism. This definition does not require inheritance. This definition of object oriented is used in referring to the original object-oriented language, Smalltalk. 5. Referring to the basic concept of the Smalltalk language, which is objects passing messages to each other. 6. Requiring encapsulation, message passing, inheritance, and late binding. This definition also fits the Smalltalk language. 7. Requiring information hiding, data abstraction, dynamic binding, and inheritance. This definition was proposed by G. Pascoe. As can be noted by the above definitions object oriented refers to more than simply a form of knowledge representation.

In object-oriented languages that conform to the stricter definitions, objects are asked to perform operations on themselves rather than simply having data passed to procedures, as is the case in conventional languages. The objects perform an active role in the execution of the program. They do not passively wait for another object to call them. Instead, they may activate themselves because of a change in the incoming data. This is the opposite of procedural languages where the counterpart of objects, functions, are passive. Data items in object-oriented programs are persistent. That is, variables maintain their values throughout the program run. One strong advantage of an object-oriented language is its evolutionary capacity: It is easy to add to the program. Object-oriented languages have a smaller semantic gap than other languages. That is, the objects defined in the program more closely correspond to the objects the program is trying to represent. This makes object-oriented programs more understandable. Object-oriented languages work best when there are a large number of similar objects which are arranged in a hierarchy. Then, inheritance can be used effectively to spawn related objects. Object-oriented languages are frequently applied to simulation problems. A frame-based system is a type of object-oriented language. Frame-based systems package data and procedures together inside of frames and possess inheritance. Two differences between frame-based systems and the classic Smalltalk paradigm are: (1) Frame-based systems generally have a more flexible inheritance scheme and they more frequently allow multiple inheritance. (2) In strict object-oriented programs data within an object may only be accessed by a message. In frame-based programs rules are frequently allowed to access and reason directly with data in a frame. This type of direct access is not allowed in a strict object-oriented type of language like Smalltalk. Perhaps the first object-oriented language was Simula(2).

When applied to data bases object oriented may also have different meanings. On one level it may simply mean the ability to represent complex objects. On a somewhat higher level it may mean the representation of complex objects along with generic operators that are used to administer to the complex objects. On a still higher level, object oriented means the use of complex objects which consists of an internal structure which includes procedures which can operate on the data within the object. *See also* Data abstraction; Encapsulation; Inheritance; Message passing; Methods; Oriented programming (Matthews Sep 1987, 83; Gomsi and Desanti Nov 1987, 60; Somsel Nov 1987, 75–76; *Knowledge-Based Systems* 1986, 2–64; Walters and Nielsen 1988, 243–246; Townsend 1987b, 5–7; Jackson 1986, 60; Swaine May 1988, 115–118; Gabriel Mar 1989, 54–65; Thomas 1989, 232; Wegner 1989, 245–253; Baker 1987, 42–43; Manola 1990, 32; Tesler 1986, 195–206.

Object-oriented data base **1.** A type of data base that emphasizes the approach used in object-oriented languages like Smalltalk, where complex objects are the focus of attention and encapsulation and inheritance are typical characteristics. In addition, object-oriented data bases emphasize very large data bases, efficiency processing, concurrency control, recovery facilities, and efficient query processing. **2.** A combination of the object-oriented paradigm with a data base management system. Such a data base has a number of advantages: (1) The data base consists of a set of objects rather than a set of flat tables. This type of data base uses an object structure which more closely mirrors the objects in the world than does a relational or hierarchical data base. (2) The objects represented can be very abstract, inheritance is available, and message passing can be implemented. (3) Integrity constraints are more easily implemented. One difficulty is that it is harder to restructure relationships with an object-oriented data base than it is for a relational data base. Some experts consider object-oriented data bases to be the next generation in data bases, replacing relational data bases. Some possible applications include CAD systems, office information systems, programming languages, and data base management systems (King 443–444; Peterson Mar 1987, 26; Manola 1990, 31–33).

Object-oriented design A type of software design that adds greater emphasis to the design and abstraction of data structures than does top-down design. It is most efficient when complex data are involved. *See also* Top-down design (Olan 1988, 37–41).

Object-oriented graphics The saving of designs in the form of calculable shapes instead of the standard bit-mapped screens (Somsel Nov 1987, 75).

Object-oriented programming (OOP) An approach to programming in which objects, rather than data and procedures, are the focus of attention. The objects in the program contain data and procedures which work with the data (encapsulation). Programming consists of objects sending and receiving messages to and from one another (message passing). Objects and their data can only be accessed through well defined procedures (data hiding). The objects operate on themselves or other objects. Contrast this with what happens in standard programming where procedures operate on data. The local state of the variables is preserved in object-oriented programming (persistence). The persistence of variable values is the opposite of what happens in a functional language where the values of variables are lost when a function is exited. Another common goal in object-oriented programming is inheritance. Advantages of the object-oriented approach are reusability of code, extensibility, the ability to handle complexity, and clarity. Since object-oriented programming is an approach to programming it can be carried out in conventional programming languages like C, though it is easier to implement this approach in a language designed specifically for object-oriented programming. *See also* Object oriented (Swaine May 1988, 115–118; Meyer 1988, 81; Baker 1987, 42; Stabler 1986, 46, 48; Tello Mar 1987, 126–134; Bharath and Sklar 1985, 49; Pascoe 1986, 139–144; Harmon and King 1985, 126; Harmon et al 1988, 37).

Object swapping A procedure used in Smalltalk languages in which objects are switched in and out of RAM memory as needed (Bernat Nov 1986, 80).

Object table A helpful tool for organizing objects in an object-oriented program. It consists of a listing of the objects, their methods, and the use to which the objects will be put.

Object term A term used in some expert systems that takes the form of (slot-name of Object). Example: (Age of John). Object term refers to the value of a slot in a particular frame.

Object type Class (Duntemann 1989, 139).

Obligatory slot entry A type of slot entry found in frame-based systems that cannot be left out while going down the specialization hierarchy. Example: a slot that holds the type of permanent data storage for a frame that represents a computer. The entry of data in this slot is necessary since all modern computers require a type of permanent data storage. Contrast with nonobligatory slot entry (Reimer 1986, 176).

Occam's razor A principle that holds that when given two equally plausible explanations for a phenomenon the simpler of the two explanations is the best. Applied in expert systems by giving precedence to relatively simple rules (Swaine May 1988, 112; Johnson 1986, 198).

Occurs check A test that ensures that a variable will not be allowed to unite with a term which holds that variable. It does permit a clause to unite with a subset of itself (Luger and Stubblefield 1989, 63, 481).

Omega-order logic An extension of first-order logic in which quantification over predicates and functions is allowed. A synonym is second-order logic.

One-input node A node used by the Rete algorithm, which is responsible for deciding if a condition in a rule is satisfied in isolation from other conditions. *Contrast with* Two-input node (Forgy and Shepard 1987, 38).

One-layer perceptron A perceptron with only one layer of modifiable connections. This is the version of perceptron that Minsky and Papert criticized as being too susceptible to combinatorial explosion ever to be able to carry out useful computations. Multilayered perceptrons were later found that are able to carry out useful computations (Rumelhart and McClelland 1986, vol 1, 111).

ON-LINE ENGLISH The language INTELLECT.

Ontological assumption The assumption made in artificial intelligence that facts can be defined, stored, and retrieved in a reasonable and efficient way. Currently, there are no methods of carrying out these processes in such a manner as to compete with the mechanisms of storage and retrieval of information of the human brain. Just one problem artificial intelligence programs face is the ambiguities which are commonly found in human language (Lawrence 1985, 165–167).

OOP *See* Object-oriented programming.

OPAL An object-oriented data base language developed by Servio Logic Corporation. Its syntax is an extension of Smalltalk (Zaniolo et al 1986, 58).

Open architecture An architecture that allows integration with other languages, conventional software programs, and graphic user interfaces.

Open-ended architecture A property of some expert system shells that lets users add capabilities to the expert system shell (Tello 1988, 147; Matthews Sep 1987, 82).

Open-ended system An expert system that allows the calling of external programs (Wolfgram et al 1987, 306).

Open loop A method of control in which there is no feedback concerning errors. Hence, the system is not self-correcting (Rosenberg 1986, 186).

Open-loop robot A robot that does not employ feedback concerning its movement. That is, there are no sensing devices that monitor if the movement has been carried out correctly (Rosenberg 1986, 131).

Open system A type of expert system that can process data concurrently, operate asynchronously in a parallel system, deal with inconsistent information, operate continuously, utilize arms-length relationships, has decentralized control, and can handle time-varying data. One approach is to use actors that operate independently of one another. Each actor can receive and send messages, change internal states, or create new actors. Such an open system is less concerned about the validity of a fact and more concerned about the impact of the fact. The concept of open systems was conceived by Carl Hewitt. Apiary is the name of the program Hewitt is working on to create an open system (Hewitt Apr 1985, 223–242; Hewitt Premier 1986, 45).

Open-world assumption The set of objects or axioms the system is aware of is not assumed to be complete. *Contrast with* Closed-world assumption (Smith 1989, 131).

Operand An object to which an operator is applied. In the function (mult 3*2), 3 and 2 are operands (Rosenberg 1986, 131).

Operationalization The utilization of the information learned to improve performance in a machine-learning system (Chabris 1989, 298).

Operationally object-oriented data base management system An object-oriented data base system that uses generic operators to handle objects. Such a system is said to be structurally object oriented. *Contrast with* Behaviorally object-oriented data base management systems (Manola 1990, 32).

Operation table A table that defines an operation by enumerating all possible combinations of values for an operand along with the outcome values (Rosenberg 1986, 132).

Operator 1. A symbol that states how an operand is to be manipulated in standard computer language. The most common operator is the + sign. The operands for this operator are the numbers it will add: 2, 3. 2. A means of changing a problem from one state to another in artificial intelligence. Rules are referred to as operators in expert systems. Likewise, in PROLOG a rule is sometimes referred to as an operator because it is a means of moving the system from one state to another. Operators are really educated guesses which one hopes will move the problem-solving procedure closer to a solution. Of course, PROLOG has standard operators like +, −, *, etc. Operators may be prefix, postfix, or infix operators (Charniak and McDermott 1985, 257; Forsyth and Naylor 1985, 139; Bratko 1986, 78).

Operator-ordering function A search function that ranks the different potential operators at each state from the best operator to the poorest operator (Charniak and McDermott 1985, 259).

Operator overloading The procedure of giving more than one meaning to an operator. The meaning selected is a function of the arguments that accompany the operator. To some extent operator overloading is present in standard program languages like C. In C the language will, for example, look at the arguments for the addition operator to see if the arguments are reals or integers and will then choose the procedure that will correctly add the numbers. In contrast to a standard C program, in C++ the programmer is able to define the meaning of the operator. The operator, +, in addition to adding integers and reals, can be given the task of adding vectors. Operator overloading takes place at compile time. *Contrast with* Polymorphism, an analogous process which takes place at runtime (Waite et al 1987, 496).

Operator schemata Operators that contain variables. Since these variables can take on different values, the operator schemata can represent multiple states (Smith 1989, 132).

Opportunistic planning A type of planning that uses a blackboard control structure. Different specialists contribute information to the blackboard and use information from the blackboard. The specialist that will be most active is controlled more by the data on the blackboard than by a rigid control structure. As a result, the system opportunistically develops different islands of knowledge. These islands of knowledge are expanded until a complete plan is achieved. A type of bottom-up planning. *Compare with* Hierarchical planner.

Opportunistic problem solving An approach to problem solving in which, if an opportunity for a quick solution to a subgoal occurs, the expert system is able to suspend what it is doing and take advantage of this opportunity. Contrast with the type of problem solving that requires that a fixed sequence of subgoals be solved no matter what new information is brought to bear (Barr and Feigenbaum 1981 vol 2, 129)

Opportunistic scheduler A type of scheduler used in blackboard expert systems, which is able to change its schedule as a function of new information. A method of coping with errorful data and large search spaces. An opportunistic scheduler uses the least-commitment principle and can move freely from top-down processing to bottom-up processing (Hayes-Roth et al 1983, 119–124).

OPS5 An expert system language developed at Carnegie Mellon by Charles Forgy. He used LISP to develop OPS5. It is a production expert system which is primarily forward chaining, although programs can be designed so that they can run in a backward-chaining mode. OPS5 consists of three parts: a rule base, working memory, and an inference engine. The rule base consists of production rules. The production rules are in the form of object attribute value triplets. (*See also* Production) The production rules resemble if/then rules but they allow for very complex pattern matching. The production rules hold relatively static knowledge. One may make an analogy between the rule base and a person's long-term memory. The second part of OPS5, working memory, holds information in a set of structures known as working-memory elements. This information is more volatile than is the information found in the rules in the rule base. The information in working-memory elements is constantly being added to, deleted, or altered through its interaction with the rules in the rule base. One may compare working memory with human short-term memory. The information in working memory is constantly being matched to the rules in the rule base. As matches are made the rules are placed in a conflict set. One rule is picked from the conflict set using what is known as a conflict resolution strategy, and this rule is executed, meaning the right-hand side of the rule fires—adding, deleting, or altering working-memory elements. The rules may be cycled through many times, in this recognize-act style, until no more information can be gleaned from the rule base. This very complex pattern matching and interaction between the rule base and working memory is what sets OPS5 apart from the simple if/then rules found in standard computer programs. The third part of OPS5 is the inference engine. The inference engine is responsible for conducting the recognize-act cycle, which takes place between the rule base and working memory. The OPS5 inference engine is known for its Rete match algorithm, which produces complex and efficient pattern matching. The Rete match algorithm also conducts the conflict-resolution strategy mentioned earlier. (*See also* Conflict resolution.) Having the control mechanism (the inference engine) as a separate module is the other distinct characteristic of OPS5 that sets it apart from standard computer programs. Most standard programs have control (do-while loops and the like,) intertwined with the knowledge (facts and rules). OPS5 does not carry out inexact reasoning, rules cannot be divided into contexts, nor does it use backtracking. A drawback of OPS languages is that it is difficult to follow the very complex reasoning process. At the same time this is one of the benefits of these languages. That is, its reasoning process is sufficiently powerful that it can solve complex problems, and actually produce correct, unanticipated answers. OPS5 was used to develop XCON, the first commercially successful expert system (Moskowitz Nov 1986, 217–224; Hayes-Roth et al 1983, 183–186, 301–308; Harmon and King 1985, 115–116; Tello 1988, 233–243).

Optimal solution   A solution arrived at by the least possible cost. That is, it searches fewer nodes in finding the quickest path than does another less optimal solution (Forsyth and Naylor 1985, 157; Smith 1989, 133–134).

Optimization   The attempt to seek the best possible solution for a given problem. While such a goal is admirable it is possible the time spent in reaching the optimal goal is prohibitive. *Contrast with* Satisfice (Schildt 1987, 19, 41–43).

Optimization model   A type of neural network model that deals with combinatorial optimization problems such as a complex freight delivery system or a manufacturing process (Josin 1987, 184, 188).

Optimized query tree   A structure produced by induction expert systems which holds the knowledge gained from examples fed to the system (Citrenbaum et al 1987, 31).

OR   A logic operator. Given a set of statements connected by the OR operator, the result is true if one of the statements is true. The result is false if all statements are false. *See also* Disjunction; Exclusive-OR; Inclusive-OR. *Contrast with* Conjunction (Brownston et al 1986, 191–193).

Oracle   A synonym for evaluation function (Luger and Stubblefield 1989, 166).

Ordered state-space search   A synonym for best-first search.

Ordered trees   A method used in eliciting data from an expert. The underlying assumption is that the objects in the domain will cluster. The domain expert is asked to recall objects. It is assumed that the domain expert will recall the objects in naturally occurring clusters (Olson and Rueter 1988, 31–32).

Ordering   A listing in logic of variables in a set of clauses such that the variables are in descending order of importance. Ordering is an important technique in semantic resolution (Dos Reis 1988, 55).

OR-parallelism   A type of parallelism that can be employed in PROLOG-based systems in which each microprocessor is assigned a goal at the same time. Each microprocessor searches its list of clauses for a match. If a match is found among any of the microprocessors, the goal succeeds.

This type of parallelism is used in programs that require more than one solution. OR parallelism in PROLOG does not use backtracking. Instead each possible solution is pursued independently and at the same time. *Contrast with* AND-parallelism (Eadline 1989, 35; Townsend and Feucht 1986, 179).

Orphan rule A rule that cannot be executed because the consequent of the rule does not appear as the antecedent of another rule. Other types of error rules include irregular rules and unfirable rules (Lane Jun 1989, 306).

Oscillating focus of attention A procedure used in expert system development in which the stage of application development should alternate with the stage of expert system tool development. Reid Smith is credited with the concept. While it has the advantage of closely tailoring the expert system tool to the application it has drawbacks. The problems encountered in oscillating focus of attention are somewhat akin to the kinds of problems one would have in developing an application in C and writing the C compiler at the same time (Firdman Oct 1986, 76).

Output connections The part of a processing unit in neural networks connected to the next processing unit, or to an output unit. The output connection is responsible for passing the output signal to the unit to which it is connected (Stevens 1985, 289; Jones and Hoskins 1987, 155).

Output contact A device used by robots to turn motors and other devices off and on (Rosenberg 1986, 133).

Output rule A rule used in neural nets, to determine the output of a processing unit (Ingraham 1988, 17).

Outstar The part of the neural net processing unit in outstar learning that sends the output signal to many other processing units (Caudill Nov 1988, 58).

Outstar activity equation An equation that defines the amount of activity of the neurodes in an outstar learning network (Caudill Feb 1989, 62).

Outstar learning A type of biological learning that has been adapted to neural networks. Outstar learning is represented by equations. There are two equations that represent outstar learning, an activity equation and a learning equation. Outstar learning can be used as a partial explanation of Pavlovian conditioning at a neural level. The Pavlovian experiment consists of presenting a bell and giving food (unconditioned stimulus) to a dog. The dog, of course, salivates. Eventually, the conditioned stimulus of the bell causes the salivation response. The following is how outstar learning explains classical conditioning: Each processing unit consists of instars and outstars. The instars of a processing unit receive input from many other processing units. The outstar of a processing unit sends the output to many other processing units. Many of the connections between processing units are responsible for relaying the unconditioned stimulus. As the conditioning process continues, certain of the other processing units become more sensitized and that accounts for the strengthening of the association between the conditioned stimulus (the bell) and the salivating response. The equation in outstar learning allows for extinction of the conditioned response as a function of time. Extinction also takes place in Pavlovian conditioning. A revised outstar learning paradigm can be used to learn the types of time-varying sequences found in speech (Caudill Feb 1989, 61–67; Caudill Nov 1988, 57–65).

Outstar learning equation A term that represents the rate of decay of the strength of association between two neurodes and a learning component (Caudill Feb 1989, 62–63).

Overlapping objects The condition in vision programs when one object partially hides another object. Controlled hallucination is one means of dealing with this problem (Schildt 1987, 136).

Overloading The process of giving an operator or function more than one meaning. *See also*

Function overloading; Operator overloading (Waite et al 1987, 496–497).

Override The ability of a slot on a frame to be able to override inherited information. Example: Mammals inherit the characteristic of live births. There are some mammals who do not have this characteristic. It is important to have the ability to override this exception. The override facility may refer to redefining inherited methods as well as inherited characteristics (Amsterdam 1987, 19; Duntemann 1989, 139).

OWL A frame-based knowledge-engineering language, which uses one knowledge base and has a flexible inheritance mechanism. It was written in LISP and developed at MIT (Hunt 1986, 188).

Own slot A type of slot whose slot will not be inherited by members of the class below the object which has the own slot. Example; In a hierarchy of automobiles a slot for number of wheels may exist. The default value is four. There may, however, be some peculiar autos which have no wheels. This slot is set up as an own slot because it is not desirable for the autos that are subtypes of this auto to inherit a wheel slot. *Contrast with* Member slot (Hu 1989, 187).

P

Packet Grouping rules according to topics. This type of grouping can increase the efficiency of an expert system. Context is an equivalent term (Michaelsen et al Apr 1985, 307).

PAM (Plan Applier Mechanism) A story-understanding system developed by Roger Shanck. It demonstrates the use of plans in comprehending stories. PAM reads a story and attempts to match what it reads with one of a set of plans PAM knows about. The plan PAM finds which matches the story has subgoals. PAM looks for the subgoals in the story. If PAM finds information in the story that verifies the subgoals, it is said PAM understands the story. It is able to summarize the dialogue and answer questions about it. It is claimed it has the capability of understanding unique events (Waldrop 1987, 81–82; Johnson 1986, 175; Barr and Feigenbaum 1981 vol 1, 313–315).

PAN A parallel associative network that has been applied to vision-processing networks and logic gates. It is being developed at IBM (Hunt 1986, 190).

Pandemonium A dynamic interactive model of perception developed by Oliver Selfridge. It uses a pattern-action demon model (Townsend and Feucht 1986, 36).

Paradigm In its most general sense it means type, pattern, or example. The term paradigm has a large number of more specific definitions—over 20. The following are the most common: **1.** A general procedure for solving a problem. Examples: a planning or diagnostic paradigm. **2.** The type of knowledge representation and reasoning procedure used in expert system shells.

Some examples are rule based, frame based, a semantic network, object oriented, forward chaining, or backward chaining. 3. Methods of representing data and methods for controlling the flow of the execution in programming (Swaine May 1988, 100; Rauch-Hindin 1988, 55; Brynjolfsson and Loofbourrow 1988, 35; Parsaye 1988, 25; Smith 1989, 135).

Parallel AI   The use of parallel processing to improve performance. *Contrast with* Distributed artificial intelligence (Gasser 1989, 27).

Parallel computation   The use of computers to solve a problem by breaking the problem down into parts and allowing a set of processors to work on each subproblem simultaneously. Neural networks are only one example of how parallel computation can take place (Zeidenberg 1987, 237–238).

Parallel deepest descent   Asynonym for back propagation (Swaine Oct 1989, 113).

Parallel-distributed model   Processing that takes place through the interactions of a large number of simple processing elements called units each sending excitatory and inhibitory messages. Each memory is represented by a unit which has mutually excitatory interactions with units standing for each of its properties. Then whenever any property of the memory becomes active, the memory tends to be activated, and whenever the memory is activated, all of its contents tend to become activated. This gives content addressability. PDP models have the ability to self-modify. They are also referred to as neural networks.

Parallel-distributed processing   A process in which massive parallel processing takes place. That is, many units are processing different parts of a set of related information at the same time, as contrasted with the type of sequential processing found in most computers. The underlying concept is that intelligence originates from the interactions of a multitude of simple processing units. This model of human intelligence comes from physiological studies of the brain. Parallel-distributed processing possesses the properties of content addressability, default assignment, and spontaneous generalization. Patterns are not stored per se; rather, connection strengths among the processing units are modified to represent the pattern. When the pattern occurs again in the environment, the internal pattern of connection strengths which represents the external pattern will be activated in a manner roughly analogous to a tuning fork being activated. The change in connection strengths is the way this system learns rather than the acquisition of new rules. All knowledge is in the connection strengths. Memory and processing are not separate entities as in conventional computer programs, instead they are closely intertwined. Such systems hold the promise of being able to carry out approximate pattern matching and unsupervised learning, activities that conventional programming techniques do poorly.

Parallelism   The firing of all instantiated rules for each recognize-act cycle in production systems. The drawback is that conflicting information may be more easily added to the accumulated facts (Brownston et al 1986, 307–308).

Parallel iterations   Multiple cells changing at a given point in time in neural networks. *Contrast with* Sequential mode (Soulie and Mejia Dec 1988, 58).

Parallel machine   A computer with more than one microprocessor and memory set aside for each processor; it is capable of doing parallel processing (Johnson 1986, 73, 245, 230).

Parallel processing   A procedure that consists of the breaking down of a problem into separate components so that the computer program and the computer can work on each component of the problem simultaneously. The kind of computer that is necessary to do this is one with more than one microprocessor. Each microprocessor is assigned a component of the problem. Each processor has its own memory. The different processors interact with one another while attempting to solve the problem. Parallel processing can greatly aid in solving complex problems which must be solved using very large bodies of knowledge. Parallel networks offer the possibility of more quickly finding the best match. This is an advantage over current AI systems which have difficulty finding the best match for the data. Parallel processing can be simulated on computers with only one microprocessor (Johnson 1986, 72–73; Townsend 1987a, 16; Mishkoff 1986, G-3; Harmon and King 1985, 59).

Parallel production systems A production system that executes all instantiations in a single cycle. XAPS, CAPS, and IntelligenceCompiler use this strategy. *See also* DoAll for an example of a conflict resolution strategy which fits this description. Contrast with the conflict resolution strategies used in OPS5 production systems (Brownston et al 1986, 307–308).

Parallel reasoning The ability of an expert system to apply a rule or a set of rules to more than one context.

Parameter 1. A constant value in a program that determines the behavior of the program. The facts in an expert system are referred to as parameters. A parameter is a fact used by an expert system to make a conclusion. 2. The attribute of an object. In the MYCIN expert system a parameter is an attribute of a context. That is, a context may be a person. One parameter or attribute is the person's weight attribute—not the actual weight of the person. 3. A symbol associated with a procedure or function. The symbol can take on a value passed to it by the calling procedure. The parameter is used as a means of receiving information from and sending information to the calling program. An example is Max(A, B, C). $A, B,$ and C are parameters for the procedure Max. The procedure decides which of the three numbers $A, B,$ and C is the maximum number. There are two types of parameters, formal and actual. The formal parameters are $A, B,$ and C. The actual parameters are the values $A, B,$ and C actually represent, which were passed to the procedure by the calling procedure.

See also San Marco LISP Explorer (Hunt 1986, 192; Parsaye 1988, 314; Walters and Nielsen 1988, 211; Wolfgram et al 1987, 306; Winston and Horn 1988, 587).

Parameter learning A type of learning used in control and pattern-matching situations in which the search method looks for the value of the parameters that produces the least error between a model and the unknown object. A type of learning that requires the calculation of parameters from data by such methods as least squares. A considerable number of trials may take place before the device finds the optimal parameters and learns the task (Barr and Feigenbaum 1981 vol 3, 375–380; Fischler and Firschein 1987, 137; Smith 1989, 136).

Parameter passing 1. The transfer of values to a function so that the function can carry out its intended computation. The term is roughly equivalent to message sending. 2. Parameter passing can refer to the ability of an expert system to pass parameters to another program. This is commonly carried out by passing pointers or by using disk-based files (Schildt 1987, 278–279).

Paramodulation A sophisticated type of resolution. An inference rule that uses two clauses. One of the two clauses must include a positive equality predicate to derive a clause which has made a substitution based on the positive equality predicate. It was developed with an eye to improved efficiency. It allows for such substitutions as follows: Assume, younger(daughter(X),X) and the relationship equal(daughter (mary), sue). Then younger(sue,mary) can be inferred (Luger and Stubblefield 1989, 439; Tello 1988, 419; Wos and Veroff 1990, 898).

Parent The object from which a child object inherits its characteristics in object-oriented programming. Mammal is a parent object for the tiger class.

Parent class The preexisting class for a newly defined class (Duntemann 1989, 139).

Parlog A relational language capable of being used in parallel programming (Miller Spring 1988, 61; Sterling and Shapiro 1986, 94).

PARRY A computer program that models a theory of paranoid belief. The program is set to be very sensitive to humiliation, interprets innocuous situations as potentially humiliating, and reacts defensively with paranoid behavior (Johnson 1986, 222, 260; Barr and Feigenbaum 1981 vol 3, 70–74).

Parser A procedure in natural-language processing that takes as input a sentence and analyzes the components in order to extract the syntactic relations in the sentence. The parser breaks down the sentence into its components and tests each component to see if it conforms to the rules of the language. It accepts correct sentences and rejects incorrect sentences. Some authorities extend the concept of a parser to include converting input text into a representation that can be used by a computer for further processing (Thompson and Thompson Dec 86, 24; Emerson 1987, 54; Rubin Jul 1985, 46; Clinger 1988, 82; Townsend 1987b, 306).

Parse tree A diagrammatic representation of a sentence which takes the form of a tree structure. This tree structure first breaks down the sentence into phrases (nonterminal nodes) and then into individual words (terminal nodes). Phrase marker is a synonym (Charniak and McDermott 1985, 176–177; Clinger 1988, 83; Forsyth and Naylor 1985, 56, 68, 69, 229).

Parsing The process of analyzing the structure of a sentence by breaking up the sentence into its components and extracting its syntax in an effort to determine if the sentence is a legal sentence and the meaning of the sentence. The parsing process usually saves useful information about the sentence. A recursive pattern matcher is generally used to analyze the sentence (Johnson 1986, 105–110, 113–114, 166; Schildt 1987, 93; Townsend 1987b, 383; Barr and Feigenbaum vol 1, 239–240; Townsend and Feucht 1986, 38; Chabris 1989, 299).

Partial binding The conditions which have been matched so far in an attempt to match all the conditions of a rule (Brownston et al 1986, 451).

Partial function 1. An operator used in a state-space search which produces a single new state. 2. Those functions that are not defined for all values in the domain range (Savory 1989, 238; Smith 1989, 136).

Partial match The ability to make a match when the two entities do not match perfectly. In a production expert system the associations between condition elements and working-memory elements that fractionally fulfill the conditions of the antecedent part of a rule. TIMM-PC is one expert system shell that uses partial matching (Tello 1988, 165; Hunt 1986, 192).

Partial pattern matching The ability of an expert system to find a match even though the match may not be perfect with respect to certain less important attributes. This is a very important characteristic since most matches in the real world are not perfect. Partial pattern matching is roughly equivalent to approximate pattern matching. *See also* the Holland classifier (Brownston et al 1986, 15, 451; Barr and Feigenbaum 1981 vol 3, 47, 283).

Partial plan A set of plan steps that does not specify all of the details of the plan; the order of steps may be left out. Variables are deliberately left uninstantiated. Partial plans leave the planning program with flexibility so that it does not have to backtrack later to make changes in the plan (Amsterdam Jan 1987, 30).

Partial test A characteristic of some expert systems which allows the execution of a rule once a given number of the condition elements is satisfied.

Partitioned knowledge base Breaking up a knowledge base into segments. With a segmented knowledge base metarules may choose to use only a particular segment of a knowledge base to solve a particular subproblem. Such an organizational structure decreases search time and improves the runtime efficiency of the expert system.

Partitioning Breaking up a problem into subtasks. For each subproblem a unique set of rules is used for solving the particular subtask. Dividing a list into smaller, more manageable parts in PROLOG (Sterling and Shapiro 1986, 56).

Pass by reference A means of passing an object on a parameter list. This method passes the address rather than the object itself. This can be a convenient feature when large, complex objects need to be passed. Pass by reference is used in C++.

Path The trail the search mechanism follows in pursuit of the goal in a state-space search. A sequence of nodes in a graph (Luger and Stubblefield 1989, 82; Chabris 1989, 299).

Pathognomonic sign A sign or symptom that is usually rare, but when it occurs it definitely confirms a particular disease process. Such pathognomic signs are very important in reaching solutions and should be used whenever possible in designing expert systems (Jackson 1986, 120).

Path queue A set of partial paths used by a search procedure to expand until a complete path is found to the goal. *See also* San Marco LISP Explorer).

Pattern An arrangement of symbols that can be used to find a match in a data base. Frequently it is a data structure with variables; and the data structure is used to find a matching entity so that the variables can take on the values of the matching entity (Barr and Feigenbaum 1981 vol 2, 58; Luger and Stubblefield 1989, 28; Anderson et al 1987, 277).

Pattern associator A type of associative learning paradigm used in neural nets in which two patterns are associated with each other. These patterns are the input pattern and the output pattern. The pattern of activation over one set of units eventually causes a pattern of activation over another set of units as a function of the change in connection strengths between the two patterns. Pattern associators learn by changes in connection strengths between individual processing units. In this type of system it is expected that after sufficient training an approximation of a given input pattern will generate the corresponding output pattern. An example of its use is to associate approximate input patterns of different planes with the ideal template pattern of specific planes. Eventually the pattern associator will be able to generate the correct ideal pattern for the different input patterns. Pattern associators do not need as input a perfect representation of the stimulus to activate the second pattern. When the representation is weak the response of the second pattern will be weak. There is no all-or-none response. *Contrast with* Auto-association, the other type of associative learning; and Classification builder and Regularity detector, two other learning paradigms (Ingraham et al 1988, 17–19 (Bayle 1988, 44; Rumelhart and McClelland 1986 vol 1, 161).

Pattern classification The process of classifying an image into a predefined category. The second phase of pattern recognition (Townsend and Feucht 1986, 184).

Pattern classifier Feature detector.

Pattern constant A nonvariable term in a pattern that may only match a term that is a variable or a term that is exactly like itself in the data base (Anderson et al 1987, 277).

Pattern-directed inference system (PDIS) Inference systems made up of independent modules that are matched with patterns found in data structures. This leads to actions being taken which modify data structures. The modules actually communicate with the data rather than with each other. A pattern-directed inference system includes an executive program called an interpreter which has some limited control over the selection and execution of modules. The interpreter is primarily responsible for starting and stopping the inference process, and conflict resolution. The most important source of control over the next module used is the data rather than the directions found in a prior module or the interpreter. A production expert system is a pattern-directed inference system. The productions or rules are the pattern-directed modules, the working memory contains the data structures, and the inference engine is the executive program which starts the inferencing process, performs conflict resolution, and stops the inferencing process. Rule-based production systems are usually thought of as pattern-directed inference systems and both predicate logic and frame-based expert systems are also considered pattern-directed inference systems. Pattern-directed inference systems typically possess a large body of knowledge. This body of knowledge may be in the modules, in the data structures, or both. Because of the modularity of pattern-directed inference systems, they can be implemented on parallel-processing computers (Jackson 1986, 30–32, 50; Michaelsen et al 1985, 305; Brownston et al 1986, 451; Bratko 1986, 390–396).

Pattern-directed invocation The ability of a pattern of data to call a procedure that will achieve a goal. Pattern-directed invocation gives artificial intelligence great flexibility with respect to flow of control. *See also* Pattern-directed retrieval, for the other major use of pattern matching in artificial intelligence (Brownston et al 1986, 451; Barr and Feigenbaum 1981 vol 2, 58).

Pattern-directed module A module that can recognize situations and respond to them. A pattern-directed module looks for a precondition, and acts when the precondition is found. A production in a production system is a pattern-directed module (Michaelsen et al 1985, 304; Bratko 1986, 390).

Pattern-directed retrieval The use of a pattern to find the desired data in a data base. A form of content addressing. *See also* Pattern-directed invocation, for the other major use of pattern matching in artificial intelligence (Barr and Feigenbaum 1981 vol 2, 58).

Pattern matching The search for similarities between symbolic expressions. The process of comparing a specific structure and a more general structure to see if the more specific structure is an instance of the more general structure. An example is matching a pattern against a data base. A pattern is a type of template that has variables. Computer programs use such a template to find an entity to match the template. An example of a template is book(Author, Title, 1988). This template has two variables, Author and Title. The template will find any book which was copyrighted in 1988, and return the name of the author and the title of the book. When a match is found an action then follows. Pattern matching usually leads to one of two important actions in artificial intelligence: As in the above example, it is used for retrieving the desired data in a data base (pattern-directed retrieval), and second, for choosing what to do next in a program (pattern-directed invocation). Pattern matching is important in vision, robotics, natural-language processing, and expert systems. In an expert system, data for the problem to be solved are compared to the facts and rules in the expert system to see if an answer to the problem can be found. Pattern matching differs greatly from one expert system to another. Some expert systems are able to recognize complex nested patterns. The ability to recognize complex patterns greatly reduces the amount of search time and costly backtracking. Some programs rely more on backtracking than complex pattern matching. Another dimension of pattern matching is how many times rules in a program run are evaluated. Some expert systems use a brute force approach in which each condition in each rule is tested in each cycle. This type of cycling continues until a complete cycle is made through all of the rules and no rule is fired. A more sophisticated approach is one that evaluates a given condition only once even though the condition may appear in more than one rule. Also, if a new value is introduced only the rules that could conceivably be fired by the new value are tested, rather than all of the rules in the rule base. The more sophisticated approach is more efficient and its positive effects can readily be seen when an expert system becomes very large. (*See also* the Rete algorithm.) Another method of limiting unnecessary pattern matching is partitioning the rule base. In logic, pattern matching is the comparison of two clauses to see if they are equal or can be made equal by the substitution of values for any variables in the clauses. Pattern matching in logic is frequently used as a synonym for the term unification. In logic-based PROLOG programs pattern matching is actually the step prior to unification. In PROLOG pattern matching is finding the correct predicate with the correct number of arguments to match the query. Then, the arguments in the query are unified with the arguments in the found predicate. This latter step is what is referred to as unification. Pattern matching is considered a type of content addressing because a pattern is used to find data rather than an address or a name. Pattern matching may also be conceptualized as search. It might be worthwhile to contrast pattern matching in data base queries with the standard type of procedural query. In a procedural data base query a list of a particular attribute such as last name is queried and all last names which are not Smith are then filtered. Then, the next attribute which may be income is used and all records are filtered except Smiths with income greater than $30,000. In contrast, a pattern matching query is more declarative and will be something like, LastName = Smith and Income > 30,000. *See also* Match (Schildt 1987, 11; Hayes-Roth et al 1983, 185, 189; Mishkoff 1986, G-3; Young 1987, 374–375; Brynjolfsson and Loofbourrow 1988, 35; Winston 1979, 323–328; Walters and Nielsen 1988, 201–207; Barr and Feigenbaum 1981 vol 1, 283–287; Barr and Feigenbaum 1981 vol 2, 58–64; Winston and Horn 1984, 253–267; *Smalltalk/V Tutorial and Programming Handbook* 1986, 56–57, 70–71; Parsaye 1988, 90; Chabris 1989, 299; Graham Jun 1989, 21; Anderson et al 1987, 277; Slagle and Gini 1990, 716–720).

Pattern of connectivity   The part of a neural net model that consists of the different connections and their associated weights (Ingraham et al 1988, 17).

Pattern recognition   1. The subfield of artificial intelligence that focuses on the recognition and classification of patterns.   2. Programs based on patterns of bits rather than reasoning. Example: Holland classifier.   3. The use of statistical techniques and templates to process and classify patterns of data. The process of classifying an image into a predefined category. The two stages of pattern recognition are feature extraction and pattern classification. The term should not be confused with pattern matching which is involved with symbolic manipulations rather than numeric computations (Frey 1986, 161; Winston 1979, 206–208; Barr and Feigenbaum 1981 vol 3, 283–291, 373–382; Townsend and Feucht 1986, 183–204; Parsaye 1988, 10; Smith 1989, 137; Kanal and Dattatreya 1990, 720–729).

Pattern variable   A variable found in patterns. Pattern variables may in some way be constrained, they may be segment variables, or they may be free to match with any object in the environment. In some implementations a pattern variable is capable of matching any constant in a data base clause which appears in the same position as does the pattern variable in the pattern. The type of pattern variables vary from implementation to implementation. Some pattern variables can be set equal to complex structures such as deeply nested lists. Some pattern variables carry restrictions with them, and such variables can only be successfully matched if the restrictions are set to true. See segment variables for a unique type of pattern variable (Barr and Feigenbaum 1981 vol 2, 58–59; Anderson et al 1987, 277; Smith 1989, 137–138).

Pearl   A natural-language front end built by Roger Schank. It is based on SAM and PAM.

Penetrance   A measure of a search algorithm's efficiency. It is computed by dividing the length of the solution path by the sum of all nodes in the search tree. *See also* Branching factor (Chabris 1989, 162).

Perception The deriving of meaningful information from incoming sensory data (Chabris 1989, 299).

Perceptron A type of early neural network whose function is to classify patterns. There are no hidden layers of processing units in a perceptron. It consists of a set of input units, a set of computation units called predicates, and a set of decision units. The input units are able to assume a value of 0 or 1. A given computation unit is connected to a subset of the input units and it computes values based on the data from the input units. The computed value is passed to a decision unit. The decision units then return a yes or no response. The perceptron-convergence procedure is the underlying learning procedure which is used in perceptrons. The system does not employ feedback as part of its internal structure. As a result, its learning ability is limited. Perceptrons could not cope with combinatorial explosion. Multilayered devices with feedback were proposed to remedy the problems of perceptrons, but initially they had no learning mechanism to substitute for the perceptron-convergence procedure. Now, there are many powerful learning procedures for complex multilayer systems—competitive learning, harmony theory, Boltzmann machines, and error propagation (Caudill Jun 1988, 56; Johnson 1986, 45–46; Barr and Feigenbaum 1981 vol 3, 376–380; Zeidenberg 1987, 240; Obermeier and Barron 1989, 219; Minsky and Papert 1969; Rosenblatt 1962).

Perceptron-convergence procedure The learning procedure developed by Frank Rosenblatt which is used in perceptrons. It emphasizes the importance of the strengthening of connections among units of a perceptron as the critical factor in learning. It does this by converging on a set of weights that produces the correct output pattern for each input pattern. In phase one of the perceptron-convergence procedure an input pattern and an associated output pattern are imposed on the perceptron. The weights of the perceptron are incremented slightly during phase one of the perceptron-convergence procedure in an attempt to find the correct weights which will produce the correct output pattern. In phase two of the perceptron-convergence procedure the perceptron is allowed to output a pattern in response to the input pattern. The weights are altered as a function of how well the output pattern matches the input pattern. The perceptron-convergence procedure is able to find the correct weights for the input pattern if there exists a set of weights that allows this. The problem with the perceptron-convergence procedure is that for most complex problems a multilayered neural network more complex than perceptrons must be used. Rosenblatt's work is an extension of that of the psychologist D.O. Hebb, who proposed the basis of learning in the human brain is strengthening of synaptic connections. Synonyms for perceptron-convergence procedure include the perceptron-convergence theorem, and the fundamental learning theorem. *See also* Perceptron-learning theorem (Brown Apr 1987, 24; Rumelhart and McClelland 1986 vol 1, 113; Hinton Apr 1985, 265–267).

Perceptron-convergence theorem See Perceptron-convergence procedure (Brown Apr 1987, 24).

Perceptron-learning theorem It was proposed by Frank Rosenblatt and states: "Given an elementary a-perceptron, a stimulus world W, and any classification $C(W)$ for which a solution exists, let all stimuli in W occur in any sequence, provided that each stimulus must recur in finite time, then beginning from an arbitrary initial state, an error correction procedure will always yield a solution to $C(W)$ in finite time." (Hinton 1985, 265–267).

Percy A robot simulation program that demonstrates learning. It is a goal-driven system whose two goals are to find food and to build a nest. It is unique in that it does not attempt to build an internal representation of its environment to carry out the tasks. Instead, Percy remembers what behaviors are necessary for building a nest and finding food. It cannot, however, re-

Performance A measure of whether or not an artificial intelligence system is able to carry out its primary objective. Can it really diagnose defects, carry out practical plans, or give sound economic advice? (Parsaye 1988, 302).

Performance grammar Semantic grammar.

Performance model An expert system that mimics an expert's behavior but does not utilize the underlying principles of the knowledge domain. *Contrast with* Competence model (Luger and Stubblefield 1989, 598).

Performance reasoning One of two types of reasoning which take place on the blackboard in the HEARSAY-III expert system tool. It is reasoning about scheduling. *Contrast with* Competence reasoning (Hayes-Roth et al 1983, 310).

Persistence The length of time data are kept during a program run. *See also* Persistent object (Wegner 1989, 253).

Persistent object An object that maintains its existence and values throughout a program run. Objects in object-oriented systems are generally persistent objects. In C, declaring a variable as a static variable makes it a persistent object. In functional languages like LISP persistent objects are rare. After a function in LISP has run its course, the variables in the function no longer exist (Peterson Mar 1987, 30; Wegner 1989, 253).

Personal construct theory A psychological theory developed by Kelly which is designed to bypass psychological defense mechanisms. It emphasizes the use of a person's private view of his or her world—one's personal constructs. Repertory grid is the method used to elicit personal constructs. The way the repertory grid is used to elicit personal constructs is as follows: Given (1) real estate, (2) stocks, (3) bonds, how is one of these three somehow different from the other two? What is the trait that characterizes this difference? What is the opposite of this trait? Such continuous comparisons can be used to identify traits that can be used to develop rule-based systems. AutoIntelligence is an induction expert system which uses repertory grids to elicit information from domain experts (Parsaye 1988, 51, 351; (Williamson 1987, 62–65; Frude 1983, 171–172).

Phenomenology A theory of intelligence that emphasizes perception, expectations, and cognitive acts. It holds certain mental abilities cannot be reduced to atomistic elements (Chabris 1989, 31, 299).

Phoneme A unit of speech which is the sound of a consonant or vowel (Johnson 1986, 137–138; Chabris 1989, 299).

Phonology The analysis of sounds that are synthesized to produce speech (Luger and Stubblefield 1989, 379).

Photometric stereo The task of using shade to define the shape of an object. Three different images of an object along with three separate illumination sources are used as the basis for processing the image (Waldrop 1987, 107).

Phrase marker A synonym for a parse tree.

Phrase parameter A type of variable found in some expert system shells which takes on as its value a piece of text (Tello 1988, 148).

Physical symbol system That type of computer program capable of manipulating symbols. GPS is perhaps the best known early physical symbol system. Expert systems are physical symbol systems. Perhaps symbol manipulation is the most important contribution of artificial intelligence (Hayes-Roth et al 1983, 45).

Physical symbol system hypothesis An assumption often made in artificial intelligence programming that thought corresponds to language and language can be captured in symbols and that by manipulating symbols one can simulate thinking. The three requirements are: (1) the use of symbols to represent the problem, (2) operations on these patterns to produce solutions, and (3) search to find the best solution from the set of solutions. It holds that a physical symbol system is sufficient to deliver intelligent behavior, and that any entity that exhibits intelligent behavior is a physical symbol system. There are two interpretations for the physical symbol system hypothesis. The weak interpretation is that this hypothesis is sufficient for explaining human thought. Certainly the physical symbol hypothesis has been useful in modeling such capacities as memory and learning. The strong interpretation is that the hypothesis is sufficient and necessary. The word necessary rules out other possible approaches to explaining human thought such as neural networks (Luger and Stubblefield 1989, 27, 580, 594).

Picture processing   A synonym for signal processing.

Piece-group pair   A type of production in which knowledge is stored as a grouping of data (Winston 1979, 152).

Pipelining   The connection of processors so that the output of one processor becomes the input of another processor (Hunt 1986, 196).

Pixel   A picture element. A single dot on the computer screen. A cell in an image (Chabris 1989, 299).

Plan elements   Elements that record information on the general problem-solving strategy in a blackboard architecture system. They are one of three types of decision elements in a blackboard system. The other two decision elements are agenda elements and solution elements (Hayes-Roth et al 1983, 16).

Planner   An early artificial intelligence language that used pattern-directed invocation and therefore was much more flexible than conventional languages. It possessed an associative data base which was able to retrieve relevant facts automatically. Planner used depth-first search and backtracking. It also used procedural programming. It was used to implement Winograd's SHRDLU. Planner is no longer used because it is too inefficient, in part because of its use of chronological backtracking. Conniver was a successor program to Planner. ACTOR and PROLOG may also be considered successors to Planner (Lagrow 1986, 84; Winston 1979, 260–261; Barr and Feigenbaum 1981 vol 1, 175–178, 295–297; Barr and Feigenbaum 1981 vol 2, 9–10).

Planning   Making preparations to take action. The ability of an expert system to organize a series of steps to reach a goal. The process of deriving a sequence of actions before proceeding with the action. The goal of planning is to reduce the search space as much as possible before problem solving begins. *See also* Hierarchical planning and repair; Least commitment; Nonhierarchical planner; Opportunistic planning (Amsterdam Jan 1987, 29; Hayes-Roth et al 1983, 84; Chabris 1989, 299; Luger and Stubblefield 1989, 551; Tello 1989, 16).

Planning and decision support   The portion of artificial intelligence devoted to designing programs that aid managers in planning and decision support.

Planning expert system   An expert system that builds a plan to reach a given goal. An expert system that can organize a series of events to reach a goal. The goal in a planning system is a future goal which will be implemented a considerable amount of time after the planning expert system has run its course. Contrast this with a diagnostic expert system whose goal is to achieve a diagnosis in the present. A planning expert system must be able to reason about events in which time is an important factor. Such expert systems must decide which events must be completed before another event can be started. Planning expert systems which are nonmonotonic and can pursue multiple lines of reasoning are especially useful. Nonmonotonic reasoning allows the program to retract certain aspects of the plan when the program finds it has pursued a part of the plan prematurely. This often happens in planning. Think of times you started a building project and then realized you must make a trip to the hardware store for a needed but overlooked part. Planning expert systems typically have much larger knowledge bases than diagnostic expert systems. Examples: configuring mainframe computers and planning to construct a nuclear power plant. The four types of planning systems are hierarchical, nonhierarchical, script-based, and opportunistic planning (Johnson 1986, 143–144; Townsend 1987a, 7; Hayes-Roth et al 1983, 84; Harmon and King 1985, 93–95; Townsend 1987b, 268–269).

Planning island An island of knowledge that is expanded as new information allows. Planning islands are exploited in blackboard planning architectures. An analogy is to think of planning islands as targets of opportunity. If new information is made available to the planning system, it may stop the current part of the plan it is working on to take advantage of the new information to expand another planning island. Planning islands can greatly reduce the search space. *See also* Opportunistic planning (Hayes-Roth et al 1983, 71).

Plasticity The degree of flexibility available in artificial intelligence programs (Reece 1987, 55).

Platform independence **1.** The ability of software such as an expert system tool to be ported to a large number of different computers. **2.** The ability of an expert system tool to run in conjunction with different versions of a particular language. Example: an expert system tool that can run with both Arity PROLOG and MPROLOG (Schwartz and Schwartz 1988, 64).

PLATO A computer-learning system developed at the University of Illinois at Urbana. PLATO programs use artificial intelligence methodology. PLATO programs have been used in genetics, rocketry, natural language, lesson planning, and math tutoring. One version of PLATO is a therapy program developed by Morton Wagman at the University of Illinois. It utilizes dilemma counseling. Dilemma counseling is based on the premise that most human problems can be cast in the model of conflicts. PLATO elicits from the client alternative solutions to the conflicts. It then provides guidelines and recommendations (Lawrence 1985, 74–76; Frude 1983, 86–87).

Plausible-move generator A procedure found in a game search algorithm whose goal is to return a list of plausible moves. It works in conjunction with a static evaluator to rank, from best to poorest, the possible operators which may be used in the next move. A synonym is forward pruning. *See also* Static evaluation (Charniak and McDermott 1985, 259; Winston 1979, 313–314; Barr and Feigenbaum 1981 vol 1, 104).

Plausible reasoning Reasoning that may not be true because the information it is based on may be incorrect. Educated guessing in the face of incomplete information to limit search space. Plausible reasoning is guided by heuristics. Abduction may be considered plausible reasoning. Default reasoning is considered a type of plausible reasoning. Reasoning which relies on pattern matching and analogical thinking is plausible reasoning. The problem with plausible reasoning is being able to find mistakes and taking corrective action. Inexact reasoning may be considered a type of plausible reasoning. Backtracking and nonmonotonic reasoning are methods of recovering from mistakes. *Contrast with* Algorithmic solution; Modus ponens (Hayes-Roth et al 1983, 110–115; Barr and Feigenbaum 1981 vol 1, 177; Wolfgram et al 1987, 306; Hunt 1986, 35; Barker and Barker Mar/Apr 1990, 48).

Playback control A technique for controlling the motion of servo robots. It consists of physically moving a robot through a task. The robot is able to remember and repeat the motion. The two types of playback control are point-to-point and continuous-path control (Mishkoff 1986, 5-18).

Pluralism A principle advocated for open systems, that holds that there is no central source of truth in the system (Hewitt Apr 1985, 239).

Plural parameter A variable that can have multiple values at a given point in time. The variable diagnosis may be a list of diseases: [diabetes, hypertension] (Tello 1988, 128).

Ply One level of a game tree. An odd ply is the opponent's move and an even ply is the user's move (Forsyth and Naylor 1985, 188).

Pointer A variable that holds the address of another memory object (Hansen 1988, 89).

Pointer representation A means of representing small sets. All members of a set are connected by pointers. Other types of representation for sets are bit and tag (Hillis 1985, 95–96).

Point-to-point Describing a type of playback control in which the robot is programmed by physically moving the robot to a series of points. The robot then remembers the positions. *Contrast with* Continuous-path control (Mishkoff 1986, 5-18).

POLITICS A natural-language-understanding program that is claimed to be able to understand stories about international events. It uses a hierarchy of goals to guide its reasoning. POLITICS takes an input political stories such as a story on the Panama Canal. It then uses a primary premise and subpremises to guide its reasoning concerning the opinions it gives. It may, for example, assume that the overall premise is to contain communism and then answer questions and make recommendations based on that premise. POLITICS is a successor to the natural-language-understanding system MARGIE (Johnson 1986, 259, 298; Waldrop 1987, 82; Tello 1988, 494–498).

POLY A vision program that interprets line drawings by reasoning about surface gradients.

Polymorphic variable A variable characterized by its flexibility, which is free to be bound to a number, a symbol, a list, or a complex structure. PROLOG regularly uses polymorphic variables and this is one of the strengths of PROLOG.

Polymorphism 1. Many shapes. 2. A characteristic of object-oriented languages in which a given message may be used with different objects and the behavior of the different objects will be peculiar to the object. An example is the message "talk." If the message "talk" is sent to a dog (dog talk), the response is different than if it is sent to a human (human talk). In other words, different objects can be sent the same message and each object will behave differently. Polymorphism depends on the ability of an object to respond correctly to directives from program codes that do not know the object's exact type. Late binding is the mechanism which makes this ability possible. Contrast with Function overloading. Polymorphism takes place at runtime while function overloading takes place at compile time. 3. The ability of a variable to be set equal to a variety of structures. (Thompson and Thompson Sep 1987, 16; Pascoe 1986, 142; *Smalltalk/V Tutorial and Programming Handbook* 1986, 63–75; Duntemann 1989, 139–140).

Poor visibility A condition in which the order in which rules are processed cannot be determined by brief inspection. This can indicate the programmer will have difficulties debugging or modifying the system. The else statement and multiple consequents contribute to poor visibility (Pedersen Apr 1989, 45).

POP-11 A highly interactive artificial intelligence language, which is a combination of Pascal, LISP, Forth, Smalltalk, and PROLOG. It inherits block structure from Pascal, and weak data typing from LISP. From Smalltalk it takes the concept of data hiding. It has a built in pattern matcher and data base, like PROLOG, but it does not have backtracking. It is like Forth in that it uses incremental compilation, access to the compiler from other programs, and the ability to interact flexibly with subprograms. Its procedures can take a variable number of inputs or produce a variable number of outputs. It has a rich set of control structures for list manipulation and pattern matching.

POPLOG A combination of LISP, PROLOG, and POP-11. It runs on VAX, SUN, Apollo, and HP computers (Harmon and King 1985, 89).

Positive example An example that fits the category and produces generalization of the concept in concept learning. *See also* Negative example (Schildt 1987, 204-206).

Positive logic Logic in which 1 represents a positive state and 0 represents a negative state (Hunt 1986, 199).

Possibility theory The theory on which fuzzy logic is based (Parsaye 1988, 223).

Post, Emil The man who laid the foundation for modern production systems (Valdex-Perez 1986, 32).

Postconditions The conditions that must be set to true after a goal has been achieved. This is useful in a production system which has many rules to achieve the same goal. Once the postconditions are set to true for a given goal the different rules that are designed to achieve the goal can be inactivated. That is, each of these rules would have the negation of the postcondition as a condition. Once the postcondition is true these rules cannot fire.

Posterior probability A synonym for conditional probability.

Postfix notation A type of notation in which the function follows its arguments.

Postgres A relational data base with extensions to support object-oriented programming, which is being developed at the University of California at Berkeley (Peterson Mar 1987, 30).

Post production system A predecessor to current production systems. It was a mathematical model of computation and was developed by Emil Post (Valdex-Perez 1986, 32; Rosenberg 1986, 142).

Power set All of the subsets of X, given a set X (Savory 1989, 238).

Practicability The degree to which an expert system is useful. There are expert systems which are accurate but not used because they do not significantly help the people they are supposed to help. One such problem could be the system asks too many questions. The user could solve the problem on his or her own in less time than it takes to use the expert system. Other important measures of the value of an expert system are adequacy, breadth, accuracy, reliability, validity, adaptability, credibility, and generality (Marcot Aug 1987, 44).

Pragmatic analysis The study of what people mean when they utter a sentence. *Contrast with* Keyword analysis; Semantic analysis; Syntactic analysis (Mishkoff 1986, 4-11).

Pragmatics 1. The part of natural-language processing that attempts to ascertain the intent of the dialogue and give a reasonable reply. 2. The field of linguistics that copes with the ambiguities found in language, like pronoun reference and intended meanings. The classic antithesis to pragmatics is replying "yes" to the request, "Can you pass the salt?" In pragmatics the surrounding sentences become important in understanding a given sentence. *See also* Semantic analysis; Syntactic analysis (Chabris 1989, 74, 299; Smith 1989, 145; Rubin Jul 1985, 44).

Precision The degree of detail the expert system is able to muster in producing an answer. In a medical expert system does it give a broad diagnosis or a highly specific diagnosis? (Parsaye 1988, 302).

Precompiled network A network of phonetic spellings for each syntactic avenue in the grammar, used in speech-understanding systems.

Precondition A condition that must be met before a goal in an expert system can be reached.

Predicate A function in LISP that returns either true or false. An example is, number$p(X)$. If the variable X is a number, then true is returned. 2. A statement in predicate calculus about an object or objects which returns a value. The predicate consists of a relation and possibly a series of arguments. Examples of predicates are likes(john, mary), is-a-color, greater-than-zero, and is-mortal. 3. What is often referred to as a predicate in PROLOG is really a function because it can return not only true or false, but a value. A predicate expresses a relationship. The following expression is an example of a PROLOG predicate: like(dogs, cats). Dogs and cats are objects, or arguments. The PROLOG program can initiate the query ?- like(dogs, cats). If the fact is in the data base, true is returned. If it is not in the data base, false is returned. The word "like" is sometimes referred to as a relation, a verb, or an operator. Now look at the example of the predicate diagnose (X), which can return X = bronchitis. PROLOG predicates can return values as well as true and false. Be aware that the definition of function as used here is not completely equivalent to the mathematical definition of function. *See also* Function (Bharath and Sklar Jul 1985, 49; McMillan 1987, 50; Minsky 1985, 138; Townsend 1987a, 32; Winston 1979, 271–274; Townsend 1987b, 383; Barr and Feigenbaum 1981 vol 1, 163, 182; Sterling and Shapiro 1986, 2; Smith 1989, 145; Hayes-Roth et al 1983, 61–62; Lane Nov/Dec 1987, 95; Lane 1988, 94).

Predicate calculus   A system of formal logic. The predicate calculus has well-defined formal semantics. The inference rules are sound and complete. Its foundation is based on propositional calculus. Like propositional calculus it is a language for representing propositions and rules to generate facts from those we already have. Propositional calculus is made up of propositions and cannot represent individual entities and their properties and relationships. That is, in propositional calculus there is no way to represent "car." A statement must be made about car—"car is fast." In predicate calculus entities such as "car" or "john" may be represented independently. Predicate calculus consists of predicates that are statements about individuals or objects, their properties, and their relationships with other objects which return a value of true or false. Predicates can have arguments. An example of a predicate is likes(john, mary). John and mary are arguments of the predicate likes. As can be seen from the example, predicate calculus specifies relationships between objects—john and mary. Predicate calculus is able to employ existential and universal quantifiers. It therefore has the capability of producing generalizations. That is, it may make the statements, "for all X" and "there exists an X." Another way to say this is that since predicate calculus uses variables it can make statements about sets of objects. Predicate calculus makes use of unification for pattern matching and substituting equivalent terms so that resolution can take place. Resolution is used to make inferences. Predicate calculus employing resolution possesses the property of completeness. If functions are used instead of predicates which simply return true or false, and the predicate "equals" is added, then predicate calculus is considered to be first-order predicate calculus. For example, likes(john, X) can be used as a query to find out who likes john. Likes(john, X) returns a value for X. X may equal mary. The language of predicate calculus includes: terms, variables, predicates, functions, connectives, and quantifiers. The terms of predicate calculus are constants, variables, and functions; this use of function is not the same as a mathematical function.) The predicate calculus also includes formulas which are combinations of terms (Mishkoff, G–3; Lane Nov/Dec 1987, 94; Hayes-Roth et al 1983, 61–66; Schildt 1987, 228–230; Barr and Feigenbaum 1981 vol 1, 163–165; Barr and Feigenbaum 1981 vol 3, 88–89, 121–122; Fischler and Firschein 1987, 91–95; Bratko 1986, 61; Smith 1989, 146; Leaman 1989, 29; Luger and Stubblefield 1989, 41, 46; Charniak and McDermott 1985, 14–21).

Predicate passing   The procedure of calling a predicate with another predicate as an argument.

Prediction expert system   A type of expert system whose conclusion is a prediction of a future event. Prediction systems must deal with errorful and incomplete data. A system which makes 100 percent accurate predictions is not considered a prediction expert system since expert systems, by definition, deal with incomplete information. Prediction expert systems must be capable of dealing with data which change over time and with heterogeneous data. *Contrast with* Diagnostic expert system (Townsend 1987a, 6; Hayes-Roth et al 1983, 84).

Preferential learning The tendency for a neural net to develop a preference for patterns to which it is exposed more frequently. It will more likely recognize an ambiguous pattern as being a pattern it has seen more often than another pattern which may be more similar to the stimulus pattern, but which has been seen less frequently (Josin 1987, 188).

Prefix notation A type of notation in which the operator precedes its arguments. LISP uses prefix notation. Example: is (+ 3 2) (Townsend 1987a, 32; Winston 1979, 265).

Premise An expression that must be satisfied to reach a conclusion. The conditional part of a rule (Dos Reis 1988, 50).

Premise-conclusion pair A type of production in which the pattern of facts is used to trigger a deduction. Many production systems are not limited to simply having deductions triggered on the right-hand side of a rule. Actions can also be triggered on the right-hand side of a rule. Such pairs are called situation-action pairs (Winston 1979, 144).

Prenex normal form A form in logic in which all the quantifiers are in front and the expression follows (Luger and Stubblefield 1989, 419).

Prepare/deliberate tradeoff The concept that highlights the tradeoff which is frequently seen in AI systems, in which the system either emphasizes large stores of knowledge or sophisticated search and reasoning. There appears to be a tradeoff that takes place in which a given program may excel in one but not both (Chabris 1989, 28–29, 299–300).

Preprocessing The initial step in visual data processing. It begins reconstruction of the image, filters out noise, and emphasizes critical aspects of the scene (Barr and Feigenbaum 1981 vol 3, 206–215).

Prescriptive knowledge Knowledge that prescribes a course of action to solve a problem. *Contrast with* Descriptive knowledge.

Prescriptive language A computer language that relies on the programmer to provide explicit procedures to compute an answer. C is a prescriptive language. Prescriptive languages are also called procedural languages. *Contrast with* Descriptive language (Townsend and Feucht 1986, 27).

Presupposition A supposition that can be used by the knowledge engineer to specify that a particular expression must be true in order for it to make sense even to seek another expression. It wouldn't make sense for the system to ask what kind of sauce is on the meat unless there actually is a sauce on the meat. This relationship between "has sauce" and "sauce" can be explicitly represented by a presupposition of the form: presupposition(sauce) = has sauce. This does away with the need for various "screening clauses" in rules that test for the presence of sauce. Presuppositions are used in the M1 expert system shell (Harmon and King 1985, 106).

Primal sketch The first of three stages in Marr's theory of vision. In this stage, the primary goal is to process the raw data by finding edges, boundaries, and regions. It divides the image into areas, and brings to the forefront the two-dimensional aspect of the different areas that make up the image (Chabris 1989, 300; Waldrop 1987, 92–102).

Primitive The basic building blocks of a language. In the English language individual words are primitives. In this vein the atoms in LISP may be considered as primitives. In LISP, the term primitive also refers to a built-in procedure. An example is the + in the function (+ 3 2). *See also* Semantic primitives and San Marco LISP Explorer.

Primitive concept   A frame that does not have a parent. *Compare with* Definitional concept (Townsend, 1987a, 124).

Primitives   The basic shape of a scene.

Principia Mathematica   A book written by Lord Alfred North Whitehead, and Bertrand Russell which demonstrated that all mathematics is founded on logic (Waldrop 1987, 16–26).

Principle of least commitment   A principle used in vision research which states, do not make a commitment as to what the object is until as much information as possible has been extracted from the object. *See also* Least commitment (Waldrop 1987, 97).

Priority   A measure of the relative importance of goals, which is used to decide which goals will be attempted first.

Priority queue   A type of nonlinked data representation that can be implemented in some production systems. The elements are assigned priorities and are recalled according to that priority.

Prior probability   A synonym for unconditional probability.

PRISM   **1.** A rule-based expert system. In PRISM, working memory holds the data which are matched with the rules in a single-rule memory. Conflict resolution is a function of rule strength and the activation level of matched elements. The conflict-resolution procedure uses a version of the Rete pattern matcher. The conflict-resolution strategy is very flexible. PRISM also has a long-term memory. Memory elements can move from long-term memory to working memory if their trace strength is high enough. Internal representations are in lists.   **2.** A constraint-based object-oriented system. PRISM uses an associative net for representing knowledge (Brownston et al 1986, 275–278, 289–296, 298–301, 341–343, 366–368; Zaniolo et al 1986, 62).

Private variable   A variable in an object in an object-oriented system. One can only manipulate or find out the value of the variable by sending the appropriate message to the object (Bernat Nov 1986, 77).

Probabilistic inference   **1.** A type of inexact reasoning developed by J. R. Quinlan which employs constraints. The inference process finds the optimum solution within the set of constraint equations by using what is known as gradient descent. It does not assume that the probabilities of the conditional factors are independent. It points out inconsistent probabilities. It is bidirectional—that is, one can generate initial probabilities from the conclusion probability.   **2.** Inexact reasoning. This includes certainty factors, fuzzy logic, and Bayesian inferencing. *Contrast with* Deterministic inference (Forsyth and Naylor 1985, 18; Thompson and Thompson Jan 1988, 15–18; Barr and Feigenbaum 1981 vol 2, 160).

Probabilistic knowledge   Knowledge that has varying degrees of certainty. Example: The user may have a .90 level of confidence concerning a fact or a rule. *Compare with* Categorical knowledge (Bratko 1986, 317).

Probability   The computation of the likelihood of an event or set of events occurring. Probability is the chance of a particular event occurring. The chance of a particular event occurring is equivalent to the number of different ways this event can take place divided by the total number of ways all possible events can occur. A probability is quantified by a number between 0 and 1. The number 0 means the event is impossible. The number 1 means the event is certain. The use of probability computations assumes the underlying process is random. The flipping of a coin is an example of a random underlying process. Applying probability computations to a process which is not necessarily random in nature introduces errors in the computation. Bayes' theorem is an example of a probability function which is used in expert systems to compute the likelihood of an event. See probability-OR, and probability-AND for information about computing conjunctive and disjunctive probabilities. Alternative approaches to the use of probability in expert systems are confidence factors and fuzzy logic. In order to use probability effectively one should have: (1) a solid causal model of the situation or (2) a good history of data. An example of the former is knowing that a die has six sides, the die is thrown fairly, and the die itself is fair. Because a thorough understanding of the model is available the probability of calculating the probability of a two can be calculated as one-sixth. If, on the other hand, you are not sure if the die is six-sided, or if the die is being thrown in a manner which facilitates randomness, or if the die is fair then knowing the history of the outcomes would be the better choice. For some situations the use of frequency histories is inappropriate. To predict the next war on the basis of historical frequencies is probably not going to be as accurate as using other available information such as economic factors, statements of national leaders, and so on. *See also* Bayes' theorem (Parsaye 1988, 213; Townsend 1987a, 172–173; Schildt 1987, 240–241).

Probability-AND Probability of event one * probability of event two. The probability of BOTH rolling a six with a die (.16) and the probability of drawing an ace from a card deck (.08) is calculated with the equation .16 * .08 = (.01). *Contrast with* Probability-OR.

Probability-OR (Probability of event one + probability of event two) − (probability of event one * probability of event two). The probability of EITHER rolling a six with a die (.16) or the probability of drawing an ace from a card deck (.08) is (.16 + .08) − (.16 * .08) = (.23). This procedure is frequently used in combining evidence to prove a given hypothesis. Assume a patient has repeated dizzy spells (.3 confidence) and spots in front of her eyes (.5 confidence). It would be appropriate to use the probability-OR to combine evidence to achieve an overall confidence of .65 for the diagnosis of epilepsy. *Contrast with* Probability-AND.

Probability propagation The change of probability at a node in an inference net because of new data, causing changes in other nodes in the net (Waterman 1986, 393; Smith 1989, 147–148; Hunt 1986, 201).

Probe Questions asked by expert systems (Wolfgram et al 1987, 306).

Problem-behavior graph A tool psychologists use to follow the thinking of a problem solver through the steps used to solve a problem. The nodes represent the state of the problem at a given point in time, and the arcs represent the means of transforming the problem from one state to another (Winston 1979, 154; Barr and Feigenbaum 1981 vol 3, 18).

Problem list A tool sometimes used in building an expert system, which lists the different possible problems which could be encountered in building the system.

Problem-reduction heuristic The process of breaking up large complex problems into smaller manageable subproblems (Winston Apr 85, 214).

Problem-reduction representation The representation of a problem as a set of subproblems. A graph can be a problem-reduction representation in which the primary data structures are problem descriptions or goals. One starts with an initial problem description, which is broken up into a set of subproblems. An AND/OR graph is a type of problem-reduction representation. Backward reasoning systems regularly use problem-reduction representations. Example: In PROLOG problems are typically represented as a set of rules in which the consequent is a goal which can be proven only by proving a set of subgoals (subproblems) in a rule. Problem reduction works if the subproblems can be independently solved. Examples of problems which can be solved in this way include route finding, symbolic integration, game playing, and theorem proving. *Contrast with* State-space representation/graph, associated with forward chaining (Barr and Feigenbaum 1981 vol 1, 24–25, 36–42; Bratko 1986, 286; Slagle and Gini 1990, 762–767).

Problem reformulation The revision of a problem so that it is in a form that lends itself to more efficient problem solving (Hunt 1986, 202; Waterman 1986, 393).

Problem scenario A problem and a proposed solution.

Problem solving The achieving of a goal state through the use of deduction, induction, analogical reasoning, or procedural analysis. In artificial intelligence the term frequently refers to employing search as a method of solving a problem. That is, moving through a problem space until a solution to the problem is found. The search space consists of nodes that represent different states, and arcs that represent operators which allow the movement from one state to the next. Problem solving may be represented as a state-space representation or as a problem-reduction representation. The two basic methods for starting the search are forward chaining and backward chaining. Forward chaining is the process of starting in an initial state and moving through a problem space to achieve a solution state. Backward chaining is beginning with a goal state and moving through the problem space in an attempt to find the necessary supporting premises of the goal. The two major methods for exploring a search space are blind search and heuristic search. Heuristic search is the more efficient of the two. The type of problem solving employed in artificial intelligence is subject to combinatorial explosion. Contrast the type of problem solving carried out in artificial intelligence with algorithmic problem solving (Johnson 1986, 47–48; Harmon and King 1985, 27; Brownston et al 1986, 15–17; Barr and Feigenbaum 1981 vol 1, 21, 153; Townsend and Feucht 1986, 9).

Problem-solving expertise The component of an intelligent computer-aided instruction system that contains the knowledge the programmer intends to impart to the student. *See also* Student model; Tutoring module.

Problem-solving function The part of an expert system that makes inferences from the knowledge in the knowledge base. The inference engine (Bratko 1986, 315).

Problem space A network of states and relations between these states which can be traversed to reach a solution. In a chess game the position of all the pieces on the board is a state. The relations between the states are usually called operators. An operator in chess is a legal chess move. The legal chess move causes a traversal to a different state—an altered chess board state. A problem space can be depicted graphically with each state being a node and the links between the states being operators. A problem space is also referred to as a search space (Harmon and King 1985, 27–29; Brownston et al 1986, 451; Townsend 1987b, 383; Barr and Feigenbaum 1981 vol 3, 13–17).

Procedural abstraction The use of predicates in logic programming to build other more abstract predicates (Parsaye 1988, 101).

Procedural attachment The process in frame-based systems in which demons are activated when a slot is accessed. In a frame-based system a demon is a set of instructions residing on a slot of a frame, which is used to compute, change, or access a value. Procedural attachment is the procedural aspect of frames (Matthews Sep 1987, 78; Harmon and King 1985, 44; Barr and Feigenbaum 1981 vol 1, 219–220; Luger and Stubblefield 1989, 362).

Procedural fever The tendency for programmers trained in conventional programming to attempt to apply excessive procedural control to a rule-based expert system. The attempt to order the execution of the rules despite the fact that the inference engine should be responsible for ordering of the execution of rules (Walters and Nielsen 1988, 206).

Procedural grammar *See* Semantic grammar.

Procedural interpretation The interpretation, to achieve X first do Y and then do Z, as applied to the PROLOG clause X :- Y, Z. *Compare with* Declarative representation (Lazarev Nov 1988, 76).

Procedural knowledge Knowledge that specifies how to solve a given problem rather than describing or specifying the problem. As a result, procedural knowledge cannot easily be scrutinized unless one traces through the different program steps. It is knowledge which is represented by a step-by-step procedure. Standard programming languages are procedural in nature. That is, they consist of procedures that work on data. A blackboard architecture is one type of expert system architecture which more readily accommodates procedural knowledge than does a rule-based or logic-based architecture. *Contrast with* Declarative knowledge (Walters and Nielsen 1988, 317–318; Brownston et al 1986, 452; Barr and Feigenbaum 1981 vol 1, 219; Rosenberg 1986, 144).

Procedural language A type of language in which built-in procedures like for-next loops operate on data items. Programs are built on these procedures. A rule-based expert system can be built using a procedural language but there are significant differences and drawbacks. In most rule-based expert systems the control procedures are separate from the rules. In a procedural language using rules there is no such distinction. One implication of this is that it is very hard to modify or maintain a procedural language expert system. That is, one must know all the implications of inserting a rule at a particular place in the program. When the inference engine is a separate component the rules are more modular—less sensitive to exactly where they are placed in the program. Procedural language emphasizes how to solve a problem. Contrast with the declarative language PROLOG which emphasizes what is known about a body of knowledge. Procedural languages include BASIC, C, Pascal, and COBOL. LISP may be considered a procedural language, although it can be used to build declarative programs. Usually LISP is referred to as a functional language (Thompson and Thompson Sep 1987, 15; Lane Nov/Dec 1987, 94; Brownston et al 1986, 451; Townsend 1987b, 384; Bratko 1986, viii).

Procedural meaning The type of meaning derived from examining the particular steps involved in how conclusions are reached (Bratko 1986, 24, 63).

Procedural query language A query language that produces a query by writing a small procedural program. *Compare with* Declarative query language (Graham 1989, 21).

Procedural representation The representation of knowledge in program statements rather than data structures. Such constructs as repeat-until are used to operate on data to arrive at an answer. In procedural representation the desired data are computed by means of a specific set of instructions, rather than explicitly using facts which can be used to infer the answer. Procedural representation gives greater search control but has less flexibility and modularity than declarative representation. (Fischler and Firschein Dec 1986, 44; Winston 1979, 390–392; Harmon and King 1985, 44).

Procedural-representation schemes The representation of a knowledge base using procedures (Luger and Stubblefield 1989, 334).

Procedural semantics 1. A methodology for representing the meaning of a set of sentences with the purpose of answering natural-language questions about the set of sentences. Production rules translate the input into procedure calls that operate upon a data base, and the answer is returned. It was first popularized in the program LUNAR. 2. The search strategy used in PROLOG (Luger and Stubblefield 1989, 476).

Procedure 1. A group of instructions for carrying out a task. 2. A collection of rules in PROLOG, each of which has the same predicate in the head of the rule. The number of arguments for the predicate in the head of the rule must be the same in all of the rules in the procedure. Each rule represents a different way of solving a problem. 3. The entity that specifies how a process is to be carried out in LISP. A list in which the first element is the name of the procedure and subsequent elements are the arguments for the procedure. Functions are procedures, but some procedures are not functions. That is, a procedure can have side effects. Functions, by definition, cannot produce side effects (Matthews Jul 1987, 37; Mishkoff 1986, 7–12; Sterling and Shapiro 1986, 11; Winston and Horn 1984, 17, 39; Parsaye 1988, 101; Shmueli et al 1986, 249; Bratko 1986, 19; Hunt 1986, 203; Winston and Horn 1988, 584).

Procedure abstraction The technique of assembling new procedures by means of building on already existing procedures. Such a process builds abstract procedures (Winston and Horn 1984, 39, 219).

Procedure-attribute property A property that specifies methods for finding the value of an attribute through procedural means instead of inferencing. Example: If an expert system cannot find the value of an attribute through inference, a procedure-attribute property may come into play which will attempt to find the value in a data base or a spreadsheet (Pedersen 1989, 50–51).

Procedure M A learning algorithm in which all examples are fed to the computer in a batch and the algorithm chooses the order in which to analyze and compare the examples. It is more powerful than procedure W. *Compare with* Procedure W (Winston 1984, 396–401).

Procedure name The first element of a list in LISP which is meant to be evaluated. *See also* San Marco LISP Explorer.

Procedure variable A variable in PROLOG which takes on the value of a goal (Jay and Knaus Jun 1989, 78).

Procedure W A learning algorithm to which examples are spoon fed in the order determined by an external source so that a concept can be built and refined. It uses the strategy of near miss. It does not remember examples once they have been used. *Compare with* Procedure M (Winston 1984, 394–396, 407).

Process-based language An object-based language that can execute objects concurrently. Such languages can be used in parallel computer architectures. ADA is a process language (Wegner 1989, 250).

Processing element The primary unit in a neural network. It has multiple input elements and a single output element. Each input element has a weight. The weights may be positive or negative. If the weight is positive, this particular input contributes to the excitation of the signal. If the weight is negative, this particular input subtracts from the total excitation of the system. The weights for the different input elements are combined with the input signals from each input to produce the output. The output may also be excitatory or inhibitory in nature depending on the type of element. That is, the output may excite or inhibit whatever unit the processing unit is connected to. Some processing elements are capable of receiving input from its output in a feedback loop. Processing elements are somewhat analogous to brain neurons (Caudill Dec 1987, 47–49; Ingraham et al 1988, 17).

Processing segmented speech The procedure used in speech-understanding systems, which divides the incoming signal according to acoustic events instead of by a fixed interval.

Processing unit Processing element.

Process model A model of implementing parallel PROLOG. The model is used to find the various parallel processes in a PROLOG program, and to ensure that the parallel executions find all solutions. *See also* AND-parallelism; OR-parallelism, for the two types of parallel processes (Eadiline 1989, 35).

Process monitoring A simulation of a real-world process. Example: monitoring a gasoline refining process. The process can be monitored by using object-oriented programming. Different aspects of the process can be represented by objects. The interaction of the objects can be monitored so that potential problems can be prevented (Somsel Nov 1987, 76–77).

Product An operation in relational algebra in which two tables are combined by multiplying the number of rows in each table. This procedure usually leaves a table which must be further refined before the table is ready for practical use (Parsaye 1988, 413–414).

Production A rule in a production system, usually of the form if/then. A production rule may be thought of as a heuristic or as an operator which moves the problem-solving process from one state to another. A production rule differs from ordinary if/then statements in that they are used by the production system interpreter to search perhaps thousands of working-memory elements for data which will match the variables in the rule. An ordinary if/then statement in conventional programs contains variables which are simply used to see if the variables have values found in specific memory locations which satisfy the conditions in the rule. Example: IF city = New Orleans AND goal is fun AND cost is unimportant THEN go to the Mardi Gras. In an ordinary if/then statement a single memory location for city supplies the value for city. If that memory location contains New Orleans and the memory location for the variable goal contains fun and the cost is unimportant the then portion of the rule is executed. If not, the rule simply fails. A production rule which has the conditions city = New Orleans and goal = fun and cost is unimportant will search through many working-memory elements for a match. There may be many failures before a match is finally found. One working-memory element may have city = New Orleans, but goal may not be fun. Another working-memory element may match all three elements and then the rule may be executed. A production rule is a modular chunk of knowledge. An ordinary if/then statement is a control construct. This is a very important distinction. An ordinary if/then rule primarily controls what statements the program will next execute. A production rule adds or deletes knowledge to the working memory. Another difference between productions and ordinary if/then rules is that productions can have negated condition elements on the left-hand side of the rule; the rule can succeed only if there are no working-memory elements that can satisfy the negated condition element. Productions vary in their format and capability: Some productions place the consequent before the antecedents (CONCLUSION IF Y AND Z). Some production systems limit their productions to a single consequent. Other productions do not allow the use of variables or the OR connective. Some productions use the ELSE condition and recursion may be allowed. Rewrite rules are referred to as productions. A production rule can represent both declarative and procedural knowledge. The term if/then rule is used interchangeably with production rule by some authorities. *See also* Production system (Chabris 1989, 300; Harmon and King 1985, 25–26, 54–55; Brownston et al 1986, 187–188; Barr and Feigenbaum 1981 vol 1, 190; Barr and Feigenbaum 1981 vol 3, 465–474).

Production expert system An expert system based on the use of productions and a production system language. (Michaelsen et al 1985, 307).

Production knowledge Knowledge that controls the sequence of problem-solving steps.

Production memory The portion of a production expert system where the rules are located. In some production systems rules may be added or deleted at runtime (Moskowitz 1986, 218; Brownston et al 1986, 13–14).

Production node A node found in OPS production systems that is responsible for combining the last condition element with the earlier set of consistent matches.

Production system A particular production-system program which includes a body of knowledge (knowledge base) as well as an inference engine (the center of control). The separation of knowledge and control is a key characteristic of a production system. Even though there is a separation of knowledge and control the inference engine is indirectly controlled by the patterns of data it finds in the knowledge base. The following is a description of a production system built with OPS5, the language most people consider the epitome of the modern production-system language: The knowledge base consists of a rule base and working memory. The rule base stores rules and working memory has data structures. The rule base is the repository of conditional knowledge. Working memory is sometimes compared to human short-term memory and it holds the facts known to the system. Working memory is dynamically changing during a program run. That is, the working memory elements may be altered, or working memory elements may be added or deleted. The rule base is sometimes likened to long-term memory. The rule base usually remains relatively stable during a program run. Patterns of facts in working memory are matched with the antecedent part of a rule. When a successful match takes place the rule is added to the conflict set. The conflict set consists of a set of successfully matched rules. Some form of conflict-resolution strategy is then used to choose a particular rule from the conflict set to fire. When this rule is executed it triggers the consequent part of the rule and the consequents are added to working memory. This process continues until no new facts can be derived. This pattern matching may be conceptualized as a search. Production systems are generally thought of as forward chaining in nature, although they can often be programmed to work in a backward-chaining mode. Production systems are very modular and allow for incremental growth. That is, with a pure production system like OPS5 the developer can be less concerned about exactly where a rule is placed in the program than one would be in a standard procedural program. This latter characteristic is a hallmark of a pure production system. Production-system languages, shells, or tools which are devoid of domain knowledge are frequently referred to as production systems, but it is best to avoid that usage and instead call them production shells, tools, or languages. *See also* OPS5, for a detailed look at a classic production-system language. Unlike other production systems, a pure production system like OPS5 has no means of backtracking from a dead end. Pure production systems like OPS5 do not use inexact reasoning. Logic-based expert systems are sometimes referred to as production systems. Logic-based systems have a great deal in common with production systems. They both use rules. Control is separated from knowledge. There are, however, a number of differences: The difference between working memory and production memory is obscured in a logic-based system. There is no Rete match algorithm or an equivalent in logic-based systems. Instead, unification is used. There is no conflict-resolution strategy in a logic-based system. Pure production systems like OPS5 generally function in a forward-chaining mode. In order to produce forward chaining in a logic-based system some effort is required since logic-based systems like PROLOG are inherently backward chaining. Logic-based programs like PROLOG use backtracking while pure production systems like OPS5 do not. The structure of the rules is quite different. In a logic-based system the rules are usually in clausal form. Finally, logic-based languages like PROLOG are more sensitive to placement of a rule than is a true production system. A comparison of a production system with state-space search is instructive. The working memory may be thought of as a node in the state-space search. The production rules are the means of transition between states. *See also* Production; Production-system language, for more information. Rule-based expert system is considered to be synonymous with production system by some authorities. Some rule-based systems, however, stray from the classical definition of production systems. See DENDRAL for such an example. *Contrast with* Frame-based expert system (Jackson 1986, 185; Valdex-Perez 1986, 30; Fischler and Firschein Dec 1986, 44; Charniak and McDermott 1985, 438–440; Winston 1979, 143–145, 151; Harmon and King 1985, 25–26; Brownston et al

1986, 9, 15–20, 23–26; Barr and Feigenbaum 1981 vol 1, 157, 190–199; Winston and Horn 1984, 269–284; Luger and Stubblefield 1989, 131).

Production-system language A language used to build a program that will match rules with facts to infer new facts. General Problem Solver was the first computerized production-system language. It used productions (rules) as a primary data structure for holding knowledge. General Problem Solver generally worked in a forward-chaining manner. Control was separate from the knowledge in GPS. These were the general characteristics of the first production-system language. See General Problem Solver for more details. OPS5 is a later production-system language. It is generally considered the epitome of modern production-system languages and is the one described here. The OPS5 language has an inference engine which is responsible for control and inference. The inference engine uses a sophisticated pattern matcher known as the Rete match algorithm which chooses the rules to be placed in a conflict set. Some form of conflict resolution strategy is then used to choose the most appropriate rule to execute. Almost all production-system languages also have a consultation shell which can answer the user's questions. Pure production systems like OPS5 generally run in a forward-chaining manner, but they can be used in a backward-chaining mode. Pure production-systems like OPS5 are not generally associated with backtracking and inexact reasoning. However, these distinctions are becoming blurred. The OPS5 language has input-output capabilities expected of a language. The user is obliged to use OPS5 to write rules and facts just as a programmer writes a program using the C language. The runtime portions of OPS5 and the rules and facts added by the user combine to make a complete production system. Production-system languages are particularly applicable in large, complex problems in which there is no fixed or apparent order in which the problem can be solved, and responsiveness to changes in data is important. *See also* Production; Production system (Tello Jul 1985, 71; Michaelsen et al 1985, 307; Moskowitz Nov 1986, 217; Brownston et al 1986, 8–9, 11–30; Hunt 1986, 3; Smith 1989, 150; Olsen 1987, 126; Luger 1989, 132).

Production-system program A program written using a production system.

Programmed learning An early version of CAI, which used feedback to tell the user if he or she was correct; it could to a limited extent individualize instruction. *Contrast with* Intelligent tutoring (Waldrop 1987, 207–208).

Programmer's Apprentice A software automation program consisting of three parts: a knowledge-based editor, interactive query, and automatic documentation. The editor can correct syntax and generate chunks of program code. The interactive query feature allows the programmer to ask questions about the execution of the program. The automatic documentation feature produces program documentation (Barr and Feigenbaum 1981 vol 2, 343–349)

Programming assistant A program that provides assistance to an experienced programmer by carrying out such activities as specification, implementation, testing, and optimization. Artificial intelligence techniques have been used to build programming assistants. Programming assistants are one step above programming environments and one step below automatic programming.

Programming environment Facilities that aid in the development of artificial intelligence programs. The tools may be libraries of subroutines, editors, and debuggers (Harmon et al 1988, 269; Roland 1987, 48; Barr and Feigenbaum 1981 vol 2, 65–71).

Program synthesis/transformation Automatic programming (Chabris 1989, 300).

Progressive deepening A procedure that repeatedly executes alpha-beta search; on each iteration the depth of the search is progressively deepened until the time allotted for the player runs out (Bratko 1986, 369).

Projection 1. The ability to reach conclusions about what could be true at one time from what is true at a different time, and to store these conclusions in a knowledge structure. This is important in planning programs that must take time into account. 2. The procedure of estimating what an artificial intelligence program will do. 3. A procedure in relational algebra in which certain columns of a table are removed (Parsaye 1988, 413; Charniak and McDermott 1985, 485; Tello 1988, 487).

PROLOG A declarative language based on logic programming. PROLOG stands for PROgramming in LOGic. PROLOG is based on predicate calculus. The clause is the primary representational scheme in PROLOG and it is used to represent relationships among objects in facts and rules (conditional facts). A PROLOG program is nothing more than a set of facts and rules represented as clauses. Within the context of clauses, PROLOG also supports the construction of complex structures like dynamic lists, recursive rules, and compound objects. The control features of PROLOG can be divided into two classes, explicit and implicit. Explicit control features include the ordering of facts and rules, the ordering of subgoals in a query, the cut, fail, true, not, call, repeat, and recursion. There are implicit control features that set PROLOG apart from other languages. The implicit control features are depth-first search and backtracking. A PROLOG programmer defines relationships among objects in facts and rules and implements the explicit control features to control the program flow partially. Then, all that is needed is to query the program. The implicit control features of depth-first search and backtracking take control of the flow of control in an effort to solve the query. Contrast this descriptive approach to programming with a conventional procedural program which consists of a sequence of procedural steps. It uses a method of inference called resolution. Part of the implementation of resolution is the unification pattern matcher. The unification pattern matcher unifies the query with the information in the facts and rules. PROLOG treats variables differently from the way conventional languages do. PROLOG variables are polymorphic. That is, a given variable may be set equal to a number, a symbol, a string, a list, or a very complex structure during a program run. The polymorphic nature of PROLOG variables gives PROLOG much of its power. Once a variable is set equal to a value there is no program command like $X = X + 1$ which will change or somehow increment that variable while attempting to solve the query. If the attempt to solve a query fails, the underlying backtracking mechanism of PROLOG automatically uninstantiates variables and then finds new values for the variables in an attempt to find an alternative solution. This loss of procedural control over variable values is an asset, but at the same time it is one of the major stumbling blocks for a programmer schooled in conventional programs. Because PROLOG cannot be used to increment or alter variables while doing a query run this makes PROLOG a good candidate for parallel processing. One other advantage of PROLOG is that it is relatively easy to build bridges to relational data bases. Programs written in PROLOG are usually smaller than equivalent programs in procedural languages. They are also easier to understand. In PROLOG, variables receive their values through the built-in unification procedure and not through assignment statements as used in procedural programs. In PROLOG programs and data are indistinguishable. This equivalence of programs and data allows for the construction of metainterpreters and self-modifying programs. PROLOG is useful in the incremental building of programs. That is, it is possible to make significant additions to a program without having to rewrite the entire program, as one must frequently do for conventional procedural programs. PROLOG can be run in a backward fashion. That is, you can construct a procedure that will append two lists. Then, you can use this same procedure to find the difference between two lists. Most computer languages will not allow you to run a program in such a backward manner. In comparison with

LISP, PROLOG is faster and does not take up as much memory. PROLOG may be considered a production-system language. It has a built-in inferencing engine, its body of facts may be considered a type of working memory, and its rules may be considered a rule base. The differentiation between working memory and the rule base in PROLOG is not as distinct as it is in most production-system languages. PROLOG like LISP uses dynamic memory management. PROLOG has a built-in definite-clause grammar. PROLOG like LISP also uses lists to represent information (Chabris 1989, 300; Bharath and Sklar Jul 1985, 49–54; Kenig Nov 1986, 59–65; Pierson 1987, 32; Lazarev Jul 1987, 59–68; Clocksin 1987, 147; Eisenbach and Sadler 1985, 192–194; Emond, and Paulissen 1986, 214; Thompson and Thompson Premier 1986, 23; Merritt Spring 1988, 64–66; Harmon and King 1985, 87–89; Brownston et al 1986, 371–374; Sterling and Shapiro 1986, 95–101; Bratko 1986, 61, 174–175; Gasser 89, 30).

PROLOG structure A functor and its arguments (Matthews Jul 1987, 37).

PROLOG II A revised version of PROLOG. The primary feature is the inclusion of infinite trees (cyclic data structures). A second feature is the ability to avoid error messages when a predicate's variables are uninstantiated. PROLOG II waits until the variables are instantiated before executing the predicate. ExperPROLOG II is the name of the Macintosh version sold in the United States (Lassez 1987, 171; Shafer 1987, 75–78).

PROLOG III A version of PROLOG that replaces the unification algorithm with constraint resolution. PROLOG III allows for the solution of systems of constraints. Variables can represent such complex entities as trees (Rettig 1988, 17; Colmerauer 1987, 177–182).

Proof All the steps involved in the extraction of a conclusion from the premises using inference rules, in logic (Dos Reis 1988, 50).

Proof by contradiction A type of proof that looks for a contradiction in order to prove a theorem. Resolution is a type of proof by contradiction (Smith 1989, 152).

Proof procedure An inference rule and the algorithm that will execute the inference rule so that it is applied to a set of propositions to produce inferences (Luger and Stubblefield 1989, 60).

Proof by refutation The procedure of negating the conclusion and then attempting to infer the empty clause from the negated conclusion and the premises (Dos Reis 88, 51).

Proof theory An approach to databases that holds that queries consist of theorems that must be proved by means of such procedures as resolution. Updates to the data base can change the underlying structure of the data base. This approach is identified with the artificial intelligence community. *Contrast with* Model theory (Brodie and Jarke 1986, 191).

Proof tree A representation of the goals and the reductions that take place in a computation. A tree-type data structure which consists of a root node and its children nodes. The root node represents the hypothesis and the children are subgoals which must be proved to prove the hypothesis. A common implementation of a proof tree is the AND/OR tree (Brownston et al 1986, 452; Sterling and Shapiro 1986, 47, 50).

Prop One item in the contents of a script. In a courtroom situation props may include the judge, lawyers, the legal charges, and the legal procedures involved (Lugar and Stubblefield 1989, 364).

Propagation method The process whereby certain problems require the application of a series of equations each of which has more than one unknown variable. The propagation method allows such equations to be held in limbo until values are discovered for the equations so that the equation may be solved. EL is an expert system that employs the propagation method (Hayes-Roth et al 1983, 111).

Property 1. The attribute of an object. Examples of attributes for an automobile may be color, engine-size, make, and so on. 2. A hashed lookup table with a built-in hashing mechanism. It can be used to build data bases. POP is one language which has properties. 3. A slot, in the expert system Nexpert (Epp et al May 1988, 824; Townsend 1987a, 119–120; Charniak and McDermott 1985, 58–59; Brownston et al 1986, 278).

Property inheritance A characteristic of most frame-based expert systems in which the properties of a parent object are automatically inherited by any newly created objects that belong to that class. An example is a Ford inheriting the properties of engine type, color, number of wheels, and so on from the parent object, automobile. This is the most common type of inheritance scheme but not the only type. Other types of inheritance include value inheritance, restriction inheritance, null inheritance, multiple inheritance, union inheritance, intersection inheritance, inheritance of methods, and after inheritance (Charniak and McDermott 1985, 405; Barr and Feigenbaum 1981 vol 1, 181–184).

Property list A structure that consists of an object and its associated properties and values. A property list is not really a LISP list and the functions that are usually used to manipulate a list cannot be used with it. It is an entity that can be used to store more than one value for a given atom. An example of a property list can be an Oldsmobile-88. Oldsmobile-88 is represented by an atom. Some of the properties of the atom are that it has an engine, wheels, and so on. Each property has a value associated with it. In the wheels property the number four is stored. In LISP, property lists are the basis for building frames. It is like an association list except that a property list is more efficient and easier to use than an association list. Another distinction is deletions; additions to property lists are destructive processes while additions made to association lists are nondestructive (Steele 1984, 165; McMillan 1987, 54; Charniak and McDermott 1985, 58–59; Winston 1979, 288–289; Barr and Feigenbaum 1981 vol 2, 7; Winston and Horn 1984, 96; Townsend and Feucht 1986, 121–122).

Proposition 1. A logic statement with a truth value, which is equivalent to the term atomic expression. 2. A well-formed statement that is employed in propositional logic and is either true or false (Luger and Stubblefield 1989, 50; Smith 1989, 153; Schildt, 1987, 224).

Propositional calculus A system of formal logic. A sequential inference system whose goal is to determine if a statement (proposition) is true or false. Common connectives found in propositional calculus include AND, OR, NOT, IMPLIES, and EQUIVALENT. Common laws that govern propositional logic include the commutative, associative, distributive, and DeMorgan's laws. The most common inference rule associated with propositional calculus is modus ponens. It differs from first-order logic in that propositional logic does not differentiate between subject and predicate, and it does not use variables. Propositional calculus is also called propositional logic. *Compare with* Predicate calculus (Schildt 1987, 224–228; Mishkoff 1986, G–3; Barr and Feigenbaum 1981 vol 1, 160–163; Townsend and Feucht 1986, 60–61; Smith 1989, 153).

Prosody The analysis of the melody of language (Luger and Stubblefield 1989, 379).

PROSPECTOR An expert system used to find ore deposits, which uses a semantic network for knowledge representation. The semantic net is divided into five models which represent the facts and relationships found in five distinct mineral deposits. The nodes in the semantic network are assertions that are either false, or true with some probability assigned to its true value. Each arc is a production rule that specifies how the probability of one assertion affects another assertion. The interface employs a natural-language interface and it is a mixed-initiative interface. It also has a good explanation system. Its best known success was finding a one hundred million dollar molybdenum deposit. Its performance is thought to be comparable to that of an expert geologist. *See also* KAS, for information on the expert system tool used to develop PROSPECTOR (Johnson 1986, 18–19; Hayes-Roth et al 1983, 54–55; Harmon and King 1985, 145–150; Brownston et al 1986, 358–359; Barr and Feigenbaum 1981 vol 2, 155–162).

PROSQL   An interface between PROLOG and SQL Data Systems, which supports either loose or tight coupling. The interface was designed at IBM.

Protocol   A synonym for method (Manola 1990, 29-32).

Protocol analysis   **1.** The systematic observation and recording of the behavior of a domain expert by a knowledge engineer.   **2.** The analysis cognitive psychologists carry out on the verbal transcripts taken from people solving problems. Cognitive psychologists use such protocols to better understand thought processes (Winston 1979, 154; Barr and Feigenbaum 1981 vol 3, 18–23; Smith 1989, 154; Olson and Rueter 1988, 24–25).

Prototype   An initial version of an expert system. A prototype represents only a very small portion of the knowledge domain. A prototype is built to see if the representation and inferencing techniques are feasible for solving the particular problem at hand. Other questions which should be faced during prototype development include: Is there sufficient knowledge? Is the knowledge consistent over time? Is there an element of uncertainty in the facts? What criteria can be used for testing performance? The prototype can begin after one case is elicited from the domain expert. Other cases are gradually added until a small sample of typical cases is included. The domain expert and knowledge engineer work together in testing and fine tuning the prototype. Prototypes are necessary in expert system development because no good principles have been developed to help knowledge engineers to decide which inference techniques or which knowledge representations should be used for a particular problem. Instead, a prototype or a series of prototypes are used in a trial-and-error process (Townsend 1987a, 249; Walters and Nielsen 1988, 16–17; Harmon and King 1985, 201–203; Townsend 1987b, 384).

Prototype development   The third of seven stages in expert system development. In this stage case studies are studied and a small expert system is developed to cover the case studies. *See also* Expert system development (Harmon et al 1988, 191–195).

Prototype language   A type of language in which it is relatively easy to build a prototype. PROLOG is frequently referred to as a prototype language, in part because it is very expressive. C is not considered to be a good prototyping language, partially because it is a compiled language.

Prototype object   An object in a frame-based system that consists of a set of instance objects. Example: mammal, which represents a set of different kinds of animals which are all mammals. *Contrast with* Instance object; Referential object (Reimer 1986, 178).

Prototype point method   A method of image understanding which emphasizes the point at which all the axes of all the features of the general example of a model meet. *Compare with* Region method; Template method (Lawrence 1985, 50).

Prototype system   An object-based language that uses delegation. That is, individual objects do not possess methods. Instead, the methods are in a parent object. When a message is passed to an individual object the message is delegated to the parent object which carries out the message request. Prototype systems make it easy for an object to be moved from one class to another (Thomas 1989, 238–240).

Pruning   The removal of a branch of a search space. Heuristic rules are used to prune a search tree (Mishkoff 1986, G-30; Barr and Feigenbaum 1981 vol 1, 60).

Pseudoprobability   The use of certainty factors in expert systems (Hayes-Roth et al 1983, 95).

Pseudoreduction The breaking up of a problem into subgoals and solving each of the subgoals independently. Care must be taken to take into account any interdependence among subgoals (Hunt 1986, 208).

Pseudo-reduction Finding a plan to solve each goal independently, when the need arises that a set of goals needs to be achieved at the same time (Hunt 1986, 13).

Pseudorule An Englishlike rule. A type of pseudocode. The pseudorule must be translated into a format the computer program can understand (Cooper 1988, 241).

Pseudorule refinement The transformation of a rule written in ordinary English into a format readily understandable by the artificial intelligence system being used (Cooper 1988, 241).

Pseudovariables A member of a certain class of variables in Smalltalk. These variables are found in methods and when activated will take on the value of the object that is receiving the message. Self and super are the two types of pseudovariables (Pascoe 1986, 144; *Smalltalk/V Tutorial and Programming Handbook* 1986, 32; 69).

PUFF A pulmonary medical expert system built using CADUCEUS, which is used for diagnosing pulmonary disorders. This expert system uses both frames and rules. The frames are called prototypes and represent different disease entities. These prototypes are arranged in a hierarchical structure, allowing effective pruning to take place. The prototypes at the upper level represent general classes of diseases. The lower-level prototypes represent specific diseases. The general control structure used in PUFF is called hypothesize and match. It is a type of approximate pattern matching and works as follows: As the initial data entering process takes place, rules are used to trigger candidate prototypes and assign values to the prototypes. The prototypes at the top of the hierarchy are compared and the most promising prototypes, those with the best scores, are chosen as the candidate prototypes. The user answers questions and fills in data for the candidate prototypes at this top level in the hierarchy, and finally the best prototype is chosen. Then, those prototypes that are subsumed under the chosen prototype are examined. That is, questions are asked that allow differential diagnosis of these lower-level prototypes. This process is continued until a final prototype is chosen. If there are symptoms not explained by the diagnosis, additional prototypes are scrutinized for a second diagnosis (Jackson 1986, 142–155; Harmon and King 1985, 150–152).

Pure object-oriented system An object-oriented language in which everything is an object. Smalltalk is a pure object-oriented language (Tello 1989, 8).

Pure production system 1. A production system that follows the OPS model. 2. A production system that does not employ backtracking (Luger and Stubblefield 1989, 131).

Pure PROLOG A logic program that efficiently uses PROLOG's problem-solving apparatus. That is, the clauses in the query and in the program are ordered to take advantage of PROLOG's problem-solving apparatus, which includes depth-first sequential search and backtracking. Extralogical features like the cut facility are not used (Sterling and Shapiro 1986, 94).

Pursue facility A synonym for what-if capability (Tello 1988, 138).

Pyramid A hierarchical representation of image features. A series of two-dimensional arrays representing the same scene in progressively greater detail. It improves the efficiency of reasoning about image features (Barr and Feigenbaum 1981, vol 3, 279–282).

Q R

QA3 A question-answering system that employs resolution to carry out deductions. Its use of unrestricted resolution made it too prone to combinatorial explosion for all but very limited problems (Barr and Feigenbaum 1981, vol 1, 168–169).

Quad tree A hierarchical representation of image features. It improves the efficiency of reasoning about image features. It is called a quad tree because each terminal node has four children. Quad trees are similar to pyramids but quad trees can store data more efficiently in some circumstances (Barr and Feigenbaum 1981, vol 3, 137, 229, 282).

Qualification problem A manifestation of the frame problem. The problem of balancing how much knowledge is needed to achieve correct inferences and how to represent that knowledge practically. In some problems the number of possible factors may be extremely large. Many of these facts may be irrelevant at one moment and then very relevant at the next moment (Eckert 1989, 52–54).

Qualitative reasoning Reasoning from first principles using nonnumeric symbolic terms, which uses verbal descriptions rather than quantitative techniques to solve problems. Qualitative reasoning has been applied to physics as an alternative to quantitative problem solving. When applied to physics qualitative reasoning provides greater insight into the underlying principles than does quantitative reasoning. A synonym is deep reasoning. *Contrast with* Rule of thumb, shallow reasoning used in many expert systems (Chabris 1989, 300; Walters and Nielsen 1988, 293).

Quanta A term associated with sponsors. A quanta limits the number of rules an expert system can fire at one time.

Quantifier A quantifier asserts set membership in predicate calculus. A method of defining the range of variables. The two types of quantifiers are existential quantifiers and universal quantifiers. The existential quantifier says there exists at least one object for a given variable for which a statement or certain conditions are true. Example: THERE EXISTS a person with red hair whose name is Smith. The universal quantifier states that for all objects represented by a variable, a statement or certain conditions are true. Example: ALL men are mortal. Variables that are in the premise of a rule, but not in the conclusion of a rule, are existentially quantified. Variables that are in the conclusion of a rule are universally quantified (Parsaye and Chignell 1988, 84–88, Barr and Feigenbaum 1981, vol 1, 164, 360; Barr and Feigenbaum 1981, vol 3, 88–89; Smith 1989, 158).

Query One of the three basic statements in logic programming. A query asks a question of a logic program. The predicate likes(john, mary) could be a query which searches the logic program data base to see if there is a matching fact. If a matching fact exists or can be deduced from the data base, the program returns true. If a matching fact cannot be found or deduced the program returns false. Queries can be conjunctive. That is, they may consist of more than one predicate. Queries frequently contain variables. The variables in queries are existentially quantified. Variables in queries open up the possibility of finding multiple solutions to a query. Multiple solutions to a query can be found by adding a fail statement to the query. Shared variables are sometimes used in a query to restrict the number of solutions (Sterling and Shapiro 1986, 3–8; Shmueli et al 1986, 249).

Query compiler A compiler that accepts a query and compiles a short program which will find all records which meet the query. It is faster than a query interpreter (Graham Jun 1989, 22).

Query generalization A method of dealing with data base query failure. This technique attempts to show why the query failed, or to show the limiting scope of the failure (Motro 1986, 597–616).

Query interpreter A procedure that interprets a data base query and produces all possible records that can meet the query. *Contrast with* Query compiler, which is faster (Graham Jun 1989, 22).

Query optimization An application of artificial intelligence technology to data base queries. Techniques that take from the user of relational data base systems the burden of having to worry about efficiency issues when preparing their queries. The process of giving a data base self-knowledge so that it can improve its efficiency in responding to a query. Assume a data base of airplanes. If the data base knows that jumbo jets are the only planes that weigh x tons, the data base can more efficiently respond to a query that asks for all planes over x tons (Parker Jr. et al. 1986, 43–44).

Query-time inference Backward chaining (Charniak and McDermott 1985, 345).

Query the user The ability of most expert systems to ask the user for an answer when the expert system has been unable to infer the answer or find the answer in its fact base (Jackson 1986, 187).

Queue A data structure that is useful for the organization of goals. It operates on the first-in-first-out principle. That is, the first goal generated is the first goal solved. The last goal generated is the last goal solved. The selection of goals in a queue cannot be altered, and because of this kind of inflexibility queues are not often used in expert systems. Other data structures used in organizing goals are tree structures, stacks, and agendas (Brownston et al 1986, 281–282; Sterling and Shapiro 1986, 252–255).

Quiescence A measure that decides if the exploration of a search tree should continue along the current path, search a new path, or terminate the search (Forsyth and Naylor 1985, 183).

Quiescence search When it finds a move that can cause critical changes, it extends the search process in this area until a state of quiescence is achieved. Example: Assume a chess program where the program is faced with losing its rook. The program can sacrifice a pawn and hold off losing the rook. However, it will lose its rook on the next move anyway, so the sacrifice of the pawn is needless. Some chess programs suffer from the horizon effect which consists of not being able to look over the horizon and see the inevitable loss of the rook. Quiescence search overcomes this deficiency by exploring in depth certain critical moves. In this way the program can foresee the inevitable loss of the rook and can avoid the needless sacrifice of the pawn (Chabris 1989, 185–187).

Quillian's Semantic Memory System A pioneering effort to come up with an operational representation of word meaning, which used an associative network. The nodes are concepts and the arcs are relations between concepts. A memory system that placed emphasis on the meaning of words in the memory process. The meaning of a word was defined in relationship to other words. The system focused on recognition memory, not recall memory.

Q'NIAL An interpreter for NIAL, which provides unification and resolution. While backtracking is provided, the user is not restricted to backtracking. It is written in C (Roland 1987, 52).

RADIX A machine-learning algorithm that analyzes time-oriented data using statistical techniques (Parsaye Jul/Aug 1989, 29–30).

RAIL A robotics-control language developed by Automatix (Mishkoff 1986, 5–19).

Ramification problem A manifestation of the frame problem, the problem of knowing all of the ramifications of a given action (Eckert 1989, 53).

Range The scope of the problems that an artificial intelligence program can handle. There is an inverse relationship between range and efficiency.

Range constriction A search that pushes each alternative as far forward as possible. When evidence is accumulated that a given alternative is not a possible solution the alternative is dropped (Winston 1979, 127).

Range finder A method for measuring depth in image analysis. Two such methods are time of flight and triangulation methods (Barr and Feigenbaum 1981, vol 3, 254–259, 272–278).

Rapid prototyping 1. An approach to expert system development that advocates the solving of a problem by developing a prototype with minimal study of the problem. 2. A method of expert system development that emphasizes the early construction of a small working expert system which works with only a small subset of the knowledge domain. The initial prototype is used as a basis for iterative expansion until a complete version of the expert system is achieved. The drawback to this approach is that the developer may become locked in too quickly to an architecture which is not the most appropriate way of dealing with the full knowledge domain (Hu 1989, 68; Walters and Nielsen 1988, 182).

Rationalization The ability of an expert system to understand and explain its reasoning (Hayes-Roth et al 1983, 48).

RCL (Robot Control Language) A language developed by RB Robot Corporation (Tello 1988, 27).

Reader An access procedure used to extract data from objects. *See also* San Marco LISP Explorer.

Read-only variable A variable used in concurrent PROLOG. When a read-only variable is established, processing is temporarily halted until the variable and all reductions that employ it are given a bound value (Luger and Stubblefield 1989, 482–483).

Real-time expert system An expert system that has its input data from an ongoing, constantly varying process.

Reasonableness The ability of an expert system to continue to function with contradictory information (Hewitt, Apr 1985, 239).

Reasoning Activities that include analyzing, classifying, diagnosing, persuading, making assumptions, problem solving, and drawing inferences. *See also* Causal reasoning; Circumscription; Common-sense reasoning; Default reasoning; Means-end; Metalevel reasoning; Nonmonotonic reasoning; Plausible reasoning; and Spatial reasoning (Henschen 1990, 822–823).

Reasoning about necessary conditions A term used interchangeably with classification (Brachman 1987, 7).

Reasoning about sufficient conditions A term used interchangeably with inheritance (Brachman 1987, 7).

Reasoning by analogy *See* Analogical reasoning.

Reasoning by circumscription A type of nonmonotonic reasoning. *See* Circumscription.

Reasoning by default The assumption that a fact is true or a variable equals a particular value unless given contradictory information. A characteristic of frame-based and object-based systems in which a value that is not specified for an object may be inherited from a parent object. Example: the variable number_legs inheriting the value of four. Reasoning by default is needed as a shortcut to reduce the amount of reasoning required. It is, of course, not guaranteed to be correct. *See also* Default reasoning (Waldrop 1987, 48–49).

Reasoning by elimination A process of entertaining all possible solutions to a problem and eliminating those solutions that are inconsistent with the information at hand. Example: eliminating all suspects in a murder case who have an alibi. Reasoning by elimination is often felt to be unrealistic in problems with large search spaces (Hayes-Roth et al 1983, 99).

Reasoning strategy A synonym for control strategy.

Reasoning under uncertainty The type of fuzzy reasoning found in the MYCIN expert system (Chabris 1989, 113).

Reasoning with intervals Reasoning with finite lengths of time. Example: Assume the following intervals of time: a, b, c. The time interval a ends when b time interval begins, and b time interval is before c time interval, then a is before c (Ladkin 1987, 62).

Reason maintenance **1.** A procedure that uses a data-dependency network to aid in adding and withdrawing facts. **2.** Monitoring assertions and the assumptions the dependencies are based on in a knowledge base. In the event an assumption is proven to be false all of the assertions it is based on can be withdrawn. Nonmonotonic reasoning and truth maintenance are terms used interchangeably with reason maintenance (Charniak and McDermott 1985, 414; Brownston et al 1986, 453; Hunt 1986, 215).

Receiver The recipient of the message in object-oriented programs. The object hexagon is the receiver in the message, hexagon findPerimeter (*Smalltalk/V Tutorial and Programming Handbook* 1986, 30).

Recency A conflict-resolution strategy used in OPS5 production-system languages. The principle of recency gives precedence to those rules that have working-memory elements which have most recently been asserted or modified. It uses time tags that are attached to working-memory elements in OPS5-type production systems. The time tag records how recently the working-memory element was asserted or modified. This information is then used in the conflict-resolution strategy. The conflict-resolution strategy chooses the rule or set of rules from the conflict set based on the recency of the working-memory elements they match. Recency is an important factor in implementing a backward-chaining expert system using OPS5. It is also important in building monitoring expert systems which must be prepared to respond quickly to alarm situations (Brownston et al 1986, 12, 43, 61–64, 453; Rosenberg 1986, 156).

Recency attribute A synonym for time tag (Brownston et al 1986, 12).

Recognition by angles A visual pattern recognizer that focuses on angles to discriminate patterns. *See also* Delta-D recognizer; Recognition by key points, for other pattern recognition approaches (Schildt 1987, 141–147).

Recognition by key points A visual pattern recognizer that focuses on that part of a pattern that uniquely discriminates it from other patterns. *See also* Delta-D recognizer; Recognition by angles, for other pattern recognition approaches (Schildt 1987, 149–153).

Recognition driven A synonym for data driven.

Recognition problem A problem in artificial intelligence in which the program must be able to recognize the meaning of the input data before it can properly be processed. Recognition can be difficult in an area like natural-language processing. Sentences can be ambiguous and the true meaning of the sentence can be missed (Feldman 1985, 278–282).

Recognize-act cycle A control procedure used in OPS5-type production systems which continually cycles through the production rules, matching, selecting, and executing rules. All rules that match the contents of working memory are recognized. Then, one rule from the set of recognized rules is selected, based on some predefined criteria, and executed. The predefined criteria may be most recent rule, most specific rule, or some other criterion. The actions that take place when a rule is executed can include adding, deleting, or altering working-memory elements. Other actions can include input and output commands. The recognize-act cycle is repeated until no more production rules can be found to be executed. The recognize-act cycle may be thought of as the inference engine for a production system (Luger and Stubblefield 1989, 302; Forgy and Shepard 1987, 36; Harmon and King 1985, 23, 55; Brownston et al 1986, 7, 60–62, 453; Rosenberg 1986, 156).

Recognize-act pair A knowledge structure that is best represented by production rules. That is, the production rule recognizes a pattern and the production rule then acts. *Compare with* Subset of (Jackson 1986, 177).

Recursion A type of control structure. An iterative technique in which a function is defined in terms of itself. The function calls itself. Each time it calls itself the parameters are altered by the function, allowing progress toward the goal the function is attempting to achieve. A recursive definition must have a means of stopping itself or it will continue indefinitely. A statement in the function monitors the changing parameters and terminates the recursion when a predetermined value is reached. Recursion was popularized in the artificial intelligence languages LISP, Smalltalk, and later PROLOG. Languages like Pascal and C, which are even more conventional, use recursion. An example of its use is to find out if a given name is a member of a list of names, and the list of names is of unknown size. Recursion is employed in production systems by a rule making a copy of the working-memory element which will satisfy the left-hand side of the rule, causing the rule to fire again. Recursion is also useful in mapping problems and in developing backward-chaining expert systems. From a more general perspective, Hofstadter's book *Gödel, Escher, and Bach, an Eternal Golden Braid* documents how recursion is frequently found in mathematics, art, music, and nature. Seeing your reflection in two mirrors facing each other is an example of recursion. Tail recursion is the most frequently used type of recursion. Developing a backward-chaining or a rule-value expert system would be very difficult without recursion, at least with some languages. *See also* Indirect recursion (Chabris 1989, 300; Harrison and Tribble 1986, 66; McMillan 1987, 52; Bharath and Sklar 1985, 52–53; Johnson 1986, 92–93, 282–283; Townsend 1987a, 95; Young 1987, 152; Brownston et al 1986, 204–206; Townsend 1987b, 14–15; Sterling and Shapiro 1986, 163–164; Winston and Horn 1984, 63–64; Forsyth and Naylor 1985, 27).

Recursive data type A data structure that allows structures to contain other structures like themselves. Lists and trees are examples of recursive data types. The use of recursive data types allows an alternative to the more standard hierarchical structuring of data (Jackson 1986, 146; Lane Nov/Dec 1987, 80).

Recursive descent parsing *See* Context-free parser (Thompson and Thompson Apr 1985, 324; Thompson and Thompson Dec 1986, 24; Schildt 1987, 107).

Recursive language A language that allows functions or procedures to call themselves. Since recursion is such an important process in artificial intelligence applications it is important that the language have recursive abilities. Languages that employ recursion include LISP, PROLOG, Smalltalk, Pascal, and C.

Recursively enumerable language A type of formal language that employs unconstrained production rules (Luger and Stubblefield 1989, 389).

Recursive pattern matcher A methodology that uses recursive techniques to find data that fit a pattern or a pattern that fits the data. Parsers are generally considered recursive pattern matchers. In some expert systems a rule can recursively call itself until it finds a match. *See also* Recursive transition network (Barr and Feigenbaum 1981, vol 1, 256).

Recursive rule A rule that can call itself. A recursive rule is a generalization of a collection of nonrecursive rules. A single recursive rule may then replace the set of nonrecursive rules. Recursive rules are helpful in dealing with nested data. The classic example is a data base that contains parents of parents, their parents, and so on. A recursive rule can burrow deeply into the data to find the appropriate parent. Without a recursive rule the user would have to have a rule for each generation. If one wanted to add another generation, one would have to add another rule (Sterling and Shapiro 1986, 28–31; Bratko 1986, 14–19).

Recursive transition network (RTN) A transition network that examines a sentence word by word to see if the sentence is syntactically correct. That is, it parses the sentence. It examines a given word to see if the word is in its vocabulary and if it is a noun, verb, or adjective. It then checks to see if the word may fit in a noun phrase, prepositional phrase, or verb phrase. If a legal order of nouns, verbs, adjective, and phrases is found, then it makes the decision that the input is a sentence. It differs from a Transition network in that some arcs may actually be a subordinate network. In this way one arc may call another network in a recursive manner. A RTN is a lobotomized mouse—it has no memory. It could not reason why something happened, or help you out if you wanted to get it to draw conclusions. Its main purpose is to decide if a sentence is grammatical. It is less sophisticated than an augmented transition network (Amsterdam Premier 1986, 15; Winston 1979, 169–172; Barr and Feigenbaum 1981 vol 1, 264–266; Tello 1988, 410; Chabris 1989, 301; Obermerer 1987, 228–229).

Red cut A cut in PROLOG that prunes the portions of the search tree that have one or more solutions. Such a procedure is useful when reducing search time is more important than finding the best possible solution. Red cuts are often used to build default rules. The NOT predicate can be used to replace a red cut, and the NOT predicate is safer. *Contrast with* Green cut (Sterling and Shapiro 1986, 168–172).

Redefinition The ability to use the same name to carry out different procedures. This ability is the basis for polymorphism (Swaine Jun 1989, 116–117).

Reductio ad absurdum Disproving a proposition by showing that its logical conclusion is absurd (Hayes-Roth et al 1983, 74).

Reduction 1. The substitution of a term by a simpler term in theorem proving. 2. The substitution of a logical expression by a simpler logical expression (Barr and Feigenbaum 1981 vol 3, 98).

Reductionism A philosophy that holds that all psychological phenomena are reducible to neurophysiology and physics (Rumelhart and McClelland 1986 vol 1, 127–129; Entsminger 1988, 96).

Reductionist A member of the school of thought in artificial intelligence that believes the mind can be explained as the sum of its parts. *Compare with* Holist (Entsminger 1988, 96; Johnson 1986, 257, 261).

Redundancy Having backup components or overlapping information that can be used to complete a task in the event of a minor failure. Memory engrams are stored in a redundant manner in the brain. Therefore, if a part of the brain is damaged, another part of the brain can take up at least part of the slack. Neural networks, which are patterned after the brain, use redundancy in the manner similar to that used by the brain. Redundancy is becoming an important architectural principle in building expert systems. A blackboard architecture expert system employs multiple knowledge sources and the knowledge in each source can be overlapping so that if one knowledge source fails in achieving a solution because of a minor discrepancy, a second knowledge source with overlapping information but with a somewhat different approach may succeed (Fischler and Firschein 1987, 54).

Reference An optional name for an object in C++. A reference is used to delineate operations for user-defined types, and as arguments to functions (Stroustrup 1987, 56–59).

Reference counting Garbage collection in which the pointers to every cell are counted, and this number is recorded in the cell. As the number of pointers decrease for a given cell the number in the cell is decreased. When this number reaches zero the cell is then a free cell and subject to garbage collection. *Compare with* Mark and sweep (Charniak and McDermott 1985, 65; Gabriel Feb 1987, 36–37).

Referent The individual to which a given concept node refers in a conceptual graph. (Luger and Stubblefield 1989, 353).

Referential ambiguity A state in which a word in a sentence may have more than one meaning. A pronoun, for instance, may refer to more than one person. Given a system that is meant to understand human language, referential ambiguity must be eliminated in the internal representation of the surface statements being analyzed.

Referential object An object in a frame-based system that refers to a single object in the real world. Example: a particular cat named Ricky which is derived from the instance object of cats. *Contrast with* Instance object; Prototype object (Reimer 1986, 178).

Referential opacity A condition in which a program is time dependent. That is, the meaning of a function in a program can change during a program run. The meaning of the function is dependent on the computational history of the program. Procedural languages like Pascal are referentially opaque. *See also* Referential transparency (Darlington 1985, 202).

Referential transparency A condition in a computer program in which the meaning of the whole can be derived from the meaning of its parts. Mathematical equations, for example, are referentially transparent. This allows expressions with the same meaning to be substituted for one another at any time. That is, 3 + 2 can be substituted for 2 + 3 or for 5. With reference to computer programs and referential transparency, the meaning of function in a program is not dependent on the computational history of the program. The meaning of the function is fixed, and an equivalent function can be substituted for the function at any time. Declarative languages are referentially transparent. PROLOG, a declarative language, is a referentially transparent language. PROLOG does not allow the expression $X = X + 1$. While this may appear to be a limitation, it is not. It allows the computer language to conform more closely to mathematics and makes the program easier to read. Referential transparency opens the door to the very important possibility of allowing the computer to break up a program into parts so that different parts of the program can be worked on simultaneously. If the value of a variable can be changed at any time in the process, the ability for this kind of parallel processing to take place would not be present. *Contrast with* Referential opacity (Eisenbach and Sadler 1985, 188, 202; Thompson and Thompson Apr 1987, 22; Lazarev Jul 1987, 62; Zaniolo et al 1986, 53).

Refinement 1. Shifting, in frame-based systems, of attention among objects in an orderly manner—from more general objects to more specific objects, or from more specific objects to more general objects. 2. Modifying the condition portion of rules so that they can handle more fine-grained situations, in production expert systems (Walters and Nielsen 1988, 218; Brownston et al 1986, 168).

Reflectance map A representation used in vision that consists of reflection constraints (Winston 1984, 380).

Reflection The ability of an AI program to reason about its own reasoning processes.

Reflection hypothesis An extension of the knowledge-representation hypothesis which was proposed by Brian Smith. A system constructed along the guidelines of the knowledge-representation hypothesis is capable of reasoning about its own processes (Chabris 1989, 27–28).

Reflective reasoning The ability of a computer program to reason about its own reasoning process (Hewitt Premier 1986, 45).

Reformulation The process of converting a problem description into a form suitable for reasoning by an expert system. An example is converting an initial problem description into a set of rules which follow the format of a particular expert system. *See also* Knowledge acquisition (Hayes-Roth et al 1983, 47).

Refraction Part of the conflict-resolution strategy used in OPS5 production systems. Refraction does not allow a rule that has already been executed to fire a second time unless another working-memory element produces a new match for the rule (Brownston et al 1986, 62–64, 453; Rosenberg 1986, 157).

Refutation complete A property of an inference rule that holds that for a particular inference rule, given an unsatisfiable group of clauses, unsatisfiability can be established (Luger and Stubblefield 1989, 427).

Region analysis The grouping of pixels of a scene according to features with common values. Pixels of a higher intensity may be grouped together on the assumption that these pixels form a discriminable surface of the object.

Region detection A segmentation process in vision in which an area with similar intensity is recognized. *Contrast with* Edge detection.

Region method A method of image understanding that uses the division of a feature space graph into regions such that the different parts of the object being analyzed need only fall within a given range around the different axes to qualify as a particular object. *Compare with* Prototype point method; Template method (Lawrence 1985, 50).

Regression testing Using a set of standard cases to test an expert system which has been modified to ensure the expert system is able to continue to solve at least a subset of cases it has

Regular expression A formalism for depicting regular languages (Chabris 1989, 301).

Regular grammar A limited context-free grammar, which permits only a single nonterminal symbol on the right-hand side of its rewrite rules (Chabris 1989, 302).

Regularity detector A type of learning paradigm that takes place in neural nets. In this type of learning the neural net is attempting to discover patterns in the input data and gain some insight into the underlying structure of the data. It is a type of unsupervised learning. Unlike the classification builder paradigm there is no predefined set of classes into which patterns are to be classified. Other types of learning paradigms include pattern associators and auto associators. The regularity detector paradigm is sometimes referred to as regularity discovery (Ingraham et al 1988, 18; Rumelhart and McClelland 1986 vol 1, 161; Bayle 1988, 44).

Regularity discovery *See also* Regularity detector.

Regular language A type of formal language in which the grammar is defined by means of a finite-state machine (Luger and Stubblefield 1989, 389).

Relation 1. An instance of a schema in a relational data base. A table of fields and records. There may be more than one relation representing a given schema in a relational data base. The different relations for the schema are found in different files. 2. A name in PROLOG, which describes the relation among members of a set of objects. It is sometimes referred to as the operator. In the predicate likes(john, mary), the relation (or operator) is likes (Townsend 1987a, 32; Townsend 1987b, 384; IXL: The Machine Learning System 1988, 24; Parsaye and Chignell 1988, 204; Lane Nov/Dec 1987, 95).

Relational algebra The method for operating on relations in a relational data base. It is made up of a set of tables and relational operations. The primary operation in relational algebra are selection, projection, product, union, difference, and join. Relational data bases and artificial intelligence methods are being integrated to produce what is known as intelligent data bases (expert data bases) (Parsaye and Chignell 1988, 412–419; Knaus June 1989, 48).

Relational clause A clause that uses comparison operators like > and <.

Relational data base A data base that organizes data in rows and columns so that data from separate tables may be cross-referenced. The five primary operations of the relational data base are union, difference, cartesian product, projection, and selection. These operations can also be implemented in PROLOG. Both PROLOG and a relational data base emphasize the relationships in data. A relational data base is better able to handle updates and concurrent users than is PROLOG. A relational data base does not possess the ability to have rules and use recursion as does PROLOG. A relational data base may be considered a special circumstance of a logic program in which rules are consequents without conditions. Various types of marriages of PROLOG and relational data bases have been proposed to produce intelligent data bases (Kowalski, 1985, 175; Sterling and Shapiro 1986, 30–32).

Relational language A language that structures data in terms of relations. An example is brother(john, mary). This means john is a brother of mary. Side-effects are avoided in relational languages. PROLOG is the best known relational language. Relational languages are a subset of declarative languages (Eisenbach and Sadler 1985, 186; Thompson and Thompson Sep 1987, 15).

Relaxation 1. The iterative assigning of values to a set of mutually constrained objects in such a way that a consistent set of values are found and no constraints are violated. Relax-

(Walters and Nielsen 1988, 136).

previously solved. Test cases should be added as new features for the expert system are developed

ation algorithms are used in vision and neural nets. It is considered to be the primary method of computation in neural nets. 2. A means of constraint satisfaction used in neural networks. It iteratively updates the values of a network until it finds a solution that satisfies the necessary constraints (Chabris 1989, 301; Rumelhart and McClelland 1986 vol 1, 135–136; Barr and Feigenbaum 1981 vol 3, 292–300).

Relevant backtracking Backtracking to the most pertinent decision location rather than the most recent decision location. Another name for dependency-directed backtracking (Hunt 1986, 13, 217).

Reliability 1. A measure of the percentage of errors an expert system produces. 2. A measure of the degree of consistency an expert system possesses. That is, given a set of reasonably stable conditions, the degree to which the expert system will give the same answer or nearly the same answer each time. Statistical measurements are commonly used to measure reliability. Other important measures of the value of an expert system are accuracy, adequacy, breadth, validity, practicability, adaptability, credibility, and generality (Marcot Aug 1987, 44; Parsaye and Chignell 1988, 302).

Remove A command in OPS production systems that removes a working-memory element from working memory (Brownston et al 1986, 51, 55–56).

Renaming The ability to carry out the same procedure using different names, in some object-oriented languages. Renaming is used to settle conflicts in multiple-inheritance schemes. *Compare with* Redefinition (Swaine June 1989, 116).

Repeated goal detection A type of problem that happens in planning programs because the program gets into a loop. An example is in a blocks program. Assume the end goal is B on A and A on C. Assume only one block can be moved at one time. The program first places B on A. It then notices it needs to move A on top of C. It takes B off A, but rather than moving A on top of C it loops and again puts B on A. This type of looping occurs frequently in planning programs (Rettig May 1987, 19).

Repertory grid analysis A method used in eliciting data from an expert. *See also* Repertory grids (Olson and Rueter 1988, 35–40).

Repertory grids Grids used to find traits and attributes which can then be used to describe objects. Repertory grids were devised by a psychologist, George Kelly. They are used in some automated knowledge acquisition systems. The expert is asked to list a set of possible elements. The computer then selects three elements and asks for a characteristic that differentiates two of the elements from the third. Then it asks for the opposite of the characteristic. This information is then used to deduce a set of rules. An example of a triad of elements is: "father," "most disliked boss," "admired person" (Parsaye May 1988, 51; Thompson and Thompson Jan 1987, 26; Williamson 1987, 63–68; Parsaye and Chignell 1988, 351–360).

Replicate the brain approach Attempts to use computers to imitate human cognitive abilities. Both the symbolists and the connectionists are classified under this rubric.

Report facility That portion of an expert system that displays the conclusions reached. While a report facility may be very simple in some expert systems, others may possess report facilities that include sophisticated graphic displays (Floyd Mar/Apr 1988, 66).

Reporting One of the four aspects of a simulation. All good simulations must be able to report on what interactions take place after the simulation has run its course (Eliot and Holliday 1988, 55).

Representation The description of an object through the use of agreed on syntactic and semantic conventions (Winston 1984, 252).

Representational indeterminacy The argument in cognitive science that holds that the representational scheme humans use to solve problems cannot be replicated using computers (Luger and Stubblefield 1989, 580).

Representation mismatch The mismatch between the way the domain expert represents a problem and the way the expert system must represent the problem (Hayes-Roth et al 1983, 153).

Representation scheme The means by which objects and their relations may be symbolized. Examples of representation schemes in artificial intelligence are semantic nets, object attribute values, attribute values, frames, objects, and predicates (Fischler and Firschein Dec 1986, 44).

Representativeness heuristic A cognitive bias in which a person bases his probability that an object belongs to a certain class on how typical the object is for that class (Parsaye and Chignell 1988, 241).

Reproduction A genetic operator that guarantees that successful structures are reproduced (Austin 1990, 49–53).

Request driven Describing a control strategy found in blackboard expert systems. The control structure chooses a knowledge source with a high probability of correctly responding to the request of another knowledge source.

Required constraint A constraint that requires solution candidates to meet certain criteria to be accepted as a possibility. *Compare with* Forbidden constraint (Jackson 1986, 21).

Rerepresentation Another name for hidden units (Touretzky and Pomerleau 1989, 227).

RESEDA A project whose goal is to retrieve information from large data bases making use of knowledge-engineering inference techniques. As in PROLOG, a uniform representation scheme is used for the fact and rules in the data base. The type of representation used in the data base is called a plane; a plane is a type of frame (Zarri 1986, 141–160).

Resolution 1. The underlying search and inference strategy of logic systems. Resolution is used to determine the truth of an assertion in logic systems. The most common version of resolution is resolution by negation. In resolution by negation, the axioms of a theorem and the negation of the theorem must produce a contradiction if the theorem is true. It makes proofs by negating the theorem to be proved and adding it to the statements that are known to be true. The resolution rule is then used to resolve the clauses until a contradiction is found. The theorem is then proved to be true. The steps for resolution refutation are summarized as follows: (1) Ensuring the information is in clausal form. (2) Adding the negation of the goal. (3) Making inferences. (4) Finding a contradiction by producing an empty clause. The resolution principle is summarized as follows: (A OR B) AND (NOT A OR C) IMPLIES (B OR C). (B or C) is the resolvent. Resolution has the property of completeness, meaning that any well-formed formula that follows from a set of well-formed formulas can in time be derived. Resolution is also sound. Resolution minimizes the number of substitutions necessary in proving a theorem. While resolution is efficient the requirement of conversion to clause form causes loss of information. The if/then statement used with modus ponens retains information better and is easier to read. Forward and backward chaining may be considered special cases of resolution. 2. The matching of a term to the head of a PROLOG clause. Full resolution, in contrast to the more limited form of resolution found in backward-chaining PROLOG systems, spends more time generating irrelevant inferences. At the same time full resolution generates more inferences and therefore may produce a needed inference which could be missed by backward chaining. Full resolution as well as the more limited form of resolution found in PROLOG both use unification. In comparison with modus ponens, resolution is more general. Modus ponens and modus tolens may also be considered special cases of resolution. *See also* Semantic resolution; SLD-resolution; *Compare with* Hyperresolution; Natural deduction; Paramodulation.   3. The number of image lines per frame height in vision that have a contrast greater than or equal to 50 percent.   4. The degree to which an expert system can discriminate patterns (Marcot Aug 1987, 44; Amsterdam Oct 1986, 18; Hayes-Roth et al 1983, 65; Charniak and McDermott 1985, 365, 378–386; Harmon and King 1985, 52–53; Barr and Feigenbaum 1981 vol 3, 77–78, 86–87, 199–200, 254–255, 279–282; Rosenberg 1986, 160; Townsend and Feucht 1986, 143–144; Waterman 1986, 324; Luger and Stubblefield 1989, 416, 435, 475; Nilsonn 1980, 161; Luger and Stubblefield 1989, 415–434; Jackson 1986, 80–85; Charniak and McDermott 1985, 324).

Resolution by refutation   *See* Resolution.

Resolution strategy   The use of certain rules that somehow restrict resolution. Examples of such rules include subsumption checking, lock resolution, unit preference, set of support, and input resolution (Charniak and McDermott 1985, 384).

Resolvent   1. The current goal at any stage of a computation.   2. A statement derived by using resolution (Amsterdam Oct 1986, 18; Sterling and Shapiro 1986, 12, 72; Barr and Feigenbaum 1981 vol 3, 77–78).

Resource identification   An important step in the identification stage of building an expert system. In this step the knowledge engineer identifies the knowledge sources, the time, and money needed for the development of the expert system.

Response   The size of the output voltage per unit of light exposure.

Response frame   The receptor of information from a knowledge source in the artificial intelligence program HEARSAY (Smith 1989, 164).

Response uncertainty   A measure of the uncertainty of a user of an expert system in answering a question being asked by an expert system. A roughly similar term is user uncertainty. Just as a rule may be assigned a certainty value, the user may assign a certainty value to his response to a question. An expert system may then use this certainty value as an aid in computing the best possible conclusion (*Knowledge-Based Systems* 1986, 1–26).

Restriction inheritance   An inheritance in frame-based systems. What is inherited is a restriction on the data to be allowed. Example: The amount of RAM for a particular class of computer and all of its children may be restricted to the range of 128K to 640K (Walters and Nielsen 1988, 230).

Rete algorithm   The pattern-matching algorithm used in OPS production systems. The word Rete means network. An algorithm that computes and processes the conflict set in an OPS expert system. It compares the rules to the working-memory elements and places all eligible rules in a conflict set. It is an extremely efficient matcher because it takes advantage of the fact that working memory changes slowly and that the "if" portion of rules generally contain many similar patterns. It keeps track of which rules have which condition elements in common and when a given condition element is satisfied. The Rete algorithm remembers this information and it does not need to test the same condition element in subsequent rules. As the matching process continues, a given rule will be reexamined only if a working-memory element which can be associated with the rule has somehow been altered. This prevents wasted time on useless matches (Forgy and Shepard, 1987, 36–40; Moskowitz Nov 1986, 221; Brownston et al 1986, 228–239, 453; Rosenberg 1986, 160; Smith 1989, 164–165).

Rete network   A complex data structure used in OPS production systems to match productions with working memory efficiently. An index for the productions in a production system. The Rete network contains information about which rules contain the common condition elements. It is the memory state that is changed as working-memory elements are added or deleted. The network enhances rule processing. Each condition need only be processed one time rather than each time a rule with the condition is processed (Forgy and Shepard 1987, 37; Moskowitz, Nov 1986, 222; Neiman and Martin 1986, 58).

Retrospective reasoning Reasoning that explains how a conclusion was reached. The explanation processor is the aspect of an expert system that is responsible for this task (Hu 1989, 162).

Return-CF A command used in the expert system tool Intelligence Compiler. It returns the certainty factors of a set of hypotheses in order of their certainty levels. Example: Diagnosis is:
  Epilepsy, CF 80,
  lead poisoning, CF 20,
  attention deficit disorder, CF 15
(Tello 1988, 78).

Reusability The ability to reuse segments of programming code. Object-oriented approaches are touted as having reusable code (Swaine Jun 1989, 117).

Revision procedure A synonym for truth maintenance (Smith 1989, 165).

Rewrite rule A production rule used in a natural-language processing program in parsing a sentence. It can be used to generate a sentence or to check the validity of a sentence. A rewrite rule permits one expression to be rewritten into another. Example: the left-hand part of the rule is matched with the sentence and the right-hand side of the rule is used as a means of subdividing the sentence into its components, as <Sentence> IF <Noun Phrase> AND <Verb Phrase> (Barr and Feigenbaum 1981 vol 1, 239–241; Chabris 1989, 301; Smith 1989, 165).

RHS The right-hand side of a production rule. The right-hand side of a production rule executes actions and functions (Moskowitz Nov 1986, 220; Neiman and Martin 1986, 57; Brownston et al 1986, 453).

Right-hand side The action portion of a rule in a production system (Brownston et al 1986, 453; Rosenberg 1986, 161).

Right memory A data structure in OPS5 production systems which consists of lists that chronicle the group of working-memory elements that match the corresponding condition element (Brownston et al 1986, 231–234; Rosenberg 1986, 161).

Rings A type of network topology found in connection machines. It is useful only for a system that employs a small number of microprocessors. Other topologies include Clos networks, trees, banyan-type networks, grids, delta networks, hashnets, shuffle-type topologies, and crossbars (Hillis 1985, 57).

RLL (The Representation Language) A frame-based language used in the EURISKO program. The framelike structure is called units. The units are capable of producing mutations of themselves. The mutated units then can produce improved performance. Programs built with RLL are able to reflect on their own behavior and discover new rules. Both representation schemes and control knowledge are explicitly represented. Since control knowledge is overtly represented, programs using RLL are able to explain what they are doing, and are able to provide self-correction when they stray from a specified course of action. RLL provides much of the extensibility and flexibility usually associated with the LISP language. RLL's knowledge representation provides flexibility and the ability to represent very complex concepts or objects. RLL is capable of deciding if the results of a computation should be saved so that they can be used again. It is known for its flexible inheritance scheme (Hayes-Roth et al 1983, 314–321; Tello 1988, 416, 511–512; Forsyth and Naylor 1985, 214).

Roberts, L. G. A vision researcher who pioneered work in the recognition of three-dimensional objects.

Robot 1. A machine which can take action without a need for close supervision. 2. An animate machine. 3. A reprogrammable, controllable mechanical device with a series of mechanical links and an end effector which can be a gripping device, a welder, or some other instrument. **4.** A machine that can be programmed to carry out manual or locomotive tasks (Schildt 1987, 168–179; Mishkoff 1986, 5–14 to 5–19; Rosenberg 1986, 161; Waldrop 1987, 106–107).

ROBOT   A computer language that evolved into the language INTELLECT.

Robotic control language   A computer language specifically designed to control a robot. It differs from other computer languages in that it controls the movements of robots.

Robotics   The field of artificial intelligence that pursues the goal of developing intelligent robots. Robots have a number of advantages: improved quality, greater productivity, ability to work in hazardous environments, and reduced costs (Mishkoff 1986, 5–14).

Robustness   **1.** The ability of an expert system to handle new, unanticipated problem situations or errorful data.   **2.** The extent to which a perceptron can continue to function despite destroyed cells (Reece 1987, 53; Hayes-Roth et al 1983, 46; Rosenberg 1986, 162; Walters and Nielsen 1988, 126–127).

ROGET   A knowledge-acquisition program that can be used in conjunction with the EMYCIN shell. ROGET is capable of developing a conceptual model of the expert system it is to construct. TEIRESIAS is a somewhat more limited knowledge-acquisition program which is used in conjunction with EMYCIN (Tello 1988, 436–443).

Role   An action that participants in a script perform (Luger and Stubblefield 1989, 364).

R1   *See* XCON.

Rooted graph   A graph that has a node with a path to all other nodes in the graph (Luger and Stubblefield 1989, 80).

Root node   **1.** In a tree, the node which has no parent.   **2.** A type of node used by the Rete algorithm. The starting node for the matcher. A nonoperational node (Forgy and Shepard 1987, 38; Forsyth and Naylor 1985, 129, 184).

Rosenblatt, Frank   The designer of the first perceptron. Rosenblatt's perceptron came to recognize all 26 letters of the alphabet but only when presented in standard form. It consisted of 400 photocells randomly connected to 512 electronic neurons called accumulators. The signals from the accumulators would go to another layer which would fire or not depending on the signals they received. It was criticized for working at too molecular a level—as in predicting the weather by observing molecules. *See also* Perceptrons.

ROSIE   An expert system that uses if/then rules which can be divided into sets of rules. It can have more than one data base, and the user controls which data base to use. The data base can hold both facts and inferences made during a program run. ROSIE contains some procedural aspects. The syntax is Englishlike and easy to understand (Hayes-Roth et al 1983, 321–326; Brownston et al 1986, 361–362).

Roster data model   A generalization of the relational data base model. It is used as the basis for the interface between inference/analysis tools and a data base implemented with NIAL (Jenkins 1987, 35).

Rote learning   The memorization of data. A type of learning in which a computer excels. *Contrast with* Interactive language; Learning by analogy; Learning by being told; Learning by example (Kolokouris 1986, 225).

Routing problem   A type of problem in which the purpose is to find the most efficient route to a number of different places. An example is finding the most efficient route a salesman should take between a given number of cities. Such problems can be very complex and difficult to solve. The application of artificial intelligence technology shows some promise in solving such problems.

RPL   A robotics control language developed by SRI (Mishkoff 1986, 5–19).

Rule 1. A type of knowledge structure that represents a conditional relationship between expressions. 2. A control construct in conventional programs as well as expert systems. The application of rules in conventional programs differs from their use in expert systems. In a conventional program the variables in the if part of the statement are checked against a particular location in memory to see if the expression is valid. If the conditional expression is valid, the then part of the rule is executed. The rule controls what statement the program will next execute. 3. A conditional statement that infers new facts. For an artificial intelligence rule, deduction, not program control, is the more important factor. A rule in a production expert system is frequently called a production. In a rule in a production expert system the pattern matching is considerably more complex, with multiple pattern matching and possibly backtracking being employed. It allows the deduction of facts from existing facts, but it also executes actions in production rules. It allows the expert system to move from one state to another. 4. One of the three basic statements in logic programming, it represents a conditional relationship between clauses. A rule in logic programming is in clausal form. Example: $A:- B, C$, which means A is true if B and C are true. 5. An operator in AI which moves the program from one state to another. The solution of problems through the use of rules is called inference, formal reasoning, or deduction. A rule is a statement that expresses a relationship between facts such that one fact is conditional on another. A rule has a condition and a conclusion. The form of the rule may be, if A then B; or it could take the form, B if A. Rules are used in both backward- and forward-chaining expert systems. Rules are less applicable in cases that involve inheritance, exceptions, and default assumptions. *See also* Backward rule; Default rule; Forward rule; If-then rule; Production; Recursive rule (Harrison and Tribble 1986, 66; Townsend 1987a, 45–49; Hayes-Roth et al 1983, 402; Harmon and King 1985, 43; Brownston et al 1986, 5–6; Sterling and Shapiro 1986, 8–12; Jackson 1986, 218; Forsyth and Naylor 1985, 127–129; Shmueli et al 1986, 249).

Rule askable Describing the type of rule that asks the user about the veracity of a premise of a rule, once the expert system has determined it has no knowledge concerning the premise (Hu 1989, 245).

Rule base The portion of a rule-based expert system that contains the rules.

Rule-based expert system An expert system in which knowledge is stored primarily in rules and facts. It consists of an inference engine and a knowledge base. The knowledge base is subdivided into a rule base and a working memory. It is typically associated with heuristic knowledge, as opposed to model-based systems which focus on deep knowledge. Rule-based systems are either forward- or backward-chaining systems. Most rule-based expert systems are production expert systems. Some authorities do not make a distinction between rule-based expert systems and production systems. The two differ in historical origins, terminology, and in some implementation details. They have more in common than differences. In a production system a rule is called a production. The inference engine is referred to as the recognize-act cycle. The archetype production system is OPS5, which is forward chaining in nature. One rule-based expert system that does not fit well in the classic production system mold is DENDRAL. As with most expert systems, a rule-based expert system includes a rule-based editor and an explanatory interface. Logic-based expert systems may be considered rule-based expert systems. A logic-based expert system uses clauses for rules and facts, and it is associated with predicate calculus. *Contrast with* Blackboard architecture; Expert system (Hayes-Roth et al 1983, 402; Mishkoff 1986, 3–22; Brownston et al 1986, 317–322; Townsend 1987b, 232–234; Smith 1989, 168; Michaelsen et al 1985, 306–307).

Rule Cluster A set of rules that are related in the sense that they are all working toward a common goal. Each rule in a rule cluster is designed to achieve a subgoal which is important in achieving the goal of the rule cluster. A production system may consist of a number of rule clusters. One rule cluster will need to achieve its common goal before the next rule cluster can be started. A synonym is rule set (Matthews Sep 1987, 82; Brownston et al 1986, 113–116).

Rule compiler A compiler used in some expert systems to transform the rules into a state in which the rules can be processed more efficiently.

Rule editor An editor used to edit the rules in an expert system. Some rule editors are able to detect syntax errors and point out contradictory rules.

Rule filtering Filtering that screens rules from the match process in production systems. Such screening achieves faster solutions. There are three types of rule filtering: controlled, goal restricted, and context restricted (Brownston et al 1986, 454).

Rule format The manner in which a rule is written. In most expert systems forward- and backward-chaining rules are formatted in different ways. The rules can then be used with only one type of chaining. This causes difficulties in applications in which it is necessary for the same rules to chain in both directions. NEXPERT is an example of an expert system that allows its rules to be used in a forward- or backward-chaining mode.

Rule interpreter The portion of a rule-based expert system engine responsible for inference and control. It is the inference engine for a rule-based expert system. It controls which rule it will next examine. The rule interpreter is responsible for the matching and execution of rules. It first matches the condition elements of the rule with data in working memory and then executes the action part of the rule. The rule interpreter is sometimes simply referred to as the interpreter (Mishkoff 1986, 3–5; Brownston et al 1986, 448, 454; Fischler and Firschein 1987, 192; Townsend and Feucht 1986, 34; Hunt 1986, 224).

Rule memory The part of a production-type expert system that stores rules, also called production memory.

Rule model A description of a set of rules in an artificial intelligence system, which includes the similarities in the rules (Smith 1989, 168).

Rule models A technique used in TEIRESIAS to aid in maintaining consistency among rules. It does this by comparing the antecedents of all rules that draw similar conclusions. The assumption is that these rules should have similar antecedents (Luger and Stubblefield 1989, 327).

Rule network An expert system aid found in NEXPERT and some other expert systems that show the links between rules in the rule base (Harmon et al 1988, 113).

Rule of inference A rule in logic that tells how to produce new expressions from a given set of expressions logically. Modus ponens and resolution are rules of inference (Dos Reis 1988, 50).

Rule of thumb A rule of good judgment. A rule developed from experience by experts. A rough approximation rather than precise scientific measurement. It reflects shallow knowledge rather than deep knowledge (Harmon and King 1985, 5).

Rule ordering A means of control used in some expert systems. The most important rules or the rules that will do the greatest amount of pruning of the search tree may be placed first. They could also be ordered by assigning tags to each rule, which would specify the relative importance of the rules.

Rule set A group of rules that are somehow related. *See also* Rule cluster.

Rule-set overload An excessive number of rules in a rule set, a condition that causes a number of problems. The time needed for pattern matching can become excessive, it is difficult to follow the logic of such rule sets, and large rule sets are difficult to maintain. About 50 rules in a rule set is considered a reasonable number (Walters and Nielsen 1988, 205).

Rule space   The set of all rules or higher-level representations that may apply to a situation, in example-driven learning. *See also* Instance space; Two-space view of learning (Barr and Feigenbaum 1981 vol 3, 360, 365–368).

Rule support   A method that improves the performance of goal-proof processes in PROLOG by augmenting the rules in the rule base with additional support knowledge. The support knowledge consists of intermediate knowledge gained from prior queries. Such information is usually discarded, but using rule support the information can efficiently compute future queries. Rule support was derived from the techniques used in view maintenance, which are employed in relational data bases (Shmueli et al 1986, 247, 267).

Rule-value approach   *See* rule-value method; Sideways chaining (Forsyth and Naylor 1985, 22–25).

Rule-value method   An improved backward-chaining expert system, which asks questions in an optimal order so that the greatest amount of uncertainty is removed. It uses the different items of information to compute the probability of the different hypotheses under consideration, and as a result of these computations it chooses which hypothesis to pursue and which questions to ask. It is relatively slow during the problem-solving process as compared with forward and backward chaining, because of the extra time needed for the computations. Its overall speed may be quicker because of the questions it is able to avoid asking. A synonym is sideways chaining (Schildt 1987, 65–66).

Runtime efficiency   The speed with which the final product of an artificial intelligence development project can carry out its task (Freedman Sep 1987, 73; Bernat Mar 1987, 42).

Runtime system   A compiled expert system. An expert system that can be executed without the support of the expert system shell or tool (Townsend 1987b, 385).

Runtime typing   Ascertaining the type of an object during a program run. The program reserves the necessary memory space for the object as it is created, and the object's type is identified. LISP is one language with this ability; this type of flexibility is an important aid in building artificial intelligence programs (Gabriel Feb 1987, 33; Luger and Stubblefield 1989, 454).

RUP   (Reasoning Utility Package) A truth-maintenance system used in Cake and the Programmer's Apprentice (Tello 1988, 480).

S

SAIL An artificial intelligence language that excels in quick lookup of multiple indexed facts in a data base. LEAP, an association-retrieval formalism, is the process at the heart of SAIL. This computer language is block structured, typed, and uses dynamic strings, arrays, and records. Its origins are from ALGOL. It is a procedural, compiler-based language (Smith 1989, 170; Johnson 1986, 20–21; Barr and Feigenbaum 1981 vol 2, 11).

SAINT (Symbolic Automatic INTegrator) SAINT is used to solve symbolic indefinite integration problems at the college freshman level. It employs a specialized pattern matcher which is tailored to the specific knowledge domain. This approach is more efficient than a general pattern matcher (Hayes-Roth et al 1983, 9, 39; Barr and Feigenbaum 1981 vol 1, 123–127).

Salience A method of ranking rules by priority. Salience is employed in the expert system tool ART (Tello 1989, 176).

SALT An induction system that deals with synthesis problems instead of analysis problems (Parsaye May 1988, 51).

SAM *See* Script applier mechanism.

Samuels, Arthur The man known for his development of the computer program Samuel's checker player. The program looks ahead a few moves, then it counts the pieces each side has, estimates control of the center of the board, and returns a number (static evaluator) for the proposed move. It continues this process for other moves and then picks the move with the highest number. It can recognize some board configurations and it learns from its mistakes. The development of computer programs to play games was an early AI field of endeavor (Johnson 1986, 48, 50; Mishkoff 1986, 2–14; Barr and Feigenbaum 1981 vol 3, 332–333, 339–344, 457–462).

San Marco LISP Explorer An on-line interactive LISP tutorial by San Marco Assoc. Available through Gold Hill Computers, Inc., 26 Landsdowne St., Cambridge, MA 02139.

SARGON III A computerized chess program which is perhaps the most powerful such program on microcomputers. The development of chess programs was one of the initial problems attacked by artificial intelligence researchers (Tello 1988, 9).

Satisfiable Describing a calculus expression in predicate calculus, for which an interpretation and values for the variables in the expression exist (Luger and Stubblefield 1989, 59).

Satisfice A solution that may not be the best solution but which is considered to be a satisfactory solution for a set of constraints. The term was coined by Herbert Simon. *Contrast with* Optimization (Waldrop 1987, 21, 35; Hayes-Roth et al 1983, 402; Brownston et al 1986, 157, 454).

Saturn Project An automated automobile manufacturing project by General Motors (Waldrop 1987, 216–220).

Save playback A feature of some expert systems that allows the user to save a portion of a consultation with an expert system. The saved portion can be recalled and used in a subsequent consultation later. This feature helps avoid the repetitious part of a consultation (Tello Oct 1987, 242).

Savvy A natural-language front end for data bases which not only allows retrieval of data but also modification of the data in the data base. It does not attempt to ascertain if a sentence is grammatically correct. Instead it uses what is known as adaptive pattern recognition. Adaptive pattern recognition avoids analysis of the sentence. Instead, it simply chooses the command in its files that most closely resembles the query (Rubin Jul 1985, 46).

Scalability A measure of the ability to increase the size of a computer system without having to redesign it extensively. Most expert systems have a high degree of scalability as compared with conventional programs.

Scalable Describing the degree to which a neural net built on a microcomputer can be scaled up to handle larger more complex real-world problems (Obermeier and Barron 1989, 222).

Scalar A data type consisting of a single entity. Examples: numbers, characters, and logical values. Lists and arrays are not scalar data types (Hunt 1986, 228).

Scanner A device used for visual pattern recognition (Rosenberg 1986, 166).

Scene A component of a script, which represents an interval of time in the script. Assume a script for flying an airplane. Such a script needs to be divided into scenes. One scene may be a preflight checkup. Other scenes may be starting the plane, taking off, and landing (Mishkoff 1986, 4–8; Luger and Stubblefield 1989, 364).

Scene analysis The processing of three-dimensional scenes (Barr and Feigenbaum 1981 vol 3, 127–138; Brice and Fennema 1990, 205–226).

Scene analysis/understanding Image analysis/understanding (Chabris 1989, 301).

Scene characteristic Intrinsic characteristics.

Scene domain The physical three-dimensional aspects of a scene. *Contrast with* Image domain (Barr and Feigenbaum 1981 vol 3, 131–135, 155).

Schank, Roger A thinker best known for his work in language processing. He developed MARGIE, SAM, PAM, and FRUMP, all of which are based on the concept of conceptual dependency (Johnson 1986, 170–176).

Scheduler One of the three basic components of a blackboard architecture. The scheduler is responsible for deciding which knowledge source is to be active at any given time. It is the primary control structure. *See also* Opportunistic scheduler (Parsaye and Chignell 1988, 145–147; Hayes-Roth et al 1983, 18, 402).

Scheduling blackboard A component of the blackboard in HEARSAY III. The scheduling blackboard is where performance reasoning takes place. *See also* Domain blackboard.

Scheduling problem An important class of problems to which artificial intelligence programs have been applied. The scheduling problem involves using scarce resources in an optimal way over a period of time. Finding scheduling solutions is important in manufacturing (Charniak and McDermott 1985, 255).

Schema 1. A term used in psychology literature which refers to memory patterns that humans use to interpret current experiences. The psychologist Jean Piaget referred to schemata as a reflection in the mind of a real situation. 2. A symbolic representation of a concept which has a means of accounting for the properties of the concept. 3. Knowledge structures that hold information about objects, words, concepts, and other complex structures. 4. A set of objects or classes of objects. 5. A description of the organization of data. 6. A frame in the languages CRL and SRL. 7. A synonym for framelike structures. 8. A sizable set of facts with accompanying variables, in the predicate calculus. Under this definition a script can be considered a special case of a schema. 9. A template used for creating a table of fields and records, in the world of relational data bases. The plural of schema is schemata (Schuler 1987, 99; Charniak and McDermott 1985, 405, 411; Walters and Nielsen 1988, 210; Brownston et al 1986, 454, Rosenberg 1986, 166; Parsaye and Chignell 1988, 49; Fox et al 1986, 161; Jackson 1986, 167; Hayes-Roth et al 1983, 230, 402; Rumelhart and McClelland 1986 vol 1, 199–213; Schildt Dec 1987, 242; Luger and Stubblefield 1989, 330).

Schema instantiation *See* Model-driven schema instantiation (Barr and Feigenbaum 1981 vol 3, 416–419).

schema-schema A high-level structure used in TEIRESIAS the function of which is to construct new schema (Luger and Stubblefield 1989, 330).

Scheme A version of LISP which differs significantly from the common LISP standard. This very powerful version of LISP has some unique features: In Scheme all objects are first-class objects. That is, any object may be returned as a result of a function call, and any object may be used as an argument to a function. Scheme uses continuation, a process that can temporarily put one environment on hold and work with another environment. Scheme uses lexical scoping. Finally, Scheme has an object-oriented extension called SCOOPS (Tello 1988, 358–364; Ward et al 1987, 74–76).

SCHOLAR An intelligent computer-aided instruction system that provides instruction in South American Geography. It uses a semantic network and a mixed-initiative natural-language interface. That is, it answers questions of the student, but it can also generate questions of its own. It is capable of generating good tutorial questions based on the responses of the user (Mishkoff 1986, 6–4; Barr and Feigenbaum 1981 vol 1, 186).

SCOOPS The object-oriented portion of the LISP language Scheme. The type of polymorphism it supports differs from Smalltalk. It implements polymorphism through name-function overloading. SCOOPS has multiple inheritance, a feature missing in Smalltalk and C++ (McGregor 1987, 49–56).

Scope The part of the program in which a given variable may be accessed. In PROLOG, a variable's scope extends only to the rule. Such limited scope is helpful because it can greatly cut down on programming error. In contrast to PROLOG's localized scoping of variables, other languages allow global variables. A global variable's value can be accessed from any point in a program. Scope frequently refers to how an implementation deals with free variables. *See also* Dynamic scoping; Lexical scoping (Thompson and Thompson 1986, 27; Sterling and Shapiro 1986, 7; Rosenberg 1986, 166; Graham Apr 1989, 27).

Scout algorithm A search algorithm for a two-game search tree which is able to decline poor moves efficiently based on an initial cursory evaluation. More promising nodes are, of course, evaluated in greater depth (Forsyth and Naylor 1985, 189–194).

Script A data structure that represents a stereotyped sequence of expected events. A description of how a sequence of events is expected to unfold. Scripts use a framelike structure. A restaurant script may consist of a series of slots that describe the procedure of going to a restaurant. Each slot represents a scene in the script. One scene may be entering the restaurant. Another may be ordering from the menu. If needed, facets monitor the changing situation and they decide what is relevant and what needs to be changed. These attached procedures allow frames and scripts to become active dynamic objects. One of the primary advantages of scripts is that they are able to continue to work in the face of incomplete information. That is, in the restaurant script the program expects to receive a menu. If a menu is not received, the program will know to ask the waiter for a menu. Scripts are frequently used as a means of understanding written stories. Scripts can be matched with sentences and once a match takes place the program then assigns meanings to the words that are appropriate for that particular script. In scripts, slots are provided for props, roles, times, location, and expected event sequences. See Charniak and McDermott 1985, 393–395, 405, for a description of how scripts can be implemented using predicate calculus. A script is similar to a frame in that it represents a set of expectations. It differs from a frame in that it represents a sequence of events. Scripts can be represented with rules (Waldrop 1987, 52–57; Thompson and Thompson Oct 1987, 19–27; Mishkoff 1986, 4–8; Barr and Feigenbaum 1981 vol 1, 216–222, 307–309; Barr and Feigenbaum 1981 vol 3, 69–70; Parsaye and Chignell 1988, 138–140; Tello 1988, 416–417; Chabris 1989, 58–61; Dyer et al 1990, 980; Schank and Abelson 1977).

Script-applier mechanism An artificial intelligence program whose aim is to understand stories. The program is frequently referred to as SAM and is based on Schank's conceptual dependency theory. It takes a story as input, and attempts to match the story with a relevant script and fills in details of the story which may not be in the input. Example: If the input text is about dining out a restaurant script may be triggered. If the input text does not mention that a menu must first be read and ordered from before eating, then the program will supply these details (Johnson 1986, 174–175).

Scruffy An AI worker who starts with a problem, and using intuition and experiment, works on finding the best way to solve the problem. *Compare with* Neats (Luger and Stubblefield 1989, vii).

SDI (Strategic Defense Initiative) A space-based defense system which is a large potential user of artificial intelligence technology. *See also* Brilliant pebbles (Waldrop 1987, 4).

Search A problem-solving procedure. The investigation of different potential solutions in the problem-solving or planning process. The procedures of exploring a search space in an attempt to solve a problem. Most search uses some form of inference. Search is used for very complex problems in which no algorithmic solution is known. Operators are used to transform the initial state into subsequent states until a suitable goal state is found. Search does not guarantee a solution. Two broad categories of search are blind search and heuristic search. Some well-known heuristic search algorithms include best-first search and A*. Range constriction is a type of search associated with machine vision. Minimax and alpha-beta are search techniques found in game search. Search techniques are frequently applied to planning and scheduling problems. *See also* Problem-reduction representation; State-space search. *Contrast with* Control (Harrison and Tribble 1986, 66; Hayes-Roth et al 1983, 66–72, 82; Mishkoff 1986, G-4; Winston 1979, 87–126; Bratko 1986, 278–283; Chabris 1989, 302; Smith 1989, 173; Charniak and McDermott 1985, 256–259; Pearl 1984).

Search space A network made up of nodes which represent problem states or subproblem states, and links which represent the means of moving from one node to another. The sum total of states that could be explored during a search. Whenever possible it is best to organize a search space in a hierarchical manner. A hierarchical search space facilitates pruning. The search space is sometimes called a search tree or a problem space. Some authorities make a distinction between a search space and a search tree. Two types of search space are state search space and an AND/OR tree. *See also* Plausible-move generator; Search tree; State-evaluation function (Mishkoff 1986, G-4; Townsend 1987a, 137–139; Schildt 1987, 15; Hayes-Roth et al 1983, 66; Charniak and McDermott 1985, 259–270; Harmon and King 1985, 56–57, Brownston et al 1986, 26–27; Townsend 1987b, 385; Barr and Feigenbaum 1981 vol 1, 26–28, 153).

Search tree 1. The tree or graph that consists of the nodes which are actually explored during search. *Contrast with* Search space, which represents all states which could be explored during a search. 2. A Christmas-tree-shaped graphic representation of a state-space search. The beginning state is the root node. The children of a particular node can be reached by the use of a single operator. The goal nodes are the leaves of the search tree (Chabris 1989, 302; Sterling and Shapiro 1986, 86–88; Barr and Feigenbaum 1981 vol 1, 26).

Secondary search The search that is conducted by some programs after a move has been decided on in a game search, to ensure that the chosen move is indeed the best one (Smith 1989, 174).

Second-level induction A type of induction that performs a limited degree of generalization. Example: In an expert system using barometric pressure if examples used the values of 25 and 32 the induction system would generalize between the numbers 25 and 32. *See also* First-level induction; Fourth-level induction; Third-level induction.

Second-order logic 1. An extension of first-order logic in which quantification over predicates is allowed. *Contrast with* First-order logic, which only allows quantification of objects. 2. The incorporation of features in PROLOG that are not considered to be a part of first-order logic. The use of set predicates and expressions which treat functions and relations as first-class data objects (Sterling and Shapiro 1986, 280–281; Fischler and Firschein 1987, 96).

Second-order predicate calculus *See* Second-order logic.

SEE The first vision computer program to use heuristics. It used vertices and junctions to discriminate among three-dimensional objects. It was able to discriminate the different objects in a scene even if the objects were not completely visible. It analyzed scenes without the aid of prestored models of objects.

Segmentation A synonym for intermediate processing (Barr and Feigenbaum 1981 vol 3, 238–242).

Segment variable A variable that can bind with a subset of a sequence of items in a data element. The order of items is not relevant. Example: assume the following function which uses the segment variable X: process (all__cars made__ in__the__USA, X). It finds the following entity: "GM, Ford, Chrysler, Toyota." X becomes bound to "GM, Chrysler, and Ford." The function finds all American-made cars and places them on a list, which is then bound to X (Barr and Feigenbaum 1981 vol 2, 59, 61; Brownston et al 1986, 295–297; Rubin May 1986, 17).

Selection   A method for operating on relations in the relational algebra. Selection chooses rows in a relational table which satisfy the criteria of a query (Parsaye and Chignell 1988, 413).

Selective backtracking   A type of backtracking that decides which variable bindings are at fault for the failure (Charniak and McDermott 1985, 361).

Selective inheritance   The ability of object-oriented systems to prevent certain characteristics from being inherited. Example: Most birds can fly, but a penguin cannot fly; so it is necessary to have a means of excluding this characteristic for penguins (Swaine Jun 1989, 117).

Selector relation   A relation in PROLOG which can be used to access components of objects (Bratko 1986, 97–99).

Self   A special variable in the Smalltalk language which represents the object that receives a message. The self variable is usually found residing in a method of an object. The message-lookup procedure is the same as the lookup procedure used if the message is sent externally, stating the name of the object. That is, the lookup procedure begins in the object's class. It is a type of pseudovariable (*Smalltalk/V Tutorial and Programming Handbook* 1986, 54; Pascoe 1986, 144).

Self-knowledge   An expert system's knowledge about its own operation and structure. Self-knowledge provides the capability for an expert system to explain its reasoning, as well as the potential to produce an expert system which is self-modifying (Hayes-Roth et al 1983, 28, 48).

Self-modification   The ability of some expert systems to alter the knowledge in their knowledge base in the light of new information. Self-modification usually refers to adding, deleting, or modifying rules (Hayes-Roth et al 1983, 28).

Self-organization   The ability of certain neural networks to learn without having to be told the right answer (Caudill Aug 1988, 61).

Self-organizing system   An artificial intelligence program that is able to modify itself by adapting to its environment without help from an outsider. It is able to profit from experience. Perceptrons are examples of self-organizing systems (Josin 1987, 184, 188).

Self-referencing rule   A rule found in PC PLUS that allows a default value to be given to a variable if the user does not specify a value for the variable, and the program is not able to derive the value, or the value specified is incorrect. Example: Perhaps the user does not know the volume of the stock market in the previous week. This value may be useful but not crucial in determining the answer to the question being asked, so it would be desirable to assign a default average value rather than have to abort the entire consultation process. Any expert system that allows variables to be instantiated to UNKNOWN can implement self-referencing rules. An expert system searches its fact base to find a value for the variable X but fails. The user is asked the value for X and he or she does not know. The variable is then assigned the value UNKNOWN. A portion of the rule can then test for UNKNOWN and if UNKNOWN is found to be present, a default value can be substituted (Tello 1988, 287; Tello Oct 1987, 243).

Self-supervised learning   Learning that takes place in neural nets. In this type of learning the neural net monitors its performance and corrects errors in its performance. *Contrast with* Supervised learning; Unsupervised learning (Obermeier and Barron 1989, 218).

Semantic analysis   **1.** The interpretation of the meaning of a sentence. Conceptual dependency is the best known theory of semantic analysis. Along with syntactic analysis and pragmatic analysis, semantic analysis is an important factor in natural-language processing.   **2.** The metamorphosis of an input sentence into a meaningful internal representation (Rubin Jul 1985, 44; Mishkoff 1986, 4–11; Smith 1989, 175).

Semantic consistency checking   The ability of some expert systems to detect inconsistencies between a rule currently being entered and previously existing rules (Hayes-Roth et al 1983, 152).

Semantic convergence   The ability of an AI system to define terms in relation to terms it has defined already.

Semantic decomposition   Building structures for concepts so that concepts with comparable meanings have similar structures (Barr and Feigenbaum 1981 vol 3, 57–61, 65).

Semantic gap   The distance that exists between the actual state of the world and the ability of a data processing tool to model the real world. An object-oriented language has a smaller semantic gap than a conventional language (Peterson 1987, 27).

Semantic grammar   A grammar that specifies task requirements. In a semantic grammar the grammar classes are not the usual <NOUN>, <ADJECTIVE>, and so on. Instead, the grammar classes are semantic categories. Assume the semantic grammar is for an expert system natural-language processor. The categories may include <CHAINING PROCEDURE>, <GOAL>, <KNOWLEDGE REPRESENTATION>. These categories would make up the rewrite rules. The categories are obviously much more restricted than <NOUN>, <VERB>, and so on, and this greatly reduces the search space. Semantic grammar is a relatively simple way of providing a natural-language interface for a variety of applications. Its basic assumption is that for most applications only a small number of words will be used for input. LIFER and SOPHIE use semantic grammars. Synonyms include performance grammar and procedural grammar (Winston Apr 1985, 218; Barr and Feigenbaum 1981 vol 1, 261, 317–320, 335; Tello 1988, 411; Obermeier 1987, 227; Chabris 1989, 302).

Semantic-grammar parsing   Analyzing a sentence according to units of meaning rather than syntactic structure (Mishkoff 1986, 4–11).

Semantic memory   Memory for concepts and their relationships with one another. Semantic memory recalls concepts based on their meaning. Semantic networks were developed to deal with semantic memory. *See also* Intersection search; Spreading activation (Chabris 1989, 48).

Semantic network   A knowledge representation based on graphs which represents relationships among objects or concepts. Semantic networks were originally created to represent semantic meaning. The meanings of the concepts represented by a semantic network are a function of their relationships with one another. Semantic networks consist of nodes and labeled directed arcs. Objects or states are represented as nodes and relationships are represented as the links of arcs between the nodes. For example, each node could be a type of clothing and the arcs between the types of clothing would describe if the next piece of clothing is a particular type of clothing (is-a), or is a part of a type of clothing (has-a). That is, a sports coat is-a coat. A suit has-a coat. What arcs can stand for is relatively unrestricted. The arcs could stand for is-a, has-a, contains, or other relations. A network can be constructed which is not a semantic network. A network with nodes labeled as X23 is not a semantic network because the labels are not meaningful. Semantic networks are capable of inheritance. Frames and attribute-value objects are restricted types of semantic networks. The types of arcs allowed with these two representation systems are limited. Semantic networks place emphasis on relationships while frames place emphasis on objects. Semantic networks are useful for very difficult types of artificial intelligence problems such as complicated taxonomies, language processing, scheduling, and planning problems. Although semantic nets are very flexible they are relatively inefficient. When large knowledge bases are involved, inference engines can have great difficulty working with semantic networks. Perhaps a more appropriate synonym for semantic network is associative network. In predicate calculus semantic networks are implemented by having nodes represented as terms and arcs as predicates. In LISP, semantic networks are implemented as structured lists. Semantic networks may be considered as derived from logic. That is, the facts in the semantic network may be considered axioms, and the deductions that take place in a semantic network can be considered theorems. Semantic networks were developed by Ross Quillian (Waldrop 1987, 53–54, Minsky, Apr 1985, 138; Miller July/Aug 1988, 27; Fischler and Firschein Dec 1986, 44; Townsend 1987a, 121–122; Charniak and McDermott 1985, 22–23, 400–405; Winston 1979, 181–184; Harmon and King 1985, 35–38, 46–48; Barr and Feigenbaum 1981 vol 1, 180–189; Parsaye and Chignell 1988, 137–138; Chabris 1989, 40–51, 65; Chabris 1989, 302; Luger and Stubblefield 1989, 33; Tello 1988, 409; Winston 1984, 253; Sowa 1990, 1011–1024; Findler 1979).

Semantic primitive 1. Any term in natural-language processing that is used but is not defined within the system. 2. An indivisible element of meaning. 3. One of a small set of meaning categories. Each semantic primitive is capable of conveying the meaning of a number of other language structures. In conceptual dependency theory there is a built-in vocabulary of semantic primitives: propel, move, ingest, ptrans, mtrans, mbuild. Each of these semantic primitives can encompass many other words. Move, for example, can include pick up, carry, load, and so on (Johnson 1986, 111–112; Barr and Feigenbaum 1981 vol 1, 207–215; Chabris 1989, 302; Tello 1988, 412–414).

Semantic resolution A type of resolution that restricts the number of resolvents generated without preventing necessary resolvents from being generated. It accomplishes this through two restrictive procedures—interpretation and ordering. The interpretation procedure evaluates the truth value of the clauses. Resolution is restricted so that no attempt is made to resolve two true clauses. The ordering procedure orders the variables in a set of clauses by priority. This allows resolution between a true and false clause only if the variable to be eliminated has the highest priority for all variables in the false clause. Semantic resolution generates more efficient proofs than does standard resolution (Dos Reis 1988, 54–55).

Semantics 1. The meaning of a logic program or an expression. 2. Paying attention to the meaning of sentences, in natural-language processing. To derive the meaning of a sentence, phrase, or word properly, the context must frequently be taken into account. *Contrast with* Syntactic (Freedman 1987, 71; Johnson 1986, 99; Hayes-Roth et al 1983, 402; Chabris 1989, 302; Tello 1988, 405).

Sembase An experimental data base management system based on an object-oriented model, which is being developed at the University of Colorado (King 1986, 443–467).

Semiexact inference A combination of inexact reasoning and standard inferential reasoning. Example: using inexact reasoning to produce five candidate diagnoses. Then, a predicate is used which selects the candidate with the highest confidence level, and this candidate is further examined using standard inference (exact-inference). If the candidate passes the scrutiny of standard inference, it is then accepted as the diagnosis. If it is rejected, then the candidate with the next highest confidence level is tested (Parsaye and Chignell 1988, 284–285; Tello Feb 1988, 76).

Sensitivity 1. A measure of the responsiveness of an expert system to a changing pattern of incoming data. The conflict resolution strategy is an important factor in sensitivity. Sensitivity is especially important with real-time expert systems. *Contrast with* Stability. 2. The minimum illumination necessary to produce a usable signal (Brownston et al 1986, 454; Rosenberg 1986, 167).

Sensor-controlled robot A robot that is intelligent in the sense it is able to use information from an external sensing device to adjust to its environment and carry out its assigned task. It is able to make plans, carry the plans out, and take corrective actions if necessary. A synonym for intelligent robot (Mishkoff 1986, 5–19; Rosenberg 1986, 167).

Sentential connective   A predicate used to connect propositions in logic. Examples: AND, OR, NOT, IMPLIES, and EQUIVALENT (Smith 1989, 176).

Sequence   A list or a one-dimensional array in LISP. Some of the functions used with sequences are length, reverse, substitute, sort, merge, and delete (Steele 1984, 245).

Sequence-dependence problem   The implicit coding of procedural information into a rule-based system which is intended to be nonprocedural. When this is done the rules in the program are less independent. That is, a given rule may become dependent on the sequential firing of other rules. This may work for the set of problems the knowledge engineer is using at the outset, but when a new case is introduced the program may mysteriously fail because the solving of the new case may involve a rule sequence that violates the implicitly coded sequence (Walters and Nielsen 1988, 128–129, 135).

Sequence robot   A robot whose movement consists of a fixed sequence of positional changes (Rosenberg 1986, 168).

Sequential closure   The consequence that a computer program cannot run when any single part of the program cannot function (Tello 1989, 21).

Sequential mode   The mode in neural networks in which the cells change in a sequential manner. *Contrast with* Parallel iterations (Fogelman, Soulie, and Mejia 1988, 58).

Sequential processing   The type of processing used in most computers in which actions are performed one at a time, in sequence. *Contrast with* Parallel processing (Mishkoff 1986, G–4).

Serendipity   A principle that is advocated for open systems, which holds that it is not crucial to the problem-solving task whether a system obtains important problem-solving knowledge before it is needed in a problem or after work has already started on the problem (Hewitt Apr 1985, 239).

Serial processing   The process whereby the standard computer carries out only one task at a time. *Contrast with* Parallel processing (Johnson 1986, 71).

Servomechanism   A device the function of which is to correct a robot's performance through the use of feedback information (Rosenberg 1986, 169).

Servo robot   A programmable robot that possesses smooth movement. Some servo robots are considered intelligent if they can change their motion in response to input from a sensing device. Servo robots have a servomechanism that can be programmed (Mishkoff 1986, 5–18; Rosenberg 1986, 169).

Set   1. A group of points, objects, or numbers which satisfy given criteria in mathematics. There can be no duplicates in the set.   2. A class in object-oriented programming which will store objects of any kind. Unlike bags there can be no copies of a particular object in a set.   3. A type of active data structure used in Connection machines. The members of a set are distinguished by either bit representation, tag representation, or pointer representation. In a Connection machine all members of the set can be marked simultaneously. Other types of active data structures are trees, butterflies, arrays, strings, and graphs (Hillis 1985, 92; Townsend 1987b, 70; Jay and Knaus Mar 1989, 20).

Set-of-support strategy   A strategy used in resolution-theorem proving. Given a group of input clauses A, a subset of A called B can be specified. The B subset is the set of support. The strategy underlying the set of support is that one of the resolvents in each resolution have an ancestor which can be found in the set of support. If A is unsatisfiable and $A - B$ is satisfiable, then it can be shown that the set-of-support strategy is refutation complete. This strategy works well for large clause spaces (Luger and Stubblefield 1989, 428).

S-expression   Symbolic expression. In LISP it includes symbols, numbers, and lists which are constructed from symbols and numbers (Charniak and McDermott 1985, 46).

Shadowing A technique in multiple inheritance in which the characteristics supplied by the highest precedence class or by the most specific class are used in the child object (Amir 1989, 30).

Shafer-Dempster theory of evidence A procedure for dealing with uncertainty. It uses belief functions as opposed to the conditional probabilities of the Bayes' formula. It assigns a degree of belief to propositions. If a measure of belief is given to a proposition, the remainder of the measure of belief does not need to be assigned to the negation of that belief. Instead, a portion of the remainder of the belief may be assigned to ignorance. This is in contrast to Bayesian probability, which insists that the probability of an event and its negation must sum to one. The proponents of the Shafer-Dempster theory argue that it works effectively with noisy, inconsistent, and incomplete data. Example: Assume two observers of an unidentified object. Observer 1 states the object was a helicopter (.3), plane (.4), and (.3) was assigned to ignorance. The second observer felt the object was a balloon (.2), a plane (.5), and the remainder (.3) was assigned to ignorance. These measures of belief can be combined to compute the value which is most likely. It uses belief functions which have weaker assumptions than those that are needed in probability theory. It also produces weaker conclusions, but proponents of Shafer-Dempster would argue that the stronger conclusions of probability theory are not justified (Borden 1987, 50–54; Fischler and Firschein 1987, 100–103; Luger and Stubblefield 1989, 314–315).

Shallow backtracking A type of backtracking that takes place when the unification of a clause and a goal fails and another clause is then attempted. *Contrast with* Deep backtracking (Sterling and Shapiro 1986, 97).

Shallow knowledge The use of external relationships to arrive at conclusions. A representation of knowledge which consists of signs, correlations, symptoms, and solutions without regard to whether or not causality is involved. The use of knowledge other than that based on the theory of the process being studied. There is no model of the underlying process present. Such correlational information is likely to be less reliable than deep knowledge. With shallow knowledge there is a lack of understanding as to why a rule is valid. As a result, shallow knowledge is limited in being able to know when a rule should not apply. Shallow knowledge is generally represented in the form of if/then statements. Most expert systems are based on shallow knowledge. A synonym is surface knowledge. *Contrast with* Deep knowledge (Townsend 1987a, 151–152; Harmon and King 1985, 33, 236, 245; Michaelsen et al 1985, 304–309, Townsend 1987b, 385; Fischler and Firschein 1987, 201).

Shannon A logarithmic measure of information used in information theory (Rosenberg 1986, 169).

Shannon, Claude The man who devised a mathematical definition for information. Shannon used boolean logic to build electronic AND/OR gates which could represent thinking. His ideas were important in the development of the binary system of information storage on which the modern computer is based. His ideas gave impetus to the field of information science (Johnson 1986, 39–41, 61–62; Mishkoff 1986, 2–7).

Shape from methods A set of methods for recovering shape from shading, contours, and textures in monocular images (Barr and Feigenbaum 1981 vol 3, 260–267).

Shape-from-shading problem The problem of finding the shape of a scene by using shading cues (Winston 1984, 335).

Shareable image A single executable piece of code that can be used by multiple programs. Example: An expert system may be considered a shareable image when it can be called by accounting programs, data bases, CAD/CAM programs, and so on.

Shared variable A variable used more than once in a PROLOG query or rule which therefore shares a common value. It is a means of restricting the range of a variable. Suppose the following query is made: likes(john, X) and likes(mike, X). X is the shared variable. This means X must represent the same entity for both likes(john, X) and likes(mike, X). The goal can be true only if an X can be found which both john and mike like (Sterling and Shapiro 1986, 7–8).

Sharing a binding A condition in which one variable is bound to another. This process is seen frequently in PROLOG and some expert systems. A variable X may be equal to bear. In the search through the data base a variable Y is found which is uninstantiated. The variable Y is then instantiated to the value of X. X and Y are then said to share a binding (Thompson and Thompson 1986, 27).

Sharpening The process of removing blurs in images. Spatial differentiation, and high-emphasis frequency filtering are two processes that carry out this task (Barr and Feigenbaum 1981 vol 3, 209–213).

Shell 1. A high-level expert system framework. Shells have a built-in inferencing system and data structure which are suitable for expert system development. A shell is an expert system without the domain knowledge. Shells also possess a module which allows the shell to interact with the user. The shell may ask the user for information. The user may ask the shell why it is asking a question or how the shell reached a particular conclusion. The advantage of a shell is that it cuts down on the development time in building an expert system. The disadvantage is that it may not be flexible enough to handle all of the problems the knowledge engineer will encounter. Some people reserve the term tool in referring to the more sophisticated expert system shells. *Contrast with* Expert system. 2. A program that accepts commands and then executes them. Interpreters and disk operating systems are shells under this more general definition (Citrenbaum et al 1987, 30; Townsend 1987a, 20–21; Townsend 1987b, 385; Sterling and Shapiro 1986, 185–187; Bratko 1986, 314–316).

SHRDLU An artificial intelligence program developed by Terry Winograd which solves problems in a restricted blocks world. It builds an internal model of the blocks world, and is able to scrutinize and modify its data structures. This introspective ability gives it a degree of understanding. It was the first program to integrate language ability with a capacity for reasoning about the world. It can respond to commands, answer questions about why it carried out an action, ask questions when it is not sure about what to do, and reason. Assume SHRDLU is faced with a situation in which it needs to place an object on top of a block. Currently a pyramid is on the block. SHRDLU can reason that it needs to remove the pyramid before placing the object on the block. It uses hetarchy in its program design. SHRDLU is procedurally oriented rather than declarative (Johnson 1986, 115–118; Barr and Feigenbaum 1981 vol 1, 295–299; Waldrop 1987, 68–71; Winston 1979, 158–167, 173–177; Sterling and Shapiro 1986, 221–224; Chabris 1989, 13).

Shrinkage by generalization The replacement of a set of rules by a smaller number of more powerful, more general rules.

Shuffle-type topology A network topology found in Connection machines which is used in fast Fourier transforms. Other topologies include Clos networks, rings, trees, banyan-type networks, grids, delta networks, hashnets, and crossbars (Hillis 1985, 58–59).

Sibling One of a number of nodes in a tree structure which have the same parent.

Side effect A program statement that modifies what was previously available rather than simply adding to what is already available. When a permanent change of a value takes place in a program run this is termed a side effect. An example of an expression that produces a side-effect is $X := X + 1$. Languages that have side effects include FORTRAN. Functional languages such as LISP are relatively side-effect free and this helps improve program maintenance and helps prevent mysterious changes in the value of variables in a program run. Side effects also prevent the use of parallel processing. Side effects can take place in rule-based expert systems. Some expert systems allow counting variables of the form $X := X + 1$. If the developer is not careful rules containing such statements can be unintentionally executed and cause a false count. Assert and retract are commands in PROLOG that cause side effects. *See also* Side-effect model (Thompson and Thompson Sep 1987, 15; Eisenbach and Sadler 1985, 186; Walters and Nielsen 1988, 329–331; Brownston et al 1986, 211).

Side-effect model A model in which the end result of a computation is to change the contents of a memory cell. FORTRAN follows the side-effect model. *Contrast with* Value model (Allen Jul 1985, 29).

Sideways chaining *See* Rule-value approach; Rule-value method (Forsyth and Naylor 1985, 22).

Sigmoid A curve shaped like the letter S (Obermeier and Barron 1989, 219).

Signal processing The transformation of an input image into a second image, which has important properties that will help in better understanding the scene (Barr and Feigenbaum 1981 vol 3, 127).

Signal-processing task A type of task given expert systems in which the system is given initial information and the expert system reasons with the data looking for patterns. It then provides conclusions and recommendations. In a signal-processing task, there is a minimum of ongoing dialogue with the user and a forward-chaining system is usually more appropriate. *Contrast with* Dialogue task (Harmon et al 1988, 187).

SIMD machine *See* Single instruction multiple data (Hillis 1985, 24–25).

Similarity The measure of the proportion of bits that match and the total number of bits that match in a pattern-matching procedure. This type of pattern matching takes place in a pattern classifier, like the Holland classifier (Frey 1986, 163).

Similarity-based learning Learning that, as opposed to explanation-based learning, must have a set of learning examples. Similarity-based learning uses the similarities and differences in these examples to form generalized concepts. Concept learning and version-space search are both examples of similarity-based learning (Luger and Stubblefield 1989, 573).

Similarity network A type of knowledge representation that consists of a group of objects connected by links. The links are given a numerical score according to the degree of similarity among the objects. This type of knowledge representation allows for powerful retrieval of information. A similarity network does not replace other types of knowledge representation. Instead, similarity networks are used as an overlay for other types of knowledge representation. Example: The objects in a similarity network can be frames. The similarity score for the object can be kept on slots of the frame. Similarity networks provide associative memory capacity. One may ask for all judicial cases which could help in a specific type of medical lawsuit. Perhaps there are certain lawsuits that are not medical lawsuits, but may, in some other way, have a bearing on this type of suit. A similarity network could pull such cases. A hill-climbing search mechanism is usually used with similarity networks (Bailey Thompson and Feinstein Jul/Aug 1988, 29–32; Winston 1979, 96–98).

Simon, H., and Newell, A. Scientists who demonstrated that the computer could be used to study the mind. Their emphasis was on symbol manipulation and search. These pioneers initiated symbolic processing with computers. Their two best known programs were Logic Theorist and General Problem Solver. Simon developed the idea of satisfice. Simon and Newell found that humans think in terms of subgoals rather than overall goals. They believe scientific discovery is a relatively simple problem-solving process in the sense that many people are capable of doing it (Johnson 1986, 47–48, 198–201; Waldrop 1987, 20–30).

SIMULA A computer language used to simulate operations that are made up of discrete events. SIMULA can be applied to such problems as the operation of a retail business, plane traffic, automobile traffic, and communication networks. It is an object-oriented language and a forerunner of Smalltalk. It introduced the concept of classes. Unlike Smalltalk, access to the internals of objects is possible in SIMULA (Walters and Nielsen 1988, 295; Rosenberg 1986, 171; McGregor Jul 1987, 56).

Simulated annealing A minimization algorithm used in neural networks, which randomly tries different weights until the errors in the system are minimized. While random search is an inefficient process simulated annealing is able to detect a global minimum. That is, it can avoid local minima so as to be able to find global minima. A good way to think of simulated annealing is with an analogy: Think of a ball that has to contend with two minima X and Y. The Y minimum is the true minimum. The X minimum is a local minimum. The force of gravity works to move the ball to one of the minima. Either minimum has a reasonable probability of being chosen by the ball. Up to this point the analogy describes gradient descent. Now, assume the entire structure is shaken. The shaking process is more likely to encourage the ball to move to the Y minimum than it is to the local X minimum, because the force of gravity will more likely allow a move to a lower level rather than allow a move to a higher level. This is how the mathematical process of simulated annealing works. Simulated annealing is used in Boltzmann machines. It is a type of supervised learning. *See also* Gradient descent (Rumelhart and McClelland 1986 vol 1, 287–289; Ingraham et al 1988, 19–20; Hinton 1985, 270; Swaine Oct 1989, 113; Colvin 1989, 62).

Simulation The attempt to emulate a process or phenomenon using a computer. A simulation consists of four parts: objects, time, inspection, and reporting. A professional who builds a simulation is not only interested in predicting but also in the assumptions and process by which predictions are derived. Spreadsheets are frequently used to build numeric economic simulations. An example of a symbolic simulation is building a model of an airport in which the arriving and departing planes are the primary objects. The program General Problem Solver is a simulation of human problem solving. Simulations usually allow what-if scenarios. Object-oriented programs are particularly well suited for simulations. An expert system is more likely to make inferences about the current state of the system while a simulation predicts a future state (Eliot and Holliday 1988, 55; Walters and Nielsen 1988, 295–296).

Simulation rule A rule that models how different components of a system are supposed to behave. Simulation rules are used in candidate generation by constraint-suspension expert systems (Chabris 1989, 124).

Simultaneous-goal principle The principle that states: Given a goal of (X and Y), the program proceeds to solve for X. It then ensures that while solving for Y no changes take place which can alter the truth value of X (Smith 1989, 179).

SIN A successor to the SAINT expert system, which is able to do calculus at very advanced levels. It employs a specialized pattern matcher which allows it to operate more efficiently than a general pattern matcher. The main improvement over SAINT is its much larger knowledge system (Hayes-Roth et al 1983, 39; Barr and Feigenbaum 1981 vol 1, 125–127).

Single instruction multiple data A type of parallel processing that has centralized control and a high degree of coordination between processing tasks. This type of architecture works best with highly structured problems with predictable patterns. *Contrast with* Multiple-instruction multiple data (Hillis 1985, 24–25).

Single paradigm Describing an expert system with one kind of knowledge representation (rule, frame, semantic networks, and so on) and one reasoning method (forward chaining, backward chaining, and so on). *Contrast with* Multiple paradigm (Rauch-Hindin 1988, 55; Matthews Sep 1987, 47).

Single-representation trick Using a consistent representation format in both the training instances and rules in a machine-learning program. If this can be accomplished it greatly simplifies programming overhead. *See also* Operationalization (Chabris 1989, 298, 302; Smith 1989, 179).

Situation A state in working memory in a production system (Hunt 1986, 237).

Situation-action pairs A production rule that uses a pattern of facts to trigger actions rather than simply a new deduction. The action triggered could be opening a file or printing to a screen. *Contrast with* Premise-conclusion pair (Winston 1979, 144).

Situation-action rule Another name for production rule (Hunt 1986, 31; Jackson 1986, 31).

Situational calculus A means of reasoning about situations that change over time. Facts are grouped according to situations and the facts are monitored so as to ascertain when these facts change. The alteration of the facts signals a transition from one situation to another. It is useful in situations in which the assumption can be made that there is only a single next situation that follows. Frames can be used to implement situational calculus. Contrast situational calculus with the more static situation of diagnosing the cause of an engine malfunction. Situational calculus has difficulty in representing continuous processes (Tello 1988, 489; Hayes-Roth et al 1983, 96–97; Charniak and McDermott 1985, 417–420; Hunt 1986, 35–36).

Situational knowledge Knowledge about what can be inferred from different groups of facts. *Compare with* Strategic knowledge (Jackson 1986, 144).

Situation semantics A language comprehension tool developed at Stanford University with which the truth of a statement is analyzed in terms of the context (Waldrop 1987, 87).

Skeletal knowledge-engineering language A computer language designed to build expert systems, which does not include domain specific knowledge (Waterman 1986, 394).

Skeletal plan An abstract plan (Smith 1989, 179).

Skeletal system A synonym for expert system shell.

Sketchiness The use of shallow rather than deep knowledge by most expert systems (Hayes-Roth et al 1983, 42).

Skill acquisition Improving a skill by practice and knowledge accumulation (Firdman Premier 1986, 84; Barr and Feigenbaum 1981 vol 3, 326, 532).

Skill refinement Learning that involves building new rules to generate more efficient performance. Skill refinement is used in OPS5 production systems. The principles used in skill refinement include generalization, discrimination, designation, and composition (Brownston et al 1986, 335).

Skolem constant A ground term that replaces an existential quantifier. Example: F16 Tomcat may be a skolem constant which replaces an existential quantifier which holds that there exists in the data base an American fighter plane with two rudders (Luger and Stubblefield 1989, 420).

Skolemization The process that eliminates existential quantifiers in resolution refutation. That is, finding a ground term for an existential quantifier. An existential quantifier that holds that there exists in the data base an American fighter plane with two rudders may be replaced by the skolem constant F16 Tomcat (Luger and Stubblefield 1989, 62, 418–420; Charniak and McDermott 1985, 349–351; Barr and Feigenbaum 1981 vol 3, 89–91, 95).

SLD-resolution The version of resolution used in PROLOG. It stands for Selecting a literal, employing a Linear strategy and using Depth-first search to peruse the search space (Butrick 1987, 30; Voda 1988, 23; Sterling and Shapiro 1986, 90).

Slew rate The top speed of a robot's manipulator joint (Rosenberg 1986, 171).

Slice The ability to describe a situation in different ways. A given perception of a problem may not be able to solve a portion of a problem, but an alternative perception may succeed. SYN is an expert system that uses this approach in solving electronic circuit problems (Hayes-Roth et al 1983, 115).

Slot A subunit of a frame. A means of storage in a frame. A part of a frame that usually contains information about the object the frame represents. It is analogous to the term attribute in a rule-based system. A slot frequently represents a characteristic of the frame. The slot contains the value of that characteristic. A simple example is a frame that represents an automobile. One slot stands for the engine. The value of the slot is the type of engine—a V8. The slot values are not restricted to numbers and simple values of an attribute. The slot may hold a constraint, a link to another frame, the object's name, a default property value, a list of values, a set of rules, other objects, or a procedure to determine a value. A slot may contain more than one of these entities. This type of flexibility in what can reside in a slot is one of the characteristics of a frame which makes it much more flexible than a record in a standard programming language (Finin 1986, 47; Townsend 1987a 125–126; Hayes-Roth et al 1983, 402; Walters and Nielsen 1988, 211–216; Harmon and King 1985, 44; Townsend 1987b, 288; Salzberg Aug 1987, 37).

Slot inheritance The inheritance of slots in a frame-based system. A particular slot not the value, is inherited. Assume a frame representing a computer with a slot called CPU. There are many types of CPUs—8088, 80386, 68000, and so on. Therefore, the user does not want a particular value inherited, just the slot CPU. This is slot inheritance. Contrast slot inheritance with the inheritance of slots and values. An example could be a frame which stands for an automobile. There is a slot called wheels which holds the number of wheels the automobile has. Almost all cars have four wheels. In this case the user wants the slot and its value inherited by any children of this frame (Walters and Nielsen 1988, 228–229).

Small expert system An expert system that is the equivalent of 500 rules or fewer (Harmon et al 1988, 20).

Smalltalk A well-known object-oriented language, developed at Xerox. In Smalltalk, objects are the center of attraction. Objects are able to inherit variables and methods from parent objects. Each object may also have its own private variables and methods. Objects may send messages to other objects and respond to messages from other objects. An object's internal state cannot be directly accessed. The access of an object's internal state can only take place through message passing. An object's values are persistent in nature. This is in contrast to the ephemeral nature of a functional language's variables values. Inheritance is another important characteristic of Smalltalk. It does not, however, use multiple inheritance. Smalltalk's advantages include code reusability, uniformity, close approximation of the world, understandability, and its incremental development capacity. One of its most fruitful applications has been in simulations. *See also* Object-oriented. *Contrast with* Frame language; Functional language; Relational language (Somsel May 1988, 95–98; Bernat Nov 1986, 77–81;

Shafer Winter 1987, 38–39; *Smalltalk/V Tutorial and Programming Handbook* 1988, 5–10).

Smart procedures manual   A program that can be constructed with an expert system shell whose primary function is to instruct a person in what procedures need to be followed in a mundane situation. Rather than working with a knowledge domain that only an expert knows, the knowledge in a procedure manual covers such everyday subjects as office procedures (Harmon and King 1985, 232–233).

Smart report   A type of report that is delivered on disk and not only contains the conclusions of the report, but also the assumptions and the reasoning involved in reaching the conclusions. The recipient of the report is able to query the smart report concerning the reasoning and assumptions. Such a report requires a knowledge-based system for development (Harmon and King 1985, 221).

Smoothing   The deemphasis of portions of a scene that has abrupt changes in intensity (Barr and Feigenbaum vol 3, 213–215; Forsyth and Naylor 1985, 80).

Snapshot   A facility found in the expert system Personal Consultant, which allows graphs drawn by external editors to be captured in an expert system (Shepard Mar 1987, 74).

SNOBOL   A general-purpose computer language oriented to the manipulation of symbols. A functional, extensional language with excellent string-processing capabilities. These characteristics make it suitable for artificial intelligence applications (Urqhart 1988, 135–149).

SNOOPE   (System for Nuclear On-line Observation of Potential Explosives) A neural net used to detect explosives in luggage at airports.

Society of Mind   An artificial intelligence text by Minsky. The thesis is that mind is not a single unified consciousness but an association of agents that work together. This is somewhat similar to Gardner's *Frames of Mind,* in which he identifies seven kinds of intelligence (Johnson 1986, 257–258; Waldrop 1987, 124–128).

Soft implication   An implication that involves a certainty or probability factor. Example: If a then b with certainty of .90 (Bratko 1986, 349).

Solid modeling   The computer representation of three-dimensional objects (Hunt 1986, 238).

Solution element   An element that holds information concerning the hypotheses and decisions a blackboard system produces. They also stand for the dependencies that link the different decisions. They are one of three types of decision elements in a blackboard system. The other two are agenda elements and plan elements (Hayes-Roth et al 1983, 16–18).

Solution graph   The solution path of a state space or an AND/OR graph (Smith 1989, 182).

Solution path   A path traversing nodes from an initial state to a goal state (Luger and Stubblefield 1989, 83).

Solution space   The body of information necessary to solve a given problem.

Soma   The body of a neuron (Stevens 1985, 288).

Sombrero filtering   A filtering procedure used in image processing. It applies a function shaped like a Mexican hat to different areas in the bitmap so as to emphasize the edges by changing them into zero-crossings (Chabris 1989, 302).

SOPHIE   An intelligent computer-aided instruction system that simulates an electronics lab in which students attempt to find faults in electronic equipment. It simulates faults in electronic circuits and aids the student in finding the faults. This program gives particular emphasis to the student exploring new ideas, thus facilitating the acquisition of the problem-solving process (Hayes-Roth et al 1983, 41; Mishkoff 1986, 6–4; Barr and Feigenbaum 1981 vol 2, 247–253, 292–293).

Sound Describing an inference for which, given a set of propositions and an inference rule, every inference made logically follows the inference rule (Luger and Stubblefield 1989, 59).

Soundness A property of propositional calculus that states that a contradiction cannot be achieved by applying the rules of inference. That is, in propositional calculus, it is not possible to derive a contradiction of a fact if that fact already exists as a fact in the system. Other properties of propositional calculus are completeness and decidability (Jackson 1986, 74).

SOUP (Semantics Of User Problem) A set of user functions that are created in the NOAH planning system to carry out the plan (Tello 1988, 481).

Spanning tree The nodes of a graph and a subset of the edges of the graph so that all nodes are connected to one another and there are no cycles in the spanning tree (Bratko 1986, 228–230).

Spanning-tree problem A type of mapping problem in which the minimum or maximum route is ascertained. Route delivery and airplane scheduling problems fit under this rubric. A language like PROLOG is well suited for solving such problems since PROLOG has lists and is capable of recursion (Townsend 1987b, 349–355).

SPARC (Scalable Process ARChitecture) Chips that are expected to run at speeds of up to 40 million instructions per second (Dunn and Knox 1988, 22).

Sparse array A type of nonlinked data representation that can be implemented in OPS5 production systems. Most of the elements have the same default value, and because of this, all values do not have to be specifically represented (Brownston et al 1986, 183–184; Winston and Horn 1984, 190–193).

Spatial differentiation Sharpening an image by subtracting the second derivative of a function from the function (Barr and Feigenbaum 1981 vol 3, 211–212, 216–217).

Spatial reasoning 1. Reasoning involving the use of visualizations about shapes, positions, and motion. Einstein is said to have gained insight into relativity by visualizing how velocity may affect shape and time. An example of an attempt to emulate spatial reasoning is an artificial intelligence program that solves geometric analogy problems. 2. The study of controlling motion in a space, in robotics (Schildt 1987, 11; Charniak and McDermott 1985, 433–437).

Speaker-dependent recognition A method of speech recognition tailored to comprehend the speech of a particular individual. *Compare with* Speaker-independent recognition (Mishkoff 1986, G–4).

Speaker-independent recognition A method of speech recognition that comprehends the speech of any individual who uses the system. *Compare with* Speaker-dependent recognition (Mishkoff 1986, G–4).

Specialization The process of discovering special cases of a general principle. The propagation or inheritance of properties from a class to an object. The inverse of generalization. An example is replacing a rule containing variables with a set of rules containing constants. The different rules handle special cases of the variable rule (Brownston et al 1986, 341–345; Barr and Feigenbaum 1981 vol 3, 408, 432, 434, 444, 502; Epp et al 1988, 825).

Specialization hierarchy Representing knowledge about objects as specializations of more general objects. A Ford Model-T is a specialization of the concept of a vehicle. This is essentially the concept of inheritance found in frame-based and object-oriented systems (Reimer 1986, 177–178).

Special variable Another name for a free variable (Charniak and McDermott 1985, 65).

Specification by example A type of automatic programming that relies on examples of program input and output. Artificial intelligence procedures are used to examine patterns in the examples and use these patterns to construct the program. *Contrast with* Formal specification; Natural-language specification (Mishkoff 1986, 6–7).

Specificity Part of the conflict resolution strategy used in OPS5 production systems. Specificity chooses the rule or rules from the conflict set with the most detail. This frequently translates to a rule that has the most variables and constants in the left-hand side of the rule (Brownston et al 1986, 454; Rosenberg 1986, 173).

Specific rule A rule that does not use variables, which can only be used with certain specific facts. *Compare with* General rule (Parsaye and Chignell 1988, 46).

Speech-acts theory A theory of speech proposed by John Searle. It is an attempt to analyze the intent of what a person says. Statements are classified in such classes as requests, promises, and orders (Waldrop 1987, 86–87).

Speech processing The field of artificial intelligence whose goal is to recognize and synthesize spoken human speech.

Speech recognition The discrimination of speech sounds by a computer. *Contrast with* Speech-understanding system (Schildt 1987, 92; Mishkoff 1986, 1–16; Barr and Feigenbaum 1981 vol 1, 325–326; Chabris 1989, 302).

Speech synthesis The production of speech by a computer (Schildt 1987, 92).

Speech-understanding systems Artificial intelligence programs whose goal is to understand human speech. HEARSAY II is the best known example (Johnson 1986, 123–126; Barr and Feigenbaum 1981 vol 1, 325–361).

Spherical-coordinate robot A robot that has horizontal and vertical motion and an arm that can be extended and retracted (Rosenberg 1986, 173).

Spinning off A type of incremental growth by refinement used in rule-based systems. An already existing rule is the basis for creating a variant of the rule which has added conditions. *See also* Fission for another version of incremental growth by refinement (Brownston et al 1986, 168–170).

Splitting Dividing a goal into subgoals. This process is used in OPS5 production systems to implement backward chaining.

Sponsor A mechanism used in the expert system tool Goldworks. A sponsor assigns resources for specific tasks. It is an entity that is responsible for choosing the search strategy and ordering the type of inferencing strategy for a set of rules. That is, a sponsor may dictate a depth-first search, which employs forward chaining, then backward chaining. Sponsors are hierarchically organized. A sponsor may have what is known as a quanta which limits the number of rules it can fire at one time (Matthews Sep 1987, 82; Flamig Spring 1988, 52; Tello 1988, 311; Tello 1989, 170–171).

Spontaneous generalization The tendency in parallel distributed processing systems to retrieve what is common to a set of memories when the retrieval cue being used is too general to capture any single memory. By activating a unit corresponding to membership in the system this unit will partially activate all the instances of the set. In this way the model can retrieve the typical values that the members of the set have on each dimension: single, age, sex, and so on. The connection strengths among units are the critical factor. The knowledge for a pattern is not stored in the connections of a special unit reserved for that pattern, but is distributed over the connections among a large number of processing units (Rumelhart and McClelland 1986 vol 1, 30–31).

Spontaneous learning Learning that takes place without a teacher. This type of learning is unique to living organisms, some neural nets, and a selected few other AI programs like EURISKO (Rumelhart and McClelland 1986 vol 1, 155).

Spreading activation 1. A method of computing and assigning the activation level of objects in an expert system. A node that is assigned a higher activation level spreads activation to connected nodes. The activation level determines the degree of attention nodes receive. 2. A procedure used in intersection search which finds common links between two concepts. In a semantic network the activation of two nodes in the net and the activation of all the nodes connected to the two initial nodes. This activation continues until a point of intersection between the two original nodes is found. The point of intersection defines the commonality between the two original nodes. 3. The application of the activation function to a neural net. The basic process by which a neural net carries out its computations. The incoming data cause alterations in the weights at the different nodes in the net until a state of stability is achieved (Obermeier and Barron Aug 1989, 218–219; Smith 1989, 185; Chabris 1989, 49; Brownston et al 1986, 455; Rosenberg 1986, 173).

Spurious knowledge False knowledge. Such knowledge can be introduced into knowledge bases as a result of coincidental events (Walters and Nielsen 1988, 187–188).

SQL *See* Structured query language.

SRL A frame-based representation language. Frames are referred to as schemas in SRL, which provides flexibility in specifying both inheritance and the procedure used in searching the hierarchy. SRL is capable of alternate-worlds reasoning. Demons and slot constraints are available. SRL uses a disk cache system which allows it to be used with data bases that are larger than primary memory (Fox et al 1986, 161–170).

S set The most specific subset of the set of hypotheses given a set of hypotheses (Smith 1989, 169).

Stability The property of an expert system which measures the system's ability to continue to focus on a goal or set of goals. The conflict-resolution strategy can greatly influence stability. *Contrast with* Sensitivity (Brownston et al 1986, 304, 455).

Stack A one-dimensional data structure that is useful for the organization of goals. It operates according to the last-in-first-out principle. The last goal generated is the first goal processed. This type of implementation lends itself to a backward-chaining architecture. Other data structures used in organizing goals are tree structures, queues, and agendas. In OPS5 the conflict resolution strategy can be used to implement a stack (Brownston et al 1986, 185).

Standard predicate A predicate that is built into a particular PROLOG implementation (Townsend 1987b, 386).

STAR procedure A procedure that uses type and structure information to generalize a single given example based on a set of constraints. It is used in the machine-learning algorithms AQ, INDUCE, and CLUSTER (Parsaye Jul/Aug 1989, 29).

State A snapshot of the condition of a data structure at a given point in time in a problem-solving situation. The data structure is a description of the state of the problem. The state may be considered a node in a problem space. For example, the situation may be a chess game. The state is the position of the different pieces at a given time. A move of one of the chess pieces is called an operator and the move changes the state of the chessboard.

State-driven inference An inference that is driven by the condition of the system. In a forward-chaining rule-based system a given rule may fire and deposit new facts in working memory. One of the facts deposited fulfills the condition for another rule to fire. *Compare with* Change-driven inference; Goal-driven expert system (Hayes-Roth et al 1983, 187).

State-evaluation function A procedure in search algorithms which is used to give an estimate of the distance of each candidate state to the goal state (Charniak and McDermott 1985, 259–270).

State graph A graph consisting of nodes and arcs which is used to represent different states in a problem-solving process. The nodes symbolize the state of a problem at a particular point in the problem-solving process (Hunt 1986, 243).

State machine parser   A language parser that uses the current state of the sentence to calculate the category of word which can come next. For example, a preposition may only be followed by an article, pronoun, or noun. A state machine parser works well in situations in which only a limited number of sentences can be expected to be processed. *Contrast with* Context-free parser; Definite-clause grammar parser; Noise-disposal parser (Schildt 1987, 95–105; Townsend 1987b, 312–318).

Statement   1. A complete program instruction. 2. The constructs of logic programs. There are three kinds of statements in a logic program: facts, rules, and queries (Rosenberg 1986, 174–175; Hansen 1988, 69).

State space   A graphic representation of all of the potential problem states of a given problem. The problem states are connected by arcs which represent operators which produce the transformations from one state to another. *Contrast with* AND/OR tree; Search space; Search tree (Barr and Feigenbaum 1981 vol 1, p. 26).

State-space representation/graph   A graphical representation of a problem consisting of a set of nodes. The graph is a directed graph and each node represents a state of the problem. The arcs represent the means (operator) to make a transition from one state to the next. A forward-chaining production system could have its problem-solving process represented in a state-space representation. In a production system the operators are rules, and working memory can represent the problem-solving state. *Contrast with* Problem-reduction representation; Search space (Rettig Mar 1987, 15; Minasi May 1988, 22; Crawford 1988, 90–92; Barr and Feigenbaum 1981 vol 1, 24, 32–36, 40–42).

State-space search   A search in which a problem and its solution are depicted as the searching for a solution path between an initial state and the final state. It consists of a starting state, a set of operations to transform one state to another, and a means of testing to see if a goal state has been reached. A state-space search is used when there is no algorithmic solution. Two types of search are blind search and heuristic search (Rettig Mar 1987, 15; Hayes-Roth et al 1983, 66–67; Barr and Feigenbaum 1981 vol 1, 46–53, 58–73; Jackson 1986, 3; Luger and Stubblefield 1989, 82–83.

State variable   A variable that records the condition of an object or the state of a problem. Examples: the temperature of a patient, the pressure in an engine, and the number of subgoals that must still be achieved (Winston 1979, 250).

Static   1. Describing an object that is created in the data segment (static object). This is in contrast to an object created on the heap (dynamic object).   2. Describing a method that is bound early (static method) as opposed to being bound late (virtual method) (Duntemann 1989, 140).

Static data   Data which do not vary over time. Dealing with static data is much easier than dealing with dynamic data.

Static data base   The portion of the data base that is not altered by a program run (Townsend 1987a, 66–67).

Static data structure   A data structure found in expert systems which is definitional, relatively fixed, and separate from the inferential knowledge base. Static data structures may be in the form of lists, tables, or a set of parameters. *Compare with* Dynamic data structures (Jackson 1986, 96–97).

Static evaluation   1. A means of computing a number for each potential move in a game situation. The highest number computed indicates the best of the available moves. The estimating of the value of a board position without looking ahead at any of that position's successor positions. An effective evaluation function may take into account up to 30 factors along with the interaction among the factors. **2.** Evaluating an expert system by examining its knowledge base. *Contrast with* Dynamic evaluation (Winston 1979, 115; Forsyth and Naylor 1985, 181–193; Barr and Feigenbaum 1981 vol 1, 96–97; Barr and Feigenbaum 1981 vol 3, 459–464).

Static frame A frame that cannot be changed during the course of a consultation. *Contrast with* Dynamic frame.

Static inheritance A type of inheritance in which the child object inherits slots and methods from the parent object, and the child object will always be a member of this class (Amir 1989, 30).

Static method A method that is bound early. The method cannot be changed after compile time. (Udell 1989, 105; Duntemann 1989, 140; Fleener 1989, 94).

Static model An expert system representation in which, in contrast to the dynamic model, input data are not changed over a period of time. That is, one set of data is given to the system and the system responds to that set of data (Walters and Nielsen 1988, 284–295).

Static object **1.** An object declared in the data declaration part of the program, which is not created while the program is running, in contrast to dynamic objects. **2.** An object and its attributes, but not its values. Instances of this object take on values for the attributes during the program run. **3.** Objects that are not affected by code execution. Static objects cannot be created, deleted, or changed at runtime. The values of the object will remain unchanged during a program run. *Contrast with* Dynamic object. **4.** A type of object found in C++ in which the object holds its value throughout the execution of the program. *Contrast with* Automatic object (Duntemann 1989, 140; Stroustrup 1987, 250; Harmon and King 1985, 39, 64).

Static representation A model-based representation in which the inputs are predictable. An example of a static representation is the modeling of an oil-refining process which may be complex but one in which the input ingredients are always the same. Generally such systems are used to analyze failures in the internal process. *Contrast with* Dynamic representation (Walters and Nielsen 1988, 289–294).

Static rule A rule that cannot be created, deleted, or changed during a consultation (Townsend, 1987a, 124).

Static scoping A free variable taking on the value it held at the time the function it is in was defined. *Contrast with* Dynamic scoping, in which the free variable takes on the value it held at the time the function was called (Charniak and McDermott 1985, 270).

Static typing Typing in which all expression types are decided at the time of compilation (Wegner 1989, 248).

Statistical logic Logic that deals with frequencies and probabilities.

Status Whether a goal has been reached, failed, or postponed.

Steamer A teaching expert system used for giving instruction concerning operating procedures of steam plants on board ships. It is a frame-based system (Michaelsen 1985, 310–311).

Stepwise refinement **1.** A design approach to expert system development, which is especially useful if the problem is not clearly defined. A small prototype is first built which works with only a subset of the domain. Then, using the information gained from the prototype the prototype is iteratively added to, until the intended goal is reached. *Compare with* Structured design which is often used in conjunction with stepwise refinement. **2.** Programming methodology in which a program is specified at an abstract level, and then successively refined until it is accounting for the details necessary to reach the goal. When used in this way stepwise refinement is interchangeable with top-down programming. The primary difference between this definition and the former definition is that, under this definition of stepwise refinement, the programmer spends a great deal of time thinking through the problem before any programming is carried out (Bratko 1986, 180–181; Brownston et al 1986, 172, 455; Townsend 1987b, 194–195; Sterling and Shapiro 1986, 53; Rosenberg 1986, 175; Hunt, 1986, 244).

Stereoscopic vision The use of two cameras separated by some distance to record the same scene (Forsyth and Naylor 1985, 82–83).

Stereotype A structure used to show the type of sentence constructions in which a word can be used. It is framelike in nature (Smith 1989, 188).

Stimulus-equivalence problem The problem faced by neural nets of not being able to ascertain the equivalence of an image when the image is compared to a rotated equivalent. Example: Assume one teaches your neural net to recognize the letter B. If the B is rotated 90 degrees the neural net cannot now recognize the B. More recent neural nets have been able to cope with this problem (Rumelhart and McClelland 1986 vol 1, 113–115).

Stimulus frame The part of the blackboard that a knowledge source uses to obtain information (Smith 1989, 188).

Stochastic Chance or probability (Obermeier and Barron 1989, 219).

Stop-and-copy storage management Program suspension during garbage collection (Wolfgram et al 1987, 308).

Store/compute tradeoff Roughly the same as prepare/deliberate tradeoff (Chabris 1989, 303).

Strategic knowledge Knowledge used to direct the general reasoning process in an expert system. The type of knowledge usually found in metarules or hard coded into the interpreter. Some authorities argue that it enhances the performance of expert systems when strategic knowledge is separated from structural knowledge. *Compare with* Situational knowledge (Jackson 1986, 144, 210).

Stratified language A language that does not allow the construction of a metalanguage. FORTRAN is a stratified language (Rosenberg 1986, 176).

Stream 1. A source of data or a repository of data. A file may be in an input stream, or an output stream depending on whether or not data are being received or stored. Data being sent to the printer or the monitor are an output stream. 2. A data structure made up of a sequence of data elements. A set of assertions in an expert system may be a stream. *See also* San Marco LISP Explorer (Luger and Stubblefield 1989, 488; Bratko 1986, 137).

String A type of active data structure used in Connection machines, which is much more efficient on Connection machines than on conventional computers because new data can be inserted efficiently into a string on a Connection machine. A conventional computer would not be able to carry out this task efficiently. Other types of active data structures are trees, butterflies, arrays, sets, and graphs (Hillis 1985, 113–114).

STRIPS A variation of General Problem Solver. The program makes plans for a robot, so that the robot can reach a goal. An early artificial intelligence program that has the capability of learning to improve on its searching ability by discovering, generalizing, and remembering macro operators. It is capable of developing a generalized plan which can be used later. STRIPS like GPS uses means-end analysis, but its application of means-end analysis is more sophisticated than what is used in General Problem Solver. STRIPS uses recursion and does not use backtracking. The representation scheme is first-order predicate calculus (Rettig May 1987, 17–21; Hayes-Roth 1983, 106; Winston 1979, 137–143; Barr and Feigenbaum 1981 vol 1, 128–134, 138–139).

Strong AI A term coined by Searle which refers to the position that AI not only simulates brain processes, but duplicates thinking. Artificial intelligence research the goal of which is to develop a computer system to produce an entity that will think and understand in the same way a human being does. *Compare with* Weak AI. *See also* High-church computationalism (Chabris 1989, 303; Waldrop 1987, 135–136).

Strongest-link method A rule of fuzzy logic. Rather than simply performing an evaluation which returns true or false, fuzzy logic allows an evaluation of a rule with a number ranging from 0 to 1. The strongest-link method returns the maximum value of the subgoals of a rule. If fruit_grows_on_a_tree (.2) AND fruit_is_red (.5) THEN fruit_is_an_apple (.5). This rule will return .5 the maximum value as the answer to the rule. *Contrast with* Weakest-link method (Schildt 1987, 251–255).

Strong link Rules that share conditions or hypothesis in the expert system NEXPERT Object. *See also* Weak link (Epp 1988, 825).

Strongly typed object-oriented language An object-oriented language that possesses strong typing and dictates all objects to be abstract data types (Wegner 1989, 248).

Strong method A problem-solving method using domain knowledge to improve performance. It includes knowledge found in rules and certainty factors. It focuses on domain-specific heuristics. *Contrast with* Weak methods (Luger and Stubblefield 1989, 596; Hayes-Roth et al 1983, 402).

Strong search A search in which information is used to choose where to go next. A synonym for heuristic search.

Strong typing Typing in which the type compatibility of all expressions symbolizing values from the static program is decided at compile time (Wegner 1989, 248).

Struct A class in which all members are public, in C++.

Structural description A description of an object based on the components of the object and the relationships among components (Rosenberg 1986, 176).

Structural hierarchy A hierarchy that consists only of the different components of an object. There is no notion of how the components are related in a cause-effect way or what is the function of the components. This type of hierarchy represents shallow knowledge. *Compare with* Causal hierarchy; Functional hierarchy (Townsend and Feucht 1986, 72).

Structural induction Another term for induction expert system. This approach has difficulty deciding which variables are important and handling noisy data and exceptions (Lenat 1988, 70).

Structural knowledge Knowledge that consists of the facts in the knowledge domain under study. Some authorities argue it enhances the performance of expert systems to separate strategic knowledge from structural knowledge (Jackson 1986, 210).

Structural similarity The phenomenon in production systems of common condition elements among rules. The Rete algorithm exploits this phenomenon to perform more efficient matching (Brownston et al 1986, 234–236; Hunt 1986, 245).

Structure **1.** An object that is defined by specifying its member parts. An object with multiple components. Example: computer (CPU, RAM, monitor, keyboard). **2.** An entity in LISP similar to a Pascal record having fields and field values. The number of fields are fixed. **3.** An expression in PROLOG that is not a program statement but does have a structure name, and that is followed by one to 255 valid expressions that are separated by commas and enclosed in parentheses. Take the following statement; likes(mary, football, fan_of(broncos). The expression fan_of(broncos) is a structure because it is a part of the full statement. If fan_of(broncos) was in the program as a separate fact, on a line by itself, it would be a statement and could not be a structure. **4.** A frame, which is useful in representing taxonomic relations. **5.** A record in a data base, which consists of multiple components. *Contrast with* Class (Jackson 1986, 52, 219; Clocksin Aug 1987, 152; Young 1987, 95–96, 370; Winston and Horn 1984, 100; Bratko 1986, 30–21; Steele, 1984, 163; Lazarev Nov 1988, 76; Steele 1984, 32).

Structured data The organization of data in a meaningful manner. That is, compound objects may be nested in compound objects. The data structure may then more closely resemble the way we conceptualize the object. It is similar to the term data abstraction (Sterling and Shapiro 1986, 25–28).

Structured design An approach to expert system design which consists of reducing the problem to a set of subgoals. A module is designed for each subgoal. *Compare with* Stepwise refinement, which is often used in conjunction with structured design (Townsend 1987b, 194–195).

Structured growth A programming style in which the necessary modules are in place at the outset and in simplified form. Program development takes place by gradually increasing the complexity of the modules. *Contrast with* Incremental development (Barr and Feigenbaum 1981 vol 2, 65).

Structured induction The breaking up of a problem into a set of small problems and then using induction procedures to build a rule base (Michaelsen et al 1985, 310).

Structured object *See* Structure.

Structured programming The organization of programs into independent modules (Smith 1989, 190).

Structured query language A nonprocedural relational data base language developed by IBM which is rapidly becoming a standard. Expert systems are becoming capable of generating structured queries, determining the state of a project, and assigning work as needed. Many projects are currently endeavoring to interface SQL data bases with expert systems (Rettig Jul 1987, 19–24; Schur 1988, 27).

Structured representational scheme A scheme in which each object is a complex object made up of slots which can hold values and procedures. Examples: scripts; frames; and objects in object-oriented programs (Luger and Stubblefield 1989, 334).

Structured rule A rule characterized by no procedural content, minimal use of the ELSE statement, and simple conclusions (Pedersen 1989, 47).

Structured rule tool A rule-based expert system that allows the rule base to be hierarchically organized. This may be accomplished in individual rules by the use of object-attribute values. It can also be accomplished by dividing the rules into separate contexts. The latter technique can increase the search efficiency of the system since all rules do not have to be searched when the program is working on a particular subproblem. *Contrast with* Object-oriented approaches, which are also hierarchically organized but unlike structured rule tools object-oriented systems possess inheritance (Harmon et al 1988, 55–58, 119).

Structured selection The use of expert systems to make hypothesis selections based on the available evidence. The term not only covers diagnosis but also decision-making processes (Forsyth and Naylor 1985, 15–16).

Structure editor An editor in LISP to operate on lists, directly modifying the contents of cons cells (Jacobs 1986, 58).

Structure inheritance The inheritance of the slots of a parent object, in object-oriented programming. It is also called slot inheritance (Gabriel Mar 1989, 55–57).

Structure inspection A set of predicates in PROLOG that analyze the structure of terms. A simple example is integer (X). If X represents an integer, then the predicate returns true (Sterling and Shapiro 1986, 134–145).

Structure knowledge One of three types of knowledge found in diagnostic expert systems. It is the knowledge of the parts the expert system is to diagnose. *See also* Event knowledge; Functional knowledge (Merritt Sep 1987, 53).

STUDENT A computer program that reads algebraic story problems, converts them to equations, and solves the problem. It was built by Daniel Bobrow (Johnson 1986, 101; Mishkoff 1986, 2–18; Winston 1979, 335–339; Barr and Feigenbaum 1981 vol 1, 284–285).

Student model The component of an intelligent computer-aided instruction system that represents the student's understanding of the knowledge (Mishkoff 1986, 6–3).

Subclass 1. A class with a parent class from which it inherits characteristics. 2. A child class. 3. A class that inherits from a more abstract class. The subclass can have its own unique characteristics. Example: the class animals and the subclass birds (Pascoe Aug 1986, 142; Stabler 1986, 54; Duntemann 1989, 141).

Subcognition The antithesis of the proposition that humans are logical-symbol manipulators. Rather than formal reasoning, the claim is that humans use a type of unsystematic, distributed, pattern matching to solve problems. This type of unsystematic, distributed pattern matching is called subcognition. Subcognition is used in Hofstadter's COPY CAT program (Johnson 1986, 279–280, 286–288).

Subgoal One of a set of goals that must be reached before a broader goal can be achieved. Breaking up a problem into subgoals is a standard means of problem solving in artificial intelligence (Harrison and Tribble 1986, 66; Townsend 1987a, 154; Brownston et al 1986, 455).

Subgoaling The breaking up of a goal into subgoals (Smith 1989, 190).

Subjective certainty A synonym for certainty factor (Bratko 1986, 347).

Subjective understanding A theory of language understanding developed by James Carbonell. An attempt to grapple with the underlying meaning of sentences. Schank's conceptual-dependency theory reaches one level of underlying meaning, but subjective understanding theory attempts to go deeper. Example: "Would you go to the ball with me?" Conceptual dependency theory may correctly interpret the question as a request concerning accompaniment to a dance. Subjective understanding attempts to interpret if the statement involves such issues as strong ego involvement, great emotional significance, and so on. A number of programs have attempted to reach these deeper levels of understanding: Cold War Ideologue uses a simple set of rules to guide understanding. SAM uses more sophisticated scripts for understanding relatively stereotyped situations. PAM uses plans, themes, and goals for understanding unique situations. Carbonell believes that more than scripts and rules are needed to endow a program with understanding. As an alternative he used a hierarchy of goals as a cornerstone of his theory of subjective understanding. He implemented his theory in the program Politics and later in Triad. In Politics, the overall goal may be that the Communists must be contained. Subgoals may include a strong intelligence network, an aggressive military posture, a sound economy, and so on (Waldrop 1987, 78–84).

Subkind link A link from a more abstract object to a more specific object in a semantic network (Salzberg 1987, 33).

Subproblem One of a set of problems that must be solved before the overall problem can be solved. Subproblems can be dependent on a particular order of solution, or independent of the order of solution of the subproblems (Barr and Feigenbaum 1981 vol 1, 81–83).

Subset of A type of taxonomic relationship in which a class is represented as a subclass of another class. In "subset of" the information is represented in a hierarchy. That is, lions are a subset of the class of cats. "Subset of" is best represented by frames (Jackson 1986, 177).

Substitution The supplanting of a variable by an expression in logic (Smith 1989, 190).

Subsumption 1. The ability of one concept to encompass another. Example: Cat is subsumed under the concept of animal. 2. When the antecedent of one rule can be found as a subset of the antecedent of another rule and their consequents are equivalent. A procedure can then be used as an inference rule to eliminate all clauses which are redundant or more specific than the most general clause available (Tello 1988, 419; Finin 1986, 47; Hayes-Roth et al 1983, 290; Arora 1990, 308).

Subsymbolic paradigm A hypothesis that states that thinking must be viewed from a more molecular level than the symbolic paradigm generally followed in artificial intelligence. The subsymbolic paradigm is employed in neural nets, and it uses such concepts and methods as spreading activation, relaxation, and statistical correlation (Rumelhart and McClelland 1986 vol 1, 195–197).

Summation function A function that combines the different input signals of a neural-net processing unit into a single activation value (Jones and Hoskins 1987, 155; Obermeier and Barron 1989, 219).

Super A special Smalltalk variable that takes on the name of the object it resides in, and allows the user to override a class method so that a method in the superclass of the object can be used. A type of pseudovariable. It is found in methods inside of objects in the Smalltalk language (*Smalltalk/V Tutorial and Programming Handbook* 1986, 69; Pascoe Aug 1986, 144).

Superclass 1. The class under which a given class is subsumed. A parent class. 2. A more abstract class. Example: Birds are a class which belong to the superclass animals (Pascoe Aug 1986, 142; *Smalltalk/V Tutorial and Programming Handbook* 1986, 142–145; Duntemann 1989, 141).

Superlogical quantifier A predicate found in some PROLOG-type expert systems that is used to achieve different types of iteration. Examples: for-all, do-until, for-every; these superlogical quantifiers are built using the predicates, fail, cut, and repeat (Parsaye and Chignell 1988, 267).

Superobject An object that uses or contains other objects (Bulman 1989, 57).

Supervised learning Learning in neural nets in which there is an outside agent that tells the neural net if its response is correct. This type of training must take place before the neural net can carry out useful tasks. Two types of supervised learning are simulated annealing and back propagation. *See also* Self-supervised learning. *Contrast with* Unsupervised learning (Colvin 1989, 62; Obermeier and Barron 1989, 218; Caudill Feb 1988, 56; Bayle 1988, 42).

Supervisory-controlled robot A programmable robot which possesses a hierarchical control structure and is capable of a reasonable degree of autonomous decision making (Rosenberg 1986, 177).

Support environment Support programs that aid a knowledge engineer in building an expert system. Examples: debugging programs and editors (Rosenberg 1986, 178; Smith 1989, 190).

Support hypothesis The assumption, in vision processing, that every object must be supported by another object or by the ground. The assumption is necessary in estimating the depth of an object.

Surface knowledge Shallow knowledge.

Surface representation Shallow knowledge.

Surprise The ability of an expert system to handle unexpected problems (Eliot Feb 1988, 71).

Syllog An expert system that can interface with a relational data base. It uses Englishlike syllogisms, is more declarative than PROLOG, provides an error-checking facility, and uses both backward and forward chaining (Packer Jr et al 1986, 38).

Syllogism 1. A statement in logic consisting of two premises and a conclusion. 2. The application of implication to reach a conclusion: If *X* then *Y*. And if *X* is true. Then *Y* is true (Parsaye and Chignell 1988, 408–409).

Symbol 1. An entity chosen to represent a person, object, concept, operation, relationship, or attribute of an object in the world. A symbol may be either a constant or a variable. 2. A fundamental LISP data type. An atom that is not numeric. More specifically, a string of letters and numbers which begins with a letter and has no spaces. Examples: john, red-block, z23. A symbol's value may be another symbol, a number, or a list. The symbol itself can consist of three parts: the name, a property list, and a package cell. The properties on the property list have property values. Example: man. The symbol man may have properties like size, age, and weight, along with the accompanying values. A symbol does not have to have properties in LISP. A symbol without properties is sometimes simply referred to as a constant. A symbol with properties may be thought of as a structure. Symbols are used as operands in LISP. What this means is that operators can be applied to the symbols. For example, the two symbols A and B may represent lists, and the operator APPEND may be used to make the two separate lists into a single list. Artificial intelligence is built on the representation and manipulation of symbols. In LISP a symbol differs from a variable in a standard programming language in that the symbol does not represent an address as a variable does. The symbol can therefore represent any object and is not constrained by allotted memory space. 3. An address in C. Example: the address of a variable. *See also* San Marco LISP Explorer (Neiman and Martin 1986, 56; Townsend 1987a, 12, 250; Charniak and McDermott 1985, 45; Townsend 1987b, 386; Rosenberg 1986, 178; Chabris 1989, 303; Steele 1984, 163; Smith 1989, 191; Cornish Aug 1988, 61; Coffee Mar 1988, 40; Winston and Horn 1988, 587).

Symbolic atom A data type that consists of alphabetic and special characters and is used to represent nonnumeric objects. Symbolic atoms are used extensively in LISP (Rosenberg 1986, 179).

Symbolic expression Either an atom or a list, in LISP.

Symbolic language A computer language that excels at symbol manipulation as opposed to numerical processing. LISP and PROLOG excel at symbol manipulation. A language should have facilities for efficient symbol manipulation available if it is to be used in artificial intelligence programming (Rosenberg 1986, 180).

Symbolic logic The different types of logic: propositional logic, first-order logic, and second-order logic (Miller Jul/Aug 1988, 28; Johnson 1986, 38–39, 61–62; Schildt 1987, 223–224).

Symbolic modeling The technique of representing a body of symbolic knowledge in a computer program so that the program can draw conclusions and answer questions about the body of knowledge.

Symbolic processing Processing that distinguishes artificial intelligence programming from other types of programming. Formal reasoning with symbols. The manipulation of symbols using strategies and heuristics, as opposed to the manipulations of numbers or the use of algorithms (Townsend 1987a, 19; Hayes-Roth et al 1983, 72–81; Townsend 1987b, 5).

Symbolic programming An alternative name for artificial intelligence. The advantages of the term symbolic programming are that it avoids the futuristic connotations and the inevitable comparisons with human beings (Johnson 1986, 237).

Symbolist A member of the school of thought which holds that artificial intelligence research should emphasize the manipulation of symbols. *Contrast with* Connectionist (Brachman Aug 1987, 7).

Symbol manipulation The recognition, assembling, and modification of symbols. It is argued by some that the primary contribution of artificial intelligence is the furtherance of the study of symbol manipulation as opposed to numerical manipulation. The thrust of artificial intelligence has been to use symbols to make inferences, and this is the core of symbol manipulation (Hayes-Roth et al 1983, 46; Barr and Feigenbaum 1981 vol 2, 3–5; Winston and Horn 1984, 3–7).

Symbol structure A data structure made up of symbols. Example: the list (parent john mary) (Hayes-Roth et al 1983, 61).

Symbol system hypothesis *See* Physical symbol system hypothesis.

Symmetry reduction Taking into account the portions of the search space that are symmetrical, which may not have to be searched. This reduces the search space. Many board games are symmetrical (Luger and Stubblefield 1989, 151).

Synapse The connection point of two neurons (Obermeier and Barron 1989, 219; Stevens 1985, 288–289).

Synchronous design A type of design found in most conventional computer systems in which all components of the system are controlled by a central clock. *Contrast with* Asynchronous design.

Synergy The concept that the whole is greater than the sum of its parts. This concept is sometimes applied to expert systems in the following manner: Whereas each individual rule may have only limited power by itself, a set of rules produces power which is greater than the sum of each individual rule. That is, the complex interactions among the rules produces the extra power (Lenat 1988, 72).

Syntactic Describing the structure of a symbolic expression (Smith 1989, 192).

Syntactic ambiguity A problem in the field of natural-language understanding, which refers to the possible multiple interpretations a sentence can have. Example: "I hit the man with the baseball." Did you use the baseball to hit the man, or did you hit the man who was holding the baseball? This type of ambiguity is very difficult for a computer (Brittain 1987, 34; Mishkoff 1986, 4–4).

Syntactic analysis The study of the structure of the sentence, which is important in natural-language processing. Parsing techniques are an important part of syntactic analysis. *Contrast with* Lexical analysis; Semantic analysis (Rubin Jul 1985, 44; Mishkoff 1986, 4–10).

Syntactic category A synonym for nonterminal symbol (Barr and Feigenbaum 1981 vol 1, 239).

Syntactic method The process of parsing pictures in vision. It is analogous to the process of parsing sentences.

Syntax 1. The order in which the symbols in an expression are arranged. 2. The rules that specify the use of symbols in an expression. 3. The rules regulating the structure of a language. 4. The part of language analysis that determines if the structure of a sentence is correct and if the sentence is therefore a legal member of the language. *Contrast with* Semantics (Chabris 1989, 303; Johnson 1986, 109, 117–118; Hayes-Roth et al 1983, 403; Townsend 1987b, 386; Rosenberg 1986, 180; Tello 1988, 405).

Synthesis expert system An expert system that combines knowledge with procedures to perform actions. Information is combined to reach conclusions. XCON is an example of a synthesis expert system. *Contrast with* Analysis expert system, which breaks up a problem into subproblems (Floyd Mar/Apr 1988, 64).

System development The fourth of seven stages in expert system development. In this stage, whatever structural changes are needed are made and knowledge is added. *See also* Expert system development (Harmon et al 1988, 168–170).

Systemic grammar A theory of grammar developed by Michael Halliday in which the analysis is based on the intended use of the language as opposed to the emphasis on structure found in transformational grammar. The types of uses the grammar attempts to discern are ideational uses, interpersonal uses, and textual uses. Each utterance is analyzed according to these three uses. The ideational use pays attention to the content. The interpersonal use pays attention to whether or not the utterance is a statement, a question, a command, or an exclamation. The textual use pays attention to the overall theme of the discourse. SHRDLU employs systemic grammar.

Compare with Case grammar; Context-free grammar; Transformational grammar (Smith 1989, 193; Barr and Feigenbaum 1981 vol 1, 249–251).

System interface   The portion of an expert system that carries out interaction with data bases, spreadsheets, and languages (Harmon et al 1988, 64).

T

Table A two-dimensional static array structure. Tables are useful for holding tabular data, like the data found in spreadsheets. Some expert systems use tables as an instance of a frame. The data in tables are uniformly structured. In OPS5 working-memory elements can be used to store tabular data (Brownston et al 1986, 142–146).

Table lookup A procedure that uses a table of values to obtain the correct value for a function argument (Hunt 1986, 250).

Table of connection A data structure used in General Problem Solver to hold the operators that are responsible for reducing the difference type in a group of objects (Smith 1989, 194).

Tactile sensing A term used in robotics to refer to the continuous sensing of variable contact forces by a set of sensors. Tactile sensing should be capable of coping with three-dimensional space. There are two phases of tactile sensing—transduction and data processing. Taction sensing is a synonym (Rosenberg 1986, 189).

Taction A synonym for tactile sensing.

Tag An entity attached to a set of data which contains information about the set of data. Information about the data type of a variable is kept in a tag (Cornish Oct 1987, 52–56; Rosenberg 1986, 181).

TAG A PROLOG-based expert system shell that attempts to refute assertions made by users (Jackson 1986, 213–214).

Tagged-memory architecture An architecture in which a part of each memory word is used to convey information about the data stored in the rest of the word. The information includes data type and format (Minsky Apr 1985, 138).

Tag representation A means of marking members of a set which takes advantage of hierarchical, nonoverlapping sets. Assume a set of different types of office equipment made up of computers and xerox machines. Each category is made up of subcategories. The primary categories of computers and xerox machines are represented by one bit. If it is a computer, the bit is 1; otherwise the bit is 0. Assume there are subcategories of computers. Then, secondary bits will be needed to distinguish between these subcategories. These same secondary bits can be used to distinguish between subcategories of xerox machines since the primary category bit will always be used to distinguish between computers and xerox machines. Other types of representation for sets are bit and pointer (Hillis 1985, 93–95).

Tail The portion of a list that remains after the head of the list is removed (Townsend 1987a, 87; Townsend 1987b, 386).

Tail recursion Recursion in which the last line of a clause contains the recursive call. Tail recursion takes up less memory space than nontail recursion. It is also easier to understand (Covington 1988, 86; Townsend 1987b, 15).

Tally A numerical weight associated with a rule or with data which reflects the degree of confidence in the rule or the data (Jackson 1986, 96).

Tangled hierarchy A situation in which a node may inherit properties and procedures from more than one parent node. It is a hierarchy in which there are exceptions. Example: Mammals give live birth but some mammals are exceptions and lay eggs (Jackson 1986, 226).

Tangled tree A tree structure in which an object can inherit characteristics from more than one subordinate object. Example: an organism that inherits characteristics from both the animal and plant classes (Harmon and King 1985, 40–41).

Tapered forward pruning In tapered forward pruning the quantity of moves kept depends on the depth of the search when the move is computed (Smith 1989, 194).

Task Goal; context (Rosenberg 1986, 181).

Task analysis The second of seven stages in expert system development. In this stage the task is delineated, the sequence of events is scrutinized, and the type of knowledge involved is identified. Tentative decisions about the type of knowledge representation and the appropriate inferencing technique are made. *See also* Expert system development (Harmon and Maus 1988, 187–190).

Task domain A field in which an expert system is applied.

Task paradigm The kind of general task an expert system is designed to perform. Examples of such tasks are diagnosis, planning, configuring, scheduling, monitoring, signal processing, and dialogue tasks (Harmon and Maus 1988, 187, 207–215).

TAU Thematic Apperception Unit is a knowledge structure used in the Boris language-understanding system. It is used to deal with interpretation errors (Tello 1988, 504–507).

Tautology A trivially true clause. The expression "X or Not X" is a tautology (Barr and Feigenbaum 1981 vol 3, 92).

Taxonomic fever The overuse of a taxonomic (frame-based) design. This happens when a knowledge engineer becomes overly enamored with a frame-based paradigm (Walters and Nielsen 1988, 248–249).

Taxonomic net A net that allows hierarchical organization of objects and inheritance of characteristics (Smith 1989, 195).

Taxonomy The classification of objects as to how they are alike and different.

Teacherless learning Learning using intelligent computer-assisted instruction programs (Smith 1989, 195).

Teach pendant   A control box used in teaching a robot a new task. The control box is used to make the robot go through the desired motions for the new task. The computer monitors and remembers the movements so that it can then carry out the task without the aid of the teach pendant (Schildt 1987, 172; Rosenberg 1986, 182).

Technology approach   An approach to expert system design which holds that one should first develop the application which is most likely to give the biggest return. Such applications are usually large, complex, and more risk prone than a business systems approach (*Knowledge-Based Systems* 1986, 2–46).

Technology transfer   Teaching a domain expert or end user how to use and do some limited modification of an expert system. Placing expert system technology in the hands of the end user and convincing the end user to use it (*Knowledge-Based Systems* 1986, 2–6 to 2–8; Harmon and King 1985, 205–206; Rosenberg 1986, 182; Harmon and Maus, 1988, 199–200 & 270).

TEIRESIAS   A facility used as an aid in collecting knowledge for rule-based expert systems. It uses an interactive question-and-answer technique to acquire knowledge. It was added to the MYCIN expert system as an aid in modifying the rule set. It handles backward chaining and inexact reasoning. TEIRESIAS also allows MYCIN to back up in its inferencing to start over (Hayes-Roth et al 1983, 39–40; Barr and Feigenbaum 1981 vol 1, 195–199; Rosenberg 1986, 182; Tello 1988, 425–435).

Template matching   The use of stored patterns that can be used in the analysis of sentences or images by comparing the templates with input patterns. This early parsing technique was first popularized in the sentence-processing program ELIZA. A template is "I X all Y." Matches for this template are: "I hate all war.", "I love all beautiful things." This simplistic form of template matching was abandoned in favor of more sophisticated techniques like Augmented transition networks (Barr and Feigenbaum 1981 vol 1, 260; Rosenberg 1986, 182; Waldrop 1987, 66–68).

Template method   A method of image understanding that uses a template which is generated during feature extraction and which is compared with objects in the computer's memory. When enough critical factors of the template match the computer memory object the computer then recognizes the object. *Compare with* Prototype-point method; Region method (Lawrence 1985, 51).

Temporal logic   Logics that allow reasoning about time. A type of logic in which time is explicitly represented (Eckert 1989, 52; Luger and Stubblefield 1989, 373).

Temporal planning system   A planning system that is able to reason about continuous processes over continuous time periods (Tello 1988, 483–484).

Temporal reasoning   The ability to represent and reason about time states. Time interval relationships such as "before" and "during" are used. Terms such as "is true", "was true", "will be true" are used. Temporal reasoning can be used to construct a series of steps in a plan. Progress in temporal reasoning is necessary if AI programs are ever to approximate commonsense reasoning. *See also* Situational calculus, a well-known temporal formalism (Fischler and Firschein 1987, 96).

Temporal redundancy   The phenomenon observed in production systems that working memory changes little from one recognize-act cycle to the next. The Rete algorithm in OPS production systems exploits this redundancy to perform more efficient matching (Brownston et al 1986, 230–234, 256; Rosenberg 1986, 182).

Temporal system analysis   A type of problem analysis in which time is taken into account. Some problems are not solvable unless time is taken into account. Certain facts may be true at certain points in time and later the fact may be false. Later, the same fact may again be true. In some problem-solving situations it is crucial to have a knowledge of the sequence of events so as to know when certain facts are true or false (Charniak and McDermott 1985, 420–429).

Term The data structure of a logic program. The three terms in a logic program are constant, variable, and compound term. It is the smallest portion of an expression to which a value can be given. A list is considered a special type of compound term (Matthews Jul 1987, 37; Townsend 1987b, 12–13, 54; *Turbo PROLOG* 1986, 53; Sterling and Shapiro 1986, 5; Bratko 1986, 31).

Term building Building facts and rules in PROLOG by using such built-in predicates, as =. and functor (Jay and Knaus Jun 1989, 78).

Terminal node 1. A node that ends a path. A node with no descendants. 2. A type of node used by the Rete algorithm. It stores information about the complete satisfaction of the left-hand side of a rule and then adds the rule to the conflict set (Minasi Jun 1988, 25; Forgy and Shepard 1987, 38; Schildt 1987, 15, 22; Charniak and McDermott 1985, 180; Barr and Feigenbaum 1981 vol 1, 38, 43).

Terminal symbol The English words in language processing that make up the vocabulary of the parsing procedure. For the nonterminal symbol <articles>, the terminal symbols may be a, an, the. *Contrast with* Nonterminal symbol (Barr and Feigenbaum 1981 vol 1, 239; Barr and Feigenbaum vol 3, 495; Chabris 1989, 303).

Testing One of five phases in developing an expert system. In this phase case studies are used to test the system and the necessary revisions are carried out. The five phases, in order, are identification, conceptualization, formalization, implementation, and testing. Recently programs have been constructed that will test expert systems for errors (Hayes-Roth et al 1983, 24; Kang and Bahill 1990, 46–51).

Text generation The process of constructing meaningful text using a computer (Barr and Feigenbaum 1981 vol 1, 273–280).

Textual scope Another, perhaps more appropriate, name for lexical scope (Winston and Horn 1988, 587).

Texture analysis Analysis used to recognize types of surfaces in objects and to differentiate among the surfaces of an object (Barr and Feigenbaum 1981 vol 3, 230–237, 264–267).

Thematic role frames A frame used to capture meaning in language. A frame for a noun could have slots for person, place, and thing. Each of these slots could be further divided into specific persons, places, and things (Forsyth and Naylor 1985, 70).

Theorem A statement that can be proved. The conclusion of a valid argument. The entities that are deduced from the axioms in predicate calculus (Dos Reis 1988, 50; Charniak and McDermott 1985, 20; Parsaye and Chignell 1988, 408).

Theorem prover A program that starts with a goal and searches for implications whose conclusions will unify with the goal. A theorem prover has a data base consisting of a set of axioms. Its inference mechanism makes inferences that lead to the satisfaction of the goal. Theorem provers are usually associated with proving theorems in propositional calculus and mathematics. Logic Theorist is the best known computer-based theorem prover. Theorem provers are frequently based on the resolution principle. The addition of such things as input-output facilities and the cut makes PROLOG a limited version of a theorem prover. *See also* Mechanical theorem prover (Barr and Feigenbaum 1981 vol 1, 22–23, 109, 116; Barr and Feigenbaum 1981 vol 3, 76–123; Bratko 1986, 396).

Theorem proving The subarea of artificial intelligence involved in using computers to prove mathematical and logic theorems. Both deductive reasoning and intuitive leaps can be employed in theorem proving (Smith 1989, 197; Parsaye and Chignell 1988, 10).

Theory of conclusions This theory is derived from decision theory and uses default reasoning.

In contrast to decision theory, it considers revising hypotheses only when substantial evidence is available to compel a revision (Smith 1989, 197).

Thermodynamic model A type of multilayered neural network that uses units which can take on the value of 0 or 1. All connections in the model must be symmetrical. The activation values in thermodynamic models are a statistical function of the inputs. Harmony theory and Boltzmann machines are examples of thermodynamic models.

Third-level induction A type of induction that performs maximal generalization from the examples. In an expert system using barometric pressure if examples used the values of 25 and 32 the induction system would generalize beyond these values to a range of 10 to 50. *See also* First-level induction; Fourth-level induction; and Second-level induction.

Thrashing The loss of efficiency as memory decreases and garbage collection increases (Wolfgram et al 1987, 309).

Threaded interpretive language A language that uses primitives in combinations to build higher-level constructs. FORTH is an example of a threaded interpretive language. C and Pascal may also be considered threaded interpretive languages, though their capabilities along this line are more limited (Tello 1988, 392).

Three-d model representation The final stage in Marr's theory of visual processing. In the previous two-and-one-half-sketch stage all of the surfaces in the images have been identified and in the three-d model representation stage individual objects are identified. This is carried out by comparing the image with previously stored images in an attempt to achieve a successful match (Waldrop 1987, 101–102).

Threshold 1. A value that must be exceeded in order to have an action take place. 2. The least amount of energy needed to excite a neuron (Obermeier and Barron 1989, 219; Reece Jan 1987, 52; Rosenberg 1986, 183).

Threshold function The function in a neural network that takes as its input the output of the summation function and decides if the value is sufficient to fire the connected neural net processing unit. A threshold function can take on one or two values: 0 or 1. It takes on the value of 1 only if a specified threshold has been exceeded (Rosenberg 1986, 183; Jones and Hoskins 1987, 155).

Threshold logic unit (TLU) A model of a neuron consisting of a Schmidt trigger, an operational amplifier, and potentiometers. The potentiometers adjust the threshold that needs to be exceeded to fire the TLU (Brown 1987, 17).

Threshold statement A specification of the lowest allowable percentage of confidence necessary for an expert system to reach a conclusion. Example: One may decide not to allow any conclusions with a confidence factor lower than .50 (Barr and Feigenbaum 1981 vol 2, 181).

Tight coupling Coupling used to bind query results to PROLOG variables from a data base. It is faster, more memory efficient, and easier to implement than loose coupling, but is not as modular as loose coupling (Missikoff and Wiederhold 1986, 388–399).

Tigre A generalized data base management system which has an interface with PROLOG. The data base is capable of storing large and complex objects which are needed in applications like CAD and office automation. Tigre can call on PROLOG for inference (Adiba and Nguyen 1986, 487–504).

Tile puzzle A puzzle consisting of a square with individual cells. Every cell but one contains a letter. The exception cell is empty, thus allowing the other cells to be moved. The goal is to move the different cells until the desired end state is reached. The desired end state is usually getting the letters in alphabetical order. Artificial intelligence programs are devised to find efficient means of solving tile puzzle problems.

Time-dependent data Data which change over time. The term is often used interchangeably with dynamic data. *Contrast with* Static data.

Time interval A representation technique used to represent time in an artificial intelligence program. Time is represented as intervals rather than as points in time (Ladkin 1987, 58).

Time-map manager 1. A program module that is used in a time-projection manager whose function is to save and recall information and the temporal relationships associated with the information. 2. A procedure for managing a data base of state and event tokens. It helps to answer questions like: Did you finish your degree BEFORE starting this project? Are you going to take a vacation AFTER school is out? *See also* Time-system analyzer (Charniak and McDermott 1985, 429–433; Tello 1988, 491–492).

Time of flight A method of estimating the depth of an object. The time it takes for a waveform to reach an object and return is used to measure the depth of an object. Commonly used waveforms are sound and lasers (Barr and Feigenbaum 1981 vol 3, 254–255).

Time-projection manager A planning program that employs a data base as an aid in dealing with more complex situations which simpler methods like situational calculus cannot handle. Two important components of a time-projection manager are a time-system analyzer and a time-map manager (Tello 1988, 490).

Time-system analyzer The part of a time-projection manager that is responsible for reasoning about time. *See also* Time-map manager (Tello 1988, 490–491).

Time tag A tag attached to working-memory elements in production expert systems to determine how recently the working-memory element has been placed in working memory or modified. The time tag is used to determine which rule to fire in the event that more than one rule is eligible to fire. Time tag is sometimes called a recency attribute (Moskowitz Nov 1986, 218; Brownston et al 1986, 43, 456).

Time-varying data Knowledge that can change as a function of time. Representing such data in an artificial intelligence program is difficult. Situational calculus is one method of dealing with time-varying data (Hayes-Roth et al 1983, 123).

Tip A node in a graph that has no children, which is the same as a leaf (Luger and Stubblefield 1989, 82).

TLU *See* Threshold logic unit.

TMS *See* Truth-maintenance system.

Token 1. A PROLOG name, a nonspace character, or an unsigned number, in PROLOG. 2. A data structure used by the Rete algorithm. Every time there is a change to working memory a token is created to represent this change (Forgy and Shepard Jan 1987, 37; Brownston et al 1986, 456; Townsend 1987b, 54).

Token node A node used to help define a type node. The token node represents the components of what is represented by the type node. Example: A type node may be a computer and the token nodes may be the keyboard, terminal, and CPU (Jackson 1986, 55).

Tool An inference engine, a user interface, and procedures for entering knowledge. It is very much like a shell but some authorities reserve the term tools for more sophisticated shells like ART and KEE (Hunt 1986, 254).

Tool kit A set of integrated tools that can be used to solve AI problems. Example: a tool that possesses a frame-based component, a logic component, and a forward-chaining component. A tool does not have a knowledge base. The programmer is expected to supply the knowledge base. A tool may be thought of as being more sophisticated and powerful than an expert system shell which may possess only one of these components (Citrenbaum et al 1987, 31).

Top-down comprehension An image-comprehension procedure. A synonym for controlled hallucination (Forsyth and Naylor 1985, 86–88).

Top-down design Software design that is based on control abstraction. It is most useful when complex flow of control is involved. *Compare with* Object-oriented design (Chabris 1989, 303).

Top-down editing The ability of object-oriented systems to define and edit objects at the class level and then at the subclass level, and finally at the object level. *Compare with* Bottom-up editing.

Top-down inference Backward chaining.

Top-down parsing Evaluating a sentence by using its expected structure (Mishkoff 1986, 4–11).

Top-down problem solving Backward chaining (Reedy and Kaplan Oct 1986, 66).

Top-down refinement A problem-solving process that starts with carrying out a complete abstract plan to solve the problem. Each subproblem at a given level is solved independently from others. After solutions have been found at a more abstract level, the problem-solving procedure moves to a less abstract, more detailed level. This process continues until a concrete detailed problem-solving plan is completed. This is also known as hierarchical planning. Top-down refinement is used in the expert system ABSTRIPS (Hayes-Roth et al 1983, 104–105).

Topic The primary structural, storage, and control unit used in the expert system shell KnowledgePro. It is extremely flexible. It can act as a procedure, system command, function, variable, frame, or a hypertext node. Topics act as a procedure in the same way as procedures are executed in a conventional language. Each procedure in turn is called and executed, and is capable of passing parameters. As a variable, a topic may be assigned a value. If the topic is incorporated into a rule as condition for executing a rule, then the rule will be executed depending on the value of the topic. A topic can also be an action in the consequent portion of the rule. The parameters passed by topics are lists. One of the ways lists can be applied is in dealing with a group of related objects. An example is condensing a series of rules with similar antecedents into one list. When the user is asked to choose one of the antecedents KnowledgePro looks up and executes the corresponding consequent in the list. Topics may be nested within topics. This type of hierarchical structuring permits inheritance of values from parent topics. Topics are dynamic in nature. That is, they may be created during the execution of the program. One of the most interesting aspects of topics is their use in creating sophisticated consultation paradigms. Example: When a question is asked to which the system does not know the answer, it can backchain to another topic which will create a window and a menu of possible answers for the question. In addition, topics can be used in hypertext mode. That is, words in the question can be highlighted so that the user can ask information about that word. Assume a question asks, which declarative language would you like to know more about? If you do not know what a declarative language is, you can ask for information about declarative languages. The amount of information can be pages in length (Shafer Jul/Aug 1988, 37; Thompson and Thompson Apr 1988, 40–43).

Top node A parent node in a tree structure, which has no parent. It is also called a root node (Minasi Jun 1988, 25).

Topological predicate A type of predicate used in predicate calculus that indicates containment, overlap, and fitting together of objects (Charniak and McDermott 1985, 324–325).

Topology-preserving map A map that duplicates the shape of the distribution pattern. Kohonen networks can produce topology-preserving maps (Caudill Aug 1988, 65–66).

TOPS A knowledge structure used in BORIS, a natural-language AI program. TOPS is used for capturing very general knowledge (Tello 1988, 503–504).

Touch sensor A sensor used in robots that senses the presence of objects when physical contact is made (Rosenberg 1986, 184).

Towers-of-Hanoi problem A well-known problem which is regularly used in artificial intelligence. It consists of three pegs, referred to as pegs *a*, *b*, and *c*. The idea is to transfer the disks on peg *a* to peg *c*. All of the disks on peg *a* are ordered by size with the largest-diameter disk being on the bottom and the smallest being on the top. The goal is to place all of the disks, in order by size, on peg *c*. During the transfer process the game player cannot place a larger-diameter disk on a smaller-diameter disk. Peg *b* can be used as a temporary storage area (Lawrence 1985, 107–111; Bratko 1986, 292).

Toy problem Problems that have no real practical application, which are useful in illustrating a particular AI procedure. Game problems like the towers-of-Hanoi problem and Knight's Tour are examples of toy problems (Waterman 1986, 395).

Tracking window The window in robotics that places limits on the freedom of movement of a robot (Rosenberg 1986, 185).

Train facility A facility found in the TIMM expert system shell which is used to tune the knowledge base by assigning certainty factors. More than one expert may be used to answer the same problem. The responses they make can then be averaged and used in future consultations (Tello 1988, 167).

Training Teaching a neural network to make an association between the input and the right answer (Obermeier and Barron 1989, 219).

Training instance A solved problem being presented to an example-driven learning system. Training instances are used to build rules (Smith 1989, 200).

Trait A distinguishing characteristic of an object. Traits are used in induction systems to devise rules.

Trajectory The motion of a robot (Rosenberg 1986, 185).

Transfer functions Differential equations used in neural nets to determine the output of each processing element based on the input. The coefficients of the transfer functions can be modified by a learning rule (Caudill Feb 1988, 56; Ingraham et al 1988, 17; Caudill Dec 1987, 48; Bayle 1988, 41–42; Fogelman and Mejia Dec 1988, 58).

Transformation The process of reducing a goal to a series of subgoals (Eisenbach et al 1985, 186).

Transformational approach A type of automatic programming that attempts to transform a previously existing program into a new program with added capabilities. Other approaches to automatic programming include the deductive approach, high-level language approach, and knowledge-based approach (Tello 1988, 420).

Transformational grammar A theory of language introduced by Noam Chomsky. The theory states that when we make a statement the receiver of the statement makes a number of transformations of that statement into simpler statements. The final transformation is a simpler transformation which retains the essential deeper meaning of the original statement. Transformational grammar uses what are known as context-sensitive, or transformational rules. A transformational rule may be used to do such things as ensure the number of the verb and the noun are the same. Context-free grammar, in contrast, concerns only the essential meaning of the sentence and is less concerned with whether or not the noun and verb of a sentence agree. Because transformational grammar deals with such contextual questions, transformational grammar is a more complex grammar than is context-free grammar. *Compare with* Case grammar and Systemic grammar (Brittain 1987, 33; Charniak and McDermott 1985, 188–194; Winston 1979, 169; Barr and Feigenbaum 1981 vol 1, 245–248; Barr and Feigenbaum 1981 vol 3, 497–498; Chabris 1989, 92, 303–304).

Transformational rule   A rule used in transformational grammar that places restrictions on the grammar. Example: The number characteristic of a subject and the verb must be identical (Charniak and McDermott 1985, 188–189).

Transition network parser   A top-down parser that consists of context-free rules, the purpose of which is to decide if a sentence is legal according to the context-free rules. It cannot, however, remember what it has parsed. *See also* Augmented transition network (Charniak and McDermott 1985, 197–198; Winston 1979, 169–178).

Transition rule   A rule used to detect a change of state in the system. Example: a rule that fires when the condition of a patient enters into a critical state (Hayes-Roth et al 1983, 97).

Transitivity   1. Relating objects so that if the first is related to the second, and the second is to the third, then the first is related to the third. 2. In frame-based languages a means of checking to see if two schemata are associated by a particular relation (Fox et al 1986, 167–168; Tanimoto 1987 92–93).

Transparency   1. The clarity of a program. The degree to which an artificial intelligence program is understandable. A related definition is the degree to which a system is able to explain its conclusions.   2. The independence of the meaning of the rule from its location. The meaning of the rule is encapsulated in the rule (Pedersen 1989, 45; Hayes-Roth et al 1983, 128; Jackson 1986, 12; Bratko 1986, 317; Bratko 1986, 179).

Transposition problem   A problem that arises in a search in which there may be many possible ways of achieving a given state. Example: In a chess game there are many ways to reach a given board pattern (Chabris 1989, 188).

Transputer   A 32-bit RISC chip used for parallel processing (Swaine May 1988, 105).

Traveling-salesman problem   The problem that states: A salesman is to visit a number of cities. Each city is to be visited only once. Once all cities are visited the salesman is to return to the starting city. Given the distances between the cities, what is the shortest possible route for the salesman? For more than 10 cities the number of possibilities is in the million range (Thompson and Thompson Jul 1987, 30).

Tree   1. A type of graphic knowledge representation. A hierarchical type of graph which resembles a Christmas tree. A tree is well suited for hierarchical information. Many games have knowledge that is arranged hierarchically. A tree is a net in which each node has a unique parent. Each node can have more than one child. There can be no arcs from offspring to parents. The top node is the root node and it has no parents. A tree structure is frequently represented inside of the computer as a list of nodes. Each node on that list in turn has a list of the children nodes. Tree structures can also be represented in one-dimensional arrays. *See also* Binary tree.   2. A low-cost network topology found in Connection machines. A problem with this type of topology is the communications bottleneck at the base of the tree. This regular data structure is especially useful in gathering information from the leaves of the tree and sending information to the leaves of the tree. Other topologies include Clos networks, rings, banyan-type networks, grids, delta networks, hashnets, shuffle-type topologies, and crossbars (Hillis 1985, 57–58, 97–100; Minasi 1988, 25; Walters and Nielsen 1988, 220–222; Brownston et al 1986, 456; Forsyth and Naylor 1985, 129–130; Chabris 1989, 304; Luger and Stubblefield 1989, 336; Winston and Horn 1984, 169).

Tree of contexts   A set of choice points.

Tree structure   A graph consisting of nodes and arcs organized in a hierarchical structure. The top-most node has no parent. The other nodes have only one parent. Each node represents a state in the problem-solving process. Each arc represents an operator which is used to transform the preceding state into the successor state. A tree data structure can be useful for the organization of goals. It is used in backward-chaining systems like EMYCIN, which seeks answers by decomposing a goal into a series of subgoals. Other data structures used in organizing goals are queues, stacks, and agendas (Harmon and King 1985, 55–56, 66, 191; Hunt 1986, 258).

Triad   A natural-language understanding program, developed by James Carbonell, which is able to comprehend and answer questions about situations involving goal conflicts (Waldrop 1987, 62).

Triangulation method   A method of estimating the depth of an object. It consists of an active light projector and a passive sensor. The active light projector moves so as to give the passive sensor different perspectives of the object. (Barr and Feigenbaum 1981 vol 3, 255–259).

Trigger   The satisfaction of the conditions of a rule so that it is ready to fire (Chabris 1989, 304).

Trilogy   A language which is a combination of logic, procedural languages, and data base languages. It is similar to PROLOG. Unlike PROLOG, it uses constraint logic rather than blind backtracking. As a result it is more of a logic-based language than is PROLOG. The procedural aspects of the language are useful in avoiding backtracking. It contains a data base and employs a number of data base commands, including procedures for inserting, deleting, and modifying records (Voda 1988, 24–26; Chapnick May 1988, 6; Reeves 1989, 34–36; Lane Mar 1988, 145–151).

Tri-valued logic   A class of logic that allows a rule to be true, false, or unknown (Thompson and Thompson Apr 1985, 328).

Truckin   An intriguing strategy board game which is played by each player writing a rule base for his or her truck. The object of the game is to move one's truck around the board, buying, selling goods, and trying to make money. After the rule base is written, the game starts and the players watch and cheer their trucks on (Waldrop 1987, 206–207).

Truth functional predicate   A synonym for connectives, like "and" and "or" (Charniak and McDermott 1985, 16).

Truth-maintenance system (TMS)   A type of belief-revision system that is capable of handling errorful information, because it keeps track of inferences being made, and the antecedents that allow the inferences to be made. If an antecedent is shown to be false, then all inferences which were based on the antecedent can be withdrawn. The objects which exist in a TMS are either justifications or propositions. Justifications are the reasons the system believes or disbelieves a given proposition. The propositions are those statements the system believes or disbelieves. The propositions in a TMS are labeled as believed or disbelieved. When a new proposition is added to the system the TMS searches for believed propositions which may now need to be disbelieved and disbelieved propositions which may now be believed. Some propositions may be labeled as contradictory, and the necessary beliefs are changed through dependency-directed backtracking so that inconsistent propositions are withdrawn (Hunt 1986, 34; Hayes-Roth et al 1983, 75–76, 403; Brownston et al 1986, 456; Barr and Feigenbaum 1981 vol 2, 72–76; Luger and Stubblefield 1989, 315; Chabris 1989, 304).

Truth symbol   The terms true or false in logic (Luger and Stubblefield 1989, 47).

Truth table   A method in logic to represent the meaning of a proposition. It can also be used to prove the equivalence of two expressions. A table that is used to list the truth of a conjunction or disjunction of statements, as different statements vary as to whether or not they are true. All possible combinations of true and false values for the statements are included in the truth table (Charniak and McDermott 1985, 16–17; Harmon and King 1985, 53; Rosenberg 1986, 186; Barr and Feigenbaum 1981 vol 1, 161–162; Parsaye and Chignell 1988, 406–407).

Turing, Alan   Acknowledged by many as the father of artificial intelligence. He argued that a machine could be built which could emulate human thinking. He devised a nonnumerical model of computation (Johnson 1986, 43–45).

Turing machine A hypothetical logic machine. A machine that uses binary code to perform algorithmic operations. An infinitely long tape divided into squares as if it were a roll of postage stamps. Each square is either blank or has a symbol on it. A scanning device moves forward and backward along the tape. Depending on what it finds it can write a symbol, erase a symbol, move one square forward, or move one square back—and that is all (Johnson 1986, 43–44, 78–80).

Turing test A method of testing to see if a computer is able to think. An examiner conducts an interview using a computer and attempts to decide if he or she is interacting with a computer or another person. If the examiner is unable to make the differentiation, then the computer passes the Turing test. It is then argued the computer is capable of thought. An analogy is throwing a bottle in the ocean, and if the bottle is able to make it to dry land then the bottle is capable of swimming. The Turing test, as it is generally described, is a superficial method of assessing the presence of thought processes. A more sophisticated approach is to delineate the details of human thought and to devise procedures that test for the presence of these specifics in artificial intelligence programs (Johnson 1986, 44, 170, 182).

Tutoring module The component of an intelligent computer-aided instruction program that selects strategies to attempt to correct the student's misconceptions. The misconceptions are discovered by the student module component of the ICAI (Mishkoff 1986, 6–3).

TWEAK A planning program developed by David Chapman. TWEAK has the characteristic that if it can produce a plan to solve a problem, then the problem can be solved using the plan. If TWEAK is unable to produce a plan, then there is no plan that exists to solve the problem. It uses a procedure known as the modal truth criterion to develop plans. TWEAK is able to solve relatively insubstantial problems, because of its limited representational scheme (Amsterdam Jan 1987, 28–32).

Two-and-a-half-degree sketch The second of three stages in Marr's theory of visual processing. This stage receives information from the first stage, the primal scene. In two-and-a-half-degree sketch the individual surfaces in the image are identified. The resulting information is passed on to the final stage—three-d model representation (Waldrop 1987, 92–102).

Two-input node A type of node used by the Rete algorithm. It is responsible for the processing necessary to decide if multiple conditions in a rule can be satisfied at the same time. It combines the matches for a condition element with the matches for all prior condition elements. *Contrast with* One-input node (Forgy and Shepard 1987, 38; Brownston et al 1986, 456; Hunt 1986, 259).

Two-space view of learning The approach to learning that involves an interaction between an instance space and a rule space. That is, the program can search the different possible examples in its data base to confirm, build, and refine rules. The rules can be used to find examples for solutions to possible problems. The two basic types of two-space learning are data-driven methods and model-driven methods (Barr and Feigenbaum 1981, vol 3, 360).

Type 1. A description of a class of values that defines the range of the values, how much storage is necessary for the elements, and the way its elements are displayed. A classification of entities. A type specifies a set of operations which can be used with these values. Examples: integer, real, boolean, and string data types. 2. A collection of terms in PROLOG (Sterling and Shapiro 1986, 33).

Type checking Ensuring that the type of the data is appropriate for the operation to be carried out (Luger and Stubblefield 1989, 451–454).

Type conversion The conversion of a data type to another data type. In PROLOG a predicate can be used to convert a string into a symbol (Stroustrup 1987, 89–90).

Typed language A language that must declare the type of all the variables in a program at the start of a program. Such typing increases the speed of the program but reduces flexibility. Typeless languages such as LISP and most versions of PROLOG are generally preferred for artificial intelligence programming because of their greater flexibility.

Typeless argument An argument of a predicate in PROLOG that is not limited to a specific data type. The data type may be a number, an atom, a list, or a complex structure. Most conventional languages limit the argument of a procedure to a particular data type. The use of typeless arguments greatly facilitates artificial intelligence programming (Jay and Knaus 1989, 77).

Type node A term used by Quillian which refers to a node that represents a concept. Token nodes are connected to the type node and are representations of components of the concept represented by the type node. Example: the concept of a computer, in which the keyboard, terminal, and CPU may be considered token nodes (Jackson 1986, 55).

Type I error Rejecting information as false when the information is actually true (Marcot Aug 1987, 46).

Type/token distinction The distinction between a class of objects and an individual object. This distinction can be important. Example: In an inheritance hierarchy a class of animals may be an endangered species, but it is not appropriate to classify a given animal as an endangered species (Chabris 1989, 61–64, 304).

Type II error Accepting information to be true which is actually false. It is important to keep type I and II errors in mind when designing expert systems. In a strategic air-defense warning system, type II errors are preferable to type I errors as long as nobody uses the system as a basis for launching a counterstrike (Marcot Aug 1987, 46).

Typical consultation A knowledge-engineering design tool. The knowledge engineer simply asks the expert to describe a typical consultation he or she may have with someone who is seeking advice.

Typicality A state in which most objects in a class possess the same properties. A structured-object approach to expert system programming has been criticized because typicality is usually used. This makes the system subject to numerous exceptions because all objects may not share the properties. An alternative approach is to make a distinction between essential properties and accidental properties (Jackson 1986, 67).

U

UIM *See* Ultra intelligent machines (Forsyth and Naylor 1985, 246–250).

Ultra intelligent machines (UIM) A hypothetical machine possessing superhuman intelligence for which supposedly all artificial intelligence researchers are striving. It is argued that we ought to be thinking about the desirability of such machines and how we would cope with them (Forsyth and Naylor 1985, 246–250).

Unary message A message in object-oriented programs which has no argument (Rubin Aug 1985, 28; *Smalltalk/V Tutorial and Programming Manual* 1986, 31).

Uncertain data Data which may not be correct. Fuzzy logic, Bayes' theorem, Shafer-Dempster theory, and certainly factors are means of coping with uncertain data (Merritt Sep 1987, 56).

Uncertain information *See* Uncertain data.

Uncertainty **1.** The inability of an expert system to obtain a value. In that event the expert system may ask the user, attempt to calculate the value, use a default value, or attempt to continue reasoning without the value. **2.** The lack of sure knowledge as to whether or not a rule, a fact, or a user response may be correct. Inexact reasoning is used to reason with uncertainty. Certainty factors, fuzzy logic, Shafer-Dempster theory, and Bayes' theorem are methods of inexact reasoning available for dealing with uncertainty (Townsend 1987a, 167–175; Schildt 1987, 239–256; Walters and Nielsen 1988, 203–204; Rosenberg 1986, 189; Hunt 1986, 260; Smith 1989, 203).

Unclear antecedents A problem with which the field of natural-language understanding must cope. Example: Mike is mad at John because he likes Sue. Either Mike or John could be the one who likes Sue (Mishkoff 1986, 4–4).

Unconditionally forward hypothesis A type of inference found in the expert system NEXPERT OBJECT. Using this strategy the next knowledge island will be tested no matter what the outcome of the current hypothesis. The other types of inference found in NEXPERT OBJECT are forward-confirmed hypotheses, forward-rejected hypotheses, forward-actions effects, and exhaustive evaluation (Tello 1988, 303).

Unconditional probability The probability of an event independent of any prior events. Example: the probability that a patient has a disease in absence of any knowledge of the patient's symptoms. Unconditional probability is used in Bayes' theorem. Unconditional probability is also called prior probability (Charniak and McDermott 1985, 457).

Unconscious A term coined by Freud which has some relevance for artificial intelligence. Freud contended much human behavior is motivated by unconscious instincts and that logic does not necessarily play an important part. One important behavior considered to take place at an unconscious level and not bound by logic is creativity. For artificial intelligence to deal with creative behavior, the hallmark of intelligent behavior, it is necessary to cope with these issues.

Undecidable Describing a proposition that has an infinite search space. That is, a proposition to test empirically that all values of π are irrational is undecidable (Luger and Stubblefield 1989, 55).

Understanding The ability to understand in the area of artificial intelligence, which is measured in terms of a program's ability to solve problems, ask intelligent questions about the problem area, and answer questions. In natural-language processing it is thought a computer is capable of understanding a situation if it is able to paraphrase the verbal description of the situation and answer sophisticated questions about the situation. When a program is able to build internal models of the world and examine its own data structures this may be considered the basis for understanding. In vision, it is held that a computer program is able to understand a scene if it can correctly classify the scene (Waldrop 1987, 138; Chabris 1989, 13).

Understanding system An artificial intelligence system that is able to use a body of textual knowledge to answer questions about the body of knowledge. The more advanced AI understanding systems do more than simply find a piece of text in response to a query. Understanding systems are able to scrutinize text, make inferences, and answer questions when the answer is not explicit but only implied. The Goldwater Machine, POLITICS, and BORIS are three understanding AI programs (Tello 1988, 495–498).

Unfirable rule A rule which cannot be executed because one of its consequents does not appear in the knowledge base. Other types of error rules include dueling rules, irregular rules, and orphan rules (Lane Jun 1989, 306).

Unification An inference rule in logic, which is used to unify two formulas to produce a clause. In PROLOG, it is frequently referred to as a pattern-matching and variable-value-assigning algorithm. Strictly speaking, unification is the actual variable-assignment portion of the algorithm. Prior to unification, pattern matching takes place. Pattern matching consists of finding a predicate that matches the predicate in the query, and ensuring that the number of arguments in the predicate and query are equal. Then, unification takes over. The unification may consist of unifying two terms that are exactly the same (equality testing), a ground term and a free variable, a bound variable and a ground term that are exactly the same, or two free variables. When a free variable and a term that is not a variable are involved, the result of the unification is the assignment of the term to the free variable so that both patterns are the same. Advantages of unification over simple types of pattern matching are (1) that substitutions can be made by very complex objects, since terms include compound objects; and (2) that variables are allowed in both the query and the data. It should be noted that the type of unification found in most versions of PROLOG are different from the type of unification found in logic. Most PROLOG implementations have made changes in unification to improve efficiency. Unification is the core of the resolution-proof procedure of PROLOG (Deering and Faletti 1986, 530; Minsky Apr 1985, 138; Deering Apr 1985, 201; Baker 87, 41–42; Eisenbach and Sadler Aug 1985, 186; Thompson and Thompson Premier 1986, 25–28; Townsend 1987a, 53; Charniak and McDermott 1985, 346; Townsend 1987b; 12–13; *Turbo PROLOG* 1986, 51–54; Barr and Feigenbaum 1981 vol 2, 61–62; Sterling and Shapiro 1986, 68–72; Parsaye and Chignell 1988, 91–92; Tello 1988, 418; Bratko 1986, 61; Young 1987, 18–22; Hunt 1986, 260; Luger and Stubblefield 1989, 62).

Uniform abstraction space. An abstraction space in an expert system that differs primarily in the level of detail involved. The knowledge in the abstraction spaces is relatively homogeneous and the vocabularies of the abstraction spaces are equivalent. *Compare with* Heterogeneous abstraction space (Hayes-Roth et al 1983, 117).

Uniform-cost search A state-space algorithm that employs a cost function to calculate the cost of paths. The least expensive path is the one chosen. When cost is uniform throughout the search tree, uniform-cost search becomes breadth-first search. It is better known as branch-and-bound search (Chabris 1989, 153–157, 304).

Uniformity The condition in which what is true about an object at one point in time remains true in the future. That is, objects retain their values.

Union An operator in relational algebra that joins two relations to produce a new relation which has all of the information from the original relations. The two original relations must have the same schema (Parsaye and Chignell 1988, 414–415).

Union multiple inheritance Inheritance of different values from two different parent slots of the same name (Walters and Nielsen 1988, 232–233).

Unit 1. A frame-like structure that has slots with unrestricted values. The value of a slot may be a number, a word, or a function. Units are used in the computer program EURISKO. 2. An object that cannot have subclasses. Example: In a hierarchy of animals, the dog next door called Rover is a unit. Rover is an end-point object in the class. Rover is a unit. Contrast with the term St. Bernard which is not a unit because there may be many objects which can inherit from the subclass of St. Bernard. Sometimes the term entity is used interchangeably with the term unit (Hu 1989, 189; Forsyth and Naylor 1985, 214; Walters and Nielsen 1988, 210; Chabris 1989, 304).

Unit clause A fact in PROLOG. A clause with no body (Shmueli et al 1986, 249; Morein 1986, 155).

Unit-preference strategy A strategy used in resolution-theorem proving. This strategy looks to perform resolution on clauses with one literal (a one-unit clause) whenever such clauses are available. This moves the resolution process quickly to the goal of a clause with no literals—the empty clause (Luger and Stubblefield 1989 428–429).

UNITS A frame-based knowledge representation system which was the forerunner of RLL and the expert system tool KEE (Tello 1988, 416; Salzberg Aug 1987, 32; Hayes-Roth et al 1983, 150–153).

Unity path A path that is forged through the use of rules that have a certainty of one (Luger and Stubblefield 1989, 319; Smith 1989, 204).

Universal entropy A term that describes the disorganization that takes place in production expert systems as rules are incrementally added. Incremental programming can encourage the addition of a rule without completely thinking through the consequences of the addition of the rule (Jackson 1986, 140).

Universal instantiation 1. A rule of inference in predicate calculus. It states if something is true of all objects, then it is true for any particular object. 2. The principle that, given a universally quantified variable in a true sentence, then any substitution by any appropriate term in the domain will produce a true sentence (Luger and Stubblefield 1989, 61; Charniak and McDermott 1985, 20).

Universalization A type of generalization that moves from "some of" to "all of." An example is the jump from "some female mammals are observed to give milk" to "all female mammals give milk."

Universal quantification The condition of most variables in rules in PROLOG, which is that if X is a variable in a PROLOG rule it means that it stands for all possible substitutions of the variable X. *Contrast with* Existential quantification (Sterling and Shapiro 1986, 6–7; Barr and Feigenbaum 1981 vol 3, 88–89, 91).

Universal quantifier The quantifier that indicates that a sentence is true for all the values in the domain. A variable in a fact or rule in a logic program. In the fact likes(X, mary), X is the universal quantifier and it will match with all queries of the form likes(john, mary), likes(mike, mary), and so on. That is, ALL X like mary. Another example is that for all X has (X, wings). This means all objects (planes in this case) in the data base have wings. *Contrast with* Existential quantifier (Charniak and McDermott 1985, 18; Luger and Stubblefield 1989, 51).

Universal specialization A rule of inference which is similar to modus ponens but it incorporates a universal quantifier. An example is "If Socrates is a man" and "All men are mortal" then "Socrates is mortal." The all in "All men are mortal" is the universal quantifier. *Contrast with* Modus ponens (Hayes-Roth et al 1983, 64–65; Barr and Feigenbaum 1981 vol 1, 164; Smith 1989, 205).

Unknown A value allowed for variables in many expert systems. Having the ability to assign unknown to a variable and still continue with the reasoning process can be an asset in some expert system applications. The value unknown can be used as a condition for an expert system to assign a default value to a variable.

Unsatisfiable Describing a group of clauses in which for every interpretation at least one clause in the group is not true. *See also* Satisfiable (Luger and Stubblefield 1989, 426; Dos Reis 1988, 50).

Unsolvable node A node that has no successor node and which is not a solution node (Smith 1989, 205).

Unsupervised learning 1. Learning that takes place in a neural net. In this type of learning the neural net has no outside agent telling the neural net if its response is correct or incorrect. In unsupervised learning the network clusters the data. Unsupervised learning is sometimes referred to as learning from observation. *Contrast with* Supervised learning. *See also* Self-supervised learning. 2. Learning found in some induction expert systems in which unclassified training instances are presented. Induction systems capable of this type of unsupervised learning use heuristics to classify the instances (Barr and Feigenbaum 1981 vol 3, 363; Caudill Feb 1988, 56; Rosenberg 1986, 189; Bayle 1988, 42; Obermeier and Barron 1989, 218).

Unwinding The return from the bottom level of the recursive process to the top level (Hasemer 1984, 39).

Upward inheritance Inheritance from the child to parent. This is opposite to the direction inheritance usually takes (Arcidiacono Nov 1988, 112).

UR resolution An inference rule that produces a simple clause from a group of clauses, one of which is a compound clause. It produces the simple clause so that the most general set of values of the variables will work for all of the clauses (Tello 1988, 418; Wos and Veroff 1990, 897).

User confidence One of two types of confidences found in an expert system. It is the confidence the user has in his or her response to a question posed by an expert system. *See also* Expert confidence (Harmon and Maus 1988, 75).

User defined Describing the ability of some programming languages to define and use new data types. Languages that have this ability include Pascal and C (Hunt 1986, 261).

User-defined inheritance strategy A strategy whereby the inheritance characteristics of an object-oriented system can be altered by the user of the system. Metaslots are used to make the alterations.

User-interaction function The part of an expert system responsible for asking questions of the user, answering questions of the user, and displaying conclusions (Bratko 1986, 315).

User interface The portion of an expert system with which the user interacts. It allows communication between the user and the expert system. The user may ask how or why questions. The expert system may ask the user for information. It may include menus, questions, text explanations, and natural-language interfaces (Harmon and Maus 1988, 63–64; Mishkoff 1986, 3–5; Parsaye and Chignell 1988, 33).

User-modified syntax A mechanism found in some expert systems by which the knowledge engineer can improve the readability of the knowledge base. The knowledge engineer can declare particular words as prefix, infix, or postfix "operators." These allow nonatomic expression names to be specified without hyphens. Example: "the-best-sweetness" can be written as "the best sweetness" if "the" and "best" are declared as prefix and postfix operators. User-modified syntax is found in the M1 expert system shell.

User response The type of response a user may give to queries by an expert system. The types of responses allowed could include yes, no, don't know, why, a natural-language sentence, a choice from a menu, multiple responses, or a mouse click.

Utility A value attached to a rule which specifies the importance of the rule. The higher the value, the higher the priority the rule will have in being used to solve the problem (Shepard Mar 1987, 76; Tello Oct 1987, 243).

Utility branch A function in robotics which is activated when a signal from an external source indicates a malfunction has taken place. The function ensures that the robot will take corrective action (Rosenberg 1986, 190).

Uttley machine A variation of a perceptron which utilizes Bayes' theorem to reduce the required input channels. The number of demons used are therefore reduced. The Uttley machine also uses a local feedback mechanism between demons which reduces the number of components necessary to classify incoming patterns. The Uttley machine is one answer to the criticism of Minsky and Papert, which stated that perceptrons were too susceptible to combinatorial explosion to be of any practical value (Reece 1987, 54).

V W

v A symbol used in logic to represent the logical operation of disjunction.

VAL A robotics-control language developed by Unimation (Mishkoff 1986, 5–19).

Valid Describing an argument whose conclusions logically come from its premises (Dos Reis 1988, 50).

Validation The demonstration that an expert system performs the tasks it is intended to perform. That is, how well the system has captured the information of the domain expert. *Compare with* Verification (Geissman and Schultz 1988, 27; Barr and Feigenbaum 1981 vol 2, 182).

Value The worth of an attribute. The worth may be quantitative or qualitative. Example: The value of the attribute color may be red (Harmon and King 1985, 38, 43; Townsend 1987b, 387).

Value inheritance Perhaps the most common type of inheritance in a frame-based system. The slot inherits the value from a parent slot. A Ford automobile would inherit the value 4 for the wheels slot from the automobile parent frame. *Contrast with* Slot inheritance (Walters and Nielsen 1988, 229–230).

Value-inheritance procedure An algorithm whose function is to determine if an object is a member of a particular class. If it is, the object inherits the properties and values of the class (Chabris 1989, 48).

Value model A model in which the intent of a computation is to generate a value. Functional languages are based on a value model. *Compare with* Side-effect model (Allen Jul 1985, 29).

Variabilization The procedure of generalizing a formula by substituting a constant with a variable.

Variable A symbolic representation of a value. The value may change during a program run. It is one of the three terms of a logic program. *Contrast with* Symbol (Harrison and Tribble 1986, 66; Townsend 1987a, 38–39; Brownston et al 1986, 456; Winston and Horn 1988, 588).

Variable quantifier A symbol that places limits on a variable and hence limits the meaning of a sentence in which the variable appears. Universal quantifiers (for all) and existential quantifiers (for some) are both variable quantifiers (Luger and Stubblefield 1989, 50–51).

Variable rule A rule that contains one or more variables. Such rules are necessary in all but the most simplistic expert systems. The use of variables in a rule greatly reduces the number of rules required in an expert system because a variety of facts can be substituted for the variables (Harmon and King 1985, 43–44).

Vector 1. A one-dimensional array. Example: #(a b c). It differs from a list in that a member of a vector can be accessed more quickly than a member of a list. The disadvantages of vectors for artificial intelligence programming include having to be declared at runtime, having a fixed number of elements, and having to contain homogeneous objects.   2. The rough equivalent of a LISP list in production systems.   3. A set of elements of the same type in C++. A vector is used as a tool for building higher-level structures, maximizing runtime efficiency, and minimizing memory overhead (Young 1987, 288–292; Brownston et al 1986, 177–181).

Vector attribute An attribute in OPS5 production systems which can take on more than one scalar value at the same time. An example is the vector attribute passengers. The names of the passengers are the different values. Another example is the attribute purse contents. The scalar values could include a mirror, comb, wallet, Kleenex, and so on (Brownston et al 1986, 457; Rosenberg 1986, 191).

Venn diagram A graph used to represent the amount of overlap among different sets of objects. Example: a set of objects that can live in the water and a set of objects which give live birth. The overlap between the two sets of objects is those objects that can both live in the water and give live birth (Harmon and King 1985, 48).

Verb The predicate in PROLOG.

Verbal learning The learning of verbal associations. EPAM is a computer program used to simulate verbal learning (Barr and Feigenbaum 1981 vol 3, 33–35).

Verbal protocol analysis A type of manual knowledge acquisition. In verbal protocol analysis the knowledge engineer requests the expert to think out loud. The knowledge engineer records the expert's statements. The knowledge engineer needs to ask questions to check the validity of the statements. In psychology, this approach is referred to as introspection (Parsaye and Chignell 1988, 344–346).

Verification Ensuring that a program has been developed in a formally correct way in accordance with a specified methodology, and that it is error free and runs as specified. The demonstration of the consistency, completeness, and correctness of the AI program. Verification is more concerned with the nuts and bolts of program development than is validation (Geissman and Schultz 1988, 27).

Version management The ability of an object-oriented data base management system to save an old version of an object and retrieve it if needed. This is frequently needed in CAD systems (Zaniolo et al 1986, 53)

Version space 1. A data structure for representing a concept. The conceptual description of a set of training examples.   2. A data structure for representing the space of all concept descriptions consonant with the current training experiences. 3. A learning methodology that uses specific training instances to establish constraints, refine the data structure, and crystallize the concept of interest. The classic example is the concept of an arch. A training instance may be presented to the program which is not an example of an arch. The program uses the characteristics of this negative example as a means of discriminating why this example is not an arch. The constraints found are used to restrict the concept of the arch. A training instance may be presented of an arch which is identified as truly being an arch. The characteristics of that arch are analyzed and these characteristics are used to expand the concept of what an arch is. Both discrimination and generalization are used to crystallize the concept (Jackson 1986, 196–200; Barr and Feigenbaum 1981 vol 2, 121; Rosenberg 1986, 192; Fischler and Firschein 1987, 147–149; Barr and Feigenbaum 1981 vol 3, 385–400; Chabris 1989, 304; Smith 1989, 206).

Version-space method A type of data-driven example-learning program. The representation technique in version space is similar for both examples and the rules which are derived from the examples. This approach greatly simplifies search and interpretation (Barr and Feigenbaum 1981 vol 3, 369).

Version-space model A model that uses a version space and the candidate-elimination algorithm to distill a concept. The version space is a combination of all possible combinations of features. The version-space model is not dependent on the order of presentation of the examples. The candidate-elimination algorithm is used to build a version space. The result of the use of the candidate-elimination algorithm and the version space is a description of a concept that has been distilled from the examples (Chabris 1989, 213–216).

Vertex 1. The point where two edges meet. 2. A synonym for node (Chabris 1989, 304; Jackson 1986, 52).

Viewpoint The ability of some expert systems to reason about a number of alternatives at the same time. Multiple worlds is a synonym (Walters and Nielsen 1988, 258; Barr and Feigenbaum 1981 vol 3, 141–142; Harmon and Maus 1988, 58–59).

Virtual A reserved word in Turbo Pascal which ensures that the method with which it is associated is a virtual method (Duntemann 1989, 141).

Virtual function A function that permits a derived class to utilize a specialized version of a base-class member function. This type of function is found in C++ and it allows the programmer to redefine the function for each subsequent derived class (Stroustrup 1987, 201–203; Miller Aug 1989, 63).

Virtual memory A procedure that keeps in memory only the portion of a program currently needed. Artificial intelligence applications typically require a great amount of memory. Virtual memory can be an important adjunct in such programs. The drawback is that there is more disk accessing, which results in a slower-running program (Mishkoff 1986, G-4).

Virtual method 1. A method created at runtime. 2. A method that is late binding. In Smalltalk all methods are late binding. A virtual method can be replaced after a compile time. In Turbo Pascal the user has a choice of late binding or early binding. *Compare with* Static method (Duntemann 1989, 141; Shafer Sep/Oct 1989, 66; Fleener 1989, 94).

Visible unit Processing elements that are directly connected to the environment in neural nets. *Contrast with* Hidden unit (Ingraham et al 1988, 17).

Vision The reception, processing, and understanding of visual images in AI. The information processing chore of comprehending a scene from its images (Ballard and Brown 1985, 245–261; Chabris 1989, 305; Marr 1982).

VISIONS A model-based vision system that uses a blackboard architecture to recognize objects (Johnson 1986, 145–146; Mishkoff 1986, 5–13).

Vocorder representation A method of encoding human speech. Speech is treated as an acoustic signal and the signal is broken up into its component wavebands. Only an approximation of the true signal is used because the true signal would be far too complicated to process. Two other methods of encoding human speech are linear predictive coding and formant representation (Forsyth and Naylor 1985, 42–45).

Von Neumann bottleneck The constraints in calculation ability brought about by the Von Neumann architecture which dictates one step at a time (Waldrop 1987, 114; Chabris 1989, 305).

Von Neumann Machine It consists of a central processing unit and memory. The CPU fetches, executes, and returns. It treats data and programs in the same way. Most current computers are based on the Von Neumann Machine. *Contrast with* Parallel machine (Lazarev 1987, 59–60; Townsend 1987a, 16; Townsend 1987b, 387).

Walkthrough The domain expert walking through a typical task with a knowledge engineer (Wolfgram et al 1987, 310).

Waltz effect The principle that holds that with more detailed description, more constraints are identified and objects are more easily recognized and more readily analyzable (Winston 1979, 70).

Waltz filtering A type of boolean constraint propagation. The use of constraints reduces size of the search space and decreases the probability of combinatorial explosion. Labeling of parts of the object is the constraint procedure utilized. Waltz filtering was first applied to vision problems (Barr and Feigenbaum, 1981 vol 3, 164–167).

Waltz's algorithm The algorithm used to ascertain the orientation of vertices in three-dimensional blocks-world images. It uses constraint propagation (Chabris 1989, 305).

WAVE An interactive robotics-control language built at Stanford. A successor program, VAL, is based on WAVE (Mishkoff 1986, 5–19; Rosenberg 1986, 195).

Weak AI AI as a means of understanding cognitive behavior and producing useful computer applications which simulate human thinking. *Contrast with* Strong AI (Chabris 1989, 305).

Weakest-link method A rule of fuzzy logic. Rather than simply performing an evaluation that returns true or false, fuzzy logic allows an evaluation of a rule with a number ranging from 0 to 1. The weakest-link method returns the minimum value of the subgoals of a rule. Example: If A (.2) and B (.5) THEN C. This rule will return .2, the minimum value, as the answer to the rule. *Contrast with* Strongest-link method (Schildt 1987, 249–252).

Weak link Rules that do not share conditions or hypotheses, in the expert system NEXPERT Object, but are still declared to be related. *See also* Strong link (Epp et al 1988, 825).

Weak methods 1. An artificial intelligence problem-solving method which does not use domain knowledge to improve performance 2. One of a class of general problem-solving methods which includes uniform representation, sound inference rules, generate and test, blind search, means end, problem reduction, and hill climbing. These methods rely more on reasoning and less on domain knowledge. Weak methods are used in GPS and resolution-theorem-proving programs. Production systems use weak methods as well as strong methods. Weak methods have been replaced, or supplemented, by pattern-directed inference systems in expert system development. Pattern directed inference systems rely more on domain knowledge for their strength. The problem with procedural problem-solving procedures is that known procedures do not exist for solving many problems. *Contrast with* Procedural problem-solving procedure which is more efficient (Hayes-Roth et al 1983, 402; Rosenberg 1986, 195; Jackson 1986, 19; Chabris 1989, 305; Luger and Stubblefield 1989, 410, 434–435, 596).

Weak search A class of search procedures which do not use heuristics. Breadth-first search and depth-first search are weak search procedures. Weak search is equivalent to blind search.

Weak typing A language that does not require the declaration of variables prior to the execution of a program. LISP, OPS5, and most versions of PROLOG are weak-typed languages. Pascal and C are strong-typed languages. Weak typing promotes great flexibility. In PROLOG, for example, a given variable may be instantiated to a simple atom, or the same variable may be instantiated to a complex structure (Kenig Nov 1986, 64).

Weight A number that represents the strength of a connection between two units in a neural net (Obermeier and Barron 89, 219).

Weighted average A method for calculating confidence factors. Assume a set of rules with the same conclusion. Each rule has confidence factors for each premise and a confidence factor for its conclusion. Multiply the confidence factors in rule one. Do the same for subsequent rules. Add the results from each rule and divide this result by the sum of the premise confidence factors. Other methods of calculating confidence factors include confirmative of minimums, confirmative of products, maximum of minimums, maximum of products, average of minimums, and average of products. The problem at hand dictates the most appropriate method for computing confidence factors (Shafer May/Jun 1989, 71).

Weighting A variant of resolution in which priorities are placed on different components of a problem. The priorities control which components will be used and how the problem will be solved (Tello 1988, 419).

Weiner, Norbert The creator of Cybernetics.

Weisenbaum, Joseph The researcher who is best known for his development of ELIZA, a famous artificial intelligence program that mimicked the advice given by a Rogerian psychotherapist. ELIZA looks for certain keywords from the input and processes the input, based on the keywords, in such a way as to make a somewhat intelligent response. More recently he has been a voice in the wilderness, warning of the dangers of artificial intelligence. He is concerned we will abandon our decision-making role and become superfluous. More optimistic voices see artificial intelligence programs as aids in decision making (Johnson 1986, 265–271; Schildt 1987, 3).

Well-formed formula (WFF) A symbolic expression in first-order logic which has been constructed using terms, atomic formulas, connectives, and quantifiers. A proposition or a compound proposition (Parsaye and Chignell 1988, 402; Hayes-Roth et al 1983, 63; Barr and Feigenbaum 1981 vol 1, 164).

Well-founded relation A relation in which no infinite descending chain exists (Savory 1988, 240).

Well-structured knowledge base A knowledge base consisting of well-structured rules (Pedersen 1989, 44).

Well-structured rule A rule that does not produce multiple conclusions, avoids the else statement, and is not procedural. Well-structured rules increase clarity and decrease debugging problems (Pedersen 1989, 44, 47).

WEST An intelligent computer-aided instructional system that tutors students in mathematics. The program has an internal model of the best moves the student can make. When the student does not make the best move it attempts to infer what mistake the student made. It then gives advice to the student and allows the student to take a turn over. The emphasis is on developing diagnostic strategies for best dealing with student errors, and tutoring strategies which best hint at getting the student back on the right track (Waldrop 1987, 211–212; Barr and Feigenbaum 1981 vol 2, 254–260).

WFF *See* Well-formed formula.

What if Describing a term most often associated with spreadsheet models but also useful in expert systems. The process is as follows: once a set of data have been entered, questions have been answered, and a conclusion has been reached, changing a portion of the data of answering a question differently to see how the conclusion would be altered.

Whencached A command used in the expert system shell M1 to start forward chaining (AI Expert Jun 1987, 27).

When-deleted demon A type of demon called into action when a value has been deleted from a slot in a frame (Matthews Sep 1987, 80).

WHENEVER A type of rule found in some rule-based expert system shells which acts as a demon. That is, a WHENEVER rule monitors all variables in the conditional part of the WHENEVER rule and the rule fires when the status of any of those variables is altered by another rule in the program. WHENEVER is similar to WHENFOUND (Shafer Sep/Oct 1988, 54–59).

WHENFOUND 1. A command used in some expert systems to cue a set of actions when a particular variable is instantiated. The expert system is temporarily suspended until the process is completed. 2. A command found in the M1 expert system tool that allows a given rule to fire any time the rule's antecedent becomes true. Usually a rule must wait its turn until the inference engine finally gets to it even though the fact needed for the antecedent was asserted into the fact base some time ago. The WHENFOUND command causes the inference engine to pay close attention to the rule, and to execute the rule as soon as the antecedents are proved true (Harmon and Maus, 1988, 112; Thompson and Thompson Nov 1986, 29).

When-modified demon A type of demon activated by a modification of a value. It may carry out such activities as sending a message to another object, or it may change the value of another slot (Matthews Sep 1987, 80).

When-needed demon A demon triggered when a value on a slot is being accessed (Matthews Sep 1987, 80).

Whitehead and Russell The authors of *Principia Mathematica*. They demonstrated that all mathematics is founded on logic.

Wholeness The degree of complexity of an expert system (Marcot Aug 1987, 44).

WHY An intelligent computer-aided instructional system that specializes in dealing with information which is not factual and which involves causal and temporal relationships.

Why processor A component of the explanatory part of an expert system which answers why a particular question is being posed by the expert system (Floyd MR/AR 1988, 66).

Widrow/Hoff rule A learning rule used in parallel-distributed processing systems, which has the capability of associating arbitrary input/output pairs and then learns to compute arbitrary input/output functions. It is also called the Delta rule and the least-mean-square algorithm (Caudill Dec 1987, 52).

Wildcard variable A type of variable used is some pattern-matching programs to match with a ground expression or another wildcard variable. The wildcard variable is not bound to the ground expression as a named variable is. A wildcard variable is usually represented as a question mark (?). A wildcard variable is used in relatively simple pattern matching (Luger and Stubblefield 1989, 270).

Wilks's machine translation system A system that can take as input simple English paragraphs and generate French. It utilizes semantic primitives. Choices among competing alternatives are made based on which alternatives satisfy the most preferences for how the words in the paragraph are most generally used.

Winograd, Terry The man known for the development of SHRDLU. It was the first program to integrate language ability with a capacity for reasoning.

Winston, Patrick The researcher who, in his doctoral dissertation, used the notions of hit and near miss to get a computer to learn the concept of an arch. More recently he devised a cup-learning program and a program called Macbeth. His textbooks, *LISP* and *Artificial Intelligence*, are considered classics (Johnson 1986, 89–91, 157–158; Schildt 1987, 204; Barr and Feigenbaum 1981 vol 3, 392–396).

Woods, W. The researcher who developed the expert system LUNAR, which was used to identify moon rocks. At the heart of LUNAR is an augmented transition network (ATN) which efficiently parses sentences. It determines if a sentence is grammatical and determines the role each word plays. This noun is the subject, this word is an adjective which modified this noun. ATNs recursively call different subprograms and use pushing and popping—putting the main program on hold while they check out a possibility. They make many decisions as they work. They remember what they discovered, including, this is a verb in the passive voice (Johnson 1986, 99–101, 108–110, 113–115).

Word-sense ambiguity The problem presented for natural-language systems by words having more than one meaning (Charniak and McDermott 1985, 13).

Word-sense disambiguation The major problem faced in machine language translation. How to compensate for the ambiguity of words (Charniak and McDermott 1985, 173).

Working memory A type of global data base for production expert systems. Working memory is considered part of the knowledge base of an expert system. It is usually the repository of data. Working memory consists of working-memory elements. A working-memory element is an object and its attribute value pairs. Working-memory elements can represent facts that are in working memory at the start of the program run, facts that are deposited as a result of the answering of a question by the user, or facts that are deposited as a result of an inference by a production rule. During a program run, working-memory elements are constantly being added, deleted, or altered. Working memory is usually more volatile than the other portion of a knowledge base, production rules. Working memory is sometimes compared to human short-term memory. A synonym is data memory. *See also* Production systems and Working-memory element (Neiman and Martin 1986, 56; Moskowitz Nov 1986, 218; Townsend 1987a, 129–132; Harmon and King 1985, 23–25; Brownston et al 1986, 457; Townsend, 1987b, 387).

Working-memory element A structure found in the working memory of a production system. The object consists of fields. The first field holds the name of the class of the working-memory element. Subsequent fields possess attribute value pairs. Example: (Person !name John !age 33 !sex male). In some production systems the working-memory elements have a time tag which tells how recently the element has been introduced into memory. The time tag can be used in conflict resolution. Time tags are found in an OPS expert system's working memory (Moskowitz Nov 1986, 218; Brownston et al 1986, 36–37, 457; Forgy and Shepard 1987, 35).

Working storage A synonym for dynamic data base.

World-dependent integrity constraint A restriction of the knowledge structure in frame-based systems which may be dynamically added or deleted from a knowledge base. *Contrast with* Model-dependent integrity constraint (Reimer 1986, 175).

World model A type of representation used in vision which focuses on information about volumes. The information is expressed in coordinates of objects. Two other types of representation are two-and-a-half-D sketch and primal sketch (Winston 1984, 335–336, 380).

Worst-case complexity Looking at a problem solution from the point of view of the most difficult case. In complex problems the worst case may be impossible to solve. In some problems the worst case occurs so infrequently it is possible to ignore it and focus only on the expected case complexity. (Charniak and McDermott 1985, 256).

Wrist The joint that attaches the robot hand to the arm (Rosenberg 1986, 197).

Wrist-force sensor A sensor used in robots that measures the forces and torque exerted on the wrist of the robot hand (Rosenberg 1986, 197).

Writer An access procedure used to write data to objects *(San Marco LISP Explorer)*.

WUMPUS An intelligent computer-aided instructional system employed as a coach in a game situation. The object of the game is to track down the dangerous WUMPUS. The skills taught are logic, decision theory, probability, and geometry. The WUMPUS game consists of four modules: the Expert, the Student Model, the Psychologist, and the Tutor. The Expert has rules which can be used to make judgments on the correctness of the move and it provides information to the Psychologist about which skills are currently needed and how the student is performing. The Psychologist uses information from the Expert to decide which skills the student is deficient in and which skills the student should next acquire. The Student Model is where information is kept about what the student knows. The Tutor uses information from the Student Model to choose the appropriate topic to discuss with the user about the game, explanations of what is happening, and what advice to give to the user (Barr and Feigenbaum 1981 vol 2, 261–267).

X, Y, Z

XCON An expert system used by Digital Equipment to configure mainframe computers. It is sometimes referred to as R1. A forward-chaining system that was developed using OPS4 and OPS5. XCON was the first commercially successful expert system. The use of production rules permits a great deal of modularity, allowing for relatively easy incremental expansion of the expert system as new computer configurations are added to the mainframe computer line. XCON is classified as a planning expert system (Townsend 1987a, 8–9; Harmon and King 1985, 155–156, 206–207; Townsend 1987b, 216; Merritt 1986, 30).

Xector A data structure used in Cm LISP in which each value of the data structure is the responsibility of a single microprocessor. Each processor holds one value of the data structure. In this way all values may be addressed at the same time (Hillis 1985, 33–37).

XPLAIN An expert system shell known for its sophisticated explanation system. The explanation system can answer three types of questions: (1) questions about the means being used by the program to solve the problem; (2) queries about the justification for certain recommendations; (3) queries about questions the expert system is asking (Jackson 1986, 210).

XSEL A successor to XCON. Like XCON it is used to help computer salespeople configure computer systems.

YAPS A production expert system shell that can have more than one data base each of which has its own set of rules. Rules may be added during a program run. Rules can act as demons.

It permits a combination of rules and object-oriented programming. The data elements are nested lists. The conflict resolution strategy is roughly similar to OPS5 (Brownston et al 1986, 362–364).

Zero-crossing A boundary line in a filtered image between two pixel groups that can be used to determine edges in the image. The boundary line is actually where the pixel points change signs from positive to negative (Chabris 1989, 305).

Signs, Symbols, and Numbers

123–tree   A balanced tree in which each internal node has either two or three children and in which all the leaves are at the same level (Bratko 1986, 233–241).

2½ dimensional sketch   A sketch that delineates the surfaces in the image and their orientation from a user-centered perspective. *Contrast with* Primal sketch (Chabris 1989, 285; Winston and Horn 1988, 335–338).

2–3 dictionary   A dictionary based on a 2–3 tree in which the data in the subnodes are stored in a left-to-right sequence. The internal nodes have labels that serve as signposts for searching the subnodes. An internal element with two subnodes contains the label of the minimal element of the rightmost subnode. An internal element with three subnodes holds the smallest elements of the middle and rightmost subnodes (Bratko 1986, 234).

2–3 tree   A tree that is empty, or one with only one node, or one in which each node has two or three subnodes and all leaves are of equal levels (Bratko 1986, 234).

$AND   A rule found in the expert system shell ACQUAINT with the unique characteristic of evaluating all premises even after one premise is proved false (Tello 1987, 266).

$OR   A rule found in the expert system shell Acquaint with the unique characteristic of evaluating all premises even after one premise is proved true (Tello 1987, 266).

&   The symbol used in logic to represent the logical operation of conjunction.

→   The symbol used in logic to represent the logical operation of implication.

Expert System Shells/Tools

Expert system shells are constantly updated, and prices change. Information that was correct at the time this book was written can become outdated. Use this appendix only as a starting point for further information.

ACQUAINT It supports forward and backward chaining, certainty factors, contextual rule sets, frames, demons, and fuzzy comparisons. There is a data base facility and a forms facility. It is possible to halt a consultation temporarily and browse through the knowledge base. As of this writing ACQUAINT has no looping capability, no facility for multiple-choice responses, and no list-processing abilities. Lithp System BV, PO Box 65, 1120 AB Landsmeer, The Netherlands (Tello 1988, 207–221; Tello Jun 1987, 265–272).

Actor An object-oriented programming language. The WhitewaterGroup, Technology Innovation Center, 906 University Pl., Evanston, IL 60201, (312) 491-2370.

ADS AION Corp., 101 University Ave., Palo Alto, CA 94303, (415) 328-9595.

AI-NET A neural net that learns by example and automatically generalizes to solve similar problems. The program has the property of graceful degradation. The expert system can be embedded into existing programs. The cost is $1,500.

AI-WARE, Inc., 11000 Cedar Ave., Suite 212, Cleveland, OH 44106, (216) 421-2380.

ALEX An expert shell based on Smalltalk/V for IBM-PC computers. It is used to build classification and fault diagnostic expert systems. Features include debugging facilities, windowing, and the ability to add new features. It can interface with Smalltalk, PROLOG\V, graphics, data bases, spreadsheets, and assembly language. Harris & Hall Associates, PO Box 1900, Port Angles, WA 98362, 1 (800) 4333-1983.

Arborist A decision-support program that utilizes operations research techniques to build decision trees. Potential fields for use include law, engineering, marketing, and financial planning. Texas Instruments Corp., PO Box 809063, Dallas, TX 75380, (800) 527-3500.

Arity/Expert A backward-chaining expert system written in PROLOG for IBM-PC computers. The program can connect to data bases. The cost is $295. Arity Corporation, 30 Domino Dr., Concord, MA 01742.

ART A high-end expert system tool. Features include: forward and backward chaining, logic-based programming, opportunistic rule application, incremental rule compilation, rule priorities, subgoaling, hypothetical scenario generation, comparative evaluation, time-based reasoning, planning, simulation, algorithms, consistency maintenance, asynchronous processing, and metaknowledge. It has a sophisticated tracing facility, color graphics, and an Englishlike language mode for rules and facts in the data base. It allows for the evaluation of different possible answers and helps select the best possible answer. The primary control mechanism is its blackboard architecture. It runs on Symbolic LISP machines. Prices range from $29,000 to $80,000. It should soon be available at C. Inference Corporation, 5300 W. Century Blvd., Los Angeles, CA 90045, (213) 417-7997 (Harmon et al, 1988, 146-154).

AutoIntelligence An induction expert system for the IBM-PC. Features include color graphic menus, graphs, and other visual aids. The rules generated can be elaborated with other expert systems. The cost is $495. IntelligenceWare, Inc., 9800 S. Sepulveda Blvd., Suite 730, Los Angeles, CA 90045, (213) 417-8896.

CxPERT This program can be embedded in C programs. It has backward and forward chaining, attribute value pairs, and rules. The rules can include multiple antecedents and multiple consequents. Rules employ the else clause. In forward chaining, the developer has flexible control over the order of execution of rules. The rules can include Englishlike descriptions of rules. Unknown is accepted as an answer. The program's frame-based component includes arrays of frames, dynamic creation of frames, multiple inheritance, and attached procedures. Text-processing capabilities are available. The latest version includes hypertext. There is no royalty fee and no copy protection. The program runs on IBM-PCs and costs $395. Software Plus, 1652 Albermarie Dr., Crofton, MD 21114, (301) 261-0264 (Wilson 1987, 73-77).

Envisage A PROLOG-based tool which is an OPS5 type of production expert system. Features include demons, simulation, fuzzy logic, and Bayesian probability. The price ranges from $8,600 to $21,000. The program runs on VAX mini- and mainframes and MicroVAX. Systems Designers Software Inc., 444 Washington St., Suite 407, Woburn, MA 01801, (617) 935-8009.

ES/P ADVISOR A text-oriented expert system. That is, the system will function well with knowledge in the form of complex instructions or regulations. It has an open-ended architecture so the user can resort to PROLOG when needed. Variable types include fact, number, category, and phrase. The program runs on IBM-PCs and costs $895 to $3,000. Expert Systems International, 1700 Walnut St., Philadelphia, PA 19103, (215) 735-8510 (Tello 1988, 146-151).

ExperOPS5+ An OPS5 expert system for the Macintosh. The program costs $500. ExperTelligence, Inc., Department P, 559 San Ysidro Road, Santa Barbara, CA 93108, (805) 969–7871.

Expert Ease A decision-support expert system. The program develops rules from examples, but can only achieve one goal. For example, all examples in one system would be directed toward the goal of transportation cost. The program runs on IBM-PC, DEC Rainbow, and Victor 9000 computers. The cost is $2,000. Human Edge Software, 2445 Faber Pl., Palo Alto, CA 94303, (800) 624–5277.

EXPERT EDGE A rule-based Bayesian probability expert system. The program will interface with popular spreadsheets and databases. EXPERT EDGE runs on personal computers. Human Edge Software, 2445 Faber Pl., Palo Alto, CA 94303, (800) 624–5227, (800) 824–7325 (in CA).

Expert-2 Mountain View Press, PO Box 4656, Mountain View, CA 94040, (415) 961–4103.

EXSYS A forward- and backward-chaining, if/then/else rule-based system. The system can handle more than 5,000 rules. Rules can have multiple antecedents and consequents. The OR connective is allowed. Knowledge is represented as object-value pairs. Depth-first search is used. The program has a command language and a rule editor. A nice variety of confidence systems are supported. The program has a limited what-if capability. External graphics and color graphics can be used. EXSYS can interface with data bases and external programs. A consultation report facility is available. The latest version includes password protection, invisible embedding, frames, blackboards, a compiler, voice synthesis support, and hypertext. A license is needed for runtime versions. Use this program with IBM-PC and AT computers. The cost runs from $395 to $5,000, depending on the level of sophistication required of the system. EXSYS, Inc., PO Box 75158, Contr. Stn. 14, Albuquerque, NM 87194, (505) 836–6576 (Harmon et al 1988, 71–79; Oxman 1989, 57–62).

1stClass HT An induction-based expert system shell. It includes hypertext, graphics, multiple help/reference windows, entry forms, a report generator, tracing, and instant replay capability. There are no royalty fees. It connects 1stClass software with other software and hardware. The program runs on the IBM-PC and costs $2,495. Less expensive versions are also available. Expert Systems, Inc., 286 Boston Post Rd., Wayland, MA 01778, (800) 872–8812 (Lane May/Jun 1989, 10–51; Marcot 1988, 77–80).

FLOPS Kemp-Carraway Heart Institute, 1600 N. 26th St., Birmingham, AL 35234, (205) 226–6697.

GoldWorks An expert system shell closely linked with Golden common LISP. The program offers frames, forward chaining, backward chaining, goal-directed forward-chaining rules, and object programming. The frame-based system uses demons and is capable of multiple inheritance. Knowledge-based partitioning and metalevel inference are present. Other features include lattices, sponsors, certainty factors, assertion relations, functional relations, LISP function relations, dependency information, truth maintenance, and agendas. GoldWorks interfaces with data bases, spreadsheets, and C. An on-line help and tutor comes with GoldWorks. It has a sophisticated editor, a frame browser, and an object inspector. Also available is a graphics module. It can address up to 15 megabytes of memory. Use with IBM-PC and AT computers. The cost is $7,000 plus. Gold Hill Computers, Inc., 26 Landsdowne St. Cambridge, MA 02139, (800) 242–LISP (Tello Jul/Aug 1989, 56–59; Somsel 1987, 75–78; Matthews 1987, 77–85; Tello 1988, 306–320; Harmon et al, 1988, 154–156).

GURU An expert system with its own data base, spreadsheet, graphics, natural-language facility, and report generator. GURU includes a wide variety of inexact reasoning. There are metarules, mixed forward and backward chaining, and multiple-rule-firing capability. Each rule can have a priority, cost, and test method. There are a variety of environment variables giving the user control over how the system responds to questions, certainty factors, strategies for dealing with unknown variables, and more. A set of rules can have its execution readiness sensitized or desensitized. The procedural instructions of the spreadsheet and data base are available through a Ready window, which allows procedural instructions to read data from a spreadsheet or data base as a result of a rule firing. Iterative loops are included. It also has a case-saving and replay facility. Calls to DOS are permitted. Data from Lotus 1-2-3 can be ported to the GURU spreadsheet. Relations among rules, variables and goals can be graphically displayed. IBM-PC, DEC-VAX 11, and DEC VAX Mate computers can use this program. Prices begin at $895. MDBS, PO Box 248, Lafayette, IN 47902, (800) 344–5832 (Tello Aug 1986, 281–285; Tello 1988, 240–265; Harmon et al 1988, 124–132).

Humble   An expert system shell based on the Smalltalk-80 language. The Smalltalk-80 language, when accessed, can extend the capacity of this expert system. The program has multiple inheritance, certainty factors, a network browser, blackboards, and frames. Use with IBM-AT computers. The cost is $1,300. Xerox Special Information Systems, 250 N. Halstead St., PO Box 5608, Pasadena, CA 91107-0608, (818) 351–2351 (Somsel 1987, 75–79).

IN-ATE   Automated Reasoning Corp., 290 W. 12th St., Suite 1D, New York, NY 11014, (212) 206–6331.

Instant-Expert   It has forward chaining, backward chaining, and mixed-inference strategies. The cost is $49.95. Human Intellect Systems, 1670 S. Amphlett Blvd., Suite 326, San Mateo, CA 94402, (415) 571–5939.

Intelligence/Compiler   A hybrid expert system with forward and backward chaining, goal-directed forward chaining, inexact reasoning, semiexact reasoning, frames, tables, and a relational data base. The rule base can be partitioned. The program includes multiple inheritance with exceptions and attached procedures as part of the package. The user can use the standard certainty factor computations that come with the system or program his or her own version of certainty factors. PROLOG users will find backtracking, the cut, fail, repeat, list processing, list processing predicates, and recursive rules. There are over 200 predicates available. These predicates are important in input/output functions. Other features of the program allow fact bases and rule bases to be saved or deleted from memory and new fact bases and rule bases to be introduced. The input/output predicates provide a wide array of text-processing and menu-building facilities. The user can define his or her own predicates, which greatly extends the power of the system. Both the AND and OR connectives are supported in rules. There is dynamic tracing. Master-scope provides a syntax checker and a means of cross-referencing rules and clauses having common predicates. The program is written in C and will interface with C and DOS. Access to dBaseIII, Lotus, and other data bases and spreadsheets is possible. Intelligence Compiler allows SQL Queries. It includes trigonometric functions. The built-in relational data base lets facts and frames be disk based, allowing very large systems to be built. Many relational commands like join, select, union, intersection, difference, and project can be used from within rules. Graphics and menu facilities can be enhanced through the purchase of programs from other companies. An on-line help facility and an on-line tutorial are included. The latest version includes hypertext capabilities. The company makes other products which can be used with Intelligence/Compiler. These products include Autointelligence, Expert Measure, Database Supervisor, Neural/Query, and IXL. The system uses incremental compilation, and no royalties are charged. The program runs on the IBM-PC. The price is $495. IntelligenceWare, Inc. 9800 S. Sepulveda Blvd., Suite 730, Los Angeles, CA 90045, (213) 417–8896 (Mercadal 1989, 66–69; Tello Feb 1988, 5–6; Tello 1988, 266–278; Oxman 1989, 57–62).

IXL A unique expert system program that uses symbolic data analysis, induction, and deduction to produce rule bases from popular data bases. The rule base derived can be further enhanced by using the company's expert system program called Intelligence/Compiler. The program runs on the IBM-PC and costs $495. Intelligence Ware, Inc. 9800 S. Sepulveda Blvd., Suite 730, Los Angeles, CA 90045, (213) 417–8896.

KBMS A knowledge-based management system for the IBM mainframe environment with the capability of working with installed data bases. It features forward and backward chaining, hypothetical reasoning, and object-oriented programming. AICorp., 100 Fifth Ave., Waltham, MA 02254–0156, (617) 890–8400.

KDS3+ A frame-based expert system which uses a blackboard. The cost runs $1,495. KDS Corporation, 934 Hunter Rd., Wilmette, IL 60091, (312) 251–2621.

KEE A high-end expert system tool. It has backward and forward chaining, frames with inheritance, object-oriented programming, limited logic programming, active values, multiple worlds, truth maintenance, multiple rule bases, and data base interfaces. It has a graphics editor which allows the construction of meters and gauges to help explain the reasoning of the system. It does not have an agenda manager. It runs on LISP machines. A new version runs on 80386-based computers. The cost is $9,990 and up. IntelliCorp, 1975 Camino Real West Mountain View, CA 94040–2216, (415) 965–5500 (Harmon et al 1988, 146–154).

KES A structured rule tool which has recently been ported to C. Facts can be single valued or multivalued. Attributes can be given a default value. It employs multiple instantiation. The condition part of the rules allows AND, OR connectives. KES uses one of three inference techniques. These techniques are production, statistical pattern classification, and hypothesize-and-test. The knowledge base contains four types of information. They are: schema, associations, actions, and free text. A schema is defined as a list of attributes in the attribute hierarchy including their values, sets, and other related information. Associations consist of the connections that associate the values of one attribute with those of another. Actions are instructions about how the data base is to be arranged. Free text includes such things as definitions and references. All variables must be declared before they can be used. User and expert confidence is available. The program has the ability to allow a user to halt the inference process temporarily so that the knowledge structure can be examined. A DISPLAY TREE can be used to examine the relationship among attributes. Its conclusion-justification facility is sophisticated, allowing for queries concerning the final conclusion, intermediate results, or all of the values that have an attribute of the same name. A Bayesian and a frame-based module should be available soon on personal computers. KES provides integration with other software programs. A KES knowledge base can be called from C. A finished expert system can be delivered on a mainframe. Software AE, 1600 Wilson Blvd., Suite 500, Arlington, VA 22209, (703) 527–4344 (Tello 1988, 180–185; Harmon et al 1988, 118–124).

Keystone Technology Applications Inc., 6621 Southpoint Dr., N. #310, Jacksonville, FL 32216, (904) 737–1685.

Knowledge Craft A high-end frame-based tool with procedural attachment. The inheritance mechanism is highly flexible and does not limit the user to the standard is-a inheritance. Logic programming, rule-based programming, object-oriented programming, and alternate worlds are all available. The logic-base component supports full resolution and the cut-and-fail predicates. There are data base management facilities. Event management is available for simulation and scheduling. A context mechanism and an agenda mechanism are included. A programmer's workbench and interface tools with graphics are present. There's a tool for developing a natural-language interface. The ability to use LISP, the underlying language, is present. The cost runs from $35,000 to $55,000. Use with Sun, Apollo, MicroVAX, and LISP computers. The Carnegie Group, Inc., 650 Commerce Court Station Sq., Pittsburgh, PA 15219, (412) 642–1900 (Harmon et al 1988, 146–154).

KnowledgeMaker An induction tool costing $99. Knowledge Garden Inc., 473A Malden Bridge Rd., Nassau, NY 12123, (518) 766-3000.

KnowledgePro An expert system with hypertext and interfaces to dBaseIII, Lotus 123, and computer languages. It can handle list processing, string manipulation, tracing facilities, menu-making facilities, procedural control, inheritance, and topics. Topics are the primary means of knowledge representation. They can contain commands like a procedure, store values like a variable, return values like a function, be assigned properties like frames, inherit values, be used in hypertext, and be placed in a hierarchy. *See* Topics, for more details concerning this unique concept. The rules in KnowledgePro are very flexible. They allow multiple antecedents, multiple consequents, and else statements. The iteration constructs "while" and "repeat until" are available. There is no built-in confidence factor system, but the user probably could construct one. The window system, on-line help, and tutorial are excellent. The Windows facility allows direct links to Excel and other programs that use Windows. There was no mention of royalty fees. The price is $495. Knowledge Garden Inc., 473A Malden Bridge Rd., Nassau, NY 12123, (518) 766–3000 (Rasmus Sep/Oct 1989, 47–49, 57; Shepard 1988, 69–71; Oxman 1989, 57–62; Shafer 1988, 37–39).

LEVEL5 There are two LEVEL5s—LEVEL5 FOCUS and LEVEL5 OBJECT. LEVEL5 was originally Insight2+, a backward-chaining, unstructured rule-based system that evolved into a more advanced system. It uses forward chaining, backward chaining, mixed chaining, complex pattern matching, methods, dynamic agendas, hyper-regions, and hybrid knowledge representations. LEVEL5 also features enhanced debugging tools, debugging facilities, a graphics user interface, external program execution, higher mathematical operations, a goal outline, confidence levels, and sophisticated connectivity with many diverse data sources including FOCUS. LEVEL5 OBJECT is capable of inheritance and now functions with Microsoft Windows. Both programs run on IBM-PCs, IBM mainframes, DEC VAC, and Macintosh computers. Information Builders, Inc., 1250 Broadway, New York, NY 10001, (800) 444–4303 (Fichtelman 1986, 75–78; Tello 1988, 137–145; Harmon et al, 1988, 71–79; D'Ambrosio 1985, 345–347; Oxman 1989, 57–62).

M1 A backward-chaining rule-based system. It does not have rule-base partitioning. Features include certainty factors, multiple instantiation, an input-forms facility, multiple windows, metafacts, presuppositions, a cache, recursion, list processing, metarules, metapropositions, a WHEN-FOUND facility, floating point math, an interactive data base, limited forward chaining, automatic question generation, and the ability to check responses for validity. The OR connective is available. M1 has the ability to define new operators. It can produce displays in ordinary English, rather than cryptic "computerese." A text-trace facility can produce a report of a consultation. There is no built-in editor making debugging difficult. A finished expert system can be delivered on a mainframe. The program runs on IBM-PCs. Prices begin at $7,500. Teknowledge, 1850 Embarcadero Rd., Palo Alto, CA 94303, (415) 424–9955 (Tello 1988, 152–163; Harmon et al 1988, 106–117).

MacSMARTS A rule-based forward- and backward-chaining system with an induction component. It has the capacity for object-oriented secondary links with HyperText and HyperGraphics. Other features include modular construction, import-export facility, an integrated editor, context-sensitive on line help, report-generation facilities, and retention of answers across knowledge-based transfers. It has graphics capabilities and takes advantage of the Macintosh interface. The program runs on the Macintosh and costs $149.

Cognition Technology, 55 Wheeler St., Cambridge, MA 02138, (617) 492-0246.

Nestor Development System A neural network system using the 36 RCE paradigm. The cost is $9,600. Nestor, Inc., One Richmond Square, Providence, RI 02906, (800) 423-DISK or (401) 331-9640.

NeuralWorks Professional A neural network system. Control strategies include Hopfield, Adaline, Madaline, Back-propagation, Counter-propagation, Perceptron, Bidirectional Associative Memory (BAM), and TSP. The program costs $495 and runs on IBM-PCs. NeuralWare Inc, Penn Center West, Bldg. IV, Suite 227, Pittsburgh, PA 15276, (412) 787-8222.

NeuroShell A neural network development shell. Use with IBM-PCs and compatibles. The cost is $195. Ward Systems Group, Inc., 228 West Patrick St., Frederick, MD 21701, (301) 662-7950.

NEXPERT OBJECT A midrange hybrid expert system tool. The program's features include object and rule representation, integrated forward and backward chaining, inexact reasoning, incremental compilation, automatic goal generation, demons, methods, rule priorities, nonmonotonic reasoning, multiple and user-defined inheritance, classes, metaslots, a rule and object network browser, input forms, windows, a graphic knowledge editor, and graphics. All rules can be used in forward and backward chaining. How and why questions can be asked. Interestingly, the OR logical connective is not used. Floating point math is supported. Multiple choice menus can be incorporated into programs. NEXPERT OBJECT has direct access to relational data bases and can make calls to DOS. The latest version provides a bridge to the NESTOR neural network system. There is a royalty fee. Computers that can run this program include: IBM-AT, Macintosh, MicroVAX, Apollo, and Sun Microsystems. The cost ranges from $5,000 to $8,000. Neuron Data, Inc., 444 High St., Palo Alto, CA 94301, (415) 321-4488 (Rasmus Jan/Feb 1989, 49-72;

Rasmus Mar/Apr 1989, 38-41; Tello 1988, 293-305; Harmon et al 1988, 106-117).

OPS83 A forward-chaining OPS5 type expert system. It is strongly typed and interfaces with C and other languages. The program incorporates a flexible control strategy and procedural abilities with speed. The user has greater control and expression over rules than with the original OPS5 language. Use with IBM-PC. Production Systems Technologies, Inc., 5001 Baum Blvd., Pittsburgh, PA 15213, (412) 683-4000 (Nieman and Martin 1986, 54-63; Tello 1988, 222-239; Czajkowski 1990, 30-33).

Personal Consultant Plus The advanced version of Personal Consultant Easy. The program is designed on a frame-based system and employs rules in either a backward- or forward chaining mode. Demons are available. The knowedge base consists of contexts, parameters, and production rules. Contexts are produced by breaking up a large problem into subproblems. Contexts are roughly analogous to frames. A context can inherit values and rules. Parameters are the facts of the knowledge base. Parameters can be multivalued. Production rules can be assigned certainty factors and priorities through the utility and dobefore commands. Rule bases can also be partitioned. Default values can be assigned to variables in rules. User responses can be given with confidence factors. Other features include methods, mapping functions, self-referencing rules, and active values. Floating point math is supported. The how and why facility is supplemented by the ability to ask for more detailed text explanations. A REVIEW facility and a PLAYBACK facility allow the user to review earlier consultations. The snapshot facility allows the inclusion of graphics into the expert system. It can access popular data bases and the underlying LISP language. A graphics facility allows browsing of the frames. There is a royalty fee of $95. Use with the IBM-PC. The program costs $2,950. Texas Instruments Corp., PO Box 809063, Dallas, TX 75380, (800) 527-3500 (Tello 1988, 279-292; Harmon et al 1988, 106-117; Tello Oct 1987, 242-244; Oxman 1989, 57-62).

Personal Consultant Easy A rule-based backward-chaining expert system patterned after MYCIN. Some limited forward chaining is available. Knowledge is represented as attribute value pairs. The program's knowledge base consists of production rules and parameters. Parameters are the facts of the knowledge base. Parameters can be multivalued. Explanation facilities are present. Production rules can be assigned certainty factors. The snapshot facility allows the inclusion of graphics into the expert system. It can access popular data bases and make calls to DOS files. A graphics facility allows browsing of the frames. The program compiles incrementally. The menu interface makes entering rules easy. Utilities include a trace facility. It is upwardly compatible with Personal Consultant Plus. There is a royalty fee of $95. The program runs on the IBM-PC and costs $495. Texas Instruments Corp., PO Box 809063, Dallas, TX 75380, (800) 527-3500 (Shepard 1987, 73-79; Harmon et al 1988, 79-83).

Rbest Titan System, Inc., 20151 Nordhoff St., PO Box 2123, Chatsworth, CA 91313, (818) 709-9685.

REVEAL A type of business-decision-making software which combines a relational data base, a natural-language front end, a spreadsheet, and fuzzy sets to analyze numerical data. The program is capable of modeling, simulation, and decision making. It runs on an IBM-PC with 640K. McDonnell-Douglas, Knowledge Engineering Products Division, 20705 Valley Green Dr., Cupertino, CA 95014, (408) 446-6553.

RuleMaster 2 It includes an induction component. Program features include: an import-export facility, fuzzy logic, the ability to generate C code and link with external C code. An end-user interface has pull-down menus, windows, and English-language explanations. It has a forward-chaining paradigm. Rules can be added directly. It can also induce rules from fault tables. There are no royalties for runtime systems. Use with the IBM-PC. The price is $495. RADIAN Corp., PO Box 201088, Austin, TX 78720, (512) 454-4797 (Tello 1988, 173-179; Harmon et al 1988, 103).

Sierra OPS5 An OPS5 expert system with windows, an editor, incremental compilation, tracing, and debugging. The expert system can be embedded in C programs. Use with IBM-PC computers. The price ranges from $129 to $495. Inference Engine Technologies, 1430 Massachusetts Ave., Suite 306-I, Cambridge, MA 02138, (800) 2555-0625.

S.1 In S.1 knowledge can be factual, judgmental, or procedural. Features include a multi-window development environment, an English-like user interface, and an explanation facility. A finished expert system can be delivered to a mainframe. Use with Xerox 1100 series computers of LISP machines. Teknowledge, 1850 Embarcadero Rd., Palo Alto, CA 94303, (415) 424-9955.

Superexpert An example-based expert system. The program has backward and forward chaining, a new induction algorithm, import-export capabilities, a text editor, help screens, and tutorials. It is not copy-protected. Runtime versions are available. The price is $199.95. Softsync, Inc., 162 Madison Ave., New York, NY 10016, (212) 685-2080.

TIMM-PC An induction-based expert system tool. It is rule based. TIMM has the ability to reach conclusions and estimate the reliability of the conclusion even with very limited information. The development and consultation environment are mixed, making it easier to update the system. The drawback is that the user cannot produce runtime systems. Other features include a training feature and the ability to use existing rules to generate new rules. TIMM has a limit of only 25 outcomes. It is written in FORTRAN. It runs on an IBM-PC and on IBM mainframes. The cost ranges from $1,900 to $19,000. General Research, 7655 Old Springhouse Rd., McLean, VA 22102 (Tello 1988, 164-172; Harmon et al 1988, 100-102).

TOPSI An inexpensive version of OPS-5. The latest version features the Rete algorithm. Use with the IBM-PC. Prices range from $125 to $250. Dynamic Master Systems, PO Box 566456, Atlanta, GA 30356, (404) 565–0771 (Moskowitz Aug 1986, 261–264).

TURBO Expert An inexpensive backward-chaining expert system shell. The program, based on TURBO PROLOG, includes the source code. Use with the IBM-PC. The price is $89. The Berkshire Software Co., 44 Madison St., Lynbrook, NY 11563, (516) 593–8019.

TWAICE A rule-based expert system shell written in PROLOG. Logicware, Inc., 237 Park Ave., Suite 2136, New York, NY 10017, (212) 551–3536.

VP-EXPERT It includes an induction facility which generates rules. It is a backward-chaining shell with limited forward chaining. It has why commands, how commands, multiple instantiation, a graphic-trace facility, intelligent help, dynamic graphics, windows, mouse support, and what-if capabilities. The variables may be plural or dimensioned. The rules are Englishlike and support the else clause. The control structures include WHILEKNOWN and ACTIONS. Data base and spreadsheet searches are not limited to single cells. It is written in C for speed. Other programs may be run from within VP-EXPERT. VP EXPERT has a built-in editor. The latest version includes hypertext and supports SQL queries. The program runs on the IBM-PC and costs $124.95. Paperback Software, Inc., 2830 Ninth Street, Berkeley, CA 94710, (415) 644–2116 (Shafer Sep/Oct 1988, 54–60; Stoddard 1988, 73–77; Harmon et al 1988, 83–85; Shapiro 1987, 321–324).

Wizdom Expert System This program supports proposition and object-oriented programming, forward and backward chaining, fuzzy logic, frames, scenario matching and scanning, a semantic-definition language, incremental knowledge definition, and interactive knowledge maintenance. It can address up to 16 megabytes of RAM. The program runs on the IBM-PC and PC/AT. Prices range from $750 to $20,000. SIL, Inc., 1593 Locust Ave., Bohemia, NY 11716, (516) 589–1676.

WizdomMice Machine Intelligence Corp., 1593 Locust Ave., Bohemia, NY 11716, (516) 589–1676.

Xi Plus Portable Software, Inc., 650 Bair Island Rd., Redwood City, CA 94063, (415) 367–6264.

References

Ackley, D.H., G.E. Hinton, and T.J. Sejnowski. 1985. A learning algorithm for Boltzmann machines. *Cognitive Science*. 9: 147–169.

Addanki, S. 1990. Connectionism. In *Encyclopedia of Artificial Intelligence*, ed. Stuart C. Shapiro, 200–205. New York, NY: John Wiley & Sons.

Adiba, Michel, and G. T. Nguyen. 1986. Handling constraint and meta-data on a generalized data management system. In *Expert Database Systems,* ed. Larry Kerschberg, 487–504. Menlo Park, CA: Benjamin/Cummings Publishing Company, Inc.

Agre, P. 1990. Control structures. In *Encyclopedia of Artificial Intelligence,* ed. Stuart C. Shapiro, 211–219. New York, NY: John Wiley & Sons.

Allen, John R. 1987. The death of creativity: Is common LISP a LISP-like language? *AI Expert*. Feb: 48–61.

———. 1985. Speaking LISP. *Computer Language*. July: 27–33.

Amir, Shawn. 1989. Building integrated expert systems. *AI Expert*. Jan: 26–37.

Amsterdam, Jonathan. 1986. Augmented transition networks for natural language parsing. *AI Expert*. Premier: 15–21.

———. 1986. Building a flexible knowledge Representation Scheme. AI *Expert*. Nov: 19–22.

———. 1986. Constructing a better theorem-prover in PROLOG. *AI Expert*. Oct: 17–19.

———. 1986. Retrieving frames from a frame data base. *AI Expert*. Dec: 19–21.

———. 1987. Planning with tweak. *AI Expert.* Jan: 28–32.

———. 1987. Solving SFRL problems with a representation language language. *AI Expert.* Feb: 15–19.

———. 1988. Creating an adventurous language. *Dr. Dobb's Journal.* 138: 18–39.

Anderson, John., A. Corbett, and B. Reiser. 1986. *Essential LISP.* Reading, MA: Addison-Wesley.

Arcidiacono, Tom. 1988. Expert system on-call. *PC Tech Journal.* Nov: 112–135.

Arora, K. 1990. Frame theory. In *Encyclopedia of Artificial Intelligence,* ed. Stuart C. Shapiro, 308. New York, NY: John Wiley & Sons.

Austin, Scott. 1990. An introduction to genetic algorithms. *AI Expert.* Mar: 48–53.

Bailey, David, D. Thompson, and J. Feinstein. 1988. The practical side of neural networks, Part I. *PC AI.* Nov/Dec: 33–36.

———. 1988. Similarity networks. *PC AI.* Jul/Aug: 29–32.

Bailey, Roger. 1985. A Hope tutorial. *Byte.* Aug: 235–258.

Baker, Louis. 1987. ADA and AI join forces. *AI Expert.* Apr: 38–43.

Ballard, B., and M. Jones. 1990. Computational linguistics. In *Encyclopedia of Artificial Intelligence,* ed. Stuart C. Shapiro, 133–151. New York, NY: John Wiley & Sons.

Ballard, Dana, and C. Brown. 1985. Vision. *Byte.* Apr: 245–261.

Barber, Gerald. LISP vs. C for implementing expert systems. *AI Expert.* Feb: 28–31.

Barker, Don, and Chia-Ling Barker. 1990. Neuro-Shell. Common sense applied to decision making. *PC AI.* Mar/Apr: 48–52.

Barr, Avron. 1988. Interview. *PC AI.* Spring: 46–48.

Barr, Avron, and Edward Feigenbaum. 1981. *Handbook of Artificial Intelligence.* vols. 1, 2, 3. Los Altos, CA: William Kaufmann, Inc.

Baskin, Cathryn. 1986. Representing knowledge. *Byte.* Nov: 147.

Bates, Madeleine, D. Meltzer, and S. Shea. 1987. Designing a practical interface. *AI Expert.* May: 60–66.

Bates, Madeleine, M. G. Moser, and D. Stallard. 1986. The IRUS transportable natural language database interface. In *Expert Database Systems,* ed. Larry Kerschberg, 617–630. Menlo Park, CA: Benjamin/Cummings Publishing Company, Inc.

Bayle, Aime. 1988. Learning in neural networks. *PC AI.* Nov/Dec: 40–44.

Bernat, Andrew. 1986. Digitalk: Smalltalk/V. *AI Expert.* Nov: 77–81.

———. 1987. Actor goes on stage. *AI Expert.* Mar: 40–44.

Bharath, Ramachandran. 1988. How much information does a message contain? *Micro Cornucopia.* 41: 42–46.

———. and M. Sklar. 1985. Learning about PROLOG. *Computer Language.* Jul: 49–54.

Biermann, A. 1990. Automatic programming. In *Encyclopedia of Artificial Intelligence,* ed. Stuart C. Shapiro, 18–35. New York, NY: John Wiley & Sons.

Bisiani, R. 1990. Beam search. In *Encyclopedia of Artificial Intelligence,* ed. Stuart C. Shapiro, 56–58. New York, NY: John Wiley & Sons.

Blackman, Michael. 1990. CASE for expert systems. *AI Expert.* Feb: 27–31.

Boisen, Sean. 1987. Language processing: Using definite clause grammars. *AI Expert.* Jun: 46–56.

Borden, Andrew. 1987. Computer, know thine enemy. *AI Expert.* Jul: 48–54.

Brachman, Ron. 1987. Knowledge Representation: A shaky keystone? *AI Expert* Aug: 7–8.

Brachman, R. J. 1983. What IS-A is and isn't: An analysis of taxonomic links in semantic networks. *IEEE Computer.* 16(10): 30–36.

———. and Hector J. Levesque. 1986. What makes a knowledge base knowledgeable? A view of databases from the knowledge level. In *Expert Database Systems*, ed. Larry Kerschberg, 69–78. Menlo Park, CA: Benjamin/Cummings Publishing Company, Inc.

———. and B. C. Smith (guest editors). 1980. Special issue on knowledge representation. *Sigart Not.* 70.

Bratko, Ivan. 1986. *PROLOG Programming for Artificial Intelligence*. Reading, MA: Addison-Wesley.

Brice, C.R., and C.L. Fennema. 1970. Scene analysis using regions. *Artificial Intelligence*. 1: 205–226.

Brittain, Skona. 1987. Understanding natural languages. *AI Expert*. May: 30–38.

Brodie, Michael L. et al. 1986. Knowledge base management systems: Discussions from the working group. In *Expert Database Systems*, ed. Larry Kerschberg, 19-34. Menlo Park, CA: Benjamin/Cummings Publishing Company, Inc.

Brodie, Michael L. and Matthias Jarke. 1986. On integrating logic programming and databases. In *Expert Database Systems*, ed. Larry Kerschberg, 191–208. Menlo Park, CA: Benjamin/Cummings Publishing Company, Inc.

Brown, James, E. Eusebi, K. Fordyce, and G. Sullivan. 1987. APL and expert systems. *AI Expert*. Jul: 72–84.

Brown, Robert J. 1987. An artificial neural network experiment. *Dr. Dobb's Journal*. 126: 16–27.

Brownston, Lee, Robert Farrell, Elaine Kant, and Nancy Martin. 1986. *Programming Expert Systems in OPS5*. Reading, MA: Addison-Wesley.

Brynjolfsson, Erik, and T. Loofbourrow. 1988. An overview of expert system building tools for PCs. *PC AI*. Sep/Oct: 31–35.

Bulman, David M. 1989. An object-based development model. *Computer Language*. Aug: 49–59.

Burg, Jerry. 1988. The umbrella analyzer. *PC AI*. Sep/Oct: 12–14.

Butrick, Richard. 1987. Logic and knowledge representation in PROLOG. *Dr. Dobb's Journal*. 129: 30–38.

Carbonell, J., and P. Langley. 1990. Learning, machine. In *Encyclopedia of Artificial Intelligence,* ed. Stuart C. Shapiro, 464–488. New York, NY: John Wiley & Sons.

Carbonell, J., R. Michalski, and T. Mitchell. 1983. Machine learning: A historical and methodological analysis. *AI Magazine*. 2: 69–79.

Carey, Michael, David DeWitt, and G. Goetz. 1986. Mechanisms for concurrency control and recovery in PROLOG—A proposal. In *Expert Database Systems*, ed. Larry Kerschberg, 271–291. Menlo Park, CA: Benjamin/Cummings Publishing Company, Inc.

Castle, Tom. 1988. Certainty factors in Turbo PROLOG. *Turbo Technix*. Jul/Aug: 70–75.

Caudill, Maureen. 1987. Neural networks primer, part I. *AI Expert*. Dec: 46–52.

———. 1988. Neural networks primer, part II. *AI Expert*. Feb: 55–61.

———. 1988. Neural networks primer, part III. *AI Expert*. Jun: 51–59.

———. 1988. Neural networks primer, part IV. *AI Expert*. Aug: 61–67.

———. 1988. Neural networks primer, part V. *AI Expert*. Nov: 57–65.

———. 1989. Neural networks primer, part VI. *AI Expert*. Feb: 61–67.

———. 1989. Neural networks primer, part VII. *AI Expert*. May: 51–58.

———. 1989 Neural networks primer, Part VIII. *AI EXPERT*. Aug: 61–67.

Chabris, Christopher. 1989. *Artificial Intelligence and Turbo C*. Homewood, IL: Multiscience Press.

Chang, C.L., and J.R. Slagle. 1971. An admissible and optimal algorithm for searching AND/OR graphs. *Artificial Intelligence*. 2: 117–128.

Chapnick, Philip. 1987. From data base to knowledge base. *AI Expert*. Nov: 7–8.

———. 1988. The positive philosophy of no. *AI Expert*. Mar: 5–6.

———. 1988. AAAI 1988. *AI Expert*. Nov: 7–8.

Charniak, Eugene, and Drew McDermott. 1985. *Introduction to Artificial Intelligence*. Reading, MA: Addison-Wesley.

Citrenbaum, Ronald, J. R. Geissman, and R. Schultz. 1987. Selecting a shell. *AI Expert*. Sep: 30–39.

Clinger, Barbara. 1988. Definite clause grammars in Turbo PROLOG. *Turbo Technix*. Sep/Oct: 80–84.

Clocksin, William. 1987. A PROLOG primer. *Byte*. Aug: 147–158.

———. and Christopher Mellish. 1984. *Programming in PROLOG*. Berlin, Germany: Springer-Verlag.

Coffee, Peter C. 1988. Why LISP? *AI Expert*. Mar: 38–41.

———. and D. J. Strauss. 1988. Conventional languages and AI. *AI Expert*. May: 38–45.

Colmerauer, Alain. 1987. Opening the PROLOG III universe. *Byte*. Aug: 177–182.

Colvin, Gregory. 1989. SYNAPSYS: A neural network. *The C Users Journal*. Apr: 59–66.

Cooper, Thomas. 1988. *Rule Based Programming with OPS5*. San Mateo, CA: Morgan Kaufman Publisher, Inc.

Cornish, Merril, 1988. The right tool for the job. *Computer Language*. Aug: 55–61.

———. 1987. Tagging LISP: Hardware or software? *AI Expert*. Oct: 52–56.

Covington, Michael. 1988. The tail recursion tiger. *Turbo Technix*. Jan/Feb: 85–91.

Crawford, Robert. 1988. State space. Turbo Technix. Sep/Oct: 90–92.

Cromarty, Andrew, et al. 1986. Distributed database considerations in an expert system for radar analysis. In *Expert Database Systems*, ed. Larry Kerschberg, 505–524. Menlo Park, CA: Benjamin/Cummings Publishing Company, Inc.

Cunningham, Ward, and K. Beck. 1987. Diagramming objects. *AI Expert*. Nov: 52–58.

Czajkowski, Alex. 1990. Three case histories. *PC AI*. Jan/Feb: 30–33.

D'Ambrosio, Bruce. 1985. Insight—A knowledge system. *Byte*. Apr: 345–347.

Darlington, John. 1985. Program transformation. *Byte*. Aug: 201–216.

Davis, E. 1990. Commonsense reasoning. In *Encyclopedia of Artificial Intelligence*, ed. Stuart C. Shapiro, 833–840. New York, NY: John Wiley & Sons.

Davis, L. 1975. A survey of edge detection techniques. *Computer Graphics Image Processing*. 4: 248–270.

Davis, L. S. 1990. Feature extraction in *Encyclopedia of Artificial Intelligence*, ed. Stuart C. Shapiro, 300–302. New York, NY: John Wiley & Sons.

Davis, L., and A. Rosenfeld. 1981. Cooperating processes for low-level vision: A survey. *Artificial Intelligence*. 17: 245–263.

Davis, R. 1982. Report on the workshop on distributed AI. *Sigart Newsletter*. 73: 42–52.

Deering, Michael F. 1985. Architecture for AI. *Byte*. Apr: 195–206.

Deering, Michael F., and Joseph Faletti. 1986. Database support for storage of AI reasoning knowledge. In *Expert Database Systems*, ed. Larry Kerschberg, 527–536. Menlo Park, CA: Benjamin/Cummings Publishing Company, Inc.

Denney, Richard. 1988. Using keys to control backtracking. *AI Expert*. Jun: 44–51.

Dietterich, T.G., and R.S. Michalski. 1981. Inductive learning of structural descriptions: Evaluation criteria and comparative review of selected methods. *Artificial Intelligence.* 16: 257–294.

Dlugosz, John M. 1989. Object-Oriented Programming for C. *Computer Language.* Aug: 103–116.

Dos Reis, Anthony J. 1988. Theorem proving using semantic resolution. *Dr. Dobb's Journal.* Apr: 50–57.

Doyle, J. 1979. A truth maintenance system. *Artificial Intelligence.* 12(3): 231–272.

Duda, R.O., P.E. Hart, and N.J. Nilsson. 1976. Subjective Bayesian methods for rule-based inference systems. Proceedings of the AFIPS National Computer Conference. 45: 1075–1082.

Duff, Charles B. 1986. Designing an efficient language. *BYTE.* Aug: 211–224.

Dunn, James W., and M. J. Knox. 1988. Power PCs. *PC AI.* Spring: 20–27.

Duntemann, Jeff. 1989. Humpty-Duntemann's handy object-oriented glossary. *Dr. Dobb's Journal.* 156: 132–141.

Dyer, M. et al. 1990. Scripts. In *Encyclopedia of Artificial Intelligence,* ed. Stuart C. Shapiro, 980–994. New York, NY: John Wiley & Sons.

Eadline, Douglas. 1989. Making PROLOG Parallel. *AI Expert.* Jul: 34–42.

Eckel, Bruce. 1988. Building MicroCad: Design with C++. *Micro Cornucopia* 44: 32–37.

Eckert, Eric. 1989. The frame problem. *PC AI.* Sep/Oct: 52–54.

Eisenbach, Susan. 1985. Declarative languages. *Byte.* Aug: 149.

———. and C. Sadler. 1985. Declarative languages: An overview. *Byte.* Aug: 181–197.

Eliot, Lance B. 1987. Machine learning, Soar, and the art of PROLOG. *AI Expert.* Mar: 61–62.

———. 1988. International cognodynamics. *AI Expert.* Feb: 71–72.

———. 1988. Neurophilosophy and mind/brain modularity. *AI Expert.* May: 74–75.

Eliot, Lance B., and F. Holliday. 1988. Go directly to ADA. *Computer Language.* May: 55–60.

Emerson, Tom. 1987. Parsing formalisms. *AI Expert.* May: 54–59.

Emond, J.-C., and A. Paulissen. 1986. The art of deduction. *Byte.* Nov: 207–214.

Entsminger, Gary. 1988. Machinery of the Mind. *Micro Cornucopia.* 41:96.

Epp, Helmut et al. 1980. PC software for artificial intelligence application. *Science.* May 6: 824–830.

Erman, L., F. Hayes-Roth, V. Lesser, and D. Raj Reddy. 1980. The HEARSAY II speech understanding system: Integrating knowledge to resolve uncertainty. *Computing Surveys.* 12, 2: 213–253.

Evanson, Steven E. 1988. How to talk to an Expert. *AI Expert.* Feb: 36–42.

Feldman, Jerome A. 1985. Connections. *Byte.* Apr: 277–284.

Fernhout, Paul D. 1989. Simulating interacting intelligent objects in C. *AI Expert.* Jan: 38–46.

Fichtelman, Mike. 1986. Level five research: Insight 2+. *AI Expert.* Dec: 75–78.

Findler, N.V., editor. 1979. *Associative Networks: Representation and Use of Knowledge by Computers.* New York, NY: Academic Press.

Finin, Tim. 1986. Understanding frame languages. *AI Expert.* Nov. 44–50.

———. and David Silverman. 1986. Interactive classifications of conceptual knowledge. In *Expert Database Systems,* ed. Larry Kerschberg, 79–90. Menlo Park, CA: Benjamin/Cummings Publishing Company, Inc.

Firdman, Henry E. 1986. Components of AI systems. *AI Expert.* Premier: 81–85.

———. 1986. The importance of being earnest in selecting an expert system shell. *AI Expert.* Oct: 75–77.

Fischler, Martin A., and O. Firschein. 1986. The central role of representation: Intelligence and the computer. *AI Expert*. Dec: 42–49.

——. 1987. *Intelligence: the Eye, the Brain, and the Computer*. Reading, MA: Addison-Wesley.

Flamig, Bryan. 1987. Object-oriented programming with C++. *PC AI*. Winter: 18–26.

——. 1988. Software review. *PC AI*. Spring: 50–53.

Fleener, Kevin. 1989. Object-oriented Pascals: The next generation. *Computer Language*. Aug: 91–100.

Floyd, Michael. 1988. Expert system design from a height. *Turbo Technix*.Mar/Apr: 64–66.

——. 1988. Suitable for framing. *Turbo Technix*. Mar/Apr: 80–88.

Flynn, Anita M. 1987. GNAT robots. *AI Expert*. Dec: 34–42.

Forgy, Charles, and S. J. Shepard. 1987. Rete: A fast match algorithm. *AI Expert*. Jan: 34–40.

Forsyth, Richard, and Chris Naylor. 1985. *Hitch-Hiker's Guide to Artificial Intelligence*. London: Chapman and Hall.

Fox, Mark S., J. Mark Wright, and David Adam. 1986. Experiences with SRL: An analysis for frame-based knowledge representations. In *Expert Database Systems*, ed. Larry Kerschberg, 161–172. Menlo Park, CA: Benjamin/Cummings Publishing Company, Inc.

Freedman, Roy. 1987. Twenty-seven product wrap-up: Evaluating shells. *AI Expert*. Sep: 69–74.

Frey, Peter W. 1986. A bit-mapped classifier. *Byte*. Nov: 161–172.

Frude, Neil. 1983. *The Intimate Machine*. New York: The New American Library.

Fulton, Steven, and Charles Pepe. 1990. An introduction to model-based reasoning. *AI Expert* Jan: 48–55.

Furtado, Antonio. and Claudio Moura. 1986. Expert helpers to data-based information systems. In *Expert Database Systems*, ed. Larry Kerschberg, 581–596. Menlo Park, CA: Benjamin/Cummings Publishing Company, Inc.

Gabriel, R. P. 1987. Memory management in LISP. *AI Expert*. Feb: 32–38.

——. 1989. The common LISP object system. *AI Expert*. Mar: 54–65.

——. 1989. Implementing OOP. *PC AI*. Sep/Oct: 40–42.

Gasser, Les. Distributed artificial intelligence. *AI Expert*. Jul: 26–33.

Geissman, James R., and R. D. Schultz. 1988. Verification and validation of expert systems. *AI Expert*. Feb: 26–33.

Giboney, Vance. 1986. Conventional programming and expert systems. *Computer Language*. Aug: 53–60.

Gibson, Michael. 1989. The CASE philosophy. *Byte*. Apr: 209–218.

Glasgow, Barry, and E. Graham. 1988. Rapid prototyping using core knowledge bases. *AI Expert*. Apr: 26–34.

Goldberg, Morton. 1988. JSB: An AL simulation. *AI Expert*. Feb: 63–65.

Gomsi, Jeff, and M. Desanti. 1987. BOOPS and the relational data base. *AI Expert*. Nov: 60–66.

Graham, Paul. 1988. Common LISP macros. *AI Expert*. Mar: 42–53.

——. 1989. LISP flexibility: Using functions as data. *AI Expert*. Apr: 23–28.

——. 1989. A LISP query compiler. *AI Expert*. Jun: 21–26.

Guthery, Scott. 1989. Are the emperor's new clothes object oriented? *Dr. Dobb's Journal*. 158: 80–86.

Haley, Paul B. 1987. The search strategy for commonsense logic programming. *Byte*. Oct: 173–175.

Hansen, Augie. 1988. *Learn C Now*. Redmond, WA: Microsoft Press.

Harmon, Paul, and David King. 1985. *Expert Systems*. New York: John Wiley & Sons.

Harmon, Paul, Rex Maus, and William Morrissey. 1988. *Expert System Tools and Applications*. New York: John Wiley & Sons.

Harris, Larry R. 1989. Hypothetical reasoning. *AI Expert*. June: 56–59.

Harrison, Mark, and D. Tribble. 1986. Five-minute PROLOG. *Computer Language*. Aug: 65–68.

Harrison, Peter G., and H. Khoshnevisan. 1985. Functional programming using FP. *Byte*. Aug: 219–232.

Hasemer, Tony. 1984. *Looking at LISP*. Reading, MA: Addison-Wesley.

Hashim, Safaa H. 1988. Metalogic and expert systems. *Turbo Technix*. Mar/Ap: 89–97.

———. and Philip Seyer. 1988. *Turbo PROLOG Advanced Programming Techniques*. Blue Ridge Summit, PA: Tab Books.

Hayes, P. J. 1973. The frame problem and related problems in artificial intelligence. In *Artificial and Human Thinking*, eds. B. Elithorn and B. Jones, 45–59. San Francisco, CA: Jossey-Bass.

Hayes-Roth, B. 1985. A blackboard architecture for control. *Artificial Intelligence Journal*. 26: 251–232.

———. 1990. Blackboard systems. In *Encyclopedia of Artificial Intelligence*, ed. Stuart C. Shapiro, 73–80. New York, NY: John Wiley & Sons.

Hayes-Roth, Frederick, Donald Waterman, and Douglas Lenat. 1983. *Building Expert Systems*. Reading, MA: Addison-Wesley.

Henschen, L. 1990. Reasoning. In *Encyclopedia of Artificial Intelligence*, ed. Stuart C. Shapiro, 822–823. New York, NY: John Wiley & Sons.

———. 1990. Theorem proving. In *Encyclopedia of Artificial Intelligence*, ed. Stuart C. Shapiro, 1115–1123. New York, NY: John Wiley & Sons.

Hewitt, Carl 1985. The challenge of open systems. *Byte*. Apr: 223–242.

———. 1986. Concurrency in intelligent systems. *AI Expert*. Premier: 44–50.

Hillis, Daniel. 1985. *The Connection Machine*. Cambridge, MA: MIT Press.

Hillman, David. 1988. Bridging acquisition and representation. *AI Expert*. Nov: 38–46.

Hinton, Geoffrey E. 1985. Learning in parallel networks. *Byte*. 265–273.

———. 1990. Boltzmann machine. In *Encyclopedia of Artificial Intelligence*, ed. Stuart C. Shapiro, 80–81. New York, NY: John Wiley & Sons.

Horak, Karl. 1988. Borland International: Turbo PROLOG 2.0. *AI Expert*. Jun: 77–79.

Hu, David. 1989. *C/C++ for Expert Systems*. Portland, OR: MIS Press.

Hunt, Daniel. 1986. *Artificial Intelligence and Expert Systems Sourcebook*. New York: Chapman and Hall.

Ingraham, Diane, G. Kandola, and M. Pillon. 1988. Neural networks. *Micro Cornucopia*. 41: 16–20.

Intelligence Compiler User's Manual. 1985. Los Angeles: IntelligenceWare, Inc.

IXL: The Machine Learning System. 1988. Los Angeles: IntelligenceWare, Inc.

Jackson, Peter. 1986. *Introduction to Expert Systems*. Reading, MA: Addison-Wesley.

Jacobs, Jeffrey M. 1986. A LISP structure editor. *AI Expert*. Oct: 58–63.

Jay, Christopher, and R. Knaus. 1989. Frames in PROLOG. *AI Expert*. Mar: 19–24.

———. 1989. Picking the best PROLOG. *AI Expert*. Jun: 75–79.

Jenkins, Mike. 1987. Intelligent data bases and NIAL. *AI Expert*. Mar: 32–39.

Johnson, George. 1986. *Machinery of the Mind: Inside the New Science of Artificial Intelligence.* New York: Random House.

Jones, William P., and J. Hoskins. 1987. Back-propagation. *Byte.* Oct: 155–162.

Jorgensen, Chuck, and C. Matheus. 1986. Catching knowledge in neural nets. *AI Expert.* Dec: 30–38.

Josin, Gary. Neural-network heuristics. *Byte.* Oct: 183–192.

Kaehler, Ted, and D. Patterson. 1986. A small taste of Smalltalk. *Byte.* Aug: 145–159.

Kanal, L. N., and G. R. Dattatreya. 1990. Pattern recognition. In *Encyclopedia of Artificial Intelligence,* ed. Stuart C. Shapiro, 720–729. New York, NY: John Wiley & Sons.

Kang, Yue, and T. Bahill. 1990. A tool for detecting expert-system errors. *AI Expert.* Feb: 46–51.

Keller, Robert. 1987. *Expert System Technology: Development and Applications.* Englewood Cliffs, NJ: Prentice Hall.

Kenig, Marc E. 1986. LEAP: An alternative AI language. *Computer Language.* Aug: 30–32.

———. 1986. Procedural programming versus PROLOG. *AI Expert.* Nov: 59–65.

Kerschberg, Larry, ed. 1986. *Expert Database Systems.* Menlo Park, CA: The Benjamin/Cummings Publishing Company, Inc.

Ketonen, Jussi A. 1989. Toward reasoning about data. *AI Expert.* Feb: 44–49.

Keys, Jessica. 1989. The Citibank pension expert. *AI Expert.* Jun: 61–65.

Kimbrell, Roy E. 1988. Fuzzy data retrieval. *AI Expert.* Jul: 56–63.

King, Roger. 1986. A database management system based on an object-oriented model. In *Expert Database Systems,* ed. Larry Kerschberg, 443–468. Menlo Park, CA: Benjamin/Cummings Publishing Company, Inc.

Kleer, J.D. 1986. An assumption based TMS. *Artificial Intelligence.* 28(2): 127–196.

Klimasauskas, Casimir, C. 1988. Neural networks: A short course. *PC AI.* Nov/Dec: 26–30.

Knaus, Rodger. 1988. Faster and smarter queries. *AI Expert.* May: 13–18.

———. 1989. Executable data. *AI Expert.* Jan: 13–19.

———. 1989. An RDBMS kernel in PROLOG. *AI Expert.* Jun: 46–54.

Knowledge-Based Systems: A Step-by Step Guide to Getting Started. 1986. Dallas: Texas Instruments, Inc.

Knuth, C.E., and R.N. Moore, 1975. An analysis of alpha-beta pruning. *Artificial Intelligence.* 6: 293–326.

Kolokouris, Angelos T. 1986. Machine learning. *Byte.* Nov: 225–231.

Kosko, Bart. 1987. Constructing an associative memory. *Byte.* Sep: 137–144.

Kowalski, Robert. 1985. Logic programming. *Byte.* Aug: 161–177.

———. 1985. The origins of logic programming. *Byte.* Aug: 192–193.

Kuipers, B. 1990. Causal reasoning. In *Encyclopedia of Artificial Intelligence,* ed. Stuart C. Shapiro, 827–832. New York, NY: John Wiley & Sons.

Ladkin, Peter. 1987. Logical time pieces. *AI Expert.* Aug: 58–68.

Lagrow, Craig. 1986. Computervisions. *Computer Language.* Aug: 81–86.

Lane, Alex. 1987. Thinking in Turbo PROLOG. *Turbo Technix.* Nov/Dec: 94–98.

———. 1988. Trilogy: A new approach to logic programming. *Byte.* Mar: 145–151.

———. 1988. Logic and Turbo PROLOG. *Turbo Technix.* Jul/Aug: 92–94.

———. 1988. Turbo PROLOG 2.0. *PC AI.* Sep/Oct: 61–64.

———. 1989. Object oriented programming in C. *PC AI*. Jan/Feb: 11–16.

———. 1989. 1st-CLASS Fusion. *PC AI*. May/Jun: 10–51.

———. 1989. An end to dueling rules. *Byte*. Jun: 303–308.

———. 1989. Lucid. *PC AI*. Sep/Oct: 28–33.

———. 1989. What is an expert system? *PC AI*. Nov/Dec: 20–22.

Lassez, Catherine. 1987. Constraint logic programming. *Byte*. Aug: 171–176.

Lawrence, Stevens. 1985. *Artificial Intelligence: The Search for the Perfect Machine*. Hasbrouck Heights, NJ: Hayden Book Company.

Lazarev, Gregory L. 1987. Solving problems with PROLOG. *AI Expert*. July: 58–68.

———. 1988. PROLOG/V: PROLOG in the Smalltalk environment. *Dr. Dobb's Journal*. 145: 68–80.

Leaman, Claire M. 1989. Rule-based structural design in C. *AI Expert*. May: 28–34.

Lecot, Koenraad, and D. S. Parker. 1986. Control over inexact reasoning. *AI Expert*. 32–43.

Lenat, Douglas B. 1988. Computer software for intelligent systems. *Scientific American Trends in Computing*. 1 Special Issue: 68–75.

———. 1988. Knowledge Representation. *RPC AI*. Jul/Aug: 33–35, 69.

Lendaris, George G. 1988. Neural Networks, Potential Assistants to Knowledge Engineers. *The Journal of Knowledge Engineering*. Dec: 7–18.

Lesser, V., and D. Corkill. 1990. Distributed problem solving. In *Encyclopedia of Artificial Intelligence*, ed. Stuart C. Shapiro, 285–251. New York, NY: John Wiley & Sons.

Levi, G., and F. Sirovich. 1976. Generalized AND/OR graphs. *Artificial Intelligence*. 7: 243–259.

Levine, Daniel. 1989. The third wave in neural networks. *AI Expert*. Dec: 27–30.

Lieberman, H. 1990. Languages, object oriented. In *Encyclopedia of Artificial Intelligence*, ed. Stuart C. Shapiro, 452–456. New York, NY: John Wiley & Sons.

Ligomenides, Panos A. 1988. Experiential knowledge engineering. *The Journal of Knowledge Engineering*. 1–6.

Lipovski, G.J. 1990. Associative memory. In *Encyclopedia of Artificial Intelligence*, ed. Stuart C. Shapiro, 16–18. New York, NY: John Wiley & Sons.

Loveland, D. W. 1990. Completeness. In *Encyclopedia of Artificial Intelligence*, ed. Stuart C. Shapiro, 131–132. New York, NY: John Wiley & Sons.

Lowerre, B.T., and R.D. Reddy. 1980. The Harpy speech understanding system. In *Trends in Speech Recognition*, ed. W.A. Lea, 340–360. Englewood Cliffs, NJ: Prentice-Hall.

Luger, George, and William Stubblefield. 1989. *Artificial Intelligence and the Design of Expert Systems*. Menlo Park, CA: Benjamin/Cummings Publishing Company, Inc.

Mackworth, A. K. 1990. Constraint satisfaction. In *Encyclopedia of Artificial Intelligence*, ed. Stuart C. Shapiro, 205–211. New York, NY: John Wiley & Sons.

Maida, A.S. 1990. Frame theory. In *Encyclopedia of Artificial Intelligence*, ed. Stuart C. Shapiro, 302–312. New York, NY: John Wiley & Sons.

Manola, Frank. 1990. Object-oriented knowledge bases. *AI Expert*. March: 26–36.

Marcot, Bruce G. 1987. Testing your knowledge base. *AI Expert*. Aug: 42–47.

———. 1988. 1st-class expert systems: 1st-class. *AI Expert*. May: 77–80.

Marr, D. 1982. *Vision*. San Francisco, CA: W.H. Freeman.

Martins, J. 1990. Belief revision. In *Encyclopedia of Artificial Intelligence*, ed. Stuart C. Shapiro, 58–62. New York, NY: John Wiley & Sons.

Matthews, M. Haytham. 1987. PROLOG and C. join forces. *Computer Language*. Jul: 34–38.

———. 1987. GoldWorks. *AI Expert*. Sep: 77–85.

———. 1987. Maintenance and Language Choice. *AI Expert*. Sep: 42–49.

Maxwell, John, and M. S. Riggle. 1989. LISP macros for backtracking. *AI Expert*. Mar: 28–39.

Mays, Eric. 1986. A temporal logic for reasoning about changing data bases in the context of natural language question-answering. In *Expert Database Systems,* ed. Larry Kerschberg, 559–578. Menlo Park, CA: Benjamin/Cummings Publishing Company, Inc.

McCalla, G., and N. Cercone (guest editors). 1983. Special issue on knowledge representation. *IEEE Comput.* 17 (10).

McCarthy, J. 1980. Circumscription: A form of non-monotonic reasoning. *Artificial Intelligence*. 13:27–40.

McClure, Carma. 1989. The CASE experience. *Byte*. Apr: 235–244.

McGregor, John D. 1987. Object-oriented programming with SCOOPS. *Computer Language*. Jul: 49–56.

McMillan, Mike. 1987. Learn Logo before LISP. *AI Expert*. Mar: 46–55.

Menzies, Tim. 1989. Domain-specific knowledge representation. *AI Expert*. Jun: 36–45.

Mercadal, Dennis. 1989. Intelligence/compiler. *PC AI*. May/Jun: 66–69.

Merritt, Bonnie. 1987. Anatomy of a diagnostic system. *AI Expert*. Sep: 52–63.

Merritt, Dennis. 1986. Forward chaining in PROLOG. *AI Expert*. Nov: 30–42.

———. 1988. Rule based programming with PROLOG. *PC AI*. Spring: 64–66.

Meyer, Bertrand. 1988. Exotic language of the month club. *Computer Language*. May: 81–87.

Michaelsen, Robert H., D. Michie, and A. Boulanger. 1985. The technology of expert systems. *Byte*. Apr: 303–312.

Michalski, R. S. 1990. Concept learning. In *Encyclopedia of Artificial Intelligence,* ed. Stuart C. Shapiro, 185–194. New York, NY: John Wiley & Sons.

Miller, Barbara H. 1988. The bookshelf. *PC AI*. Spring: 61–63.

———. 1988. An overview of knowledge representation. *PC AI*. Jul/Aug: 27–28.

Miller, William M. 1988. Error handling in C+. *Computer Language*. May: 43–46.

———. 1989. Multiple inheritance in C++. *Computer Language*. Aug: 63–71.

Minasi, Mark. 1988. The AI-approach to problem solving. *AI Expert*. May: 21–24.

———. 1988. Water jugs in the arboretum. *AI Expert*. Jun: 21–25.

———. 1988. Making searches more efficient. *AI Expert*. Dec: 21–26.

Minker, J. 1971. An overview of associative memory or content-addressable memory systems and a KWIC index to the literature. *Comput. Review*. Oct: 453–504.

Minsky, M. 1974. A framework for representing knowledge. *Artificial Intelligence Memo 306. MIT AI Lab.*

———. 1985. Communication with alien intelligence. *Byte*. Apr: 127–138.

———. and S. Papert. 1969. *Perceptrons: An Introduction to Computational Geometry*. Cambridge, MA: MIT Press.

Mishkoff, Henry. 1986. *Understanding Artificial Intelligence*. Ft. Worth, TX: Radio Shack.

Missikoff, Michele, and Gio Wiederhold. 1986. Towards a unified approach for expert and database systems. In *Expert Database Systems,* ed. Larry Kerschberg, 383–400. Menlo Park, CA: Benjamin/Cummings Publishing Company, Inc.

Morawski, Paul. 1989. Understanding Bayesian belief networks. *AI Expert.* May: 44–48.

Morein, Robert. 1986. PD PROLOG. *Byte.* Oct: 155–165.

Morrill, Jane. 1989. CASE. *Byte.* Apr: 296.

Moskowitz, Leonard. 1986. TOPSI 2.0. *Byte.* Aug: 261–264.

———. 1986. Rule-based programming. *Byte.* Nov: 217–224.

Motro, Amihai. 1986. Query generalization: A method for interpreting null answers. In *Expert Database Systems*, ed. Larry Kerschberg, 597–616. Menlo Park, CA: Benjamin/Cummings Publishing Company, Inc.

Nachsheim, Philip R. 1989. Solving constraint satisfaction problems. *AI EXPERT.* Jun: 30–35.

Neiman, Dan, and J. Martin. 1986. Rule-based programming in OPS83. *AI Expert.* Premier: 54–63.

Newell, A., and H.A. Simon. 1972. *Human Problem Solving*. Englewood Cliffs, NJ: Prentice-Hall.

———. J.C. Shaw, and H.A. Simon. 1960. Report on a general problem-solving program. Proceedings at the International Conference on Information Processing. UNESCO House, Paris: 260–264.

Newquist, Harvey P., III. 1987. American Express and AI: Don't leave home without them. *AI Expert.* Apr: 63–65.

———. 1987. Machinery of medical diagnosis. *AI Expert.* May: 69–71.

———. 1987. Will the real AI language please stand up? *Computer Language.* Jul: 58–59.

———. 1988. Intelligent data: Getting to first base. *AI Expert.* Jan: 21–24.

———. 1988. Braining the expert. *AI Expert.* Feb: 67–69.

Newton, Mike, and J. Watkins. 1988. The combination of logic and objects for knowledge representation. *Journal of Object-Oriented Programming.* Nov/Dec: 7–10.

Nilsson, Nils. 1980. *Principles of Artificial Intelligence*. Palo Alto, CA: Morgan Kaufman Publisher, Inc.

Nutter, J.T. 1990. Default reasoning. In *Encyclopedia of Artificial Intelligence,* ed. Stuart C. Shapiro, 840–848. New York, NY: John Wiley & Sons.

Obermeier, Klaus K. 1987. Natural-language processing. *Byte.* Dec: 225–232.

———. and J. J. Barron. 1989. Time to get fired up. *Byte.* Aug: 217–224.

Olan, Michael. 1988. Unconventional design. *Computer Language.* May: 36–41.

Olsen, Bruce, B. Pumplin, and M. Williamson. 1987. The getting of wisdom: PC expert system shells. *Computer Language.* Mar: 117–146.

Olson, Judith R., and H. Rueter. 1988. Extracting expertise from experts: Methods for knowledge acquisition. Heuristics. *The Journal of Knowledge Engineering.* Dec: 21–41.

Oman, Paul. 1988. IEEE Software. Moscow, ID: Computer Science Dept., University of Idaho.

OOP in the real world. *PC AI.* Sep/Oct: 37–38, 66.

Oxman, Steven. 1985. The quiet revolution in the expert system area. *Heuristics.* Jun: 57–62.

PAO, Yoh-Han. 1989. Functional link nets: Removing hidden layers. *AI Expert.* Apr: 60–68.

Parker, D. Stott, Jr. et al. 1986. Logic programming and databases. In *Expert Database Systems,* ed. Larry Kerschberg, 35–48. Menlo Park, CA: Benjamin/Cummings Publishing Company, Inc.

Parsaye, Kamran. 1988. Acquiring and verifying knowledge automatically. *AI Expert.* May: 48–63.

———. 1989. Machine learning: The next frontier. *PC AI.* Jul/Aug: 26–32.

———. and Mark Chignell. 1988. *Expert Systems for Experts*. New York: John Wiley & Sons.

References

Parsaye, Kamran, Mark Chignell, Setrag Khoshafian and Harry Wong. 1990. Intelligent databases. *AI Expert*. Mar: 38–47.

Pascoe, Geoffrey A. 1986. Elements of object-oriented programming. *Byte*. Aug: 139–144.

Pearl, J. 1984. *Heuristics: Intelligent Search Strategies for computer problem solving*. Reading, MA: Addison-Wesley.

———. 1990. Bayesian decision methods. In *Encyclopedia of Artificial Intelligence,* ed. Stuart C. Shapiro, 48–56. New York, NY: John Wiley & Sons.

Pedersen, Ken. 1988. Connecting expert systems and conventional environments. *AI Expert*. May: 26–34.

———. 1989. Well-structured knowledge bases. *AI Expert*. Apr: 44–55.

———. 1989. Well-structured knowledge bases, part II. *AI Expert*. Jul: 45–48.

Perlis, D. 1990. Circumscription. In *Encyclopedia of Artificial Intelligence,* ed. Stuart C. Shapiro, 100–103. New York, NY: John Wiley & Sons.

———. 1990. Nonmonotonic reasoning. In *Encyclopedia of Artificial Intelligence*, ed. Stuart C. Shapiro, 894–853. New York, NY: John Wiley & Sons.

Peterson, Robert W. 1987. Object-oriented data base design. *AI Expert*. Mar: 26–31.

Peterson, Wayne. 1987. Simulation with OOP. *PC AI*. Winter: 33–37.

Petrick S. 1990. Parsing. In *Encyclopedia of Artificial Intelligence,* ed. Stuart C. Shapiro, 687–696. New York, NY: John Wiley & Sons.

Phillips, Jack S., and P. Sanders. 1988. First steps in prototyping. *AI Expert*. May: 64–68.

Pierson, Dan L. Four PROLOGS for the MacIntosh. *Dr. Dobb's Journal*. 126: 30–41.

Pohl, Ira. 1989. Data hiding in C++. *Computer Language*. Sep: 67–77.

Pountain, Dick 1986. Object-oriented Forth. *Byte*. Aug: 227–233.

Pugh, Kenneth. 1986. Abstraction in C. *Computer Language*. Feb: 26–28.

Quillian, M.R. 1969. The teachable language comprehender. CACM 12: 459–475.

Rapaport, Matthew. 1988. Designing with data bases. *Computer Language*. Oct: 91–98.

Rasmus, Daniel W. 1989. Nexpert object part I. *PC AI*. Jan/Feb: 49–72.

———. 1989. Nexpert object part II. *PC AI*. Mar/Apr: 38–41.

———. 1989. Knowledge pro. *PC AI*. Sep/Oct: 47–49, 57.

Rauch-Hindin, Wendy B. 1988. Problems with paradigms. *AI Expert*. Mar: 55–60.

Reece, Peter. 1987. Perceptrons and neural nets. *AI Expert*. Jan: 50–55.

Reedy, Matt, and R. Kaplan. 1986. Writing expert systems with Small-X. *AI Expert*. Oct: 64–72.

Reeves, Ray. 1989. Trilogy. *PC AI*. Sep/Oct: 34–36, 58.

Reimer, Ulrich. 1986. A system-controlled multitype specialization hierarchy. In *Expert Database Systems,* ed. Larry Kerschberg, 173–188. Menlo Park, CA: Benjamin/Cummings Publishing Company, Inc.

Reiter, R. 1980. A logic for default reasoning. *Artificial Intelligence*. 13(1&2): 81–132.

Rettig, Marc. 1987. Using Smalltalk to implement frames. *AI Expert*. Jan: 15–18.

———. 1987. Heuristic state space search. *AI Expert*. Mar: 15–19.

———. 1987. GPS: A simple planning algorithm. *AI Expert*. Apr: 15–19.

———. 1987. Planning with STRIPS in a simple domain. *AI Expert*. May: 17–21.

———. 1987. Marrying logic programming and data bases. *AI Expert*. Jun: 15–19.

———. 1987. PROLOG and SQL: A happy union. *AI Expert*. Jul: 19–24.

———. 1987. LISPs with class: Three object-oriented LISPs. *AI Expert*. Nov: 15–23.

———. 1987. Programming with constraints. *AI Expert*. Dec: 17–24.

———. 1988. Bertrand: A general-purpose constraint language. *AI Expert*. Feb: 15–18.

Reymann, Joseph. 1988. C inherits inheritance: A handful of C++ tools. *Computer Language*. May: 89–93.

Richards, Bradley L. 1988. When facts get fuzzy. *Byte*. Apr: 285–290.

Ricketts, Grant V. 1988. How to do more in less time. *AI Expert*. Jan: 46–52.

Roach, David, H. Berghel, and R. Rankin. 1989. PROLOG programming pitfalls I. *PC AI*. Mar/Apr: 46–47.

Roach, David, H. Berghel, and J. Talburt. 1989. Intelligent problem solving with strings. *PC AI*. Sep/Oct: 24–27.

Robinson, J. A. 1965. A machine oriented logic based on the resolution principle. *Journal of the ACM*. 12: 23–41.

Roland, Jon. 1987. C on the horizon. *AI Expert*. Apr: 46–55.

Rosenberg, Jerry. 1986. *Dictionary of Artificial Intelligence and Robotics*. New York, NY: John Wiley & Sons.

Rosenblatt, I.F. 1962. *Principles of Neurodynamics Perceptrons and the Theory of Brain Mechanisms*. Washington, D.C.: Spartan Books.

Rothman, Peter. 1988. Knowledge transformation. *AI Expert*. Nov: 28–35.

Rovira, Charles A. 1988. Creating back-chaining expert systems. *AI Expert*. Nov: 67–69.

Rozier, Laurence and Dan Shafer. 1989. Building a learning expert system in dBase and framework. *PC AI*. Jul/Aug: 40–47.

Rubin, Darryl. 1985. Natural language software. *Computer Language*. July: 43–47.

———. 1985. Smalltalk comes to the Micro. *Computer Language*. Aug: 27–33.

———. 1986. Pattern matching languages. *Computer Language*. May: 17–24.

Rumelhart, David, and James McClelland. 1986. *Parallel Distributed Processing*. vol 1. Cambridge, MA: MIT Press.

Salzberg, Steven. 1987. Knowledge representation in the real world. *AI Expert*. Aug: 32–39.

———. 1988. Machine learning moves out of the lab. *AI Expert*. Feb: 44–52.

Savory, Stuart. 1988. *Artificial Intelligence and Expert Systems*. New York, NY: John Wiley & Sons.

Schank, R.C. 1972. Conceptual dependency: A theory of natural language understanding. *Cognitive Psychology*. 3: 82–123.

Schank, R.C., and R.P. Abelson. 1977. *Scripts, Plans, Goals, and Understanding*. Hillsdale, NJ: Erlbaum.

Schank, Roger, and L. Hunter. 1985. The quest to understand thinking. *Byte*. Apr: 143–155.

Schildt, Herbert. 1987. *Advanced Turbo Prolog*. Berkeley, CA: Osborne/McGraw-Hill.

Schrodt, Philip A. 1986. Predicting international events. *Byte*. Nov: 177–192.

Schubert, L.K. 1990. Memory, associative. In *Encyclopedia of Artificial Intelligence*, ed. Stuart C. Shapiro, 593–594. New York, NY: John Wiley & Sons.

Schuler, Doug. 1987. Knowledge representation with CRL. *Computer Language*. Jul: 99–103.

Schur, Stephen. 1988. The intelligent database. *AI Expert*. Jan: 26–34.

Schwartz, Tom J., and D. Schwartz. 1988. AI trade trends. *AI Expert*. Mar: 62–65.

Sciore, Edward, and D. S. Warren. 1986. Towards an integrated Database-PROLOG system. In *Expert Database Systems*, ed. Larry Kerschberg, 293–306. Menlo Park, CA: Benjamin/Cummings Publishing Company, Inc.

Shafer, Dan. 1987. Expertelligence's PROLOG for the MAC: ExperPROLOG II. *AI Expert.* Jan: 75–78.

———. 1987. Interview with Dr. Adele Goldberg. *PC AI.* Winter: 38–39.

———. 1988. The ultimately flexible knowledge representation scheme. *PC AI.* Jul/Aug: 37–39.

———. 1988. Ask the expert. *PC AI.* Sep/Oct: 10–11.

———. 1988. VP-Expert 2.0. *PC AI.* Sep/Oct: 54–60.

———. 1989. Ask the expert. *PC AI.* May/Jun: 70–71.

———. 1989. Ask the expert. *PC AI.* Sep/Oct: 55–57.

Shafer, Dan, and P. C. Anacker. 1986. Micro data base systems: GURU. *AI Expert.* Nov: 83–87.

Shafer, Dan, and M. Golden. 1990. Rules to objects: A case study. *PC AI.* Jan/Feb: 55–60.

Shammas, Namir C. 1985. Cross thoughts. *Computer Language.* July: 11–12.

Shapiro, Ezra. 1987. AI, AI, oh! *Byte.* Jun: 321–324.

Shapiro, Stuart, editor. 1990. *Encyclopedia of Artificial Intelligence.* New York, NY: John Wiley & Sons.

Shaw, George. 1988. Forth shifts gears. *Computer Language.* May: 67–75.

Shepard, Susan J. 1987. Expert system tools: TI's personal consultant. *AI Expert.* Mar: 73–79.

———. 1988. AI insider. *AI Expert.* Feb: 9–12.

———. 1988. Knowledge Garden Inc.: KnowledgePro. *AI Expert.* Oct: 69–71.

Shepherd, Allen, and Larry Kerschberg. 1986. Constraint management in expert database systems. In *Expert Database Systems,* ed. Larry Kerschberg, 309–332. Menlo Park, CA: Benjamin/Cummings Publishing Company, Inc.

Shmueli, Oded, Shalom Tsur, and H. Zfira. 1986. Rule support in PROLOG. In *Expert Database Systems,* ed. Larry Kerschberg, 247–271. Menlo Park, CA: Benjamin/Cummings Publishing Company, Inc.

Shoham, Y., and D.V. McDermott. 1990. Reasoning, temporal. In *Encyclopedia of Artificial Intelligence,* ed. Stuart C. Shapiro, 870–874. New York, NY: John Wiley & Sons.

Simpson, Patrick. 1988. Bidirectional associative memory systems. *Heuristics, the Journal of Knowledge Engineering.* Dec: 50–57.

Skelly, Chris. 1987. Object-oriented programming in C: Objective-C. *Ai Expert.* Apr: 81–86.

Slagle, J., and M. Gini. 1990. Problem reduction. In *Encyclopedia of Artificial Intelligence,* ed. Stuart C. Shapiro, 762–767. New York, NY: John Wiley & Sons.

———. 1990. Pattern matching. In *Encyclopedia of Artificial Intelligence,* ed. Stuart C. Shapiro, 716–720. New York, NY: John Wiley & Sons.

Sleeman, D., and J. Seely Brown, editor. 1982. *Intelligent Tutoring Systems.* London: Academic Press.

Smalltalk/V Tutoring and Programming Handbook. 1986. Los Angeles: Digitalk Inc.

Smith, Raoul. 1989. *The Facts on File Dictionary of Artificial Intelligence.* New York: Facts on File.

Somsel, Joseph. 1987. NEXPERT Object and HUMBLE: Object-based shells. *AI Expert.* Nov: 75–79.

———. 1988. Smalltalk/V. *Computer Language.* May: 95–98.

Soulie, Fogelman, and C. Mejia. 1988. Connectionist learning networks. *Heuristics, the Journal of Knowledge Engineering.* Dec: 58–71.

Sowa, J. 1990. Semantic nets. In *Encyclopedia of Artificial Intelligence,* ed. Stuart C. Shapiro, 1011–1024. New York, NY: John Wiley & Sons.

Stabler, Edward P., Jr. 1986. Object-oriented programming in PROLOG. *AI Expert.* Oct: 46–54.

Stapleton, Lisa. 1988. Embedding intelligence: The new AI paradigm. *Computer Language* Aug: 97–98.

Steele, Guy L., Jr. 1984. *Common LISP*. Bedford, MA: Digital Press.

———. 1987. LISP: Stayin' alive. *AI Expert*. Feb: 5–6.

Stefik, M. 1981. Planning with constraints. *Artificial Intelligence*. 16: 111–140.

———. 1981a. Planning with constraints (MOLGEN:part 1). *Artificial Intelligence*. 16: 111–139.

———. 1981b Planning meta-planning (MOLGEN:part 2). *Artificial Intelligence*. 16: 141–169.

Stein, Jacob. 1988. Object-oriented programming and databases. *Dr. Dobb's Journal*. 137: 18–34.

Sterling, Leon, and Ehud Shapiro. 1986. *The Art of PROLOG*. Cambridge, MA: MIT Press.

Stevens, John K. 1985. Reverse engineering the brain. *Byte*. Apr: 287–299.

Stoddard, Joan. 1988. Paperback software: VP-Expert v.2.0. *AI Expert*. Oct: 73–77.

Stroustrup, Bjarne. 1987. *The C++ Programming Language*. Reading, MA: Addison-Wesley.

Suits, David B. 1988. Sometimes true and unequivocally indeterminate. *Computer Language*. Aug: 39–43.

Swaine, Michael. 1988. Programming paradigms. *Dr. Dobb's Journal*. 139: 100–118.

———. 1989. Babbit's guide to OOP. *Dr. Dobb's Journal*. 152: 114–117.

———. 1989. Parker's perceptions. *Dr. Dobb's Journal*. 156: 112–121.

Szpakowicz, Stan. 1987. Logic Grammars. *Byte*. Aug: 185–195.

Tanimoto, S. 1987. *The Elements of Artificial Intelligence*. Seattle, WA: Computer Science Press.

Tank, David W., and J. J. Hopfield. 1987. Collective computation in neuronlike circuits. *Scientific American*. 257: 104–114.

Tello, Ernest R. 1985. Knowledge systems for the IBM PC, part I. *Computer Language*. Jul: 71–83.

———. 1985. Knowledge systems for the IBM PC, part II. *Computer Language*. Aug: 87–102.

———. 1986. Guru. *Byte*. Aug: 281–285.

———. 1987. Object-oriented programming. *Dr. Dobb's Journal*. 125: 126–134.

———. 1987. The GCLISP 286 developer. *Byte*. Apr: 241–244.

———. 1987. Object-oriented programming in AI. *Dr. Dobb's Journal*. 126: 146–150.

———. 1987. Acquaint. *Byte*. June: 265–272.

———. 1987. Personal Consultant Plus. *Byte*. Oct: 242–244.

———. 1988. Intelligenceware: Intelligence compiler. *AI Expert*. Feb: 75–78.

———. 1988. *Mastering AI*. Indianapolis, IN: Howard W. Sams & Company.

———. 1989. Goldworks II. *PC AI*. Jul/Aug: 56–59.

———. 1989. *Object Oriented Programming for Artificial Intelligence*. Reading, MA: Addison-Wesley.

Tennant, H. 1981. *Natural Language Processing*. New York, NY: Petrocelli.

Tesler, Larry. 1986. Programming experiences. *Byte*. Aug: 195–206.

Thomas, Dave. 1989. What's in an object? *Byte*. Mar: 231–240.

Thompson, Beverly A., and W. A. Thompson. 1985. Inside an expert system. *Byte*. Apr: 315–330.

———. 1986. Finding rules in data. *Byte*. Nov: 149–158.

———. 1987. Hyping text: Hypertext and knowledge representation. *AI Expert*. Aug: 25–28.

———. 1987. Scripts and stories. *AI Expert*. Oct: 19–27.

———. 1987. Structure, bottlenecks, and knowledge acquisition. *AI Expert*. Nov: 25–28.

———. 1988. Numerical Experts. *AI Expert*. Jan: 15–18.

Thompson, William A., and B. A. Thompson, 1986. Knowledge + control = expert systems. *AI Expert*. Nov: 25–29.

———. 1986. LISP and Pascal: A tale of two languages. *AI Expert*. Dec: 23–29.

———. 1986. PROLOG from the bottom up. *AI Expert*. Premier: 23–28.

———. 1987. Creating expert systems from examples. *AI Expert*. Jan: 21–26.

———. 1987. Using Pascal to implement functional LISP. *AI Expert*. Apr: 21–28.

———. 1987. Building new functions from old. *AI Expert*. May: 23–28.

———. 1987. Neurons, analog circuits, and the traveling salesperson. *AI Expert*. Jul: 27–32.

———. 1987. Programming with objects. *AI Expert*. Sep: 15–20.

———. 1988. Topics in knowledge-based languages. *Dr. Dobb's Journal*. 138: 40–49.

Touretzky, Davis S., and D. A. Pomerleau 1989. What's hidden in the hidden layers? *Byte*. Aug: 227–233.

Townsend, Carl. 1987a. *Mastering Expert Systems in Turbo PROLOG*. Indianapolis, IN: Howard W. Sams & Company.

———. 1987b. *Advanced Techniques in Turbo PROLOG*. San Francisco: Sybex.

Townsend, Carl, and Dennis Feucht. 1986. *Designing and Programming Personal Expert Systems*. Blue Ridge Summit, PA: Tab Books.

Trelease, Robert B. 1987. The Forth Wave in AI. *AI Expert*. Oct: 58–66.

Turbo PROLOG. 1986. Scotts Valley, CA: Borland Communications.

Turing, A. M. 1936. On computable numbers with an application to the entscheidungs problem. Proceedings of the London Mathematical Society 42: 230–265.

Tzvieli, Arie. 1989. Emulating OPS5 with a database. *AI Expert*. Feb: 32–41.

Udell, Jon. 1989. Clash of the object-oriented Pascals. *Byte*. Jul: 104–106.

Urqhart, Russ. 1988. Two Snobols: Snobol4+ and Minnesota Snobol4. *Computer Language*. Oct: 135–149.

Valdex-Perez, Raul E. 1986. Inside an expert system. *AI Expert*. Oct: 30–37.

Van Der Gaag, L. C., and P. J. F. Lucas. 1988. Hepar: An expert system in PROLOG. *AI Expert*. June: 34–43.

Vita, James P. 1987. The knights' tour. *AI Expert*. Jun: 30–36.

Voda, Paul J. 1988. The logic of programming language. *Micro Cornucopia*. 41: 22–28.

Waite, Mitchell, Stephen Prata, and Donald Martin. 1987. *C Primer Plus*. Indianapolis, IN: Howard W. Sams & Co.

Waldrop, Mitchell. 1987. *Man Made Minds*. Walker Publishing Co.

Walters, John, and Norman Nielsen. 1988. *Crafting Knowledge Based Systems*. New York, NY: John Wiley & Sons.

Wang, Yulun, and S. Butner. 1987. Robot motion control. *AI Expert*. Dec: 26–32.

Ward, Harold, L. Winston, and S. Shepard. 1987. LISP on the micro, part I. *AI Expert*. Feb: 67–78.

Waterman, Donald. 1986. *A Guide to Expert Systems*. Reading, MA: Addison-Wesley.

Watkins, M. 1990. Episodic memory. In *Encyclopedia of Artificial Intelligence,* ed. Stuart C. Shapiro, 275–280. New York, NY: John Wiley & Sons.

Wegner, Peter. 1989. Learning the language. *Byte*. Mar: 245–253.

Williams, Kent. 1989. Tables within tables. *Computer Language*. Aug: 36–45.

Williamson, Mickey. 1986. Project costing with COCOMO1. *AI Expert*. Nov: 52–57.

———. 1988. Breaking the expert system bottleneck. *Computers in Science*. Nov/Dec: 62–65.

Wilson, Lynwood H. 1987. Expert systems and C: CxPERT. *AI Expert*. May: 73–77.

Winston, Patrick H. 1979. *Artificial Intelligence*. Reading, MA: Addison-Wesley.

———. 1984. *Artificial Intelligence*. 2nd ed. Reading, MA: Addison-Wesley.

———. 1985. The LISP revolution. *Byte*. April: 209–218.

Winston, Patrick H., and Berthold Horn. 1984. *LISP*. 2nd ed. Reading, MA: Addison-Wesley.

———. 1988. *LISP*. 3rd ed. Reading, MA: Addison-Wesley.

Wolfgram, Deborah. 1987. In search of a solution. *PC AI*. Winter: 64–68.

———. T. Dear, and C. Galbraith. 1987. *Expert Systems for the Technical Professional*. New York, N.Y.: John Wiley & Sons.

Woods, W. A. 1973. Progress in natural language understanding: An application to lunar geology. AFIPS Conference Proceedings 42, National Computer Conference and Exposition.

Wos, L., and R. Veroff. 1990. Resolution, binary: Its nature, history, and impact on the use of computers. In *Encyclopedia of Artificial Intelligence*, ed. Stuart C. Shapiro, 892–902. New York, NY: John Wiley & Sons.

Young, Richard. 1987. *PROLOG A Primer for Logic Programming*. Mississauga, Canada: Logicware Inc.

Zaniolo, Carlo. 1986. PROLOG: A database query language for all seasons. In *Expert Database Systems*, ed. Larry Kerschberg, 219–232. Menlo Park, CA: Benjamin/Cummings Publishing Company, Inc.

———, et al. 1986. Object oriented database systems and knowledge systems. In *Expert Database Systems*, ed. Larry Kerschberg, 49–66. Menlo Park, CA: Benjamin/Cummings Publishing Company, Inc.

Zarri, Gian P. 1986. Constructing and utilizing large fact databases using artificial intelligence techniques. In *Expert Database Systems*, ed. Larry Kerschberg, 141–160. Menlo Park, CA: Benjamin/Cummings Publishing Company, Inc.

Zeidenberg, Matthew. 1987. Modeling the brain. *Byte*. Dec: 237–246.

MAR 22 1991